Birds
of Chew Valley Lake
ECOLOGY | HISTORY | TALES

Keith Vinicombe

Compiled and edited by
John Rossetti

Cormorants flying to roost on Denny Island | Laurel Tucker

Typical Chew scene, with Shoveler, Ferruginous Duck and Spotted Crake in the foreground | Ray Scally

Our local sponsors

This book is a celebration of the wonderful habitat that is Chew Valley Lake, and so we contacted local organisations who had most involvement with the lake itself, and with the lake's bird and other natural life. We are very grateful to them for their sponsorship which has aided the production of this book.

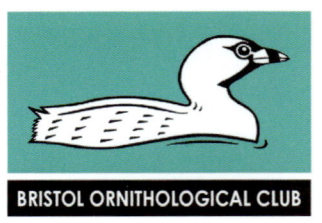

Bristol Ornithological Club

Bristol Ornithological Club (BOC) is delighted to be a main sponsor for *The Birds of Chew Valley Lake*. The Club formed in 1967 as the first organisation locally to focus on birdwatching. From the outset, it issued a monthly bulletin of sightings from the Bristol area, *Bird News*, in which the two reservoirs serving Bristol – Blagdon Lake and Chew Valley Lake – feature prominently. The very first issue of *Bird News* included records from Keith Vinicombe, Andy Davis and Dick Senior, all contributors to this book. The Club has been a training ground for many members who went on to become well-known figures in the birding world, including Dr Mark Avery and the late Tim Cleeves who started birding at the lake. It is also fitting that the cover of this book includes the Great Crested Grebe: Dr Ken Simmons' observations of them, based on his field work at Chew, were published in our journal *Bristol Ornithology* in 1968. The author later became the editor for Bird Behaviour in the monumental *Handbook of the Birds of the Western Palearctic*.

The Club exists to promote, encourage and co-ordinate the scientific study of ornithology in the Bristol area, primarily through field and indoor meetings and *Bird News*. It welcomes everyone with an interest in birds, especially young members and beginners. The 'Tuesday Group' organises weekly bird walks at a wide range of local sites. The BOC supports and assists conservation projects by active co-operation with local organisations and individuals. In 2019 the Chew Valley Ringing Station, based at the lake, acquired a thermal imaging camera with a grant from the BOC. The annual *Avon Bird Report* is produced jointly with the Bristol Naturalists' Society. Our website (bristolornithologicalclub.co.uk) contains information on our activities as well as the top local birdwatching sites. Daily bird sightings can be found on the Avon Birds blog (avonbirding.blogspot.com).

The BOC logo is a Pied-billed Grebe. The first example of this American species to be seen anywhere in the Western Palearctic was discovered at Blagdon Lake in 1963, and seen at Chew in several subsequent summers.

Bristol Naturalists' Society

Bristol Naturalists' Society, founded by a group of natural history experts in 1862, is extremely pleased to be sponsoring *Birds of Chew Valley Lake.* This book matches perfectly with the Society's everyday studies of the flora, fauna and geology of the Bristol area and with the recording undertaken through, for example, structured surveys, monitoring, etc., and also meets our aims of supporting projects that involve natural history research, education or conservation. The 'Bristol Area' reaches up into the Cotswolds, down onto the Somerset Levels, west to the Severn (including Steep Holm Island) and east to the Wiltshire border.

To this day, the Society remains a group of learned experts in Natural History and Geology, supported by knowledgeable members. All members will wish to continue to learn about their natural surroundings, and we are sure that many will have bought *Birds of Chew Valley Lake*, a book that will surely inspire deeper enquiry.

Chew Valley Lake is an extraordinarily important site for our native and migratory fauna, such as birds, and it provides the conditions for some of our rarer botanical, invertebrate and mammal species which all sections of the BNS study. Created in the 1950s to provide water for the City and County of Bristol, it is the fifth largest artificial lake in the UK covering an area of 1,200 acres. Opened by Queen Elizabeth II in 1956, it is a spectacular Site of Special Scientific Interest (SSSI), and also a Special Protection Area (created under the European Union's Directive on the Conservation of Wild Birds) plus a national centre for birdwatching, which the Ornithology Section of the Society visits the most frequently of all. Away from the public and picnic areas, Bristol Water only allows entry to members of ornithological and naturalist societies recognised by Bristol Water in order for the flora and fauna to remain undisturbed. While Bristol Water owns and manages the fish stocks and surrounding reed beds and islands, the areas of once rich farmland on its shores are maintained with the help of organisations such as the Avon Wildlife Trust. This came in to being in 1980 following the preparatory work necessary for its existence being undertaken by the Bristol Naturalists' Society and especially the late, great Richard Bland. E. M. Forster's directive of, '*Only connect'* in his novel, *Howards End,* has most certainly been fulfilled by this Society in its lifetime and it will continue to do so. We hope you will enjoy this lovely book.

Bristol Water

We are very pleased to support this excellent and attractive book, which celebrates the many aspects of the unique environment which is Chew Valley Lake.

The book not only focuses on the species of birds of the lake, but it also gives a comprehensive analysis of their distribution, habits and trends over a period of about 70 years since the lake was first built. We're pleased to see that the book also covers the history of the lake, its ecology and celebrates all lakeside activities such as family access, fishing and sailing. We believe it is important for all communities to engage with the natural environment and we strive to strike a balance between managing a drinking water resource with the provision of space for wildlife and people to thrive in.

We have a long history in the Mendips, supplying local populations with water from sources such as Blagdon Lake, Cheddar springs and the Line of Works. Chew Valley Lake is in fact the newest of the Mendip reservoirs opened in 1956. Our supply network is interconnected and by careful resource management we keep all our communities in a continuous supply of wholesome water. These resources are managed for people and the environment on a timescale that must consider the impacts of climate change, environmental pressures and changes in population across our region.

Water supply for our local community and our natural environment has always be our main objective. We invest in maintaining and developing the Chew Valley Lake catchments and its habitats to encourage wildlife to flourish. We are supportive of the continued data collection taking place around the lake, including at Chew Valley Ringing Station and from the bird hides which we have established for safe viewing of wildlife at Chew. The information provided by Keith demonstrates the passion so many people share for this special space. We hope that many more budding ornithologists and ecologists develop a love of the environment and continue to access our publicly accessible picnic areas, a great place for all the family to enjoy and experience this wonderful lake environment.

We look forward to this book increasing public awareness of this wonderful natural asset as it demonstrates our collective affection for our natural environment.

Mel Karam *Chief Executive Officer*

Ann Cleeves

I'm delighted to sponsor this book in the name of my late husband Tim Cleeves. Chew was his first birding destination; it inspired him and made him the ardent birder he would become. It wasn't easy to get there from his home – it took a couple of bus journeys or a lift from a sympathetic relative – but the lake represented freedom. More importantly, it represented friendship. His very early notebooks contain sketches, records (that might occasionally have been dodgy), and the initials of his companions. On most pages, there was a mention of one of the people behind this project. They remained his friends until he died and he would have cherished this book.

Keith Vinicombe, on the left, with John Rossetti at the lake, September 2020

Published in 2020 by Keith Vinicombe and John Rossetti

© Copyright Keith Vinicombe and John Rossetti 2020

All rights reserved. No part of this publication may be reproduced, stored in any retrieval system or transmitted in any form for or by any means, electronic, mechanical, photocopying, recording or otherwise, without the prior written permission of the publishers. The publisher, Author, Artists and photographers assert their moral rights to be identified as creators of this work.

Author
Keith Vinicombe

Compiled and Edited by
John Rossetti

Principal Contributors
Rupert Higgins, Mike Bailey, John Rossetti, Dick Senior, Andy Davis,
Rich Mielcarek, Martin Cottis, Chris Craig.

Illustrators
Laurel Tucker and Ray Scally

Main Photographers
Gary Thoburn, Rich Andrews, Lucy Masters and Ian Stapp

Copyeditor
Julian Thomas

Design and Production
Chris Gaughan
Designwing
info@designwing.co.uk

Printers
Swallowtail Print Limited
sales@swallowtailprint.co.uk

British Library Cataloguing-in-Publication Data.
A catalogue record for this book is available from the British Library.
ISBN: 978-1-5272-6368-0

Acknowledgements
and how this book developed

This is very much Keith Vinicombe's book; it was his idea and his very many years of knowledge, records, charts and graphs, along with a great deal of research on other records and information, that went into this manuscript, and which he was constantly updating.

This had been an exhausting process, and he was inclined to 'just self-publish as is' and get it behind him. But then his good friend Andy Middleton got involved and pulled together meetings with William Earp and Ken Carruthers of the Bristol Ornithological Club to see how they, with their experience, could help. I got pulled in, partly as a birding mate with a business background, and a group of us met up at the Robins Pub at Ashton Gate. Not because we were Bristol City supporters, which we mostly weren't, but because it was situated between those who lived in North Bristol and those who lived closer to the lake. I foolishly agreed to take the minutes and ended up with the privilege of being able to compile and edit this book.

This group of seven decided to extend the scope of the book and widen its appeal, which we hope we have managed. As well as Andy Middleton and myself, there was Andy Davis, Rupert Higgins, Rich Mielcarek, Chris Craig and of course Keith. I would like here to especially thank the many other people who have given their time and expertise to help in this project.

Bristol Ornithological Club have been especially helpful as well as being a major sponsor, and the new chairman Alastair Fraser, along with William Earp, have had several meetings with us and invited us to present the concept of the book to a meeting of the club's members. William suggested to us that we could try to engage with what he described as 'The A-Team', by which he meant Chris Gaughan for graphic design, Ray Scally for original illustrations and Swallowtail Print's Mike Dawson for production. It has been excellent to be able to work with this talented and knowledgeable group who have produced such excellent and attractive publications. I would also like to thank Roger White, who has self-published many birding guides himself, for being so willing to explain the rather daunting processes involved in publishing, marketing and distributing.

With a book like this, the visual impact provided by quality artwork and photographs was always going to be vital. I would like to thank Nigel Tucker, who, as well as Keith, provided many original line drawings and some colour plates that were done by the late (and outstanding) local artist Laurel Tucker. The excellent local bird photographers Gary Thoburn and Rich Andrews gave us free use of their superb work. Rich also introduced me, via Instagram, to Lucy Masters. She lives and works near the lake and has provided many of her beautiful scenic shots, along with bird and insect photos, that adorn this book throughout.

We are also extremely grateful for the support, including significant sponsorship, from the Bristol Naturalists' Society, and especially their honorary secretary Lesley Cox. I am also very appreciative of the support and significant donation from my good friend and well-known author Ann Cleeves, wife of the late and great Tim Cleeves, who started his birding at the lake.

During the editing of the substantial bird list section of the book, Rich Mielcarek had been superb in his speedy and detailed response to all matters relating to bird records. Andy Davis has also helped with this, as well as contributing to chapters on the history of the lake and memorable birding moments. Chris Craig has helped with the records and shared his knowledge of the ringing records in particular. Rupert Higgins, as well as writing the expert ecology sections, has put up with my repeated requests for even more photos, as indeed has Mike Bailey who also wrote the chapter on the history of the ringing station. And our great friend Dick Senior has written the poem about the swifts, as well as his amusing story of him and Keith finding, and mis-identifying, a rare bird at the lake in the early days. I would also like to thank my friend Debbie Cole who has freely given her time, and significant editorial expertise, in advising, copyediting and often substantially improving the text.

I would like to thank Bristol Water for their support and in particular the Environment Manager Natasha Clarke who has been extremely positive in supporting and promoting the book, and also a special mention for Dan Barwise, the Communities and Conservation Officer, who has given his time in meetings and also assisted in providing access to photographs from the Bristol Water archives.

We are grateful to the young volunteer Connor Stansfield and assistant warden George Dunbar who have managed to work on social media advertising and on-line ordering systems, while also working on Bardsey Island, managing to find time in between catching storm petrels, I imagine.

A special mention has to go to the Harptrees History Society and their editor Lesley Ross, for allowing us to make significant use of the reference material, including quotations, from the excellent and interesting book *Before the Lake – Memories of the Chew Valley*, which we use especially in the chapter on the History of the lake.

Lastly, we are grateful to Roger Riddington of *British Birds*, who gave us permission to re-print much of the article by Keith that appears in the book *Best Days with British Birds*, which is the copyright of British Birds Ltd.

John Rossetti

A tribute to our mentors

I have been incredibly lucky to have been introduced to birdwatching at a young age and been able to gain so much from it over the years. Not only has it been a totally immersing hobby that has provided great fun, travel and entertainment, but it has also provided me the opportunity to serve on national committees and write books that have achieved some worthwhile recognition.

While reflecting on this in the light of my work on this book, it brought me to think about all the good Chew birders back in the old days, who were mentors and great influences on us when we were young kids. I thought that it would be important to recognise them officially.

During the early days of the lake, particularly in the 1960s, a number of keen birders and ringers were very willing to pass on their knowledge and wisdom to the younger generation. My own mates – Andy Davis, Dick Senior and Keith Fox – taught me a lot.

As time went by, we got to know all the regular Chew birders, who are listed below in alphabetical order, with apologies to those that I may have inadvertently omitted.

These include *Roy Curber, Dorothy Crampton, Paul Chadwick, Tim Cleeves, Pete Doulton, Pete Garvey, Roger Harkness, Ken Hall, Roger Hemmings, Helen Highway and her husband (who was always referred to as 'The Colonel'), Bernard King, Norman Lacy, Ron Lewis, Derek Lucas, Antony Merritt, Don Ladhams, Sid and Olive Mead, Steve Moon, Roger Palmer, Robin Prytherch, Brian Rabbitts, Colin Selway, Trevor Silcocks, Ken Smith, Wally Stone, George Sweet, Roy Thearle, Maurice Tibbles and Keith Young*.

Sadly, but inevitably, a number of the above are no longer with us.

Keith Vinicombe

Mute Swan from a page of Laurel's notebook | Laurel Tucker

About the author

Keith Vinicombe is a very well-known and respected national birdwatcher, who started his interest at Chew Valley Lake where he has been studying and recording birds since 1962. This book is his brainchild, as he wanted to produce a detailed account of all the birds of Chew, using his own records while also researching all other published sources.

Keith is an expert in bird identification, which stems from thousands of hours observing both common and unusual birds in all plumages. He has served on the British Birds Rarities Committee and the British Ornithologists' Union Records Committee. Locally he has found many rare birds at Chew as well as nine county first records for Avon. He found the first Lesser Scaup and Blyth's Reed Warbler for the Isles of Scilly (a very well-watched location) and confirmed the identification of Britain's first (and only) Lesser Short-toed Lark at Portland Bill in 1992.

Keith authored **The MacMillan Field Guide to Bird Identification** (1989), which continues to be a reference book for identifying difficult species, providing much more detail than in traditional guides. He also wrote **Rare birds in Britain and Ireland, a photographic record** (1996). Keith has been the identification consultant to the highly regarded monthly magazine *Birdwatch* and has written numerous articles and papers for other titles such as *British Birds* and *Birding World*. He lives in Bristol but also enjoys annual stays at Portland Bird Observatory and the Isles of Scilly, plus of course the odd twitch.

John Rossetti

ruff like stance when nervous or alarmed.

Pectoral Sandpiper. juv.
Crown warm brown streaked black. Nape to mantle brown tightly streaked. Mantle blackish with bordered with thin white V. Scapulars similarly lined. Greyish buff supercilia not as noticeable as in Wood Sands. Lores smudged dark. Ear coverts faintly edged darker. Lesser coverts greyish brown, with less contrasting pale edges. Greater covs. + tertials dark with whitish on edges to outer covs. + tertials, and rich brown almost chestnut to outers. Prims. dark, extending to tip of tail. Chin pale, breast washed buff tightly streaked dark brown. Pec. band not obvious on side view as streaks extended for a short way along sides of belly; then most obvious face on. Bill dark brownish, paler at base of lower mandible? Legs muddy, yellow ochre. STRUCTURE. Vaguely like common sand, with short bill + legs, and tapering body. Fed very close to ground with fast pecking movements. Pecked several times from one position. Not a prober covered small area only, fairly slow walker pecked mostly in one area. In flight, pointed wings, very thin wing bar not extending to outer prim. covs. Dark rump + central tail feathers, and dusky edgings to underwing, especially on carpal joint.

Kestrels *(top)* **and a page from Laurel's notebook** | Laurel Tucker

Laurel Tucker

I am very pleased that we have been able to include many line drawings and a few plates by Laurel Tucker, which have been supplied both by Keith and by Nigel Tucker.

Although originally from the Channel Islands, Laurel really got interested in birding when she moved to Bristol, spending much time at Chew as well as enjoying dashing off on a twitch or three! She was a very detailed artist and birder, as you can see from this page from her notebook. Those of us lucky to have known her will always remember her energy and enthusiasm, her sense of fun, wicked sense of humour and infectious laugh. She also travelled on many foreign trips to see and study birds that were hard or impossible to see in the UK.

She was already an established and highly regarded bird artist when she tragically died suddenly from a brain tumour on 20 June 1986 at the age of 35. Without doubt she would have had an illustrious career ahead of her.

We have chosen many of her drawings to decorate this book. These are all of birds that have occurred at Chew, but I hope you will allow the inclusion of some that may have been drawn elsewhere.

John Rossetti

Black-headed Gull | Laurel Tucker

Contents

Preface 18

Introduction 21

The history of Chew Valley Lake
The Chew Valley before the lake 38
Excavations and prehistory 47
Construction 51
The Inauguration and later developments 57

Leisure at the lake
Picnic areas and walks 65
Fishing 70
Sailing 78

Ecology of the lake
Flora – Vegetation and other non-animal life 88
Non-avian Fauna – Insects, amphibians, reptiles, mammals, fish and others 101

Memorable birding moments and tales
How Keith got into birding 118
Being an account of finding a rare bird 120
Swifts 122
Mervyn the Merganser 123
The ones that got away 125
Special events and years including: 128
    The 'Great Fall' of 1966 130
    Keith's best day 138
    2011 – the ultimate year? 150

The Ringing Station
Sixty years of ringing 156

Complete species list and charts 172

Index 460

Preface

Ever since I started birdwatching as a young lad, Chew Valley Lake was my main local patch, and despite having travelled and birded far and wide, it has always been my special place and where I have spent thousands of hours of pleasure watching birds, common and rare alike.

Nestled as it is at the foot of the Mendip Hills and some way from the coast, it has still managed to attract a wide number of species. I have been recording and studying them for well over 50 years. I did not want all that information to be lost, and so I decided to compile it, along with all other published sources that I could find, into a manuscript. Apart from a short introduction, this work was basically a list of all the birds of the lake, together with discussion, charts and records.

I would really like to thank my friend John Rossetti who, despite my frequent attempts, has refused to put himself down as a joint author. He has almost single-handedly conceived the wider scope of the book and sourced not only the funding but also all artwork, photographs, promotion, design and publication, as well as writing several of the pieces.

I hope that people will enjoy this book as a celebration of a wonderful, albeit man-made, environment. I also hope that another generation will become inspired to see the importance and the joy of protecting our natural environment.

Keith Vinicombe

View over Chew Valley Lake | Lucy Masters

Introduction

John Rossetti

Birds of Chew Valley Lake is not just a book about birds. Admittedly there are a lot of birds in it. But it also charts the history of the valley of the river Chew from the Stone Age up to today. It describes the development of this man-made environment, still within living memory, and explores its ecological journey. It describes the enjoyment and activities that so many people get from being at or in this place. This short chapter allows you to dip your toes in the water, before you dive in!

Great White Egret surrounded by Cattle Egrets | Ian Stapp (July 2020)

The history of Chew Valley Lake

We may view the history of the lake as starting with its construction, leading to the official opening by the Queen in 1956. However, prior to the works and the flooding, archaeological excavations were made showing evidence of earlier inhabitants from the Old, Middle and New Stone age periods.

More recently, the valley of the river Chew had its own communities and way of life, and we are indebted to a wonderful book (*Before the Lake*) which has provided reference information. There is always a human and natural cost to major construction projects all over the world.

The need for this lake to supply enough water for Bristol had been known for a long time, with plans starting before the Second World War. But much earlier Bristol had already been reported as one of the worst large towns in England in respect of water supply according to a commission from 1844. Bristol Waterworks Company was formed in 1846 when also a 'line of works' was authorised. This old chart shows the levels of potential water supply from both Barrow and the Chew Valley Head, compared with the Clifton and Bristol harbour, also showing the famous Clifton Suspension Bridge. Those who know Bristol will see that this drawing was produced before the Suspension Bridge was built (in 1864 after Brunel's death), as the design is different from how it ended up!

Chew Valley Lake – a place to study and treasure

A newly created man-made reservoir provides a unique opportunity to see the development of a new environment over time and its effect on wildlife. At Chew, we have had the opportunity to study this for over 65 years and to enjoy all it has to offer.

One of the most conspicuous ways of seeing the development and changes to this natural environment is by studying and enjoying the very many species of bird that visit the lake over different seasons and years, and this is a main focus of the book. The changes in birds over this time have been dramatic and give an insight into the rapid speed of these changes, almost certainly due to man-made effects on the wider environment. Who would have thought, in the early days, that that we would today see a Great White Egret on Herriott's Pool, let alone being surrounded by Cattle Egrets?

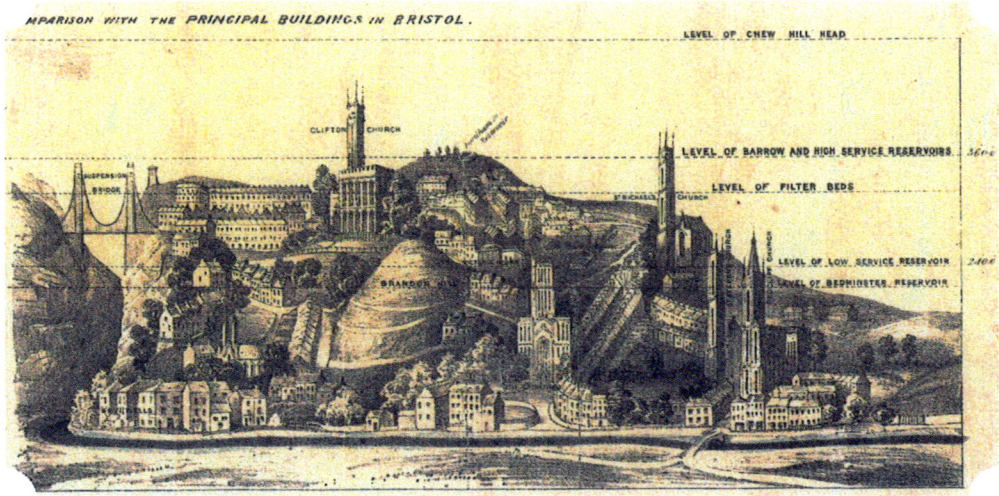

This illustration shows the old harbour, Clifton, and levels of the proposed water supply | Courtesy of Bristol Water

Transformation

From this:

Early Construction | Courtesy of Bristol Water

To this:

The lake today | Lucy Masters

Leisure at the lake

While we emphasise the natural environment of the lake, people can also celebrate its use as an open and attractive location for other pursuits. As well as a place to simply enjoy the scenery, paths and picnic areas, it is also enjoyed for other pursuits such as fishing and sailing. Sometimes these may be seen as in conflict with the wildlife, but in general it works well and agreed separations are in place where needed. All basically share the same love of the outdoors. Most simply come to enjoy being in such a beautiful place and close to nature.

Fishermen return on a misty morning after 2020 lockdown | Lucy Masters

A beautiful environment in which to learn to sail | Lucy Masters

INTRODUCTION

Ecology of the lake

Flora

Rupert Higgins has enjoyed and surveyed the lake's plant life for many years and is an expert in his field. The plantations and meadows support over 200 species of flowering plants, ferns and associated groups with fine flower-rich meadows. These meadows are an environment protected by the prohibition of the use of fertilisers since the reservoir was formed. Perhaps this can give us an insight into what might have been, in the rest of our present countryside. Those plants that live around or beneath the water line are of particular importance and their response to the changing environmental conditions have driven many of the changes in the lake's birdlife.

This section provides a fascinating and expert account of these changes over time and their effects on various bird species. Rupert has also been uniquely able to compare the surveys of the mid 1970s with a survey undertaken in 2015, highlighting their dramatic differences. He also discusses the improvements caused by a reduction in pollution as a result of reduced phosphate pollution from fertilisers and also from the improvements made to local sewage treatment facilities.

The expansion of the extent of the reedbeds has been important for many birds but can also diminish the variety of plant species. At certain seasons and in some years, the water level of the lake drops significantly and exposes the muddy lake floor. This can lead to a colonisation by specialist plant species, some of which are the most uncommon plants recorded at the lake. These include the North American Slender Mugwort, the appearance of which at the lake remains a mystery.

Even the stone banks on the lake's main dams provide a habitat that is surprisingly rich in plants. There is much still to be discovered about the so-called 'lower plants', the algae, mosses, liverworts, lichens and fungi (the last two not being actual plants at all in fact), offering an opportunity especially for those who are prepared to get down on their hands and knees in the wet 'inundation' zone.

Non-avian Fauna – other animal life at the lake

Four-spotted Chaser | Rich Andrews

Green-winged Orchids at The Parkland | Rupert Higgins

Many birdwatchers in quieter moments, and others with an interest in wildlife, have studied and recorded the other animal groups around the lake. Rupert points out, however, that there is very much yet to be categorised and studied. There is a reasonably complete knowledge of groups such as dragonflies, grasshoppers, butterflies, moths and bats, but very little about, for example, the interactions between the fish and aquatic invertebrates.

The top predator fish is the Pike, with the largest so far caught weighing in at 44lb 6oz. Impressive, but also with an impact on other fish as well as on bird populations.

There is much to be learnt about many animal groups, including the planktonic micro-crustaceans which have not been studied since the mid-1970s. Flies, midges and lesser water boatmen are also discussed as regards their effects on the birdlife. The aquatic molluscs are often identified from their shells and form an important part of the diet for several duck species.

The lake is locally important for grass snake, and also has 37 species of mammal recorded, of which 13 are bats, with exceptionally high occupancy rates for the bat boxes that have been put up around the lake. Two mammal species that have colonised this millennium are Polecat and Otter.

Volucella inanis | Ian Stapp

Common Toad | Ian Stapp

Roe Deer | Rich Andrews

Memorable birding moments and tales

Birdwatching is not just about seeing as many species as possible, although it is of course great to see a species that is rare, and especially so if you have never seen one before. So although all the records of birds recorded at Chew Valley Lake are covered in the main list, we have tried to pull out special days and years to provide insight into the excitement, joy and even humour of everyday birding.

Bird behaviour is also endlessly fascinating, and the renowned Dr K E L Simmons, who edited the 'Social Pattern and Behaviour' sections in the monumental *Handbook of the Birds of the Western Palearctic*, spent a lot of time observing at Chew Valley Lake. In particular he describes in great detail the courtship rituals of the Great Crested Grebe (along with the drawings of local legend Robin Prytherch), which features prominently on the cover of this book. Members of the crow family are especially intelligent and can often indulge in what we can only describe as play.

Keith's introduction to bird watching started with the commoner species, using his set of wartime binoculars, and persuading his dad to give him lifts.

There are two special contributions in this section from Dick Senior, who was one of Keith's earliest mentors. One is the account of both finding and mis-identifying a rare bird, and the other is the poem about swifts which is beautifully illustrated by Ray Scally.

Swift over the reedbeds *(top)* **and Carrion Crows** | Laurel Tucker

'Mervyn' on his own | Ray Scally

And who cannot feel sympathy for Mervyn, the Red-breasted Merganser, who came to the lake every winter for an incredible 34 consecutive years. It seems that he thought he was in fact a Goosander, as he spent all these years displaying, unsuccessfully of course, to female Goosanders.

More controversial perhaps is the little section entitled 'the ones that got away'. Again beautifully illustrated, we dare to suggest that, just possibly, three different species seen at Chew and which have never been accepted onto the British List, just might have been genuinely wild birds. Who knows?

Based around an extraction of interesting records provided by Andy Davis, we highlight special years and events. The 'Great Fall' of 1966 is not, as you might expect, about the failings of the West German defence, but relates to a remarkable 'dropping in' of migrating birds in a snowstorm.

The account of Keith's 'best day' relates to a remarkable weekend in September 1983 when a gale brought seabirds into the lake. This piece also shows the sheer excitement of seeing birds that are new to one's local patch, even though they are by no means rare birds. This account first appeared in the book *Best Days with British Birds* that was published by British Birds Ltd and is included with their permission. Here it is accompanied by beautiful vignettes from Ray Scally, and also includes the hilarious account of what we call 'The Gannet in the Bath'.

Talking of humour, Keith sent an email describing a conversation that was overheard in one of the public bird hides, with his questioning comment 'One for the book?'

Did you hear the one about?

Overheard conversation between an elderly couple at the public 'Bernard King' hide opposite Denny Island.

She: *'Hey, do you get Dolphins here?'*

He: *'Don't be stupid, it's not deep enough!'*

Sunrise at the lake | Lucy Masters

The Ringing Station

Mike Bailey's brief history of the Ringing Station at the lake gives a real insight into the momentous efforts by a dedicated group of volunteers since the first bird was ringed at the lake in 1961. Up to the end of 2018, about 210,000 birds of 144 species had been ringed. This includes a nationally important 40,000 Reed Warblers, as well as several rare species such as Temminck's Stint, Red-backed Shrike, Aquatic Warbler, Savi's Warbler and Little Bunting.

The Ringing Sation is situated close to the main reed bed areas, with much of the ringing taking place early in the morning. At the start, ringing was carried out in the open, or from the back of a car! Mike describes the development of the Ringing Station from a garden shed up to the more extensive and more modern facilities in use today. Generous support from Bristol Water and other local firms and volunteers has also been important in this development.

Having a long-standing ringing station allows the identification of trends over time, and the ability to reflect on circumstances such as climate change and conditions in wintering areas such as West Africa. Also of note is a male Cetti's Warbler, first trapped as a juvenile in 1989 and last recorded in October 2008, making him hold the longevity record for this species in the UK at 9 years, 3 months and 28 days. In a similar vein, a Reed Warbler caught as a juvenile in 1989 and last seen in May 2001 must have done 12 return trips to Africa in his more than 11 years of life.

Many birds have been found, seen or trapped elsewhere in the world, with the longest distance being 9,700 km for Swallows recorded in South Africa. The information provided from birds caught, sexed, aged and weighed feeds into national schemes to track the productivity and survival rates for 24 species of common songbird. This data is also fed into mathematical calculations of 'catching effort' which were studied at the lake when they decided that Net Foot Hours (length of nets times duration) was the best of the three methods they used.

Mike also describes the computerisation of the records, and the training that they provide for novice ringers, typically taking about five years to become a fully qualified 'C' ringer. The Ringing Station now also runs an annual British Trust for Ornithology (BTO) sponsored ringing course.

In addition to ringing, a lot of general work is undertaken by the station, including running about 200 nest boxes and habitat management. Mike provides contact details for anyone who is inspired to contact the ringing station and who may wish to join in with some of the activities.

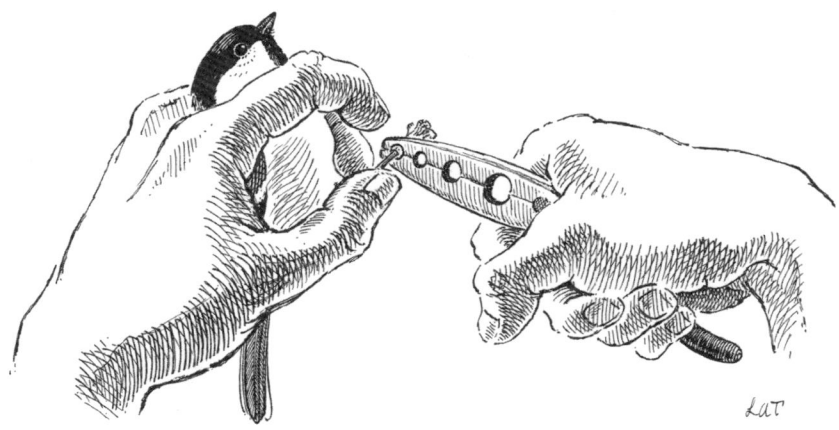

Ringing a bird | Laurel Tucker

Complete species list and charts

This section is the original and main basis for the book, written by Keith Vinicombe from his many years of experience and observations at the lake. As such it gives great insight into not only the details of the seasonal and yearly fluctuations, but the background in terms of changes in vegetation, water levels, climate change and other factors. Many of his discussions on unusual numbers or sightings also refer to movements going on elsewhere in Europe at the time and are often referenced to his own books and other publications such as *British Birds* and *Birding World*. Chew has also been an important breeding site for many species, especially wildfowl, where Keith discusses the remarkable suspected breeding of both Ferruginous Duck and Goldeneye.

Local, national and international trends are discussed, as well as recent dangers such as the large numbers of predatory Pike that now live in the lake and predation by Mink. There is also a considerable movement of wildfowl between other local reservoirs, especially Blagdon but also Cheddar and Barrow Gurney, where different conditions in those places affect numbers at Chew. Keith describes how the first record of Pied-billed Grebe for the Western Palearctic in 1963, initially at Blagdon but later at Chew, was met with incredulity that such a small and weak-flying grebe could cross the Atlantic. Since then however there have been over 45 additional records. It is interesting to see some of the long-term changes to bird populations over the 65 or so years covered here. See for example Keith's comment that there were no breeding data for Lapwing between 1954 and 1964, probably because at that time it was considered a common species and 'not worth monitoring'. How times have changed, although they are sometimes brought in by cold weather in winter. The sad declines in other species such as Cuckoo and Turtle Dove are also covered. However, a few good numbers of other species have occurred in recent years, such as the estimated 9,000 Swallows on 30 April 2018.

The lake has been a notable site for gulls, where there is a winter roost of over 20,000 birds, mostly Common Gulls. Many other species and sub-species of gull have been seen, and it can be expected that this will develop, as the studies of gulls from foreign breeding grounds and by DNA analysis continue to be an area where our knowledge is rapidly changing.

As well as his own observations, Keith has referred to all other published sources, in particular the *Avon Bird Report,* and also *Somerset Birds* that was formerly the main report that covered the area including Chew.

Very much time has been spent by other local birders and recorders to ensure all the data in this book is as accurate as possible. In many cases the graph data is up to date as of the end of 2019. It has also been possible to include all scarce or rare sightings up to the end of 2019, and we have also been able to include some records for 2020, the year of publication.

It is a truism that any book that provides records for a local area will be out of date as soon as it is published. Our hope is that this record of Chew Valley Lake, its history and the pleasure it has given to so many, will provide a more enduring legacy and encourage others to protect and develop our precious environments in the UK and beyond.

Gulls departing at dawn | Lucy Masters

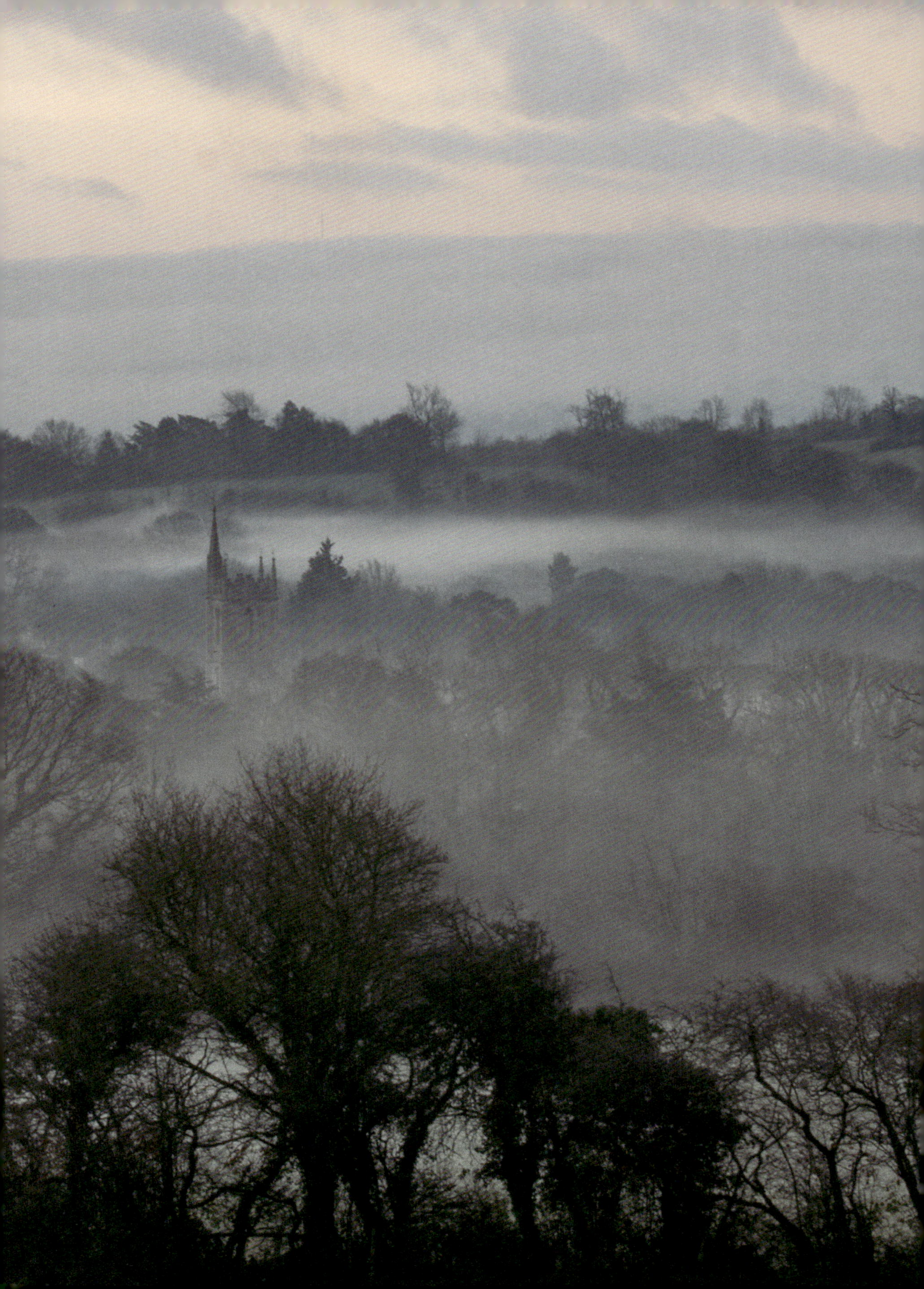

The history of Chew Valley Lake

John Rossetti
with additional material from Andy Davis and Rupert Higgins

The Chew Valley before the lake
Excavations and prehistory
Construction
The Inauguration and later developments

You might think that the lake's history starts with its construction. But here we also discover the Chew Valley before the lake, its earlier history back to the Stone Age, and of course the celebrations at its opening by the young Queen in 1956.

The Chew Valley before the lake

The countryside

Quite a lot is known about the countryside and the people of the Chew Valley over time. Many sources have been used here, but the main reference has been the publication *Before the Lake – Memories of the Chew Valley*, which provides a fascinating and detailed account of life in the valley. We thank The Harptrees History Society for permission to use this source. In addition, many of the personal quotes have come from this book.

In many ways the landscape will not have changed for many years, and the view of St Andrews Church, although taken recently, would have looked remarkably similar hundreds of years ago. Even at the end of the Roman Period, up to about the middle of the 4th century AD, the environment was said to be much like that of the 1950s although more marshy, with periodic flooding of the river and slight changes in its course. The Roman villa that was discovered at Chew Park was on a sandy promontory as close to the river as possible without being too wet. The woodland nearby would have been mostly of oak and ash, with hazel scrub, hawthorn and fruit trees. Crops would have included wheat and barley, and fallow deer were common. People kept domestic fowl, dogs and horses and the diet would have included vegetables, beef, pork and mutton as well as shellfish and snails.

Most of our extensive knowledge of much earlier periods, from Neolithic societies up to the Roman Period, came in fact during the early construction phase of the lake when remarkable excavations took place. This is therefore covered in the following section.

It is no accident that this part of the valley of the River Chew was chosen for the site of the reservoir. Not only was there a clearly identified need for larger supplies of drinkable water to the wider Bristol area, it had the geological advantage that there was a quite narrow gap at the north end where the sides of the valley came together and so the river had to flow between steep banks. This is where the main dam of the lake is now.

The river fell about 35ft (from 185ft to 150ft above sea level) from Herriotts Bridge to the dam site. It flowed northwards, with many twists and turns, and was joined by small tributaries including one from the hills behind what is now Herons Green Bay, and one from Hollow Brook joining from the east near the dam. There were four mill leats along the way from the sites of mills at Herriotts Bridge, Stratford Lane, Moreton and Woodford. The river could be low in summer but full in spring, and often flooding the low-lying fields and nearby buildings after heavy rain. Downstream from Moreton the bank was generally lined with undergrowth, while upstream towards Stratford Mill the banks were more open, which was an important feature for fly-fishermen. Local people remember the large variety of wildlife, including otters, water voles, kingfishers, moorhens and other birds. There were lots of dragonflies and the meadows were rich in flowers, including kingcups, buttercups and daisies.

There were many small to medium-sized fields in the valley, and some still showed the boundaries of medieval field systems. Most were used for meadow or pasture, with some arable on the higher, drier ground. The amount of arable was increased of necessity during the Second World War. The fields were mostly hedged, and elms were the commonest trees. Almost every farmhouse had an orchard close by, and grass verges full of wildflowers bordered the lanes. Often the high hedges would meet overhead.

There are very few written bird records from the Chew Valley before the lake, but records from nearby villages give us an indication of several of the species that may have been present. The *Bristol Bird Report* records the Corncrake in nearby Hinton Blewett and Compton Martin in the late 1940s, so this species may well have been heard calling from the valley meadowlands in summer.

The Cirl Bunting bred in Chew Magna, East Harptree and Compton Martin before 1907, so the fields bordered with elms in the Chew Valley would have been ideal habitat for this species. This species has not been resident in Somerset for three decades.

The Red-backed Shrike, according to Palmer and Ballance, was a widespread summer visitor to all parts of the old county of Somerset before the decline in numbers after the 1920s, so this species could well have been part of the avifauna.

The Turtle Dove, which is now in steep decline in the UK, was a breeding bird in the Chew Valley and the species persisted as a summer visitor into the 1960s at the lake.

Tree Sparrows were still breeding in at least one orchard in the early 1960s and Palmer and Ballance note that by 1925 the species was still breeding in the lower Chew Valley.

Lesser Spotted Woodpeckers, now quite a scarce bird, were widespread but local on lower areas in Somerset, in woodlands, hedgerow trees and orchards. There are breeding records since 1950 for Bishop Sutton and Stanton Drew and generally they were probably commonest in apple-growing areas. Until about 1920 it was thought to be the commonest woodpecker in Somerset.

A typical shot of the countryside before the lake | Courtesy of Bristol Water

Male Cirl Bunting in the foreground, with Turtle Doves flying behind | Ray Scally

Great Spotted Woodpeckers were scarcer than the former species during most of the mid to late 19th century but between 1900 and 1930 it greatly extended its range in Somerset so this species may have been present in the valley, together with the Green Woodpecker.

The Chew Valley may have been home to the Common Redstart, as it is clear the 19th-century observers knew it as a garden bird. At Wells, Somerset, in 1839, Dean Goodfellow saw a juvenile from a nest near his garden, and around Cheddar, Stanley Lewis found this species regularly breeding in walls, outhouses and dilapidated properties.

Life in the Chew Valley and the eventual need for water

It does seem that life in the valley changed very little for a considerable time, at least up until the construction of the lake. As with a lot of UK history however, there is a big gap in our detailed knowledge. Following the Roman withdrawal in the 4th century AD, no evidence was found of the use of the valley during the next seven centuries – the 'Dark Ages' and the Anglo-Saxon period. This is not to say that there could not be evidence to be found at other unexplored sites in the area. There are probably a great many more sites under the water. And, of course, these are fairly safe now from disturbance, at least for a long time!

The next detailed source of information comes from the Domesday Book which was completed in 1086. This tells us who the chief lords were that held the estates which were to be affected by the construction of the reservoir over 850 years later.

Compton Martin plus the manor of Moreton, and Chew Stoke, were both held by Serlo de Burci. He was from Calvados in Normandy and held several estates in Somerset, with some coming directly from the King (such as Blagdon and Ubley) and some as a tenant of the Bishop of Wells. To the east, Chew Magna, Bishop Sutton and Stowey were held by the Bishop of Wells. To the south, West Harptree, which was split into two manors, one held by Walter de Douai (a Fleming who had been given many estates in Somerset, particularly along the River Parrett), and the other by the Bishop of Coutances, also a major land holder in Somerset. These manors were later identified as West Harptree Gournay and West Harptree Tilly respectively.

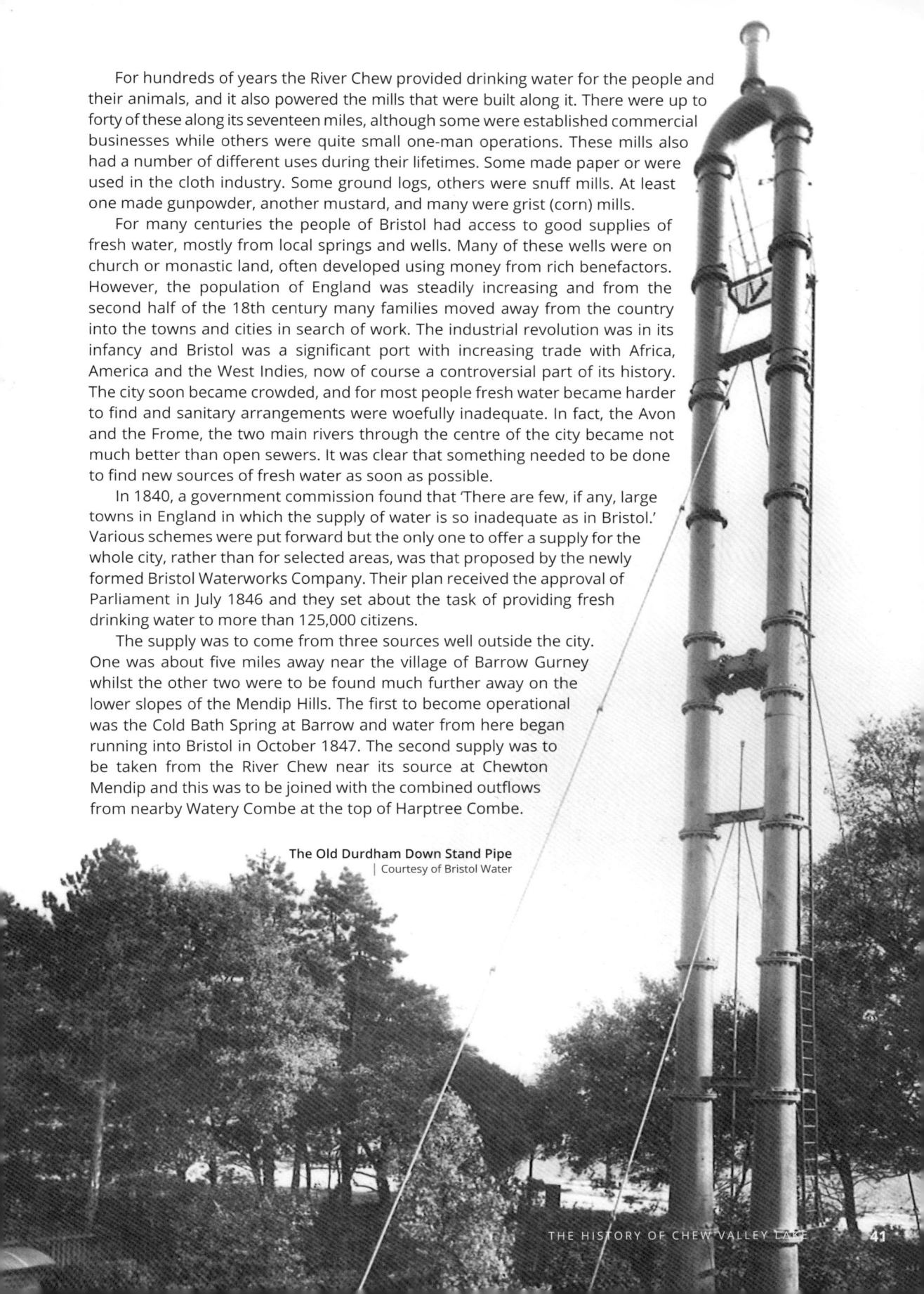

For hundreds of years the River Chew provided drinking water for the people and their animals, and it also powered the mills that were built along it. There were up to forty of these along its seventeen miles, although some were established commercial businesses while others were quite small one-man operations. These mills also had a number of different uses during their lifetimes. Some made paper or were used in the cloth industry. Some ground logs, others were snuff mills. At least one made gunpowder, another mustard, and many were grist (corn) mills.

For many centuries the people of Bristol had access to good supplies of fresh water, mostly from local springs and wells. Many of these wells were on church or monastic land, often developed using money from rich benefactors. However, the population of England was steadily increasing and from the second half of the 18th century many families moved away from the country into the towns and cities in search of work. The industrial revolution was in its infancy and Bristol was a significant port with increasing trade with Africa, America and the West Indies, now of course a controversial part of its history. The city soon became crowded, and for most people fresh water became harder to find and sanitary arrangements were woefully inadequate. In fact, the Avon and the Frome, the two main rivers through the centre of the city became not much better than open sewers. It was clear that something needed to be done to find new sources of fresh water as soon as possible.

In 1840, a government commission found that 'There are few, if any, large towns in England in which the supply of water is so inadequate as in Bristol.' Various schemes were put forward but the only one to offer a supply for the whole city, rather than for selected areas, was that proposed by the newly formed Bristol Waterworks Company. Their plan received the approval of Parliament in July 1846 and they set about the task of providing fresh drinking water to more than 125,000 citizens.

The supply was to come from three sources well outside the city. One was about five miles away near the village of Barrow Gurney whilst the other two were to be found much further away on the lower slopes of the Mendip Hills. The first to become operational was the Cold Bath Spring at Barrow and water from here began running into Bristol in October 1847. The second supply was to be taken from the River Chew near its source at Chewton Mendip and this was to be joined with the combined outflows from nearby Watery Combe at the top of Harptree Combe.

The Old Durdham Down Stand Pipe
Courtesy of Bristol Water

The remaining water then started a journey of more than ten miles, mainly by gravity, to Number 1 reservoir at Barrow Gurney. The route was known as the 'Line of Works' and for its time was certainly a remarkable feat of engineering, and still forms the basis of a large part of today's supply.

In Bristol itself three service reservoirs were built; at Bedminster Down for the area south of the River Avon; Victoria Reservoir at Oakfield Road for the lower areas north of the Avon; and the Durdham Down Reservoir for the higher districts. The water flowed from the Barrow Reservoir to Oakfield Road by gravity where there was a pump driven by a steam engine to raise the water to the Downs level.

The Durdham Down reservoir water surface is at 328 feet above Ordnance Survey datum but originally a more distinctive feature was an iron standpipe 70 feet higher. The reservoir with a capacity of 625,000 gallons was in use by October 1850. It has walls of stone blocks with an outer layer of clay supported by an earthen embankment. The inner walls slope outwards and have buttresses to provide added strength.

By local repute, the bungalow at 46 Upper Belgrave Road was owned by BWW (Bristol Water Works) and was of reduced height so that the man in charge of the pump at Oakfield Road could see the standpipe and stop pumping when the reservoir was full!

After the Second World War there were problems in maintaining adequate water pressure in supplies to the new higher suburbs of Bristol, for which one solution was a raised water tower at the Downs. The first proposal came before the Downs Committee in June 1947. The start of work on site was expected to be authorised on 1 April 1953 but it was agreed that nothing would be done until after the Coronation Celebrations in June (the national ones, not the inauguration of the lake which was in 1956). Work started in July 1954 and by June 1956 the outside surface of the tank was reported to be silver grey with a coarser grade finish on the tank. The reinforced concrete structure has a 21 feet deep tank raised on twelve columns to 100 feet above the Downs surface. The capacity of the tank is 250,000 gallons. The 'Water Tower', as it is known locally, remains a prominent feature on the Bristol downs.

A condition of the assent for the 1846 bill was that none of the homes, farms or businesses along its course was to suffer by the diversion of water from the River Chew. However, this water extraction from the river was to change the river forever and contribute to the gradual decline in the numerous businesses that had used these waters for centuries to turn their millwheels. Many rural industries were eventually to be put out of business by the rapid development of machinery and the growth of large factory mills during the industrial revolution.

As regards detailed information about who was living in the Chew Valley, we can refer to the 1901 census, which provides a snapshot at the turn of the 20th century, including the families, servants and others resident on the day of the census. This brings us, more or less, up to the period when personal memories come into play.

Durham Downs Water Tower, built in 1954 and in use today
| Courtesy of Bristol Water

THE HISTORY OF CHEW VALLEY LAKE

Rural life before the start of the construction of the lake

In the early part of the last century the population of the hamlet of Moreton was around 70, which is much the same as it is believed to have been in Roman times. The whole of the valley was farmed, though some of the low-lying land was still on the wet side.

The land was split between many farms. Some of these were owned by the people who farmed them, but the majority were tenanted. Some farmers employed a cowman and although that was his main responsibility, he would be called on to help at haymaking and harvest too. In those days, when operations were so labour intensive, farmers would help each other out on a reciprocal basis at peak times. At haymaking and at harvest and when there was threshing to be done the same people would be asked to come in and help and they could always be relied on. The whole family would give a helping hand, as described in the quote below.

> *In those days it was just picks (forks) and loose hay. We used to go round with a hand rake and go all round the hedge. Then the baler came in and I used to sit on the baler because some of them would miss and I would have to tie them. I remember once when I got off my face was so dirty all they could see was my eyes. And the blouse I was wearing, I never got it out of the seams!*

At harvest and at haymaking time local men were also available to work. Men from the local coal pits would sometimes help when they were off shift. Most of the valley land was rich pasture grazed by the cattle in summer, or meadow that provided hay. In the winter, this was the staple diet of cattle as well as horses. On livestock farms therefore, the health and very survival of the animals depended on a supply of good hay.

The land was rich and, if set aside for hay early in the season, produced a heavy crop. It was essential to choose the right day to cut it when the 'glass' was set fair.

Traditional hay making, 1923
| Photographer unknown

Other trades and businesses

In the 1930s there were still plenty of horses working on the farms and plenty of work for local blacksmiths. There were one or two in every village as well as a saddler in Chew Magna. The blacksmith was Spear, where the Co-op is now in Chew Magna. There was also Monty Ball in Winford and there had been two in Chew Stoke; all the villages had them. It is interesting the way some of them adapted to changing times. For example, Brent's at Sutton started as a blacksmith, then did bicycles and gradually moved up to motorbikes.

Blacksmiths had always made and repaired agricultural metalwork. Gradually, tractors and trailers were replacing horses and for a while the local blacksmiths were being asked to convert horse-drawn implements for use behind a tractor. Shoeing horses was no longer the mainstay of their business, but it was still needed.

The last village blacksmith at Chew Stoke | Photographer unknown

The stink factory

On the old West Harptree to Chew Stoke road, close to Ben Bridge, was one other small business, the 'stink factory'. This was the local name for the building where the carcasses of dead animals which were not fit for human consumption were rendered down for fertiliser. This was an essential service in a livestock area. Many of the people described the appalling smell which emanated from the plant and its one-man workforce. Here is a typical quote:

> *On the way to Chew Stoke each day on my bike I would pass the man on his way to work. Even first thing in the morning the smell was awful!*

General stores

There were several general stores, and others that were specialists such as butchers, bakers and saddlers. It became important to be able to offer a delivery service, which would originally have been by horse and cart. With so many outlying farms and cottages, some people commented that *'you never went shopping. It was all brought to your doors years ago.'*

Being in general an area based around agriculture, there was nowhere to buy many items such as nails, cartridges or specialist drapery. Many of these would have to be sourced from warehouses in Bristol.

The West Harptree shop and its delivery van | Photographer unknown

Many of the local people looked back at their rural childhood as an idyllic period of innocence. When the research was being done for the book *Before the Lake* at the start of this current century, they were fortunate in being able to share the reminiscences of many whose early years were spent among the fields and farmsteads of Moreton and the wider valley.
Here are some typical quotes.

❝I had a very happy childhood. It was a lovely place to live and there was always something going on. We had good parents and it was just all happiness.❞

❝Happy childhood? Oh God, yes, really and truly. We were free to go all across the fields. We had our chores to do, but on a Saturday when we'd done what we had to, we were free. Oh yes, we had a lovely time. We didn't have luxuries but we had what mattered.❞

The war and its impact

As with the rest of the country, the whole way of life changed during these times. Night-time blackouts, petrol and food rationing, the introduction of 'Red Petrol' and so many other changes. Many men and women went off into the armed forces, although some farmers needed to do what they could to hold on to sons and other farm labourers.

Home-grown agricultural produce was extremely important, so some land had to be ploughed up to increase crops, sometimes instructed by the War Agricultural Committee. There was also a very active Home Guard.

Many of the local households took on the responsibility of housing evacuees, often from the East End of London. This could be a culture shock for both sides, as the children were from such different backgrounds. Often it worked really well, and some evacuees remained in touch with their Somerset families for many years afterwards. However, some evacuees felt so out of touch in a country environment that they only stayed for a very short time.

Bristol was an important industrial city and was badly hit in the Blitz. People came out of Bristol for short breaks to escape the bombings. The following is an account from a Bristol woman who remembered those times.

> *Part of Stratford Mill farmhouse was a separate cottage. During the War it was made available to Bristol Waterworks staff to take a break away from the bombing. My father was an accountant with the Company and I spent several holidays there with my parents. I was approximately thirteen at the time. Our luggage was sent out by Bristol Waterworks and so we didn't have to worry about that. We cycled out from our home in Stoke Bishop and spent time exploring the Mendip area, walking and cycling. I think we stayed for a week in the summer but it might have been a fortnight.*
>
> *I went to visit a friend from school in Bristol who was staying in a house on the main Blue Bowl to Chew Stoke road. I think her family were there to get away from the bombing too.*
>
> *It was such a lovely old farm and such an idyllic situation with the pond and the river.*
>
> *During the War they used to have lots of scouts and messenger boys come out from Bristol to camp. They used to have big camps. We used to have marvellous times actually. We all went swimming. I went on a tandem with one of the lads to his home for a week. So it really opened up quite a few opportunities.*

The bombings in Bristol continued to cause problems to the water supply, and during the air raid of 24 November 1940 all water supply to Victoria Pumping Station was lost, so an alternative emergency supply to the Durdham Down reservoir was arranged from the 27-inch diameter water main running under the Portway to Avonmouth. (It was the failure of this water main in September 2001 which caused the retaining wall of the Portway to fall into the river at the bottom of Bridge Valley Road.) Work started in December 1940 and the installation was in use in two severe raids in February 1941. The pipe remained until August 1945 when the pumps were recovered, but it took another five years to remove the cast iron main and refill the trench.

The winter of 1947

The winter of early 1947 was particularly harsh, especially when the country was still recovering from the Second World War. Starting in January, several cold spells brought large drifts of snow, blocking transport routes and energy supplies. Animal herds froze to death and towards the end of February, there were fears of food shortages as supplies were cut off and vegetables frozen into the ground.

Bristol Water workmen and their van | Courtesy of Bristol Water

Excavations and prehistory

How it came about

It might seem that 'Prehistory' should come before 'History', which seems logical, but as mentioned before our knowledge of this period only came about as a result of excavations carried out in the early stages of the lake's construction.

These excavations started off on a very small scale, as it was thought that the area was of little archaeological interest. It developed into one of the most exciting, and unexpected, series of discoveries in the country. The site of the lake was of course very carefully planned, but who would have known what lay beneath the land that was to be submerged?

The only significant site that was known about in the early 1950s was the Roman Road at Stratford, although a trial dig had been carried out by Mr F C Jones of Bristol Water in 1949 at Nunnery Fields, where some medieval remains were found, thought to be of a small nunnery.

The reservoir project was the trigger for the archaeological excavations that started during the construction in 1953 and ended two years later when the water rose to cover all the sites. The archaeologists (employed by the Ministry of Works) who carried out most of the excavations were Philip Rahtz and his colleague Ernest Greenfield. They were helped with the digging by four paid labourers (including one local farmer) and, at Chew Park, by 30–40 volunteers.

The quotes below are from Philip Rahtz himself.

"Originally I was only engaged for a week or two to dig the Roman road and then of course we went on continuously for two years."

"The history of the valley was virtually a blank before that and written off as archaeologically barren. It was in fact a wonderful sample of everything from about 10,000 BC onwards. And so the most interesting thing was to have a piece of landscape of 1200 acres whose history could be taken from the earliest prehistory right the way through to the flooding. It was the first time that anybody in England had actually done a whole landscape. The two years in the Chew Valley was the equivalent of a lifetime of experience because every period was represented and different kinds of sites. You wouldn't get such an opportunity now, over two years, to find out about archaeology."

The dotted white line shows where the lake will go, with Denny Island near the top right | Courtesy of Bristol Water

The plant and machinery used by Bristol Water to clear the vegetation and to scrape the top layer of soil exposed the initial evidence of possible early occupation. This covered a far larger area and far more quickly than traditional methods would have done, although laborious hand digging was still needed afterwards.

❝*When we were digging the Roman road with a trench across it, workmen came over from Herriott's Bridge and said, 'Oh you chaps should be over there'. Other things were turning up there, skeletons and pottery. So we straight away dropped what we were doing and went over, and there was the site of Herriott's Bridge all stripped by the Water Works - a lovely dry pond. And of course all the red clay had been exposed over fifteen acres and there was a huge Roman site, so the whole thing took on a very different complexion then.*❞

The excavations in 1949 at Nunnery Fields | Courtesy of Bristol Water

Eight separate sites were excavated within the lake area: at Chew Park (near Chew Park Farm); Herriott's Bridge; Ben Bridge; Moreton; St Cross Nunnery (near Whitehall Farm); Stratford Mill; Stratford Lane; and Denny Moat (near Denny House Farm).

The results of the work, and that of the many experts that examined, identified and interpreted the features, objects, soil and pollen samples are set out by Philip Rahtz and Ernest Greenfield in their book *Excavations at Chew Valley Lake, Somerset*. Due to the vast scale of the excavations, a large number of experts were needed to record and identify the various finds and it was twenty years before the book was published by the Department of the Environment (the successor to the Ministry of Works) in 1977.

The prehistoric and Roman remains discovered, with the exception of wooden writing tablets, are all held as part of the archives at the Bristol Museum and Art Gallery.

The early excavations and heavy machinery used by Bristol Water revealed some of the interesting archaeological areas for further investigation | Courtesy of Bristol Water

What was discovered?

Prehistory

The prehistoric period was from about 10,000 BC until 'Romanisation' around the middle of the 1st century AD. The excavations found evidence of people belonging to the consecutive periods known as Upper Palaeolithic, Mesolithic and Neolithic (Old, Middle and New Stone Ages), Bronze Age and Iron Age. In broad terms, the late Neolithic and early Bronze Ages are about 3000 to 2000 BC, and in England, the Iron Age is dated from about 500 BC.

For the Upper Palaeolithic and Mesolithic periods, various stone implements were found. These included a knife at Herriott's Bridge; a number of flint blades at Chew Park, similar to those found in the Mendip caves; and the head of a mace at Moreton.

Firm evidence of occupation in the Neolithic period was only found at Chew Park: a ring of post holes for a small circular hut or house about ten feet in diameter, and a small pit containing fragments of pottery and flint and other domestic refuse. Other tools, including fragments of polished flint axes were found at other sites.

Chew Park and Ben Bridge are the main sites where Bronze Age features were found. At Chew Park a circular grave dated around 1800 BC was discovered. This contained the burnt bones of a man aged perhaps 30 years old when he died. There was also a flat stone quern for grinding corn. This was of special interest, as it was the earliest evidence of cereal cultivation in the valley.

With the Iron Age, it was possible to identify three separate phases of settlement in the area. At Chew Park the first phase was represented by a long straight ditch and several pits, which were thought to represent either the fringe of a farmstead or an outlying granary or barn connected with a farm. There was also a ditch system which appeared to indicate drainage for growing crops. Similar drainage ditches to those at Chew Park were also found at Herriott's Bridge and Moreton, which, together with pottery found in all three sites, enabled these to be dated to the third Iron Age phase.

The Roman period

The Roman period initiated a sudden change to the Iron Age way of life, and lasted until near the end of the 4th century, when the barbarian invasions occurred.

Interestingly, mineries for silver and lead extraction were thought to be under way in the Mendips just south of the lake as early as AD 49, this being only six years after the Roman invasion. They also are thought to have grown grapes there. The road that later connected them to the Chew Valley is the track leading to Stratford Bay. It is impressive that it is still the parish boundary!

There was a large rectangular timber house discovered at Chew Park. It appears to have been the nucleus of the early Romanised occupation of Chew Park, and by the end of the first century full Romanisation had taken place. The villa at Chew Park and the Charterhouse mining were interlinked, with lead smelting and de-silverisation taking place at the villa. A network of roads has been traced linking the villa with the mines to the south and the Roman port of Abonae (Sea Mills, now part of Bristol) to the north.

The now submerged Chew Park Villa also yielded evidence for major corn production, as well as soft fruit including grapes, cherries and plums. There were cattle grazing and horse breeding, as well as evidence of light industry such as leatherworking from the resulting cowhide, and also the extraction of lead from sources on Mendip. It also seems likely that this area was used for the production of salt-beef, and there were salt-pans at Banwell (on the Severn Estuary to the West); this staple army foodstuff must have been, with grain, an important and profitable enterprise for the villa.

By the 3rd century there were signs of small-scale industrial activity such as iron smelting, a lime kiln and the quarry at Denny Moat. A villa was built solidly of stone on good foundations by early in the 4th century and probably used as a farmhouse. Although the villa was not luxurious, from the evidence of coins and other finds, its owner would have been reasonably wealthy. There were also signs of a much smaller dwelling there for a short time, before abandonment not much later than AD 350. Much of the evidence of the villa's existence would have been lost when the stones from the ruins disappeared into the kilns of the medieval lime burners.

The villa had a good water supply provided by a well, and it was here that one of the most important finds was made, being the first discovered in this country. As Philip Rahtz said:

❝The most exciting thing was the discovery of the writing tablets. They have rather been overtaken, because quite a lot of other writing tablets have been found since, especially at Vindolanda. When Ernest was down the well, he sent up a bucket and he said, 'I think this is a writing tablet'. When it came up on the bucket in bright sunshine I could see there was writing on it. We realised that it all might have faded away in the sunshine and so it was hastily put back in the wet mud and sent straight away to London.❞

After being deciphered some time later, the writing proved to be part of a legal document about the transfer of land – perhaps for the villa itself, though this could not be proved.

Construction

Getting the go-ahead

To get approval to build the lake, the Bristol Waterworks Company submitted a bill to Parliament in 1938 for a reservoir, to be called The Chew Stoke Reservoir, in the parishes of Chew Stoke, Chew Magna, Compton Martin, West Harptree, East Harptree and Hinton Blewett, or some of them, to be formed by means of an embankment across the River Chew commencing in the parish of Chew Stoke.

It was not until a competition was held by the Bristol Waterworks company in 1954 that the reservoir acquired its present name of Chew Valley Lake.

The bill was passed and became an Act of Parliament in 1939. However, the Second World War and the more urgent priorities of the post-war years meant that the scheme had to be put on hold.

Water consumption continued to increase and, in 1947, Bristol Waterworks Company was given permission to construct a temporary intake and pumping station near the proposed site of the dam at Chew Stoke. This supply was connected into the 'Line of Works' aqueduct built in 1846 to carry the water to the treatment works at Barrow.

The reservoir scheme was eventually sanctioned in 1949. The construction then entered the more detailed design and tendering stage for all the work needed on the surroundings, as well as on the lake itself. The contract to construct the reservoir was awarded in 1950 to A. E. Farr & Co. ('Farrs'); a family firm originally founded in Hereford but based at Westbury in Wiltshire by the 1950s. The firm had been carrying out civil engineering contracts in Bristol from soon after the Second World War, clearing up the legacy of the war years and contributing to the rebuilding of Bristol.

Building the reservoir

Work started in November 1950 with building a road to the site of the dam which included widening the first part of Walley Lane. The objective was to complete the reservoir by 1955. It was also hoped to start extracting some water for use by 1953, once the reservoir had started to fill sufficiently. Construction of the dam and the other major earthworks were clearly critical to achieving this.

Excavating the draw-off tower | Courtesy of Bristol Water

Hard work

The work on the dam's foundations was very hard, and conditions difficult. But labouring work was very different in those days, as is evidenced by some of these quotes from the workmen.

Negotiations

❝Well I went in there. They couldn't get men to go down in that trench. One time they give them all a rise but we didn't get a rise so old Stan Chidzey from Sutton, he said, 'Right, let they go down for a week and we'll come up on the sunshine'. And he went up and saw the head bloke and he said, 'No, they won't go down in there'. Stan said, 'Well, we want more money.' So we had more money than the men on the top.❞

❝We worked in water. The stream was still going through but they put the stream up a lot higher so that they could get through this trench. One night they had a hell of a flood and that stream busted through and that stream went back on its same track. It took wheelbarrows, everything with it.❞

Health and safety

❝They never had no ladders, down there. They put the diesel ready for night time to fill it up and you had to get up and down there at night. A lot were half afraid to go down 'cause there weren't no lights much. No Health and Safety in those days. No compensation if you got hit. That was it.❞

❝Not many was injured. There was no first aid on the spot at all. There was one I took to hospital, he'd cut his hand when they were mixing the cement. There was nobody there to do it. They come down and asked me to take him to hospital because I had a car.
   Down there by the pump house one day Farrs had to go down and dig a trench. Well this chap didn't realise electric wires were up over. Of course he swung the ruddy bucket round and all caught on the wires. All went flash, the ground were on fire. He were ruddy lucky he weren't electrocuted.❞

Other tasks

Work, lots of it manual, was going on all around the lake site.

Working on the Outlet Tunnel
Courtesy of Bristol Water

Clay puddling

On top of the concrete, the core of the dam was made of puddled clay, nearly all of which was taken from near Stratford Mill. The clay was mixed with sand in a twin-shafted pug-mill near the site offices, where the concrete blocks to face the dam were also made. This again was hard and dirty work, as the quotes below testify.

> We did bring the clay back and tip it up. There be three of us hauling it and that had to go up an elevator, through the machine. It would come out in a long line but a bloke with a spade would be there cutting it as it came out in blocks. Then into a Fergie trailer and that had to be took down to where they were putting the clay. The blocks had to be placed clean in a layer in the trench; there would be two or three blokes throwing it and then they had to make heel marks all over that in proper lines. That was where all the work came in. We didn't call it puddling.

> The banks had to be made up in thin layers and they had to go over it rolling it with holes in the soil and then they did water it. There was a tanker there. Every load had to be rolled properly 'cause the Waterworks people would be there watching. I know one or two people who did drive the 'happy wagons'.

(These were the caterpillar tractors pulling trailers of red marl for the bank fill.)

> When they did go on to that bank they could tip either side. They had a lever in there to pull as they drove along. In the summer time when they did stir up the dust, you could see the dust for miles. And you would come home covered red.

Laying the core for the Puddle Clay for the dam | Courtesy of Bristol Water

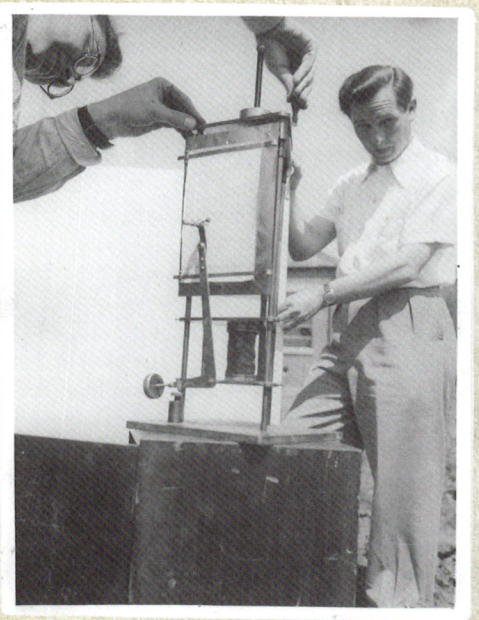

Testing the strength of the Puddle Clay with a compression device | Courtesy of Bristol Water

OK, ready to start puddling! | Courtesy of Bristol Water

The Puddle Clay is in the trench awaiting compression | Courtesy of Bristol Water

Roads and countryside

New roads had to be built, including any embankments that were needed, and lanes that crossed the lake had to have their access barred. The present road across the dam and round the north-east side of the lake was built to connect Chew Stoke and Chew Magna with the lanes to Bishop Sutton. A temporary road diversion was needed for a couple of years until the road over the dam was ready.

Parts of the road from Chew Stoke to West Harptree were below the top water level of the lake (the 185 ft contour line) and so the section of the road between Stoke Villice and the turning to Nempnett and Ubley were moved further to the west.

Rather amusingly, if unconventionally, the engineer who designed the new Chew Stoke to West Harptree road section was a keen motorcyclist. He designed the camber on the bends so that on a motorcycle you could take the bends at high speed and accelerate into the straight.

Because such a large area of farmland had to be cleared, over 25,000 trees and 100 miles of hedges were removed and five and a half miles of county roads were diverted. The site is approximately 4 km from north to south and 2.5 km from east to west. It has a surface area of 500 hectares and the shoreline is about 16 km in length. The average depth is 4.25 m.

It was important to allow fish from the River Chew access to the lake, and so a fish pass was constructed at Herriott's Bridge.

Stratford Mill

The last mill site to be flooded, and the only one still in working condition up until the 1950s, was Stratford Mill in West Harptree. The last miller was Arthur Wilson, and two of his daughters gave the quote below of their memories. The overwhelming feeling that comes across when listening to them is that of a wonderfully happy childhood in a peaceful rural haven.

'It was a great old place and such an idyllic situation with the pond and the river. Lovely – and always something going on. We had a beautiful house. It was to the right of the mill. There were four bedrooms with a little annex down in, like we used to call a little box room. It was very primitive, you know, at Stratford, but the house was in very good condition. It wasn't damp and Mother always had a lovely fire. But I didn't care for the winters; it was very, very cold. There was no running water and no electric light. It was all candles and in the kitchen we had to pump the water up from outside.'

The Mill was carefully taken down stone-by-stone and was then re-erected in the grounds of Blaise Castle Museum in Bristol, where it remains to this day.

The fish pass being constructed | Courtesy of Bristol Water

The Inauguration and later developments

A Golden Day – The Inauguration

17 April 1956 was a memorable day, remembered very happily by all who were there. Villagers from five parishes gathered on the stands; it was a very grand occasion. Lots of plants had been brought in for the day from Bristol Zoo, and primroses adorned the banks. These had been dug up from the lanes around Bishop Sutton and had to be returned after the Queen's departure. It was a bright but cold day, and they had to wait a long time, but they all said it was well worth it.

The Queen and Prince Philip had arrived at Bristol Temple Meads station to large crowds, and they also toured Bristol docks, so it was quite late when the royal party travelled through the villages on their way to the lake.

Extensive preparations had been made, with the Royal Guards doing three weekends of drill training; some of them had come up from St Ives in Cornwall. The Wrens gave a display of semaphore with their bright flags, which included a message of congratulations to the Queen.

Rows of stands were constructed, and 2500 guests were invited in addition to local villagers. Children were at the front. There were lots of fur coats and tall hats. Workers had to buy new clothes if they were to meet the Queen.

The royal party travelled due south from Bristol and over Dundry hill, which gave a fine distant view of the lake, before travelling at some speed through the local villages. In Chew Magna the party had to slow down, over the hump-backed bridge by the fire station and by the sharp bend at Hayes Pond corner, so the crowds could get a good view of the Queen and Prince Philip.

The villages were decorated in bunting, flags and flowers, transformed in preparation for the royal visit. Some even hung out 'Father's Pyjamas', which was a local joke. In Chew Magna, huge arches were covered in evergreens and banners, and there was a decorated maypole.

The Queen and party then drove down Denny Road from Bishop Sutton to the lake.

The Lord Bishop of Bath and Wells gave the dedication.

The Queen stopped to have a special word with Miss C M Rees-Mogg, who was the Chairman of the Clutton Rural District Council.

The Queen, crowds and bunting in the background, with the Chairman of Bristol Water | Courtesy of Bristol Water

The Queen and Prince Philip, with the Royal Guards and the band in the background | Courtesy of Bristol Water

After viewing the plaque and commemoration stone, the Queen was introduced to several of the workmen. She then left for Woodford Lodge, which is named after an old lodge that was then submerged under the lake. The Queen said that the Chew Stoke Reservoir (as it was then called) 'will be one of the most extensive man-made lakes in the country.'

The national anthem was played to the cheering crowds.

As some there said, it was a wonderful day, nothing like it will come again.

One of the official invitations to the event | Courtesy of Bristol Water

The Queen walks down the impressively straight lines of Royal Guards | Courtesy of Bristol Water

THE HISTORY OF CHEW VALLEY LAKE

Some later developments

It wasn't until 1958 that the lake was finally filled up.

Very soon, wildlife discovered the new habitat and began to colonise the wetlands. There was an influx of wild geese and various breeds of duck, as well as other water birds such as coot. Migrating birds discovered the lake and rarities began to crop up from time to time, bringing early twitchers and local birdwatchers alike. Warblers started breeding in numbers, as the waters and adjoining fields were enriched by the insect life and decaying vegetation that was drowned by the rising waters.

Swarms of midges and other flies hatched on spring and summer days. These were an unexpected nuisance to local people, as shown by various articles in the newspapers at the time. Various ingenious means were attempted to reduce the problem, but the trout also fed on them and quickly grew to a great size. Some bird hides were put up, and the ringing station was started near to Herriott's Bridge, close to the main reedbeds. Sir Peter Scott came down from Slimbridge and worked with local naturalists, and local children were encouraged by him to take an interest. A television recording first shown in 1971, 'Man Made for Nature', exists as a record of these early days.

In 1972, the first picnic and car park areas were made to provide access for the general public. The ground on the eastern end of the dam was landscaped and first a visitors' centre and a toilet block and snack bar were built. Later a café was added.

The Bristol Water staff used a specially designed raft around this time to assist in moving heavy material around the lake, and this was given the name 'Kon-Tiki' after Thor Heyerdahl's famous raft that navigated the Pacific.

February 1958, the first time the water actually overflowed the dam and the spillway | *Courtesy of Bristol Water

The Picnic Area in the early days, August 1973. Very different to how it is today | Courtesy of Bristol Water

In addition, an area further to the south was developed, complete with nature trails. The whole of this side of the lake is an attractive viewing area, as are the lay-bys at Herriott's Bridge and Herons Green. Finally, at Woodford Lodge a restaurant has been added.

With such an attractive environment and body of water, it is not surprising that people wanted to use it for other pursuits, and these are covered in the next chapter.

And finally...

The Chew Valley has seen many changes in its long history of human settlement, but few have been more dramatic than the creation of the lake. It is now seventy years since its creation, and there were of course those that were adversely affected by the flooding of a pretty and productive valley. What we have now, however, is a beautiful and priceless asset that is enjoyed by thousands of people every year.

References

The Harptrees History Society (2009). *Before the Lake, Memories of the Chew Valley*. (Note first published 2004.)
P A Rahtz, E Greenfield, et multi alii. (1978). *Excavations of Palaeolithic to post-medieval material at Chew Valley Lake, Somerset Avon*.
Peter Harris (2006). *Clifton and Durdham Downs: a place for Public Resource and Recreation*. Local history pamphlet. The Bristol Branch of the Historical Association. **ISSN 1362 7759**
Emily La Trobe-Bateman (1999). *Avon Extensive Urban Survey*. Archaeological Assessment Report for Bath and Northeast Somerset Council.
A History of the County of Somerset, volume 1. Originally published by Victoria County History, London, 1906
David Higgins (2005). *The History of the Bristol Region in the Roman Period*. Bristol Branch of the Historical Association.
Peter Ellis (1992). *Mendip Hills: An Archaeological Study of the AONB*. Report to Somerset County Council and English Heritage.
Chew Valley Lake and other civil engineering contracts, A.E.Farr, Westbury, Wiltshire, 1958.
Bristol Bird Reports, Bristol Naturalists' Society
E M Palmer and D K Ballance (1968). *The Birds of Somerset.*Longmans.
David K. Ballance (2006). *A History of the Birds of Somerset*. Isabelline Books.
A Golden Day at Chew. Memories of the day the Queen came to open Chew Lake, 17 April 1956. DVD, a Chew Valley Films Production, © Bristol Water 2006.

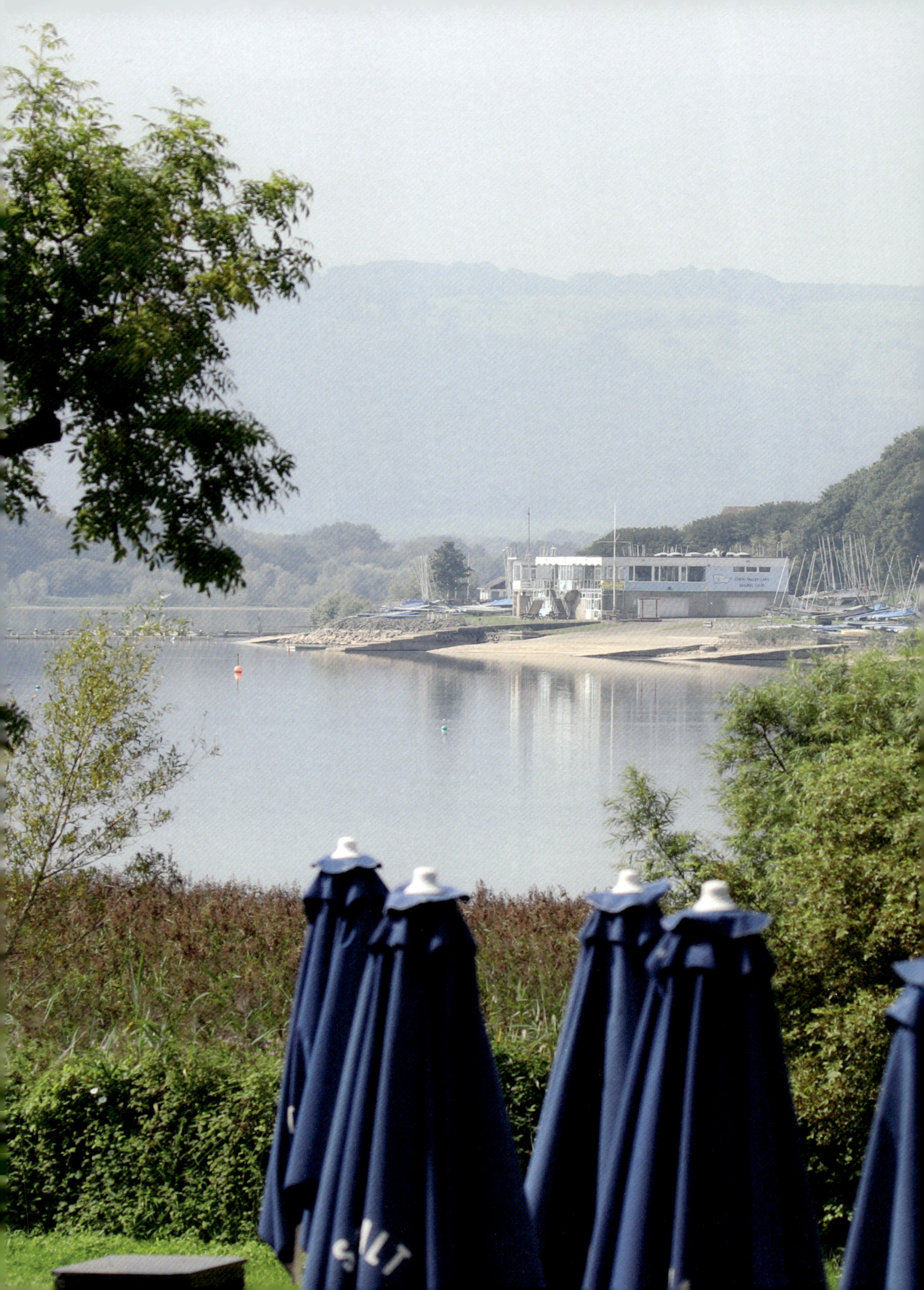

Leisure at the lake

John Rossetti

Additional information from Martin Cottis and Bristol Water, and historical details taken from the book '*Before the Lake*' (see the 'History of Chew Valley Lake' chapter).

Picnic areas and walks
Fishing
Sailing

Many people come to the lake every year simply to enjoy the beautiful surroundings. Some may be looking for a peaceful walk and to get close to nature, maybe to escape from the hustle of modern life. Others may want a family picnic or a spot of lunch. While some will test their skill at fishing, or take on the excitement of sailing, in every type of weather.

LEISURE AT THE LAKE

Picnic areas and walks

There are many areas from where you can access or look over the lake, and these are shown on the map opposite. By car, the parking areas at Herriott's Bridge and at Heron's Green Bay allow great views; many birds are seen from here, and if you're lucky you can also see other wildlife such as Roe Deer and even Otters. On most days you can also treat yourself to an ice cream.

If you want to get closer to the lake, the two picnic areas on the North Shore are wonderful places, and Woodford Lodge on the West side has free parking, and a great terrace on which to eat and drink while having a panoramic view of the lake. The lodge also has a restaurant that may be booked and is the centre for the fly-fishing activities and permits. The grounds also include the peaceful 'life for a life' memorial woodlands.

The lodge is also where you can get daily or annual birdwatching permits, available to members of recognised ornithological and naturalist societies. This will allow access to the hides and routes that are marked in red on the map.

Picnic Area 1 is also home to 'Salt & Malt', which is a great place for inside eating or takeaway, as well as outside under the umbrellas to provide protection from sun or rain.

As the name suggests, the staple is great British fish and chips. You can get a meal any time of day, be it breakfast favourites from poached eggs and the full English, through to lunch, serving quiche, soup and of course fish and chips. They also offer afternoon tea with a range of cakes, tray-bakes, scones and hot drinks. It is normally open from Wednesday to Sunday, best to check on their web site.

Parking is metered, free for permit holders and with discounts offered if you use the services of Salt & Malt. If you are a regular visitor, you can also get an annual parking ticket for both areas (currently £20) and get your car sticker from here or Woodford Lodge. From here you may walk along the path by the lake towards the other picnic area and its walks, or you may simply drive a couple of minutes to arrive there under the shade of the trees.

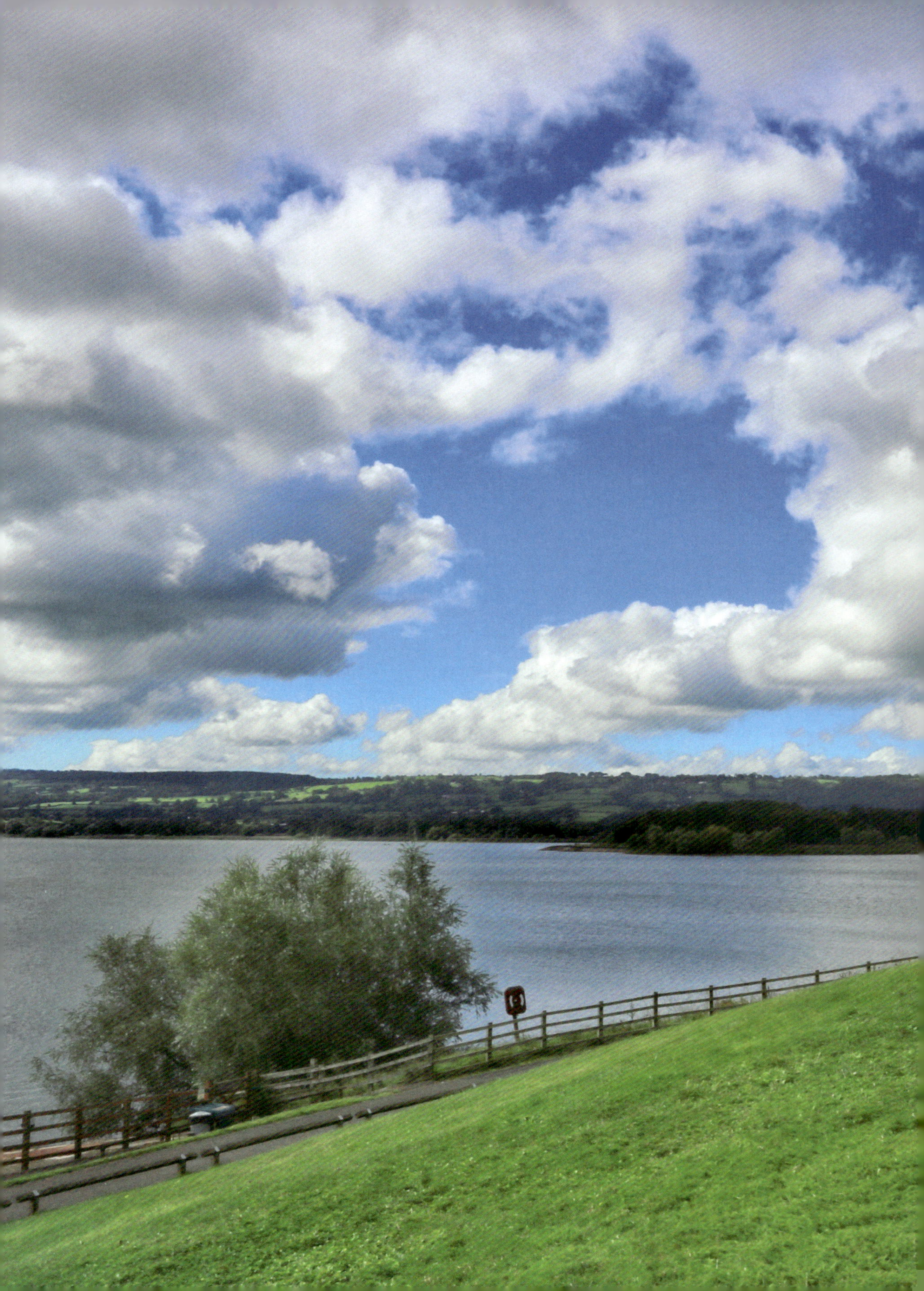

Woodford Lodge | Lucy Masters

No wind for boats? Becalmed sailing club from Picnic Area 1 | John Rossetti

Quiet relaxation at Picnic Area 1 | Lucy Masters

Picnic Area 2 and the trails

The lake is designated as an SSSI (Site of Special Scientific Interest) and is also a Special Protection Area (SPA). You can explore part of this environment by trails from this parking area. The first one you come to is the Grebe trail, which starts from the south end of the car park. This is a hard-surfaced, all-weather path, suitable for pedestrians, pushchairs and wheelchairs. It provides a 1.2 km circuit.

View of the lake from the Grebe trail | Lucy Masters

    The Bittern Trail is accessible as an extension to the Grebe trail. Following the footbridge over Hollow Brook, the path is not surfaced and can be wet and muddy, so boots or wellies are advisable.
    This trail runs along Twycross and the East Shore and is the route to the open bird hide which overlooks Denny Island. This is a great spot to see many species of bird both in the water and in the island's trees, often also wading birds when the water levels are not too high. But look out all along the trail, there is lots to find.
    You may then go back the way you came or complete the 1.5 km circuit. Don't forget to bring a picnic in good weather and enjoy being beside the lake.

Some leisure activities are occasional visitors! | Lucy Masters

Fishing

Today and yesterday

Fishing has always been an important activity at the lake for many years, and at the nearby Blagdon reservoir.

Chew is well renowned for its scenic beauty and top-quality fly-fishing. The size and condition of the trout caught here is second to none, and anglers find success using a wide variety of fishing methods and fly patterns making it a popular competition venue. Chew is a relatively shallow reservoir with an average depth of only 14ft at top level and a maximum depth of just 37ft. The area it covers, once rich farmland, is now fertile ground for the aquatic life necessary for sustaining quality trout fishing.

But we also know that the River Chew had been fished for very many years before the lake was even thought about. The Chew Valley, because of its proximity to Bristol, has always attracted city dwellers to its quiet leafy lanes and the tranquillity of the river. On Sundays and public holidays, walking and cycling in the countryside were popular escapes from the noise and grime of weekday life.

In fact, not all visitors to the valley returned to Bristol after their day out, as several farms took in paying guests. Denny House Farm was always popular. People used to come for holidays, not just for bed and breakfast, and would stay for a week with full board.

Locals had always fished in the river, but strictly speaking this was poaching. The right to fish in the Chew had belonged to individuals for many years. Originally, these would probably all have belonged to the lords of the manors, and in 1630 the lord of the manor of East Harptree had fishing rights extending from Sherborne to the church bridge in East Harptree. However by the 1930s the fishing rights to most stretches of the river and its tributaries were rented by clubs. For example, the Knowle Angling Association's rights included most of the stretch of the Chew now under the lake. Other clubs included the Golden Carp, the City of Bristol, and Avon and Tributaries. The fishing was mainly for coarse fish and some trout.

In fact, the river held almost every type of freshwater fish. People recalled that you wouldn't find any water that did not have Pike in it, and they were a menace because they love fish.

Patient perseverance on the quiet waters | Ian Stapp

> *I can remember the dace. Now dace will go for your fly, but if you think trout fishing with a fly is difficult then try catching dace. You could drop the fly on the water; the dace will come, take hold of it and spit it out before you can blink. I reckon you might catch one for every 100 fish. There were chub in the river. I can remember that because chub is quite a nice fish.*

> *It was of course very different times in those days. If you were coming from Bristol, it meant cycling all the way. If your half-day was Wednesday and you didn't catch a fish on Wednesday afternoon, then Thursday lunch was egg and chips!*

This quote gives us a feel of how it was before the fish were stocked, and about the environment, much of which has returned in recent years.

> *You would often catch a trout that weighed say a pound and a quarter. The further upstream you went, the stream got narrower and shallower. It was much more difficult to catch the trout. Part of the joy of fishing was the environment. One great thing in those days – we had Otters and we used to curse them. I was sat on the river bank one day, minding my own business, fishing quietly in this cow drink as we called it (where the cows went in to drink – a good place to fish because the cows stirred up the mud and therefore food for the fish) and I heard this curious barking noise. I turned round – an Otter. That Otter wanted to go in the cow drink and he was letting me know. Eventually the penny dropped and I moved away and that blasted Otter went in there and within two minutes he was out with a trout, walking back up the bank.*

There was at least one benefit though.

> *I've also fallen asleep and lost food to water creatures, water voles. Some of them were quite big. Stoats were very prevalent in those days and if you wanted to see Kingfishers, go to the Chew, but we didn't have Cormorants in those days, thank God.*

LEISURE AT THE LAKE

Cormorants today are not the fishermen's friends | Ian Stapp

Today's fishing in the lake

We are indebted for this section to Martin Cottis, who has provided many of the photographs, sometimes taken by clients on his camera! He started fishing the lakes in 1976 when he was teaching in London, but then more regularly from 1980 onwards after moving to Devizes. He set up as an instructor and guide in 1999 and now organises and runs beginners' classes as well as a mentoring scheme, as many beginners just cannot get into the fishing without some sort of help. He also organises 'Family Fishing' weekends on behalf of Bristol Water.

There are few anglers in England who can match Martin's expertise on Chew Valley and Blagdon Lakes. He is an undisputed expert and renowned throughout the country for his dry-fly fishing skills. He has an unmatched record of having won the Bristol Reservoirs Fly Fishers' Association's Orvis competition four times and represented England at Loch Style Home International level.

He considers that he has a fantastic 'office' at Chew and Blagdon Lakes, and considers himself very lucky to have such a job.

Buzzers

Collectively referred to as 'buzzers' by fishermen, the chironomid or non-biting midges consist of over 400 species, and buzzers are the most important insect group to stillwater trout and fly fishermen.

As the water starts to warm in the early season buzzer hatches can be prolific, before giving way to a rich larder of non-hatching aquatic insects later in the season such as corixa, snail, hoglice and shrimp. Many trout fishers look forward to the buzzer season, the tell-tale signs being the clouds of buzzers rising like smoke from the bushes. They swarm and sway in the lightest of breezes above treetops and hedges.

The other and often best indication is to watch the migratory swifts and swallows. The birds majestically cover the skies, often hundreds of feet up, then within minutes they glide inches above the surface at incredible speeds and turning like high-speed bikes on a double chicane. The hatch has started. As buzzers can make up 90 per cent of the trout's natural diet, there is no more important method to perfect than this – and it truly is the most exciting method to fish.

With such an abundance of natural feed at the lake, fishing imitative dries, emergers and nymphs on floating lines prove very popular to regular fishermen here. Chew has an excellent capacity for producing grown-on fish, and the lake records stand at 22lb 7oz for Brown Trout and 14lb 9oz for Rainbow Trout.

Martin Cottis with a fine brown trout.

The largest Brown Trout Martin has caught. At 34 inches would have been about 15 lbs in weight. Immediately returned to the water, with photo taken by a Canadian client.

The fishing areas at the lake

The deepest part of the lake is by the Dam and the outlet tower, where the steeply sloping shores of Walley Bank and the North Shore put depths of up to 20ft within the reach of bank anglers. Southwards the lake gets progressively shallower towards Herriott's, where the upper River Chew enters the Lake. Chew is fortunate that it does not only rely only on the lake shore to contribute towards its productivity, as large offshore areas around Little Denny and the Roman Shallows grow dense weed beds in the warmer months providing further valuable habitat for insect life.

Day and afternoon bank fishing permits are available at Woodford Lodge. No fishing is allowed from the Dam or stone embankments, the Sailing Club, in front of the Picnic Areas and in the Nature Reserve.

There is also a Wheely Boat at Chew. This boat, specially designed for use by anglers in wheelchairs, is available by advance booking only. Lifejackets must be worn by all boat fishermen, and these are available for loan on request. Anchoring is not permitted from the Dam to the line of yellow buoys between the North Shore and Walley Bank. No boats are allowed in the area marked off by white buoys in front of the Stratford bird hide.

Pike fishing

Chew Valley Lake is home to monster pike with the lake record currently sitting at 44lb 6oz. A previous lake record pike of 40lb 8oz was caught by Mike Green on the fly and must represent one of the most unusual captures of fly-caught pike in the United Kingdom.

Chew Valley Lake is an ideal venue for fly fishing for pike. Large areas of reeds and weed beds combined with shallow depths over the majority of the lake means there is always the possibility of getting your flies near a pike. The most successful method for fly-caught pike is to drift over the large shallow areas around Stratford, Moreton and Herriott's and concentrate on getting your flies down to the correct depth. Popular line choices are intermediates and Di3 type lines with flies fished slowly a few feet above the bed of the lake.

Pike fly fishing is available throughout the trout fishing season on Chew Valley Lake. During periods of extreme water temperature or water quality issues, fishing for pike may be suspended to protect the welfare of the fish.

Pike fishing on the lake follows the Sustainable Pike Fishing approach set out by the Pike Anglers Club.

A Pike of 18 lbs taken on fly at Chew. What was also taken was this photo of Martin, by a client.

Other fish at the lake

Chew can also have very high densities of Roach.
It appears that this often leads to an increase in the Perch population, and these are also caught by the fishermen.

Two fine Perch. These were actually caught by Martin at Blagdon.

Mayfly evening | Martin Cottis

And finally ... It seems some even like to dress up! | Courtesy of Bristol Water

LEISURE AT THE LAKE

Sailing

With such a large and attractive lake close to Bristol, there are several activities that are enjoyed by many people. The picturesque surroundings make it a popular destination for walkers, picnickers, anglers and sailors as well as birdwatchers. So all have to work together and try as much as possible to minimise their effects on other lake users.

As regards the sailing, there are restrictions on sailing times, especially as regards leaving the lake in the evenings so that roosting birds are not disturbed. Additionally, the sailing area is designed to avoid disturbance to the SSSI areas such as reed beds. Inevitably there is disturbance to waterfowl in particular, especially at weekends, with movements between the other reservoirs in the area in particular Blagdon, Cheddar and Barrow.

Chew has a large sailing area, approximately 3 km long. It is divided into two areas, the restricted area and the full area. The full area can be used throughout the winter and on Sunday afternoons, although in recent years this restriction has not been applied, enabling the use of the whole sailable area all year round.

Sailing Club history

There is in fact a long history of sailing at the lake, with the club starting in 1967.

In 2012, a book was produced called *The First 45 Years of Chew Valley Lake Sailing Club 1967 to 2012*. This was put together by three club members of many years, who wanted the history to be recorded before it was too late. Those three guys were the late Peter Cheek, a founder member of the club, David Macklin, also a founder member, and Brian Brooks. They set about putting plans in place that would hopefully chart the history of the C.V.L.S.C. Whilst writing about the very early days, David Macklin spent many hours sifting through available early minutes, some of his own, and some of those fortunately saved and given to him by Frank Webb, another of the initial founders.

Sailing, rain or shine | Errol Edwards

Laser Class dinghies | Errol Edwards

In it they describe some of the colourful political history that gave rise to the club's formation. The first Commodore of the club, John Norman, said that things started with a government decision to encourage water companies to be less restrictive in access to their properties. Interest started from the Pegasus Sailing Club who were based at Uphill on the rather inhospitable Bristol Channel. They felt that sailing on the lake in the Chew Valley would be a dream worth pursuing.

Following an approach to the then Bristol Waterworks Company, they received the response of 'Over my Dead Body!' from the Fisheries officer of the time. However, in 1964 the Labour Government appointed Dennis Howell as the first Minister of Sport, who said '*Inland waters are to be made available for recreation, or the general public will take them over*'.

To the surprise of the newly formed club, they received a government grant to help build the clubhouse, and the club launched its first boats in December 1967. The very first race was started by a government minister with a shotgun; sadly, there is no photograph of this event!

The book concentrates on a club owned and run by its members, who have all in one way or another played their parts in the development of this club and put it where it is today; a premier sailing club in Britain.

Current members may be rather jealous of the early costs to join the club:

	Guineas	Shillings	Pence
Entry fee:	10		
Single:	3		
Family:	5		
Non-sailing:	1		
Junior:		30	
Cruising non-members:		2	6

(A Guinea is £1 and 1 Shilling, i.e. £1.05 today)

LEISURE AT THE LAKE

Chew Valley Lake Sailing Club

The club celebrated its Golden Anniversary in 2017 and a number of special activities took place. This also included the launching of the new logo and corporate identity. Fifty years before, when the Chew Valley had only recently been flooded, the colours of green and gold had been relevant. But with the club having established its reputation as one of the leading professional sailing organisations in the South West, the shiny blues of the new logo seemed much more appropriate. Indeed, the club has gone from strength to strength over the years and, if you look in detail at the graphic you will see that the boat is now sailing on the 'crest of a wave'.

On the water, the club can easily cater for fleets of over one hundred boats and has in the past been called upon to host many large events. Five separate slipways enable easy launching. Off the water, the clubhouse facilities include large changing rooms, hot showers, a galley run by professional caterers (serving hot and cold lunches, light refreshments and drinks) at the weekends, a fully licensed bar and terrace overlooking the lake.

The club also caters for disabled people, with facilities on both floors and a lift.

The club is open for sailing on Wednesdays, Thursdays (limited hours) and every weekend with racing held on Wednesday evenings and Sundays. Various sailing courses are held at the club including RYA training, various youth training, powerboat training, race officer training as well as more informal training run within each fleet. A selection of dinghies is also available for members to try.

Club races may be started from the race hut at the south end of the terrace or from a committee boat anchored on the lake.

There is a sailing gate off the southern end of the clubhouse building, the transit of which is marked by two red and white poles in front of the race hut. The inner and outer distance marks have blue flags.

Having fun on the water. Sometimes looks more like a 'Wild Swimming' club | John Rossetti

LEISURE AT THE LAKE

Sailing Club events and activities

The Sailing Club is very active, caters for all types of people and boats, and also has well over one hundred races per year.

Handicap fleet

The Chew handicap fleet attracts a wide range of dinghies ranging from International 14s and RS800s all the way to Mirrors. We have recently divided the fleet into Fast Asymmetric and Conventional divisions allowing them to race over different courses, so the Fast Asymmetrics will sail on their preferred Windward/Leeward courses where practicable, whilst the rest of the fleet can enjoy a more varied course with a mix of beats runs and broad and tight reaches. The split is at PY 952, though we will allow the RS400s to choose which fleet they sail in and RS600s may opt for the conventional courses if they prefer.

The club boasts a number of sailors who are well placed in their respective open and national competitions including classes such as the RS800, RS700, RS600, Musto Skiff, Cherub, Fireball, Contender, Blaze, Scorpion and Finn. We are keen to encourage newcomers and there are a number of less complex and possibly more stable classes active at the club including the Buzz, Phantom, Kestrel, RS200, Laser 3000, Laser 2000, National 12, Wayfarer, Laser Vago, Europe, Miracle, Mirror and others.

Flying Fifteen Class

Chew Valley Lake provides a magnificent setting for sailing Flying Fifteens. The lake was formed when the valley was flooded to form a reservoir. The surrounding countryside is very beautiful and the lakeside is a nature reserve. The Mendip hills form a backdrop to the south and the local terrain alters the wind a little.

The club has a long history of producing distinguished sailors including the 2000 National Champion and the 2003 and 2007 Classic World Champion. It hosted the 2000 and 2007 Inland Championships – and the 2017 Flying Fifteen Inland Championships.

'Flying Fifteens' on the lake | Errol Edwards

Lasers at Chew Valley

Lasers at Chew have traditionally been a strong fleet and ex-members include Keith Wilkins (a former Olympic sailor with 12 world titles to his name) and Chris Gowers (former Olympic and Great Britain head coach). Current members include past and current champions at both European and National Masters level, backed by a strong racing fleet of over 50 boats taken from a current fleet of around 125 Lasers. There are usually in excess of 10 Lasers on the start line on a Sunday, and 25–35 on Wednesday evenings, with a full range of abilities. So, whether you are a hot-shot or a beginner you are sure to have someone to race against.

The one-design nature of the Laser class means that you don't need huge sums of money in order to buy a boat with winning potential. Second-hand Lasers can be picked up for as little as £500, and as long as the sail is fairly decent, you will be on a level playing field with the others in the fleet. This results in close and competitive racing at all levels. The Laser has additional advantages of being exceptionally quick to rig, requires virtually no maintenance and is cheap to insure. The smaller and interchangeable 4.7 and Radial rigs make the boat just as suitable for teenagers and light helms.

Solo

The National Solo is a classic, one-design, single-handed dinghy designed by Jack Holt in 1956 to be built in wood so that private builders could compete on a national basis with a recognised design and handicap rating. The Class Association now permits both individual constructors and commercial builders to produce the dinghy in a wide range of materials and construction methods, including the latest sandwich composites, while still complying with the class rules. The fully battened sail gives good performance in all weathers; the wide choice of rigs, foils and controls allows individuals to select the combination that best suits their sailing style and can be sailed competitively by a wide range of ages and weights.

The Chew Valley Lake Sailing Club has a well-established Solo fleet with about 30 members and a small racing fleet that competes throughout the year. It is a dinghy that provides close racing and Chew Valley has consistently produced a number of successful helms in both local and national events.

Short course

The short course racing group is specifically for the club's novice racers, and junior and youth sailors. As the name suggests the courses are generally shorter than the main club fleet courses, and the short course fleet is also the last start of the regular start sequence. This results in a much emptier, quieter start line, and a shorter overall race; perfect for the novice and younger racers at the club.

The short course is used in the main Sunday series throughout the year. Typical junior and youth boats racing in the Short Course start are Optimists, Teras, Fevas, Mirrors and Toppers. The Topper has fleet status at the club; historically this start was known as the Topper start, and that name is still often used around the club. The junior and youth boats are often joined by the club's novice racers. Any novice racer, sailing any class of boat, is welcome to sail in the short course group.

Disabled sailing

Chew Lake Association of Disabled Sailors (CLADS) is based at Chew and is a club for people with physical disabilities. We are linked to RYA Sailability. The club meets most Saturdays from April to October and welcomes new sailors and volunteer helpers

RYA training for members

Chew Valley Lake Sailing Club is an RYA (Royal Yachting Association) recognised training centre for dinghy sailing courses and powerboat courses. Training takes place on the lake in our fleet of training dinghies and RIBs, and in our dedicated training room. We have a friendly team of instructors ready to welcome you. Please note that CVLSC is not a commercial training centre, so courses are only available to club members.

Solo Sailing | Errol Edwards

Open events
Chew Valley Lake Sailing Club is situated just south of Bristol and is an ideal venue for open meetings and other sailing events. The sailing area is large enough to set Olympic style courses from either a shore or committee boat start, and large inflatable marks are used to avoid navigational confusion.

Members' experiences
Here are a couple of many stories from recent members of the club.

Anna's story
Since learning to sail in my late teens I've been completely hooked and can't get enough of it. So when I moved to Bristol a big priority was to find a sailing club and get out on the water. But having loved my previous club I was worried if I would find somewhere as friendly and fun – I need not have feared! I turned up on my own on a Saturday wondering with some trepidation if anyone would say hi. Unknown to me I was arriving just at the start of the ladies 'lake and cake' so was greeted by an enthusiastic bunch of about 15 ladies ready to spend a social afternoon sailing and then eat surprising amounts of cake. I got stuck in (to the cake that is!) and the rest, as they say, is history.

Becky & Jim – Returning to sailing
On one sunny summer afternoon six years ago, we stumbled into the sailing club and as luck would have it, bumped into an old friend. He grasped the nettle and showed us round; the convivial, friendly nature of the club was plain to see. So, we joined, albeit with a little apprehension. Jim was just fifty, Becky of an undisclosed, but younger, age! Becky has spent a lot of her life sailing, Jim less so but neither of us has sailed for a few years to any extent. The club boats combined with the help of friendly members got us on the water.

Membership places are currently available at Chew Valley Lake Sailing Club. We recommend that you visit the club to meet some of our members and see what we have to offer as we would be delighted to show you around. All membership applications are subject to an approval process which usually takes up to 2 weeks. You will be kept up to date by email regarding the status of your application. Membership runs from 1st April each year but you are welcome to join at any stage during the year.

Frostbite individual membership
This is available to members of other sailing clubs that do not offer racing during the winter. You may join Chew Valley Lake Sailing Club temporarily for the club racing which runs from 1st January to 31st March and includes the only scheduled races on Sundays (normally two – am and pm).

Out in the blue | Errol Edwards

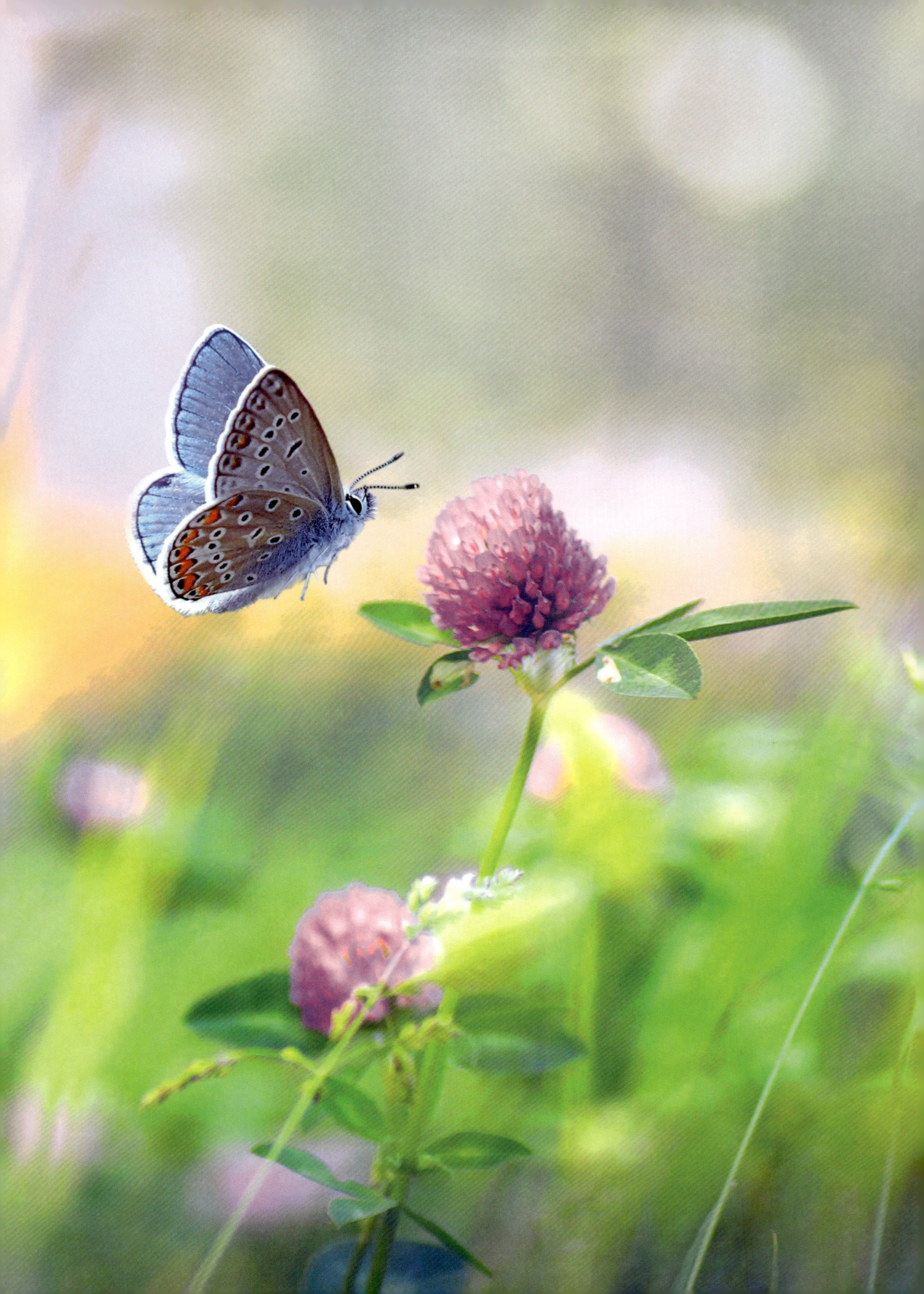

Ecology of the lake

Rupert Higgins

Flora
Vegetation and other non-animal life

Non-avian Fauna
Insects, amphibians, reptiles, mammals, fish and others

We have been able to watch and study the transforming ecology of the Chew Valley within a single lifetime. From the pleasure of flower-rich meadows to getting down close to investigate lower plants. All supporting a huge variety of animal life, beautiful damselflies and other insects as well as smaller life forms. Impressive fish, and even a glimpse into the world of bats.

Flora

Vegetation and other non-animal life

This section gives an overview of some of the many plant species to be found in and around Chew Valley Lake, focusing on flowering plants but with a mention also of so-called lower plants. I have been surveying, studying and simply enjoying the lake's plants for over thirty years, following in the footsteps of earlier botanists, and have seen much to interest both the casual naturalist and the expert botanist.

Chew Valley Lake and its associated hedges, plantations and meadows support in excess of 200 species of vascular plants (flowering plants, ferns and allied groups). This is not in itself an exceptional total, but populations of some species are regionally important, and those of many others are of ecological or historical interest, or are simply beautiful, increasing the pleasure of visits to the lake.

The plants of most significance to the birds are those growing within, on, or above the lake: submerged, floating and emergent species. It is changes in the populations of these plants, themselves a response to changing environmental conditions, that have driven many of the changes in the lake's birdlife. Submerged plants are important in providing food for species such as Mute Swan, Gadwall and Pochard, as well as habitat for the invertebrates that are fed on by species such as Tufted Duck. They also provide shelter for fish.

Dramatic changes in the abundance of various submerged plants have occurred in the last two decades, but unfortunately their populations are difficult to survey with any accuracy. The species diversity can be roughly monitored from fragments washed up on the lake's edge, but a systematic boat-based survey is required to assess the distribution and abundance of submerged vegetation. One such series of surveys was carried out by University of Bristol biologists, who were commissioned to investigate water quality in the mid-1970s. They found an extremely limited diversity of water plants growing in small patches only. Areas dominated by Fennel-leaved Pondweed *Stuckenia pectinata* were present off the East Shore, over Denny Shallows, in the mouth of Heron's Green Bay and off Moreton Point.

Patches of Amphibious Bistort *Persicaria amphibia* were noted on the edges of Villice Bay, Heron's Green Bay, Moreton Bank and Spring Bay. The rest of the lake was barren, in contrast to the nearby but much older Blagdon Lake, which had extensive mixed underwater lawns of pondweeds and stoneworts.

Flower-rich meadows, one of the lake's foremost botanical treasures. Ox-eye Daisy, Black Knapweed and Dyer's Greenweed are the most obvious here | Rupert Higgins

The authors attributed the paucity of Chew's submerged vegetation to phosphate pollution, exacerbated by wave action. During the 1990s it became apparent that this situation was changing drastically: large growths of plants could be seen in late summer in areas such as Villice Bay and Herriott's End and new species were colonising the lake. One of these, Fan-leaved Water Crowfoot *Ranunculus circinatus*, first appeared in 2003 and rapidly became so abundant that sheets of its flowers could be seen, if not identified, from as far away as Dundry Hill.

In some years, growths of water plants in Heron's Green Bay and Herriott's End are now sufficiently dense to support the weight of birds such as Lapwing and Black-headed Gull. I was fortunate enough to be commissioned by Bristol Water to carry out a survey of invasive non-native plants at the lake in 2015 and took the opportunity to record and map submerged vegetation in the process. This survey confirmed that the underwater environment at Chew no longer bore any resemblance to that described in 1975. Only small areas off Whalley Bank, where the lake is at its deepest, were unvegetated. Stoneworts, complex and large algae whose absence was commented on in the earlier study, were abundant in deeper water, and included the nationally rare Starry

Some marginal vegetation at Sutton Wick, most prominently Creeping Thistle, Meadowsweet, Marsh Woundwort and Water Mint | Rupert Higgins

Stonewort *Nitellopsis obtusa*, which covered large areas. In shallower waters there were mixed patches of Canadian and Nuttall's Pondweeds *Elodea canadensis* and *Elodea nuttallii*, Rigid Hornwort *Ceratophyllum demersum*, Spiked Water-milfoil *Myriophyllum spicatum*, various water crowfoots and five species of fine-leaved pondweeds (*Potamogeton pusillus, Potamogeton berchtoldii, Potamogeton trichoides, Stuckenia pectinata* and *Zannichellia palustris*). The obvious explanation for this drastic change is a gradual decline in phosphate and other pollution as sewage treatment in the catchment area has been improved, and as fertiliser use on farmland has decreased. However, the chemical balances that influence the growth of these plants are very complex. The possibility remains that a small change could shift the lake back into an ecosystem dominated by planktonic and filamentous algae, which would have severe consequences for water quality and wildlife alike.

A typical mixture of plants on the lake's late summer muddy margins: Golden Dock, Water Mint, Corn Mint and Gypsywort are all visible here | Rupert Higgins

Marsh Ragwort at Moreton Bank | Rupert Higgins

ECOLOGY OF THE LAKE

Bearded Tit is one of the species that occurs almost exclusively in reed beds | Lucy Masters

The changes in the emergent vegetation around the lake's edge have been equally significant. The most obvious has been the dramatic spread in Common Reed *Phragmites australis*, which typically forms virtually mono-specific stands that are of low botanical interest but are of immense importance for birds. Large reed beds had formed by the 1970s and these have now spread to dominate virtually the entire shoreline of the lake.

The potential for further spread into deeper water is ecologically limited since Common Reed cannot survive in water more than around one metre deep. There are, however, small areas of shore it has yet to colonise, notably around Villice Bay. The vegetation in these remaining areas is much more diverse than it is within the reedbeds. It includes stands of Amphibious Bistort *Persicaria amphibia* and Marestail *Hippuris vulgaris* in shallow water and mixed patches of sedges *Carex spp*, Flowering Rush *Butomus umbellatus*, Branched Bur-reed *Sparganium erectum*, Sea Club-rush *Bolboschoenus maritimus*, Purple Loosestrife *Lythrum salicaria*, Horse Radish *Armoracia rusticana* and other plants on the water's edge.

A further habitat becomes available when the lake's water level drops and bare mud is colonised by a mixture of plants known as an 'inundation community'. Some of these are specialists of this unusual habitat and they include several of the most uncommon plants recorded at Chew. These include Round-fruited Rush *Juncus compressus* and Golden Dock *Rumex maritimus*, which are widely distributed around the lake and appear annually amongst more common species such as Water Forget-me-not *Myosotis scorpioides*, Marsh Cudweed *Gnaphalium uliginosum* and Water Chickweed *Stellaria aquatica*. Mudwort *Limosella aquatica*, Northern Yellow-cress *Rorippa islandica* and Orange Foxtail *Alopecurus aequalis* are nationally scarce and are more sporadic in their occurrence. All three have been discovered at the lake since 1995; it is hard to know whether this indicates that species-richness is increasing or that it is a reflection of the difficulty of finding and identifying these plants.

One oddity of the lake's plant life is the presence in the inundation community of Slender Mugwort *Artemisia biennis*, first found here in 1961. This plant is native to North America, and elsewhere in Britain it has generally been recorded at sites such as docks and grain warehouses, where it has failed to persist for more than a single growing season. How it reached Chew, and why it has found it so much more to its liking than the rest of Britain, remains a mystery. In 2015 it appeared at Blagdon; it will be interesting to see how it fares there.

Many other species growing in the inundation community are far more widespread, often exploiting bare soils on agricultural land and in places such as development sites. They include Corn Mint *Mentha arvensis* and Scarlet Pimpernel *Lysimachia arvensis*, as well as various mayweeds, oraches and goosefoots. These species' adaptation to rapidly and opportunistically colonise an ephemeral habitat whose appearance is unpredictable, means that many of them produce enormous quantities of seed. As rising water levels drown the vegetation, usually in the early winter, this seed can be enormously important for dabbling ducks, especially Teal.

Away from the lake itself, the most botanically significant habitats within the reservoir enclosure are the meadows and other grasslands. In order to protect water quality, the use of fertilisers on these areas has not been allowed since the reservoir was established. This has meant that they have escaped the destructive agricultural practices, known as 'improvement', that caused the loss of almost all of our species-rich grassland in the second half of the twentieth century.

Flowering Rush grows in the few places that have not been invaded by reeds on the lake's margins | Rupert Higgins

A scarce plant that appears as water levels drop: Orange Foxtail | Rupert Higgins

Purple Loosestrife and Meadowsweet dominate a patch of wetland vegetation by the Bittern Trail | Rupert Higgins

A nice old pollarded Pendunculate Oak.
This is a vestige of a far older landscape, on the north shore of Heron's Green Bay | Rupert Higgins

Patches of Heath Spotted Orchid, sometimes with the rare hybrid with Southern March Orchid, have grown in size in recent years | Rupert Higgins

The fate of unimproved grassland is exemplified by Green-winged Orchid *Anacamptis morio*, which is present in very large numbers in grasslands on the western side of the lake. This has been put forward as the British plant that has undergone steeper population declines in recent decades than any other species. It was formerly sufficiently widespread to gather numerous vernacular names – one local version was the inexplicable goosey-ganders – but it is now restricted to a few select sites, with Chew supporting the largest colony I have ever seen. Green-winged Orchid seems to be holding its own at the lake but some other orchid species appear to be spreading. These include the closely related trio of Common Spotted *Dactylorhiza fuchsii*, Heath Spotted *Dactylorhiza maculata* and Southern Marsh *Dactylorhiza praetermissa* orchids, with puzzling plants appearing intermediate between all three species.

Other attractive plants that remain abundant in the species-rich grasslands around the lake include Dyer's Greenweed *Genista tinctoria*, Saw-wort *Serratula tinctoria*, Betony *Betonica officinalis*, Devil's-bit Scabious *Succisa pratensis* and Adder's-tongue Fern *Ophioglossum vulgatum*, all of which have disappeared from most farms.

One oddity of the grasslands at Chew is that several areas have a mixture of herb species that are characteristic of neutral grassland but their dominant grass is Upright Brome *Bromopsis erecta*, which is characteristic of calcareous grassland. This unusual combination, which is also evident around Blagdon Lake, presumably reveals some unusual characteristic of the underlying soil.

Betony is one of the characteristic meadow flowers at Chew | Rupert Higgins

ECOLOGY OF THE LAKE

Stump Puffball is a common saproxylic (feeding on dead wood) fungus in woodlands around the lake | Rupert Higgins

The hedges can be divided into two categories. Many were planted when the lake was flooded and are generally dominated by a single species, often either Hornbeam *Carpinus betulus* or Hawthorn *Crataegus monogyna*. The more interesting are those that pre-date the creation of the lake. These generally have a wide variety of shrub and tree species, the most frequent of which is Hazel *Corylus avellana*. Hedges such as this are typical of the wider Chew Valley and provide evidence that the field systems and hedges here are of medieval origin and were established well before the better known 18th and 19th century enclosures. The ground flora of these hedges also provides evidence of their ancient origin and plants such as Bluebell *Hyacinthoides non-scripta*, Greater Stitchwort *Stellaria holostea* and Sweet Violet *Viola odorata* are abundant in spring. Primroses *Primula vulgaris* in the hedges have crossed with Cowslips *Primula veris* in the grasslands in several places around the lake, resulting in striking clumps of the hybrid False Oxlip *Primula x polyantha*.

A dense growth of Devil's-bit Scabious at Villice Bay | Rupert Higgins

False Oxlip, the hybrid between Primrose and Cowslip, adds early spring colour to hedge banks around the lake | Rupert Higgins

The lake's rarest flowering plant, Bithynian Vetch, with Dyer's Greenweed,
a declining indicator species of unimproved grassland, in the background | Rupert Higgins

One of the rarest plants found around the lake, Bithynian Vetch *Vicia bithynica*, is present on a hedge bank near Villice Bay. It seemed to have disappeared and despite annual searches was not seen between 1985 and 2017. It then reappeared after the adjacent hedge was re-laid, presumably profiting from increases in light levels and disturbance to the soil, and showing impressive seed longevity. A larger colony is present on a nearby road verge, forming a fine display with Dyer's Greenweed *Genista tinctoria*, Grass Vetchling *Lathyrus nissolia* and Zig-zag Clover *Trifolium medium*.

Nearly all of the woodlands around the lake are plantations that were designed by a landscape architect in order to blend the reservoir into its surroundings. A variety of species were used, resulting in blocks dominated by poplar cultivars, European Larch *Larix decidua*, Corsican Pine *Pinus nigra*, Silver Birch *Betula pendula* and other species. To the contemporary eye many appear rather alien and intrusive.

Ivy *Hedera helix* covers the floor of many of the plantations but several are becoming more species-rich as woodland plants slowly colonise, usually from remnant hedges. These plants include Bluebell *Hyacinthoides non-scripta*, Primrose *Primula vulgaris*, Moschatel *Adoxa moschatellina* and various ferns. Species present in smaller quantity include Spurge Laurel *Daphne laureola*, Wood Anemone *Anemone nemorosa* and Broad-leaved Helleborine *Epipactis helleborine*. More ecologically valuable are the woodlands that have developed close to the water's edge and are dominated by Alder *Alnus glutinosa* and various willow species. The ground flora of these areas is not exceptionally diverse but includes an unusual community of sedges and other wetland plants.

The woodlands around Chew are not especially rich in plants but *Colchicum autumnale* grows in a few places. Its distinctive appearance has earned it several English names, including Meadow Saffron, Autumn Crocus and Naked Ladies | Rupert Higgins

Wood Avens, a locally uncommon plant that occurs rarely in wet woodlands around the lake | Rupert Higgins

Cavernous Crystalwort is an uncommon liverwort that grows abundantly in late summer if the lake level drops | Rupert Higgins

The final habitat that should be mentioned are the stony banks forming lake edges at the dam, Heron's Green Bay and Herriott's Bridge. These are surprisingly rich in plants, including a strange mixture of wetland species such as Marsh Woundwort *Stachys palustris* and Purple Loosestrife *Lythrum salicaria*, plus species such as Biting Stonecrop *Sedum acre* and Rue-leaved Saxifrage *Saxifraga tridactylites* that are characteristic of very dry habitats. Several non-native species can be seen on these highly artificial habitats. Some, such as Snow-in-Summer *Cerastium tomentosum* and Lucerne *Medicago sativa*, seem permanently established here. A rarely seen plant, Bristly Hawkweed *Crepis setosa*, persisted at Herriott's Bridge for many years but now seems to have disappeared. Other species appear for one season and then disappear; most are introduced with bird seed and have included oddities like Blue Woodruff *Asperula arvensis* and Chia *Salvia hispanica*, as well as more frequent species such as Sunflower *Helianthemum annuus*, Millet *Panicum miliaceum* and Cockspur *Echinochloa crus-galli*.

The accounts above have focused on vascular plants and make little mention of the so-called lower plants: algae, mosses, liverworts, lichens and fungi, the last two not being plants at all. The lake has interest for all these groups.

The inundation zone is of particular importance for mosses and liverworts, with huge populations of Spreading Earth-moss *Aphanorrhegma patens* and Cavernous Crystalwort *Riccia cavernosa* obvious to anyone prepared to get down on their hands and knees, as well as less conspicuous populations of several other species. Lakeside willows have luxuriant and very species-rich populations of mosses, liverworts and lichens, which thrive in humid air. They used to include the descriptively named String-of-sausage Lichen *Usnea articulata* but this has unfortunately disappeared, presumably as a consequence of rising levels of nitrate pollution.

The Alder woodlands probably have the most value for fungi due to the presence of specialist species such as Alder Bolete *Gyrodon lividus*. The grasslands do not appear to be exceptionally rich in fungi, but several species of waxcap *Hygrocybe spp* can be seen on the Parkland and elsewhere. With all these groups there is doubtless much to be discovered.

Fly Agaric is a well-known species of fungus, one of many that forms a close association with trees. The fruiting bodies only appear every few years at Chew, when weather conditions are favourable | Rupert Higgins

Non-avian Fauna

Insects, amphibians, reptiles, mammals, fish and others

Birds are the star element of Chew Valley Lake's fauna but they are by no means the only animals of interest found around the lake. This section briefly describes some of the more important and obvious groups, and also highlights some significant gaps in our knowledge.

No group of animals at Chew Valley Lake has been as well studied as the birds, and none is of such importance. However, many birdwatchers have filled in quiet moments with observations of insects, and there have been some dedicated studies, notably of moths and bats. It is probably fair to say that we have reasonably complete knowledge of the lake's dragonflies (and damselflies), grasshoppers and related insects, moths, butterflies, hoverflies, reptiles and bats. However, little is known about many other animal groups. In particular, it would be good to have more information about the lake's fish and aquatic invertebrates, the relationships between fish and invertebrate populations, and the influence these have on bird numbers and diversity.

The lake is stocked annually with approximately 40,000 Rainbow Trout *Oncorhynchus mykiss* and Brown Trout *Salmo trutta*, the former massively outnumbering the latter. In the past some of these Brown Trout would breed in the lake's tributaries, but only sterile triploid fish are now stocked. The most numerous coarse fish is Roach *Rutilus rutilus*, a small species that forms shoals in open water and feeds largely on invertebrates. Its numbers fluctuate greatly from year to year, and there are also marked annual variations in the proportion of different age groups. There are no estimates of the numbers involved, but a visiting fish biologist told me in 2015 that the Roach densities are the highest he had ever seen, and some individuals have reached an exceptional size (for this species). Booms in the Roach population often seem to lead to large numbers of Perch *Perca fluviatilis*, which in turn are a favourite prey of herons and egrets.

The top predator within the lake is Pike *Esox lucius*; this species was introduced here in the mid-1990s and the early generations have reached an astonishing size: the largest caught to date weighed in at 44lb 6oz. There is some evidence that these monsters are suppressing younger cohorts, presumably by cannibalism. The Pike have almost certainly had an adverse impact on birds, particularly on breeding wildfowl. This is both by direct predation, especially of chicks, and also by supporting a much-increased population of Great Black-backed Gulls, which feed on dead Pike and also predate young birds.

One of the huge Pike that are now being caught at the lake | Martin Cottis

A photo of Caddis Flies during evening fishing on the lake | Martin Cottis

There is no denying, however, that the sight of huge Pike cruising through shallow water during their spring spawning season is highly impressive. Numbers of other fish are relatively low and include Tench *Tinca tinca* and Rudd *Scardinius erythrophthalmus.* Common Eel *Anguilla anguilla* just about clings on at the lake and has been the subject of recent conservation efforts by Bristol Water plc.

The fish are sustained by huge populations of aquatic invertebrates but, as mentioned above, frustratingly little is known about these species. Studies carried out by University of Bristol biologists in the mid-1970s revealed much about groups such as planktonic micro-crustaceans, but it is likely that there have been enormous changes since then. A feature of the lake's early decades was huge emergences of non-biting midges (chironomids); the males of several species would lek in dense clouds over prominent features such as tall trees, where they resemble plumes of smoke. It appears that, after many years of decline, this spectacle is once again becoming more frequent. A systematic study of this group could reveal much about the lake's ecology.

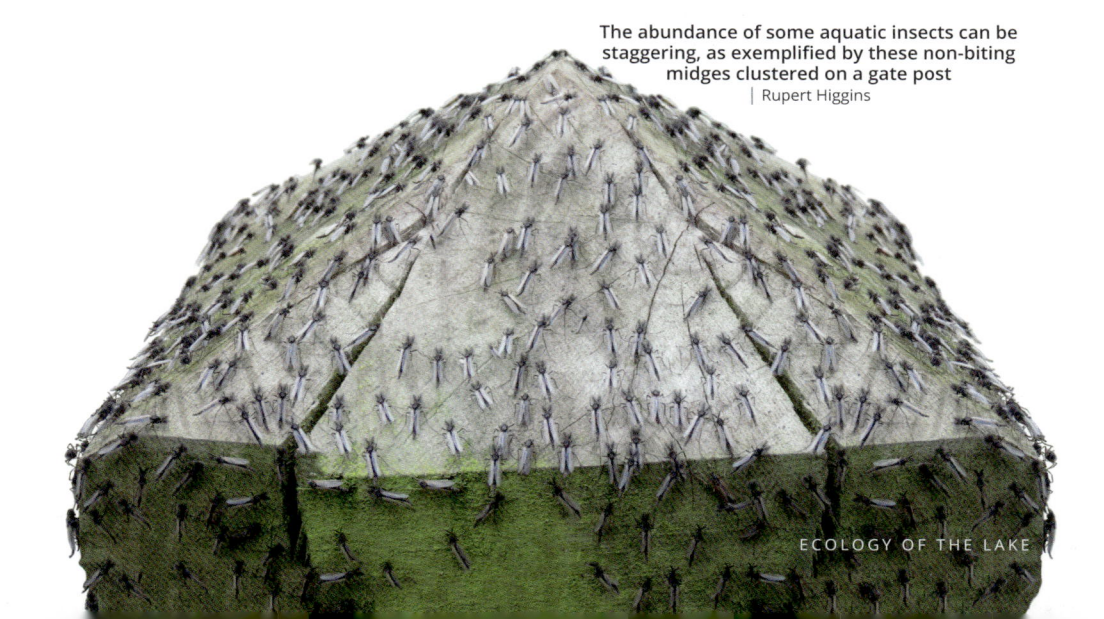

The abundance of some aquatic insects can be staggering, as exemplified by these non-biting midges clustered on a gate post
| Rupert Higgins

It is possible that some species of insect have become less abundant, and that this accounts for declines in passage waders, but this is pure speculation. Another abundant group are the lesser water boatmen (corixids). Very casual observations suggest that the frequency of these bugs varies enormously from year to year and that good boatmen years result in high counts of Tufted Duck. Caddisflies are a conspicuous element of the aquatic fauna; the adults can often to be seen fluttering over the reedbeds or at rest on wood. Several species are numerous, the most abundant being the Grousewing *Mystacides longicornis*.

Another insect that can be highly conspicuous on walls and vegetation around the lake is the Alderfly *Sialis lutaria*. Aquatic molluscs probably form an important component of the diet of several waterfowl species. Judging by the lines of shells that appear when water levels drop several species are numerous. These include pond snails such as *Bithynia tentaculata, Lymnaea stagnalis* and *Radix peregra;* ramshorns such as *Planorbis planorbis, Planorbis carinatus* and *Anisus leucostoma*; and pea mussels *Pisidium spp*. The large shells of swan mussel *Anodonta cygnea* sometimes turn up around the lake but seem to be less frequent than formerly.

The group that provides the exception to the rule of aquatic invertebrates being poorly studied is the Odonata (dragonflies and damselflies). These insects are attractive to birders (including myself), being large and colourful; the fact that several species are migratory, or are undergoing rapid range expansions, adds to their appeal. Chew supports enormous populations of some species, notably Azure Damselfly *Coenagrion puella* and Common Blue Damselfly *Enallagma cyathigerum*, which drift over the lake margins in incalculable numbers. Later in the year the dragonflies Common Darter *Sympetrum striolatum*, Southern Hawker *Aeshna cyanea* and Migrant Hawker *Aeshna mixta* are conspicuous.

An example of the difficulty of analysing population trends in insects is provided by the Ruddy Darter *Sympetrum sanguineum*. This species began to appear at the lake in large numbers in the mid-1980s, before then becoming scarce towards the end of the decade, but has since become more frequent again. No reason for these changes is apparent.

The dark green damselfly: Beautiful Demoiselle *Calopteryx virgo* is frequently seen around the lake's edges in late summer, having wandered from its breeding sites in nearby rivers and streams | Lucy Masters

Migrant Hawker *Aeshna mixta* would have been, at best, a rare visitor in the lake's early decades but is now an abundant resident. Adults emerge in mid-summer and can survive into November, favouring sheltered hunting areas including the hedges around the Stratford Bay car park | Lucy Masters

Emerald Damselfly *Lestes sponsa* appeared to be lost from the lake with no records for ten years, but has recovered in 2019 and 2020 | Rupert Higgins

A Great Pond Snail in shallow waters at the edge of the lake | Rupert Higgins

Ruddy Darter is abundant around the lake in some years but can then become rare for long periods | Rupert Higgins

Purple Hairstreak *Favonius quercus* is probably widespread around the lake but is difficult to spot owing to its habit of sticking to the tops of oak trees | Gary Thoburn

Emerald Damselfly *Lestes sponsa* has shown a similar but more pronounced trend. It was one of the lake's most abundant damselflies through the 1980s and 1990s but was then not seen for ten or more years before it reappeared in 2018. The same year saw colonisation by Small Red-eyed Damselfly *Erythromma viridulum*, although the sudden appearance of thousands of adults suggests strongly that individuals must have been present in at least one previous year. There have also been records in several recent years of Lesser Emperor *Anax parthenope*, and females have been seen ovipositing, suggesting that it might now be an established part of the lake's fauna. These insects are highly responsive to changes in climate and water quality and we can expect further arrivals, and perhaps departures, in coming years.

Canary-shouldered Thorn *Ennomos alniaria* is one of many moth species that is unlikely to be seen except at a light trap. It is a fairly widespread but seldom abundant species of hedges and woodlands | Rich Andrews

Orthoptera (grasshoppers and related insects) are another group showing a rapid response to climate change: Short-winged Conehead *Conocephalus dorsalis* and Lesser Marsh Grasshopper *Chorthippus albomarginatus* were first recorded in the early 1990s, and Long-winged Conehead *Conocephalus fuscus* and Roesel's Bush-cricket *Metrioptera roeselii* have colonised since. It is harder to identify species that have disappeared, but Common Green Grasshopper *Omocestus viridulus* appears much less numerous than previously.

Lepidoptera (moths and butterflies) are well-studied at the lake. The meadows support large numbers of widespread grassland butterflies including Marbled White *Melanargia galathea*, Meadow Brown *Maniola jurtina*, Common Blue *Polyommatus icarus* and Small Copper *Lycaena phlaeas*. Small Heath *Coenonympha pamphilus* was lost in about 1995 but Brown Argus *Aricia agestis* colonised at about the same time; this reflects wider and contrasting trends in the fortunes of the two species. Silver-washed Fritillary *Argynnis paphia* was formerly a rarity at the lake but small numbers are now regularly seen, suggesting recent colonisation. Its larval foodplants, violets, are reasonably frequent on hedge banks around the lake.

The mid-summer abundance of grassland moths such as Six-spot Burnet *Zygaena filipendulae*, Narrow-bordered Five-spot Burnet *Zygaena lonicerae*, Burnet Companion *Euclidia glyphica* and Shaded Broad-bar *Scotopteryx chenopodiata* in meadows around the lake is often striking. Other day-flying grassland moths, including Small Yellow Underwing *Panemeria tenebrata*, Mother Shipton *Callistege mi* and Chimney Sweeper *Odezia atrata*, are more localised around the lake and there is one record of Narrow-bordered Bee Hawkmoth *Hemaris tityus*. Latticed Heath *Chiasmia clathrata* is surprisingly absent.

Large Wainscot is one of several wainscot moths found in the lake's reedbeds; although similar in appearance they are not necessarily closely related taxonomically | Rupert Higgins

This hoverfly *Volucella inanis* is a relatively recent colonist of the lake. Its larvae are ectoparasites of social wasps and hornets | Lucy Masters

Common Green Colonel *Oplodontha viridula* is a more widespread species of freshwater habitats | Rupert Higgins

Nocturnal moths associated with the species-rich grasslands include Feathered Gothic *Tholera decimalis* and Slender Brindle *Apamea scolopacina*. Reed bed moths have been well studied by Mike Bailey, revealing significant populations of the following wainscots: Southern *Mythimna straminea*, Obscure *Leucania obsoleta*, Twin-spotted *Lenisa geminipuncta*, Brown-veined *Archanara dissoluta*, Large *Rhizedra lutosa* and Silky *Chilodes maritima*. Several other localised species associated with wetland habitats have been recorded; they include Crescent *Helotropha leucostigma* and Double Lobed *Apamea ophiogramma*. Light trapping has shown that a representative range of widespread moths associated with other habitats is present whilst daytime searching has turned up several scarce species of micro-moth.

Note that many species of insects, such as flies and beetles, do not have unique common English names and therefore are only described by their Latin or scientific names, although we provide the English names where we can.

Hoverflies are another group to attract interest and a wide variety of species has been recorded. Most are widespread but they include wetland specialists such as *Tropida scita*, *Lejogaster metallina* and *Riponnensia splendens*. Also relatively easy to find and identify are soldierflies, which include the large Flecked General *Stratiomys singularior*, a nationally scarce species more often associated with brackish ditches. Identification of most other flies is a specialist business and virtually all of our knowledge comes from surveys commissioned by David Gibbs of Bristol Water plc. He found several flies amongst the exceptional diversity of rare species he recorded. Snail-killing flies, another wetland group, were particularly well represented.

Searching flowerheads of umbellifers and composites in mid-summer can turn up a good variety of beetles, especially soldier beetles and longhorn beetles; the latter included the first record locally of Pear Shortwing Beetle *Glaphyra umbellatarum*. More conspicuous and widespread longhorn beetles that can be found around the lake include Spotted Longhorn *Rutpela maculata* and Black-spotted Longhorn *Rhagium mordax*. Bloody-nose Beetles *Timarcha tenebricosa* are often conspicuous, as both adults and larvae, and Black Oil Beetle *Meloe proscarabaeus* and Violet Oil Beetle *Meloe violaceus* can both be seen on occasion; the larvae of both are parasites of solitary bees. Beetles that can be found in the reedbeds include Water Ladybird *Anisosticta novemdecimpunctata* and the attractive red and black *Anthocomus rufus*. Exposed mud on the water margins provides rich hunting for ground beetles, including Copper Peacock *Elaphrus cupreus* and Green-socks Peacock *Elaphrus riparius*.

ECOLOGY OF THE LAKE

Spotted Longhorn Beetle *Rutpela maculata* is a familiar sight on flowers, especially Hogweed, around the lake. Its larvae develop in dead wood, a key habitat for many invertebrates | Gary Thoburn

Golden-bloomed Grey Longhorn Beetle *Agapanthia villosoviridescens* is a recent colonist of the lake's margins | Rupert Higgins

Perhaps the most obvious beetles at the lake are the leaf beetles, *Lochmaea caprea*, *Plagiodera versicola* and *Phratora vitellinae*, which defoliate many of the lakeside willows in some years, with the last-named being perhaps the most voracious. The trees always recover, either later in the summer or in the following year. Another conspicuous leaf beetle is the attractive green and red *Chrysolina polita*, which feeds on Water Mint and other wetland plants.

The lake is not exceptionally diverse in bees, lacking the crumbly soil that many mining species need, but those present include Large Carder Bumblebee *Bombus muscorum*, a declining species that requires extensive areas of flower-rich grassland. Several species of solitary bee can be found feeding on sallow flowers early in the year. Probably the most striking insect from the order Hymenoptera (bees, wasps, ants and allied groups) present is the Hornet *Vespa crabro*, another recent colonist that now nests in trees around the lake.

Grass Snake *Natrix natrix* is a declining species that is found in good numbers right around the lake; its most important prey species is Common Frog *Rana temporaria* | Gary Thoburn

The lake's margins support large breeding populations of Common Frog *Rana temporaria,* and large numbers of Common Toad *Bufo bufo* migrate each year to the north-western part of the lake. Smooth Newt *Lissotriton vulgaris* occurs in small numbers and Great Crested Newt *Triturus cristatus* breeds in ponds close to the lake margin. The only reptile present is Grass Snake *Natrix natrix*, which is locally frequent, making the lake locally important for this declining species.

Thirteen of the 37 species of mammal that have been recorded around the lake are bats. Large numbers of bat boxes have been provided and monitored by Nigel Milbourne. By far the most common species is the Soprano Pipistrelle *Pipistrellus pygmaeus*, and several maternity roosts have been identified in villages surrounding the lake. Soprano Pipistrelles are also the most frequent bat species found in the bat box scheme put up in 2015. This suggests that feeding conditions for bats are good around the lake but that there is a shortage of roosting opportunities.

A Lesser Horseshoe Bat in flight | Nigel Milbourne

Natterer's Bat in flight | Nigel Milbourne

Daubenton's Bat over water | Daniel Hargreaves

Moth's eye view of a Brown Long-eared Bat | Daniel Hargreaves

Other species found in the box scheme include Nathusius' Pipistrelle *Pipistrellus nathusii*, Brown Long-eared *Plecotus auritus*, Natterer's *Myotis nattereri* and Noctule *Nyctalus noctula*. Additional species confirmed as present during research trapping since 2015, include Greater Horseshoe *Rhinolophus ferrumequinum* and Lesser Horseshoe *Rhinolophus hipposideros*, Common Pipistrelle *Pipistrellus pipistrellus*, Daubenton's *Myotis daubentonii*, Whiskered *Myotis mystacinus*, and Serotine *Eptesicus serotinus*.

All bats are protected species, in the UK and also within the European Union, and so great care must be taken to avoid any disturbance, with licences required for research studies and other activities.

There is a monitored maternity roost of Lesser Horseshoe Bats at the lakeside that, albeit small, is probably increasing in size, which reflects the most recent published assessment that suggests the Lesser Horseshoe is undergoing a population increase and range extension from the southwest of England and Wales. However, the report also suggests that the current British population is only around 50,000 individuals. Lesser Horseshoe feed mainly in woodland and low over meadows but are rarely seen at dusk, preferring to emerge after dark.

Natterer's Bats are also recorded regularly during survey work at the lake, and although they will feed over water, they are usually associated with woodlands where they glean insects from foliage. They emerge well after dusk, so are unlikely to be seen by the public. This is another species for which there is no reliable population estimate in Britain.

Daubenton's Bat is frequently seen at dusk, flying low over the water surface while it is trawling for insects with its large hairy feet and tail membrane. The water bat, as this species is also known, is widespread across Britain but its population isn't known with any degree of confidence. It is however, a resident that is recorded regularly at Chew Valley.

The Noctule is one of the largest British species, and is readily seen flying high over the lakeside before dark in a characteristic direct flight on narrow wings, occasionally swooping down to chase an insect. It is widespread in England and Wales, but the latest estimates of population size are unreliable due to insufficient data.

A Mink popping into view at Herriott's | Gary Thoburn

Other mammals recorded include a colony of Harvest Mouse *Micromys minutus*, although it is not known whether this persists. Water Shrew *Neomys fodiens* is occasionally seen, more often dead than alive, and is probably fairly widespread. Polecat *Mustela putorius* and Otter *Lutra lutra* have both colonised the lake since the millennium; the latter can occasionally be seen during the day, its presence usually betrayed by the reaction of nearby birds.

American Mink *Neovison vison* appears to have become slightly less common, as do Stoat *Mustela erminea* and Weasel *Mustela nivalis*, which are seen very occasionally. Brown Hares *Lepus europaeus* do not appear to be resident but are occasionally seen, mostly in spring in the Heron's Green area. There are several Badger *Meles meles* setts around the lake and Foxes *Vulpes vulpes* are a familiar site, particularly in the late summer when they forage on exposed mud. Roe Deer *Capreolus capreolus* have become much more numerous in recent years and there have been records of Muntjac *Muntiacus reevesi*, although this species does not yet appear to have become permanently established.

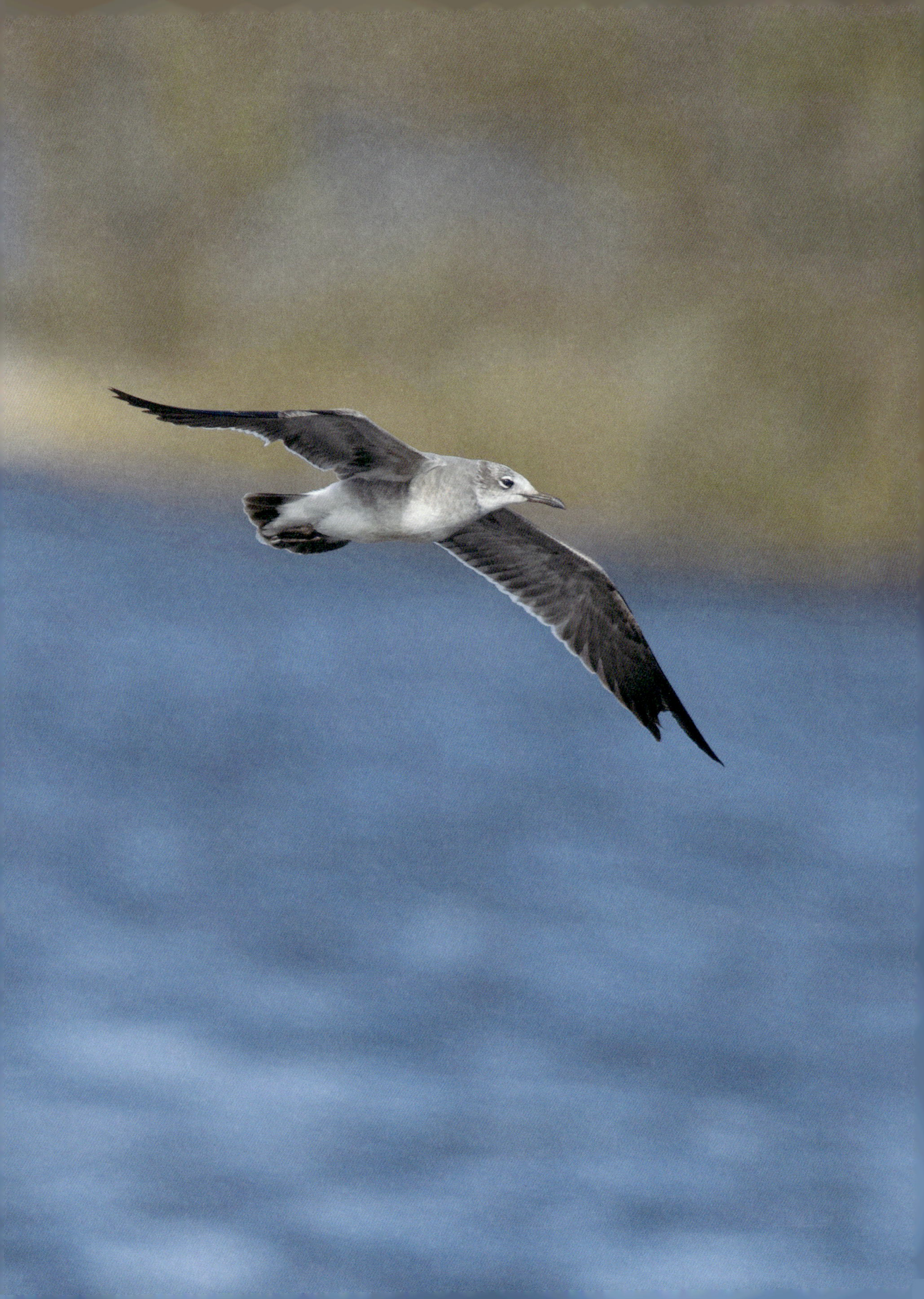

Memorable birding moments and tales

John Rossetti
Major contributions from Keith Vinicombe and from Dick Senior.
Andy Davis provided the list of annual notable records.

How Keith got into birding
Being an account of finding a rare bird
Swifts
Mervyn the Merganser
The ones that got away
Special events and years
including: The 'Great Fall' of 1966 | Keith's best day | 2011 – the ultimate year?

Many may think that birding is a quiet pursuit, requiring patience and careful observation. Which of course it is. But it also has moments of great excitement as well as disappointment, giving rise to many tales that get told and re-told, often with their own black humour. Lots of early starts and long days. And so many wonderful friendships and memories that last for years.

How I got into birding

Keith Vinicombe

Me, a pair of binoculars, my mum, and our Morris Minor

As a kid, I lived in a prefab in Whitchurch, on the south edge of Bristol, only about five miles from Chew Valley Lake. Apparently I first visited the lake in the spring of 1956, when I was only two years old. My parents had driven there to see the new reservoir, which was to be opened by the Queen on 17 April. Needless to say, I can't remember seeing any birds.

I became interested in birds in 1962, all thanks to a lad in school called Graham Sims. Graham's auntie had bought him a bird book for Christmas, and he brought it into school to show his friends. One of these was Jack Bennett, who lived just around the corner from me. I went round to his house one day to see if he fancied a kick about with the football but, he said 'No, I'm not coming out because I'm watching the birds'. I thought this was a bit odd but we both became interested and we soon gathered a whole gang of fledgling birders. We used to wander round the nearby fields, looking for both birds and their nests, although we never interfered with the nests. The interest blossomed and, pretty soon, we had a little gang of kids, all looking at the birds. My interest became particularly strong on our summer holidays, which involved a week or so in a caravan park. Croyde Bay in North Devon was a favourite destination but that soon changed to a caravan at Weymouth, which was owned by my cousin, who was a lot older than me – probably well into his thirties. I used to spend time at Ferrybridge, watching the waders and the terns, and we also went up to Portland Bill to look at the sea and the lighthouse. I remember on one occasion having a picnic just across the road from the old lighthouse. I wandered up a nearby path where I found my first ever Meadow Pipit. But my little walk came to an abrupt start when I came face to face with an adder! I came running back to my mum and dad, frightened to death!

A real turning point occurred on 17 July of that year, when I looked out of the kitchen window and saw a Goldfinch only a few feet away on my dad's bean sticks. It was a stunning bird and, from that point onwards, I was hooked on birds. My interest blossomed, especially on family holidays, but I also began to pester my dad into taking me to Chew Valley Lake.

My first birding visit there was on 28 July 1963, squinting through a pair of old wartime binoculars that my Auntie Nell had loaned me. Towards the end of 1964, a series of acrimonious letters appeared in the *Bristol Evening Post*, protesting about duck shooting at the lake. This so called 'sport' was common in those days. But what really grabbed my interest was a comment that rarer species, such as Scaup and Smew, were likely to be in the firing line. The thought of seeing such amazingly rare birds led me once again to pester my dad into taking me there. But what I really needed was a half decent pair of binoculars. On Christmas Day 1964, a pair of Viper 8x30s appeared, along with three Beatles LPs.

On 10 January 1965, my poor old dad was cajoled once again into another trip to the lake, but this was his, and my, big break. We were standing on Herriott's Bridge when three teenage lads climbed over the reservoir perimeter fence and walked across the road. They were Brian Crabb, Andy Davis and Dick Senior, all of whom were about 15. It transpired that Dick also lived in Whitchurch and he got talking to my dad. He said that, if he could get me to the bus stop in Whitchurch at 9 o'clock the following Sunday, they would be happy to take me with them.

Our stomp around the lake became a weekly event, and we soon met other birders, most notably Paul Chadwick, Keith Fox and Tim Cleeves, as well as Bernard King, at that time one of Britain's top birders, and Roy Thearle, who ran the Chew Valley Ringing Station. The latter two in particular were great mentors to us. We soon joined the Bristol Naturalists' Society and started to go on their monthly coach trips, to such exotic places as Dawlish Warren and Slapton Ley, in Devon, and also to Portland, in Dorset, where we stayed at the bird observatory twice a year.

I hate to think how many thousands of hours I've spent at Chew. Counting ducks, monitoring breeding birds and scanning through the huge bird flocks, always on the lookout for something unusual. Recently, I began to think that all this data needed analysing; hence this book.

As the 60s generation vanishes into the sunset, it would be nice to think that, at some time in the future, another, younger generation, will eventually come to realise that there is actually more to life than staring at a computer screen.

Goldfinches on my dad's bean sticks
| Ray Scally

Being an account of finding a rare bird

Dick Senior

We were eleven and fifteen when Keith and I became friends in the mid-sixties, shaking off the adults, school and home, going out birding around Chew Valley Lake under billowing clouds, with the Mendips green and soft in the distance.

Friday 8 September 1967 was our last day of freedom that summer, following which we would be reduced again to a measly single day at the weekends. However, this day was warm and bright, the light sharp after weeks of strong westerlies and we set off tramping the muddy, pungent margins, weaving our way around the water. I had just returned from Cape Clear and my head was full of Ireland. I had stories of great, grey stone crosses topping hills, the Fastnet Rock, Roaringwater Bay, dippers, shearwaters, Otters and whales watched from magnificent headlands with magical names, Blannanaragaun, Pointabullaun and Pointabullig. Keith had been too young to be included on this trip.

Despite the end of holiday gloom, we were having a fine day, relishing the sun and quiet walk around the empty lake shore with no shortage of birds. Moreton bank, late afternoon, busy with insect buzz, was flat and stony with cracked mud and exposed willow roots. We were checking out the waders when we saw a stand-out pale bird feeding with Dunlin. There was a moment's silent shock as we realized this was a bird we could not name. Slender and graceful, it resembled a miniature Greenshank. Both its neck and legs seemed proportionately long but when feeding it would often crouch with its neck retracted and sometimes it would jump up in the air to catch an insect or run very fast after one. Its black bill was long and fine, its legs yellow and in flight it recalled a Wood Sandpiper as it jinked and twisted in the air.

Near speechless, feeling a bit panicked and having not the faintest clue what we were looking at, we knew we needed help. Luckily, we also knew where there was a handy grown up within hailing distance. The Ringing Station, a mile or so away, was manned that day, so one of us had to go back and seek assistance while the other kept watch on the bird. Off Keith went and, having consulted a ringer and the *Handbook of British Birds*, returned half an hour later with the speculation that it might be a Marsh Sandpiper. I don't think we'd ever heard of one of those, our bird books being rather rudimentary, so this was a moment beyond wonderful. We knew that some people were prepared to drive hundreds of miles and go to enormous lengths to see a rare bird and here we were, having walked into one completely by chance just down the road from home. Brimming over with excitement and pleasure, we could barely sit still, or stop grinning, on the bus back that evening. A Marsh Sandpiper! Just fabulous!

Sadly, however, we'd got it wrong. Later that evening we telephoned Bernard King, our local guru, and he put out the news. The following morning, we returned to the lake to be told that the bird had been re-identified as a Lesser Yellowlegs because it had a square, white rump. Subsequent to that, it was then correctly identified as a Wilson's Phalarope, the first for Somerset and only the twenty-first British record. Well, we hadn't heard of a Wilson's Phalarope either and, although it was a little disappointing to have someone else name our bird, it was still terrific, not least because it was American and it had flown all the way across the Atlantic to our small patch in north Somerset.

During the next couple of weeks 'tickers' arrived from all over and our bird was seen by a good number of people. For us, it has stayed powerfully in our minds for over fifty years and, on each anniversary, one of us will usually remind the other of the significance of the date. In this way personal histories have been given shape and meaning and friendships maintained over lifetimes. Just brilliant!

A page from Laurel's notebook. At Chew, but not this bird! | Laurel Tucker

Swifts

Dick Senior

Swifts mate in mid-air,
a stunning fact I learned as a boy
but try as I might
I've only had sight of this once
in nearly sixty years
of watching the flights of Swifts.
High, high above Chew Valley Lake
perhaps in 1966
I saw a couple join and drop
like black sickle-winged stones
through the sharp blue sky
and then so elegant, so elegant
wheeling, curving and swooping up like a song
and parting above the glassy reflections of water.

Speed and sex can appeal to a boy
and, pondering rule breakers,
I thought, not even a Hell's Angel
bolting like a blur in a storm
on his Harley Davidson down Route 66,
a blond girl curving into him
like a second skin
could get anywhere near
as wild and glorious as a Swift,
a careering, screeching dagger.

Mervyn the Merganser
A eulogy to a duck

Keith Vinicombe

In the early days of Chew Valley Lake, there were very few records of Red-breasted Mergansers *Mergus serrator*. The first were three (two males) on 19 February 1956, with a 'redhead' until 11 March. Back in those days, there was often uncertainty regarding the separation of 'redhead' merganser from 'redhead' Goosander *M. merganser* which, being a freshwater species, was much the more abundant at the lake. It was 12 years before the next merganser records in 1968 but, by 1972, the species had become an annual visitor, usually in ones and twos, although rarely staying for any length of time.

On 31 October 1981, another 'redhead' merganser arrived, remaining with the Goosanders until 20 February 1982. What is assumed to have been the same bird, now in adult male plumage, reappeared on 18 January 1983, uncharacteristically remaining for over two months until 26 March. At this point, it must be stressed that Red-breasted Mergansers in full adult male plumage are extremely rare at the lake, most records relating to 'redheads', a term that encompasses females and males in juvenile/first-winter plumage (they do not acquire their full adult male plumage until their second winter). But, right from the outset, what was odd about this bird was that he frequently and persistently displayed to female Goosanders.

What was clearly the same bird reappeared the following winter, and every winter since, until he was last seen on 5 January 2016. He settled into the same predictable routine of tagging onto the Goosander flocks and relentlessly displaying to the female Goosanders. On the odd occasions when female mergansers did appear, he fastidiously ignored them. This behaviour lasted a remarkable 34 years.

During his stay, he occasionally commuted with the Goosanders to the other local reservoirs (particularly, and rather appropriately, Barrow Gurney) these forays usually occurring during the occasional cold spells when Chew froze over. In February 1987, during a particularly severe cold period, he was seen with the Goosanders on the River Avon in Keynsham. He usually appeared at Chew in October, the earliest arrival date being 8 October, and his latest departure date was 26 March.

The most likely reason for his attraction to female Goosanders is that, when a duckling, he became imprinted onto a female Goosander. This could have happened as a result of a female merganser 'egg dumping' into a Goosander's nest, this leading him to believe that he was actually a Goosander. Although he enlivened our winter birding for 34 years, in many respects Mervyn was a sad individual, presumably spending his entire adult life in a state of permanent sexual frustration – a situation to which many humans could also relate!

Mervyn's dates at the lake

1981:	31 October	**2001:**	17 Feb; 28 Oct
1982:	20 Feb	**2002:**	2 Mar; 14 Dec
1983:	15 Jan to 29 Mar; 30 Dec	**2003:**	16 Mar
1984:	4 Jan to 27 Mar; 24 Dec	**2004:**	4 Jan; prob 6 Nov
1985:	to 2 Mar; from 20 Dec	**2005:**	from 20 Oct
1986:	25 Jan to 15 Mar; from 11 Nov	**2006:**	13 Mar; 20 Oct
1987:	to 28 Feb; 21 Oct	**2007:**	6 Mar; 9 Nov
1988:	6 Feb; 30 Oct	**2008:**	18 Mar; 22 Oct
1989:	from 12 Nov	**2009:**	14 Feb; 8 Oct
1990:	11 Mar; 27 Oct	**2010:**	17 Jan; 13 Nov displaying to f Goosander
1991:	10 Nov	**2011:**	30 Jan; 13 Nov apparently paired to a f Goosander
1992:	2 Feb; 21 Nov	**2012:**	13 Mar; 10 Oct
1993:	17 Jan; 6 Nov	**2013:**	13 Mar (when paired to a female Goosander); 17 Oct
1994:	27 Feb; 20 Oct	**2014:**	23 Feb; 3 Nov
1995:	15 Jan; 11 Nov	**2015:**	3 Mar; 29 Oct
1996:	20 Feb; 9 Nov	**2016:**	5 Jan still displaying relentlessly to a f Goosander
1997:	9 Feb; 9 Nov		
1998:	1 Jan; 11 Jan		
1999:	15 Nov		
2000:	5 Mar; not seen at end of year but at BG Res in Nov		

'Mervyn' displaying to a female Goosander, a pair of Goosander in the background | Ray Scally

The ones that got away

John Rossetti

There is probably one thing that a birder really hopes to achieve, but very rarely does. And that is finding a bird that has never before been seen in Britain: a new bird for the British List. Remarkably there have been three species that have been correctly identified at the lake that are not on the list as at time of writing but could have a case to be so.

These have of course been carefully adjudicated by the BOU Records Committee and placed in Category D, birds that would have been on the list, but there is reasonable doubt that they have ever occurred in a natural state. We fully accept this decision, but it would be a shame to forget them. Who knows, they may be reviewed in the future. And though it may be controversial to include them, it does make a great story!

Marbled Duck

Formerly known as a Marbled Teal, one was at the lake between 24 August and 18 September 1984 and seen by many. An interesting sight, normally close to the reedbeds. This is now a threatened world species, mostly due to habitat destruction and hunting. It formerly bred in large numbers in the Mediterranean region, and would have been more widely distributed in 1984, but is now restricted in Europe to a few sites in Spain and Italy, including in Sicily as well as in Sardinia where it bred at least up to 2016. It is more common further east, however, in Iraq and Iran. A nomadic species, normally in small flocks outside the breeding season, and probably highly unlikely now to be seen in the UK.

It was commented about the bird at Chew that 'there was nothing in its behaviour to suggest it was anything other than a wild bird.'

Marbled Duck, White-headed Duck and a Booted Eagle overhead | Ray Scally

White-headed Duck

An iconic and rare European species, which in Europe breeds mainly in Southern Spain. This is a globally threatened species, mostly due to habitat loss and shooting. However recently another danger has come from occasional interbreeding with the introduced North American Ruddy Duck. A result of this threat has been a programme to eliminate Ruddy Ducks in the UK (and elsewhere in Europe), which has been particularly noticeable at Chew, which used to have a large population of these rather amusing birds.

Chew had an un-ringed male White-headed Duck in 1995, which also commuted between Abberton and Hanningfield reservoirs in Essex. Chew also had two records of young or female White-headed Ducks in 2003. These coincided with nine others elsewhere in Britain, as well as several records in Northern Europe. One in North-west France was only 300 miles south of Chew. See the account in the main species list for more details.

Booted Eagle

A second-winter pale phase Booted Eagle was a stunning sight at the lake in February 2000. I well remember seeing it hovering high over the edge of Herriott's Pool, before dropping to land on, and then eat, a hapless Coot that was innocently minding its own business in the undergrowth. Being a first for Britain, many people had made their way to the lake. The bird had a well-watched journey, starting in Southern Ireland and travelling via Cornwall and the Somerset Levels, finally being seen in Kent in April.

Booted Eagles are rare in captivity, and despite its impressive journeys that also included a visit to Orkney, it was subsequently rejected as a proven wild bird. The early arrival date and prolonged stay in the UK were among the factors leading to this decision.

At the time, and also when Keith wrote the first draft of his bird list, no one thought it would not be accepted as a first for Britain. With some recent records just across the channel, it probably won't be long!

Special events and years

Every year at the lake is special in its own way. Different weather patterns and water levels, and the wonders of bird migration, make sure that this is so. Some years are of course more special, and we have tried to pick out some of the more outstanding records and moments, mostly but not exclusively in chronological order. It has a very impressive list for an inland location that is away from the East coast, and almost always has a wonderful variety of birds on offer. Not a regular location for extreme rarities in general, but it has had the occasional twitch.

The construction of the lake was mostly complete in 1954, and as water started to slowly come into the valley and rise over the grassland, bird records started. It was a very different environment then, no reed beds and before the lakeside habitats had developed. There were, for example, very high counts of Coot initially as the water rising over the grass fields made great feeding for them. But the birds found the lake pretty quickly, as they are wont to do. 1954 saw an influx of 170 Black Terns. 1955 brought the first record of Ferruginous Duck – a rare bird, but one for which Chew has been very special with about 30 records, including what was thought to have been the first breeding record in the early 2000s, although no young were ever seen.

Black Terns appeared again in numbers in 1957, with a high UK count of 480 of these wonderful marsh terns on 21 September.

It wasn't until February 1958 that the lake was finally full for the first time, more than two years after it had been opened by the Queen, but the birds kept coming. In April that year, the first record of Common Scoter arrived, a duck of the seas that is far from common inland. A flock of 15 was seen on 6 April.

The lake was starting to get recognised despite the relatively few birdwatchers at the time, most of whom could only come out at weekends. 1959 saw Whiskered Tern and Stone Curlew, and 1960 brought a Savi's Warbler and the arrival of autumn waders with 25 Little Stints. And from then to 1964 we had Montagu's Harrier, Gyr Falcon, Little Crake, Golden Oriole, Shore Lark, Spotted Crakes and Black-winged Pratincole.

1965 was also an iconic year. Not for the two Black-winged Stilts in May, but for the famous Pied-billed Grebe in the autumn. It had in fact been found in December 1963 at the nearby Blagdon Reservoir, the first ever record for the Western Palearctic, and to this day it forms the logo for the Bristol Ornithological Club.

Part of a flock of Black Terns over the lake | Ray Scally

Common Scoters | From a plate by Laurel Tucker

MEMORABLE BIRDING MOMENTS AND TALES

The 'Great Fall' of 1966

Some of us may remember 1966 for a famous football match. In fact, on the day of the match, Keith had already arranged to go with Tim Cleeves to do a bit of birdwatching (it wasn't called 'birding' in those days) around Marshfield, which involved a long bus ride. Keith didn't have a telephone so he felt he would have to keep to the arrangement; after all it was just another football match. He recalls that when they returned, the part of Bristol where they lived was like a ghost town. They walked past houses where the occupants were all glued to their black-and-white TV sets. (Yes, it was the World Cup final, which England won, against what in those days was called West Germany.)

The 'Great Fall' was in fact earlier that year, in April. As birders will know, a fall is when very many migrating birds are 'downed' by especially adverse weather conditions, resulting in the ground and bushes being literally alive with large numbers of wet and bedraggled birds. Falls are not common, even less common in the west of the country, and are especially unusual away from the coasts. Birders never forget if they are lucky enough to witness one.

The following (edited) article appeared in the Chew Valley Ringing Station 3rd report. Note that almost all these records relate purely to the south end of the lake. It is not known who wrote it, but it is most likely to have been Roy Thearle, the Honorary Secretary of the Ringing Station.

Spring migration in April 1966

During the spring of 1966, there was fortunately continuous trapping from the 3rd until the 24th of April. This proved to be a period of unusual numbers of birds, and unusual weather conditions.

The 3rd was very cold as the wind was northerly but, by dusk, this had veered to an easterly (force 3). There had obviously been an arrival of migrants the previous week. On the 5th, the wind was still moderate from a south-easterly direction and it was generally overcast. There were few birds of note, with only about 500 hirundines over the lake and a flock of 80 Meadow Pipits. The period of 6th–8th saw the wind backing from south-west to south and generally dull conditions with rain at times. On the 8th, 20 male Yellow Wagtails appeared. On the 9th the wind backed to south south-east (force 4–5) and this was accompanied by drizzle. The 10th was marked by thunderstorms and by a south south-east wind, force 1–2, with large numbers of *Phylloscopus* species present and one '*acredula*' trapped (the sub-species of Willow Warbler found in northern Norway and north and central Sweden, eastwards into Siberia).

On the 11th, the wind had backed to a light north-easterly and it was generally dull. The first Common Sandpiper was recorded and a very early Reed Warbler was caught; the first Whitethroat also appeared. On the 12th, conditions were similar and the first Grasshopper Warbler was heard, hirundines increased to around 500, including three House Martins, and Yellow Wagtails increased to about 20 from the previous day's total of five. One Tree Pipit was also recorded.

On the 13th, the wind changed to a strong easterly and 'vast' numbers of Swallows and Sand Martins were present; there were also two more House Martins. The only birds of note were 30 each of Meadow Pipit and Yellow Wagtail. On the 14th, the wind was still easterly force 5 and this was accompanied by a blizzard which produced 12 inches of snow. 'Vast' numbers of hirundines were again present. There were now at least 20 Redstarts, 10 Tree Pipits and 20 White Wagtails and there had also been a fall of Willow/Chiffs. On the 15th, the wind was still light easterly with showers. Both hirundines and Willow/Chiffs were still present in large numbers. A male Pied Flycatcher and a flock of 100 Meadow Pipits were also recorded.

Redstart in a snowstorm, part of the 'Great Fall' of 1966 | Ray Scally

The weather on the night of the 15th/16th was unfortunately not recorded. Observers present on the 16th wished to stress the 'vast numbers of birds present': *Phylloscopus* species were everywhere, including large numbers in the reed beds. Many Blackcaps and Redstarts in all cover. This applied to the whole area of the lake and not just Herriott's Bridge End. Other birds present included 12 Whinchats, 15 Redstarts, a male Pied Flycatcher, 200 Yellow Wagtails and an Osprey and a Marsh Harrier. The latter two species were very rare at that time.

On the 17th, there were not as many birds present as the previous day although large numbers were still in the area. The Pied Flycatcher was again recorded and many Willow/Chiffs. About 20 Tree Pipits were present in addition to a Nightingale, a very unusual bird for Herriott's Bridge, and 40 Yellow Wagtails. The wind was still easterly. On the 18th several thousands of hirundines were feeding over the lake. The first Swifts appeared with 10 on the 20th and about 40 the next day.

The rest of the 1960s

1966 continued to be special, with the only currently acceptable Kentish Plover for the lake, a Bee-eater and the second Aquatic Warbler, the first having been trapped the year before.

It was also a year that saw the first White-winged Black Tern. Chew has an exceptional record for these beautiful birds, with 22 being recorded between 1966 and 2014, but unfortunately none since.

South-westerly gales in September 1967 brought the start of the American waders to the lake, with a Wilson's Phalarope on the 8th and a Lesser Yellowlegs the next day. A Bluethroat turned up in 1968, and 1969 brought a Red-necked Phalarope and the lake's first Pectoral Sandpiper.

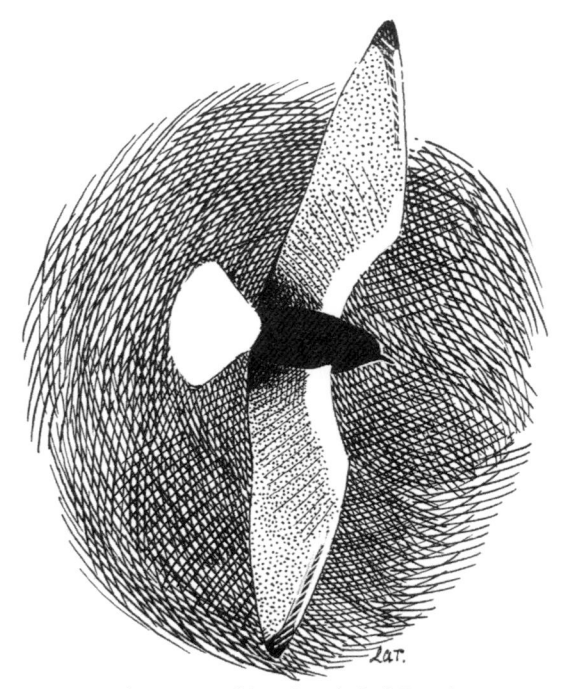

Second-summer White-winged Black Tern | Laurel Tucker

The Seventies

This was a particularly good decade for waders and established the lake as a place to see American waders especially. At times the water levels were low, with lots of exposed mud, which is certainly a help.

Chew has also been a location for American duck, with the first American Wigeon in 1977 and the first Ring-necked Duck was recorded in 1971. Since then it has occurred in 26 of the 44 years up to 2019, the majority of which have been males.

It wasn't just waders in the 70s, with Purple Heron in 1970 and the first records of Great Grey Shrike and Nightjar occurring in 1973, when there was also a female Red-backed Shrike. Other notable records included a Rough-legged Buzzard in 1974, a Little Bunting in 1976, and Twite, Marsh Warbler and Red-throated Pipit in 1979, while 1976 saw the largest wildfowl count at the lake with a total of 9,190 birds. This must have been quite an effort and lots of clicking on duck-counters.

Male Ring-necked Ducks have been a regular sight at the lake | Ray Scally

When the water levels are very low, the old road between West Harptree and Chew Stoke becomes exposed, revealing the lake's history | Courtesy of Bristol Water

But the years between 1973 and 1980 were exceptional for waders. Just lots – for example a count of 46 Little Stints in 1973 and large numbers of others such as Ringed Plover (record count of 114 in '74), Ruff (71 in '74), Common Sandpiper (46 in '74), Curlew Sandpiper (29 in '75), Greenshank (29 in '74) and Green Sandpiper (29 in '74). There were also seven Wood Sandpipers in 1974, this being, apparently, Keith's favourite bird!

Wood Sandpiper, Keith's favourite bird | Ray Scally

The Killdeer | 12 January 1976

At 14.45 on 12 January 1976, I was looking through a large flock of Lapwings on Moreton Point (there were 2,200 at the lake that day) when I noticed a 'Ringed Plover' amongst them on the stones. I couldn't believe it when it turned round and revealed two thick breast bands – a Killdeer! I watched it for about five minutes before it disappeared behind some stones. After about five minutes it reappeared and fed in a small puddle, before being chased off by a Lapwing, landing out of view in a dip.

I ran back to the Ringing Station to put out the news and, luckily, I found Sid and Olive Mead, Tim Cleeves, Malcolm Sainsbury and Dorian Buffery. By the time I got back to Moreton, the Killdeer was back on view, but a lot closer. But it then flew across the inlet in front of the point and was never seen again! Fortunately, Tim, Sid and Olive, Malcolm and Dorian all managed to see it.

The sheer shock of finding this bird lasts with me to this day, and it still rates as one of the best birds ever!

Keith Vinicombe

Killdeer – 'it turned around and revealed two thick breast bands' | Ray Scally

MEMORABLE BIRDING MOMENTS AND TALES

The Greater Sand Plover | 17 November 1979 to 10 February 1980

The Greater Sand Plover *Charadrius leschenaultii* breeds in semi-desert lowlands and plateaus from central Turkey and Jordan eastwards through Turkestan and into south-eastern Russia, Mongolia and China. It has a large winter range from the eastern Mediterranean, South and East Africa eastwards to Taiwan and Australia.

The first British record was in the winter of 1978–79 when one was present in Pagham Harbour, Sussex, which I twitched. One was then seen in Orkney from 9th to at least 14th June 1979. The third, however, was a first-winter at Chew from 17 November 1979 to 10 February 1980. The discovery of this bird stemmed from a conversation between myself and Chris Newman. We bumped into each other in the fishermen's car park at Sutton Wick, where I asked him the inevitable question: 'seen anything'?' He rattled off a few common birds and, almost as an afterthought, said 'oh yeah..... and a Ringed Plover'. Although Ringed Plovers are regular spring and autumn passage migrants at the lake, their numbers depend almost entirely on the water levels. Occurrences as late as November are unusual, with only eight recorded in that month in the 62 years from 1955 to 2016 inclusive.

I asked Chris where he'd seen it and he told me that it was on the mud in nearby Spring Bay. Rather intrigued by this, I suggested that we should go and have a look at it. I soon found the bird and I immediately felt my pulse rising. I turned to Chris and said 'You know what this is, don't you? It's a Greater Sand Plover!' 'No!' he said, in utter disbelief. But it was, indeed, a Greater Sand Plover! We watched it for some time before it was flushed by a Peregrine. We returned to the car park where we were, literally, dancing up and down and doing roly-polies. Trouble was though, when I finally decided to head for home, I couldn't find my motorbike keys. They had obviously fallen out of my pocket when I was doing my gymnastics! We embarked upon a forensic search of the car park and surrounding areas but with no success. We drove off in Chris's car and found a phone box, but I could hardly put in the coins in the slot as my hands were shaking so much from the excitement. I had another set of keys at home and Chris very kindly drove me back out there again the next day so that I could rescue my bike!

To cut a long story short, the bird stayed for three months, being last seen on 10 February 1980. Towards the end of its stay, it was also seen in the Parkland as well as in the field next to the Main Dam, in which Picnic Site 1 now resides. During the time it was present, it was enjoyed by hundreds of birders from far and wide.

Keith Vinicombe

Greater Sand Plover | Laurel Tucker

Three Americans
Buff-breasted Sandpiper, Pectoral Sandpiper and Wilson's Phalarope

But when were they all at the lake together? Well actually this 'sort of' happened twice.

In 1975, they were all there in September. Two Buff-breasts, two Pectoral Sands and a Wilson's Phalarope. But while the Buff-breasted and Pectoral Sandpipers were there at the same time, this did not coincide with the phalarope.

However in 1980 it was different, as all three species, including two Pectoral Sandpipers, were at the lake on 16 September. We are not sure, however, if anyone actually saw them all together or from the same place!

Three Americans
Buff-Breasted Sandpiper, Pectoral Sandpiper and Wilson's Phalarope | Ray Scally

Dowitcher wanderings

When it comes to Long-billed Dowitchers, they seem to prefer coming to the lake in couples. Apart from one in 2009, the two in 1977 and the two in 2011 both spent their time commuting between Chew and Blagdon Lake. In fact, the two in 2011 carried on to the Somerset Levels and on to Dorset, visiting Lodmoor and The Fleet. One remained at The Fleet, while the other moved to various parts of the Somerset Levels before, rather remarkably, being joined by the other seven weeks later. Two individual wandering Americans seemed to find each other again after being 50 miles apart in Southern England. How did that happen?

Two Long-billed Dowitchers at the lake | Ray Scally

Don't forget about White-rumped Sandpipers

Not wanting to be left out among their American cousins, two White-rumped Sandpipers were at the lake in late October 1978, with one staying into November. A further one was seen in October 1991.

Adult Marsh Sandpiper at Chew | Laurel Tucker

Juvenile White-rumped Sandpiper | Laurel Tucker

On to the 1980s

It is not really appropriate to categorise a decade of course, although somehow they do seem to have their own themes. If the 70s were about waders, particularly American ones, the 80s seem to have been about storms. These are more likely to bring gulls and birds associated with the high seas, which is what did in fact happen.

1980 saw the first Ring-billed Gull at Chew, although this was to be the first of many, with the species then recorded in 30 of the following 40 years up to 2019. 1981 saw north-easterly gales and blizzards in late April, bringing in six Arctic Terns, a Fulmar and 50 Kittiwakes. In 1982, the first British record of Kumlien's Gull was seen at the lake, and there was an influx of Arctic Terns at the end of September with up to 31 birds present. Chew's one and only Tawny Pipit was seen on 2 October.

The waders were however not to be outdone, as 1982 also saw the first Marsh Sandpiper as well as the first Spotted Sandpiper.

While 1983 started gently, with two Whiskered Terns in May, the storms in early September were quite a different thing.

Keith's best day

Keith's account of the storm of 1983, as provided for *Best Days with British Birds*
(*Included with permission from British Birds Ltd.*)

'A Big Blow and a Gannet in the bath'

Back in 1989 I was asked to contribute to a book, published by British Birds Ltd, entitled *Best Days with British Birds*. As its title indicates, the book was comprised of a number of articles by well-known birders of the time, a period of great advances in bird identification. My contribution related to an exceptional influx of seabirds at Chew on 3–5 September 1983, which stands out as probably the best weekend's birding I have ever had. Not a single tick, not a single rarity, but the birds I saw meant much more to me than that.

Since the age of 11, I have been obsessed with Chew Valley Lake, a beautiful lake and a superb place for birds. I have counted the ducks, surveyed the breeding birds, checked the roosting gulls and recorded the comings and goings of its transient migrants. By September 1983 I had seen 213 of the 250 species recorded there.

Most birders are 'listers' to a certain extent and a great many, myself included, will sometimes travel hundreds of miles to see a wind-blown vagrant blown thousands of miles off course. Although I keep a British list, I have always been more obsessed with my 'Chew' list. There is a great challenge in keeping a local list, as birds that are common elsewhere may be extremely rare locally, and the only way is to put in the maximum effort in the field.

Unlike national listing, it is not necessarily a function of one's ability to drive all night or sit by a telephone waiting for the news of someone else's discovery. The trouble is that keeping a Chew list can be an extremely frustrating experience. Passing migrants may drop in for a very brief period, never to reappear for years on end. I'll never forget when some 'friends' of mine saw both me and a Short-eared Owl in the same field of view, and on my birthday! Short-eared Owl was a Chew 'bogey bird' for me at the time, and it took me over 3 years to recover it. However, one of the big advantages is that rarities take on a whole new perspective: a Nuthatch or a Black Redstart, for example, would be great rarities at the lake and finding a 'Chew first' is an extremely satisfying experience indeed.

Seabirds are among the most difficult groups of birds to catch up with at Chew. Being 20 miles inland (or 70 if you ignore the murky waters of the Bristol Channel), we don't come across many. However, on the night of Friday 2 September 1983, there were classic conditions: torrential rain and a howling westerly gale of an intensity not normally expected so early in the autumn.

Leach's Petrel low over the lake, with House Martins | Ray Scally

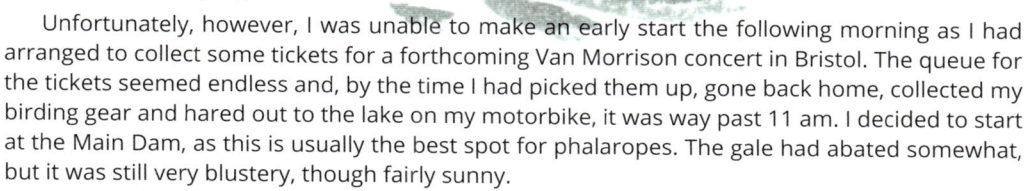

Unfortunately, however, I was unable to make an early start the following morning as I had arranged to collect some tickets for a forthcoming Van Morrison concert in Bristol. The queue for the tickets seemed endless and, by the time I had picked them up, gone back home, collected my birding gear and hared out to the lake on my motorbike, it was way past 11 am. I decided to start at the Main Dam, as this is usually the best spot for phalaropes. The gale had abated somewhat, but it was still very blustery, though fairly sunny.

As is usual in such conditions, the lake was a seething mass of House Martins when, as a result of strong winds and rain, their insect food becomes scarce over the adjacent countryside. I checked the shorelines for phalaropes, but there was nothing doing. I then checked out further, but still nothing. I am, above all, persistent, so I scanned the lake a second time and then a third time, bending in a suitably contorted position with my telescope resting on the dam wall. Suddenly, about a quarter of a mile out, amongst the thousands of flashing white rumps, there was a small dark bird pattering slowly across the surface of the lake with its wings raised. I couldn't believe it: a petrel! I zoomed my telescope up to 40 times magnification. It looked small, but it was difficult to see the rump and tail clearly as it was side-on. I was beginning to think that it must be a Storm Petrel when it turned and revealed a forked tail, a thin dark line down the middle of the white rump and a broad grey band down the centre of the upper wing: a Leach's Petrel!

Leach's Petrels are the rarer of our two breeding petrels with just a few thousand pairs nesting on St Kilda and a few other Scottish and possibly Irish islands. However, despite their rarity, they are more prone to being 'wrecked' by gales than the more numerous Storm Petrels. In November 1953, for example, there was a huge wreck, with some 2,500 in Bridgwater Bay, Somerset, alone. Because of the large numbers in the wreck, it is thought that many of the autumn birds that occur off our coasts originate from the much larger colonies on the western side of the Atlantic, mainly in Newfoundland.

I drooled over the petrel for some time before I became aware of a figure waving at me from the nearby picnic site. It was a friend of mine, Chris Newman, and I waved back in a gesture to indicate my intense excitement. I tore myself away and rushed round to meet him. He, too, had seen the Leach's and he excitedly told me that there was a second individual at the south end of the lake. After exchanging the inevitable superlatives, I decided to go round to Nunnery Point, a good vantage position on the west side, to try to see the other petrel. Once there, I soon found another Leach's close in shore, but, as I scanned further, there was another … and another … and another!

Five! I couldn't believe it. At this point I was watching more Leach's Petrels than I had ever seen in my entire life, and 20 miles inland and on my local patch to boot! The petrels were all feeding in a very distinctive manner, half flying and half walking on the water, with their long, angled wings raised, but slightly bowed. Occasionally, when moving position, they would zap off over the lake with a powerful but erratic, Nightjar-like flight action.

I was still engrossed with the Leach's when I was joined by another local birder, Jeff Holmes. Needless to say, Jeff was more than surprised when I told him what I was watching but, during our subsequent conversation, it transpired that his 'bogey bird' was Storm Petrel. We were discussing how unusual it would be to see a 'Stormie' inland when, as if by magic, there, amongst the House Martins, was a small, fluttering, bat-like petrel. 'Hey, have a look at this', I yelled, checking the features as I did so: large white rump, square tail and a prominent white line down the underwing, a diagnostic feature of a Storm Petrel! Jeff was soon on to it and we followed it as it disappeared into the distance and vanished amongst the mass of House Martins. Its rapid, fluttering wing-beats and its bounding flight were in marked contrast to the slow, lazy, Nightjar-like flight of the Leach's. The two species were as different as chalk and cheese, even to an inexperienced land lubber like myself. Jeff had had a life tick and I had had two Chew ticks! What a day!

I watched the Leach's Petrels for a couple of hours before I decided to check Blagdon Lake, two miles to the west of Chew. It's much smaller than Chew, but always worth a look after a gale. An initial scan produced nothing but, half way down the lake, I picked out a small dark brown bird sitting on the water; another small petrel. It looked too small for a Leach's and, after fluttering a short distance it revealed itself as another Storm Petrel. 'There must be more' and I drove to the dam where, inevitably, there was a Leach's feeding close in. It was at this point, however, that I became decidedly paranoid: I was wondering what was being seen back at Chew. I jumped on my motorbike and raced back to Moreton Hide on the west shore. There I found Chris Newman, Antony Merritt and Pete Hopkin avidly scanning the lake.

'How many Chew ticks have you had?' asked Anthony as I entered.

'Two' I replied. 'Thank God for that' said Chris. 'We've been trying to find you all afternoon to tell you about the Storm Petrels'.

They had seen two Storm Petrels and seven Leach's' all in view at once. I felt well 'gripped' but, at this point, two Leach's appeared in front of the hide as well as a Storm Petrel, which seemed to be a second individual as it had a somewhat less abraded tail than the first.

By the time I got home it was dark. And I only had an hour or so in which to cook tea and get ready for a celebratory drink. During that hour, the phone was ringing constantly.

'Two Grey Phalaropes, three Leach's and a Stormy at Cheddar'.
 'Sixty Leach's, five Sabine's and an unidentified all-dark petrel at New Passage'.
'Twenty Sabine's at Steart.' This was incredible.

Then came the news that we had all been waiting for: 'Have you heard about St Ives?'………10,000 Stormies, 100 Sabine's, five Leach's (!), 40 Great Shearwaters, one Cory's, Long-tailed Skua, a Pomarine Skua down to two yards, possible South Polar Skua and a Wilson's Petrel on view for an hour.

When I regained consciousness, I felt pretty sick, but there again St Ives was 200 miles away and, from what I heard, there were so many people there that, whenever anybody spotted anything, all the tripods fell over! I would never have forgiven myself for missing such a good day at Chew and I was glad that I had stayed local. That evening, in the pub, a trip was hastily arranged for the Sunday: Steart, Cheddar and Chew was the planned route.

We set off early with Chris Newman, Chris Stone, Tony Merritt, Pete Hopkin and myself, all intensely buoyed up with anticipation. We decided that Steart might not be such a good bet after all as the tide would be miles out. We therefore headed to Chew but, on arrival, there was no sign of any petrels. They had obviously departed overnight which, in a way, was a good sign as it meant that the birds were well enough to leave. It all seemed fairly quiet compared with the previous day: just a couple of Garganey, four Little Gulls, three Arctic, one Common and two Black Terns. We were parked in Villice Bay, however, when an unknown birder came up to ask us if we had seen the Spotted Crakes. 'What Spotted Crakes?' we asked. 'There's two at Herriott's Bridge'.

We piled into the car and tore off to Herriott's Bridge at the south end where we found a small gang of birders watching a superb Spotted Crake at point blank range, creeping along the edge of the reeds below the bridge. After a while, a second bird came into view and we even thought that there might have been a third, a fact confirmed later in the day by other observers. Spotted Crakes are probably fairly regular at Chew in the autumn, but their secretive behaviour makes them very difficult to see. I had only seen four there before, so to have three in view at the same time, at such close range, was a pretty unique experience.

We were engrossed with the crakes when Antony casually turned to me and asked': 'Hey Keith, do you want to see a Chew tick?'

'What?' I asked incredulously.

'There's two Bonxies out over the lake!'

There, high in the sky were two meaty, brown, gull-like birds, flashing huge white wing patches. They somehow looked even more menacing than they do at sea! They circled around for several minutes, disappeared, but then came back for a repeat performance. I was ecstatic! There were only five previous records at Chew and, by sheer bad luck, I had managed to miss all of them, except for a dead one which, of course, you can't count.

Two menacing Bonxies over the lake | Ray Scally

MEMORABLE BIRDING MOMENTS AND TALES

After a celebratory round of ice creams, we eventually decided to tear ourselves away from Chew and make our move to the coast. We decided on New Passage, just below the Severn Bridge. Brian Lancastle and a small group of locals cover this area, week in, week out. Quite frankly, it's a grot hole; miles of gooey mud, acres of spartina, and a sickly backdrop of chemical works and smelters, all spewing nauseating brown and orange smoke into the atmosphere. If the earth had piles, it would be at New Passage. What's more, there's not even many birds, apart from black ones, and even the locals have dubbed it 'No Passage'.

With a frenzied attack of misplaced optimism, we leapt out of the car and rushed up to Brian, who was rooted to his spot on the sea wall, sheltering from the inevitable wind. He looked shell-shocked. 'You should have been here this morning' was the all too predictable greeting. 'Three Sabine's, two adults in summer plumage'. Black-headed Gull would normally be a good bird at 'No Passage'. We resigned ourselves to having missed the best of the movement, but we sat down on the wall and peered resolutely seawards into the brown murk. We had, however, only been there a couple of minutes when, suddenly, Antony shouted: 'Sabine's, going left'.

There, right before our eyes was a superb summer-plumaged Sabine's Gull, slowly and gracefully heading down river, its black head and grey and white triangles on its wings making it a particularly stunning gull. Within minutes, somebody else had picked up a Storm Petrel, then a

MEMORABLE BIRDING MOMENTS AND TALES

Gannet, then some Manx Shearwaters, then a Leach's Petrel. The atmosphere was electric. 'I never thought I'd live to see the day' mused a bewildered Brian. Another Sabine's was picked up, then an Arctic Skua and more petrels close in. A small gull in the middle of the channel revealed itself as a juvenile Little Gull, just as it was joined by another Sabine's. What a comparison! They were then passed by an Arctic Skua, another good bird so far up the estuary. As we drove home, the final tally was added up: seven Storm Petrels, six Leach's, five Gannets, three Sabine's Gulls, 26 Manx Shearwaters, five Arctic Skuas, a Little Gull, four unidentified petrels and a Fulmar – an amazing total by local standards.

At work the following day, I spent most of my time, as usual, making tea and staring out of the window. I was on cloud nine and couldn't concentrate at all. Suddenly, about 3 pm, I was woken by the telephone: 'Hello, Keith, it's Antony. There's another Chew tick for you: Manx Shearwater in front of Moreton Hide, and there's a Gannet too! And we had another Storm Petrel this morning, being chased by a Hobby!'

...there was even a Manxie and Storm Petrel being chased by a Hobby! | Ray Scally

You're joking! What am I going to do? I had to go to that bloody Van Morrison concert at the Colston Hall at 7 pm. There was only one thing for it. I put the phone down, took a deep breath and calmly walked into my boss's office.

'I forgot to tell you: I've got a dental appointment at 4 o'clock: 'Is it all right if I go?'

He pondered for what seemed like an eternity and eventually nodded. I was off like a shot, down the stairs, into the car park, on my bike, up the hill and into the house. I grabbed my 'scope and bins and, half an hour later, I was back in Moreton Hide. I frantically scanned the lake – I only had an hour – no sign of anything, no Gannet, no shearwater, no petrel. 'Aaah'! I was beginning to panic. I scanned further to the right and there, large as life, was the Gannet!

It reminded me of the last Gannet, and what happened next

Like my only previous Chew Gannet, eleven years earlier, it was an adult. That too had been an exhausted storm-driven bird and I remember it vividly for a very good reason: I gave it all my ham sandwiches before I caught it, put it in in a cardboard box (which I scrounged from a nearby farm), took it home on the bus and plonked it in the bath!

I then slipped out and bought it a tin of sardines, which the Gannet proceeded to flick all over the bathroom wall. Fortunately, my mother was out shopping, though she eventually returned and I took her upstairs to proudly introduce her to the biggest rubber duck she'd ever clapped eye on.

Needless to say, she didn't share my enthusiasm for sharing a bath with a Gannet. In fact, she went berserk; she threw about 48 nervous breakdowns and ordered me to take it to the dogs' home where, no doubt, they put it in a kennel. I never did find out what happened to it.

So back to 1983...

The 1983 individual was altogether a much healthier bird and, eventually, it launched itself into the air and proceeded to fly up and down the lake, high above the surface.

'I wonder if it will...'

Then, after several circuits, it did. It stalled, turned, swept back its wings and plunged headfirst into the lake – what a superb sight! It even made the fishermen look up. I really felt that I had seen the lot – a Gannet fishing 20 miles inland! Just then, I glanced out of the hide to the left and there, close inshore was the Manx Shearwater. It swept back and forth, low over the surface and disappeared into Heron's Green Bay just as suddenly as it had appeared. Brilliant! I skipped back to my bike and hared off to Bristol, just in time to make the concert.

As I sat there in the Colston Hall, waiting for the lights to go down, I couldn't help pondering about all the people who spend their weekends digging the garden, reading the papers or cleaning the car.

Birding is generally portrayed as an eccentric, cranky or trivial pastime. But I bet there weren't many people in that audience who had experienced such an exhilarating, satisfying and enjoyable weekend as I had!

Keith Vinicombe

Keith's mum was definitely not amused

'Gannet in the Bath'

I then slipped out and bought it a tin of sardines, which the Gannet proceeded to flick all over the bathroom wall. Fortunately, my mother was out shopping, though she eventually returned and I took her upstairs to proudly introduce her to the biggest rubber duck she'd ever clapped eye on.

Needless to say, she didn't share my enthusiasm for sharing a bath with a Gannet. In fact, she went berserk; she threw about 48 nervous breakdowns and ordered me to take it to the dogs' home where, no doubt, they put it in a kennel. I never did find out what happened to it.

The first Red Kite was not until 1990, but they are getting commoner now | Ray Scally

The 1980s continued to bring gulls and storms, with up to 5 Iceland Gulls in 1984 in the early part of the year, 74 Little Gulls in May, six Ring-billed Gulls in 1986 and then another storm in 1987. This one brought Leach's Petrel, an Arctic Skua, three Sabine's Gulls and five Grey Phalaropes. Other notable birds were another Marsh Sandpiper and three trapped Aquatic Warblers. A Savi's Warbler was trapped in 1986 as well as the lake's first Yellow-browed Warbler later that year. 1988 finished things off with Black Stork and Caspian Tern.

The 1990s

They might seem very common now, especially in some parts of the country, but the lake's first Red Kite was seen in 1990. Still such a great bird to see, and taking their time to colonise the local area, although they are now seen very regularly over Burledge Hill and at other places around the lake.

Also in 1990 there was a Red-rumped Swallow and the lake's first Lapland Bunting.
A juvenile Long-tailed Skua was part of an unprecedented influx of this species in the country during September.

The rest of the 90s continued to produce many good birds, including at least three that were new to the lake, although there was the impression that it was waiting for the millennium.

Great White Egret – now an iconic sight at the lake | Ray Scally

MEMORABLE BIRDING MOMENTS AND TALES

The first Great Reed Warbler was seen and heard in May 1992. 1993 saw a male Little Bittern and a Black-winged Pratincole, but maybe the most unexpected new bird for the lake was an Eider in November. Normally a bird only of the sea, there was in fact an unprecedented inland movement of Eider across the Midlands and some northern English counties at the time.

1994 saw another Marsh Warbler trapped, and there were also five Ruddy Shelduck in June and July. While records of this species are often thought to be of questionable origin, they did coincide with an invasion of this species into Scandinavia at the time. The year ended with the lake's first, and so far only, record of an American Golden Plover in October.

An excellent five Spotted Crakes were seen in August and September 1995, while in 1996 the lake had Little Bunting and Citrine Wagtail.

The largest ever count of Smew, 21, was recorded in February 1997. It was thought that these may have been driven westwards from the continent, due to the freezing conditions at the time.

1998 saw the lake's first Alpine Swift on the early date of 18 February. Also in that year, a pair of Black-necked Grebes bred and raised two young, although unfortunately they did not survive for long.

The decade ended with a passage of Bitterns, up to 6, in March. This number was very rare here.

The Noughties – do we have any REgrets?

When we look out at the lake today, it is very hard to miss the wonderful white birds that adorn our views. And we are not talking here about the excellent swans.

It is really quite astonishing that the first Great White Egret was seen in 2002, and it was not until October 2011 before the second one arrived. Now in 2020, we are starting to get them even in the summer months, so who knows what will be next.

And of course, the egret theme has not ended. Presumably influenced by global warming and the resulting climate change, although we must not forget the fantastic and developing environment of the Somerset Levels and Avalon Marshes. The Levels always were a superb environment, even though a lot of the area was set over for peat extraction. Many of the older birder generation will remember that Shapwick was dry heathland and the place to go to see Nightjars and Glow Worms on warm summer evenings.

Enter the Cattle Egret in October 2007. The next ones were in 2009, but by September 2018 there were 29 seen, then a record for the county. These numbers will surely rise, as they continue to breed successfully in the Somerset Levels.

Cattle Egret. Now a regular sight in surrounding fields and meadows, especially in winter | Ray Scally

Other things were of course going on in the first decade of the new century, some of which were with American birds helped along their way by Hurricane 'Wilma' in 2005.

Two Honey-buzzards were an unusual sight as they passed over the lake in September 2000, but later that year strong winds brought in both Storm and Leach's Petrels.

In 2002 there was a record flock of Common Scoter, 115, in October. This seemed remarkable for a sea duck, but recently a night-time migration of these birds from Cardigan Bay over to the North Sea in spring has been picked up by sound recording, and keen-eared Bristol birders have been out in the evening getting Common Scoter on their garden lists!

The American Hurricane in 2005 and its remnants may well have been responsible for three Grey Phalaropes and three Ring-necked Ducks in November, and maybe also for the first Laughing Gull in April 2006. The second Laughing Gull was in fact in 2020.

Following the probable breeding of Ferruginous Duck in 2006 (see report in the main Bird List), the first English breeding record of Goldeneye occurred in 2008, with a brood of 3 being seen in June. These attractive ducks nest remarkably in holes or cavities of large trees near water, but also in tree stumps as well as nest boxes, and have been recorded nesting in rabbit burrows.

2008 also brought three more species to the Chew list, with a Franklin's Gull in January, the first of several Lesser Scaup records in April and a Quail in June. There were also a remarkable eight Ring-necked Ducks in November.

In addition to second, and then more, records of Cattle Egret in 2009, were up to four Glossy Ibis in September when there was also a Long-billed Dowitcher. Later that year, two Pomarine Skuas were seen at the lake in November, following gales.

Female Goldeneye with her three chicks, the first English breeding record, in 2008 | Ray Scally

The second Laughing Gull, March 2020 | Brian Thompson

2010 to 2020

A decade, as well as a bonus bit at the end.

Also one which, following the autumn of 2010 which brought a Citrine Wagtail as well as four Ferruginous Ducks, then introduced us to 'Keith's Ultimate Year' of 2011. This account includes Blagdon as well as Chew, and demonstrates that birds often move between them, separated as they are by only a few miles and no significant hills.

(Reproduced from the article that appeared in the 2011 Avon Bird Report, with their kind permission.)

Chew and Blagdon in 2011–12 – The Ultimate Year?

Many birders judge the quality of a year's birding by the number of rarities they see. At Chew and Blagdon, most years manage to turn up one or two 'BB Rarities'. But 2011 was in a class of its own. Why was this?

The numbers of birds at the lakes and the quality of the birding is determined by a number of factors, the most important of which is the water level. Being drinking water reservoirs, summer pumping means that levels usually start to fall in early summer so that, in a 'normal year', a muddy, food-rich margin soon starts to appear. This of course attracts waders, which are undoubtedly the most sought after of all the lakes' migrants. Not only are we enamoured by the beauty of their plumage and the delicacy of their structure, but we are in total awe of their phenomenal globetrotting capabilities. The earliest migrants are relatively local: Lapwings, Redshanks and Common Sandpipers from Britain and Green Sandpipers from Scandinavia. But, as the autumn progresses, species arrive from more distant and exotic lands: Iceland, Greenland and the tundras of Siberia. But what really raises the adrenaline are the 'Yanks'. In a good year, we can usually expect one or two trans-Atlantic vagrants, but the autumn of 2011 produced an astonishing eleven individuals of five species. But it wasn't just the waders. At Chew, in the twelve months from June 2011 to May 2012, we had the phenomenal total of 22 American birds of eleven species, not allowing for possible duplication with two of the duck records. Ironically, however, the 'bird of the autumn' came not from

A Semipalmated Sandpiper, one of many 'Yanks' in 2011 | Laurel Tucker

America, but from Russia. A superb juvenile Sharp-tailed Sandpiper discovered by Nigel Milbourne at Blagdon on 18 November and relocating to Chew the following day. This bird, which breeds in eastern Siberia, should have been in Australia! Needless to say, it attracted hundreds of birders from far and wide.

In 2011 the water levels fell quickly, producing large areas of mud by early July. Low water levels do not just benefit the waders, they also benefit grebes, ducks, coots, even terns and passerines. They do this by concentrating the food supplies (fish and invertebrates), and by bringing the weed closer to the surface, they expose muddy food-rich margins. This could also give rise to an increase in invertebrate numbers by raising the water temperature. In addition, the exposed shoreline benefits a disparate bunch of passerines that includes pipits, wagtails, wheatears and finches.

But three other important factors also come into play. Firstly, a good wader passage depends on the summer's breeding success on the Arctic tundras. Success rates are cyclical, dependent largely on the Lemming cycle. In a good Lemming year, the predators eat the Lemmings, allowing the birds to rear their young unmolested. This certainly seems to have been the case in 2011, at least for the Canadian breeders. Secondly, to produce falls of birds, we need poor weather as in calm, anticyclonic conditions, they simply fly straight over. But to receive American waders, we need westerly gales. Not only that, but the gales need to coincide with the time that the birds are migrating, around the September full moon. The weather in September 2011 was spot on. It was a changeable month, with frequent south-westerly and westerly winds. It was in fact the sixth most 'south-westerly' September in 139 years of record keeping. The first gales struck on 6th (remnants of Tropical Storm 'Lee') with further strong winds on 12th (remnants of Hurricane 'Katia'). The latter hit bang on the full moon and caused a major arrival of American waders, right across Britain and Ireland. The huge scale of the displacement was confirmed by events on the island of Bermuda, 640 miles off the coast of North Carolina. A contemporaneous arrival there included up to 100 American Golden Plovers, 180 Pectoral Sandpipers and a record 1,000 Semipalmated Sandpipers, followed by an astonishing 1,000+ Yellow-billed Cuckoos in the first week of October (*Bermuda Audubon Society Newsletter* Vol. 22. No. 3).

The final piece of the jigsaw is observer coverage. When my friends and I used to cover Chew in the 1960s and 1970s, during school and university holidays, we soon began to realise the potential for finding good birds on weekdays, when most of the older birders were at work. But we also realised just how much we were missing. Factor into the equation our relative inexperience, poor optics and inadequate literature, and it was obvious that we were missing as much as we were finding. What would be achieved with good optics, better ID guides and blanket coverage? The autumn of 2011 surely answered that question. It just so happens that, in recent years, a number of the most active and experienced local birders have reached retirement age, several having taken early voluntary retirement. In the autumn of 2011, the lake was covered on a daily basis by a number of seasoned regulars, all of whom were on the look-out for rarities. The first 'autumn' rarity at CVL was found by Sean Davies on 13 June : the lake's sixth Blue-winged Teal. This was followed by a Lesser Yellowlegs on 8 July and then the lake's third Spotted Sandpiper on 24 September. The excellent range of the more normal species present ensured that from late August onwards we had blanket coverage and we never looked back! On 10 November, the lake's first and long overdue Semipalmated Sandpiper arrived.

Eight days later, when hundreds arrived to see the Sharp-tailed Sandpiper, it was possible to stand on Herriott's Bridge and see Spotted Sandpiper, two Long-billed Dowitchers, Semipalmated Sandpiper and Sharp-tailed Sandpiper! With water levels remaining low, the spectacular run continued unabated into the New Year, the final rarity being discovered on 2 May 2012: CVL's second Squacco Heron. A quick scan of the list below confirms what an incredible twelve months it was.

Apart from Shetland and Scilly, could anywhere else in Britain boast such an amazing list of records? Will it ever be bettered? I hate to be a pessimist, but as I write this in mid-July 2012, having endured three of the wettest and most miserable months on record, with the water at the reservoirs cascading over the overflows, I somehow doubt it!

Rare birds recorded at Chew and Blagdon from June 2011 to May 2012

CHEW	BLAGDON
Whooper Swan (2)*	Whooper Swan*
Pink-footed Goose (4)*	Pink-footed Goose (4)*
Lesser Canada Goose*	Lesser Canada Goose*
Green-winged Teal (2)	
Blue-winged Teal	
Ring-necked Duck* (2)	Ring-necked Duck* (2)
Ferruginous Duck*	Ferruginous Duck*
Lesser Scaup (3)	
Long-tailed Duck*	Long-tailed Duck*
Fulmar (4)	
	Manx Shearwater
Great Northern Diver	
Spoonbill (9)	
Squacco Heron*	Squacco Heron*
Great White Egret	Great White Egret
Slavonian Grebe	Slavonian Grebe
	Common Crane (2)
Black-winged Stilt	
Semipalmated Sandpiper	
Temminck's Stint	
Pectoral Sandpiper (6)	
Sharp-tailed Sandpiper*	Sharp-tailed Sandpiper*
Long-billed Dowitcher (2)*	Long-billed Dowitcher (2)*
Spotted Sandpiper	
Lesser Yellowlegs	
Grey Phalarope (5)	Grey Phalarope (5)
Pomarine Skua	
Ring-billed Gull (2)	Ring-billed Gull (2)
Iceland Gull (3)	Iceland Gull*
Glaucous Gull	
Bearded Tit (2)	
Yellow-browed Warbler	
Siberian Chiffchaff	
littoralis Rock Pipit	

* = same bird seen at both Chew and Blagdon

Keith Vinicombe

A stunning adult Black-winged Stilt turned up in April 2012 almost bringing to an end a spectacular run of excellent birds, waders in particular | Ray Scally

The rest of the decade continued to add new birds to the lake. These were a Bonaparte's Gull in April 2013, a month which also brought a Woodchat Shrike to Widcombe Common. This was actually just outside the lake boundary, although Keith did also see the bird on the fence which bounds the lake itself. 2013 also saw an unprecedented skua passage in September, including eighteen Bonxies, four Arctics, a Pomarine and a possible Long-tailed. The final new entry to the list for the decade was a Roseate Tern in May 2019.

2020 also started on an exciting note, with the Laughing Gull in March and a stunning adult female Red-necked Phalarope swimming around on Herriott's Pool on a lovely warm June evening.

Finally, and immediately before going to print, the lake's first Dusky Warbler was trapped on 28 November. You will forgive us for not being able to add a new species entry or reflect this in the index, but we have managed to get its photo into page 160 in the chapter on the Ringing Station.

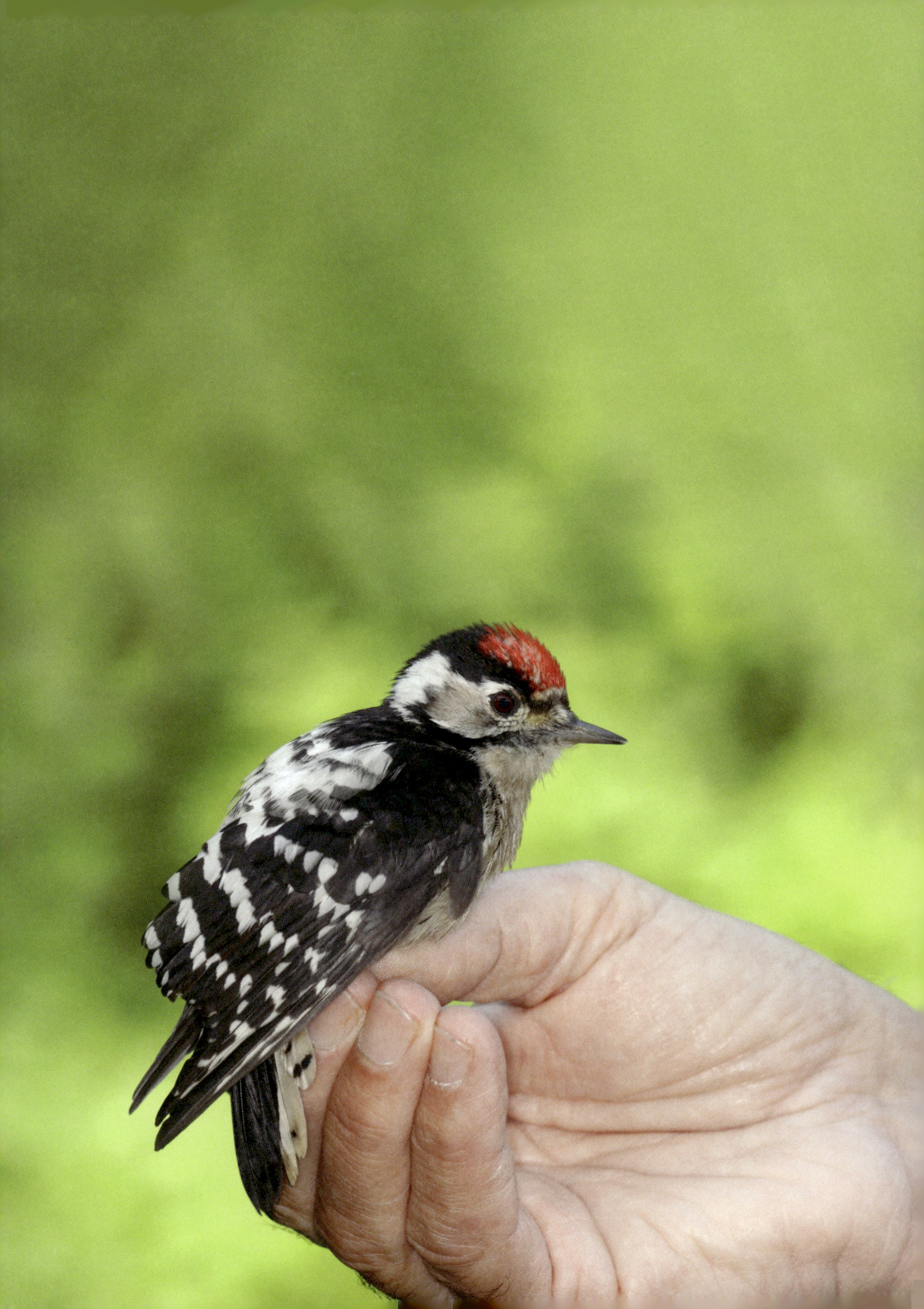

The Ringing Station
Mike Bailey

The bird ringing station at Chew Valley Lake has an impressive history and is entering its 60th year of operation. Starting in the open or in the back of a car, it has progressed through various huts to its relatively comfortable building today. It has ringed over 200,000 birds over that time, with a totally impressive 40,000 Reed Warblers.

Sixty years of ringing

Ringing at Chew Valley Lake began on 4th June 1961 when eight Reed Warblers and one Reed Bunting were caught in mist nets. Further visits to the lake that year provided a total of 226 birds of 24 species, heralding the lake's potential as a ringing site.

The Mendip Ringing Group was formed in the following year and began operating at a number of sites, particularly the Saltford Sewage Works. Permission was given by Bristol Waterworks Company to ring at the lake and although ringing was held up by the severe winter of 1962/63 it restarted in April 1963.

The ringers tried various sites around the lake and by mid-summer had decided that the southern end of the lake, around Herriott's Bridge, was the most suitable area in which to base their activities. It was realised that the lake margins were an important breeding site and feeding area for warblers in the summer and autumn, and the emphasis on this aspect of ringing at Chew Valley Lake continues to this day. It soon became obvious that the lake offered so much potential that ringing at other sites would have to be abandoned. It was therefore decided to re-name the group to fit its single-site status as the Chew Valley Ringing Station (CVRS) and the new name was officially adopted from the beginning of 1964.

Ringing was carried out in the open or from the back of a car, but in 1965 a 3m x 2m garden shed filled the triple role of laboratory, equipment store and shelter. In 1968 a larger hut measuring 7m x 4m had four small rooms, including a laboratory, an office, kitchen and lobby, plus a loft for the storage of poles. Services included electricity, Calor gas and running water.

In 1988 Bristol Water provided a much larger hut (13m x 7m) and laid the breezeblock foundations. The hut then had to be moved in sections from Bristol, at Old Sodbury, and CVRS members took on the challenge of rebuilding it. £2,000 was raised by a sponsored birdwatch and donations from local natural history societies and CVRS members. Local firms were very generous in donating plywood sheets and preservative and the hut was operational by April 1989.

In the years covered by this history, the catching effort has been dominated by the use of mist nets although various traps have also been used. A large Heligoland style trap was erected in 2007 with 50% of the funding coming from the Bristol Naturalists' Society. In this style of trap, birds enter a wider 'mouth' and are driven to a catching area, a technique originating on the island of Heligoland in Germany.

Mike Bailey, on the right, mending net with volunteer. October 2020 | John Rossetti

The newly constructed Heligoland trap in 2007 | Mike Bailey

THE RINGING STATION

Which birds have we caught and how many?

We have compiled a table that shows how many birds, and of which species, have been caught and ringed at CVRS between the start in 1961 and 2018.

Over this period, approximately 210,000 birds of 144 species were ringed: an average of 3,754 birds per year. The highest annual total was 7,091 in 1995.

Ringing Total list by CVRS, 1961–2018

SPECIES	Total Ringed
Canada Goose	5,609
Barnacle Goose	1
Greylag Goose	6
Mute Swan	212
Egyptian Goose	1
Shelduck	3
Garganey	2
Shoveler	2
Gadwall	6
Wigeon	60
Mallard	501
Pintail	2
Teal	147
Pochard	3
Tufted Duck	37
Goldeneye	2
N.A. Ruddy Duck	1
Little Grebe	27
Great Crested Grebe	21
Grey Heron	1
Cormorant	1
Sparrowhawk	98
Buzzard	9
Water Rail	202
Spotted Crake	6
Moorhen	781
Coot	234
Lapwing	19
Ringed Plover	114
Little Ringed Plover	10
Whimbrel	5
Curlew	6
Black-tailed Godwit	1
Knot	1
Ruff	12
Curlew Sandpiper	6
Temminck's Stint	1
Little Stint	8
Dunlin	298
Jack Snipe	4
Snipe	219
Common Sandpiper	258
Green Sandpiper	28
Redshank	15
Wood Sandpiper	11
Spotted Redshank	4
Greenshank	17
Black-headed Gull	84
Great Black-backed Gull	1
Herring Gull	3
Lesser Black-backed Gull	11
Black Tern	1
Little Auk	1
Stock Dove	40
Wood Pigeon	88
Collared Dove	1
Cuckoo	27
Barn Owl	88
Tawny Owl	45
Little Owl	1
Long-eared Owl	1
Short-eared Owl	1
Swift	1,802
Kingfisher	674
Wryneck	3
Lesser S Woodpecker	9
Great S Woodpecker	190
Green Woodpecker	18
Kestrel	25
Hobby	3
Jay	56
Red-backed Shrike	1
Magpie	59
Jackdaw	370
Rook	118
Carrion Crow	82
Raven	4
Coal Tit	757
Marsh Tit	136
Willow Tit	4
Blue Tit	18,888
Great Tit	9,269
Bearded Tit	83
Skylark	11
Sand Martin	4,897
Swallow	18,344
House Martin	3,669
Cetti's Warbler	774
Long-tailed Tit	3,757
Wood Warbler	5
Yellow-browed Warbler	3
Willow Warbler	6,161
Chiffchaff	14,201
Aquatic Warbler	10
Sedge Warbler	18,678
Reed Warbler	40,857
Marsh Warbler	1
Grasshopper Warbler	59
Savi's Warbler	1
Blackcap	9,449
Garden Warbler	2,794
Lesser Whitethroat	2,118
Whitethroat	1,798
Firecrest	14
Goldcrest	1,655
Wren	5,213
Nuthatch	33
Treecreeper	896
Starling	2,311
Blackbird	2,528
Fieldfare	79
Redwing	435
Song Thrush	1,147
Mistle Thrush	17
Spotted Flycatcher	165
Robin	3,394
Bluethroat	1
Nightingale	6
Pied Flycatcher	4
Redstart	68
Whinchat	41
Stonechat	22
Wheatear	4
House Sparrow	247
Tree Sparrow	250
Dunnock	3,273
Yellow Wagtail	535
Grey Wagtail	29
Pied Wagtail	1,548
Meadow Pipit	143
Tree Pipit	17
Water Pipit	3
Rock Pipit	6
Chaffinch	3,986
Brambling	34
Bullfinch	1,290
Greenfinch	5,163
Linnet	190
Redpoll	186
Goldfinch	1,434
Siskin	144
Yellowhammer	2
Little Bunting	1
Reed Bunting	4,181
TOTAL RINGED	**210,238**

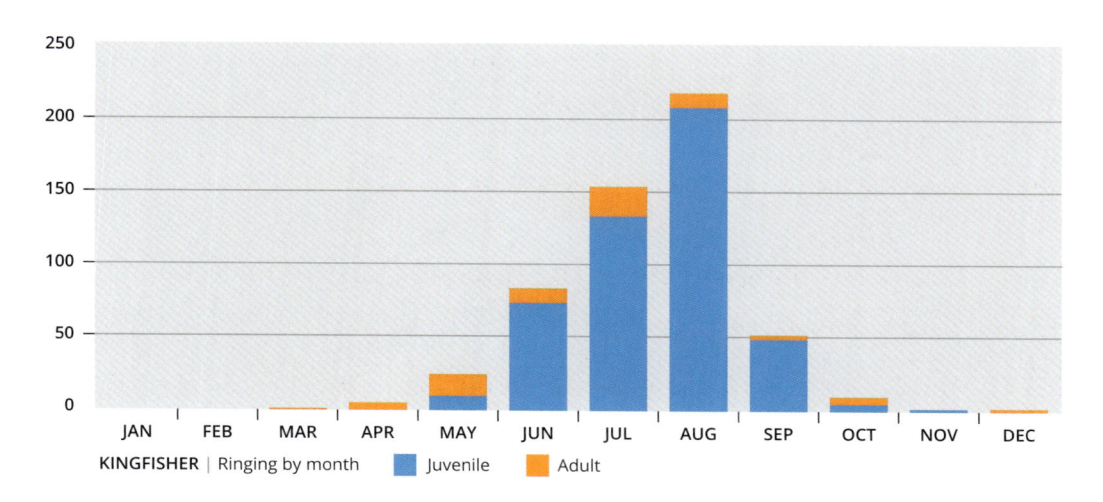

KINGFISHER | Ringing by month — Juvenile / Adult

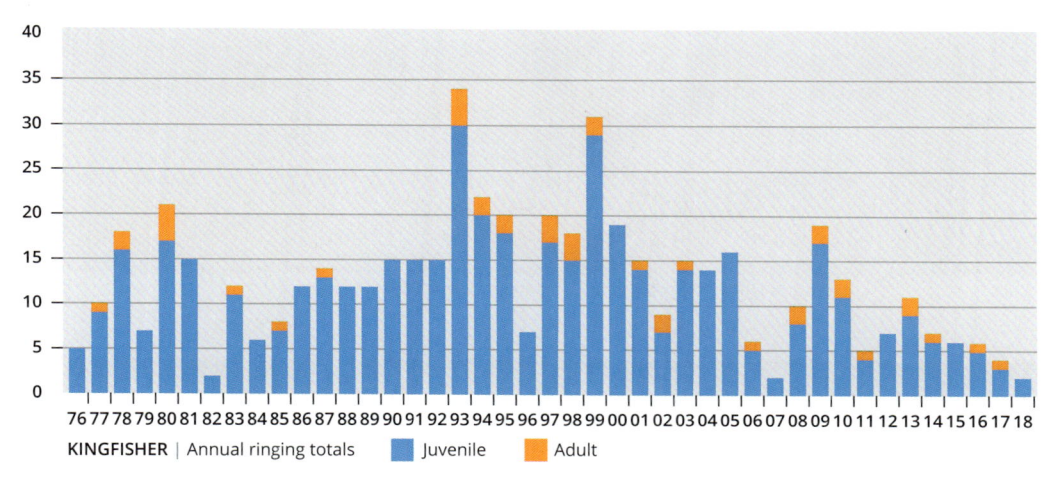

KINGFISHER | Annual ringing totals — Juvenile / Adult

Rare birds ringed

Of course rarities, by their very definition, rarely turn up, but nevertheless it does happen and surprises have included the following species: Bluethroat (1968), Little Bunting (1976), Savi's Warbler (1986) and Marsh Warbler (1994). Other species such as Wryneck, Aquatic Warbler and Yellow-browed Warbler have even occurred on more than one occasion.

However, it is the 'common' birds that are the mainstay of the ringing station's activities, as this chart of our 'top ten' species shows.

TOP TEN SPECIES RINGED 1961–2018		
1	Reed Warbler	40,857
2	Blue Tit	18,888
3	Sedge Warbler	18,678
4	Swallow	18,344
5	Chiffchaff	14,201
6	Blackcap	9,449
7	Great Tit	9,269
8	Willow Warbler	6,161
9	Canada Goose	5,609
10	Wren	5,213

A Dusky Warbler caught in November 2020 | Rich Andrews

Yellow-browed Warbler retrap October 2016 | Mike Bailey

As a major reed bed site, it is not surprising that Reed and Sedge Warbler are high on the list. In the mid-1960s there were more Sedge Warblers than Reed Warblers, by the mid-1970s their numbers were approximately equal, and from the mid-1980s Reed Warblers were more numerous.

The ups and downs in the totals reflect both the conditions they face in their winter quarters in Africa and the variation in catching effort at the lake. That the Reed Warbler now dominates the CVRS ringing totals is thought to be caused by the gradual development and expansion of the reed beds around the lake margins. This provides conditions that are ideal for Reed Warbler and less so for Sedge Warbler, as their preferred fen-scrub-swamp habitat has become increasingly restricted due to the expansion of the *Phragmites*.

For both these species, especially Sedge Warblers, their high numbers are due to birds that have bred elsewhere but use the lake as a stopping off and fattening up site in readiness for migrating. The nest recorders might also admit that the Sedge Warbler nests are much harder to find!

Blue and Great Tits form a significant proportion of the overall total as a large number are ringed as nestlings in the spring, and when coming to feeding stations in the autumn and winter months.

Although only a small number of Swallows are ringed locally during the early part of the breeding season, large catches are possible as they come in to roost in the reed beds during July and August.

Blackcap, Chiffchaff and Willow Warbler are our other commonest summer visitors. The CVRS totals for the years 1963–2018 reflect the long-term national trends.

Especially noticeable is the reduction in Willow Warbler numbers, reflecting their decline as a breeding species locally. Wren (5,213), Reed Bunting (4,181), Long-tailed Tit (3,757), Robin (3,394) and Dunnock (3,273) represent the common resident passerines at the lake.

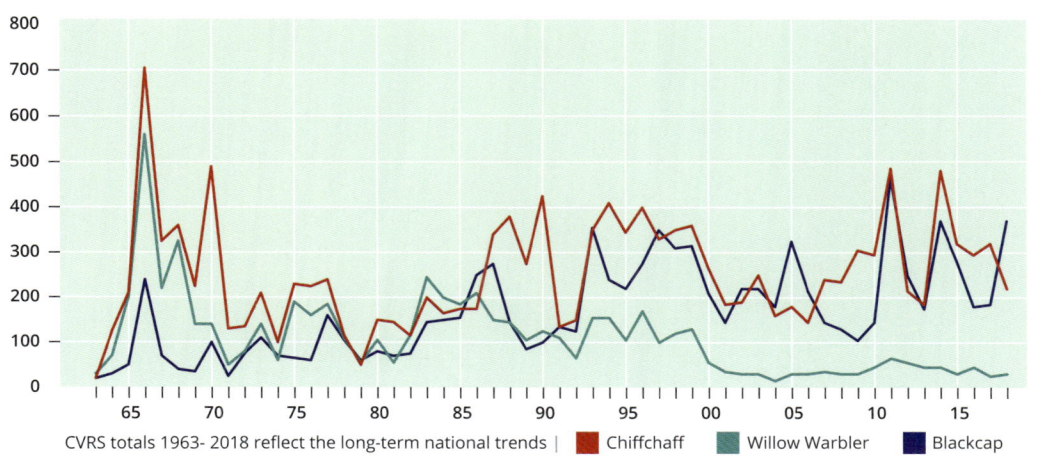

Annual ringing totals 1963- 2018 | Sedge Warbler | Reed Warbler

CVRS totals 1963- 2018 reflect the long-term national trends | Chiffchaff | Willow Warbler | Blackcap

THE RINGING STATION

Canada Goose's appearance as 9th on the list is thanks to the annual Canada Goose roundup during their flightless period. Traditionally this takes place on a Tuesday, either at the end of June or early in July. The most frequently reported ringed species (i.e. seen, trapped or recovered elsewhere) is Canada Goose with 600 records (25% of the total). A large majority of these are noted as being shot for crop protection in Devon and Somerset.

CANGO-processing 09-07-2013 | Mike Bailey

Exceptional individuals

There are two individual birds that deserve special mention, and both were almost certainly born at Chew. Cetti's Warbler N482152 was ringed as a juvenile male on 20th June 1999 and retrapped 28 times until it was last trapped on 18th October 2008. A couple of years after initial capture he moved from the east side of the reserve and settled in the area of our constant effort site in front of the ringing station, having lived for at least 9 years, 3 months and 28 days. He holds the UK longevity record for this species.

The other exceptional individual was Reed Warbler F088114, which was caught as a juvenile on 17th July 1989 and sexed as a male by cloacal development in subsequent years. He was recorded once or twice every year until last seen on 13th May 2001 having lived for at least 11 years, 3 months and 15 days. He remained in approximately the same area of the reserve throughout his life except that remarkably he must have made 12 return trips to Africa!

Cetti's Warbler | Gary Thoburn

Recoveries and controls

There are 2,400 records of birds that have been found elsewhere (recoveries) and of ringed birds found at the lake (called controls). The table below is a summary of CVRS's foreign recoveries.

SPECIES	Austria	Belgium	Corsica	Denmark	Estonia	Finland	France	Ireland	Germany	Italy	Latvia	Morocco	Netherlands	Norway	Poland	Portugal	Scotland	Senegal	Spain	S. Africa	Sweden	Syria	USSR
Wigeon				1	1																		1
Teal				1		2	2																
Tufted Duck													1										1
Cormorant																2							
Coot							1																
Ringed Plover												1											
Jack Snipe						1																	
Snipe							2												1				
Black-headed Gull			2	1		2				1			1	6							1		1
Lesser Black-b Gull							1																
Short-eared Owl															1								
Swift										1					1								
Sand Martin							3											5	3	6			
Swallow							3						3							12			
House Martin									1														
Willow Warbler							2									1							
Chiffchaff		1					2												1	1			
Aquatic Warbler															1								
Sedge Warbler		3							3		1	1						8	1	4			
Reed Warbler	2					28				7			1			8			2	13			
Blackcap			1							4						2				2			
Garden Warbler						1				1										1			
Lesser Whitethroat	1							2													1		
Whitethroat										1													
Starling					1																		
Blackbird				2						1													
Fieldfare							2																
Redwing		2																					
Song Thrush				1			1																
Yellow Wagtail																				2			
Pied Wagtail		1					1											3	2				
Chaffinch		2									2	1											
Linnet							1																
Goldfinch		1					2	1												4			
Siskin															1								

Nearly all of these recoveries will have come from birds wearing conventional metal rings that were found either dead or captured by other ringers. In a few cases though, especially the Black-headed Gulls, the reports come via colour rings being read 'in the field'. At 9,700 km the Swallow records from South Africa make this species our most distant migrant. Nine of these were reported in the early years of the ringing station from 1967 to 1969. There are seven birds, Chiffchaff (1), Reed Warbler (2), Sand Martin (3) and Sedge Warbler (1), reported from Senegal. This is thanks to a team of UK based ringers who visited the Djoudj National Bird Sanctuary in the 1991/1992 winter.

THE RINGING STATION

Catching effort

Clearly, if there is to be any means of calculating changes in bird populations by general ringing, then it will be necessary to adjust for catching effort. Three measures were proposed by Roy Smith (published in the CVRS 6th Report covering 1976–1978 pp 20–25). These were 'Operational Days', 'Ringer Days' and 'Net Foot Hours'. Of these the net foot hours have proven to be the most useful.

Net foot hours are based on a standard full height net so that, for example, two sixty-foot nets operated for 5 hours = 2 x 60 x 5 = 600 NFH. You can see from the chart below that the 1990s stand out as a period of much greater ringing activity in the use of mist nets (peaking in 1993). This period coincided with visits in the summer months by the West Wilts Ringing Group and several very active CVRS members.

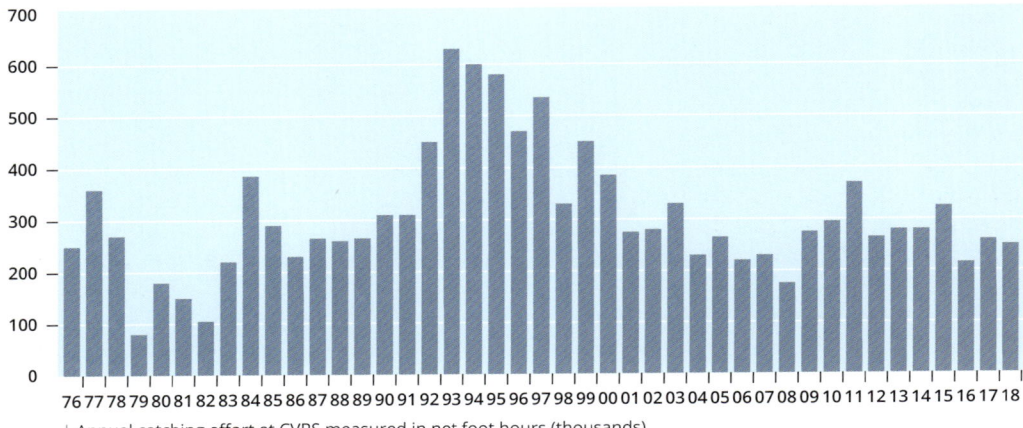

| Annual catching effort at CVRS measured in net foot hours (thousands)

Constant effort ringing

To help address the question of the variability of catching effort at different places, the ringing station takes part in the British Trust for Ornithology (BTO) 'Constant Effort Scheme' (CES). This has been in operation since 1983 with the first four years being used to test and validate the scheme. Ringers operate the same nets in the same locations over the same time period at regular intervals through the breeding season at over 140 sites throughout Britain and Ireland. The Scheme provides long-term trend information on the abundance of adults and juveniles, productivity and also adult survival rates for 24 species of common songbird.

Of these, two are on the 'Red list' of the Birds of Conservation Concern (BOCC), namely Song Thrush and Willow Tit, and four are Amber-listed: Dunnock, Willow Warbler, Bullfinch and Reed Bunting. The other species are Wren, Robin, Blackbird, Cetti's Warbler, Sedge Warbler, Reed Warbler, Whitethroat, Lesser Whitethroat, Garden Warbler, Blackcap, Chiffchaff, Long-tailed Tit, Blue Tit, Great Tit, Treecreeper, Chaffinch, Greenfinch and Goldfinch. All, apart from Willow Tit, occur annually at our CES sites at Chew Valley Lake and are included in the national figures for population trends.

Computerisation

The use of computers by CVRS began in the mid-1980s with ringers experimenting with various home computers and databases. However, no real progress was made until 1993 when the British Trust for Ornithology produced a standardised programme called B-RING. This was originally based on the BBC B home computer and could be used for sending records to their headquarters on a disc and subsequently by email.

Despite the setbacks of two burglaries and theft of the computer the data group, which for some unknown reason became known as 'The Tufty Club', held regular meetings on Tuesday evenings for data entry. By 2003 two computers were in operation and a switch was made to using the BTO's

IPMR (Integrated Population Monitoring Recorder). This involved not only entering the current data for submission to the BTO but work also began on catching up with historical records back to 1976! This was a rather monumental task that was completed by 2007. The CVRS database now holds records for approximately 275,000 birds. This includes 95,000 recaptures that provide some of the most informative data for analysis. Currently the ringing scheme is setting up a new system called DemOn (Demography On-line) which will allow data to be input directly via the internet into the BTO's central database.

Training

By its very nature ringing is a practical activity, and the training is akin to an apprenticeship. For someone interested in becoming a ringer it probably begins by seeing it taking place, perhaps at a nature reserve or when visiting a bird observatory, and it also gets wide coverage these days with television programmes such as Autumnwatch and Springwatch.

Having made contact, usually through the BTO's website, the progress is from helper, through a series of permit grades and endorsements, to finally becoming a fully-independent 'A' ringer and possibly a Trainer. There is no hard and fast rule about how long it takes to become a qualified ringer, but typically, for people that are taking it up recreationally, a couple of months are spent as a helper, two years as a trainee and two to three years as a 'C' ringer, making it around five years in total.

The training at Chew Valley Ringing Station can provide enough experience for a permit to ring passerines and near passerines, ducks, birds of prey and rails. However, for other species such as seabirds and waders, the appropriate training has to be obtained elsewhere. However, the ringing scheme can be flexible, and it is possible to qualify quite quickly for a 'restricted' permit for projects not involving the use of mist nets. For example, an experienced nest recorder may wish to broaden their study by ringing nestlings, or a carer at a bird hospital could qualify to ring rehabilitated birds on their release.

Training is a core activity for the ringing station. Some trainees will move on to run their own sites and projects while others remain as part of the established crew of around 50 members. Since 1991, thanks to the larger hut, CVRS has been able to organise an annual BTO-sponsored ringing course. This takes place over a long weekend at the end of July, and aims to give ringers from other parts of the country the experience of reed bed ringing and an opportunity for an independent assessment for permit upgrades.

Participants at one of the CVRS ringing courses in 2011 | Mike Bailey

Nest recording

Although a small number of nests may be recorded in March, the main focus begins in April and is split between checking boxes and searching for open nests. As the ringing of chicks requires different sets of skills, it is necessary to obtain separate permit endorsements for nest box passerines, open nest passerines, birds of prey, wader chicks and at seabird colonies.

CVRS runs about 200 nest boxes; of these 170 are small ones used mainly by tit species and the occasional Robin, and 30 are large boxes used by owls, Jackdaws and Stock Doves. These need to be checked at least once per week to give full nest histories and outcomes. Of course, the advantages are that the position of the nests are known and the details for the nest recording card (orientation, height, tree species, site and habitat codes) can be transferred from one year to the next. The tit pulli are ringed at around 10–16 days old when the primary feathers are between just breaking out of pin and one-third grown.

First year male Sparrowhawk 18 November 2010. Their hunting technique usually results in a few being ringed each year, having been caught in mist nets | Mike Bailey

Two 'branching' Tawny Owlets near Moreton Hide, 4 May 2014 | Mike Bailey

What do Barn Owls eat?

Some of the nest boxes that are used by Barn Owls have been used to give a fascinating study of what they eat, which has also provided interesting data on some of our less frequently seen small mammals around the lake.

In March 2015 and April 2016, students studying biology and zoology dissected 212 Barn Owl pellets collected from three Barn Owl boxes at Chew Valley Lake on 10th February 2015. These were from the areas near the southern and western sides of the lake, Herriott's Bridge, Heron's Green and the Parklands. This was part of the students' 'Diversity of Life' course at the School of Biological Sciences at the University of Bristol.

Barn Owls commonly eat Bank Voles, Field Voles, Common Shrews and other small rodents and insectivores. Their prey is a good indicator of what species of small mammal are living in the hunting range of the Barn Owl. In this exercise not only did the Barn Owl pellet dissections reveal the expected prey items but also species which are under-recorded. These included the Water Shrew and the Harvest Mouse. The Mole is an interesting prey item too – one was an adult and the other a young animal.

Barn Owls are indicators of how well local populations of small mammals are faring. In this case, the study of the pellets on this scale has helped reveal that Harvest Mice, in particular, are living and perhaps thriving around the Chew Valley Lake area.

The following pie chart shows the analysis that was found from carefully identifying small bone fragments.

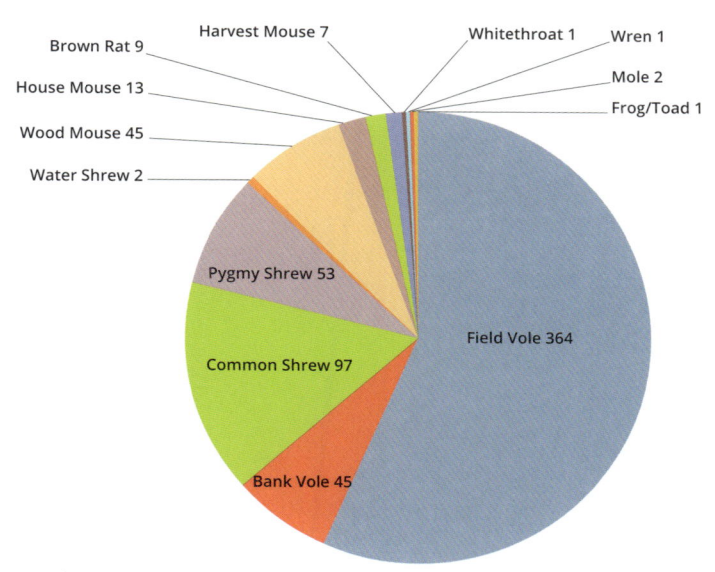

- Brown Rat 9
- Harvest Mouse 7
- Whitethroat 1
- Wren 1
- House Mouse 13
- Mole 2
- Wood Mouse 45
- Frog/Toad 1
- Water Shrew 2
- Pygmy Shrew 53
- Common Shrew 97
- Bank Vole 45
- Field Vole 364

Prey of Barn Owls from Chew Valley Lake (212 pellets collected from nest boxes 10/2/15)

Other nests

Finding and then ringing passerine nestlings in open nests is definitely more of a challenge, and great care needs to be taken not to disturb vegetation and draw the attention of predators. There is also a smaller 'window of opportunity' to ring the nestlings of around four days between when they are large enough to ring and yet young enough that they sit tight and do not 'explode' when the nest is approached.

A Reed Warbler brood – ready for ringing | Mike Bailey

And a couple of other species not often caught at Chew:

Male Redstart, 14 April 2017. An uncommon passage migrant at Chew Valley Lake. The plumage indicates a bird in its second calendar year | Mike Bailey

Water Pipit, 3 November 2012. Noted in small numbers around the lake in the autumn/winter, this bird was only the 4th ringing record. The others were in 1979, 1988 and 1999 | Mike Bailey

The CVRS year

Apart from the general mist netting and training, a pattern of activities has emerged. In the winter months the lake level usually rises to such an extent that much of the reed bed is inaccessible and there is a greater use of feeding stations and the Heligoland trap.

A recent winter project in conjunction with Aberdeen University has been to investigate which sub-species of Chiffchaff occur at the lake between November and March. By using mitochondrial DNA, it has been possible to identify three subspecies *Phylloscopus collybita collybita* (nominate), *Ph. c. abietinus* (Northern) and *Ph. c. tristis* (Siberian). All three have been shown to be present.

By April nest recording gets underway. The 200 boxes need to be checked once per week and searching for open nests is undertaken by a small band of very dedicated recorders. CVRS contributes approximately 650 nest records annually to the BTO's Nest Recording Scheme. The constant effort scheme begins on May 1st and runs through until the end of August. The two CES sites are operated from 6.00 am until 12 noon with three sessions per month at approximately 10-day intervals.

The end of June is the 'traditional' time for the Canada Goose roundup and the BTO-sponsored ringing course takes place at the end of July. In the autumn and winter more time is taken for habitat management, sometimes helped by groups of volunteers. In between these activities the ringing station plays host to various interested groups to demonstrate and explain the rationale behind the bird ringing process.

Further information about the activities of the Ringing Station may be found on our website at www.chewvalleyringingstation.co.uk which gives a monthly update on ringing activities.

More immediate news is tweeted via our Twitter account @CVRSnews.

Bristol Water

And finally, no account about the history of Chew Valley Ringing Station is complete without a special mention of our relationship with Bristol Water. From the outset Bristol Water has always been supportive of our activities. Not only by supplying our present accommodation but also every year, with donations for various items such as rings, producing reports and help with reed bed management. Above all, though, allowing us access to one of the best reed bed ringing sites in the country!

Habitat management with help from a team of volunteers, October 2018 | Mike Bailey

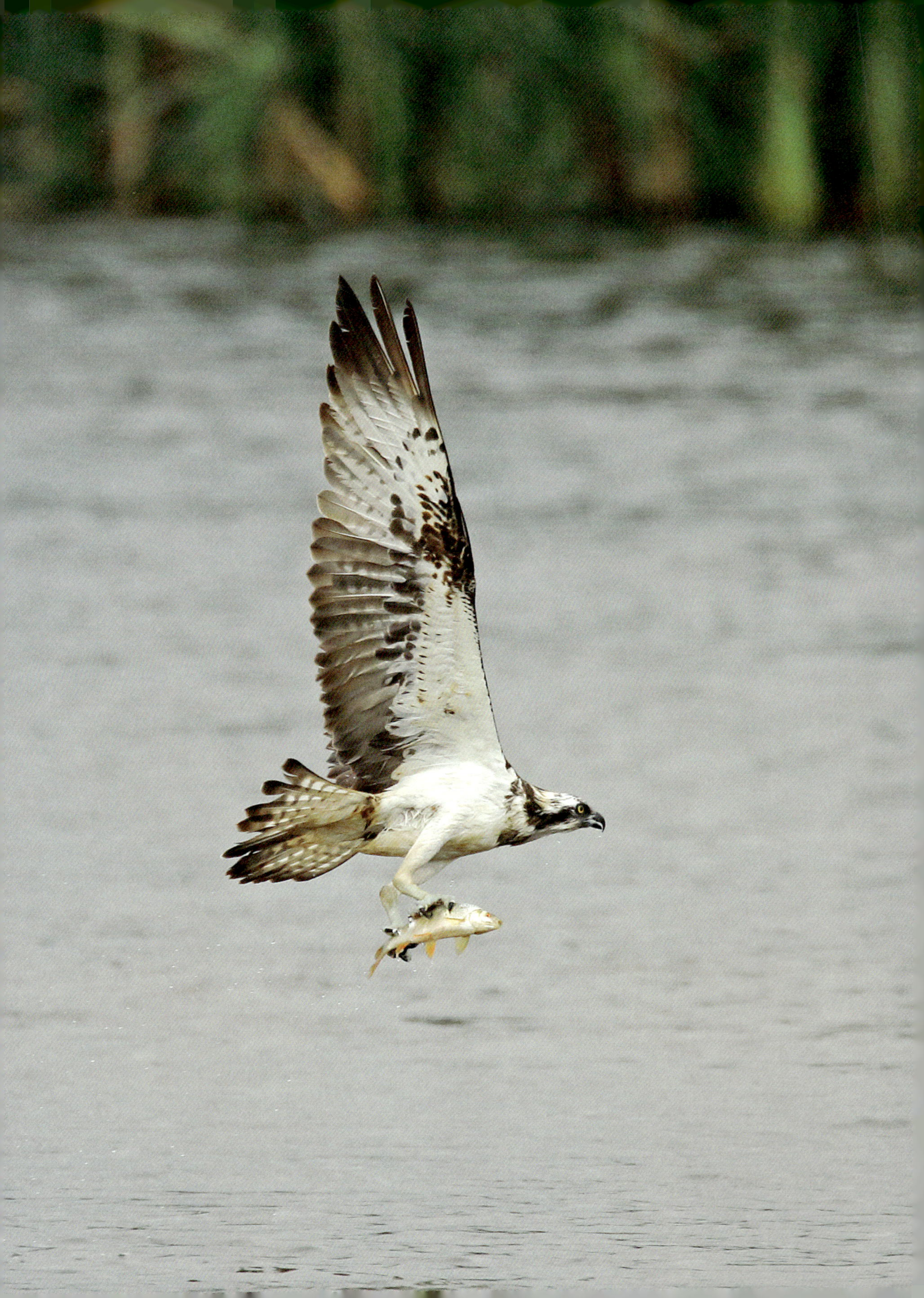

Complete species list and charts

Keith Vinicombe

This is the full list, with records from 1954 to 2020. Every species recorded at the lake is included, even some controversial ones, with many charts for quick summaries. Published records are supplemented by personal observations and analyses. It's all here.

This part of the book is illustrated with many photographs from local photographers as well as many line drawings from the late Laurel Tucker. We have not attempted to show every species, this is not intended as an identification guide. We have chosen images for their quality and interest. Every photograph will have been taken at the lake, or very close to its boundary.

For ease of locating a species, we are including an alphabetical index for this chapter.

Summary

This section comprises a full and detailed account of the birds recorded at the lake and is the result of the comprehensive analysis produced by Keith Vinicombe. Including his own records and available published sources, it aims to provide details of all records since the development of the lake itself, covering over 65 years. For most species, charts show how they have increased or declined over this period, with additional charts showing the months of the year in which they occur. As such this goes well beyond a simple list of species for a single locality, but also adds interesting comments and insights as well as showing trends that will tend to mirror changes in national bird populations over the years, conditions on the lake and other factors such as local and national weather events.

As with other books about a local 'patch' and one without a clear county boundary, we have had to make certain decisions about what we should include in this list.

Area boundary

Chew Valley Lake is managed by Bristol Water, and so the boundaries of their land form a technical boundary. However many birds that are attracted to the lake will also visit fields nearby, adjoining farmland and other areas that are not strictly within the Bristol Water boundaries, and birders will tend to go around the lake by the circular road as it is no longer possible (or desirable) to walk around the edge. So notable birds from other locations on the circuit and/or the immediately surrounding villages (Chew Stoke, West Harptree and Bishop Sutton) may be included, but any unusual or scarce records that are outside the Bristol Water boundary will be mentioned as such in the text.

Bird order and nomenclature

We have followed the order used by the Ninth Edition of the British List (BOU 2017) as updated 24 Jan 2020, and we have used the British (English) vernacular names.

Included records

These records have been checked against the accepted records from local and national recorders. As part of the work on this book, there has also been a process to review some of the older records and some have been re-circulated within the recorder's committee. As a result, some previously accepted records have been removed where it is now considered that insufficient evidence was provided. For example, Goshawk has been removed from the list, as all records prior to 1980 are considered to relate to escaped falconer's birds, or as no longer proven. Rare and scarce records are included up to the end of 2019, so that on first publication the book is as up to date as practicably possible. A few records are also included from 2020, the year of publication.

There will always be debate about certain occurrences – take for example the Booted Eagle which toured the UK in 2000 and was thought by many to be a great candidate as a wild bird. Other records fall into similar categories, such as records of Marbled Duck and other species that appeared to tie in well with other movements across Europe or had been (controversially) categorised as escapes from captivity.

To add interest and colour, as well as allowing for any future review of the records, some of these controversial records are included and debated, but their status as regards their acceptance and categorisation is clearly indicated at the end of the species entry.

Specifically, the relevant nationally agreed categories are:

Category A
Species recorded in an apparently natural state at least once since 1 January 1950.

Category C
Species that, although introduced, now derive from the resulting self-sustaining populations.

Category D
Species that would otherwise appear in Category A except that there is reasonable doubt that they have ever occurred in a natural state. Species placed in Category D **only** form no part of the British List, and any included here are clearly indicated.

(Technically Category D is a holding category between C and E, where Category E are known escapees from captivity and introduced populations that are not considered to be self-sustaining.)

Records of national rarities are adjudicated by The British Birds Rarities Committee (BBRC). Local rarities are assessed by the Avon Recorder's Committee.

Species charts and graphs

Where relevant, many species will have graphs or charts associated with the recorded numbers. These are calculated as follows:

Monthly distribution charts
These are taken from the *average* of the maximum counts for the month, over the years indicated and for which data is present. In the case of rarer species with fewer records, *total* monthly numbers may be used.

Annual broods
This is taken from the number of broods (not nests), i.e. individual family parties. This is NOT the total of young, which will be much higher (before predation and other losses).

Annual maxima
This is the largest count in the year, irrespective of month. Note that, especially for wildfowl, birds may stay over the year end and appear in 2 different yearly figures.

Abbreviations
ABR – *Avon Bird Report*
BWP – *The Handbook of the Birds of the Western Palearctic*

Observers
In general and when known, observers are noted only for the first record of the species. However, for rarer or difficult to identify birds, observers may be included on subsequent records. As many records are from Keith Vinicombe, the initials KEV are used in the list.

Species recorded at the lake

RED-LEGGED PARTRIDGE *Alectoris rufa*
There have been five records:
- **1988:** a party of seven was seen on 13 November in a field at Hollow Brook. Six were seen there again on 17th, followed by five on 17 December (KEV *et al.*). These followed a record of one on nearby Knowle Hill on 4 June (*ABR*).
- **2005:** one was seen feeding with Pheasants on the East Shore 5–24 December (R. J. Palmer *et al.*).
- **2007:** one in the Heron's Green Bay/Parkland area on 9 April.
- **2010:** one was seen at several sites on the west shore between the Parkland and Stratford Bay on three dates between 11 March and 4 April.
- **2013:** a male calling near Herriott's Bridge on 12 and 19 February.

GREY PARTRIDGE *Perdix perdix*
This species was not mentioned in *Somerset Birds* until 1963, it presumably being too common to list. There was, however, a comment that stated: 'it seems to have become rare or extinct in many parts [of Somerset] even before the severe winter of 1962–63'. Since then, the species has undergone a severe decline in Britain and Ireland, with a population decline of 91% in the UK between 1967 and 2010 (see *Bird Atlas* 2007–11). The Chew records since 1963 are as follows:
- **1963:** seven on 9 February (K. L. Fox) and two pairs on 18 May (B. E. Slade).
- **1964:** 'reported'.
- **1965:** two on 27 February, one on 30 July, and singles on 6th, 17th and 22nd August (KEV); also two on 9 September.
- **1967:** six on 26 July (KEV).
- **1970:** juvenile flushed twice on 23 July (KEV).
- **1973:** mentioned in *Somerset Birds* as 'bred' or 'seen in a covey', but no details.
- **1985:** a pair in a field behind the Sailing Club on 15 July (KEV).
- **1986:** 'noted in breeding season' (*ABR*).
- **1988:** ten on 19 November and 11 on 10 December, in fields behind the East Shore (A. H. Davis, KEV).

There were also records claimed in 1992, 1994 and 1997 but details are lacking.

QUAIL *Coturnix coturnix*

There is one record. A calling male was heard in an un-cut hay field behind Stratford Bay on 14–15 June 2008 (A. R. Ashman *et al.*) and it was also seen in flight. On 16 June it moved a mile north to the Parkland where it was also seen well in flight. Remarkably, it then commuted between the two sites until 23 June, presumably moving at night.

PHEASANT *Phasianus colchicus*

Pheasants are present around the lake in small numbers but, except for when the males are calling, they can be surprisingly difficult to see. There have been eight double figure counts, all since 1989, with maxima of 14 in October 2009, 15 in December 2010 and 20 in October 2011. The highest count, however, was of 42 on 6 December 2005, the birds feeding on colonising vegetation in a year of low water levels.

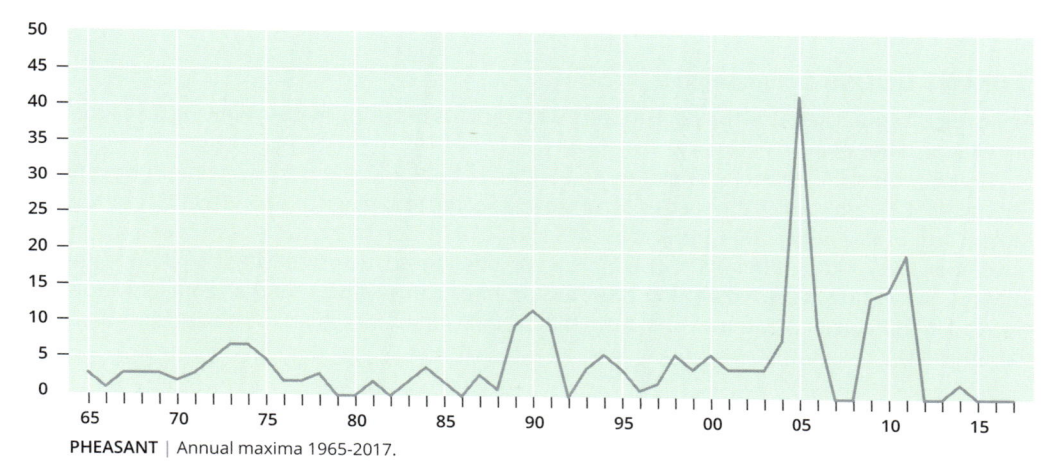

PHEASANT | Annual maxima 1965-2017.

The second graph shows the numbers of calling males during 1990-2015, the numbers clearly increasing during that 26-year period. The reasons for this are almost certainly related to releases of birds for shooting purposes, there occasionally being a large shoot on nearby Burledge Hill, to the south-east of the lake. The average number of calling males has been 13 (based on 24 out of 26 years from 1990 to 2015) but with as many as 34 in 2011.

Broods have been recorded between 12 June and 28 July but they are difficult to detect, the highest total being three in both 1994 and 2010. In 1975, a half-grown juvenile was seen as late as 17 October.

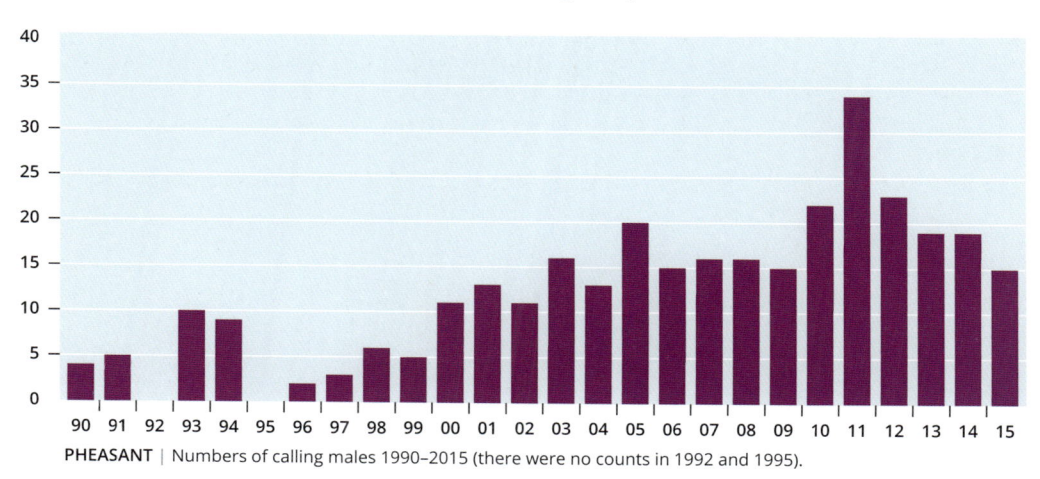

PHEASANT | Numbers of calling males 1990–2015 (there were no counts in 1992 and 1995).

The final graph shows that Pheasants are present all year round, with the largest counts in April and May, when the males are most vocal, and again in autumn and early winter, when the water levels are low and the birds are more visible.

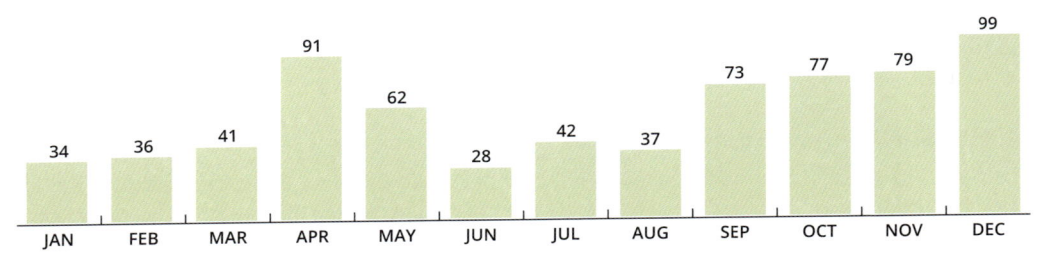

PHEASANT | Monthly maxima (combined) 1965-2015.

JAN	FEB	MAR	APR	MAY	JUN	JUL	AUG	SEP	OCT	NOV	DEC
34	36	41	91	62	28	42	37	73	77	79	99

| BRENT GOOSE *Branta bernicla*

An erratic visitor. October is the peak month, with records reducing in the following three months, but with another peak in February.

The first record involved a singleton on 23 March 1969 and the next was one in November–December 1975, after which the species occurred in 22 of the following 40 years. Recently more scarce, with records in November 2009 and also in 2015 and 2018. The highest counts have been eight in both November 1988 and October 2001. There have also been three records of single birds in May–June: 21 May 2002, 1 June 2003 and 14 May 2004. It is perhaps conceivable that the same individual was involved in this cluster of late records. Note that all individuals identified to sub-specific level were 'dark-bellied'.

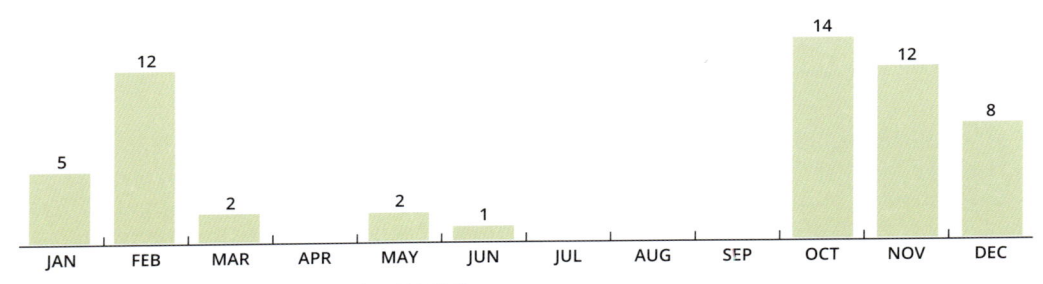

JAN	FEB	MAR	APR	MAY	JUN	JUL	AUG	SEP	OCT	NOV	DEC
5	12	2		2	1				14	12	8

BRENT GOOSE | Monthly distribution (totals) 1969-2015.

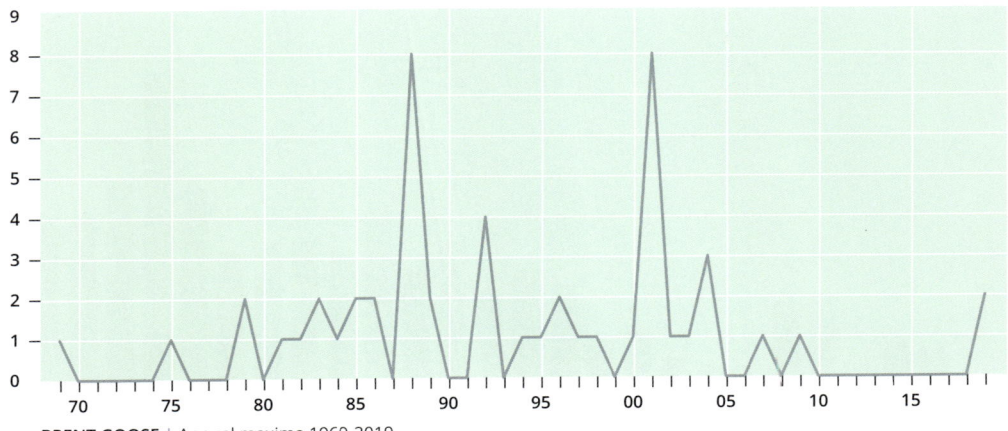

BRENT GOOSE | Annual maxima 1969-2019.

CANADA GOOSE *Branta canadensis*

The first Canada Goose to be recorded at Chew was on 4–25 March 1956, followed by two in April–May 1957, which tried to breed unsuccessfully (per H. J. Boyd). In January 1962, however, up to 48 were present from 6 to 21 January. Small numbers were again recorded in 1963 (2), 1964 (1), 1968 (3) and 1969 (3).

It wasn't until 1971 that colonisation finally began, when three appeared on 25 July. These involved a female with two juveniles and these birds went on to form the nucleus of the current Chew flock. The female left in March 1972 and it seems that in 1973 the two juveniles went on to breed together, producing a brood of two – the first breeding record for the lake. From that point onwards, numbers increased slowly, with up to five in 1973 and eight in 1974. Six new arrivals in July 1975 boosted the flock size even further and the species then increased almost exponentially, eventually reaching an unbeaten 905 in June 1996.

By 1991 however, Bristol Water were receiving complaints about the geese from local farmers, so during 1991 a control programme under licence was instigated which lasted at least until 2005. This involved various methods (dipping eggs in paraffin, nest and clutch destruction and egg pricking). This was successful, and in 1994 an astonishing 78 nests on Denny Island were destroyed under licence (*ABR* 1994). The Canada Goose breeding population started to decline and, since 1993, annual brood totals have fallen to single figures, with as few as two in 2000. There was a slight recovery from 2017 to 2019 when at least 10 successful nests were located at the south end of the lake.

Every year in late summer, large numbers of Canada Geese arrive at the lake to moult, when they become flightless for a period of about three to four weeks. During this period they are rounded up by CVRS (the ringing station) and as many as possible are ringed. This has given us a useful insight into the origins of our moulting birds. As to be expected, most come from Glamorgan, Gloucestershire, Wiltshire, Hampshire, Dorset and also Devon, but two adventurous birds reached Lancashire and Yorkshire (*ABR*).

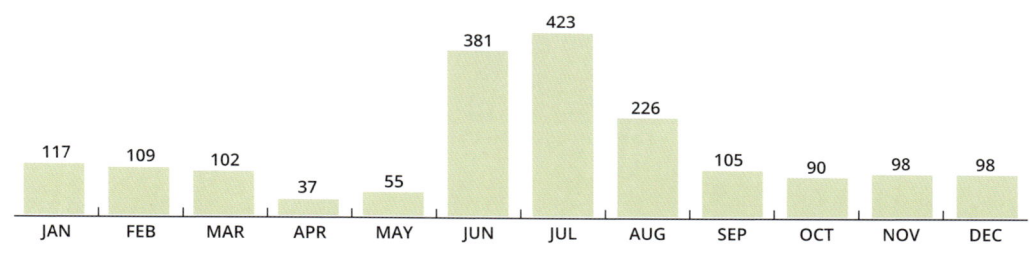

CANADA GOOSE | Monthly distribution (average) 1971–2016. Note the June to August moult influx.

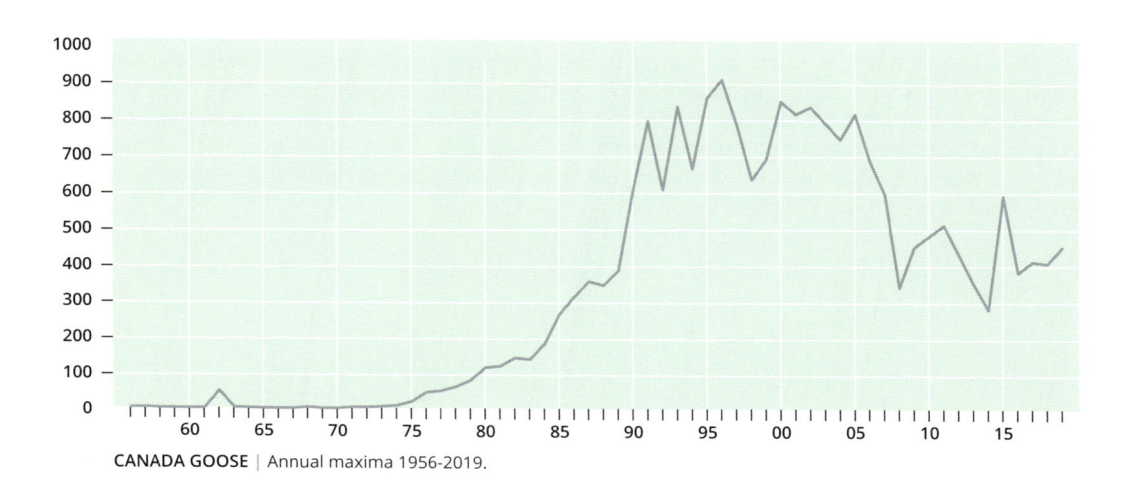

CANADA GOOSE | Annual maxima 1956–2019.

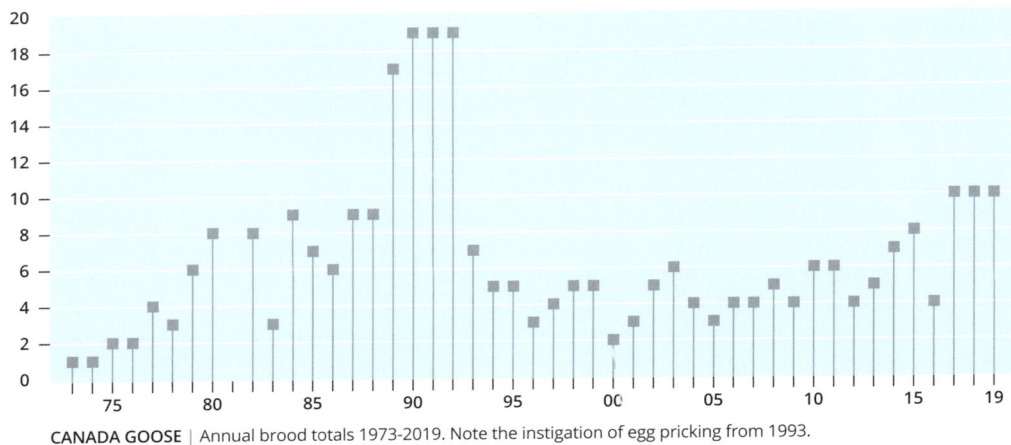

CANADA GOOSE | Annual brood totals 1973-2019. Note the instigation of egg pricking from 1993.

Canada Goose chick | Ian Stapp

BARNACLE GOOSE *Branta leucopsis*

The first records involved one on 8 November 1959, and five from 1 December 1959 to the third week of February 1960. They were initially described as 'un-ringed and wary' but were later seen to be carrying *Wildfowl Trust* rings (B. King). It is therefore unlikely that they were wild. The next record involved an un-ringed individual from 26 September to 20 October 1964 (B. E. Slade *et al.*), which would appear to have had better credentials.

None was then seen until a single from 26 June to 2 September 1976, with a second from 25 August to 16 September. These were escapes from captivity and feral Barnacle Geese have been present every year since, with the exception of 1982, 1989 and 1990. On 23 May 1997, a nest with three eggs was found on Denny Island, but it seems that they did not hatch. The species has attempted to breed in most subsequent years, with broods every year except 1999, 2000 and 2004–2006. However, fledged juveniles occurred in only eight of those years.

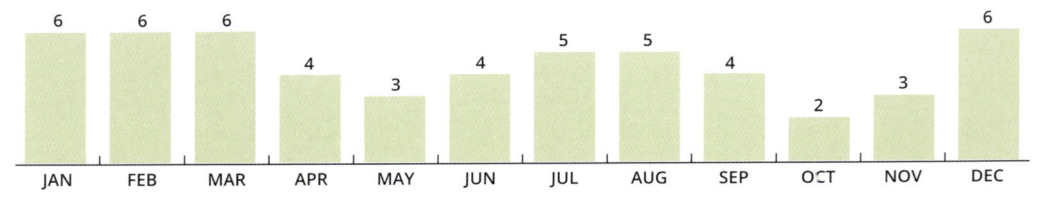

BARNACLE GOOSE | Monthly distribution (average) 1976-2016.

It remains a moot point as to whether genuinely wild Barnacle Geese have ever occurred at Chew, but perhaps the best candidate was a calling bird circling very high on 2 January 1995, before flying off to the east.

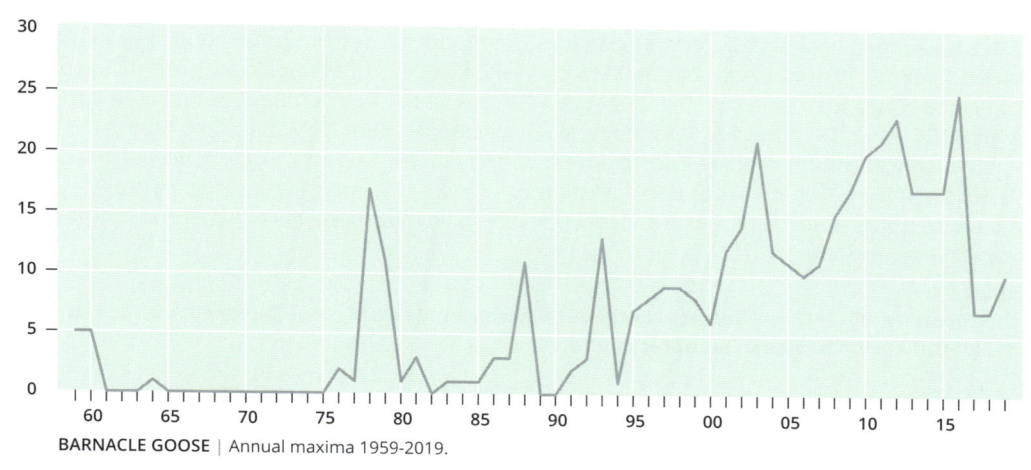

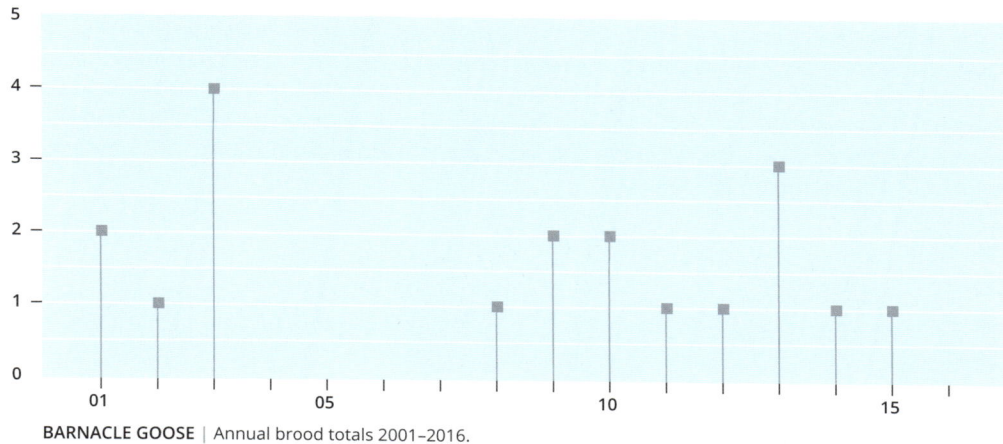

BARNACLE GOOSE | Annual maxima 1959-2019.

BARNACLE GOOSE | Annual brood totals 2001–2016.

Barnacle Geese | Ian Stapp

CACKLING GOOSE *Branta hutchinsii*

Two early records in 1982 and 1999 were presumed to be escapes from captivity.

One arrived at Blagdon Lake on 1 November 2011 (N. R. Milbourne *et al.*) and moved to Chew from 2 to 5 November. It then relocated with Canada Geese to Torr Reservoir, Somerset, where it was seen up to 22 April 2012. It was also seen at Chew on 15–28 March 2012 and again on 15 April. This record coincided with a first-winter on the Gwent Levels from 12 to 24 November 2011 (**record currently with BBRC**) and with a third at Slimbridge, Gloucestershire, from 25 March to 10 April 2012.

This concentration of three records in the vicinity of the Severn Estuary followed the classic 'American Autumn' of 2011 (see under *Memorable Birding Moments*) and despite controversy over their true status as wild birds, many local birders believe that these were quite probably genuine transatlantic vagrants.

Note:
The record in 2011/12 has not currently been accepted by BBRC as a Category A bird. However, the identification has been accepted.

GREYLAG GOOSE *Anser anser*

The first record involved two adults and a juvenile from 21 March to 13 April 1954 (B. King, P. Scott). It seems likely that these were wild birds. The next was an un-ringed individual from 7 to 22 May 1972 and, since then, it has occurred in every year except two (1973 and 2007). A flock of 25 was seen on 7 November 1982 but numbers increased sharply from 1989 to 2003, the result of a moult migration that developed in mid-summer. This reached a peak of 43 in June 1996, before falling sharply thereafter. Single figure counts only were then recorded from 2004 to 2016 but, in 2017, a flock of 14 appeared on 18 August.

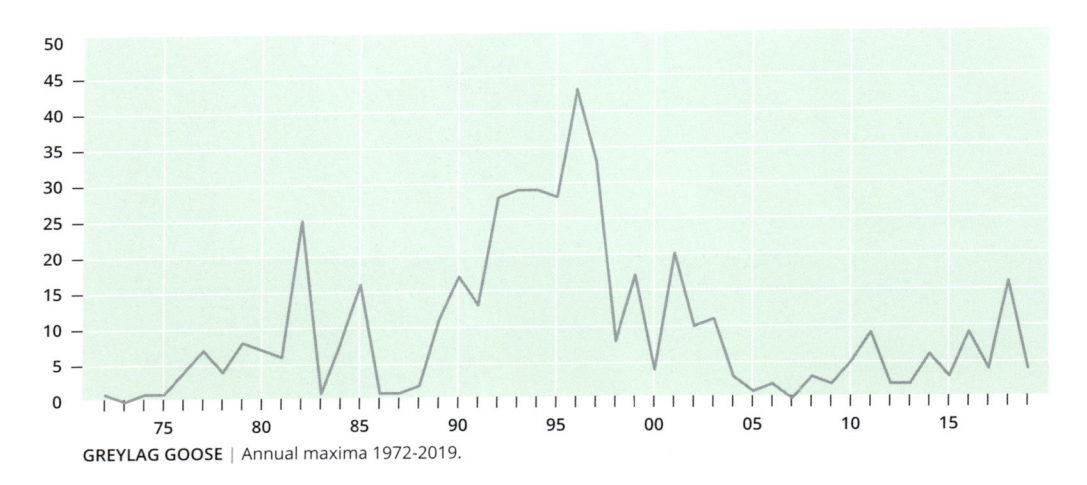

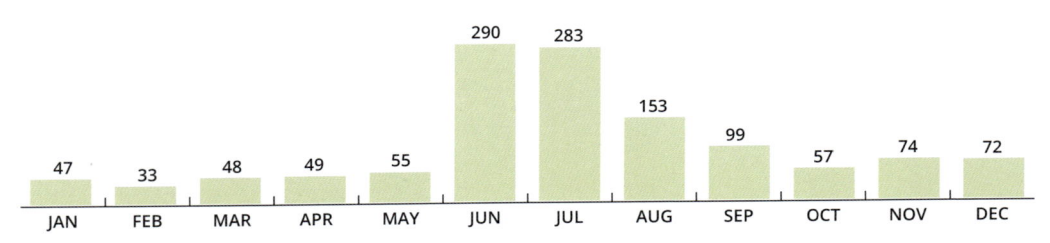

GREYLAG GOOSE | Annual maxima 1972-2019.

GREYLAG GOOSE | Monthly distribution (totals) 1972–2015.

JAN	FEB	MAR	APR	MAY	JUN	JUL	AUG	SEP	OCT	NOV	DEC
47	33	48	49	55	290	283	153	99	57	74	72

The monthly distribution totals show that the peak months are June–July, with numbers dropping quite strongly from late summer and autumn through to the early winter. Special mention, however, must be made of a flock of nine on 17 November 2011 that flew in from the north at considerable height. A flock of five was also seen at Blagdon during the morning. These were considered to have been genuinely wild birds, some of which showed characters of the race *rubrirostris*, which originates in eastern Europe and western Asia. Significant numbers were seen around the country at that time, having been displaced by easterly winds. These included several over Portland, Dorset, and also on the Channel Islands, as well as 'thousands' past various sites in Normandy; it is likely that these involved birds that were heading for their wintering grounds in Spain.

Greylag Goose | Gary Thoburn

PINK-FOOTED GOOSE *Anser brachyrhynchus*

The first record was of a ringed individual with White-fronted Geese *A. albifrons* on 26 January and 2 February 1958 (M. A. Wright, P. Chadwick and B. King). There was then a 15-year gap before the second: one with five White-fronts on 18 February 1973. There have since been another 10 records involving 14 individuals. These included a family party of four (a pair with two juveniles) between December 2011 and March 2012.

Inevitably, the peak months have been from November to March, with the earliest date being one on 24 October (in 1999). There was also a single on 19–20 June 1985 while, the following year, one that arrived on 23 February remained until 13 May. The June date may, on the face of it, suggest a captive origin but, each year, small numbers of Pink-feet do in fact remain in Britain during the summer (*Bird Atlas* 2007–11).

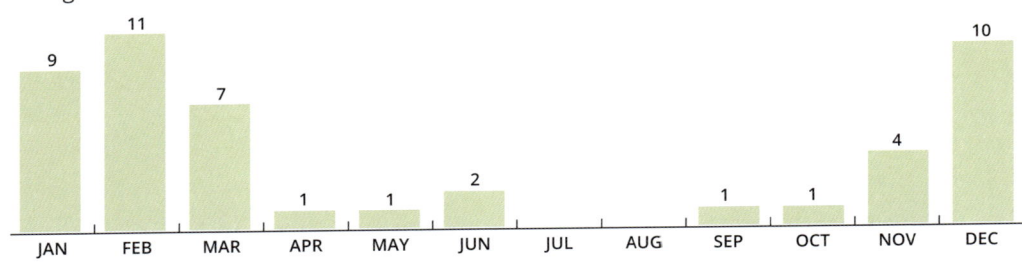

PINK-FOOTED GOOSE | Monthly distribution (totals) 1958–2019.

JAN	FEB	MAR	APR	MAY	JUN	JUL	AUG	SEP	OCT	NOV	DEC
9	11	7	1	1	2			1	1	4	10

PINK-FOOTED GOOSE | Annual maxima 1958-2019.

Pink-footed Goose (*right*) with Canada Geese | Laurel Tucker

The full list of records is as follows:

1958:	26 January and 2 February.
1973:	one with five White-fronted Geese on 18 February.
1974:	two on 9 December.
1979:	one from 22 November to 10 February 1980.
1985:	one on 19–20 June.
1986:	one from 23 February to 13 May.
1996:	one on 2 March.
1999:	one, originally at Blagdon on 22–23 October, was seen at Chew on 24 October before returning to Blagdon. It reappeared at Chew from 27 December to 13 February 2000.
2002:	one at Blagdon from 31 May to 9 June was seen at Chew with Canada Geese on 6–8 June.
2011:	four (2 juvs) at Blagdon from 10 December to 23 February 2012 visited Chew on 27 December and then relocated there from 24 February to 22 March 2012.
2013–14:	two ads from 22 November to 28 December when they moved to Blagdon. They returned to Chew from 6 January to 23 February 2014 with just one from 8 to 21 March.
2019:	one adult, at Blagdon from 24 to 26 November, briefly seen at Chew on 26th.

TUNDRA BEAN GOOSE *Anser serrirostris*

A bean goose, not identified to species level, was seen with White-fronted Geese *A. albifrons* on 26 January 1958 (Paul Chadwick, Bernard King *et al.*), with two from 2 to 9 February. Given that they were with White-fronts, it seems highly probable that these were Tundra Beans. The only record identified to species level was an adult from 28 January to 21 March 1996 (R. M. Andrews), originally seen at Blagdon on 27 January. This bird occurred during an unprecedented arrival of 400+ in early 1996, mainly on the east coast.

There are also two records of tame escapees: 16 May 1987, remaining into June, and 22–30 March 1990 and intermittently to 11 August. Neither of these was identified to species level (i.e. Tundra or Taiga Bean *A. fabalis*).

Tundra Bean Goose (*left*) with White-fronted Goose | Keith Vinicombe

White-fronted Goose | Keith Vinicombe

WHITE-FRONTED GOOSE *Anser albifrons*

In the very early days, this species was a regular winter visitor to the lakeside fields at the north end, with annual numbers increasing from 16 in February–March 1954 to a record 350 on 10 March 1956. There were further high counts of 120 in February 1958, 70 in January 1962, 60 in January 1970 and 89 in February 1979. At least some of these totals were related to cold weather. Since then, only four winters have produced double figure counts (1982–83, 1983–84, 1984–85 and 1998). This situation mirrors a huge decline in Britain's main wintering site at Slimbridge, Gloucestershire. This is thought likely to be a consequence of climate change. Milder winters enable the birds to remain on the Continent, rather than travelling further west – a phenomenon known as 'short-stopping'. A first-winter in February–March 2011 was the last to be recorded at the lake, apart from an intriguing record of an adult on the unusual dates of 22–27 May 2017. Although initially dismissed as a likely escape, it followed close on the heels of one at Weston-Super-Mare Sewage Treatment Works, preceded by one in Portugal and one in the Canary Islands. Could all these records have related to the same bird?

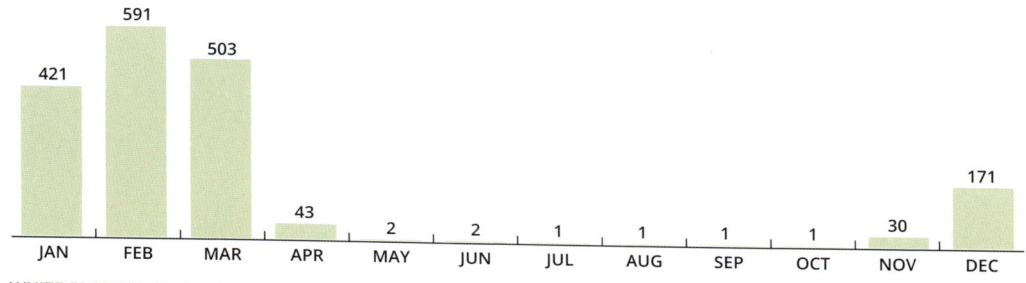

WHITE-FRONTED GOOSE | Monthly distribution (totals) 1954–2016.

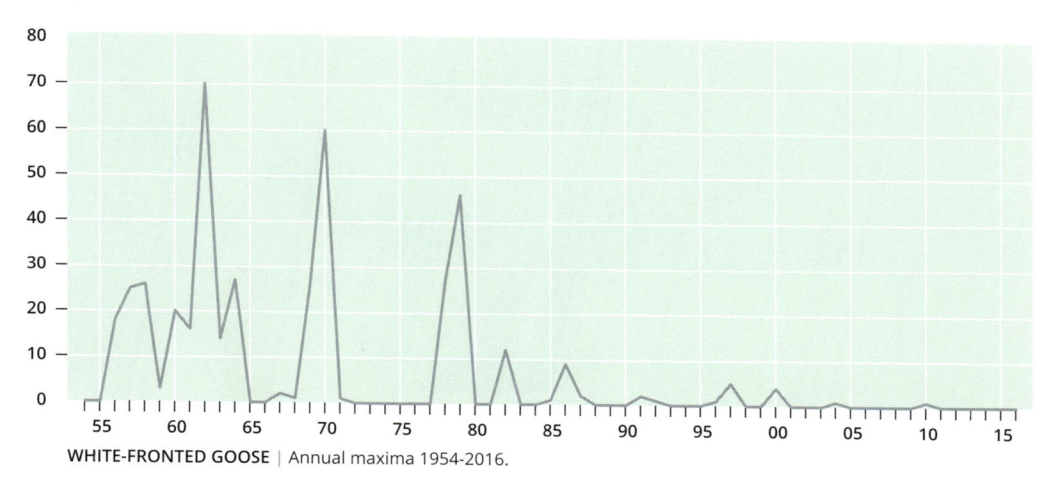

WHITE-FRONTED GOOSE | Annual maxima 1954-2016.

GREENLAND WHITE-FRONTED GOOSE *Anser albifrons flavirostris*

One with Eurasian White-fronts on 21 December 1964 (R. S. Harkness).

LESSER WHITE-FRONTED GOOSE *Anser erythropus*

An un-ringed adult was present from 18 October 1991 to 15 February 1992 (M. C. Powell *et al.*). Its arrival coincided with several other records in Britain and on the near continent.

An escaped adult was also seen on 12 and 13 June 1998, and one intermittently from 5 June to 5 August 2001.

Note: The record in 1991/2 was never accepted by BBRC as a Category A bird.

Mute Swan | Laurel Tucker

MUTE SWAN *Cygnus olor*

Numbers of Mute Swans are at their lowest in mid-winter, the average January and February counts being 20. At this time of year, the waterweed is at a low ebb and many of the swans that remain eke out a living from the people who feed them by the roadsides at Herriott's Pool and Heron's Green Bay. Numbers gradually increase from March to a peak in July–August when larger numbers arrive at the lake to moult. However, these higher counts are also boosted by the recruitment of the lake's juveniles that hatched during the spring and summer. Numbers decline steadily from September to the mid-winter low.

The numbers of breeding swans have increased since 1967, when the broods were first counted, with a marked up-turn from the early 1990s, with maxima of 14 in both 1996 and 2011. The lowest modern total was just four broods in 2012, the nests apparently being washed out in heavy rain.

The annual maxima graph indicates that the species has generally increased since 1956, the first year for which counts are available. This may relate partly to the spread of reeds around the lake, these providing the necessary nesting habitat.

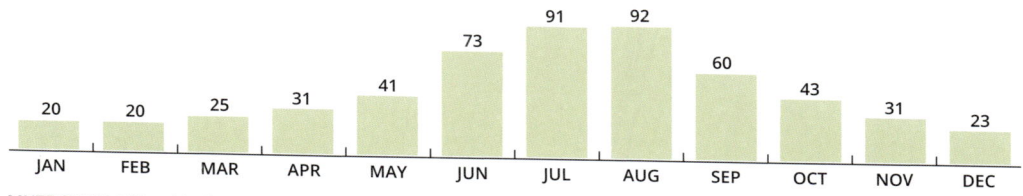

MUTE SWAN | Monthly distribution (average) 1956–2015.

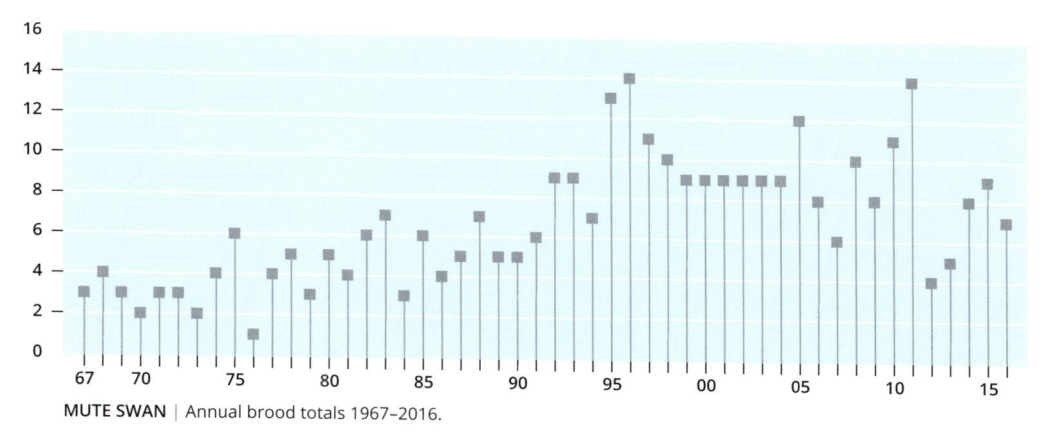

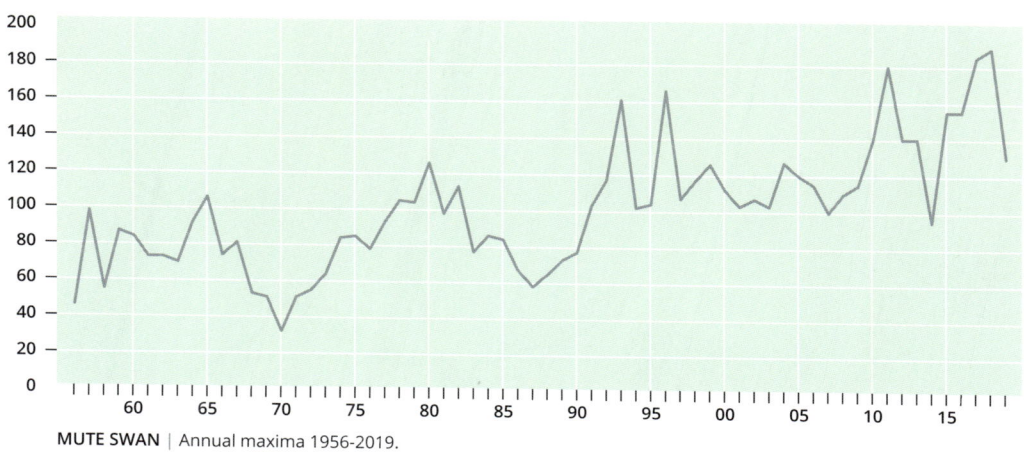

MUTE SWAN | Annual brood totals 1967–2016.

MUTE SWAN | Annual maxima 1956-2019.

COMPLETE SPECIES LIST AND CHARTS

BEWICK'S SWAN *Cygnus columbianus*

A winter visitor, mainly from October to March. The first record involved six in January 1956 but, in the following month, there were *joint* Chew and Blagdon counts of up to 88. There were no records in 1957 or 1959 but it has otherwise occurred in every year except 2002 and 2015. As the annual maxima graph shows, double figure totals were the norm until the early 1990s, with the highest counts being 54 in January 1971, a remarkable 127 in December 1976 and a record 141 in January 1977. These exceptional numbers were related to the infamous 'drought year' of 1976, when severely low water levels enabled huge areas of shoreline to be colonized by ruderal plants. During the 1976–77 winter, rising water levels flooded into these areas, providing exceptional feeding conditions for a whole range of vegetarian wildfowl, including the Bewick's Swans. Since then, as the annual maxima graph shows, numbers have been in steady decline, with maxima of just one in 2000, two in 2001, none in 2002, one in 2008 and two in 2012. Whilst some swans are no doubt 'short-stopping' on the continent (related to climate change) there is increasing concern for the long-term conservation of this iconic species.

Note that there have been three April records (21 individuals) with the latest record involving 11 on 15 April 1964.

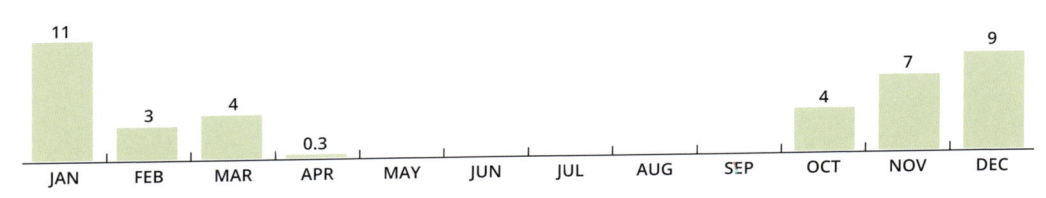

BEWICK'S SWAN | Monthly distribution (average) 1956-2016.

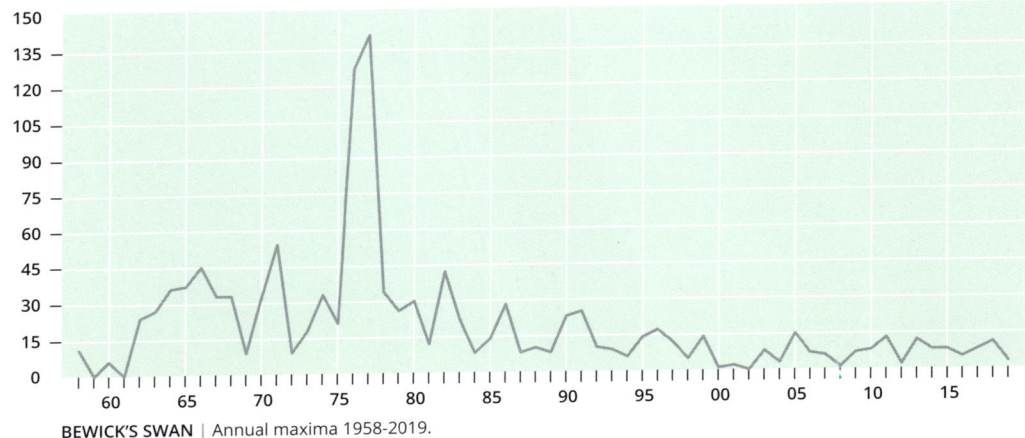

BEWICK'S SWAN | Annual maxima 1958-2019.

Bewick's Swan | Laurel Tucker

WHOOPER SWAN *Cygnus cygnus*

A surprisingly rare autumn and winter visitor, with records from 28 October to 24 March. There have been just 15 records in total, involving 35 individuals:

- **1959:** one on 3 January (B. King).
- **1961:** five (two ads, three juvs) on 29 January.
- **1962:** eight on 11 November.
- **1963:** two ads from 10 to 24 March.
- **1965:** two ads on 20 November.
- **1969:** two on 9 December.
- **1970:** two calling in flight, 13 January.
- **1973:** ad from 17 to 25 November.
- **2008:** ad on 28-29 October. **2009:** 3 ads on 23 February.
- **2010:** ad from 14 to 25 November. **2011:** ad on 23 December.
- **2012:** two ads on 19 January. **2015:** 4 adults on 21 November.
- **2016:** two ads (male, female) on 7 November.
- **2019:** ad 18 November.

Whooper Swans | Ian Stapp

EGYPTIAN GOOSE *Alopochen aegyptiaca*

The Egyptian Goose was introduced into England in the 18th century. It has long been found in a feral state in several parts of the country, but mainly in East Anglia. It was added to Category C of the British List in 1971 (BOU 1971).

The first Chew records were in April 1957 (6th and 20th, B. King) and 20 December 1959 until a record of three on 30 May 1984, followed by another three on 31 December of that year. Yet another trio appeared on 9 September 1988, followed by a single on 13 and 23 April 1989. A very tame escaped male was then present from May to November 2004. There was then a gap of seven years before a female was present from June 2011 to March 2013 with a second (sex unknown) being briefly present on 11 June 2012. The lonesome female was at last joined by a male on 11 April 2013 and, on 4 June, they produced a brood of six young, five of which fledged. From that point onwards, the species became a regular feature at the north end of the lake, where they scrounge food from visitors at the Picnic Site, next to the Dam.

Further broods hatched in 2014, 2015 (two broods in each year) and 2017 (one). However, not being very bright, they tend to nest to the north of the Dam and then attempt to bring their goslings up the Dam overflow, only to be met by the high steps on the back side of the spillway. On two occasions the young have been fortuitously rescued by birders and released onto the lake.

As the monthly distribution shows, numbers tend to dip in late winter when the birds appear to go wandering.

Reference
British Ornithologists' Union. 1971. *The Status of Birds in Britain and Ireland.* Blackwell.

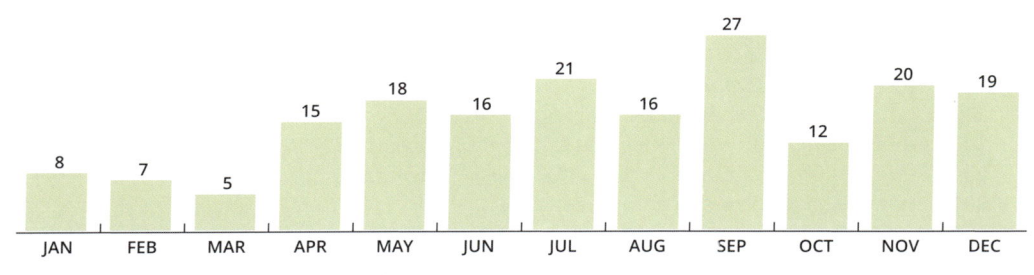

EGYPTIAN GOOSE | Monthly distribution (totals) 1984-2015.

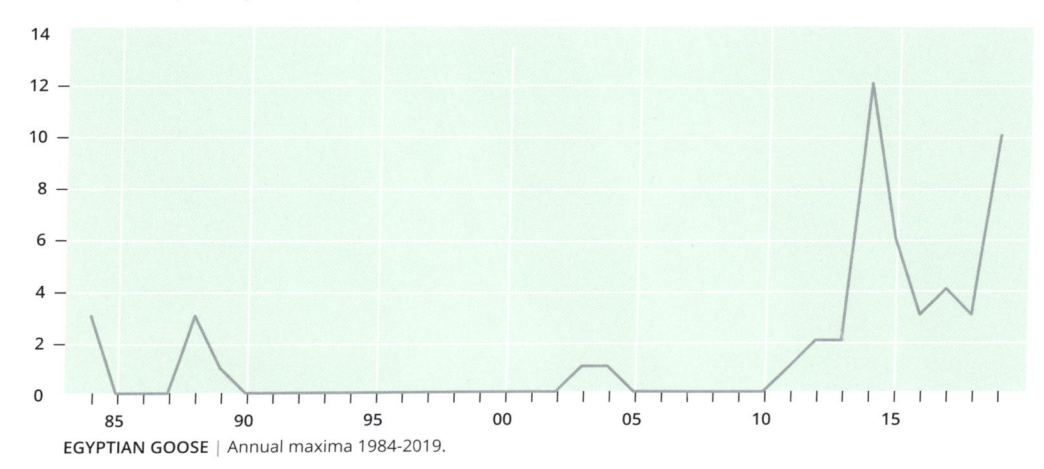

EGYPTIAN GOOSE | Annual maxima 1984-2019.

Egyptian Geese with chicks | Ian Stapp

SHELDUCK *Tadorna tadorna*

The first records were up to five from January to March 1955 and an adult was seen with a juvenile on 17 July, presumably the first breeding record at the lake. A pair also bred in 1957 and breeding has since taken place in 45 of the 51 years to 2016. In most years, only one or two broods are produced but, since the late 1990s, productivity has increased, with as many as four broods in 2009, 2011 and 2015.

The peak months are from March to June, numbers gradually reducing to a low point in September–October, when the adults leave the lake to moult, presumably in Bridgwater Bay. Only a few juveniles normally remain during this period. The adults start to return from November, gradually increasing during the course of the winter.

The annual maxima have broadly increased from the mid-1950s right through to 2013, when there were a record 48 on 31 May.

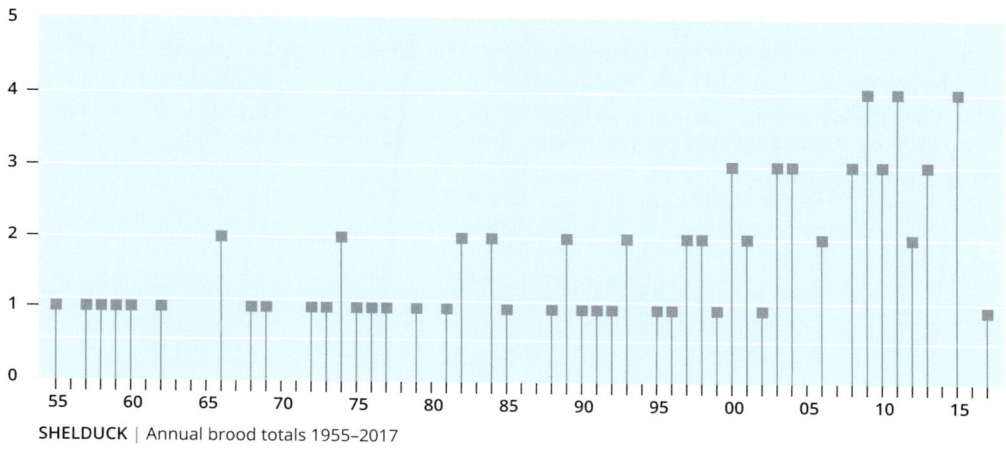

SHELDUCK | Annual brood totals 1955–2017

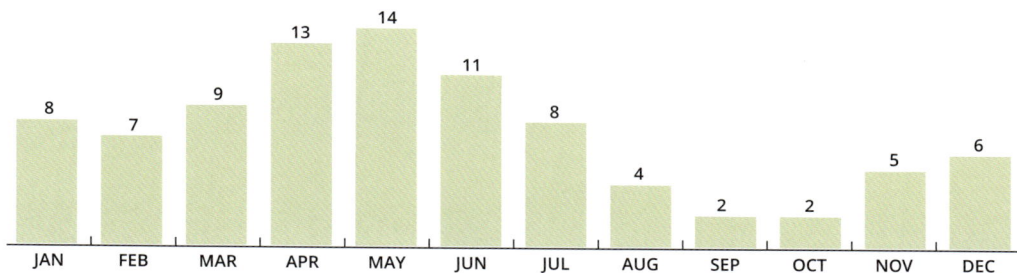

SHELDUCK | Monthly distribution (average) 1955–2017.

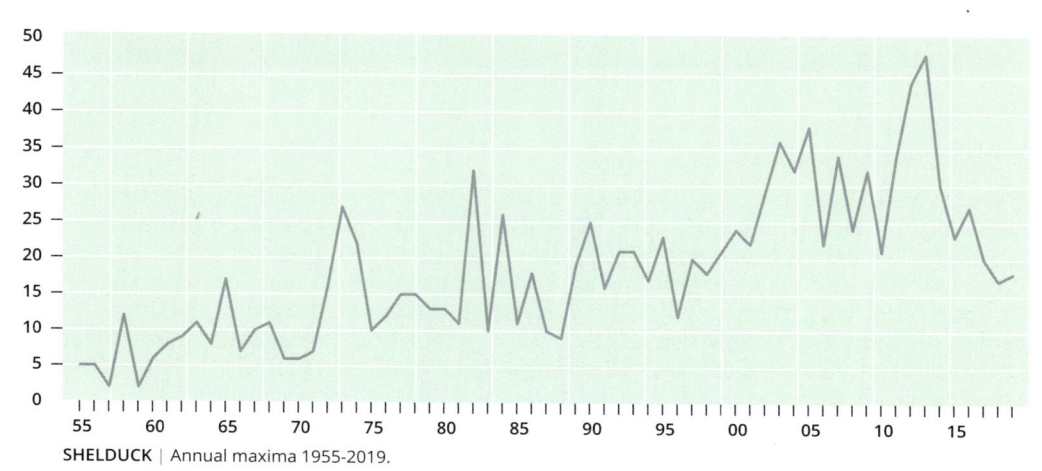

SHELDUCK | Annual maxima 1955–2019.

RUDDY SHELDUCK *Tadorna ferruginea*

The first record involved an escaped female from 20 July to 29 December 1982. It had its right wing pinioned but was capable of weak flight. Then, in 1986, a male arrived on 6 June and it moulted annually at the lake until 1994. In 1995 two were seen on 31 May, remaining until 1 July, when they were joined by a third, increasing to four on 3 August with the last two seen on 5th. There were then two moulting in 1996, four in 1997, three in 1998, four in 1999, three in 2000 and then just singles every year until 2003, the last year that they were seen. Needless to say, these birds were generally regarded as escapes from captivity and, indeed, a tame individual was seen coming to bread in 2002 and one the following year was also tame. After leaving Chew in late summer, some were then seen at various sites on the Severn Estuary (in 1988, 1990 and 1991).

Although these records are mostly considered to be of captive birds, it is intriguing to note that, in the peak year of 1994, there was an exceptional influx into Fenno-Scandia, with about 100 reported in Finland, at least 50 in Sweden and 75–100 in Denmark (Vinicombe 1996 and *Birding World* 7: 309). In addition, around this time a large moult gathering of feral birds was developing at Eemeer in the Netherlands. For further information on this subject, see Vinicombe & Harrop (1999).

Note: While Ruddy Shelduck is on the British List (Category B – records prior to 1950) and most of these records relate to escapes from captivity, the origin of others is uncertain.

References
Vinicombe, K. E. 1996. *Rare Birds in Britain and Ireland. A Photographic Record*. Collins.
Vinicombe, K. E. and Harrop, A. J. H. 1999. 'Ruddy Shelducks in Britain and Ireland, 1986–94'. *British Birds* 92: 225–255.

Ruddy Shelducks | Keith Vinicombe

MANDARIN DUCK *Aix galericulata*

There have been 22 records involving 34 individuals (to 2018). All the records have been of ones and twos with the exception of three (2 males) on 8 November 1987, six (4 males) on 22 November 2010 and 4 in 2018. They have been recorded in all months except July and August, when they are moulting. The origins of these birds are not known. Some may well have been escapes but there is now a large feral population in the Forest of Dean, Gloucestershire, and the species also breeds in many other parts of the county (Kirk and Phillips 2013). Given that the British population is now estimated at about 7,000 individuals, it is of course possible that some come from much further afield. Of those sexed, 18 have been males and 11 females. One on 29 June 2015 was a juvenile male.

Reference
Kirk, G. and Phillips, J. 2013. *The Birds of Gloucestershire*. Liverpool University Press.

Mandarin Duck | Ian Stapp

GARGANEY *Spatula querquedula*

The first record was of a male in May 1954 and the first breeding record was in 1955, when a female was seen on 18 June with 11 ducklings (B. King). The species has been annual since then and the first double figure count was 11 in August 1963. Such counts then occurred in 19 of the 33 years until 1995. The highest were 25 on 11 August 1967, 22 on 20 August 1971, a record 34 on 2 September 1978 and 21 on 2 August 1992. The last double figure count was 13 in August 1995. The annual maxima graph shows that it was most numerous in the 1960s and 1970s, with a smaller peak in the early 1990s, but it has since shown a long downward decline, with a peak of just two in 2015.

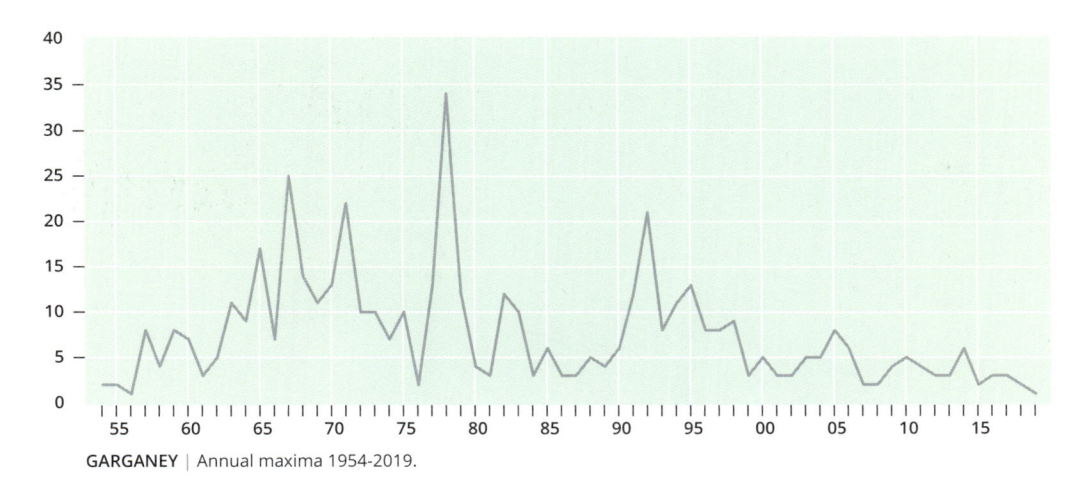

GARGANEY | Annual maxima 1954-2019.

The monthly distribution totals show the first spring records are in March, the earliest date being the 8th (in 1961). Spring passage peaks in April and May and the autumn passage peaks in August. There have been six November records and, in 1992, a first-winter male remained until 13 December. In 2011, however, a female, first seen on 11 October, remained until 20 April 2012, when she was paired to a male; she also visited Blagdon during that period.

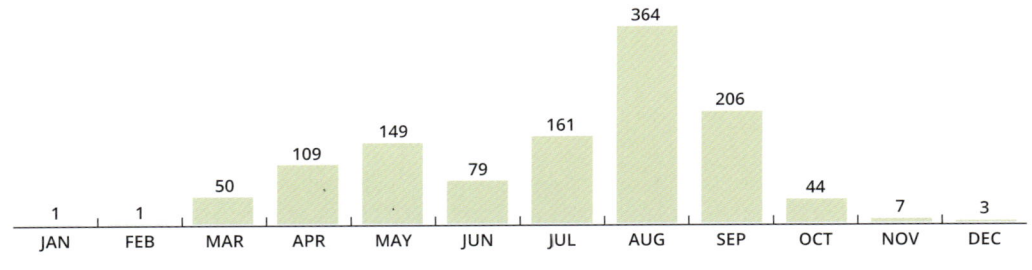

GARGANEY | Monthly distribution (totals) 1954-2017.

JAN	FEB	MAR	APR	MAY	JUN	JUL	AUG	SEP	OCT	NOV	DEC
1	1	50	109	149	79	161	364	206	44	7	3

The annual brood totals show that Garganey has bred in 13 years: 1955, 1959 (two pairs), 1962, 1963, 1964, 1966, 1967, 1969, 1970, 1978, 1988, 1991 and 1992.

Numbers of this charismatic duck have decreased significantly since the turn of the century. Given that, twice a year, it has to endure the barrage of duck shooting in southern Europe, one seriously wonders about its long-term future.

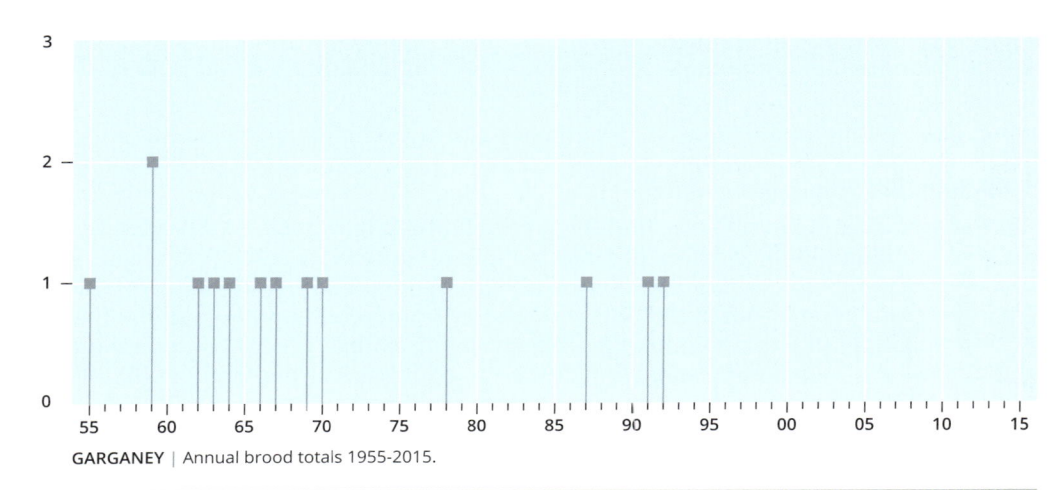

GARGANEY | Annual brood totals 1955-2015.

Garganey | Gary Thoburn

COMPLETE SPECIES LIST AND CHARTS

BLUE-WINGED TEAL *Spatula discors*
There have been six records.
- **1979:** female or juvenile male at Sutton Wick on 18 November (D. G. H. Mills, L. A. & N. A. Tucker and V. R. Tucker *et al.*).
- **1992:** female at Twycross from 29 July to 13 August (K. L. Fox, KEV *et al.*).
- **1993:** first-winter male at Stratford Hide and later at the Main Dam on 9–11 October (KEV *et al.*).
- **1995:** adult female in Villice Bay from 2 to 5 September (R. M. Andrews, KEV *et al.***).**
- **2003:** adult female at Stratford Hide from 12 to 30 August (R. M. Andrews, G. Jones *et al.*).
- **2011:** female at Hollow Brook and Denny Island from 12 to 24 June (S. Davies *et al.*).

SHOVELER *Spatula clypeata*

The first record was of 60 on 20 March 1954. Numbers then increased, reaching 875 in November 1995, followed by counts of 805 in both December 2001 and January 2002 (the December 1981 count involved about 10% of the entire British wintering population). Peak numbers have, however, fallen since the turn of the century, with the maximum count being as low as 180 in 2007. Shovelers are omnivorous, but they feed particularly on planktonic crustaceans, small molluscs, insects and larvae, seeds and plant debris (*BWP*) so it seems likely that environmental conditions must significantly influence their numbers.

There were some particularly high counts in the early years, the highest being 1,138 on 1 January 1961. However, in those days, large numbers of Shoveler often fed by surface feeding at the north end of the lake, this activity almost certainly taking place mainly during the hours of darkness. They continued feeding during the early morning but then moved to the southern end of the lake for the rest of the day. It seems highly probable that the exceptionally high counts were the result of double counting. Such counts have, therefore, been excluded from the graphs.

The annual maxima show that numbers fluctuate considerably from year to year, no doubt relating to water levels and the prevailing ecological conditions. However, the graph seems to indicate a distinct down-turn since the turn of the century.

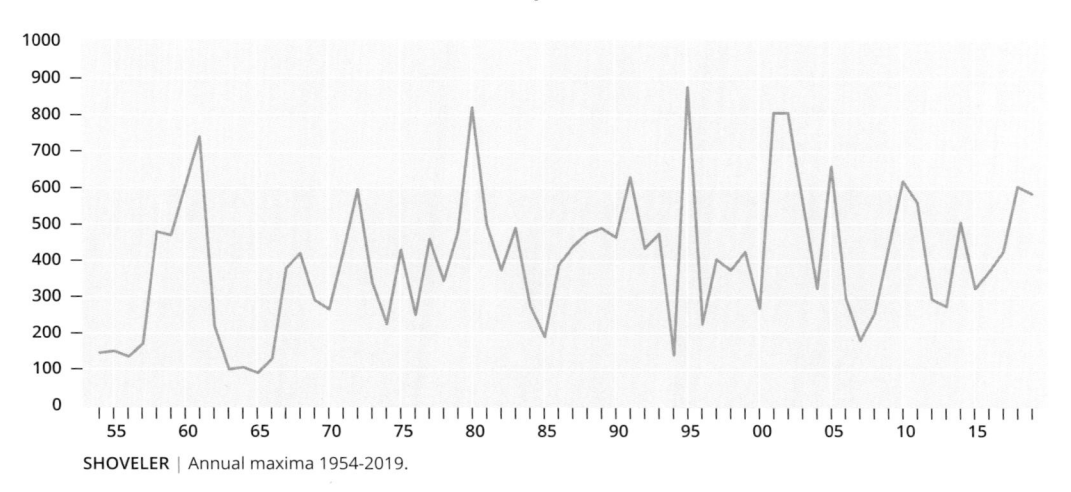

SHOVELER | Annual maxima 1954-2019.

The monthly distribution show that numbers are at their lowest in May, but the first returning birds appear as early as 19 May, rising into June (e.g. eight on 29 May 1999, 26 (23 males) on 9 June 1993 and 54 on 14 June 1992). Most of these early arrivals are males, which, no doubt, have completed their breeding activities. Numbers increase very slightly in July, followed by a large influx in August, peaking in September and October. Numbers remain high but gradually decline during the winter.

In the early years, Shovelers were regular breeders, with five broods in 1958, 1960 and 1965 and a record nine broods (59 ducklings) in 1959. In those days, the banks were covered in grass and young plantations, ideal nesting habitat for Shoveler, but, as time passed, the vegetation matured into reed beds and woodland, reducing their potential nesting sites. In addition, most of the northern end of the lake has now been opened up to the public, whilst the increase in mammalian predators, such as foxes, badgers, mink and otters, probably hasn't done them any favours. This decline is shown well in the graph below. They continued to breed almost annually until 1980, but successful breeding occurred in only six years between 1983 and 2012. However, there has been a recent improvement, with two broods in 2013 and single broods every year from 2014 to 2016.

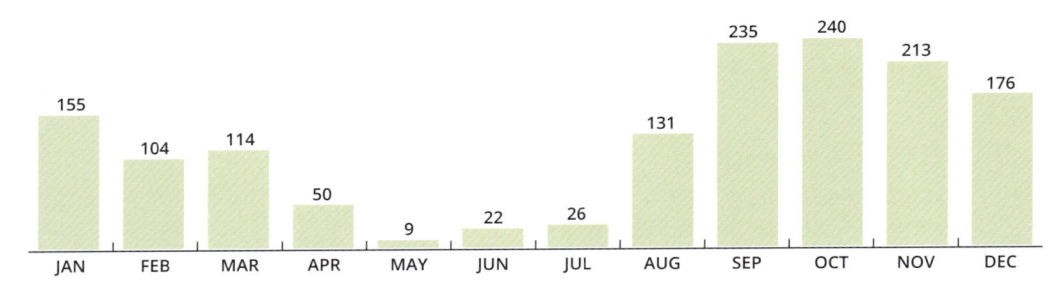

SHOVELER | Monthly distribution (average) 1954-2019.

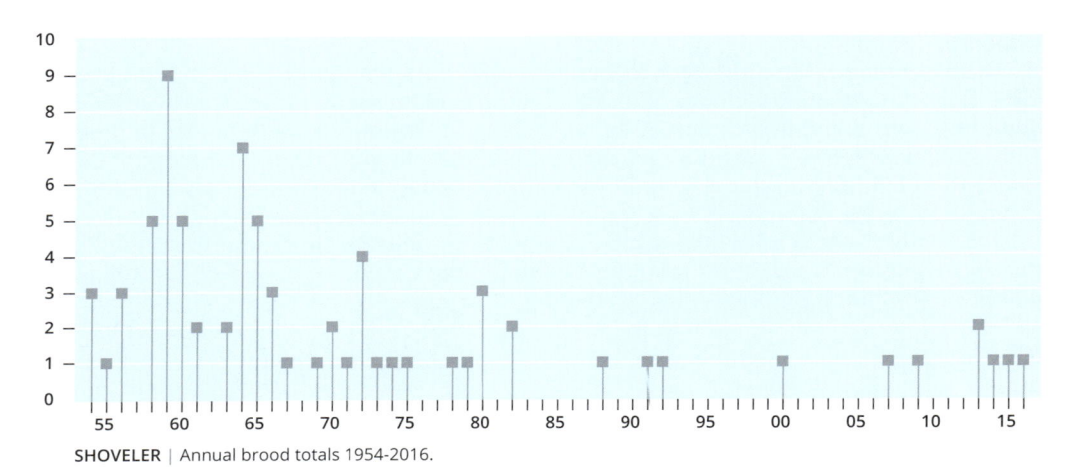

JAN	FEB	MAR	APR	MAY	JUN	JUL	AUG	SEP	OCT	NOV	DEC
155	104	114	50	9	22	26	131	235	240	213	176

SHOVELER | Annual brood totals 1954-2016.

Shoveler | Rich Andrews

GADWALL *Mareca strepera*

The monthly distribution average graph shows Gadwall reach their lowest point in February, but numbers gradually rise to a small spring peak in April. They dip slightly in May when the females are nesting. Numbers increase significantly in June, this mid-summer peak being the result of an influx of males, which come to the lake to moult. However, as they become flightless (for about four weeks) they become very secretive and difficult to see in the lakeside vegetation, this producing the apparent dip in numbers in July. They finish their moult by August, when numbers are augmented by an influx of Gadwall that take full advantage of the large amounts of waterweed present at this time. Numbers remain fairly high through September but they drop significantly in late autumn and early winter, when the weed is at a low ebb.

Gadwall was a scarce bird nationally in the 1950s, and this is reflected in the annual maxima graph. Just two were recorded at Chew in 1955 and the decadal peak was just 30 (in 1958). Numbers increased significantly through the 1960s, before stabilising at a higher level in the 1970s and 1980s. As the graph shows, annual peaks varied significantly, but counts reached 425 in September 1991, 410 in August 2003 and a record 650 in September 2011.

Gadwall | Gary Thoburn

Gadwall first bred at Chew in 1955 and it is thought likely that these early pioneers originated from The Wildfowl Trust at Slimbridge (*Report on Somerset Birds* 1955). Breeding numbers increased significantly through the 1960s and 1970s, with a peak of 29 broods in 1970. Since 1994, however, the numbers of broods have crashed, with a current average (1994–2015) of just three. What is odd is that this crash in breeding numbers corresponds with record numbers of autumn adults!

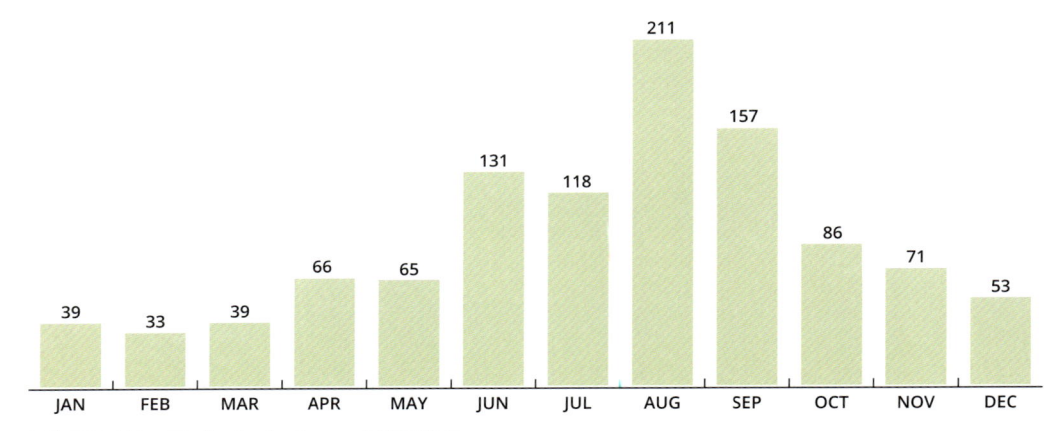

GADWALL | Monthly distribution (average) 1965-2015.

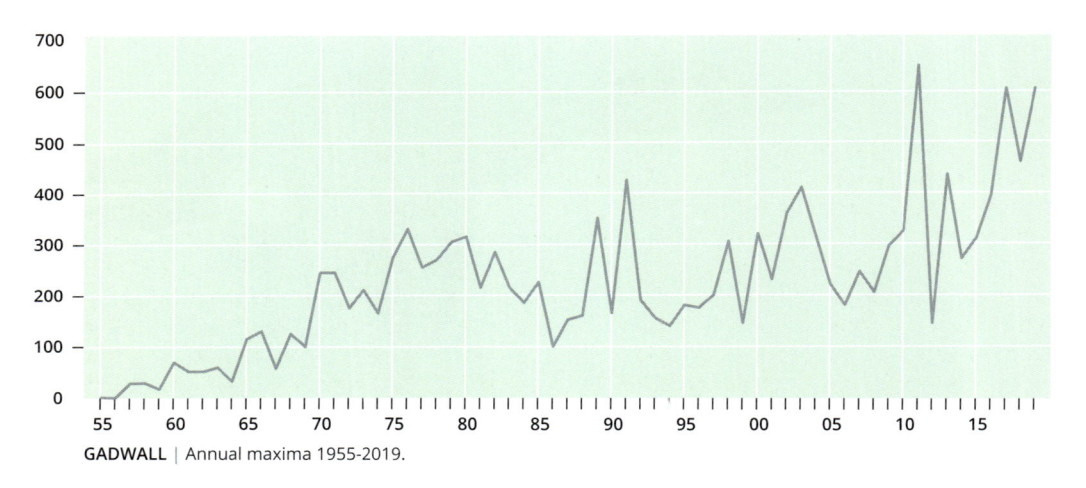

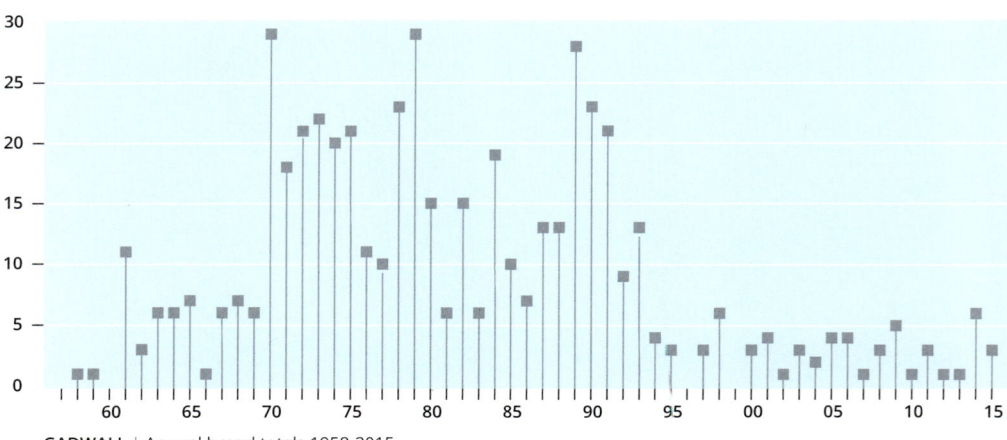

Month	JAN	FEB	MAR	APR	MAY	JUN	JUL	AUG	SEP	OCT	NOV	DEC
Value	39	33	39	66	65	131	118	211	157	86	71	53

GADWALL | Annual maxima 1955-2019.

GADWALL | Annual brood totals 1958-2015.

WIGEON *Mareca penelope*

Traditionally, the Wigeon has been a numerous winter visitor, with peak numbers in January. The first returning birds sometimes appear as early as July, gradually increasing through August and September to the January peak. Numbers then gradually declined through February and March, with just a few remaining into April. Ones and twos are sometimes present in May and June (occasionally as many as five). Small numbers of returning birds usually appear in July, slowly increasing through the late summer and autumn to December. Despite the frequent presence of small numbers in mid-summer, there has never been any suggestion of breeding.

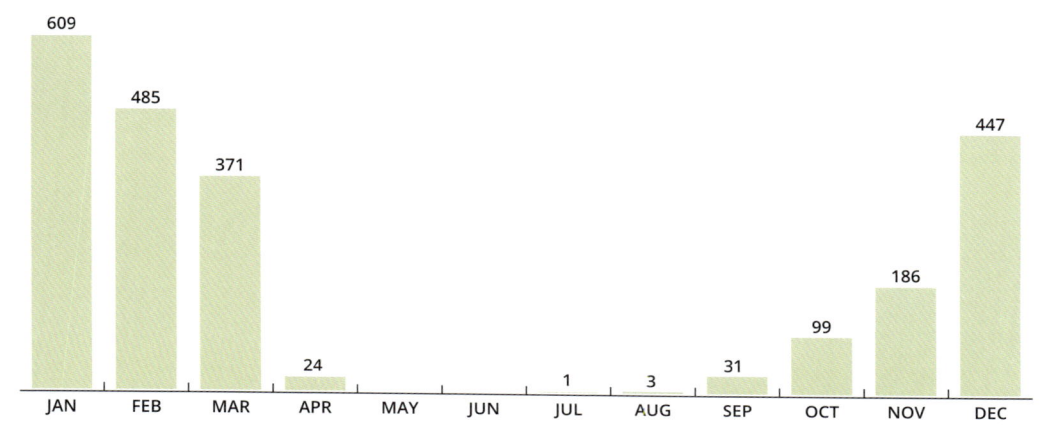

Month	Count
JAN	609
FEB	485
MAR	371
APR	24
MAY	
JUN	1
JUL	
AUG	3
SEP	31
OCT	99
NOV	186
DEC	447

WIGEON | Monthly distribution (average) 1954-2009.

In the early days, the Wigeon used to congregate in large flocks at the north end of the lake, where they grazed on grass on the lakeside banks and adjacent fields. However, this wintering population declined significantly from the 1970s, this being a direct result of the opening up of the northern part of the lake to the public. The development of sailing, two picnic sites (with their connecting pathway) and, more recently, the opening up of the Woodford Bank and Woodford Lodge area, combined to produce a general decline in the wintering population. Nowadays, the mid-winter counts are normally in double figures only, with a January count as low as 18 in 2007. It is fortunate that a number of significant bird reserves have been developed on the Somerset Levels, some of these – such as the RSPB's West Sedgemoor reserve – holding huge numbers of wintering Wigeon. The annual maxima shows the decline in numbers following the opening up of the north end of the lake to the public.

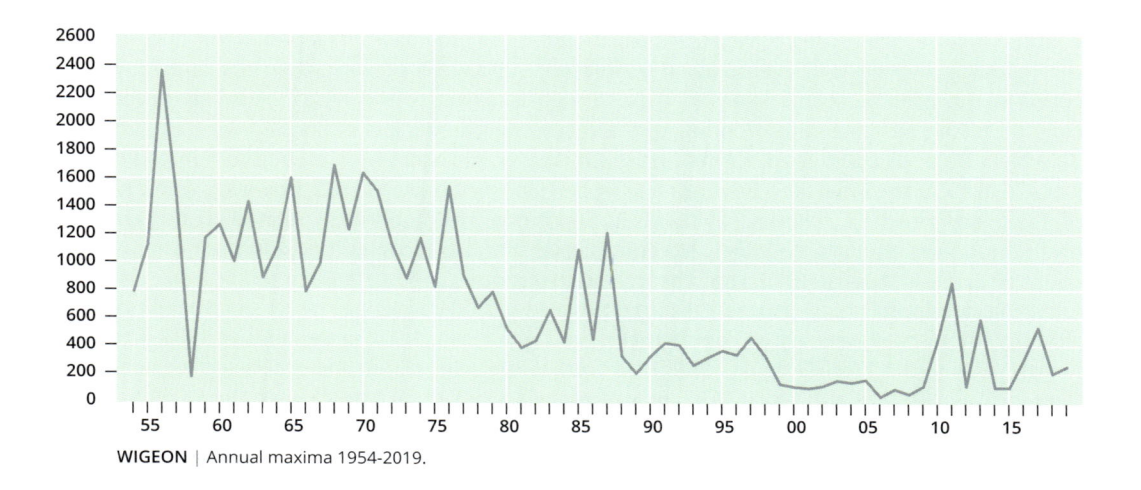

WIGEON | Annual maxima 1954-2019.

Interestingly, however, since the demise of wintering Wigeon, their overall occurrence patterns have changed. The graph below shows the recent monthly maxima during the period 2010–2015. Instead of being a grass-grazing wintering species, the peak month for Wigeon is now October, the birds taking advantage of the large amounts of water weed in the lake at this time. They then surface-feed with other species such as Gadwall *Mareca strepera* and Coot *Fulica atra*. The highest count during this period was an exceptional 855 in November 2011. Once the water levels rise (usually in late autumn) the Wigeon gradually leave, many no doubt relocating to the Somerset Levels. The monthly distribution (average) 2010–2015 is below, following the changes described in the wintering population. Compare this graph with the one (previous page) relating to 1954–2009.

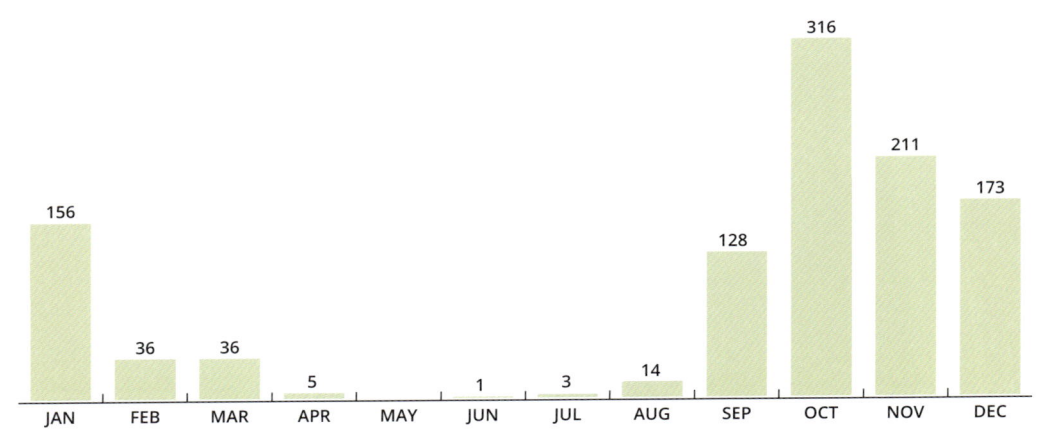

Month	JAN	FEB	MAR	APR	MAY	JUN	JUL	AUG	SEP	OCT	NOV	DEC
Count	156	36	36	5		1	3	14	128	316	211	173

WIGEON | Monthly distribution (average) 2010-2015.

AMERICAN WIGEON *Mareca americana*

An adult male from Moreton Hide on 2 April 1977 was considered to have been a bird that had been present at Cheddar Reservoir, Somerset, from 13 October 1976 to 21 February 1977 (T. A. Box, A. Pay). Another adult male was found at Hollow Brook on 10 December 1978, remaining until 20 January, latterly relocating to Herriott's End (KEV, A.H. Davis).

On 25 October 2018, a poorly marked female was found in Heron's Green Bay (KEV et al.) and photographed the following afternoon. It was then reported daily until the end of the month.

MALLARD *Anas platyrhynchos*

Inevitably, this was one of the first species to arrive at the lake after its initial flooding, with 220 counted in June 1954, rising to what was described at the time as an 'exceptional number' of 600 the following month. By December, an estimated 1,000 were present, then the largest inland count in the area. It seems likely that these high totals were the result of excellent feeding conditions following the initial flooding of the valley, there being lots of flooded vegetable matter on which the birds could feed. As the first graph shows, numbers then dipped to a maximum of just 425 in 1958, the intial food bonanza having perhaps died back. In 1959, however, a new record of 1,390 was reached, followed by 1,440 in September 1961, perhaps related to the gradual diversification of the lake's ecology. Maxima of over a thousand then became the norm, with a count of 2,160 in August 1980, thought to have been due partly to a large influx from Blagdon following excessive fishing distubance at that time. The 2,000 barrier has never since been broken, although there have been three counts that have come close: 1,900 in September 1982, 1,885 in August 1984 and 1,970 in August 1990. However, as the annual maxima graph shows, numbers then took a nose dive and, since 1997, only seven years out of 19 have broken the 1,000 barrier, with peak numbers being as low as 590 in 1996 (in August).

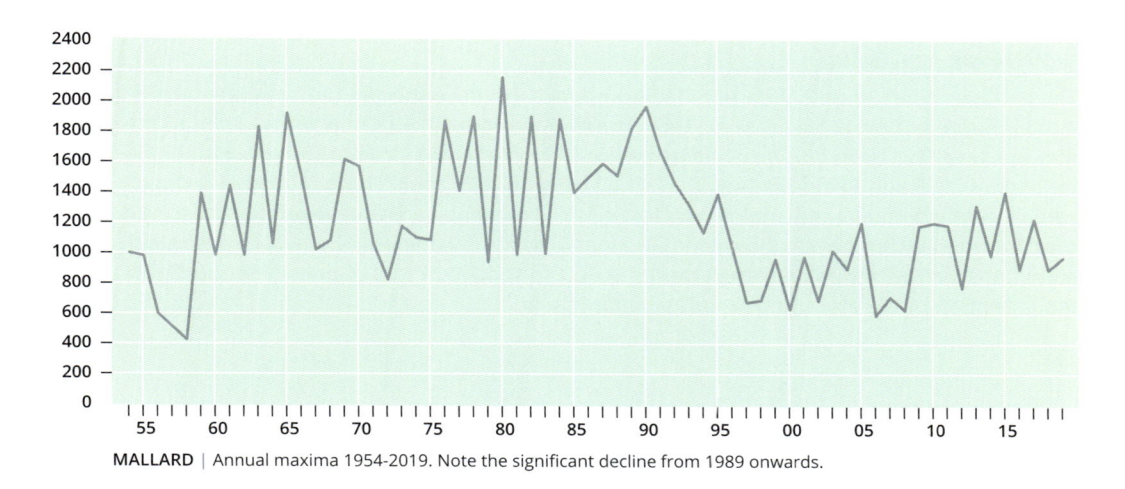

MALLARD | Annual maxima 1954-2019. Note the significant decline from 1989 onwards.

The reasons for this decline are not obvious, but, as the graph showing annual brood totals clearly reflects, it seems likely that the problem relates to breeding productivity. The increase in predators – particularly mink, pike and large gulls – is thought to be the most obvious cause, although the relentless spread of reeds around the lakeside margins may well have reduced the amount of suitable feeding and nesting habitat available for this species.

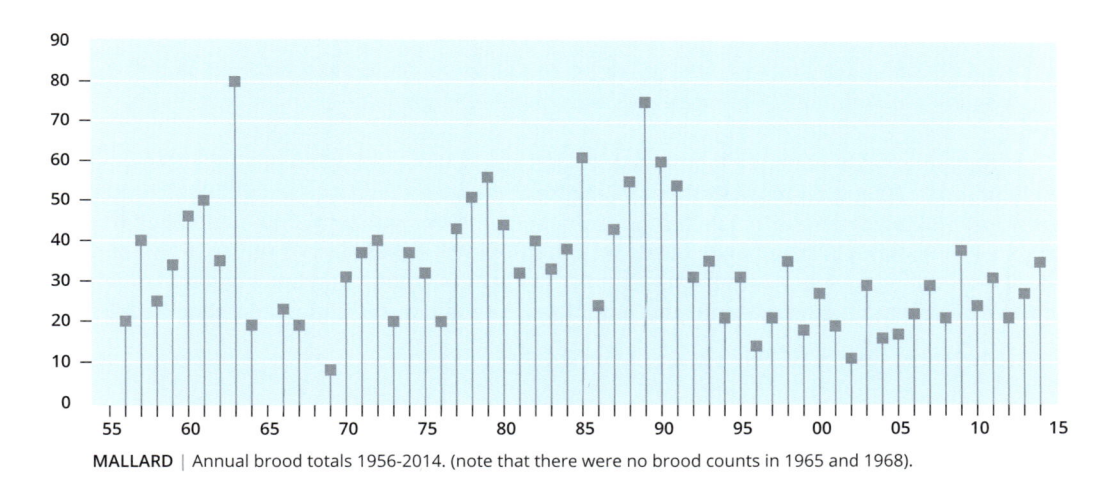

MALLARD | Annual brood totals 1956-2014. (note that there were no brood counts in 1965 and 1968).

The monthly distribution graph shows that numbers are at their lowest in April, when the birds are breeding, but they gradually increase through May, June and July, reaching a peak in August and September, before dropping through October to a mid-winter plateau around the 600–700 mark.

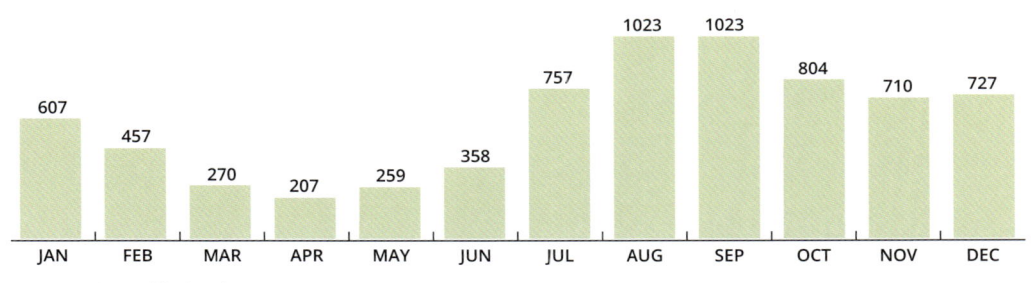

JAN	FEB	MAR	APR	MAY	JUN	JUL	AUG	SEP	OCT	NOV	DEC
607	457	270	207	259	358	757	1023	1023	804	710	727

MALLARD | Monthly distribution (average) 1954-2015.

PINTAIL *Anas acuta*

The first count was 28 on 27 February 1954 but, since then, the species has been recorded annually although, oddly, there are no data for 1959. The average of the annual maxima is 41 but, as the graph shows, there have been four three-figure peaks: 119 in December 1965, 188 in November 1976, 140 in October 2005 and 110 in October 2013. The 1965 and 1976 counts both related to 'drought years', when low late summer and autumn water levels allowed huge areas of vegetation to grow around the lake's margins. This was subsequently inundated by rising water levels, providing excellent feeding conditions. As the annual maxima graph shows, the species occurs mainly in double figures with the exception of the aforementioned 'drought years'.

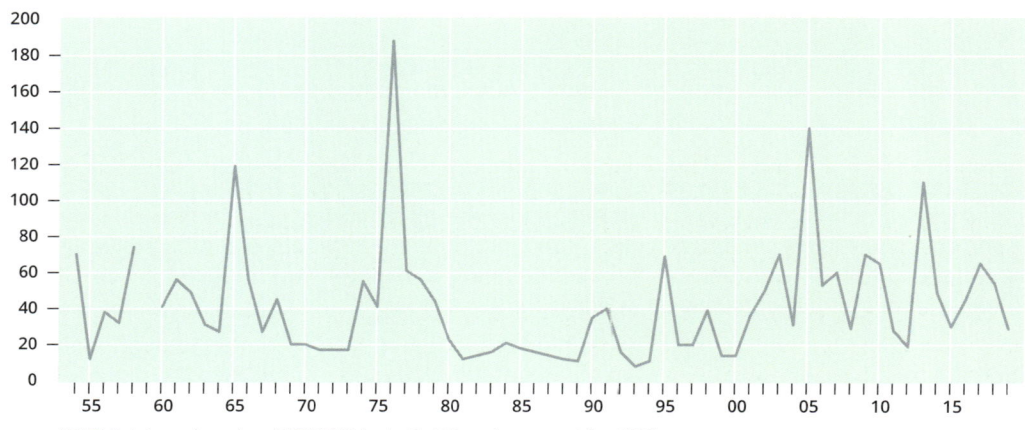

PINTAIL | Annual maxima 1954-2019 (note that there is no count for 1959).

Although not visible on the monthly distribution graph, there are seven records for May and 12 for June and, in 2008, it seems likely that a pair nested. They were seen on Herriott's Pool throughout April until 16 May, when the female disappeared, presumably incubating. She reappeared from 30 May to 7 June, having presumably failed. Small numbers of Pintail start to return in July and this accelerates during the late summer and autumn to a peak in October. Numbers then decline slightly, dropping further in the New Year as the water levels rise and as the spring migration beckons.

Pintail | Gary Thoburn

It should be mentioned that, in 'normal' years, the favoured site for Pintail is Herriott's Pool, these long-necked ducks being a dependable sight as they up-end along the back of the pool.

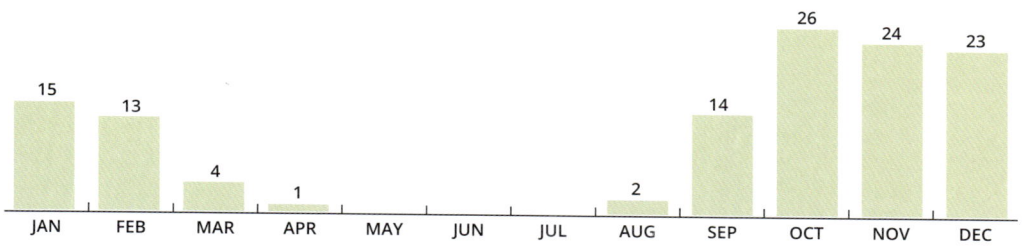

Month	JAN	FEB	MAR	APR	MAY	JUN	JUL	AUG	SEP	OCT	NOV	DEC
Count	15	13	4	1				2	14	26	24	23

PINTAIL | Monthly distribution (average) 1954-2015.

TEAL *Anas crecca*

Teal are present all year round but, despite regular summer records, the species has never bred at the lake. Numbers are at their lowest in May (with an average of just two) but they increase slowly through June and July. Larger numbers appear in August (with an average of 306) but the peak counts occur from September to January with December being marginally the best month, with an average of 849.

In 1988, a pair was present from mid-April to mid-June and the female disappeared for much of May, but she reappeared in late May/early June, suggesting a failed breeding attempt (*ABR*). Interestingly, the first returning Teal appear during May, the earliest date being 13th (in 2000). The average May maximum is just two, but this rises to 18 in June and 36 in July. In recent years, relatively small numbers have carried out their annual wing moult, the birds gathering on Herriott's Pool from late May, becoming flightless by mid-July. In 1993, for example, of 90 that were present on 14 July, about 75% were flightless; similarly, of 50 present on 31 July 2002, about 90% were flightless, and, of 72 on 26 July 2003, virtually all were flightless. In 2014, two flightless birds were also seen in Villice Bay on 13 August. The earliest juvenile recorded was one on 30 July 1999.

The average annual maximum is 1,314 but, as the graph below clearly shows, there were four years with very high numbers: 5,600 in 1984, 5,500 in 1991, 3,050 in 2005 and 3,500 in 2010. These peaks occurred during 'drought years' when, as a result of low water levels, the lake's banks were colonised by huge numbers of ruderal plants. When the water levels then flooded into these areas in winter, large numbers of Teal descended on the lake, feeding on the huge amounts of seeds produced by these plants.

The annual maxima graph shows that numbers vary quite considerably from year to year, being dependent almost entirely on the water levels and the aforementioned drought years. Relatively few are present when the levels are high, but large numbers occur when they are low, the birds then feeding by siphoning the soft lakeside mud.

A Teal ringed at Chew in October 2016 was recovered in the Pryazhinsky district of Karelia in north-western Russia. This gives us an insight into how far some of our Teal travel.

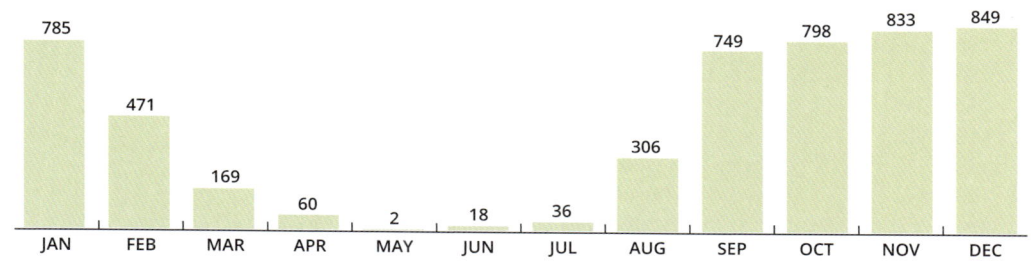

Month	JAN	FEB	MAR	APR	MAY	JUN	JUL	AUG	SEP	OCT	NOV	DEC
Count	785	471	169	60	2	18	36	306	749	798	833	849

TEAL | Monthly distribution (average) 1958-2015.

TEAL | Annual maxima 1955-2019.

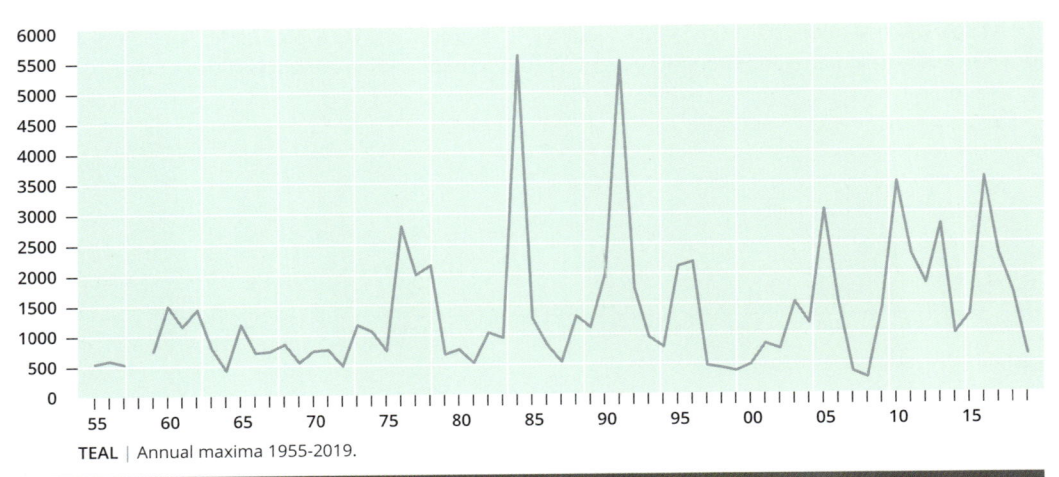

Teal | Rich Andrews

GREEN-WINGED TEAL *Anas carolinensis*

There are eight records in total, all relating to males (females are almost impossible to separate from female Common Teal). Note that a single adult male was present for six winters from November 1989 to April 1995.

1977–1978: 17 November to 26 January (KEV *et al.*).
1986: 28 October to 13 November (KEV *et al.*).
1989–1995: what was considered to have been the same returning male was seen as follows:
1989: 26 November to 7 December (KEV *et al.*).
1990–91: 3 February; 29 September to 9 December; 30 December to 23 February.
1991–92: 9 November to 7 March.
1992: 22 September to 5 December.
1993–94: 23 January; 3 October to 22 January.
1994: 3 October to 11 December.
1995: 18 February and from 26 March to 1 April, when paired to a female Teal. It failed to reappear in the autumn.

Subsequent males were recorded as follows:

- **1991:** a first-winter from 13 January to 23 February; both this bird and the returning adult male were present in Villice Bay (KEV *et al.*).
- **1998:** one, originally seen at Newton Park Lake, near Bath, from 27 January to 14 February, was seen at Chew on 21–22 March (A H Davis, R J Higgins *et al.*). Note that this bird was unusual in having faint horizontal scapular lines.
- **2000:** 8–15 April (R. M. Andrews, A. H. Davis *et al.*).
- **2010:** 17 December (R. J. Higgins *et al.*).
- **2012:** at Twycross on 17–18 April (C. J. Stone *et al.*) and perhaps the same bird at Heron's Green Pool on 30 April and 1 May (KEV *et al.*).
- **2019:** 13 November to 6 December.

Green-winged Teal | Gary Thoburn

MARBLED DUCK *Marmaronetta angustirostris*

One was present from 24 August to 18 September 1984 (A. Whatley, A Merritt *et al.*). It then moved to Cheddar Reservoir from 23 September to 27 October but was back at Chew on 28th. It then moved to Blagdon from 8 to 26 December before returning to Chew again from 1 to 5 January 1985. There was nothing in its behaviour to suggest that it was anything other than a wild bird. This bird arrived in a spell of easterly and southerly winds. See 'The ones that got away' in the chapter on 'Memorable Birding Moments and Tales'.

Note: Marbled Duck is in category D (reasonable doubt that it has occurred in a natural state) and therefore does not currently form part of the British List.

Marbled Duck (*This drawing was done in Israel*) | Laurel Tucker

RED-CRESTED POCHARD *Netta rufina*

The first record was of an eclipse male from 10 July to 28 August 1967 (C. C. Davis, B. King, D. E. Ladhams *et al.*). It has since been recorded in 35 of the 49 years to 2015, although there have been some significant gaps in its occurrences, most notably 1980–1983 inclusive.

The highest counts were five in March 1974 and four in September 1986 but, since 2009, higher numbers have been recorded, with maxima of seven in both 2009 and 2010 and six in 2013 and 2014 (see annual maxima graph below). The recent upsurge may relate to the increase in Red-crested Pochards in the Cotswold Water Park on the border of Gloucestershire and Wiltshire, breeding having first occurred there in 1975. Kirk and Phillips (2013) suggested that this population totalled about 20 breeding pairs in 2008, this amounting to about 50% of the national population, which was estimated at 320 birds.

Whilst the wild status of Red-crested Pochard records is often in doubt, it is worth noting that, over the years, several birds in autumn have arrived at the same time as numbers of Black Terns, perhaps indicative of a continental origin.

It has been recorded at Chew in every month except February, with a small spring peak in March and April, rising through June and July to a strong autumn peak in September; numbers then tail off into January.

Reference
Kirk, G. and Phillips, J. 2013. *The Birds of Gloucestershire.* Liverpool University Press.

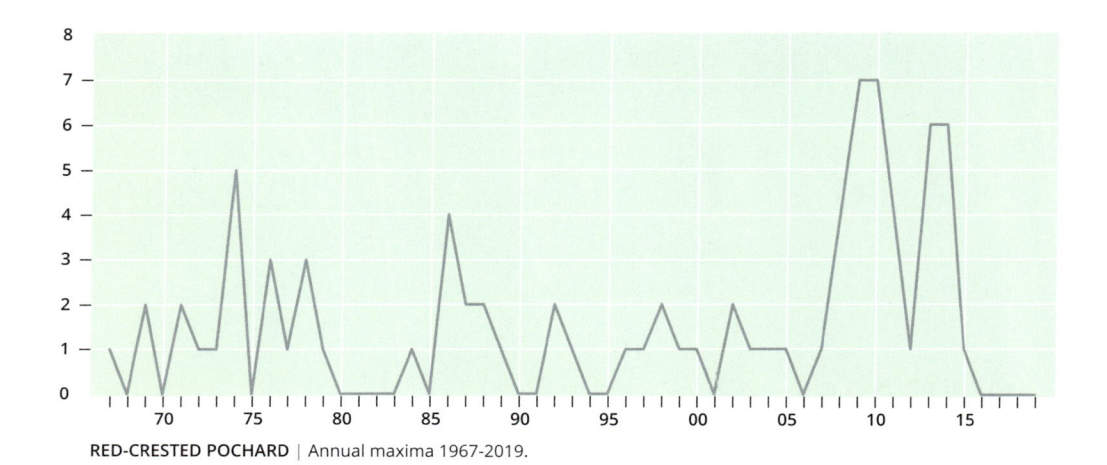

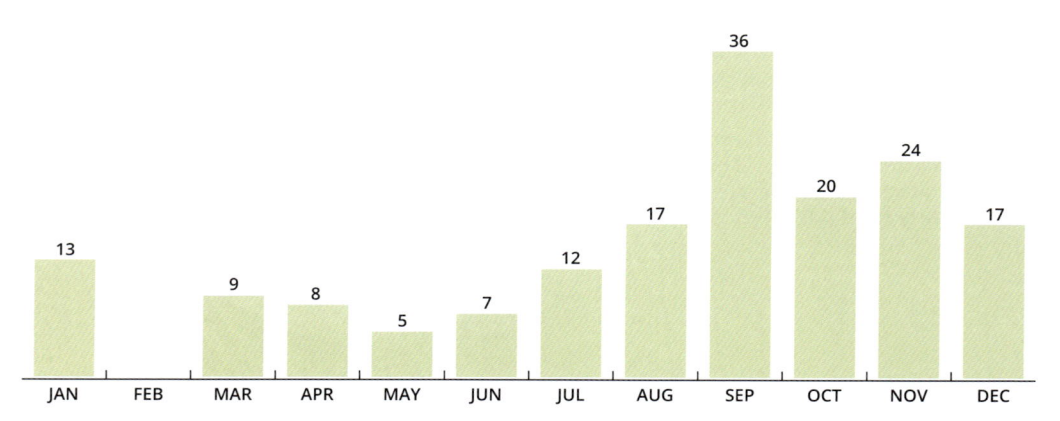

RED-CRESTED POCHARD | Annual maxima 1967-2019.

RED-CRESTED POCHARD | Monthly distribution (totals) 1967-2015. There are no February records.

POCHARD *Aythya ferina*

The monthly distribution (average) graph shows that Pochard is essentially a winter visitor, but numbers start to increase from mid-May onwards, rising during the summer and autumn to a strong winter peak from November to December. Numbers remain high into January but decrease steadily during February and March, with only small numbers remaining in April and May. However, the first returning migrants start to appear as early as mid-May, these being mostly males that have finished their courtship duties. It should be noted that, unlike other ducks, Pochards do not form discrete pairs; instead, they have a lekking system when several males – sometimes in double figures – display to a small number of females. It is noticeable that, at Chew, males always significantly outnumber females, but it is worth noting that females tend to winter further south than males.

Annual maxima at Chew average 783, with 15 years having counts of over a thousand. The graph indicates fluctuating numbers, the highest winter counts being 1,770 in January 1967, 3,095 in January 1997, 2,450 in November 1988 and 1,580 in January 2006. The highest counts are normally associated with drought years, when large areas of ruderal plants colonise the lake's margins, providing ideal feeding conditions once the water levels have flooded into them in mid-winter. The annual maxima graph shows a decline in numbers since the late 1980s.

Pochard is a fairly regular breeding species, with the first broods recorded in 1959. They have bred in 43 of the 59 years since (to 2017) with 135 broods recorded in total. The best year was 2000, with 12 broods. As they often build their nests actually in the water, years with high and stable summer water levels suit them best. Worryingly, there were no broods in 2015–2017, the increase in predators, particularly mink and pike, being the most likely suspects.

Surprisingly, the numbers of Pochards occurring at Chew also hinge on sailing activity at Cheddar Reservoir in Somerset (eight miles to the south-west of Chew, beyond the southern side of the Mendip Hills). Large numbers of Pochards winter there, the birds being attracted by algae and large populations of flowering plants such as *Elodea spp.* which are abundant in the reservoir. The birds feed there in large numbers and, when sailing activity is at its peak (usually on weekends) most of them cross the Mendips to sit out the daylight hours at either Blagdon or Chew.

Pochard | Rich Andrews

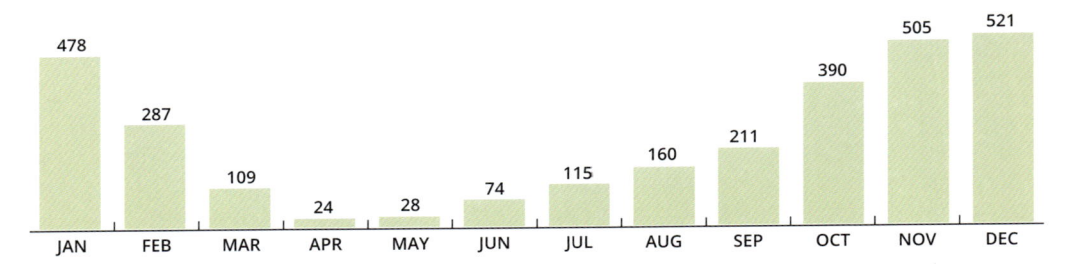

POCHARD | Monthly distribution (average) 1955-2015.

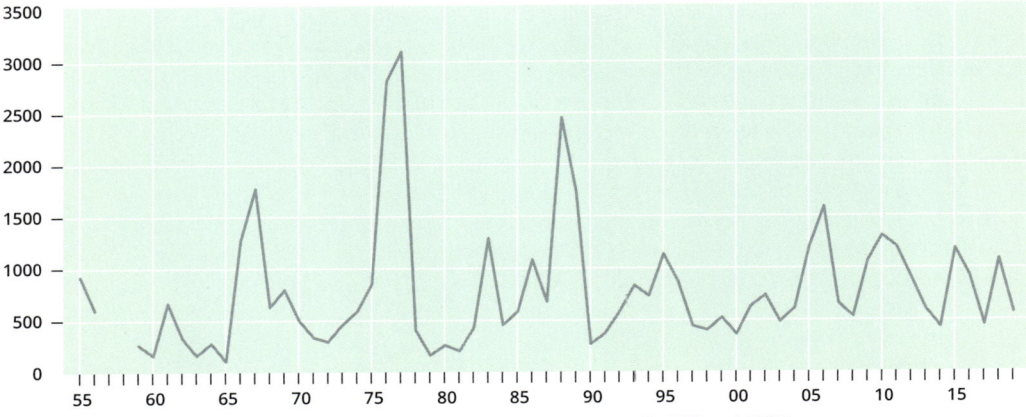

Values by month: JAN 478, FEB 287, MAR 109, APR 24, MAY 28, JUN 74, JUL 115, AUG 160, SEP 211, OCT 390, NOV 505, DEC 521.

POCHARD | Annual maxima 1955-2019 (note that there were no counts in 1957 and 1958).

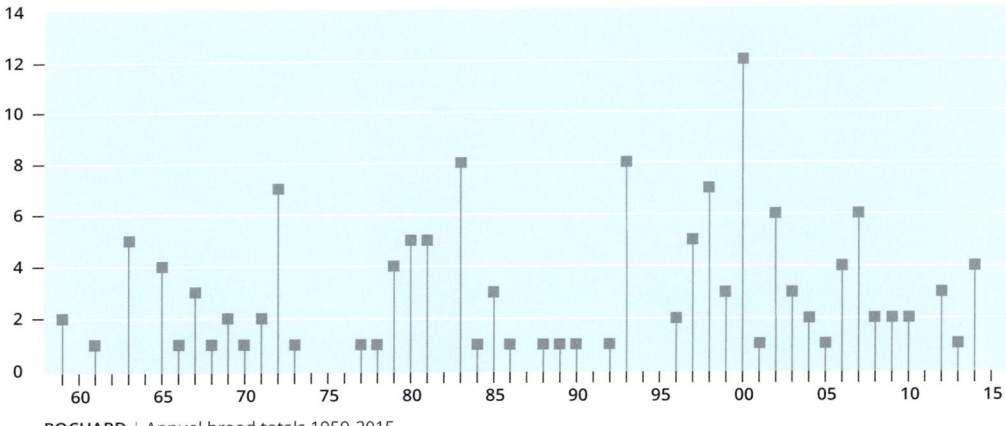

POCHARD | Annual brood totals 1959-2015.

An interesting variation on this theme occurred during the winter of 1988–89, when up to 2,450 were recorded at Chew. This high count related to the draining of the rather small Tank 2 at Barrow Gurney Reservoirs, four miles to the north-west of Chew. The draining of the tank allowed huge numbers of plants to colonise the reservoir floor and, when it refilled later in the autumn, it provided excellent feeding conditions for the Pochards, which clearly commuted back and forth from Chew and Blagdon during the hours of darkness. There are two intriguing questions relating to this: (1) how did the Pochards discover this small but abundant food source, and (2) more especially, how were the pioneers so quickly able to communicate this significant discovery to the rest of the Pochards that were present in the area?

Another interesting Pochard story is of the female with a nasal saddle that was seen at the lake on 5 June 2010. It transpired that it had been fitted south of Nantes in north-west France. This gave us an unexpected insight into the movements of this species once they leave Chew. Since then other birds with a nasal saddle have been seen, with one for example on 17 December 2019.

FERRUGINOUS DUCK *Aythya nyroca*

The first record was of a female on 2 January 1955 (B. King, E. G. Richards). The second involved an adult male that was present at Orchardleigh Lake, Somerset, from 20 December 1968 to 30 March 1969. It visited Chew on 29 December 1968 and on 5 and 19 January 1969 (J. B. O. Rossetti, G. P. Threlfall, A. H. Davis, KEV), following shoots at Orchardleigh.

The next was a male on 10–17 January 1976 (A. Merritt, KEV *et al.*). Following a 24-year gap, the species was then recorded annually from 2000 to 2016.

It has occurred in every month but, as the graph below shows, records gradually rise from January to June. They dip in July before rising to another peak in August–September, dropping slightly in October and November, with the smallest monthly total in December.

A pair is thought to have nested in 2003 and they were again seen in 2004 when, following mating, the female was again thought to have nested. Unfortunately, however, no young were ever seen. The pair was again present in 2005, 2006 and 2007. A male and a female were seen separately in 2008, up to two males were present in 2009, and three males and a female in 2010. For full details of this saga, see Davis & Vinicombe 2011.

A male was seen in 2011, a male and a female in both 2012 and 2013 and a female in 2015. A female was seen in 2016.

There is no evidence that any of the breeding activity was successful but, intriguingly, a juvenile male appeared in October–November 2006, feeding in the channel in front of Herriott's Bridge.

Reference
Davis, A. H. and Vinicombe, K. E. 2011 'The probable breeding of Ferruginous Ducks in Avon'. *British Birds* 104: 77–83.

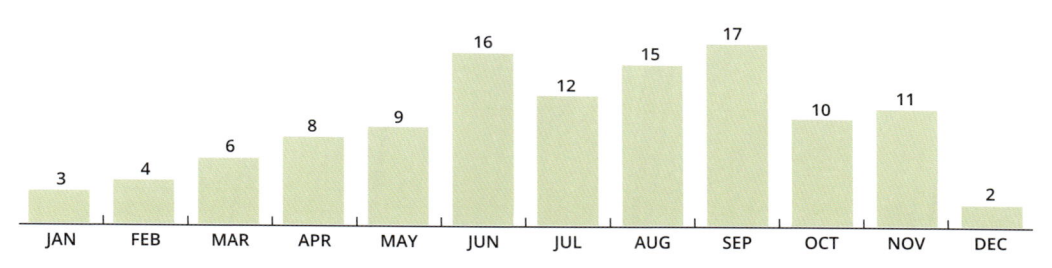

FERRUGINOUS DUCK | Monthly distribution (totals) 1955-2015.

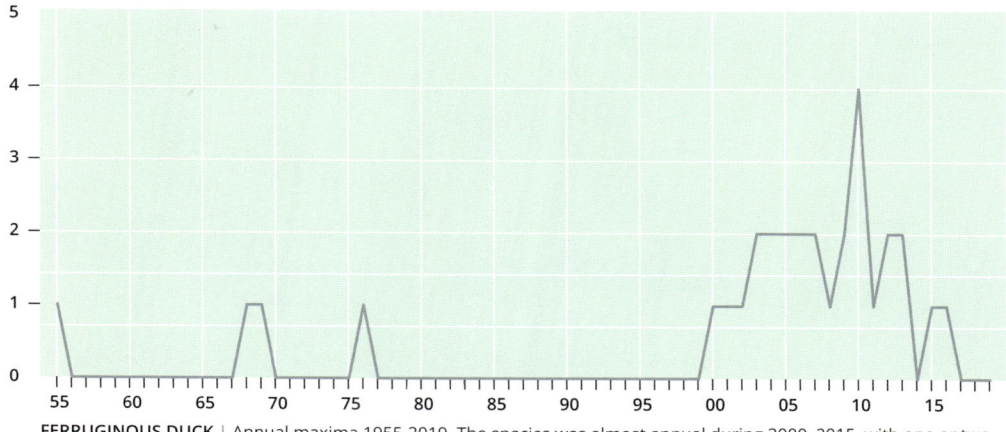

FERRUGINOUS DUCK | Annual maxima 1955-2019. The species was almost annual during 2000–2015, with one or two in every year except 2014, but with four in 2010.

Ferruginous Duck | Rich Andrews

RING-NECKED DUCK *Aythya collaris*

The first record was of a male on 2–23 May 1971 (KEV *et al.*), this bird having originally been seen at Blagdon on 4–21 April. What was undoubtedly the same individual returned in May 1972 and May 1973. The next record involved an unprecedented influx of up to three males (two adults and a 1st-winter) from 29 December 1976 into 1977, numbers increasing to four males on 6–12 February, with one to 27 March. There was also a hybrid Ring-necked x Tufted Duck *A. fuligula* present from 29 December 1976 to early April 1977.

Since then it has occurred in 25 of the 42 years from 1978 to 2019. As the annual maxima graph shows, most of the records relate to single birds, but with two seen in six years, three birds in two years, four birds in 1976 and a record eight (six 1st-winter males and two females) on 9 November 2008. It is thought possible that this last record related to the remnants of a remarkable flock of 15 that was seen on 8 October on Inishmore on the Aran Islands, off the west coast of Ireland. All of these birds were juvenile/first-winters.

Of all the Ring-necked Ducks seen at Chew, only five have involved females: one from 5 November 2005 until 22 April 2006, the aforementioned two in 2008, and one from 15 June to 9 August 1980, with a second present from 3 August to 21 September; the latter, however, was colour-ringed and was therefore likely to have escaped from captivity.

The monthly distribution totals show that it has occurred in every month, but with a spring/early summer peak in May–June and a late autumn/early winter peak in November–December.

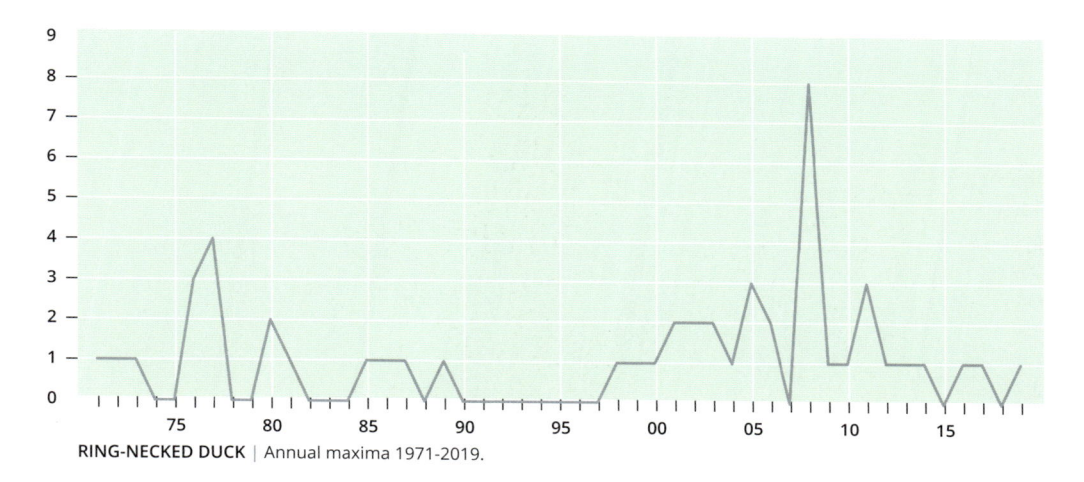

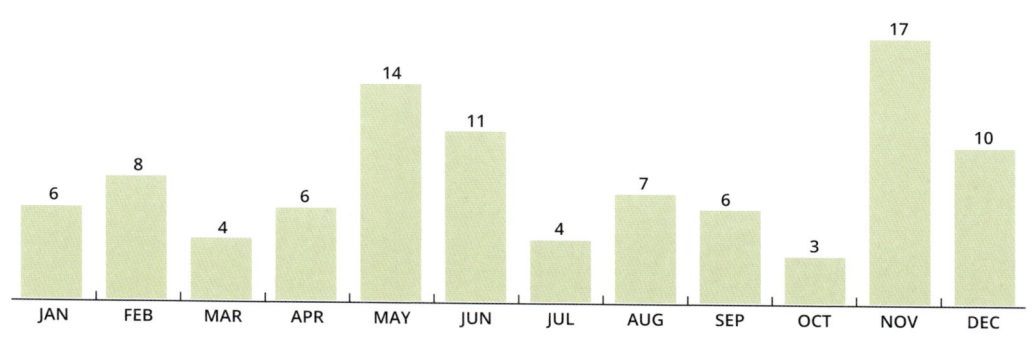

RING-NECKED DUCK | Annual maxima 1971-2019.

RING-NECKED DUCK | Monthly distribution (totals) 1971-2019.

TUFTED DUCK *Aythya fuligula*

Tufted Duck is a common species all year round, with a population of about 300–400 from November to April. The monthly distribution (average) shows that numbers dip in May and June, when the birds are off breeding, but they increase significantly in July and August as large numbers – mainly males – arrive to moult. They peak in September, numbers gradually reducing during the winter.

Annual maxima were fairly stable from 1954 to 1995, the annual average being 504. Numbers have increased spectacularly since then, averaging 1,479 during 1996–2015, with annual maxima of over 2,000 from 2010 to 2014, including a record 2,585 in September 2016, which was then beaten with 2,614 in September 2018. The reasons for this increase are unknown, but it must surely be due to an increase in aquatic invertebrates, on which they feed.

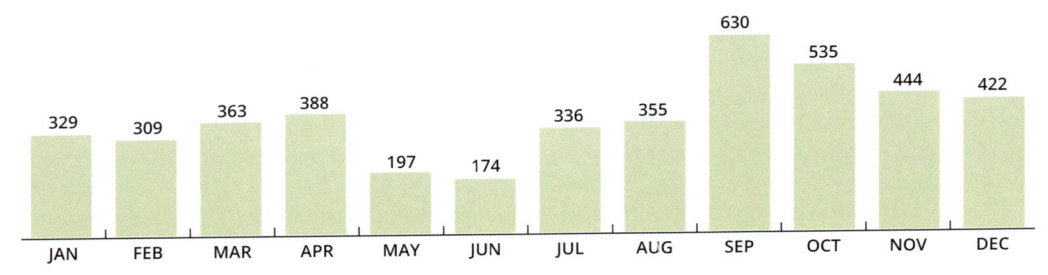

TUFTED DUCK | Monthly distribution (average) 1954-2015.

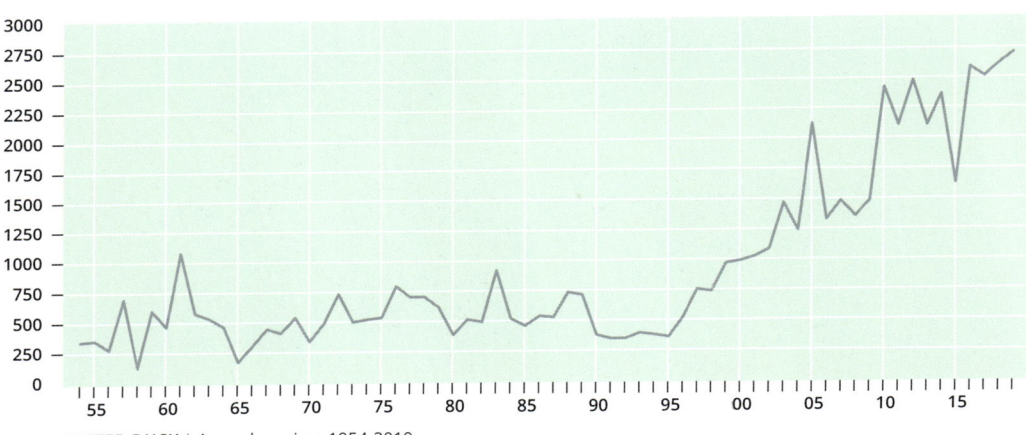

TUFTED DUCK | Annual maxima 1954-2019.

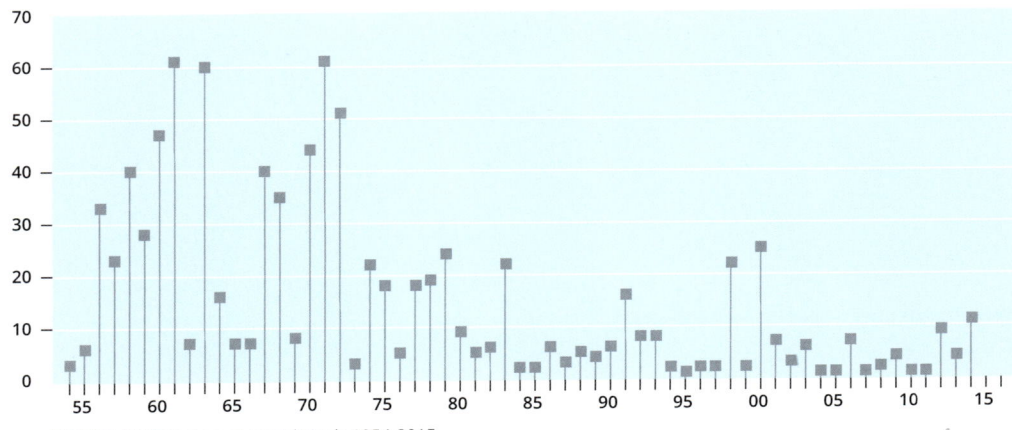

TUFTED DUCK | Annual brood totals 1954-2015.

What is odd, however, is that the increase since the mid-1990s corresponds with a crash in breeding numbers that has taken place since the mid-1980s (see annual brood totals graph). In the early days of the lake, the species was a numerous breeder, with peaks of 61 broods in 1971 and 51 in 1972. Breeding numbers then dropped, with an average of 16 broods during 1973–1979. From 1980 to 2015 the average was just six but with double figure totals of 22 in 1983, 16 in 1991, 22 in 1998, 25 in 2000 and 11 in 2014. No broods were seen in either 2015 or 2016. To emphasise the current breeding nadir, in 2015 there were more broods (two) on the tiny concrete-sided Portishead Boating Lake than there were at Chew! Given the huge numbers of Tufted Ducks that visit the lake, the contemporaneous downward trend in breeding numbers is difficult to understand. Food shortages can be ruled out but an increase in reed beds around the lake may be a problem for a bank-nesting species, as could increased predation of nesting females. Another simpler explanation is that the breeding range of Tufted Ducks could be shifting northwards.

But there is another answer: can Tufted Ducks actually moderate their own breeding when the population is high? Unlike human beings, whose population is increasing exponentially, Tufted Ducks – and other bird species – seem to have the ability to moderate their own populations, so that only a small minority of the adults produce any young on an annual basis. How do they do this? Maybe the humble Tufted Duck can achieve something that us oh-so-clever humans cannot.

Tufted Ducks | Gary Thoburn

SCAUP *Aythya marila*

The first record was of a female on 5–8 December 1954 (B. King). Since then, it has been recorded in every year except 1982 and 1991. Numbers are usually in single figures, but 12 were present in March 1966 and ten in February 1994. However, these totals were surpassed during the winter of 2016–17 when unusually large numbers were present, with 12 on 4 January, 14 on 13th, 18 on 1 February and an exceptional 21 present on 28 March (12 males and 9 females).

The monthly distribution totals show that winter visitors start to appear in October, the first date for juveniles being 14th (in both 1989 and 1990). Numbers then rise to a distinct peak in November before declining to a mid-winter low point in January, before increasing again to a spring peak in March. Numbers drop slightly in April then fall to a low point in June, when the species is rare (just seven records). Intriguingly, however, records increase in July, with 18 recorded. In 1988 there was an interesting June–July influx, with an adult male on 19–25 June, a female from 25 June to 11 July and two adult males on 4 July. This would appear to have been part of a more widespread influx, as there were also four males on the Severn Estuary at New Passage from 8 to 11 July (*ABR* 1988). Records then reduce to a low point in September (just eight). Interestingly, a flightless moulting male was seen on 1 September 1979 (KEV).

Close scrutiny in recent years suggests that about half the birds are adults and the other half juvenile/first-winters, but these ratios no doubt depend on annual breeding success in Iceland, where it is assumed that most of the Chew birds originate.

Scaup , Gary Thoburn

SCAUP | Annual maxima 1954-2019.

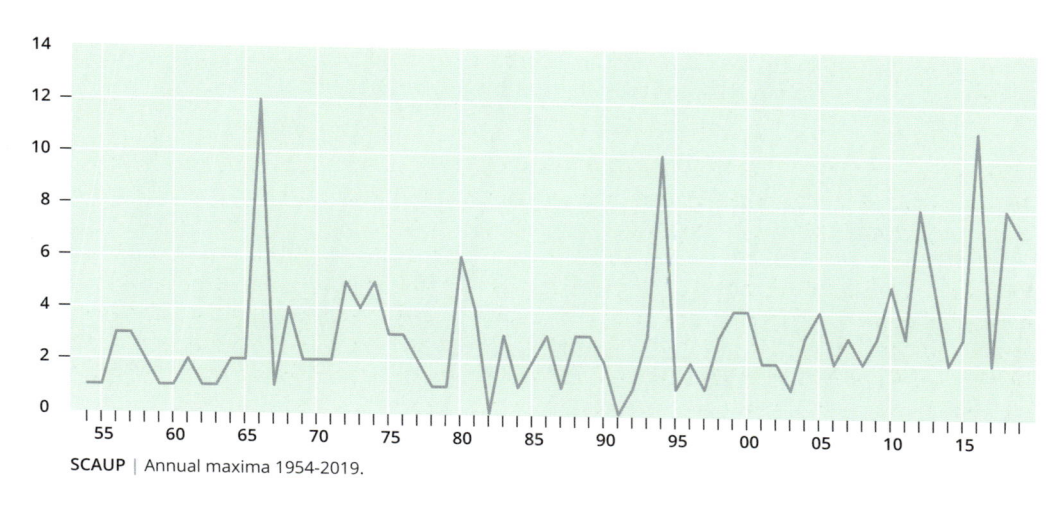

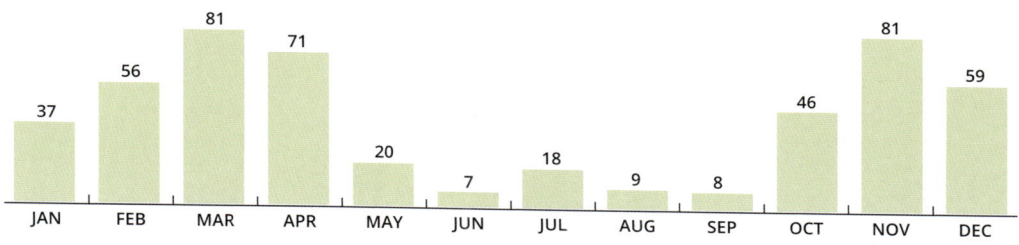

SCAUP | Monthly distribution (totals) 1954-2016.

LESSER SCAUP *Aythya affinis*

This American duck, first recorded in Britain in 1987, occurred almost annually from 2008 to 2019. Exactly how many individuals have been involved is difficult to determine, but the best estimate is six. All except one have involved males, one of which regularly commuted back and forth across the Bristol Channel to various sites in Glamorgan.

The following records, other than the bird in 2018, relate to males:

2008:	7 April to 1 May (A. H. Davis, R. Mielcarek *et al.*). Prior to this, it was at Blagdon Lake from 15 to 20 March, then at Barrow Gurney Reservoirs from 21 March to 5 April.
2010:	7 March and again from 17 March to 8 April (R. M. Andrews, G. Jones *et al.*).
2011:	3–4 November (KEV *et al.*).
2012:	23 February (KEV *et al.*); 11 and 23 March (C. J. Stone); from 28 August to 16 November (KEV *et al.*); 11–30 October (R. J. Higgins, R. Mielcarek *et al.*).
2013:	4–20 November (KEV *et al.*).
2014:	19 August to 3 September (KEV *et al.*).
2015–2016:	30 August to 28 September and again from 12 November to 7 January (S. Davies *et al.*).
2017:	12 November and another 8 December into 2018 (up to 1 February) (A. H. Davis, R. Mielcarek).
2018:	a female was present from 28 September to 8 October (A. H. Davis, R. Mielcarek *et al.*). Adult male (possibly the bird from 2017) from November 26 into 2019.
2019:	male from 2018 present until 18 January, and it or another 13–14 March. Possibly same male 25 October to 7 November.

The monthly distribution totals show that the records span the periods February to May, with a peak in March, and again from August to December, with a peak in November.

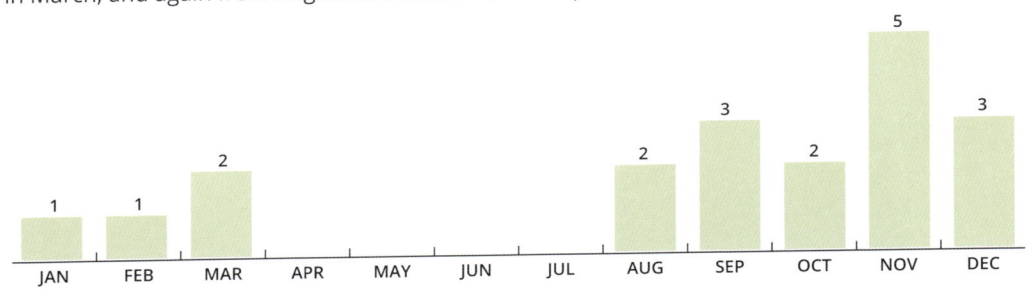

JAN	FEB	MAR	APR	MAY	JUN	JUL	AUG	SEP	OCT	NOV	DEC
1	1	2					2	3	2	5	3

LESSER SCAUP | Monthly distribution (totals) 2008-2015.

Lesser Scaup | Rich Andrews

| EIDER *Somateria mollissima*

A first-winter male was seen in Heron's Green Bay in foggy conditions on 2 November 1993. It flew off west towards Blagdon (J. P. Martin).

| VELVET SCOTER *Melanitta fusca*

There have been nine records involving 24 individuals:

- **1983:** two (adult male and a female) on 12 November (L. A. Tucker, KEV *et al.*).
- **1984:** an adult male on 21 January (J. Aldridge, A. H. Davis *et al.*); five juveniles (3 males and 2 females) on 10 November (A. H. Davis, R. Medland *et al.*).
- **2005:** three juveniles from 19 October to 9 November (M. Jenkins); another juvenile from 18 November to 9 December (A. H. Davis *et al.*).
- **2007:** five juveniles/first-winters on 16 December (R. M. Andrews *et al.*).
- **2008:** two juvenile males on 6 December (R. M. Andrews, C. Craig, KEV *et al.*).
- **2013:** four first-winters (2 males, 2 females) on 12 April (S. Davies *et al.*).
- **2016:** three juveniles/first-winters on 28 November (A. H. Davis, R. Mielcarek *et al.*).

COMMON SCOTER *Melanitta nigra*

The first record involved a flock of 15 on 6 April 1958 (B. King and T. Silcocks). It was then a somewhat erratic visitor until 1972, but it has occurred annually since then. Rather surprisingly, the fewest records have occurred from December to February, but there is a small and erratic spring passage in March and April, with totals of 39 and 72 respectively; there have been just seven May records (16 individuals). The peak months are in fact June and July, with totals of 146 and 156 respectively. Of these, 78% were males and it is clear that the birds at this time are on their moult migration. It is almost certain that they are heading to Carmarthen Bay, this being supported by the fact that, on 2 July 2017, a flock of eight males and a female headed off from the lake in a westerly direction.

There is then an autumn peak from September to November but the high total for October relates to an extraordinary event on 31 October 2002, when a flock of 115 appeared, eventually flying off south over the Mendips (A. H. Davis). These were all female-types and it is thought that they were in fact juveniles. Excluding that flock, the overall counts reveal that 52% of the scoters recorded at Chew were males but, of course, it is not known what proportion of the so-called females were actually juvenile males.

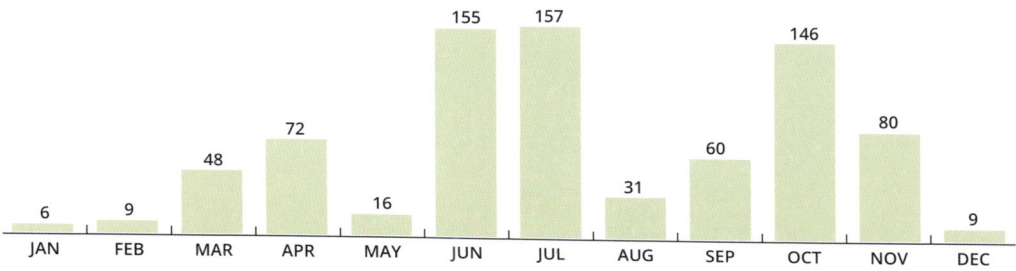

COMMON SCOTER | Monthly distribution (totals) 1958-2015.

COMMON SCOTER | Annual maxima 1958-2019.

Common Scoter | Laurel Tucker

Long-tailed Duck | Rich Andrews

LONG-TAILED DUCK *Clangula hyemalis*

The Long-tailed Duck is an erratic winter visitor. The first record involved two first-winter males on 29 March 1958, these being joined by three females on 19 April (B. King). The next was a juvenile on 15–19 December 1962. There was then a four-year gap until three in 1967. Since then, it has been recorded in 37 of the 50 years to 2016. Most records have involved single birds, but there have been four records of two and two records of three. The highest numbers, however, occurred during the winter of 1988–89. A juvenile was present from 13 to 20 November, increasing to six on 27 November and seven from 4 December to 8 January (3 1st-winter males and 4 1st-winter females). Up to six were then present until the end of March, numbers increasing further to a record eight first-years (4 males + 4 females), the last of which was seen on 28 April.

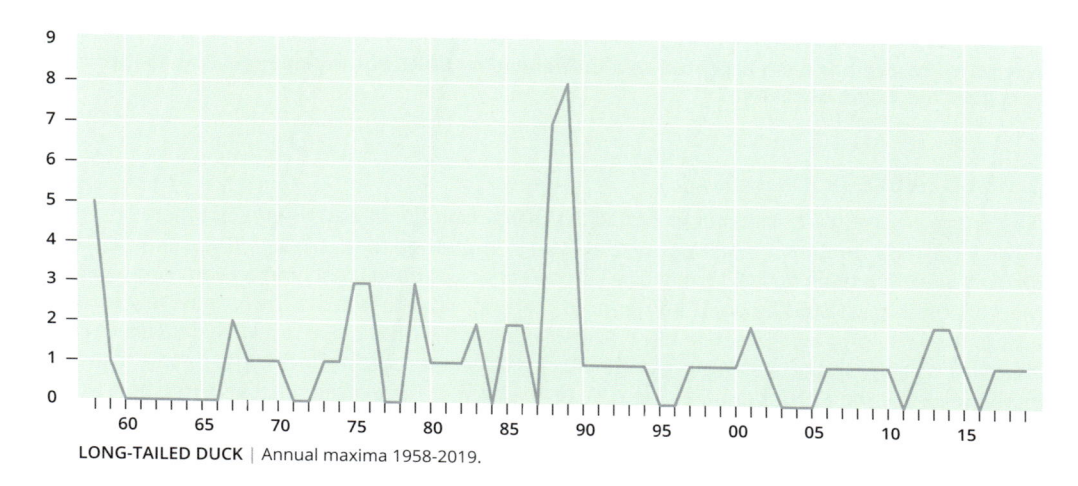

LONG-TAILED DUCK | Annual maxima 1958-2019.

As the monthly distribution totals indicate, they first arrive in October or November, the earliest date being 19 October (in 2008). The main arrival is in November, numbers then stabilising through the winter until April, when there is sometimes a further increase that seems to relate to individuals from other reservoirs in the area. The birds move to Chew at that time to take advantage of the good feeding conditions, when there are huge numbers of chironomids hatching from the lake. The latest date involved a female that stayed until 1 June (in 1969).

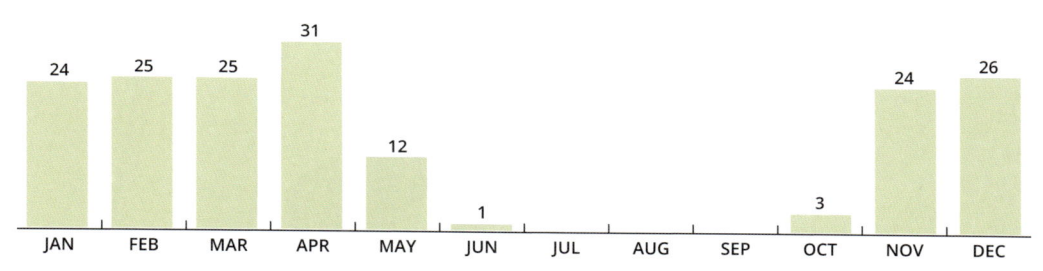

LONG-TAILED DUCK | Monthly distribution (totals) 1958-2016. Note that one in 1969 stayed until 1 June.

On 11 November 2017, a stunning adult male turned up off the Main Dam, having been present earlier at Barrow Gurney Reservoirs. This is the first time an adult male has occurred at the lake and it was present from 11 November to 29 December. What is assumed to be the same bird again turned up on 19 November 2018 and remained till 26th before moving on to Barrow Gurney Res where it remained into 2019. It then returned 3–13 November 2019, before moving again to Barrow Gurney.

BUFFLEHEAD *Bucephala albeola*

An elusive adult female was present in Stratford Bay on 1–3 May 2018 (M. Jenkins *et al.*). It was ringed but it is not known whether it was a plastic or a metal ring. Records of this species in Britain are frequently dismissed as escapes from captivity, particularly if the bird is ringed. However Reeber (2015) indicated that the species is quite rare in captivity (especially in Eurasia) and is unlikely to escape. In addition, captive birds are quite demanding, requiring deep, clear and flowing water, and the species is difficult to breed if these conditions are not met.

A search of the internet also came up with the following information: the North American population was estimated at about 500,000 individuals in 1960 but it had increased to 1,200,000 in the early 2000s. There were an estimated 1,000,000 in 2011, when stable or slightly increasing, following a sharp increase. In addition, over 22,000 have been ringed. The negative attitude towards UK records of this species is clearly not supported by the statistics.

Note: This record has been accepted as a Bufflehead by BBRC but in Appendix 3 as 'identification accepted but origin uncertain'.

GOLDENEYE *Bucephala clangula*

Goldeneye is, essentially, a winter visitor, with the first traditionally arriving in October. Since 1970, however, small numbers (up to four) have arrived in September and, since 1979, as early as August (up to three). The main arrival takes place in November, gradually reaching an early spring peak in March, possibly assisted by good numbers of Chironomidae larvae. As they are widely scattered across the lake, and also because they dive so frequently, Goldeneye are very difficult to count. However, on early spring evenings they often form a large pre-roosting flock in the middle of the lake, enabling an accurate count to take place. Since 1982, these have often reached three figures, with a record 210 on 26 March 1999. It is not certain whether these large counts are simply the result of easier counting at this time of year or whether they are due to a genuine pre-migratory influx. The latter seems more likely. Good numbers remain into early April but they drop off considerably by the middle of the month, but with small numbers (up to 20) remaining into early May.

Summer records started to occur from 1981 onwards, culminating in a pair breeding in 2008 and again in 2012, 2013, 2015 and 2017, the first English breeding records.

The annual maxima graph clearly shows that the species has steadily increased from the 1950s through to the present time, with annual maxima of over a hundred now being the norm.

Reference
Reeber, S. (2015). *Wildfowl of Europe, Asia and North America*. Helm.

Goldeneye | Laurel Tucker

Goldeneye | Ray Scally

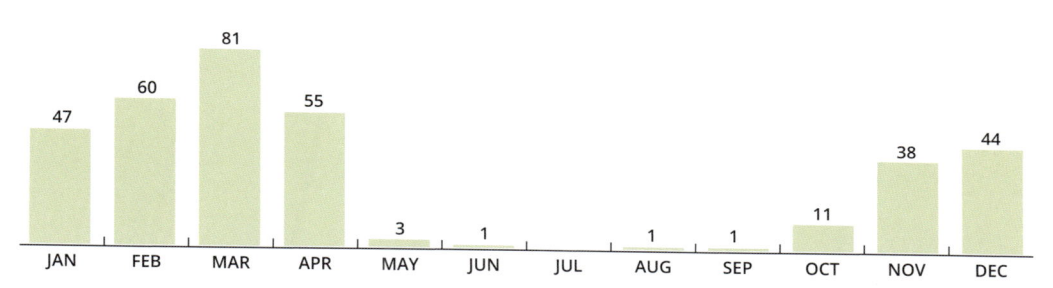

GOLDENEYE | Monthly distribution (average) 1954-2015. From 1981 onwards, there were irregular summer records and it was annual in summer during 2005–2015.

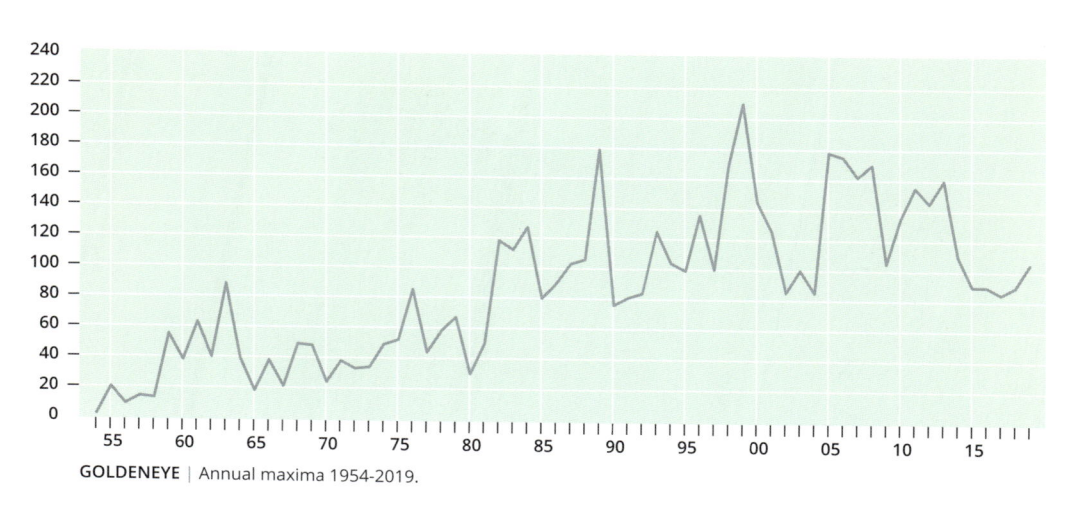

Month	JAN	FEB	MAR	APR	MAY	JUN	JUL	AUG	SEP	OCT	NOV	DEC
Count	47	60	81	55	3	1		1	1	11	38	44

GOLDENEYE | Annual maxima 1954-2019.

SMEW *Mergellus albellus*

The first record was of a 'redhead' (female or immature) on 27 February 1954 (B. King). The species then became an annual winter visitor until 2008, when none was recorded. Since then, its appearances have been erratic, with none seen during 2008–2011 or 2015–17. The recent decline may be the result of 'short-stopping' on the Continent, a consequence of climate change. Locally, however, there is a strong belief that the species' current absence at Chew (at least for the time being) is linked to the Ruddy Duck *Oxyura jamaicensis* shooting in the early years of the 21st century. The superficial similarity between a winter plumaged male Ruddy Duck and a female or juvenile Smew would hardly be apparent to a hunter squinting down the barrel of a rifle. The similarity in the trends from the mid-1990s to 2015, shown in the two annual maxima graphs, does nothing to refute this suggestion.

The monthly distribution totals clearly show that Smew was a winter visitor from October to April, the earliest autumn arrival being 25 October (in 1979). This record, however, related to an adult male that returned to the lake for six winters from November 1974 to December 1979. Each winter he arrived in eclipse plumage, gradually moulting into his full white finery during the course of the early winter.

Smew Rich Andrews

January was the peak month, with numbers dropping slightly in February and into March, although, in late winter, some moved to Blagdon Lake and probably to Cheddar Reservoir in Somerset. Small numbers – usually ones and twos – sometimes remained into April, but the latest were a female on 14–16 May 1961 and a wintering female that remained until 3 May 1980.

The last to be recorded was in 2014: a first-winter male from 2 January to 5 February.

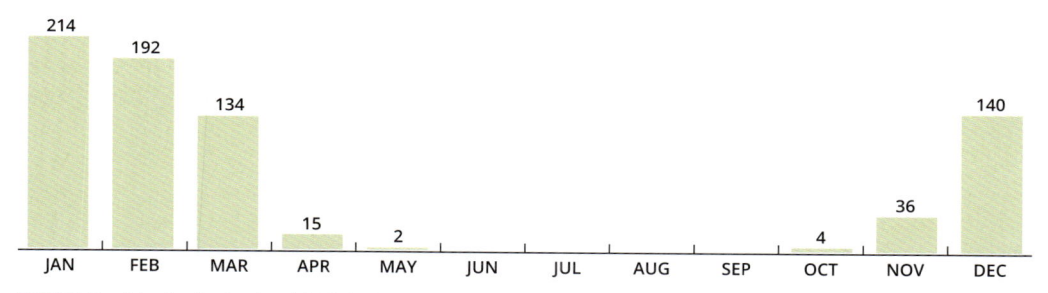

SMEW | Monthly distribution (totals) 1954-2015.

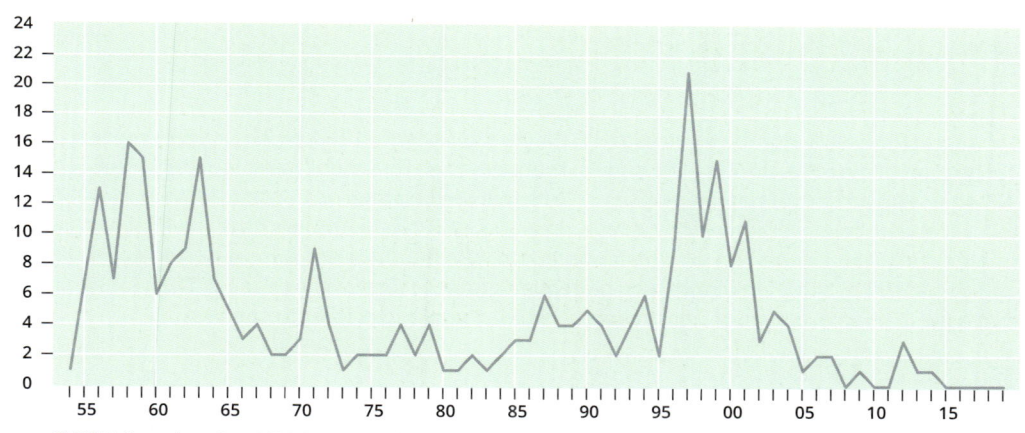

Values: JAN 214, FEB 192, MAR 134, APR 15, MAY 2, JUN 0, JUL 0, AUG 0, SEP 0, OCT 4, NOV 36, DEC 140.

SMEW | Annual maxima 1954-2019. Note the crash in numbers after 2000 following the Ruddy Duck shooting.

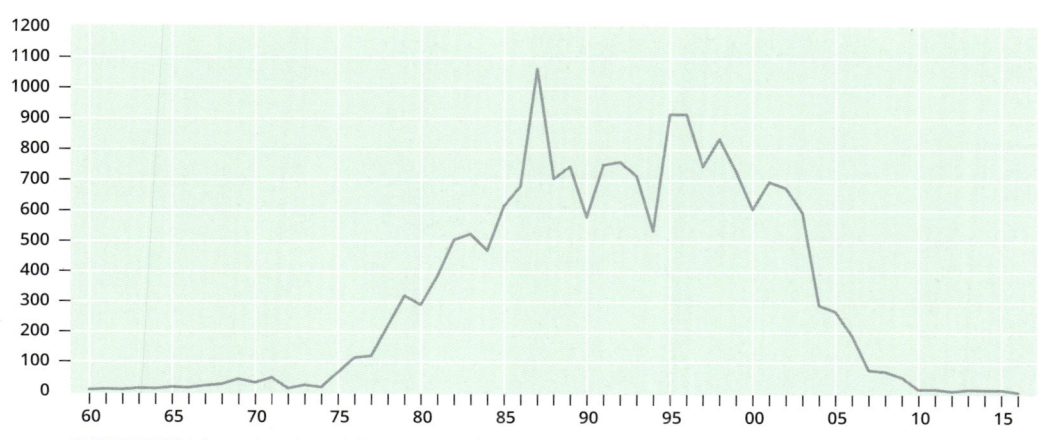

RUDDY DUCK | Annual maxima 1960-2016. Note the similar decline since the turn of the century.

GOOSANDER *Mergus merganser*

The first record was of two on 27 February 1954 (B. King). Numbers steadily rose from that point to a record 43 in January 1963, during the infamous severe winter. As the first graph shows, winter visitors usually arrive in October but, from 1980 to 1999, September arrival dates became the norm, with the earliest on 6th (in 1982). Since then, the earliest dates have largely reverted to October. Numbers reach a peak in December–January, followed by a gradual decline into March, by which time most will have left, although single figures are sometimes present into April. A female with an injured wing summered in both 1980 and 1981, when she was joined by another female with a similar injury. In 2010, there was a very strange record of seven off Herriott's Bridge on 16 and 18 July.

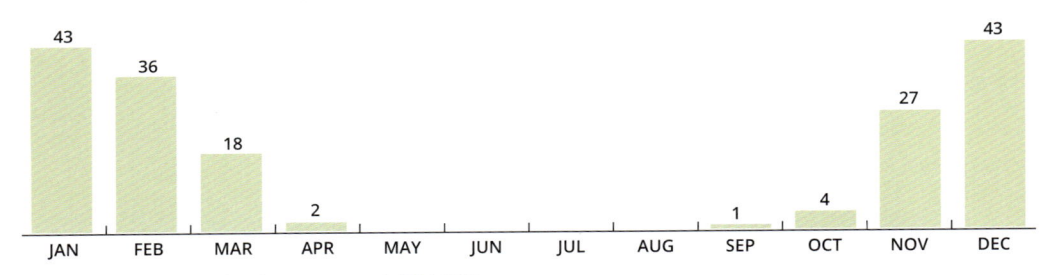

GOOSANDER | Monthly distribution (average) 1954-2019.

JAN	FEB	MAR	APR	MAY	JUN	JUL	AUG	SEP	OCT	NOV	DEC
43	36	18	2					1	4	27	43

Apart from 1963, numbers remained in single figures until 1968, when 14 were recorded, but, as the annual maxima graph below shows, numbers then rose significantly to the winter of 1995–96, when 208 were counted in December 1995, followed by a record 283 on 3 February 1996. The following year, however, there was a large drop to just 49 and numbers have never since reached treble figures. It is interesting to note, however, that the numbers of Cormorants increased sharply during the 1990s, but then dipped and plateaued after the turn of the century. This would suggest that a fall in coarse fish stocks was responsible for the declines of both species.

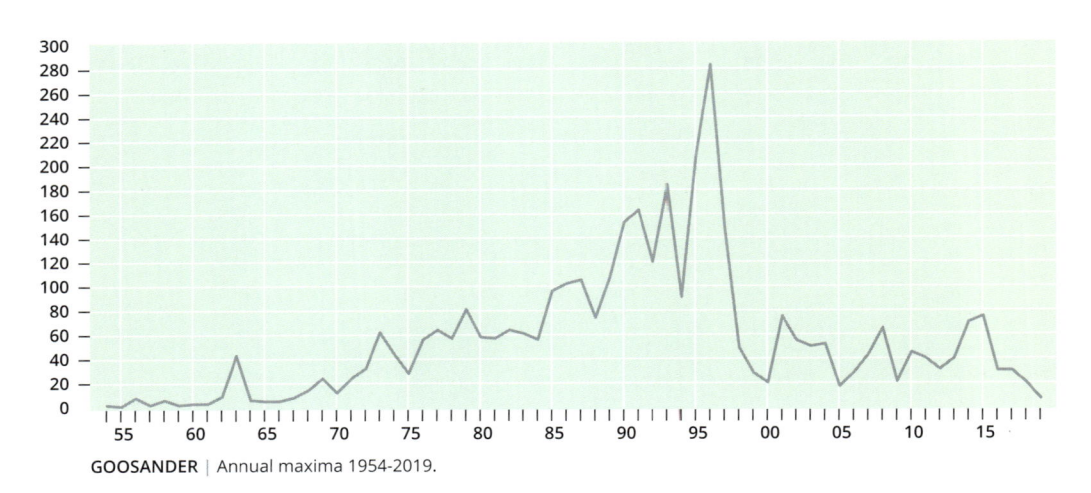

GOOSANDER | Annual maxima 1954-2019.

Goosander | Rich Andrews

RED-BREASTED MERGANSER *Mergus serrator*

The first record was of a party of three (two males) on 19 February 1956 (B. King), with the female/immature remaining to 11 March. It was 12 years before the next records, in 1968: two in March, three in April and two in November. The twelve-year gap between these sightings may have related to the fact that there was considerable uncertainty at the time concerning the separation of female and juvenile mergansers from Goosanders *Mergus merganser*. From 1968 onwards, it was recorded annually, with the highest counts in the late 1980s and early 1990s, including a record six (two adult males) in November 1989 and five in November 1991. Records declined through the 1990s with just a single bird wintering from 2004 to 2011 (see annual maxima graph below). This was followed by an up-turn during 2012–2015.

The monthly distribution totals clearly show that Red-breasted Merganser is essentially a winter visitor from October to April, with a strong peak from November to January before gradually declining towards spring. Although barely visible on the graph below, there have also been three summer records from May to July, all relating to females: on 29 July 1970, 28 June 1972 and 29 May 1992. The only month never to have had a record is August.

Mention must be made of 'Mervyn the Merganser', a very special drake that spent 35 winters at the lake between 31 October 1981 and 5 January 2016. For some reason, he appeared to be imprinted on Goosanders *Mergus merganser*. (A more detailed write-up can be found in the chapter on Memorable birding moments and tales).

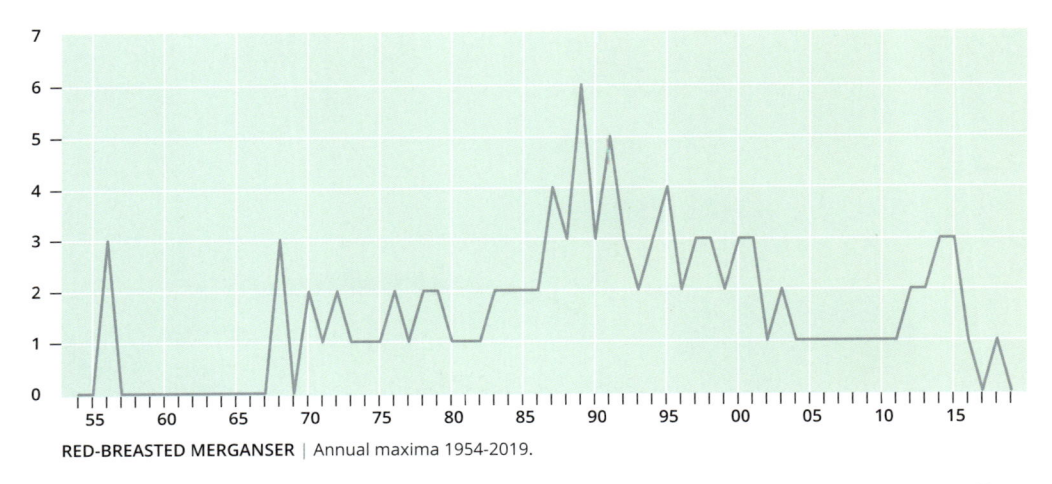

RED-BREASTED MERGANSER | Annual maxima 1954-2019.

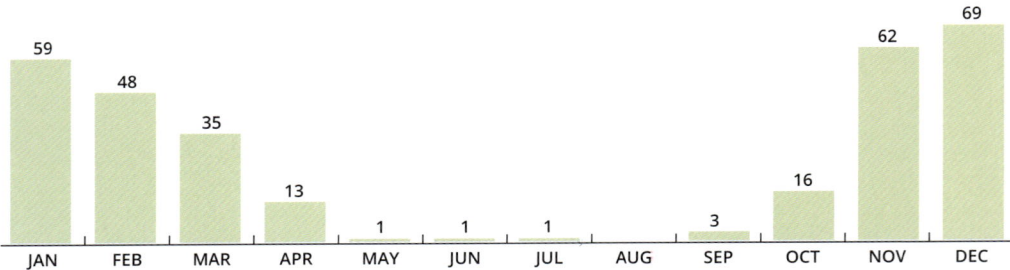

RED-BREASTED MERGANSER | Monthly distribution (totals) 1958-2015.

JAN	FEB	MAR	APR	MAY	JUN	JUL	AUG	SEP	OCT	NOV	DEC
59	48	35	13	1	1	1		3	16	62	69

226 COMPLETE SPECIES LIST AND CHARTS

RUDDY DUCK *Oxyura jamaicensis*

The first Ruddy Ducks were seen at Chew in 1957 (*Somerset Bird Report* 1960) having escaped from the then Wildfowl Trust at Slimbridge. But was that the full story? Bernard King told me that, on hearing that Ruddy Ducks were present at Chew, Peter Scott sent down his best breeding female to boost the population. Bernard told me this story on two separate occasions, and I have no reason to doubt its veracity.

The annual maxima graph clearly shows the meteoric rise in numbers from 1960 to the mid-1990s, the highest count being 1,064 on 1 March 1987 (A. J. Merritt). Numbers remained high throughout the 1990s, with maxima of 915 in both 1995 and 1996. This was followed by a sharp decline from 2000 onwards, following a sustained series of nationwide culls, as part of an international initiative to conserve the White-headed Duck.

The rationale for these culls was the research indicating that Ruddy Ducks were a threat to the endangered White-headed Duck *O. leucocephala*, the nearest populations of which are in southern Spain. The problem was both the fear of inter-breeding between the two species and also the possible displacement of the White-headed Duck by the Ruddy Duck. The Ruddy Duck was also starting to spread across the continent.

The cull eventually succeeded, and the last Chew record was of a male from 12 to 14 September 2016, when it was shot.

Ruddy Duck | Rich Andrews

RUDDY DUCK | Annual maxima 1960-2016.

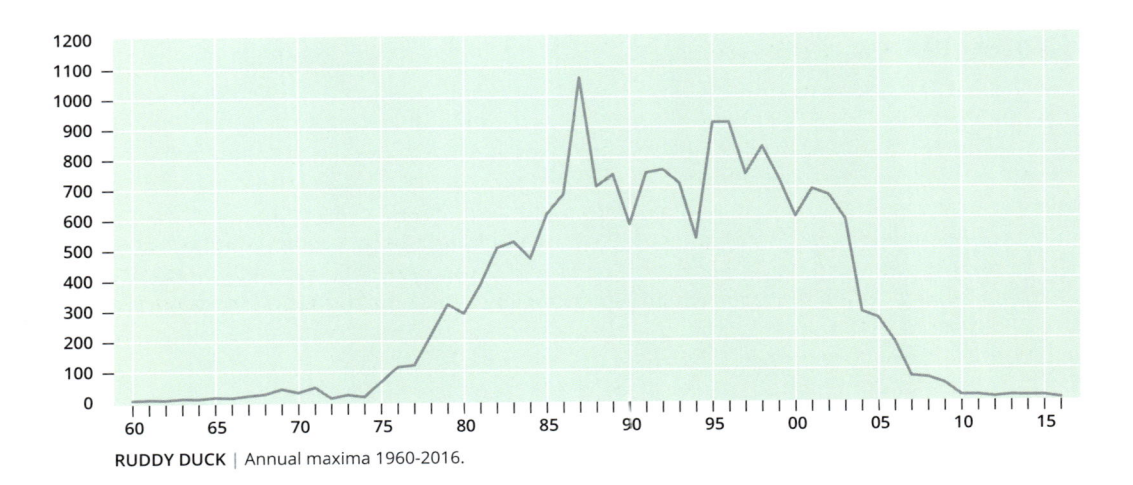

The monthly distribution average shows that the Ruddy Duck was essentially a winter visitor, most of the birds leaving in late winter and spring to breed on small lakes, mainly in the Midlands. As a consequence, numbers at Chew were low in summer, the average May and June counts being just four, although the species was very secretive at this time of year.

Ruddy Ducks first bred in 1961, when a brood of seven was seen on 3 June. They then bred in 32 of the 48 years from 1961 to 2008 as shown in the annual brood totals graph.

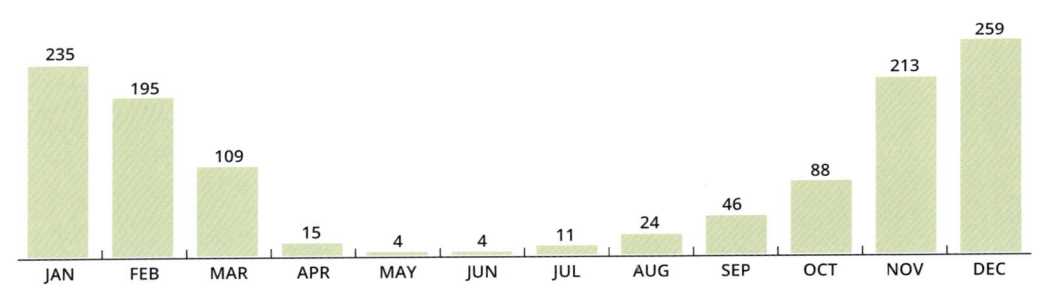

RUDDY DUCK | Monthly distribution (average) 1960-2016.

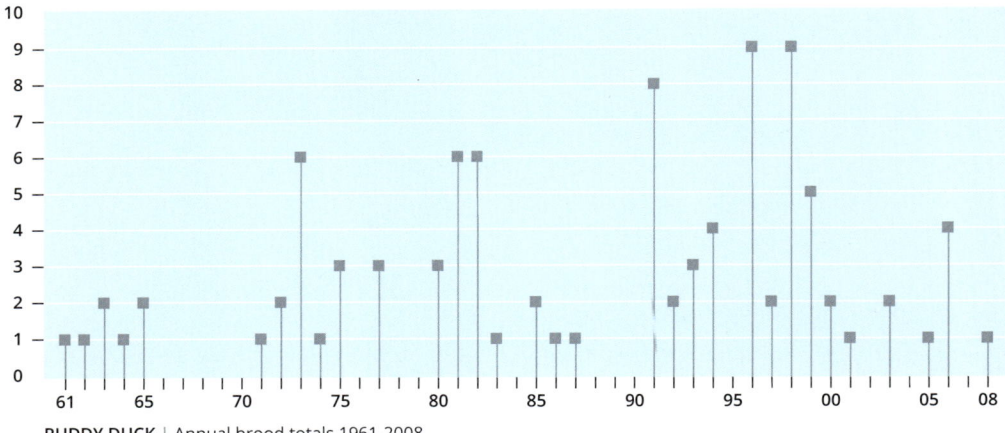

RUDDY DUCK | Annual brood totals 1961-2008.

COMPLETE SPECIES LIST AND CHARTS

WHITE-HEADED DUCK *Oxyura leucocephala*

There have been three records:

- **1985:** a very tame female at Herriott's Bridge on 9 and 19 June was considered to have been an escape from captivity (L. A. Tucker, KEV).
- **1995:** an un-ringed male in winter plumage was present from 11 November to 25 December (KEV *et al.*). It was considered to have been a bird that was first seen at Abberton Reservoir, Essex, on 2 January 1995. It was last seen there on about 4 November. After leaving Chew, it was present during the first week of January at Hanningfield Reservoir, Essex. It then commuted between there and Abberton over the next few months (*ABR*).
- **2003:** a female type, probably a juvenile, from 26 August to 3 September and what was presumably a different juvenile on 12 October (KEV *et al.*).

The records in 2003 coincided with nine others elsewhere in Britain: in Gloucestershire, Cambridgeshire, Leicestershire, Hertfordshire, Kent and East Sussex. In addition, between August 2003 and February 2004 there were ten records (11 individuals) in continental Europe outside its normal range, including six in France, one in Germany, one in Belgium and one in the Netherlands (*Birdwatch* 2004: Issue 145, page 27). The pattern of the occurrences in France and Britain was very similar to those seen in the 2016 influx of Western Swamphens *Porphyrio porphyrio* north into France and Britain. Despite these patterns of occurrence, the species has not been admitted to the 'official' British List. Many birders have pointed out the inconsistency in the approach to these two species, which may still be reviewed.

As background to the Chew records, White-headed Ducks have also occurred in France, with 15 records during 1981–1999, followed by peaks of up to 12 from 29 September to 11 November 2000. Subsequent records in north-west France occurred at Lac de Grand Lieu (west of Nantes), a site only about 300 miles south of Chew, as the duck flies. (*British Birds* 95: 179). Also, the species has increased in Spain, where there was a population of 2,400 in 1999. On 5 June 2009, a female Pochard was seen at Chew with a 'nose saddle' with the inscription 'C1B'. It transpired that the bird had been marked at Lac de Grand Lieu. This gives a clear indication of the kind of movements that many of our ducks undertake and it provides strong support for the assumption that most of the White-headed Ducks recorded in Britain are indeed wild birds.

There have also been records in Germany (a female on 29 November 1999) and one in the Netherlands (from 17 January to 14 February 1998) where there are also 12 previous records (see *British Birds* 94; March 2001, page 131).

See 'The ones that got away' in the chapter on 'Memorable Birding Moments and Tales'.

Note:
White-headed Duck is in category D (reasonable doubt that it has occurred in a natural state) and therefore does not currently form part of the British List.

NIGHTJAR *Caprimulgus europaeus*

There are two records: a male was flushed from the edge of the Main Reeds on 19 May 1973 (A. H. Davis, KEV) and a male on 27 May 1996 landed on a gate at Hollow Brook car park before flying off (D. Warden).

ALPINE SWIFT *Tachymarptis melba*

One flew north over Stratford Hide on 18 February 1998 (D. J. Angell). This is the earliest-ever British record, but it coincided with February sightings of Great Spotted Cuckoo *Clamator glandarius* in Devon on 22 February, and Red-rumped Swallows *Cecropis daurica* in Scilly on 15–16 February, Pembrokeshire on 20–23 February and Dorset on 26 February. Another Alpine Swift was seen in Cheshire on 4 March. Presumably, all these birds were early spring overshoots from Iberia.

SWIFT *Apus apus*

The first Swifts arrive at the end of April, the average first date during 1959–2015 being 21st; the earliest ever was on 8 April in 2001. As the average monthly maxima graph shows, following their arrival, numbers are high from May to July, with a peak in June. They decline considerably in August as they head south for the winter and few, if any, are left by September. The average last date is 31 August and the latest ever was one on 28 September (in 1976).

Numbers of Swifts visiting the lake vary enormously from day to day. On hot sunny summer days hardly any are to be seen; in fact it is possible to go all day without seeing one. It is in cool wet weather that the lake attracts the largest numbers, bringing in birds from the surrounding villages, towns and cities. In such conditions, there have been several estimates of up to 10,000. The birds then feed at low altitude in order to catch tiny flying chironomids that hatch from the lake in vast numbers. This creates a spectacular sight. Accurately counting such highly mobile birds is, of course, impossible, but estimates are made by counting across roughly defined transects and then estimating totals accordingly. This is not an exact science, but the rough counts achieved have proved surprisingly consistent.

Breeding Swifts have declined in recent decades as modern buildings are not generally suitable for them. This decline is hinted at in the annual maxima graph below, which indicates a distinct down-turn in numbers since the early part of the 21st century.

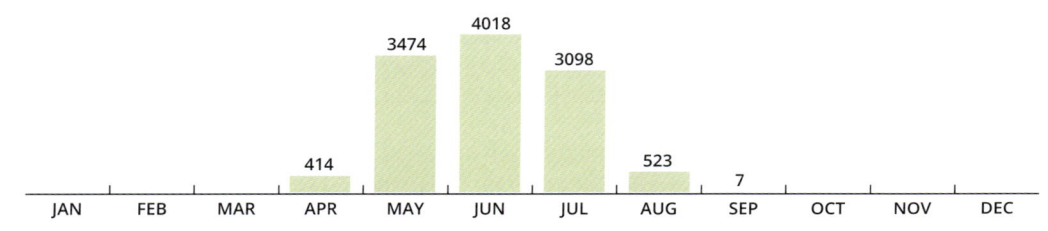

SWIFT | Monthly maxima (average) 1954-2015.

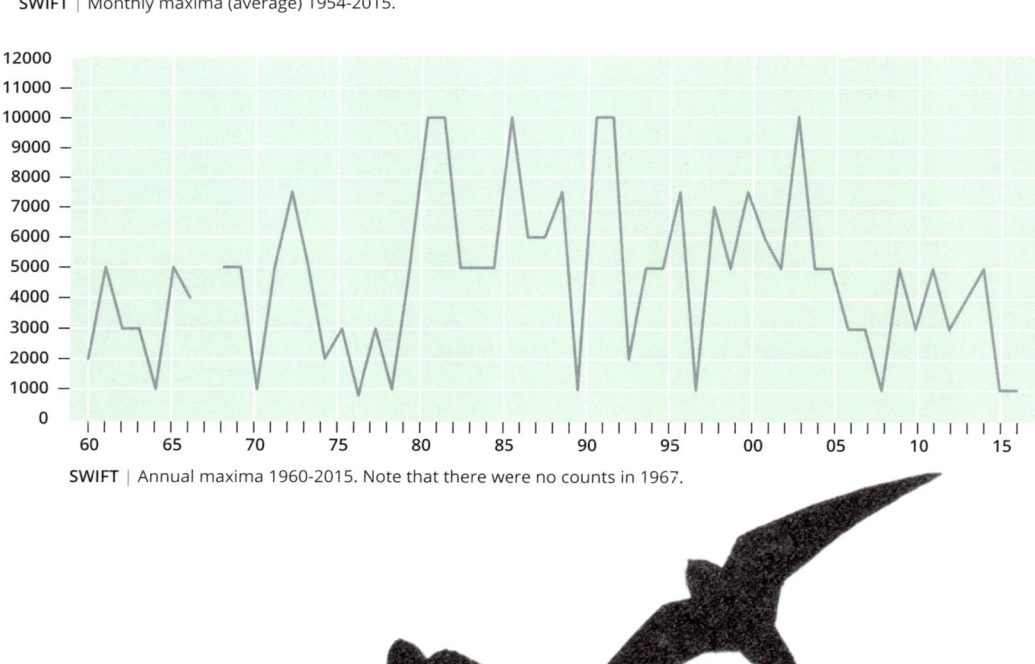

SWIFT | Annual maxima 1960-2015. Note that there were no counts in 1967.

Swifts | Laurel Tucker

230   COMPLETE SPECIES LIST AND CHARTS

GREAT BUSTARD *Otis tarda*

In West Harptree (close to the lake) – one on 30 Jan 2009, sporting a 'pink' tag on the right wing, was presumed to be the same as one at North Widcombe on 7 February, wing-tagged red 28. It then flew south over Chew and landed behind Herriott's Pool. Rupert Higgins recalls driving out to see this bird with Keith, but getting stuck in a snowdrift!

This female had been released in 2008 as part of the re-introduction programme. Note that at Puxton Moor, red 28 was seen again on 8 June 2009.

There was also one in 2017 photographed near Hollow Brook and this appeared in the 'Mendip Times'. This one was presumed to be the bird, released in 2016, that was also seen in West Harptree and summered around Chewton Mendip.

Note: These records are almost certainly from the Salisbury Plain re-introduction project and do not therefore relate to genuinely wild (European) birds. If this population becomes self-sustaining, this situation may change for any future records.

CUCKOO *Cuculus canorus*

Cuckoos have been recorded in every year. Inevitably, the main host species at Chew is the Reed Warbler *Acrocephalus scirpaceus*. The earliest arrival date is 9 April (in 1998) but the average is 21 April. Working out the number of singing males is extremely difficult, but as many as ten were recorded in 1983 and 1985. However, these counts are undoubtedly overestimates, the reason being that Cuckoos are extremely mobile around the lake, prone to calling persistently at one site before flying off – sometimes right across the lake – to call at another. In recent years, and apart from four calling males on 8 May 2016, evidence suggests that no more than one or two calling males have been present, but it is not known whether this is due to a decline or to a better understanding of their behavior. Ringing totals would seem to confirm that only small numbers are indeed present, although these will be underestimates as they are difficult to catch. A total of 26 has been ringed but with annual maxima of only three in 1984 and 1997 and four in 1999. Last dates have varied from 9 June (in 2014) to 22 September (in 1983). There has in fact been a wide spread of last dates, with eight in June, seven in both July and August, and nine in September.

Cuckoo | Gary Thoburn

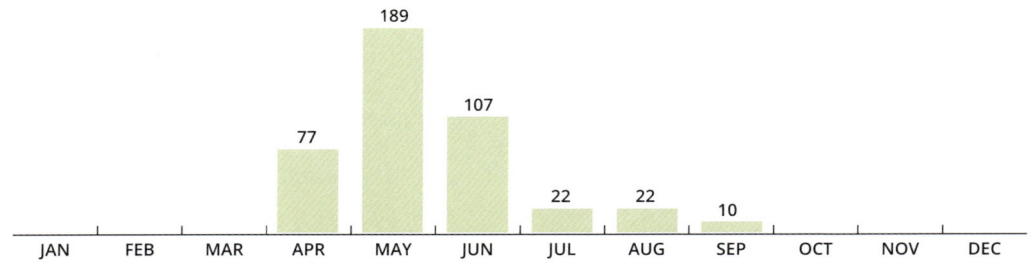

CUCKOO | Monthly maxima (combined) counts 1969-2015.

The annual maxima graph below indicates a distinct decline in numbers but it has to be borne in mind that the earlier counts, from the 1960s through to the 1990s, were almost certainly overestimates. One thing that is clear is that nothing about this species is straightforward!

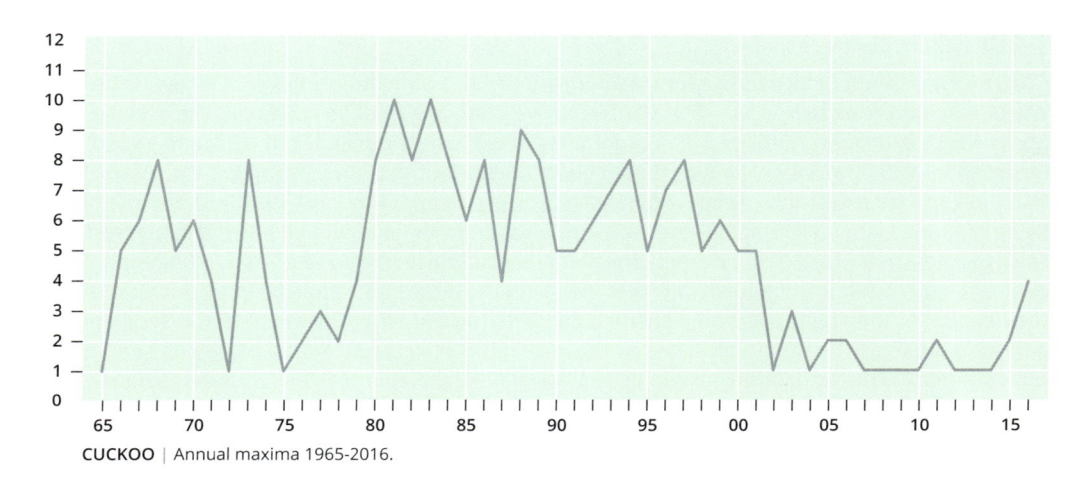

CUCKOO | Annual maxima 1965-2016.

FERAL PIGEON *Columba livia*

Feral Pigeons, or feral Rock Doves as they are also known, are scarce at the lake. Most records relate to birds that stop for a rest during a pigeon race. In line with their normal behaviour, grounded individuals usually gravitate towards humans and, as a consequence, most of the sightings have been at Herriott's Bridge, Heron's Green Bay and Picnic Site number one, next to the dam.

Wild un-ringed Feral Pigeons are occasionally attracted to places such as the Parkland Track or the dam walls, but sightings are few and far between.

STOCK DOVE *Columba oenas*

Stock Doves are normally present around the lake in small numbers. Most of the sightings relate to pairs in flight, the female (one assumes) normally taking the lead. In fact this distinctive habit makes it possible to identify flying Stock Doves at considerable range.

Some high counts have been recorded from November to February, with peaks of 170 in December 1973, 310 in February 1974, 410 in December 1980 and 400 in November 1982.

Since 1982, the only treble figure counts were 100 in January 1993 and December 2000. The highest counts corresponded with low water levels, when large areas of the lake are colonised by ruderal plants. The highest count since the turn of the century has been 40 in December 2013.

Small numbers (one to three pairs) breed at the lake, or in its immediate vicinity, but with peaks of five pairs in 2013 and six pairs from 2012 to 2015.

STOCK DOVE | Annual maxima 1962-2015.

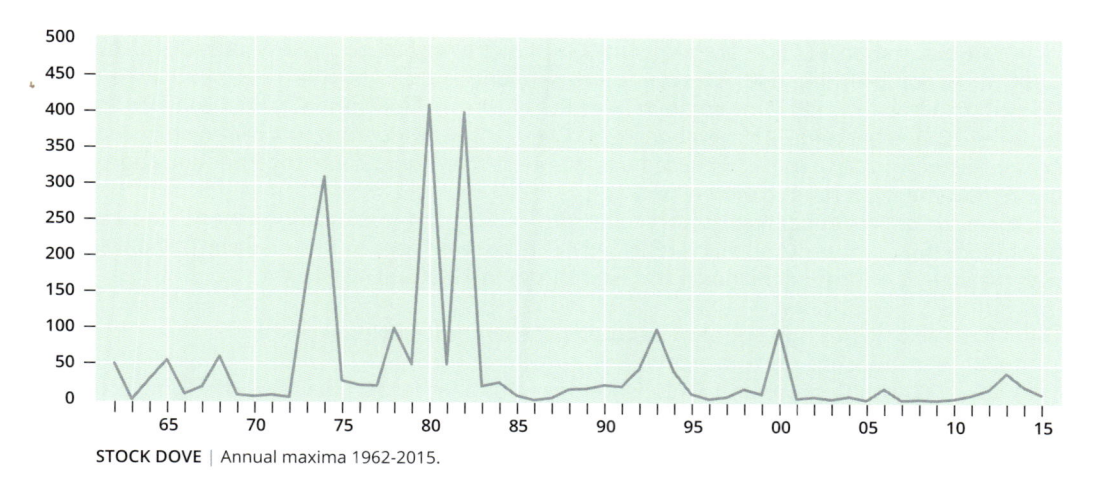

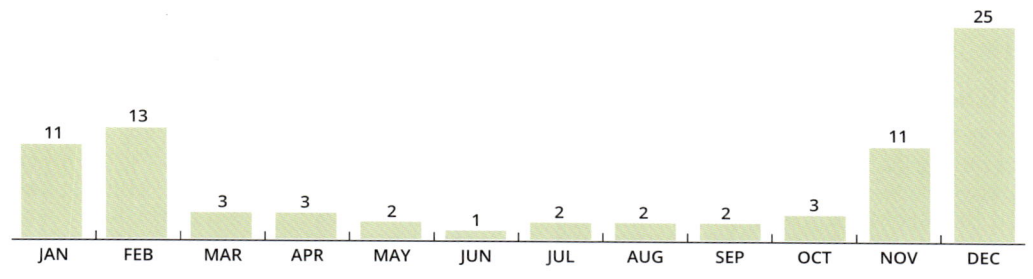

STOCK DOVE | Monthly maxima (average) 1962-2015.

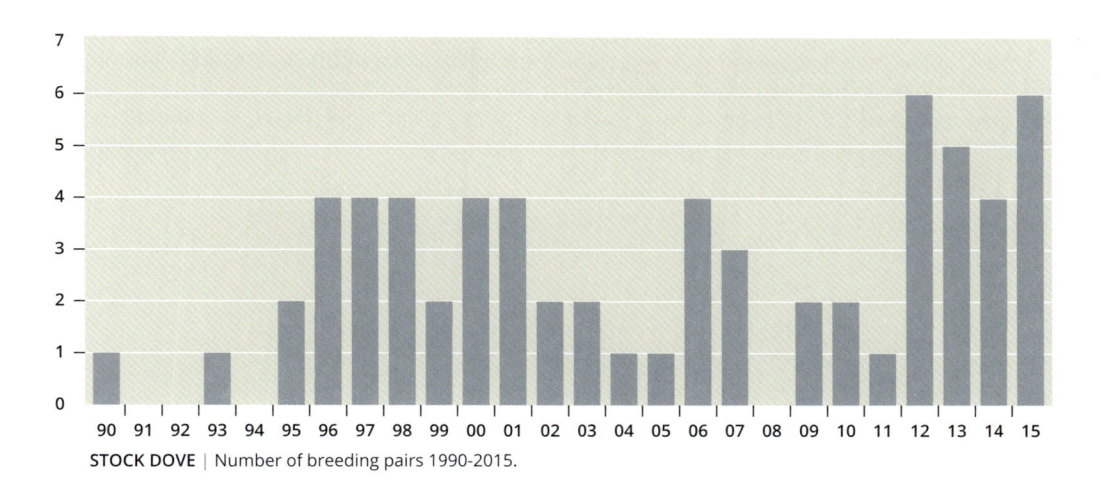

STOCK DOVE | Number of breeding pairs 1990-2015.

| WOODPIGEON *Columba palumbus*

Being such an abundant species, there have been relatively few counts. In fact there were no counts at all until 1967, when 65 were counted in April. Since then, there have been 43 counts made on random dates, most of these being in response to high numbers and/or large movements. Larger numbers sometimes congregate in lakeside fields or, in years with low water levels, on the lakeside shore. These included 200 on the East Shore in March 1989 and 400 in a maize field at Villice Bay in December 2012 and January 2013, plus another 100 behind the East Shore.

In late autumn, small flocks are sometimes seen migrating but, on 16 November 2015, a record 6,500 were counted flying south. This count corresponded with exceptional movements at Portland, Dorset, the birds there heading south in large flocks across the English Channel and into France. Between 22 October and 22 November, 54,000 were counted (*Portland Bird Observatory and Field Centre. Report for 2015*). Just how these huge numbers manage to come together and coordinate these movements, is hard to understand.

There can be little doubt that, as a breeding species, Woodpigeons have increased as the lakeside plantations have matured and this is reflected in a number of nest counts made by David Warden, with maxima of 41 around the north and east shores in 1993 and 40 in 1994.

There have also been a number of roost counts, the largest as follows:
- **1978:** 500+ roosting on 10 December.
- **1980:** 1,000 on Denny Island on 22 November plus another 500 the same day flying south over Sutton Wick.
- **1988:** 1,500 roosting on Denny Island on 6 February.
- **2013:** 1,400 roosting on 10 December (including 600 on Denny Island and 750 at Nunnery Point).

TURTLE DOVE *Streptopelia turtur*

Turtle Doves were undoubtedly present at Chew during the 1950s and the early 1960s, but there are no specific records listed in the bird reports from that era. The only comments were in the *Report on Somerset Birds* for 1961 and in the *Bristol Bird Report* for 1962, both of which say 'Breeding season records'. Specific Turtle Dove records started at the lake in 1965, with three seen on both 2 June and 22 August, while, in 1966, five were seen on 8 May followed by singles on 12 June and 10 August, with two on 17 August. They continued to be seen annually to 1979, with the exception of a blank year in 1975. On 26 May 1978, a pair was present at Hollow Brook, with the male giving its distinctive purring song. A third individual was also present the same day at Stratford Bay (still present on 27th).

There were then just three further records (four individuals) in the 1980s and eight records (nine individuals) in the 1990s, with the last being one on 13 June 1999. That would have been the last ever record had it not been for one found on 16 May 2006, along the track behind Moreton Bank (J. Aldridge *et al.*). This bird attracted a mini twitch, many of the local birders needing it for their Avon lists.

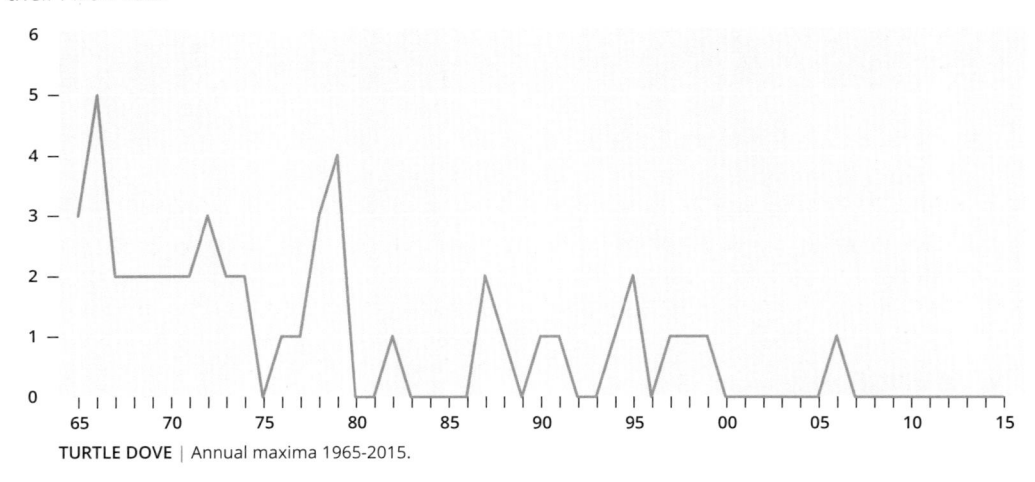

TURTLE DOVE | Annual maxima 1965-2015.

The combined monthly maxima shows there was a single record in April (on 23rd in 1995) but May was the peak month, with 19 recorded between 1966 and 2006. Fifteen were recorded in each month from June to August. The latest records were in September (on 15th in 1972 and on 10th in 1973) followed by one on 3 October 1976 (BOC *Bird News*).

Given its nationwide demise, it seems highly unlikely that this iconic species will ever again be seen at the lake – a sad indictment of modern farming practices coupled with the relentless shooting of the species during its migrations over the Mediterranean.

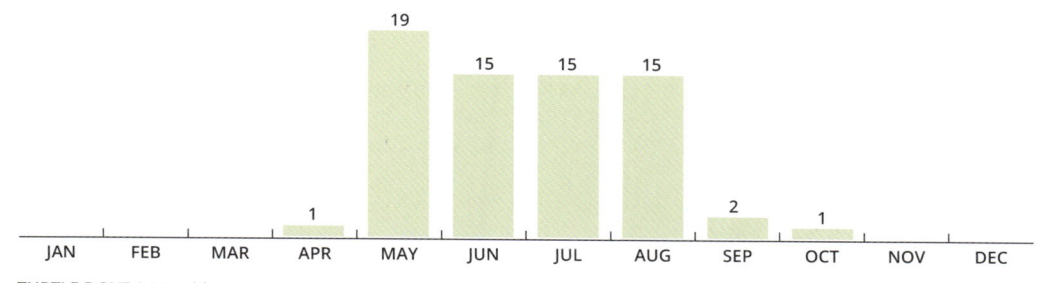

TURTLE DOVE | Monthly maxima (combined) 1965-2016.

Monthly maxima: JAN –, FEB –, MAR –, APR 1, MAY 19, JUN 15, JUL 15, AUG 15, SEP 2, OCT 1, NOV –, DEC –.

Turtle Dove | Gary Thoburn

COLLARED DOVE *Streptopelia decaocto*

The first record for Somerset was one in Bishop Sutton on 30 April 1962 (Palmer & Ballance 1968). There were then five there on 10 May 1964 and, apparently, it was first recorded at the lake in that year. There were three records of singles in 1967 and it has since been recorded in 36 of the 58 years to 2015. The vast majority of records have related to ones and twos flying across the lake, but sightings are erratic. Three years have produced double figure counts with maxima of 35 at Knowle Hill Farm on 16 October 1993, 30 at a nearby farm on 14 November 1998 and 40 there on 13 March 1976. The record count, however, was in the infamous drought year of 1976, when 78 were counted on 17 November (*Somerset Birds* 1976). No doubt they were attracted to the lakeside margins, which became covered in vegetation, producing ideal feeding conditions.

Note that, with this species often associated with human activity, we have included counts from nearby farms and also from Bishop Sutton.

COLLARED DOVE | Annual maxima 1962-2015.

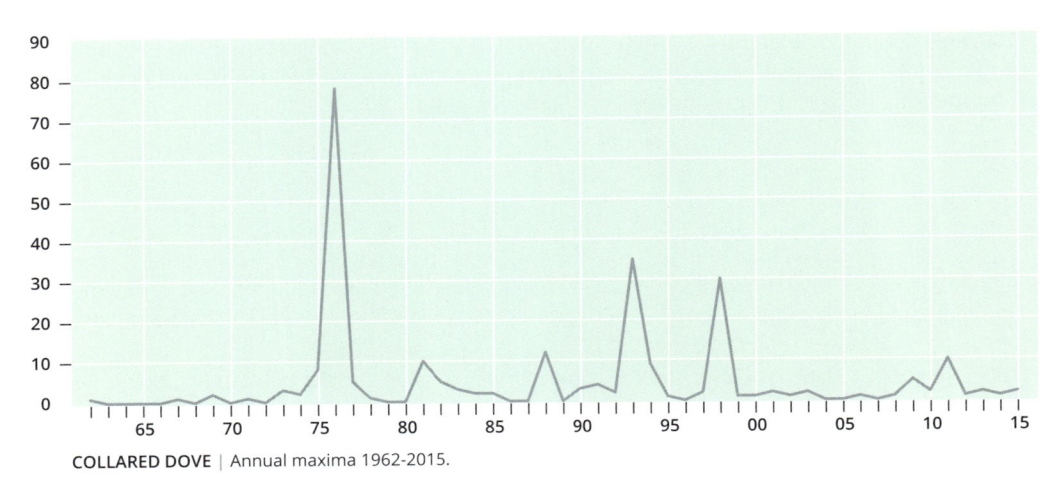

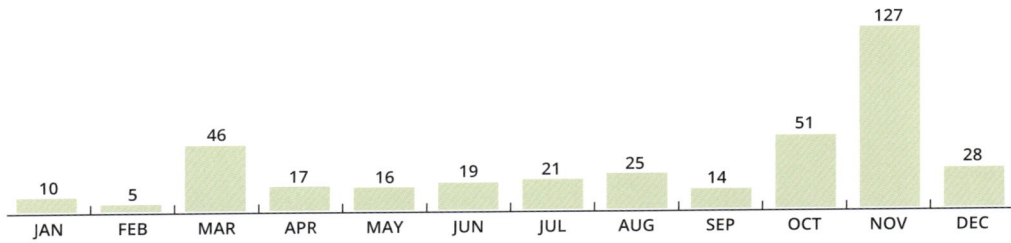

COLLARED DOVE | Monthly maxima (combined) 1962-2015. Note that the very high November total is caused by the presence of the exceptionally large flock of 78 on 17 November 1976.

JAN	FEB	MAR	APR	MAY	JUN	JUL	AUG	SEP	OCT	NOV	DEC
10	5	46	17	16	19	21	25	14	51	127	28

Collared Dove | Laurel Tucker

WATER RAIL *Rallus aquaticus*

The combined monthly maxima graph shows that Water Rail is essentially a winter visitor, with peak numbers recorded in November and December, declining gradually into the spring. Small numbers remain to breed during the summer. Being a highly secretive bird, Water Rails are difficult to survey, but some sterling work by Mark Dadds has shed considerable light on the Chew population (see final paragraph below).

It seems likely that the species has been breeding at the lake since at least 1959, when one was heard on 23 May and two were seen on 14 June. Further birds calling in summer were recorded in seven years during the period 1961–1973, with three calling on 18 May 1963 (*Report on Somerset Birds* 1963). Juveniles were seen in 1964 (2), 1966 (1), 1971 (1) and 1973 (2). Since then, broods have been recorded in 1985 and in eleven years to 2014.

The annual maxima graph shows, few were present in the early years of the lake, this undoubtedly relating to the lack of reeds at this time. As the reeds spread, numbers of Water Rails gradually increased, with high counts from the mid-1990s onwards. Being a highly secretive species, the only way to obtain useful data is by mapping calling birds and the highest totals based on this were 42 in 1998 and 41 in both 2000 and 2001, both these high counts being in November–December. As the above graph indicates, numbers decline somewhat in the New Year, and it seems likely that some of the lower late winter totals may be the result of birds leaving during the occasional cold spell. Numbers decline further into March and April, low numbers continuing towards the mid-summer nadir.

In a paper by Mark Dadds entitled *Breeding Water Rails at Chew Valley Lake in 2012* (*ABR* 2012) it was estimated that there were at least ten successful breeding attempts involving a minimum of eight pairs; they were also heard calling in another four distinct areas. In 2013, nesting activity was recorded at six sites, with juveniles being seen at three of these, while in 2014, a playback survey detected 15 pairs plus a further 22 individuals. A less thorough survey in 2015 detected 16 pairs and a further 12 single birds (M. Dadds, *ABR* 2015). Further comments in the 2015 *ABR* stated that the breeding season was poor, as reflected in the proportion of birds caught that were either pulli or juveniles, which was 36%, compared with 61% in 2012, 59% in 2013 and 64% in 2014).

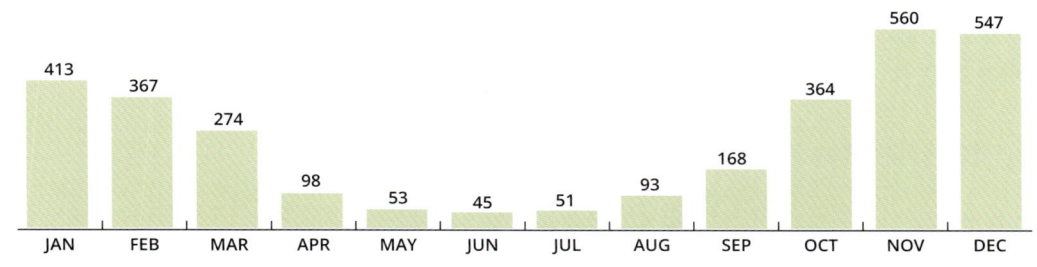

WATER RAIL | Monthly maxima (combined) 1954-2016.

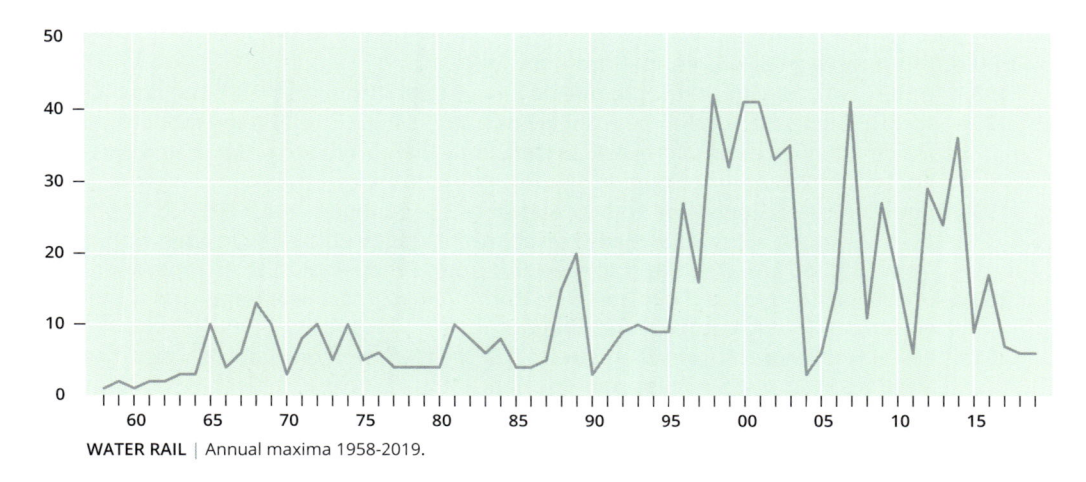

WATER RAIL | Annual maxima 1958-2019.

Water Rail | Rich Andrews

CORNCRAKE *Crex crex*
On 10 October 1965, one was flushed from rough vegetation on the East Shore during a year of low water levels (D. Cottle, A. H. Davis, R. Hemmings, R. J. Senior, KEV).

LITTLE CRAKE *Porzana parva*
There are two records: a male seen twice, but briefly, on 5 November 1961 (M. A. Wright) and a male on 10 May 1967 (D. Warden).

SPOTTED CRAKE *Porzana porzana*
The first record was on 28 October 1961 (R. S. Harkness) and a bird was also seen on 5 November in that year (J. A. McGeoch). There were then four recorded in 1963: a juvenile from 18 to at least 24 August, another juvenile caught and ringed on 19 August, an adult on 24–31 August and one on 10 October. It was suspected at the time that Spotted Crakes had bred at the lake, the habitat being much more conducive to the species than it is now. Since then, it has been recorded in 25 years to 2017.

All the records have been of singles apart from the following:
- **1983:** three (two trapped) on 4 September, with two until 11th and at least one until 20th.
- **1995:** records along the edge of the Main Reeds from 13 August to 22 September with a maximum of three on 21 August; subsequently there were up to two at Heron's Green Pool during 5–22 September.
- **1998:** one at Heron's Green Pool from 27 August to 3 September; one at Herriott's Pool 11–13 October, with two on 12th; two at Stratford Hide on 13–15 October, with one from 18th to 23rd. One was also seen at Heron's Green Pool 21 to 25 November.
- **2003:** one along the front of the Main Reeds from 17 August to 4 September and a juvenile at Heron's Green Pool 10–27 September.
- **2013:** two at Hollow Brook from 28 August to 4 September, with one until 9th. Also, two at Stratford Hide 14–15 August, with one until 24th.
- **2016:** one on 26 September and another 9–26 October.
- **2018:** one ringed bird 9–20 October.

The combined monthly maxima shows the peak months are from August to October with most in September. The earliest date is of one calling in June 1989 and the latest dates involved one in a ditch in the north-east corner of Herriott's Pool from 17 to 20 November 1984 and another at Heron's Green Pool from 21 to 25 November 1998, although there are also December records in 1964 and 1965.

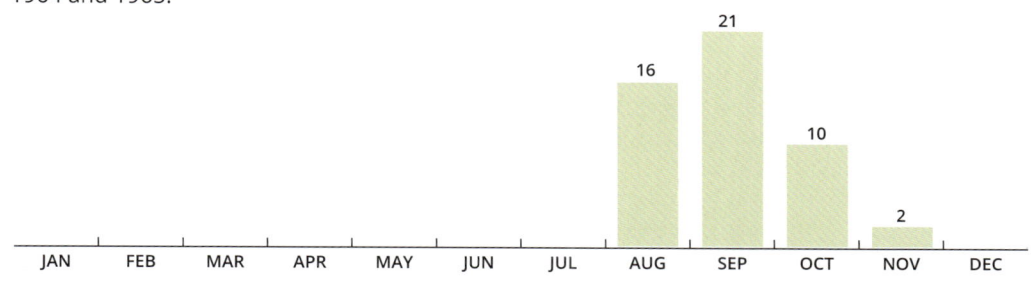

SPOTTED CRAKE | Monthly maxima (combined) individuals 1963-2016.

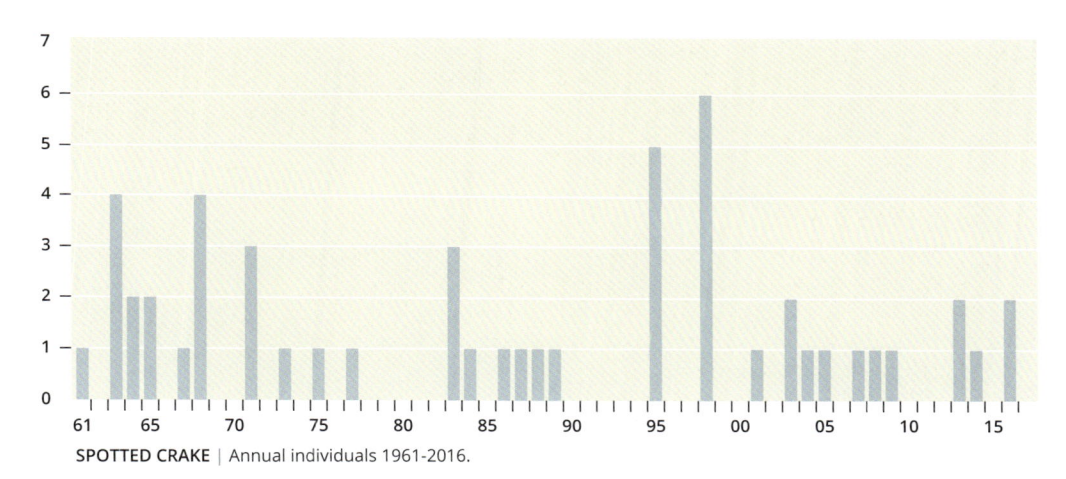

SPOTTED CRAKE | Annual individuals 1961-2016.

Spotted Crake (*left*) and Water Rail | Laurel Tucker

MOORHEN *Gallinula chloropus*

The average monthly maxima graph shows that Moorhens occur in relatively small numbers during the winter, dipping further in spring to a low point in May. The reason why there appear to be so few in the early part of the year probably relates mainly to the fact that water levels are normally high at this time, giving the species plenty of cover in which to disappear. Numbers reach a low point in May but start to increase in June, rising sharply through late summer to a peak in August–September. The species breeds in numbers, although this is hard to quantify. It has however declined, due to vegetation succession and, probably, predation. The record count is 245 in September 2003, with a similar total of 230 in August 2015. They then fall away to the end of the year.

It seems likely that the August–October peak is due to two reasons: (1) the year's young inflate the numbers and (2) falling water levels at this time render the birds far more visible. However, there is also a third factor: is there a late summer/early autumn moult influx, as there is with Coot *Fulica atra*, grebes and wildfowl?

The annual maxima graph shows the maxima from 1964 to 2015. The trend is clearly upwards but with occasional large dips, particularly in the late 1970s and early 1980s and again in the period from 2005 to 2012, when peak counts in September–October reached just 35 in 2008 and 2012.

Moorhen / Gary Thoburn

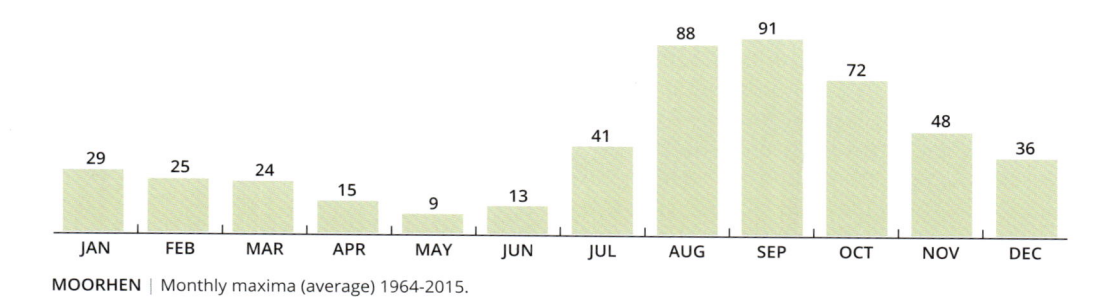

MOORHEN | Monthly maxima (average) 1964-2015.

Jan 29, Feb 25, Mar 24, Apr 15, May 9, Jun 13, Jul 41, Aug 88, Sep 91, Oct 72, Nov 48, Dec 36.

MOORHEN | Annual maxima 1964-2019. (No counts in 1965 and 1980).

COOT *Fulica atra*

The average monthly maxima graph shows that numbers of Coot from January to April are fairly stable at around the 300–400 mark but they dip slightly in May when the females disappear into the reeds to breed.

Numbers increase strongly in June, rising to a peak in August before gradually dropping from September to November. This annual peak relates to the species' moult migration, when there is a large influx that takes full advantage of the huge amounts of waterweed in the lake at this time of year. This coincides with their vulnerable period of wing moult, from mid-June to early September (*BWP*), when they are flightless for a period of about three or four weeks. Many move on once they have grown new flight feathers – this exodus accelerates through the late autumn as the waterweed starts to decline and water levels rise. At this time of year, large numbers from both Chew and Blagdon fly over Mendip to Cheddar Reservoir in Somerset, where they feed on huge banks of a moss called *Fontinalis antipyretica*. By mid-winter, those that remain at Chew had formerly been reduced to grazing on the lakeside grassland, although changes to this habitat suggest this no longer happens.

The Coot is an abundant bird but the highest ever count of approximately 4,000, in February 1960, was made by Bernard King. There was an earlier but lower count of 2,000 in December 1954. These high early counts were not very long after the valley was flooded for the first time in October 1954.

Coot | Laurel Tucker

It seems likely that the rising water level flooded a huge area of 'unimproved' grassland, providing a massive source of food for the Coots. Numbers fell as the inundated grass eventually died off, but counts of up to 2,700 persisted until 1963. As the annual maxima graph shows, maximum numbers in the 1960s were generally in the region of 1,000–2,000, but they have gradually increased since, reaching a modern record of 3,715 in 2002. Peak numbers have remained at around this level ever since, with 3,250 counted in November 2015. There are, however, signs of an increase in recent winters, probably due to an increase in water plants.

The annual brood totals graph shows that breeding numbers have been erratic, the annual fluctuations traditionally being related to water levels – they need high levels when nesting. There has, however, been a distinct decline in breeding numbers since 2000.

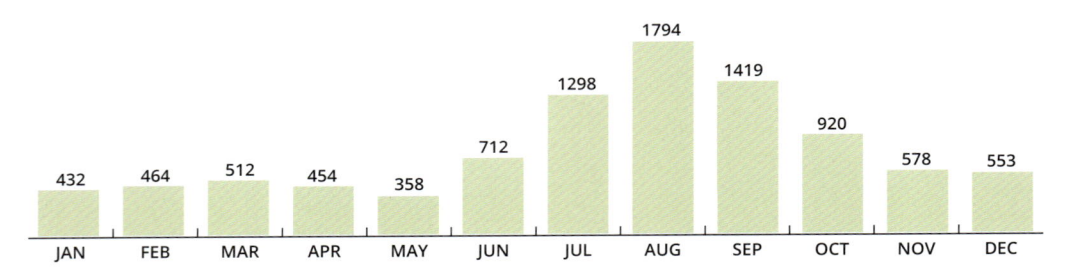

COOT | Monthly maxima (average) 1954-2015.

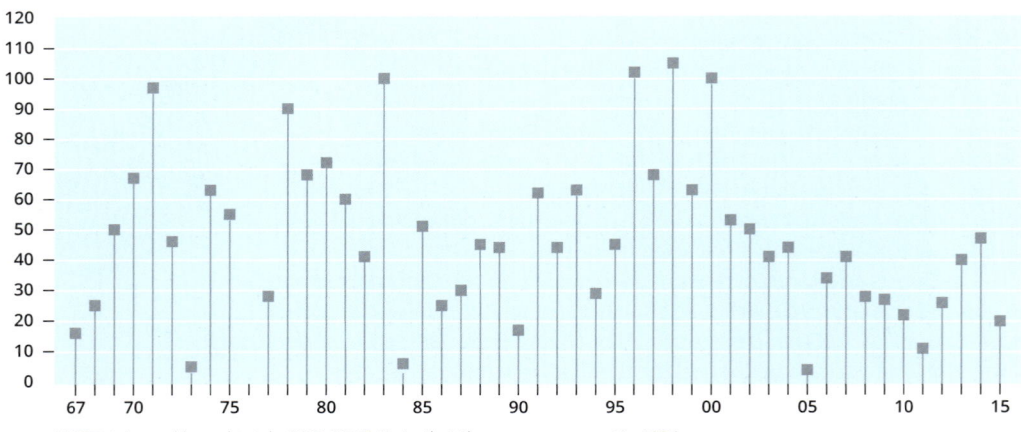

COOT | Annual maxima 1954-2019.

COOT | Annual brood totals 1967-2015. Note that there was no count in 1976.

242   COMPLETE SPECIES LIST AND CHARTS

Coot | Gary Thoburn

CRANE *Grus grus*

It seems highly probable that the following records relate to released birds from 'The Great Crane Project', which is introducing Cranes onto the Somerset Levels. Since they are not yet self-sustaining, they cannot be counted as wild, although, if everything goes according to plan, it seems highly likely that they will be in due course.

- 2013: two flew south on 10 October (C. Craig, M. Bailey, M. Dadds).
- 2016: four circled the lake on 1 April and departed to the south-west; two arrived from the east on 5 April, circled and departed high to the north-west; four were seen in flight on 18 May, then flew off north-east, and two circled on 12 June.
- 2017: three flew south-west on 11 August; an adult arrived from the north-east on 11 October and drifted south.

Note the status of these records as wild birds, as mentioned in the first paragraph.

LITTLE GREBE *Tachybaptus ruficollis*

The first count produced a total of 111 in August 1954, followed by 147 the following month. In September 1961, 97 were counted but annual maxima then dropped through the 1960s and 1970s, with the exception of a count of 103 in October 1969. From that point onwards, maximum counts usually fluctuated between 50 and 100, but there were 13 counts of over 100. The annual maxima graph shows the highest totals were all in September, with maxima of 152 in 1996, a record 180 in 2009 and 150 in 2010. However, peak numbers from 2012 to 2016 have been lower (averaging 62).

As the monthly maxima graph indicates, numbers are at their lowest in January, increasing to a small spring peak in March and April, when birds are easily located by their trilling breeding calls. After a slight dip in May and June, numbers rise to a strong peak in August–September, which corresponds with their flightless moult period (*BWP*). As the early winter water levels rise, numbers gradually drop to their mid-winter low.

Little Grebe | Rich Andrews

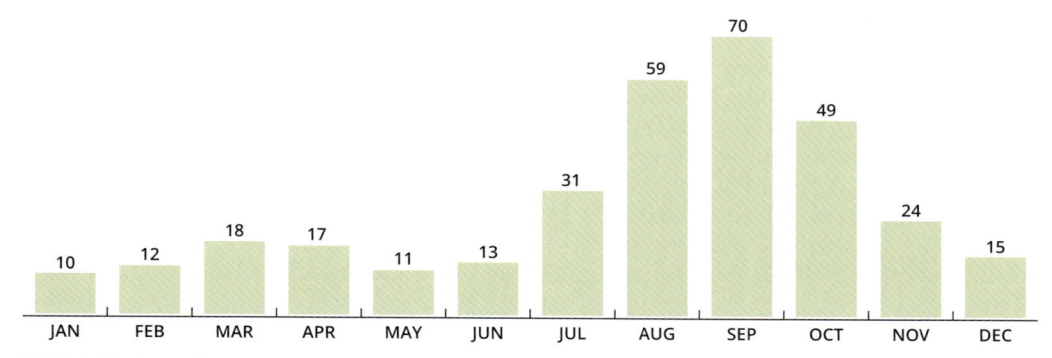

LITTLE GREBE | Monthly maxima (average) 1966-2015.

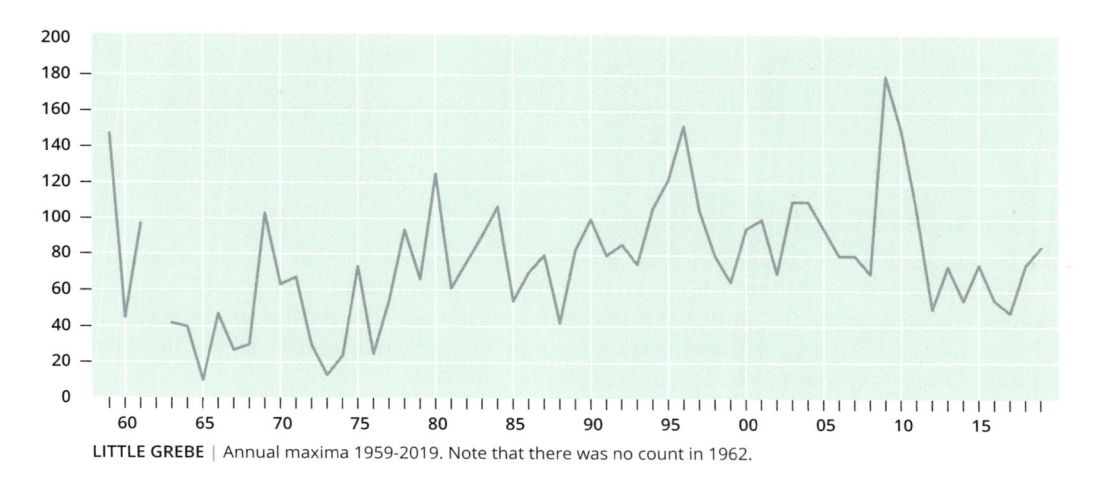

LITTLE GREBE | Annual maxima 1959-2019. Note that there was no count in 1962.

The species was first recorded breeding in 1955 (three broods) with at least nine broods in 1957. Breeding counts were then erratic until 1966, after which they were annual. As the annual brood totals graph shows, the number of broods fluctuated, with peak counts of 28 in 1971 and 1980, 25 in 1981, 26 in 1996 and 27 in 1998. Worryingly, however, there has been a strong down-turn since 2000, with no broods recorded in 2010, 2011 or 2013. The species is now teetering on the edge of extinction as a breeding bird at the lake. It is thought likely that an increase in predation is primarily responsible, most likely the result of the introduction of Pike.

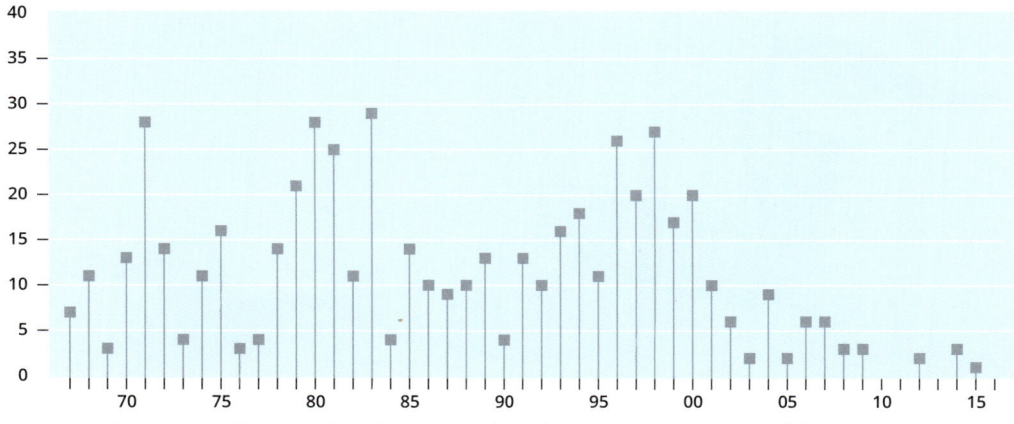

LITTLE GREBE | Annual brood totals 1967–2016. Note the parlous situation since the turn of the century.

COMPLETE SPECIES LIST AND CHARTS

PIED-BILLED GREBE *Podilymbus podiceps*

The first Western Palearctic record was one seen and, remarkably, filmed at Blagdon Lake on 22 December 1963 (R. J. Prytherch, H. A. Thornhill). At the time, this was considered to be an exceptional record, there being widespread astonishment that a seemingly weak-flying grebe could cross the Atlantic (see Prytherch 1965). What is generally considered to have been the same bird re-appeared at Chew from 17 August to 23 October 1965, taking up residence in Heron's Green Bay and attracting large numbers of birders. It reappeared off Stratford Bay on 15 May 1966 (D. Shepherd, R. F. Thearle) before appearing again in Heron's Green Bay from 21 July to 2 November (D. E. Ladhams, R. J. Prytherch, K. E. L. Simmons *et al.*). It reappeared again on 14 May 1967 and was seen intermittently in Heron's Green Bay to 2 October (A. H. Davis, E. G. Holt, Robert A. Richardson, N. T. Lacey *et al.*). It was last seen at the Ubley end of Blagdon Lake from 23 May to 6 June 1968, where it was frequently heard calling in a vain attempt to attract a mate. (D. E. Ladhams, R. J. Prytherch. K. E. L. Simmons). Since then, there have been a further 44 British records (to 2015). As the appearance of the Pied-billed Grebe coincided with the formation of the Bristol Ornithological Club (in 1967) it was adopted as the club's logo.

Reference
Prytherch, R. J. 1965. 'Pied-billed Grebe in Somerset: a bird new to Great Britain and Ireland'. *British Birds* 58: 305–312.

RED-NECKED GREBE *Podiceps grisegena*

The first was one on 18 March 1956 (G. L. Boyle). Since then it has proved to be a rare and erratic visitor, with 22 individuals from 1957 to 2016. As the monthly maxima (combined) graph shows, it has been recorded in every month, but with peaks in November–January and spring passage birds in March and April. One on 28 March 1972 was a stunning individual in full summer plumage and one on 24 August 1968 was moulting out of summer plumage.

The annual maxima graph shows that just five were recorded until 1978, all of which occurred during the period 17 February to 5 April, apart from one unusual August record. Its status changed considerably during the period 1979–1995, there being 12 records during that time.

Three were recorded in 1979 and two in both 1986 and 1992, one of the latter went on to summer. It was seen from 17 April to 25 July, when it moved to Blagdon Lake. It then returned to Chew from 20 December to 2 April 1993.

Also in 1992, a juvenile was present at Chew 12–13 September, relocating to Blagdon on 20 September, where it found the adult. They then accompanied one another until 22 November, when the juvenile moved to Cheddar Reservoir.

Red-necked Grebe | Laurel Tucker

Since 1992, it has reverted to its former status as a rare and erratic visitor, there having been just five further records:

1995: first-winter on 12 November.
2002: first-winter from 23 November to 21 December.
2004: first-winter 1–10 November.
2006: one (un-aged) on 7 December.
2012: summer-plumaged adult in Stratford Bay and Heron's Green Bay 7–8 September.

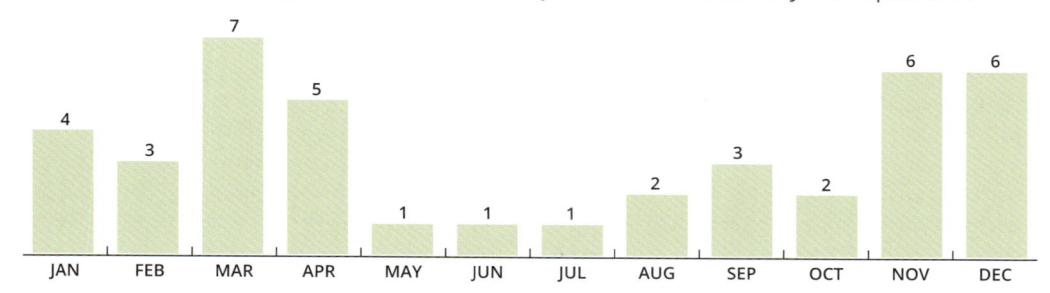

RED-NECKED GREBE | Monthly maxima (combined) 1956-2012.

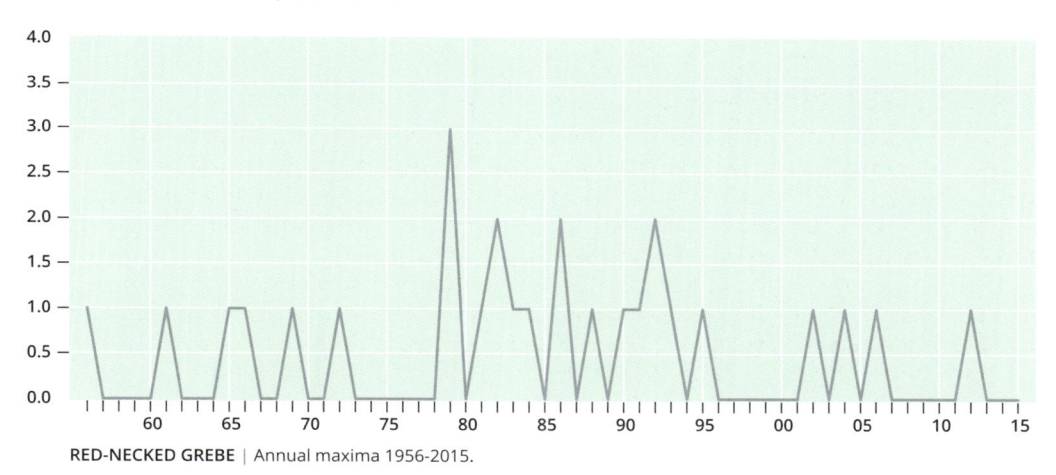

RED-NECKED GREBE | Annual maxima 1956-2015.

Red-necked Grebe | Gareth Jones

GREAT CRESTED GREBE *Podiceps cristatus*

The average monthly maxima graph shows that numbers are fairly stable from January to May, but a large annual moult migration starts in June and increases sharply through July and into August. They become flightless during August–September and perhaps beyond. As they are vulnerable at this time, they arrive at the lake because it is a safe location with huge amounts of fish fry. Numbers peak in September, then gradually decline to the end of year, dropping fairly abruptly as the water levels rise in winter (this decreases the density of the fish on which they feed).

The annual maxima graph shows that numbers were low in the 1950s and early 1960s, but they rose sharply to a record 660 on 2 November 1969, with a similar total (655) in October 1970. Peak numbers then dipped to just 205 in September 1972 but gradually increased again to a new record of 675 in September 1993. These high annual maxima persisted until 2000 when there was yet another record count of 690 on 14 October. Peak numbers then declined to 275 in July 2005, before bouncing back yet again to high numbers during 2007–2009, with another count of 690 in August 2008. Numbers then crashed to just 105 in August 2012 before increasing yet again to 575 in August 2015. The reasons for these recent fluctuations are not known but they are most likely to relate to the abundance of fish fry.

Great Crested Grebe | Rich Andrews

As the annual brood totals graph indicates, breeding numbers show large fluctuations; their success depending on water levels and, presumably, the abundance of fish fry, which clearly varies from year to year. Breeding numbers have declined strongly from a record 83 broods in 1996, with 36 broods in 2000, 38 in 2007 and 27 in 2014, but none at all in 2005, 2011, 2012 and 2016, one in 2017, and 4 in 2018. This recent turn of events is worrying. The reasons may relate to the introduction of Pike plus, perhaps, to an increase in other predators such as Mink and Otters.

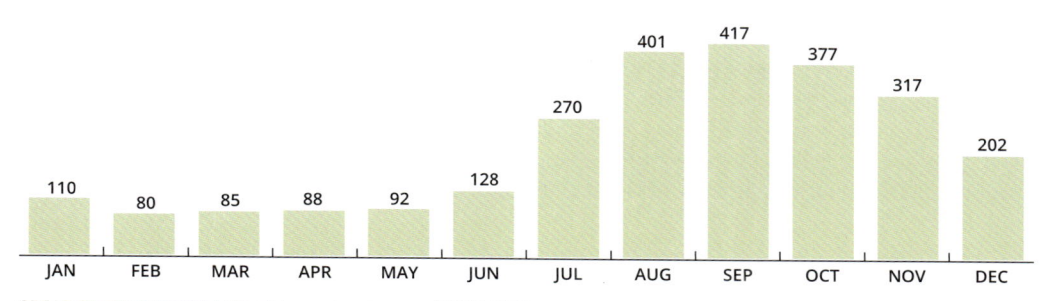

GREAT CRESTED GREBE | Monthly maxima (average) 1966-2015.

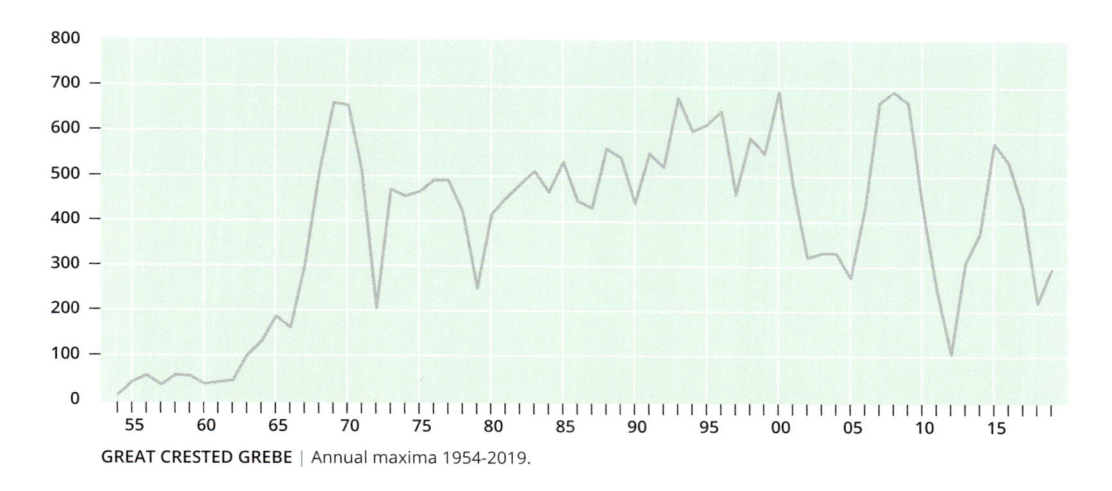

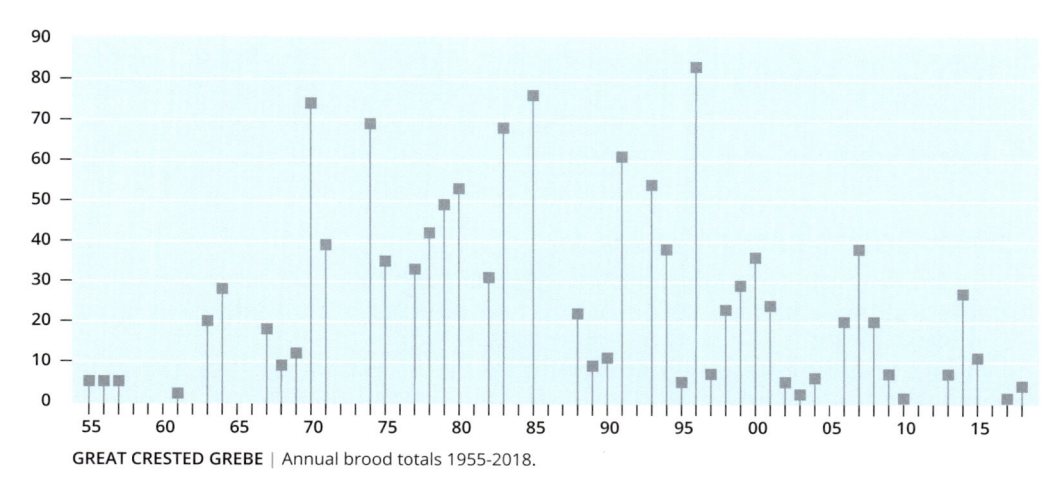

GREAT CRESTED GREBE | Annual maxima 1954-2019.

GREAT CRESTED GREBE | Annual brood totals 1955-2018.

SLAVONIAN GREBE *Podiceps auritus*

The first record was of one from 12 February to 11 March 1956 (G. C. Buxton, G. L. Boyle, B. King, R. H. Poulding). Since then, it has been recorded in 36 of the 63 years to 2016. The annual individuals graph shows that most of the records relate to single birds, but with twos recorded in 12 years. The highest totals were four in 1971 (including three on 24 January) and three on 24 November 1991, but the best year was 1996, when at least seven individuals were recorded.

As the monthly individuals graph indicates, it is essentially an erratic passage migrant and winter visitor. The earliest record was one on 4–7 September (in 1987) with records increasing through October to a peak in November (13 records, 16 individuals) falling through the winter to March. There is then a distinct spring passage in April (nine records involving 12 individuals).

In 1986, a female appeared on 18 April and was joined by a male from 23 April to 6 May, with full display seen on 3 May. Another summer-plumaged individual was present from 11 June to 14 October 2000, joining a large flock of Great Crested Grebes on 6–12 July.

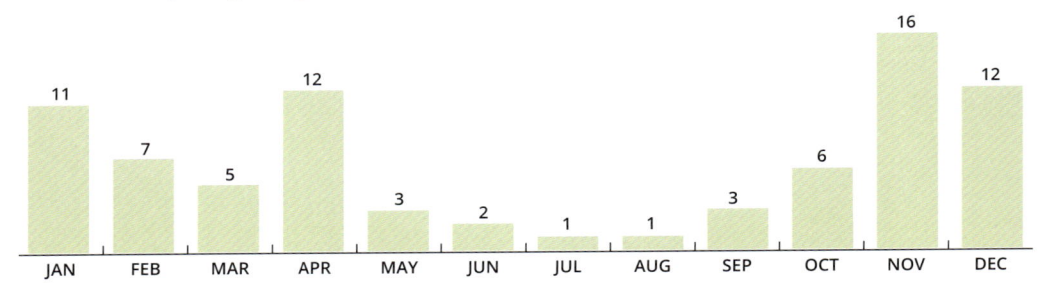

SLAVONIAN GREBE | Monthly individuals 1956-2016.

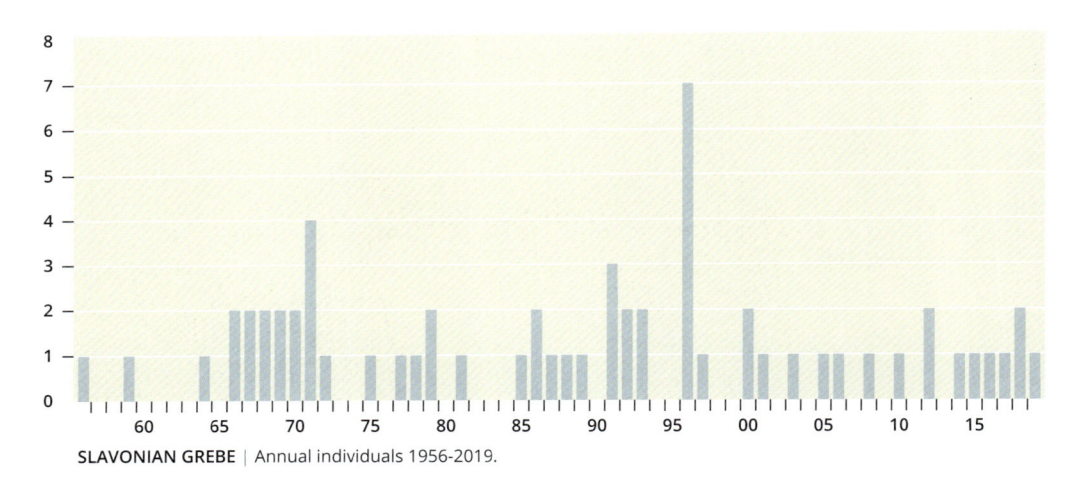

SLAVONIAN GREBE | Annual individuals 1956-2019.

BLACK-NECKED GREBE *Podiceps nigricollis*

The first record was one on 14 August 1955 (R. H. Poulding), but it was not until 1959 that the species started to occur more regularly. Since then it has been recorded in 88% of the years, with peaks of five in 1998, six in 2010 and 9 on 17 November 2018.

Although it has occurred in every month, most are seen from March to May, with a peak in April, and again from August to November, with a peak in September. Inevitably, spring and summer birds have been in summer plumage, whereas those in late summer and autumn have related mainly to juveniles. A pair bred in 1998, with two small young seen on 13 June, but, unfortunately, they failed to survive. It is interesting to note that this event followed a year that saw large numbers of lesser water boatmen *Corixidae* spp. in the lake.

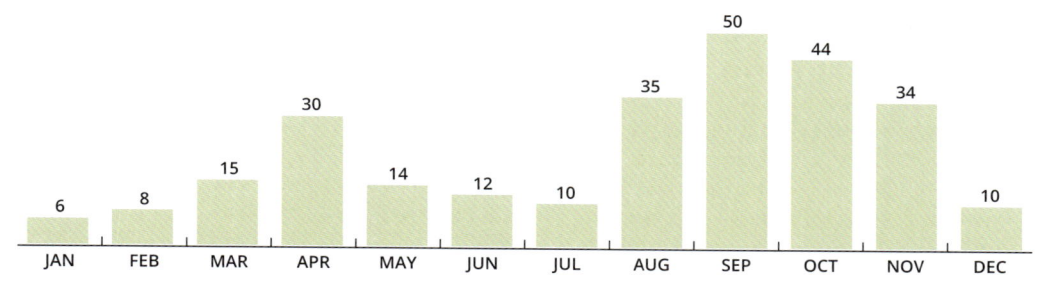

BLACK-NECKED GREBE | Monthly maxima (combined) 1954-2016.

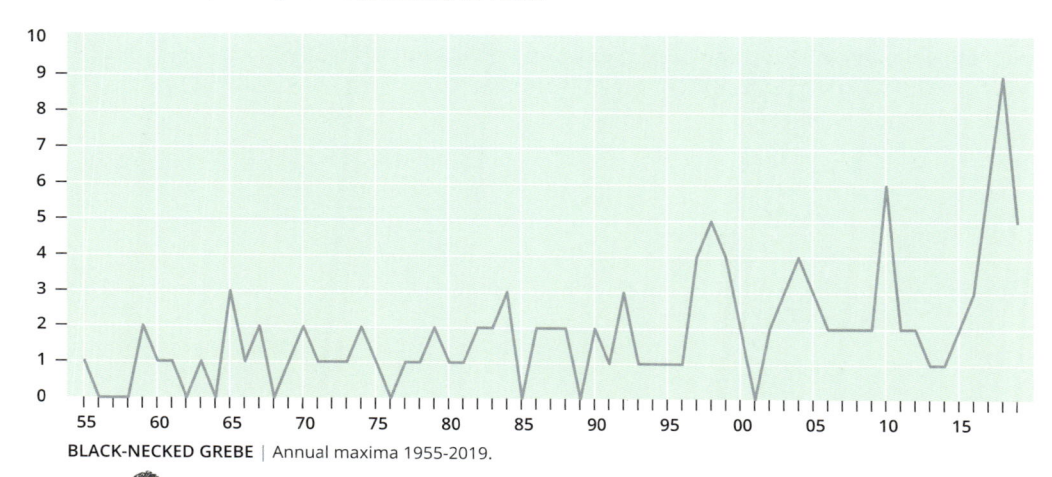

BLACK-NECKED GREBE | Annual maxima 1955-2019.

Black-necked Grebes | Laurel Tucker

| **GREATER FLAMINGO** *Phoenicopterus ruber*

There is one record.

    1992:   an un-ringed adult was seen and photographed between 18 and 21 January (KEV *et al.*).

This species is not part of the British list, being retained in Category D. A review in 2002 concluded that sightings in Britain relate to escaped birds or from a feral breeding population on the Dutch–German border, and that wandering birds of the wild Spanish population have not been seen in countries bordering the north-east Atlantic. However, in August 2020, one of seven Greater Flamingos in Nord Holland had a Spanish ring. We include this record from the lake for completeness.

| **STONE CURLEW** *Burhinus oedicnemus*

One in the Twycross/Denny Island area on 3 October 1959 (S. E. Chapman).

OYSTERCATCHER *Haematopus ostralegus*

This first record related to three on 3 August 1954 with three also on 26 September, followed by eight in August 1956. The only blank years since then were 1955 and 1959. Being essentially a coastal species, single figures are the norm but there have been four records involving double figures: 12 on 17 August 1977, 11 on 24 August 1979, 21 flying through on 6 August 1980 and 20 on 21 August 1984. Although most fly through or stay for short periods, some have lingered: one remained from 1 October to 28 November 1974 and, unusually, one in 1978 fed in lakeside fields from 8 January to 4 March. As the annual maxima graph shows, the highest numbers recorded were from the mid-1970s to the mid-1980s, counts otherwise not reaching double figures.

It has been recorded in every month, with a very slight 'spring' peak from February to May, followed by a strong post breeding peak from July to September, with August being the best month (197 recorded in total). Records then drop in October and November to a December low.

Oystercatcher | Lucy Masters

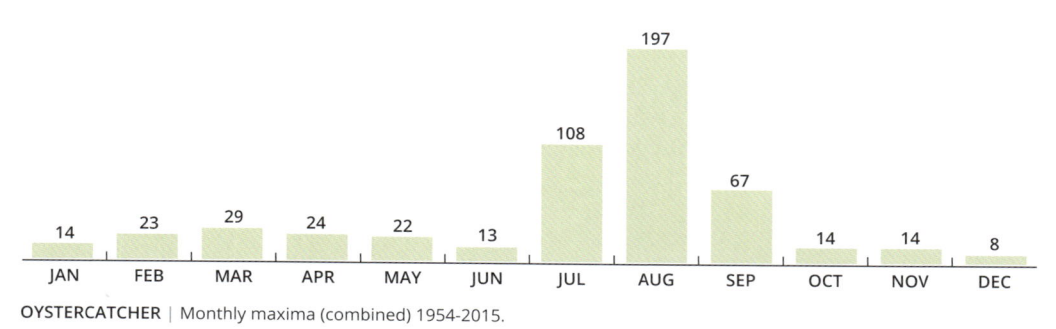

OYSTERCATCHER | Monthly maxima (combined) 1954-2015.

Month	JAN	FEB	MAR	APR	MAY	JUN	JUL	AUG	SEP	OCT	NOV	DEC
Max	14	23	29	24	22	13	108	197	67	14	14	8

OYSTERCATCHER | Annual maxima 1954-2019.

BLACK-WINGED STILT *Himantopus himantopus*

There are two records: a pair at Herriott's End 22–25 May 1965 (R. Brock, R. J. Prytherch, R. F. Thearle *et al.*) and a male at Stratford Hide on 10 April 2012 (R. J. Palmer *et al.*).

Black-winged Stilt | Gary Thoburn

AVOCET *Recurvirostra avosetta*

A rare and erratic visitor with 15 records from 1972 to 2014 (23 individuals) and with a perceptible increase from 2005 onwards. There has been a wide temporal spread with a small peak in May and a large one in November. A record seven were recorded on 31 August 2018.

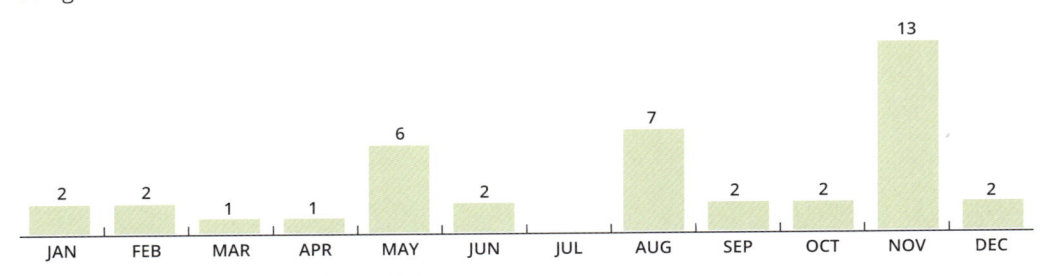

AVOCET | Monthly maxima (combined) 1972-2018.

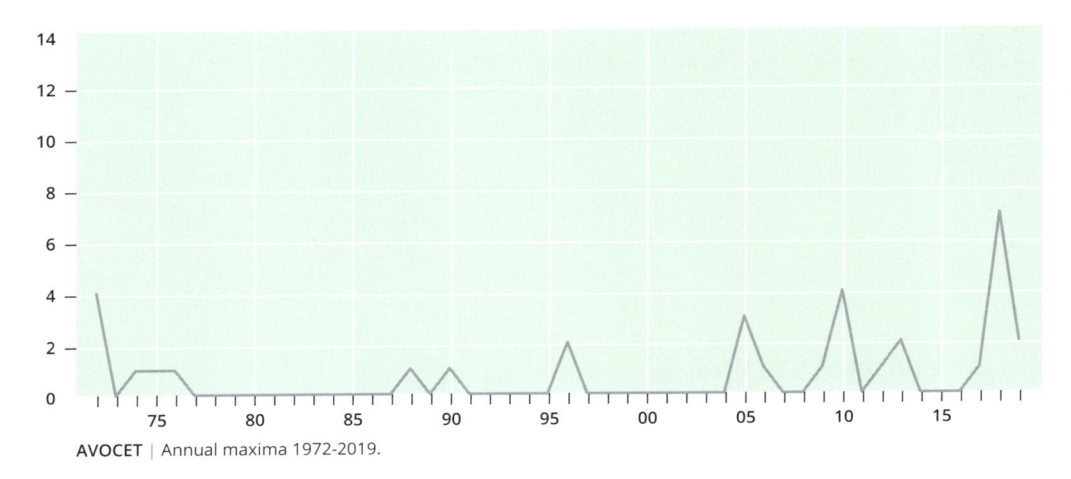

AVOCET | Annual maxima 1972-2019.

Avocets | Ian Stapp

LAPWING *Vanellus vanellus*

As the monthly maxima (average) graph shows, the Lapwing is a common bird at the lake with, traditionally, small numbers breeding – either at the lake itself or, more usually, in adjacent fields. Unfortunately, there are no breeding data from 1954 to 1964, probably because, at that time, it was regarded as a common species that was not worth monitoring. It was certainly breeding in 1965, as a nest with four eggs was found on 20 April (KEV).

For the next 50 years (1966–2016) it was present in the breeding season in 31 of those years, with nesting in 17 of them, but with successful breeding in only nine. In the drought year of 1976, however, there were about 17 pairs present on 24 April, with at least two of those incubating.

The decline of breeding Lapwings at Chew probably has many causes. Most importantly, the lake margins – with their woods and reed beds – have matured to the point where there is simply no habitat for them. Those that have nested in the lakeside fields are susceptible to predation by crows and, perhaps in more recent years, by Buzzards *Buteo buteo*, not to mention Foxes and Badgers. But certain members of the local farming community haven't exactly helped. For example, in 2012 a Lapwing's nest was shown to a farm hand who promised to avoid it during ploughing. This he did, but he ploughed to within six inches of the nest on all sides, resulting in the bird deserting. Another nest in the same year was destroyed by muck spreading.

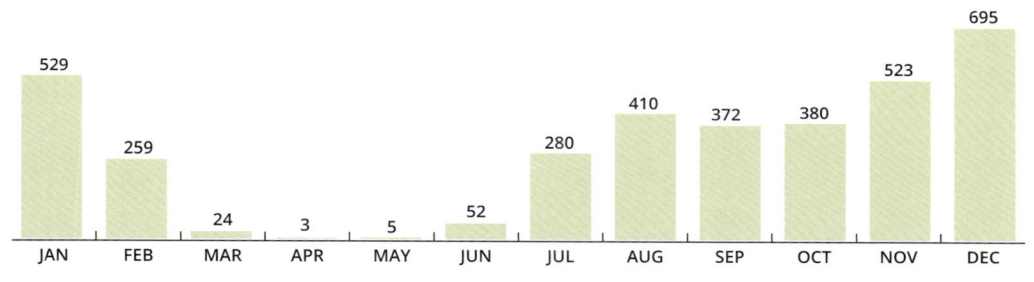

Month	Value
JAN	529
FEB	259
MAR	24
APR	3
MAY	5
JUN	52
JUL	280
AUG	410
SEP	372
OCT	380
NOV	523
DEC	695

LAPWING | Monthly maxima (average) 1964-2015.

As the graph above shows, the first returning post-breeding migrants usually appear by the middle of June, but the earliest returning date was one on 31 May (in 2010). Numbers increase to a peak in August, dropping slightly in September–October, before rising to a yearly peak in December. They decline slightly in the New Year, but fall sharply through February and into March, with April–May being the low point.

It should be noted that the figures in the graphs include birds that were counted during cold weather movements. With the gradual amelioration of our climate, such spectacles have become few and far between but, in the 1950s and 1960s, they were quite frequent. The highest such counts were as follows:

- **1961:** a southerly movement of 2,900 on 27 December.
- **1965:** 1,200 on 28 December.
- **1969:** 1,930 on 23 February flying north-east in a return cold weather movement.
- **1971:** 875 flying north-east on 6 January and a heavy southward passage of 1,000 on 28 December.
- **2009:** 1,000 moving south in a cold weather movement on 15 January. This proved to be the last count at the lake of over a thousand.

The annual maxima graph clearly illustrates the long-term decline in Lapwing numbers. They gradually increased after the 1962–63 winter, reaching a peak in the late 1970s and early 1980s, but a gradual and relentless decline has then persisted to the present day. There has also been a recent lack of breeding and almost total disappearance from the surrounding area.

LAPWING | Annual maxima 1964-2019.

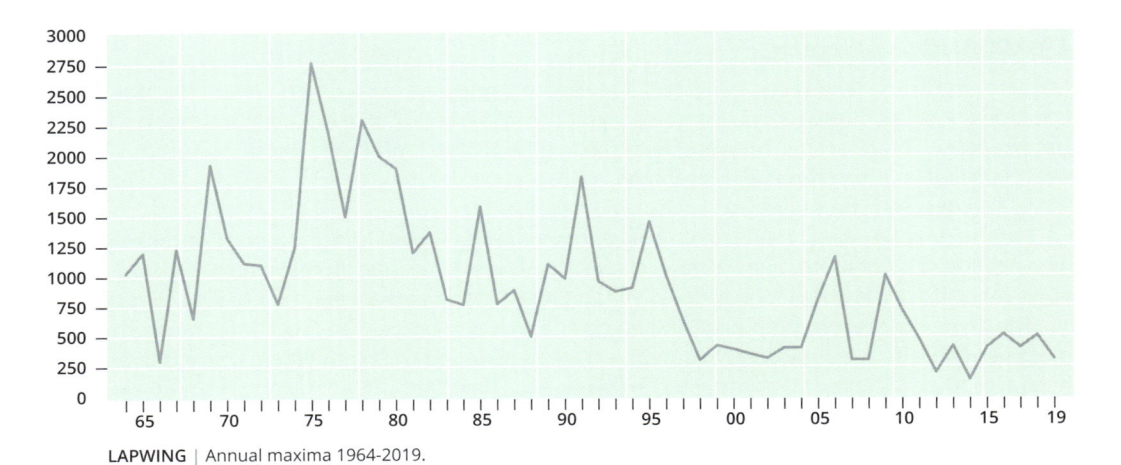

Lapwing | Ian Stapp

| GOLDEN PLOVER *Pluvialis apricaria*

Traditionally, Golden Plover was a numerous but erratic winter visitor. There are two July records – one in 1959 and seven on 29 July 1961 – but small numbers start to arrive in August and September. As the average monthly maxima graph shows, they arrive in earnest in October, increasing to a peak in November, but numbers then decline from December onwards. The latest spring record was of eight on 16 April 1987.

As the annual maxima graph shows, it has always been an erratic visitor, with annual totals varying from as low as one to a record 330 in November 1988. Traditionally, they were most numerous when late autumn water levels were low, but these birds did not feed at the lake to any great extent. Instead, they commuted between grassland areas on Marksbury Plain (between Pensford and Keynsham) and perhaps also to sites on Mendip.

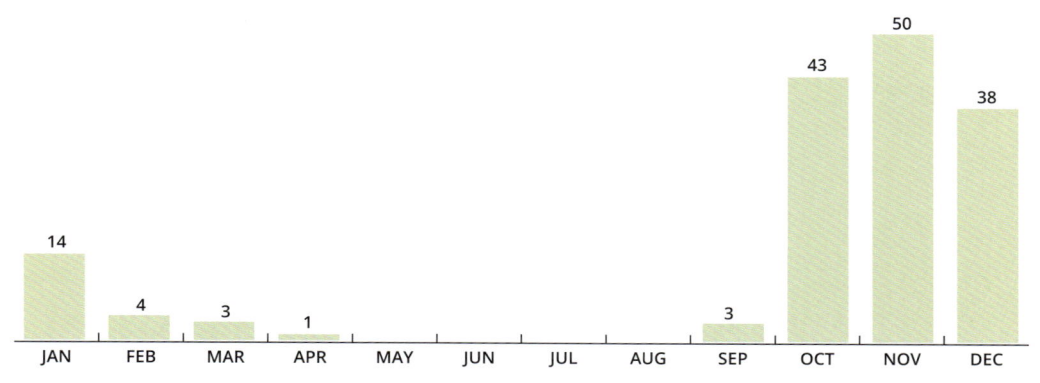

GOLDEN PLOVER | Monthly maxima (average) 1956-2015.

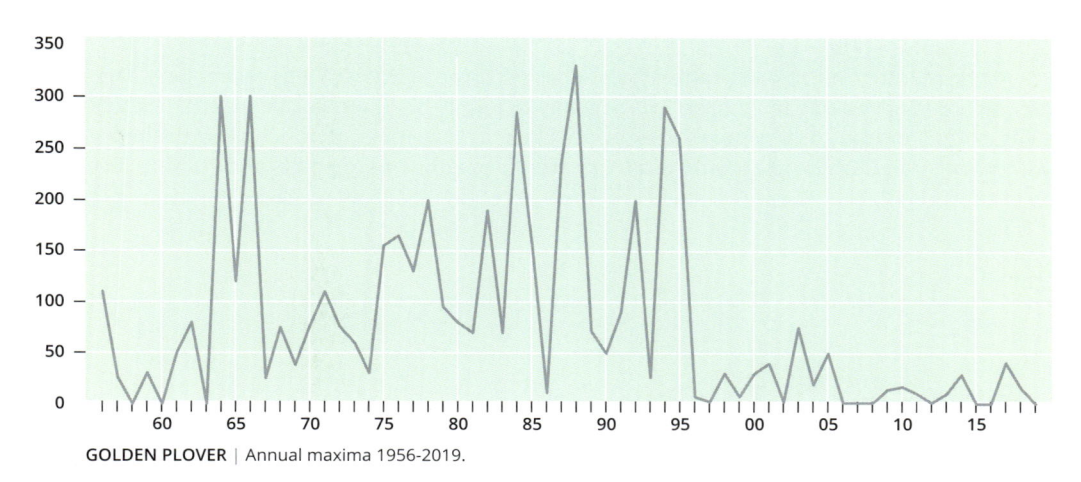

GOLDEN PLOVER | Annual maxima 1956-2019.

As the annual maxima graph above shows, numbers plummeted from 1996 onwards, with the maximum counts during the period 1996–2015 being 75 in November 2003 and 50 in December 2005. Just single birds were seen in 2006, 2007 and 2012. The reasons for this decline are not known, but it may well relate to the recent trend of higher late autumn water levels, combined with so-called agricultural 'improvements' affecting their feeding areas.

An interesting bird was present on 21 November and 26 December 1987. At face value it resembled a Pacific Golden Plover *Pluvialis fulva* but a number of features, particularly white underwing-coverts, suggested that it may have been a Golden Plover x Pacific Golden Plover hybrid.

| AMERICAN GOLDEN PLOVER *Pluvialis dominica*

An adult moulting out of summer plumage was present with up to 240 Golden Plovers *P. apricaria* at Herriott's Bridge 23–27 October 1994 (R. M. Andrews, S. Preddy *et al.*).

| GREY PLOVER *Pluvialis squatarola*

The first record for the lake was of one in 1957 (E. G. Brain, P. Tibbs). This was followed by two on 13 October 1962 (J. A. McGeoch), followed by one on 2 December. Apart from blank years in 1964 and 1988, it was recorded annually from 1962 to 1995. Since then it has become much scarcer, with no records during 1996–2001, but it has appeared in most years since. The peak counts have been nine on 13 October 1973, five on 10–16 December 1978 and five again on 3 November 1991.

GREY PLOVER | Annual maxima 1962-2019.

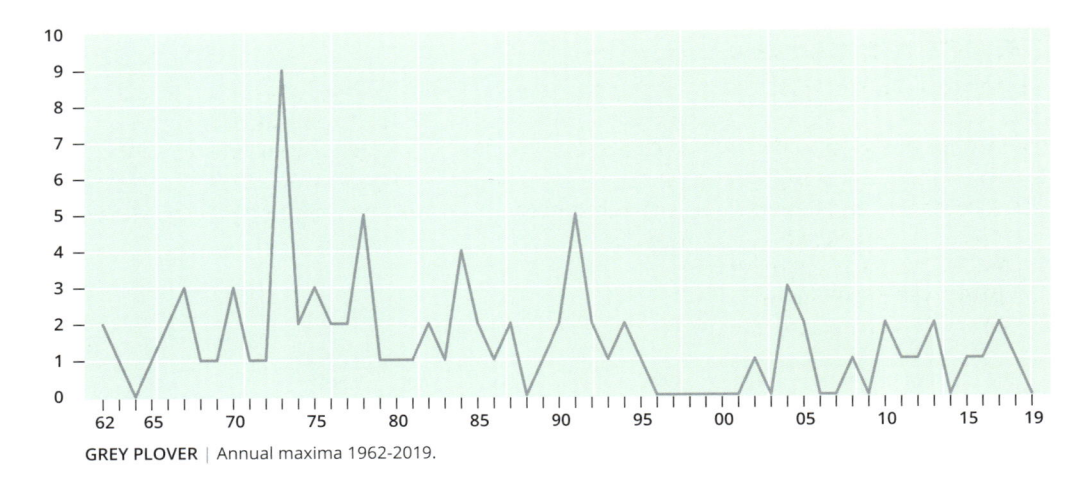

As the monthly individuals graph shows, it has occurred in every month except June. The single July record involved one in summer plumage on 28 July 1973. There is a small but distinct spring peak in April and May but numbers peak from August to November, October being the best month with 47 recorded. Of those autumn birds that were aged, four were adults and 20 were juveniles.

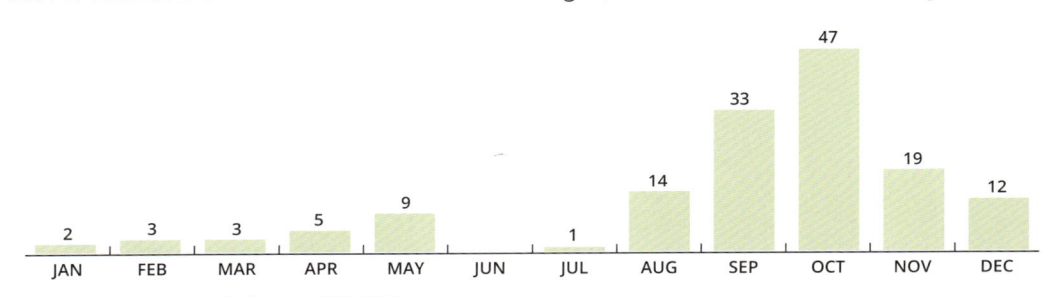

GREY PLOVER | Monthly individuals 1962-2015.

Grey Plover | Ian Stapp

RINGED PLOVER *Charadrius hiaticula*

The first report was of 'up to 14' in May 1954 followed by a record of 23 on 23 August 1955. Since then, it has been recorded annually, although the numbers vary considerably from year to year. They fell through the latter half of the 1990s and into the 2000s (see annual maxima graph below) but then peaked at 110 in September 2011. There have been eight years when the annual maximum has exceeded 50 and four years when it has exceeded 100, the following being the highest counts:

1970: 112 (9 juveniles) on 21 August.
1974: 114 on 4 September.
1989: 150 on 19 August.
2011: 110 on 9 September.

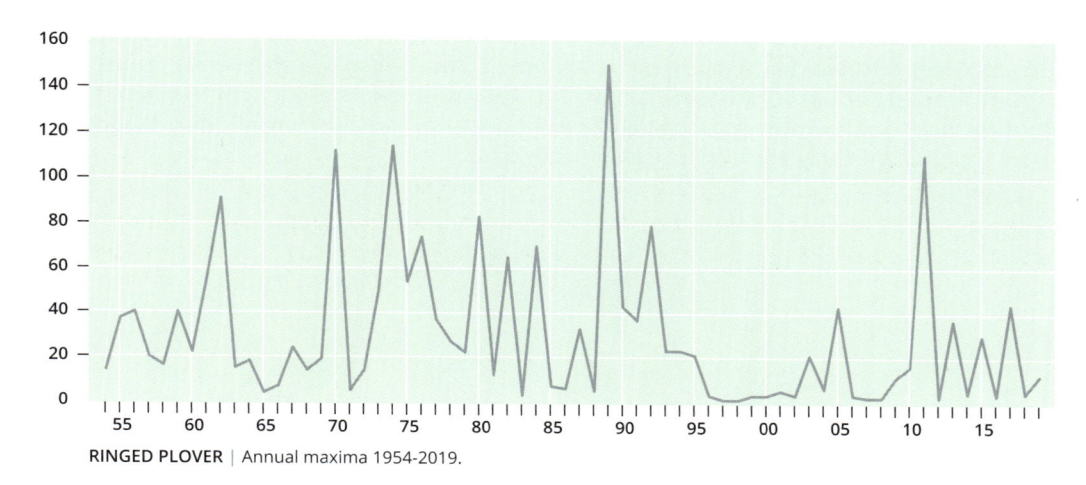

RINGED PLOVER | Annual maxima 1954-2019.

As the combined monthly maxima graph shows, the species has been recorded in every month. The earliest records have been four in February and 12 in March, but the main spring passage is in April and May, the birds at this time usually being seen on the Main Dam or along the dam at Heron's Green Bay. Spring migrants occur in single figures, with the exception of ten in both May 1959 and May 1973. It is difficult to know whether June records relate to north-bound or south-bound birds, but autumn migration clearly gets underway in July, the earliest juvenile being one on 17th (in 1982). Autumn migration reaches a strong peak in August–September before dropping significantly in October. Only twelve have been recorded in November and just singles in December and January. It is assumed that the vast majority of the Ringed Plovers recorded at the lake originate in north-eastern Canada, Greenland and Iceland.

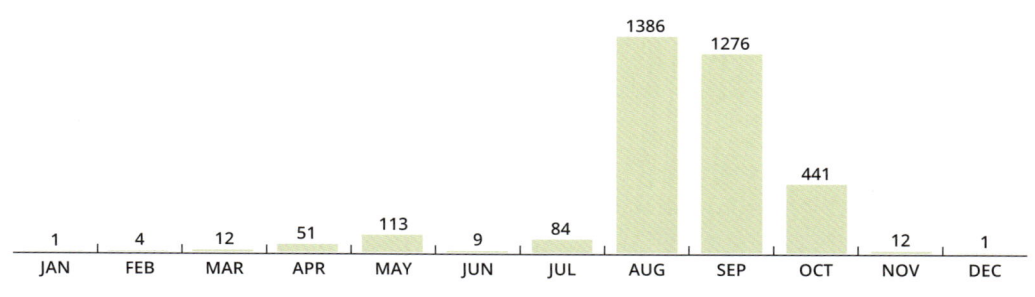

JAN	FEB	MAR	APR	MAY	JUN	JUL	AUG	SEP	OCT	NOV	DEC
1	4	12	51	113	9	84	1386	1276	441	12	1

RINGED PLOVER | Monthly maxima (combined) 1954-2019.

LITTLE RINGED PLOVER *Charadrius dubius*

This species first bred in Britain in 1938, taking advantage of the large number of gravel pits that were created at the time. The first record for Chew was on 9 May 1954 (B. King), this being only the second record for Somerset and the first for what is now the Avon area. The next was on 7–8 August 1958, but it became annual from 1961, with the exception of the 'flood year' of 1968. Most counts are in single figures – usually less than five – but there have been double figure counts in two years: ten juveniles together on 16 August 1989 and 16 on 2 August 2011, the highest Avon count.

It has occurred in March in ten years, the earliest date being one from 18th to 20th (in 2005). As the combined monthly maxima graph shows, the peak spring month is April, numbers then declining into June. Autumn migration starts with a vengeance in July, peaking in August before declining through September into October, with the last date being the 5th (in both 1975 and 1982).

The species has never bred at the lake but in 1997 there was an interesting series of records from Heron's Green Pool, which was then much larger than it is now. Up to two males and a female were present from 10 to 23 April, with some song heard. A pair was again present from 16 May to 1 June, the male, which was heard 'singing', apparently being a first-summer. Unfortunately, they disappeared in early June when the water level rose after heavy rain.

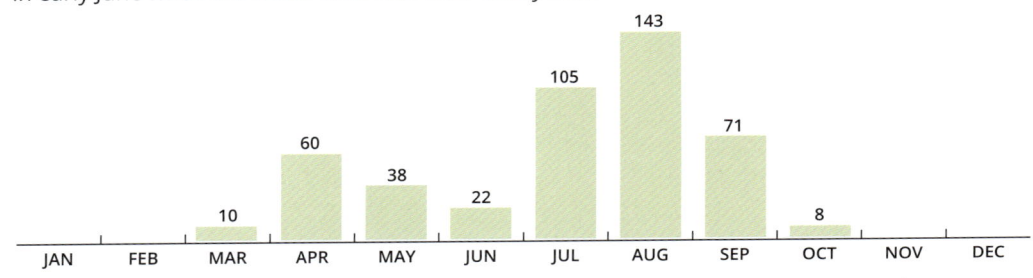

LITTLE RINGED PLOVER | Monthly maxima (combined) 1954-2015.

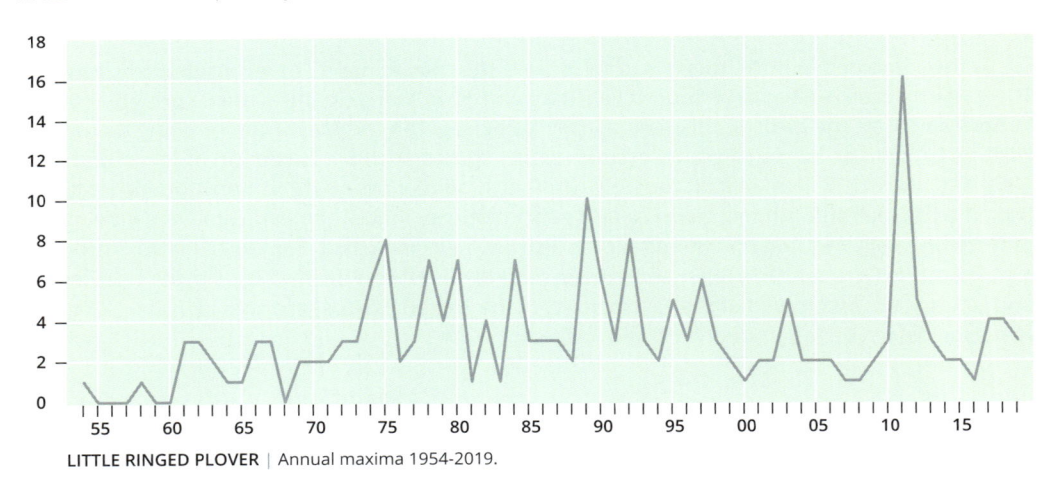

Jan 0, Feb 0, Mar 10, Apr 60, May 38, Jun 22, Jul 105, Aug 143, Sep 71, Oct 8, Nov 0, Dec 0.

LITTLE RINGED PLOVER | Annual maxima 1954-2019.

KILLDEER *Charadrius vociferus*

One was seen well at Moreton Point and Moreton Hide on 17 January 1976 before it was flushed by a Merlin *Falco columbianus* (KEV *et al.*).

KENTISH PLOVER *Charadrius alexandrinus*

Although there are published records of this species at the lake in 1967, 1972 and 1974 the documentation for these can no longer be found. The 1966 record can still be scrutinised and is acceptable.

A male at the western end of the Main Dam on 13 April 1966 (P. J. Curry, D. J. Perriman).

GREATER SAND PLOVER *Charadrius leschenaultii*

One was discovered in Spring Bay on 17 November 1979 (C. J. Newman, KEV et al.) remaining until 10 February 1980. It was only the third British record, following singles at Pagham Harbour, West Sussex, from December 1978 to January 1979, and one on Orkney in June 1979. Towards the end of its stay, it joined flocks of Lapwings *Vanellus vanellus* that fed in the Parkland and also in the field that now hosts Picnic Area 1.

The species breeds in Asia, from Turkey east to south-east Kazakhstan and Azerbaijan. It normally winters on the coasts of the Middle East and southern Asia, as well as south along the coasts of eastern and southern Africa and in Australia.

WHIMBREL *Numenius phaeopus*

The Whimbrel that pass through Britain in spring and autumn breed in Iceland. The peak months are April and May and the earliest date is 11 April (two in 2012) and the latest is 16 May (1965 and 1971). The autumn passage is more protracted, with a strong peak in August. The earliest and latest autumn dates are 8 July (1975) and 3 October (2011).

As the annual maxima graph indicates, most records involve single figure parties flying through. However, larger flocks have been recorded, the biggest being 21 on 9 May 1970, 36 flying south on 5 August 1975 and 32 in May 1996 (no precise date in *ABR*).

It has recently been discovered that, when on spring migration from West Africa, Whimbrel make a stop-over in northern France or Britain. On their autumn migration, however, the majority make a single non-stop transoceanic flight from Iceland direct to either western Iberia or West Africa (between Mauritania and Benin). This explains why, unusually, the species is commoner in spring than it is in autumn (see *Wader Study*, Volume 123, Issue 1, June 2016).

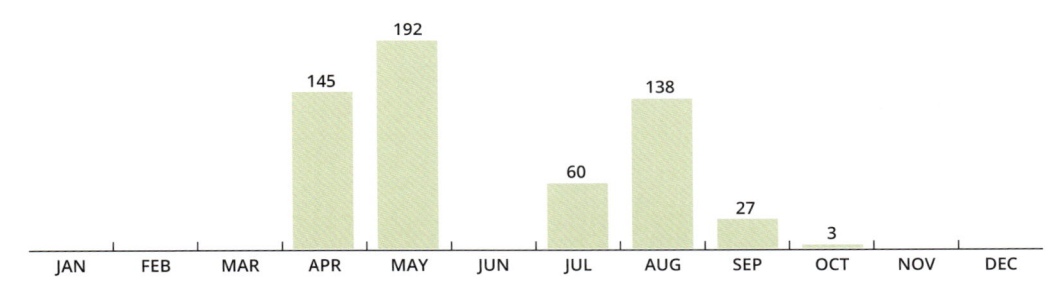

WHIMBREL | Monthly maxima (combined) 1954-2015.

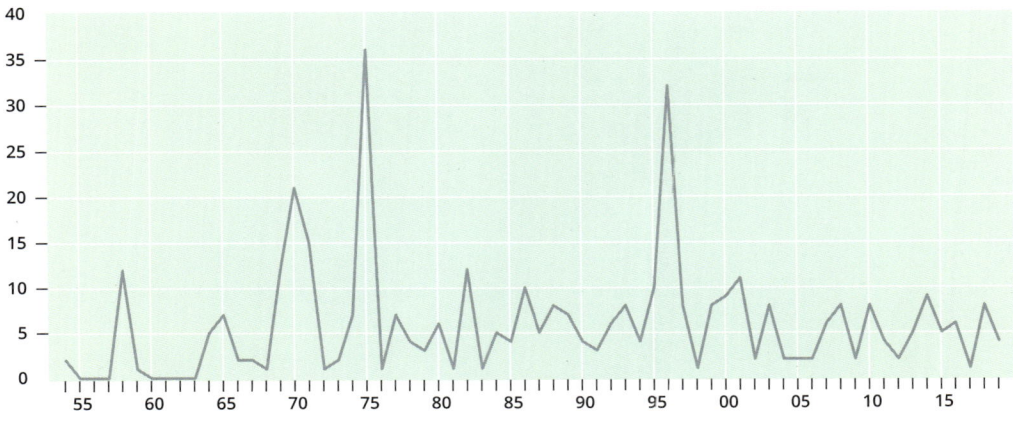

Monthly maxima: JAN —, FEB —, MAR —, APR 145, MAY 192, JUN —, JUL 60, AUG 138, SEP 27, OCT 3, NOV —, DEC —.

WHIMBREL | Annual maxima 1954-2019.

Whimbrel | Gary Thoburn

CURLEW *Numenius arquata*

The first record is of 20 on 6 January 1957 followed by two singles in 1959 and nine on 14 June 1962. From 1964 onwards, the species has been recorded annually, with peaks in May and from July to September. The highest counts have been 12 on 24 September 1967, 13 on 24 August 1969 and 16 on 6 September 1982.

Most of the records have involved birds flying over but, from September 1979 to January 1980, a small flock took up residence, feeding in the fields around the north end of the lake. The peak count was ten on 18 November. The annual maxima graph shows the erratic nature of the species' occurrences, with high peak counts during 1962–1981 but with much lower numbers since. This downward trend is also apparent nationally and this vulnerable species has recently been listed as 'Near Threatened'.

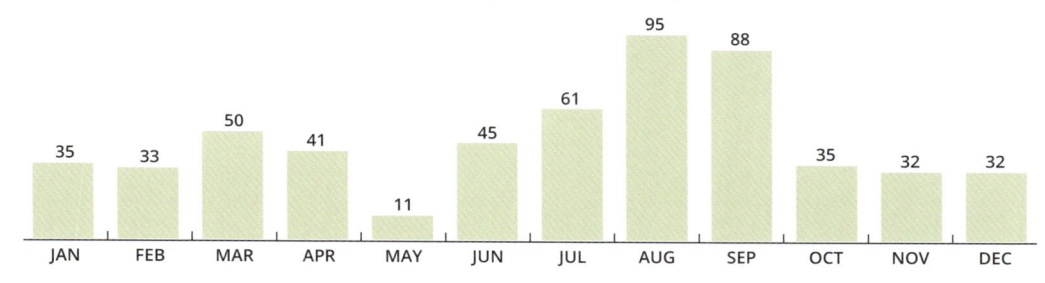

CURLEW | Monthly maxima (combined) 1957-2015.

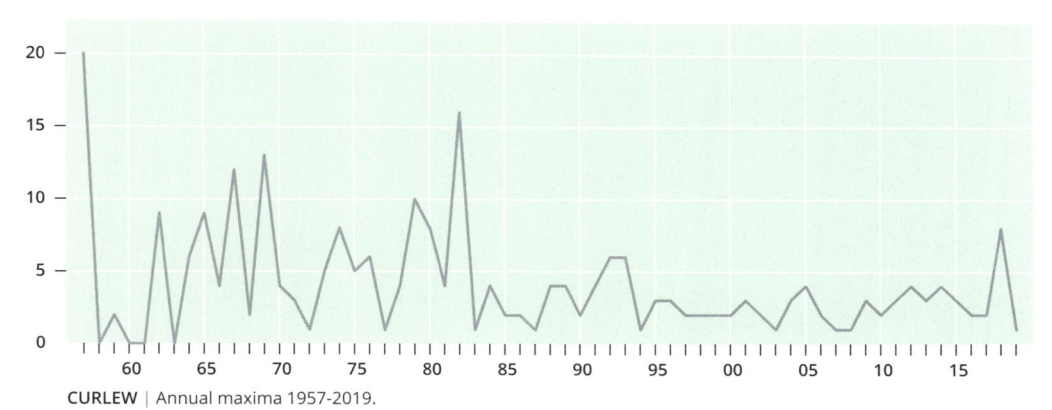

CURLEW | Annual maxima 1957-2019.

Curlew | Lucy Masters

BAR-TAILED GODWIT *Limosa lapponica*

First recorded in 1954, Bar-tailed Godwit has remained an erratic visitor, with records in all months except June. As the monthly maxima graph shows, the peak months are May and September. All counts have been in single figures except for the following:

- **1975:** 23 flew west on 4 September and 31 flew west on 6th.
- **1976:** 15 on the unusual date of 23 February; 25 flew through on 31 August.
- **2006:** by far the largest flock was of 80 that flew across the lake in bad weather and south-east winds on 2 May, eventually departing to the north-west.

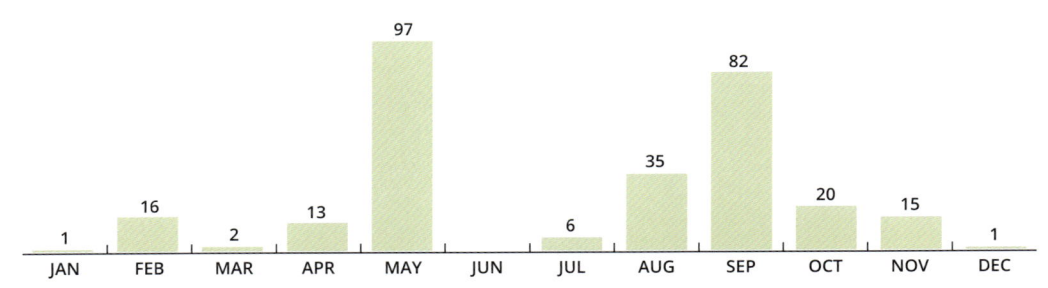

BAR-TAILED GODWIT | Monthly maxima (combined) 1954-2015.

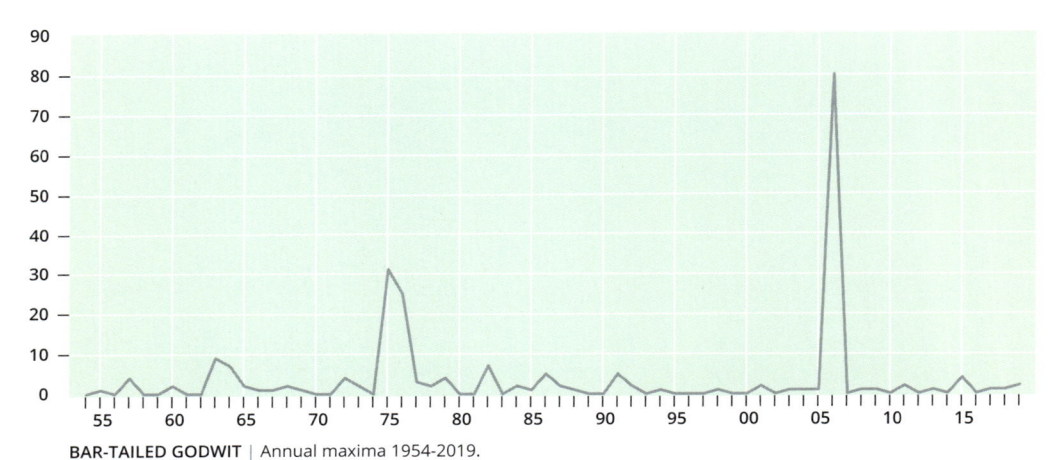

JAN	FEB	MAR	APR	MAY	JUN	JUL	AUG	SEP	OCT	NOV	DEC
1	16	2	13	97		6	35	82	20	15	1

BAR-TAILED GODWIT | Annual maxima 1954-2019.

Bar-tailed Gowdit | Laurel Tucker

Bar-tailed Gowdit | Rich Andrews

BLACK-TAILED GODWIT *Limosa limosa*

The first record was of 14 on 3 April 1954 (B. K. Brooke) and this count was not bettered until 1974, when 40 were seen on 9 April. In 1968, none was recorded at all, a consequence of high autumn water levels brought about by the infamous July floods of that year. Numbers increased through the 1980s and 1990s, reaching a peak of 37 in September 1996. Following three poor years in 1997–1999, numbers increased again from the turn of the century, reaching a new peak of 33 in 2003 followed by 58 in 2005. Apart from a poor year in 2008, when only one was recorded, peak numbers have remained high with a record flock of 62 flying west on 31 August 2012. This was followed by a count of 52 in Villice Bay on 13 August 2014. A record 65 were recorded on Herriott's Pool on 31 August 2018.

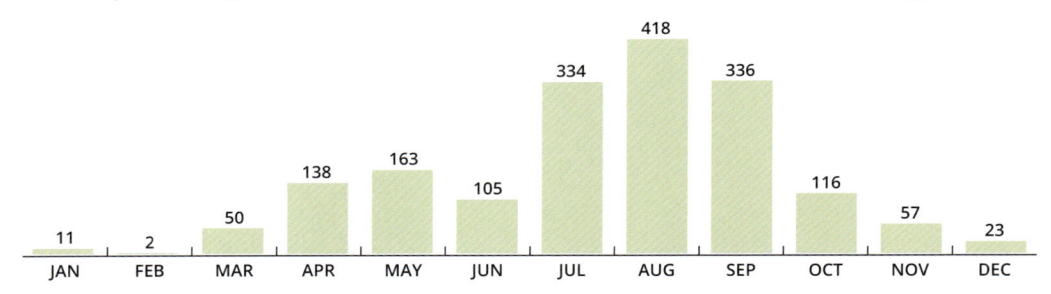

BLACK-TAILED GODWIT | Monthly maxima (combined) 1954-2015.

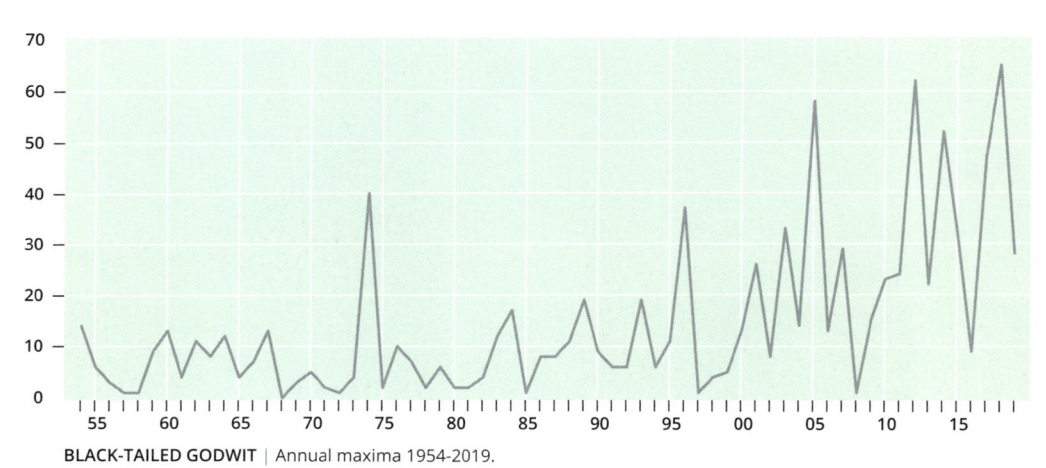

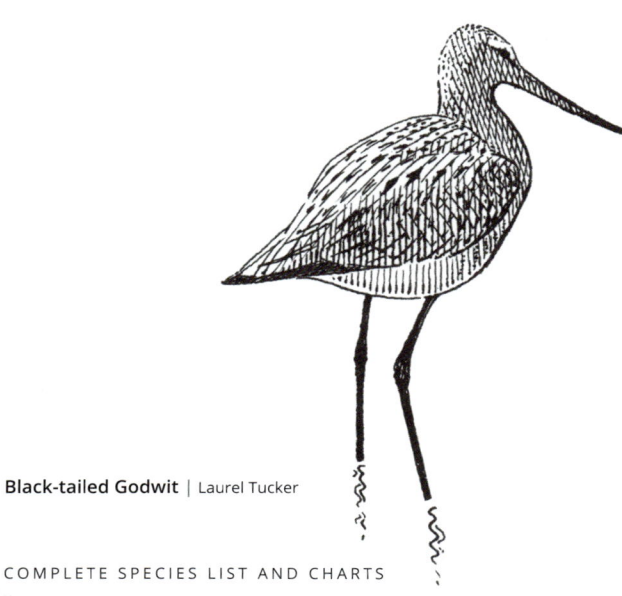

BLACK-TAILED GODWIT | Annual maxima 1954-2019.

Black-tailed Godwit | Laurel Tucker

The recent high counts at Chew are related to the fact that the Icelandic race *islandica* has increased significantly in recent years, in contrast to the nominate continental race which has been declining. Indeed, the occurrence of the latter at the Chew has never been confirmed, although two on 21 June 1989 were considered possible candidates, particularly as they included a bird that was ringed above the knee (a ringing trait normally associated with Continental birds). Current thinking is that only juveniles can be separated as regards race.

As the combined monthly maxima graph shows, it has been recorded in every month, with a small spring peak in April and May and a late summer/autumn peak from July to September, with August being the best month. Few are seen in winter, February being the poorest month with just two records.

A colour-ringed individual on 14 December 2014 had been ringed in Iceland on 10 July 2002, and so was at least 12 years old.

Black-tailed Gowdit | Rich Andrews

TURNSTONE *Arenaria interpres*

Turnstones have occurred in every month except March and December. There is a spring passage from April to early June, the first recorded date being 18 April and the last being 5 June. The first presumed returning birds have been seen as early as 24 June, with numbers increasing in July to a large peak in August. The first juveniles have appeared on 4 August (in 1984). Numbers drop in September and few are recorded in October and November, the latest autumn date being 21 November. It is assumed that most, if not all, the Turnstones that appear at the lake originate in Greenland and north-eastern Canada, rather than being Scandinavian birds.

The annual maxima graph shows that passage Turnstones occur in small numbers, usually along the dam walls in spring. The only double-figure counts were ten on 4 September 1984 and 12 on 22 August 2005, but the largest total involved 31 that flew through to the south-west on 12 September 2016 (in groups of 15, four and 12).

Two unusual records involved one in cold weather on 11 January 2011 that fed along the roadside on Herriott's Bridge; but even more bizarre was one found feeding in the yard of nearby Sutton House Farm on 15 May 2008.

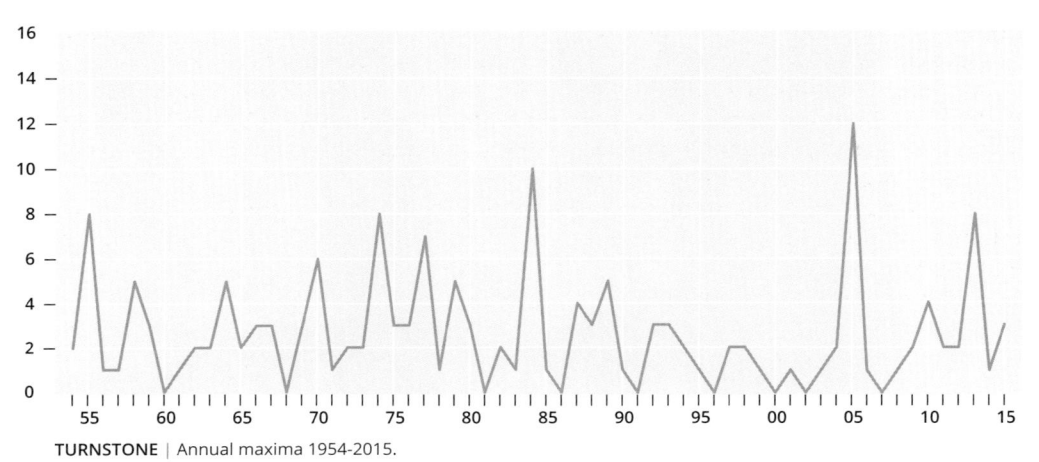

TURNSTONE | Annual maxima 1954-2015.

Turnstones | Laurel Tucker

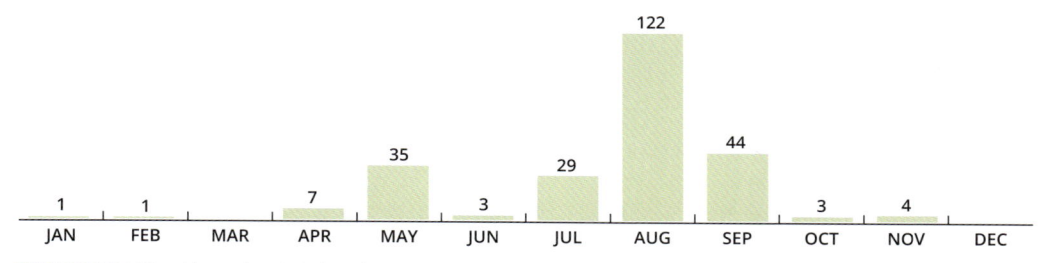

TURNSTONE | Monthly maxima (combined) 1954-2015.

Monthly values: JAN 1, FEB 1, MAR —, APR 7, MAY 35, JUN 3, JUL 29, AUG 122, SEP 44, OCT 3, NOV 4, DEC —.

KNOT *Calidris canutus*

The annual maxima graph indicates that Knot is an erratic visitor, recorded in 45 of the 63 years from 1954 to 2016. Annual totals vary considerably, with single figures in 39 of those years. The higher counts involved 35 (mostly summer-plumaged adults) on 27 August 1977, 21 after gales on 16 October 1987, 15 on 9 September 1995 and 25 briefly on 9 September 2016.

The only March record involved a winter-plumaged individual on 23 March 2012. It was with a flock of nine Black-tailed Godwits *Limosa limosa* feeding on Herriott's Pool. As its legs were not as long as the godwits, it spent the entire late afternoon swimming around, doing a very passable impression of a Wilson's Phalarope *Phalaropus tricolor*!

Of the autumn birds that were aged, 36% were adults and 64% were juveniles. The June records related to summer-plumaged adults on 10th in 1988 and on 12th in 2011 and the July record to an adult on 31st (in 1960).

There was a very good record of 26 adults on 9 August 2019.

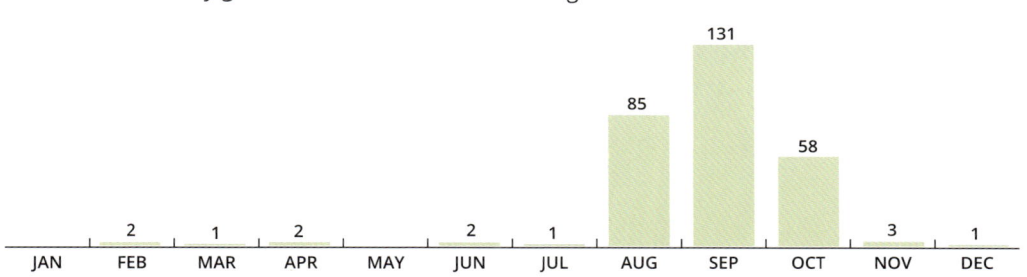

Monthly values: JAN —, FEB 2, MAR 1, APR 2, MAY —, JUN 2, JUL 1, AUG 85, SEP 131, OCT 58, NOV 3, DEC 1.

KNOT | Monthly maxima (combined) 1954-2015.

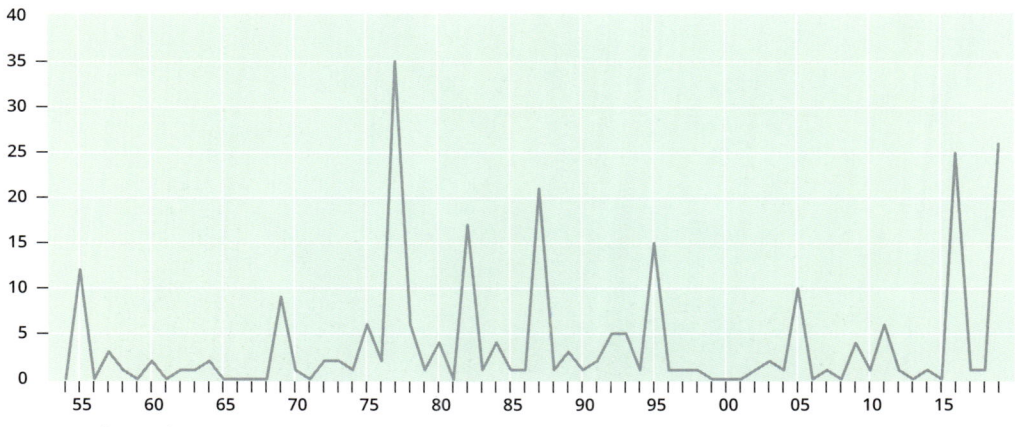

KNOT | Annual maxima 1954-2019.

Ruff | Rich Andrews

RUFF *Calidris pugnax*

As the combined monthly maxima graph shows, Ruffs have been recorded in every month. There have been seven records in June (11 individuals) the earliest involving two on 12th (in 1966) and one on 16th (in 1990), but it is not certain whether these were late spring migrants or early returning autumn ones. A male on 16 June 1990 was in full summer plumage, suggesting a late spring migrant, whereas a pair on 26 June 1995 showed only remnants of summer plumage, suggesting that they were already heading south. As can be clearly seen on the combined monthly maxima graph, the peak time is August and September, declining sharply in October to a low point in November. The average maximum annual counts have been 13, but the highest were 71 on 31 August 1973 and 63 on 21 September 1980.

Winter records are unusual, but there were as many as 25 in January 1968. In 1976, however, there was an unprecedented influx in February and March: 35 were seen on 14 February and 56 on 29th, rising to a phenomenal 101 on 13 March. These involved 16 at the Main Dam, three at Twycross, and 82 along the west shore between Herriott's Bridge and Villice Bay. This coincided with an exceptional influx onto the Somerset Levels, with 190 on Tealham Moor on 14 February and 300+ on West Sedge Moor on 29 February (see *Somerset Birds* 1976). The reasons for this unseasonal influx are not known.

The annual maxima graph shows there has been a worrying decline from the mid-1990s, the current average being just five (based on the ten years from 1996 to 2015).

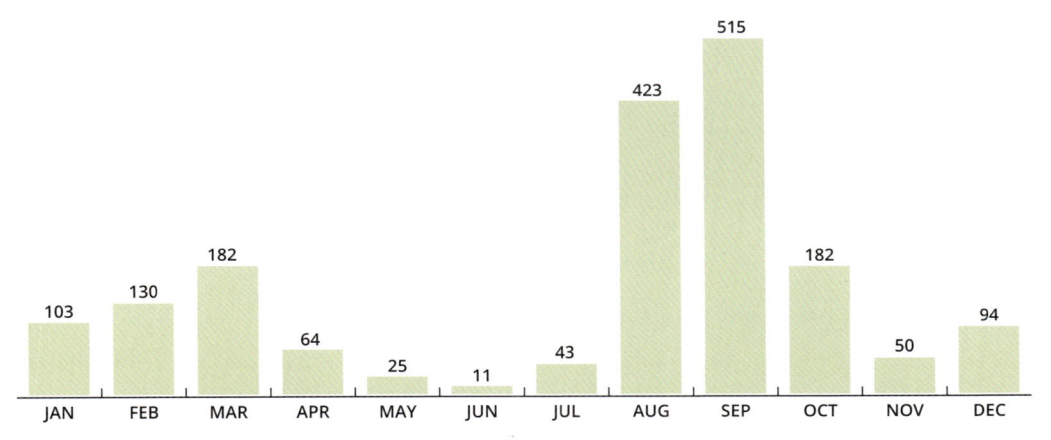

RUFF | Monthly maxima (combined) 1954-2015.

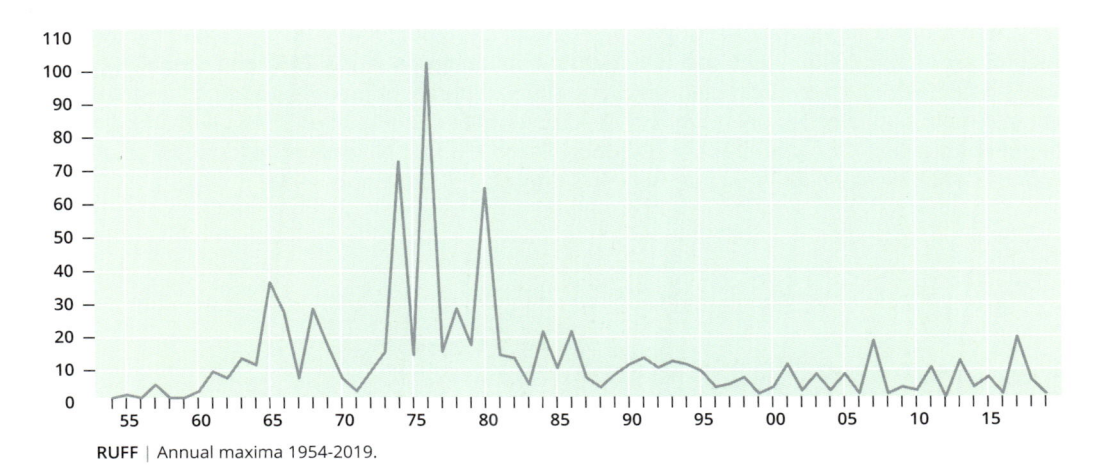

RUFF | Annual maxima 1954-2019.

SHARP-TAILED SANDPIPER *Calidris acuminata*

A juvenile that was found at Blagdon Lake on 18 November 2011 (N. Milbourne *et al.*) moved to Chew on 19th, where it remained until 11 December (apart from a day trip to Blagdon on 30 November). It finally returned to Blagdon again on 12–16 December, disappearing when the water level rose.

Sharp-tailed Sandpiper | Rich Andrews

CURLEW SANDPIPER *Calidris ferruginea*

This is a scarce and erratic visitor, numbers being dependent on breeding success in the Siberian Arctic. The vast majority of records relate to autumn juveniles. As the annual maxima graph shows, the species is scarce at the lake, although there was a definite but erratic upsurge from the mid-1970s into the early 1990s. Annual totals then dropped considerably from 1994 onwards, with eleven blank years from then until 2016.

There are two spring records: singles on 30 April 1962 and 26 May 1973. The earliest autumn records are one on 13 July 1969, an adult in summer plumage on 26 July 1980 and a moulting adult on 25 July 1990. The main passage, consisting almost entirely of juveniles, begins in August, the earliest record of juveniles being two on 18 August 1975. The migration shows a strong peak in September, tailing off considerably in October. There are four November records, all of singles, with the latest being a first-winter on Herriott's Pool on 1–5 December 1984.

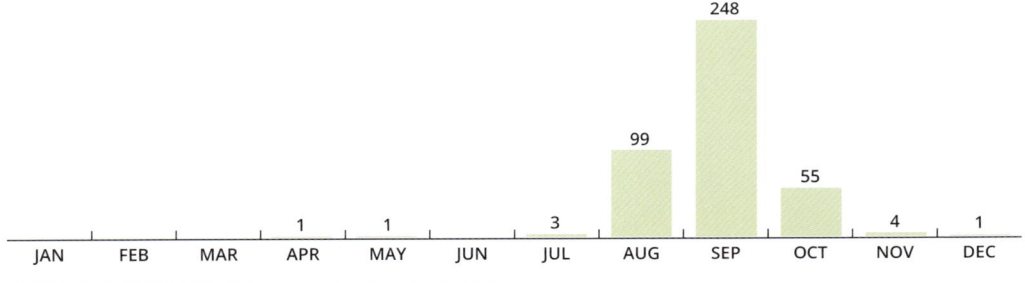

JAN	FEB	MAR	APR	MAY	JUN	JUL	AUG	SEP	OCT	NOV	DEC
			1	1		3	99	248	55	4	1

CURLEW SANDPIPER | Monthly maxima (combined) 1956-2015.

CURLEW SANDPIPER | Annual maxima 1954-2019.

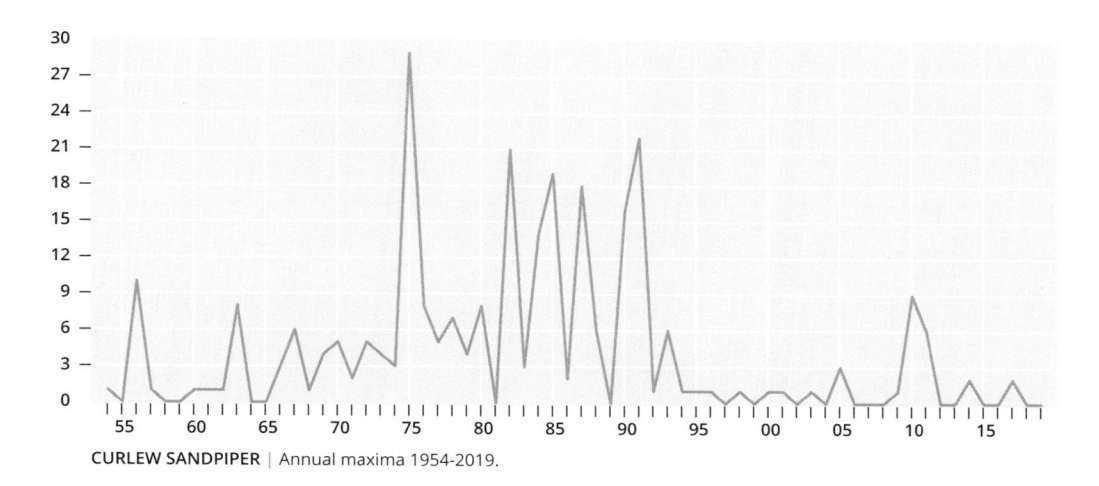

It is also worth noting that, in the autumn of 1969, there was an unprecedented westward movement of juvenile Curlew Sandpipers into Britain, with an estimated 3,500 present in the country on 31 August (see Stanley and Minton 1972). However, despite low water levels at Chew, the maximum count in that year was a paltry four, with the estimated annual total being just 13 individuals. This disappointing situation was undoubtedly due to the fact that the weather for much of the autumn was warm, sunny and anticyclonic. In such favourable conditions, migrating waders tend to over-fly the lake.

Reference
Stanley, P. I. and Minton, C. D. T. 1972. 'The unprecedented westward migration of Curlew Sandpipers in autumn 1969'. *British Birds* 65: 365–380.

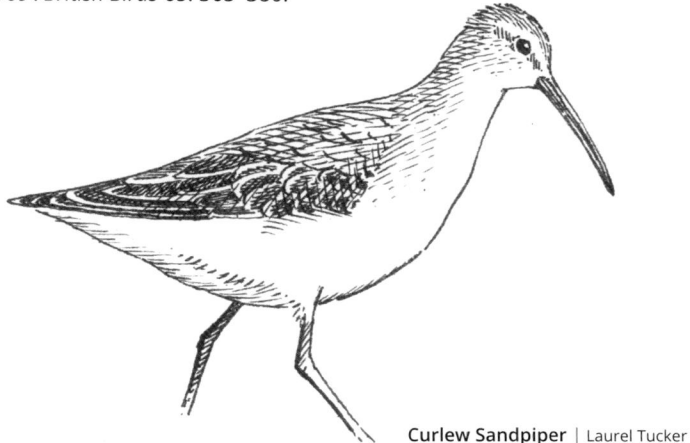

Curlew Sandpiper | Laurel Tucker

TEMMINCK'S STINT *Calidris temminckii*

This is a rare and irregular visitor, with 15 records. The first was one on 29 August 1954 (R. H. Poulding). As the annual maxima graph indicates, there was a cluster of five records between 1959 and 1964, followed by another series of six from 1972 to 1987. Since then, however, there have been only three further records (to 2015), the last being a juvenile on 26–27 August 2011. Only four of the autumn birds were aged: an adult on 30–31 August 1980, juveniles on 12–22 September 1972 and 26–27 August 2011, and a first-winter in 2002 from 22–24 September and again from 4–9 October (it was at Blagdon on the intervening dates and there again until 10 November).

There are two spring records, both on 20 May (in 1987 and 2009). The autumn records have occurred from 26 July to 22 October, with peaks of five in August and six in September.

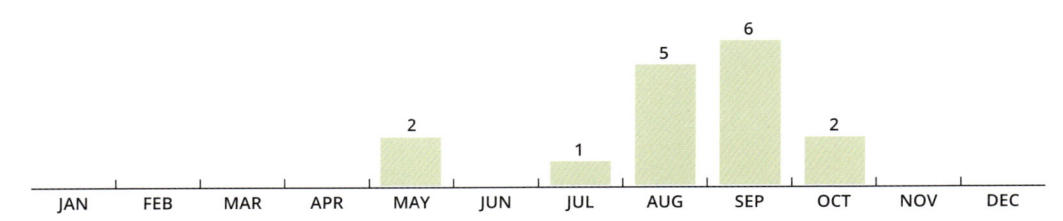

TEMMINCK'S STINT | Monthly maxima (combined) 1954-2011.

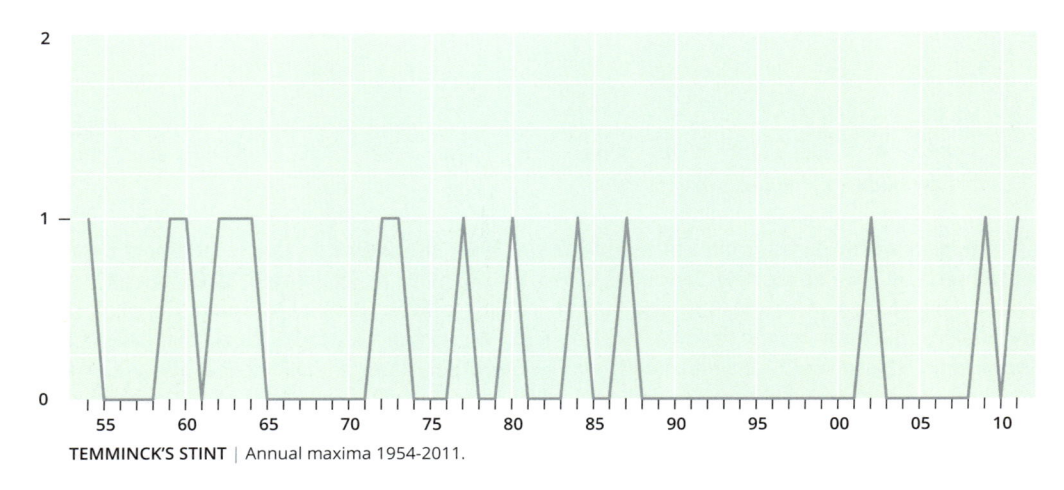

TEMMINCK'S STINT | Annual maxima 1954-2011.

SANDERLING *Calidris alba*

The first records were of singles on 1 and 29 August 1954, followed by four in May 1955. It became much more regular from 1960 onwards, being recorded in 49 of the 59 years to 2016. There were distinct peaks in the 1970s and early 1980s (see annual maxima graph).

As the combined monthly maxima graph shows, there is a single March record (a winter-plumaged bird on 15th in 2012) and four April records between 12th and 27th. By far the best month, however, is May, with a total of 84 recorded, all counts being of one to five except for nine on 13 May 1973 and ten on 5 May 1976. At this time of year, most of the records have related to summer-plumaged individuals on the Main Dam or along the dam at Heron's Green Bay. The latest spring migrants have been singles on 1 and 2 June.

The first returning adults appear as early as 15 July, with the earliest date for a juvenile being 28 July (in 2003). As the combined monthly maxima graph shows, August and September are the peak autumn months, with maxima of six (un-aged) on 31 August 2015 and nine juveniles on 15 September 2014. There are just four October records, the latest being a juvenile on 15th in 2011 and two (un-aged) on 19th in 1966. There is a single December record: one in winter plumage on 4 December 2010, during a period of freezing weather.

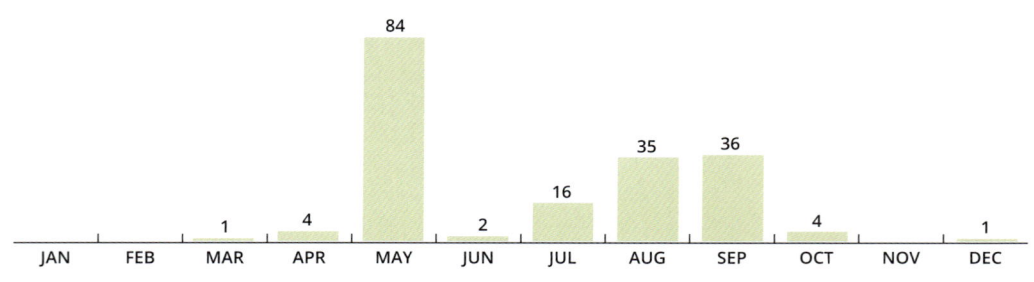

SANDERLING | Monthly maxima (combined) 1954-2015.

COMPLETE SPECIES LIST AND CHARTS

SANDERLING | Annual maxima 1954-2019.

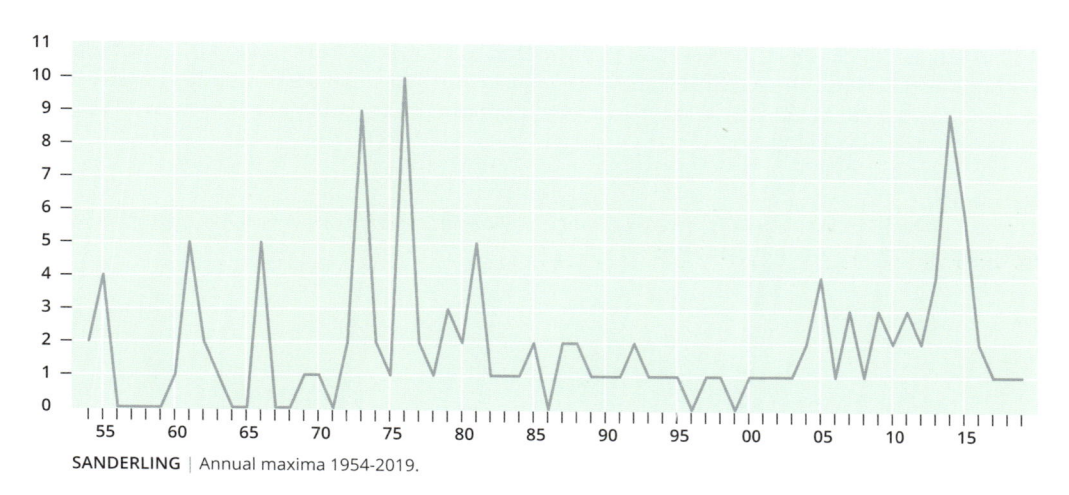

Sanderling | Rich Andrews

| DUNLIN *Calidris alpina*

As the average monthly maxima graph shows, numbers of Dunlin peak in winter, from November–January, but this winter peak is not typical as large numbers at this time occur only when water levels are exceptionally low. Such conditions were fairly frequent until 1991 but, since then, they have become much less so. The highest counts recorded were 430 in December 1964, 270 in November 1970, a record 765 in December 1973, 660 in in January 1976 and 360 in December 1978. Since then, there have been only two counts of over a hundred (260 in November 1991 and 125 in November 2010). These mid-winter Dunlin are considered to be of the nominate race *alpina*, which breeds in Scandinavia and eastwards into western Russia. This is the common winter visitor in Britain, including those on the Severn Estuary.

At other times of the year, there is a small spring passage in April and May followed by a strong autumn one from July to September, with a peak in August. The highest count at this time of year was

110 in August 1989. These, however, are considered to be mainly from Iceland (race *schinzii*) and perhaps also from north-east Greenland (race *arctica*) – an individual on 14 May 2011 was formally accepted as a *arctica* (*ABR* 2011). These two races continue south to winter in Morocco, Mauritania and perhaps even Mali (*BWP*).

Reference
Cramp, S. et al. 1983. *Handbook of the Birds of Europe, the Middle East and North Africa. The Birds of the Western Palearctic.* (*BWP*). Oxford University Press.

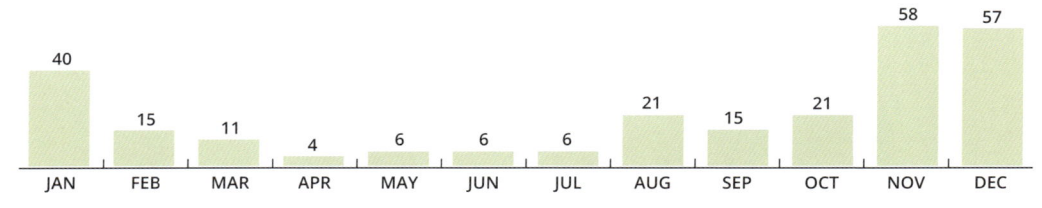

DUNLIN | Monthly maxima (average) 1954-2015.

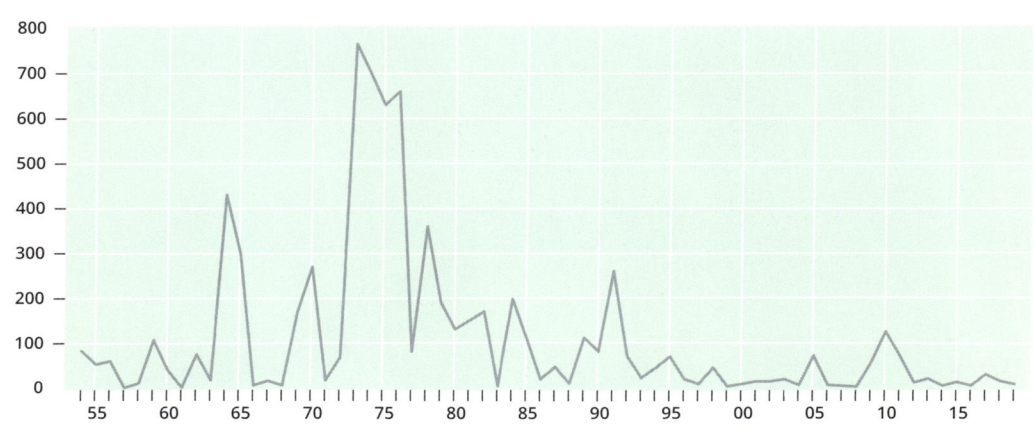

JAN	FEB	MAR	APR	MAY	JUN	JUL	AUG	SEP	OCT	NOV	DEC
40	15	11	4	6	6	6	21	15	21	58	57

DUNLIN | Annual maxima 1954-2019. Note that there were no records for 1957 or 1961.

Dunlin | Rich Andrews

PURPLE SANDPIPER *Calidris maritima*

There have been five records:
- **1969:** one on 1 December (C. R. Cuthbert).
- **1979:** one on 11 December (A. J. Merritt).
- **1991:** a first-winter in Heron's Green Bay from 29 September to 5 October (R. M. Andrews, KEV *et al.*).
- **2005:** one in Heron's Green Bay on 6 November (C Craig, A. H. Davis *et al.*).
- **2009:** a first-summer in Heron's Green Bay on 18 April (KEV *et al.*).

Of interest with respect to these records, it has recently been discovered that most of the Purple Sandpipers that winter in western Britain originate in north-east Canada and Greenland.

Purple Sandpiper | Laurel Tucker

LITTLE STINT *Calidris minuta*

The first record was one on 11–15 August 1954 (B. King), followed by two on 11 September. It has been recorded in 51 of the 61 years since to 2015. As the annual maxima graph shows, annual numbers vary considerably. There have been nine blank years but there have also been 12 years when double figures were recorded. The highest totals (over 20) were 25 in September 1960, a record 46 on 27 September 1973 (with 40 at Blagdon the same day) and 28 on 27 September 1976.

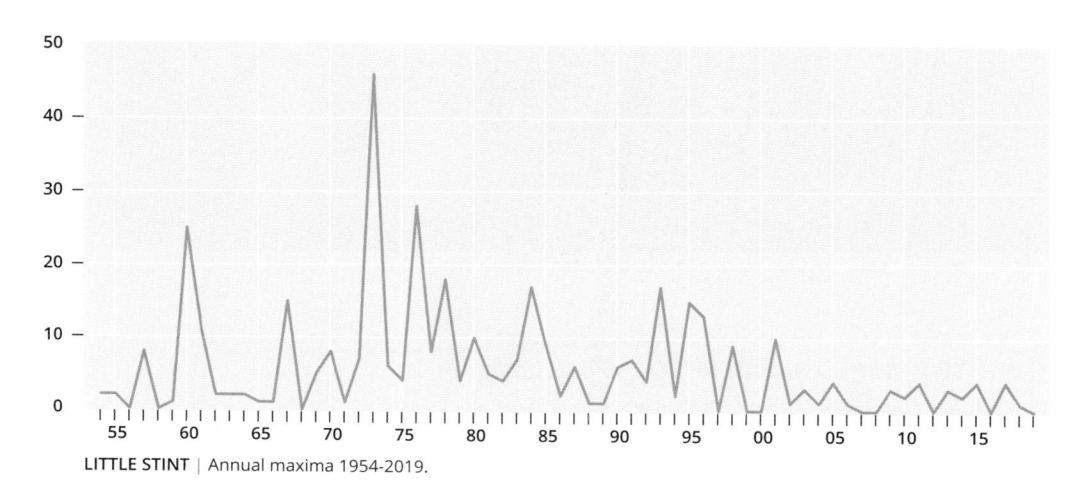

LITTLE STINT | Annual maxima 1954-2019.

Annual numbers fluctuate according to breeding productivity on the Arctic tundra, chick survival apparently peaking in Lemming years, on which the predators then concentrate. Since the turn of the century, however, numbers appear to indicate a more general downturn, the highest counts since 2000 being just four in 2005, 2011 and 2015.

The combined monthly maxima graph shows that most occur from August to October, with a strong peak in September. Numbers drop sharply in November but, in years of low water levels, small numbers sometimes attempt to over-winter, with totals of 12 in December, eight in January and three in February. March and April are the only months that have never produced a record.

Although there have been spring records, these are very few and far between: two on 25 May 1955, one on 1 May 1965 and one on 2 June 1987. Two summer-plumaged adults were also seen on 30 June 1986 but it seems most likely that these were already heading south.

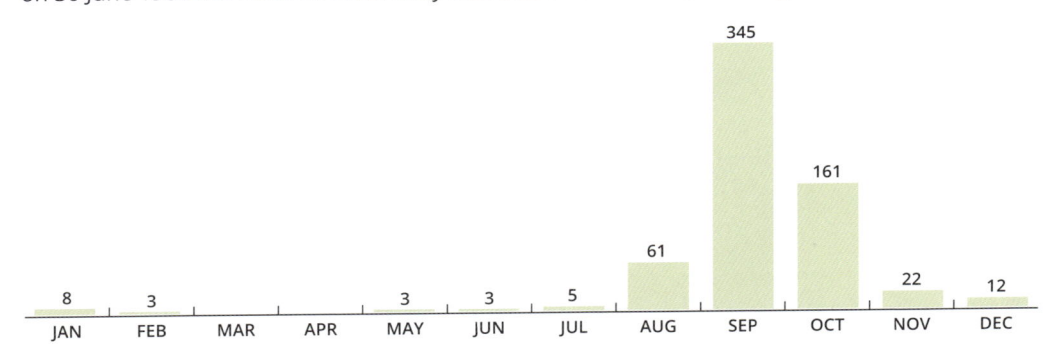

JAN	FEB	MAR	APR	MAY	JUN	JUL	AUG	SEP	OCT	NOV	DEC
8	3			3	3	5	61	345	161	22	12

LITTLE STINT | Monthly maxima (combined) 1954-2015.

Little Stint | Rich Andrews

WHITE-RUMPED SANDPIPER *Calidris fuscicollis*

There have been two records involving three individuals: two juveniles on 27–28 October 1978, with one remaining to 2 November (A. H. Davis *et al.*) and another juvenile on 5–19 October 1991 (A. J. Musgrove, M. G. Prince *et al.*).

BUFF-BREASTED SANDPIPER *Calidris subruficollis*

There were seven records of eight individuals from 1973 to 1980, all of which were juveniles. It seems remarkable that there has been none since:

- **1973:** 3 October (D. Buffery)
- **1975:** two on 1 September, with one until 12th (T. R. Cleeves, A. J. Merritt, T. Nichols *et al.*); another on 20–22 September (D Buffery, A, J. Merritt *et al.*) and a bird accepted as a different individual from 26 September to 1 October (D. Buffery, J. B. O. Rossetti, KEV).
- **1976:** one from 29 September to 6 October (P. J. Chadwick, L. A. & N. A. Tucker *et al.*).
- **1978:** one on 14 and 15 October when pursued and killed by a Carrion Crow *Corvus corone* (A. H. Davis).
- **1980:** one on 16 September (C. Hurford, J. P. Martin, M. C. Powell, E. V. Southam).

PECTORAL SANDPIPER *Calidris melanotos*

The first record was of one – un-aged – on 29 September 1969 (R. S. Harkness). Since then, the species has occurred in 14 of the 47 years to 2015.

As the combined monthly maxima graph indicates, there are two August records: single adults on 21–22 August 1987 and 18–20 August 1988. Given that these are the only adults ever to have been recorded at the lake and, given that they appeared in consecutive years on almost exactly the same dates, it seems probable that the same returning individual was involved.

The peak month of occurrence is September, the earliest date being a juvenile on 2nd (in 2011). Seventeen have been recorded in this month, plus seven in October and one in November: the latter a juvenile on 8th in 1970 (M. W. A. Martin, KEV). In 2011, up to three juveniles were present between 2 September and 15 October but it seems likely that as many as six individuals were involved in total (R. Mielcarek/*ABR*).

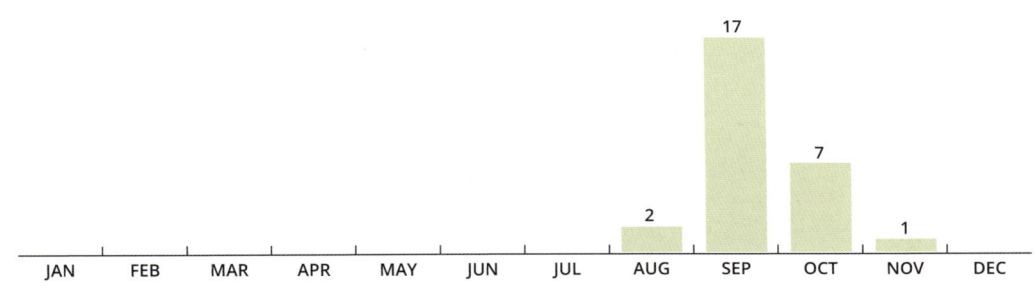

PECTORAL SANDPIPER | Monthly maxima (combined) 1969-2011.

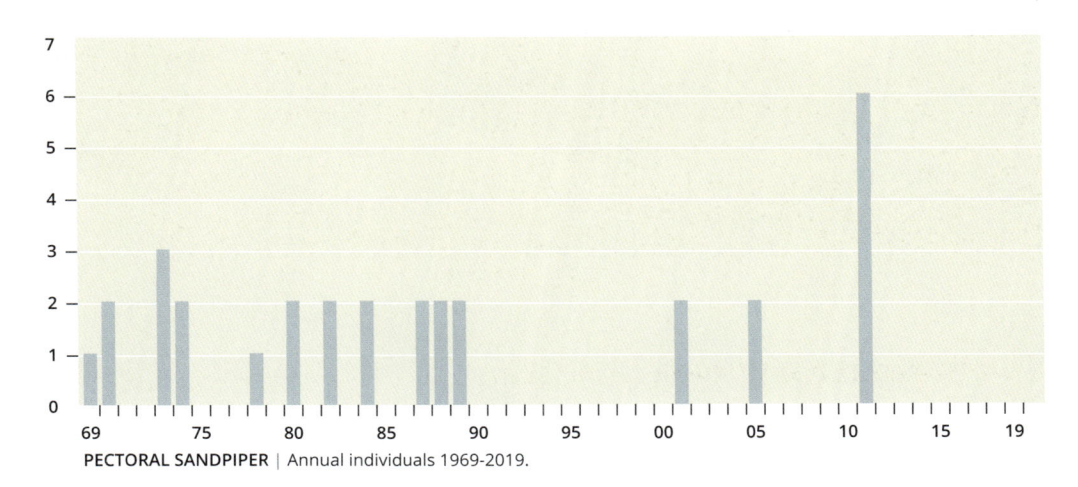

PECTORAL SANDPIPER | Annual individuals 1969-2019.

Pectoral Sandpiper | Rich Andrews

SEMIPALMATED SANDPIPER *Calidris pusilla*

There are two records, both in 2011. A juvenile on 12–13 September (KEV *et al.*) and another juvenile on 10–20 November (R. M. Andrews, KEV *et al.*).

(Note the September record was classed as 'not proven' by BBRC).

LONG-BILLED DOWITCHER *Limnodromus scolopaceus*

There have been three records (five individuals), all of which have been juvenile/first-winters:

- 1977–78: two on 30 September, later moving to Blagdon Lake where one remained until 11 January, the other to the 12th (KEV *et al.*). Both returned to Chew on several dates: 1 October (one), 26 and 29 October (two) and, finally, one on 21 January.
There is also an accepted (BBRC) record of a 'dowitcher sp.' on 28 October 1978 (A.R. Ashman, R. W. Webber and S. Wilkinson).
- 2009: a juvenile from 23 September to 2 October (D. J. Angell *et al.*).
- 2011: two were found at Blagdon Lake on 9 October (M. Pearce, R. Mielcarek *et al.*) but they moved to Chew on 11 October, regularly commuting between the two lakes until 13 December. Remarkably, this was almost exactly the same behaviour as the two in 1977–78. After leaving Blagdon, they visited Catcott Lows, Somerset, on 30 November, eventually moving to Lodmoor, Dorset, from 2 January 2012 before moving to the Fleet, Dorset, until 1 February, with just one remaining until 5 March. One then returned to Somerset, being seen at Greylake, Meare Heath and Catcott Lows during 7–19 March. Remarkably, it was then re-joined by the other bird from 20 March to 30 April. It seems amazing that they re-found each other having been separated for seven weeks in various parts of southern England. Spooky or what?!

Long-billed Dowitcher | Laurel Tucker

WOODCOCK *Scolopax rusticola*

The first traceable records were in 1965: singles on 6 November and 28 December (R. Angles, B. King). It may be that records during the 1950s simply weren't published in the bird reports, although it is equally likely that, in the early days, there was very little suitable habitat for the species, the lakeside woodland being in its infancy. This latter theory is supported by the annual maxima graph, which shows that only four were recorded prior to 1978, after which they were recorded in 31 of the 39 years to 2016. Given that very few birders tramp through the woodlands in winter, there must be far more present than are actually recorded.

As the combined monthly maxima graph shows, the first records are in October, the earliest date being 20th (in 2007). They then rise to a peak in January, with much smaller numbers from February to April, the latest recorded date being on the 10th.

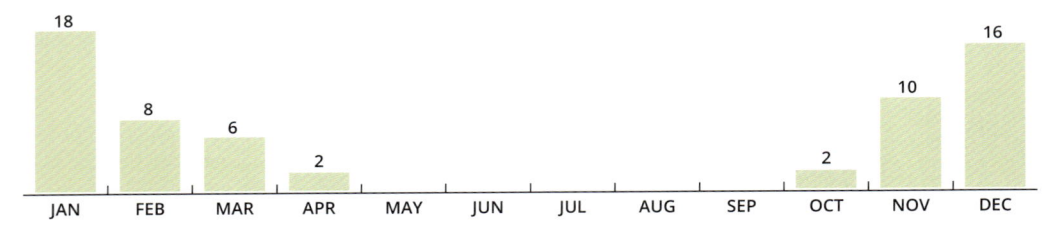

WOODCOCK | Monthly maxima (combined) 1965-2016.

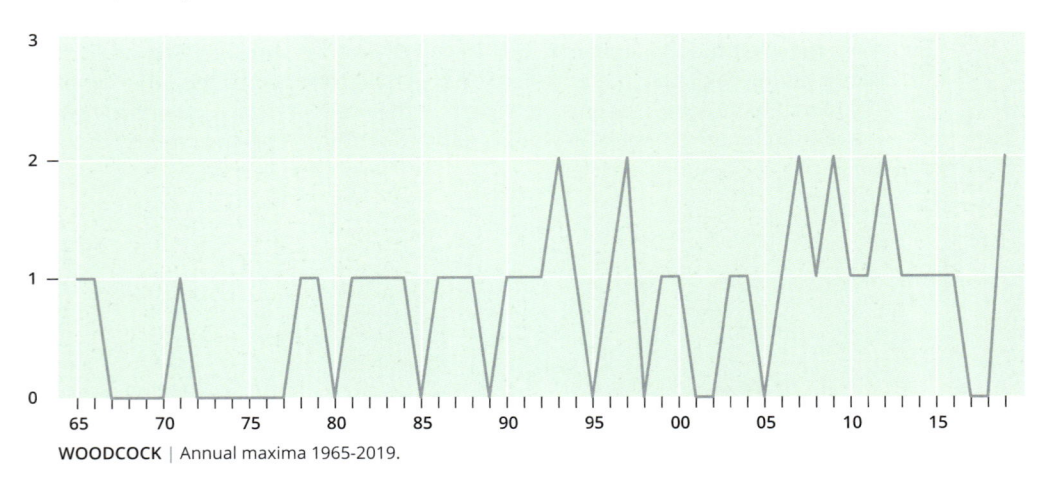

WOODCOCK | Annual maxima 1965-2019.

JACK SNIPE *Lymnocryptes minimus*

This peculiar cryptic bird is a winter visitor from late September to early April. The earliest date was one on 19 September 1973 and the latest was on 13 April 2010. As the combined monthly maxima graph shows, October is the peak month, with numbers gradually dropping to April as the water levels rise during the winter.

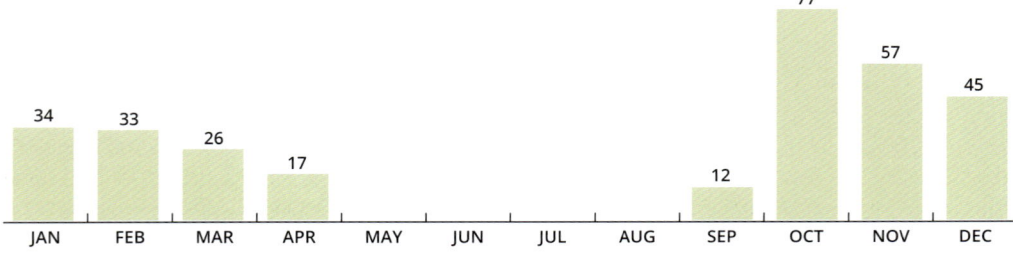

JACK SNIPE | Monthly maxima (combined) 1954-2015.

As the annual maxima graph indicates, all the counts have been in single figures apart from 15+ on 30 October 1962. The second highest was nine on 27 October 1966. Although this species can sometimes be seen feeding on the ground, most of the older high counts were the result of birders slogging through the lakeside vegetation. Since birders are now largely confined to the hides, counts of this species have diminished accordingly.

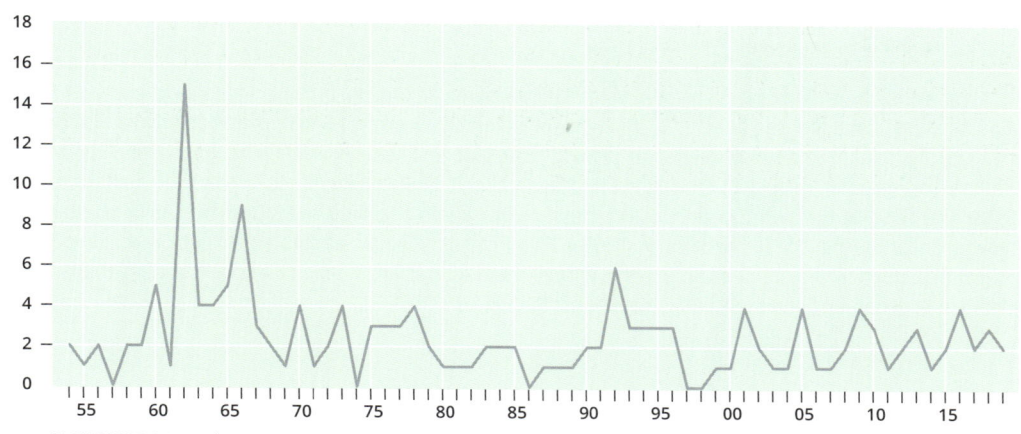

JACK SNIPE | Annual maxima 1954-2019. (None was seen in 1957, 1974, 1986, 1997 and 1998).

Jack Snipe | Rich Andrews

SNIPE *Gallinago gallinago*

As the average monthly maxima graph shows, the first returning Snipe normally appear in July, with numbers reaching a peak from September to November. There is a moderate decline in December before falling steadily from January to April, when the water levels are normally at their highest. There are five May records, the latest being one on 19 May 1979, and there is just one June record, on 16 June 2001. Surprisingly, this was a very rich buff individual that appeared to be of the race *faeroeensis* (KEV). Another such bird was seen on 9 February 2012.

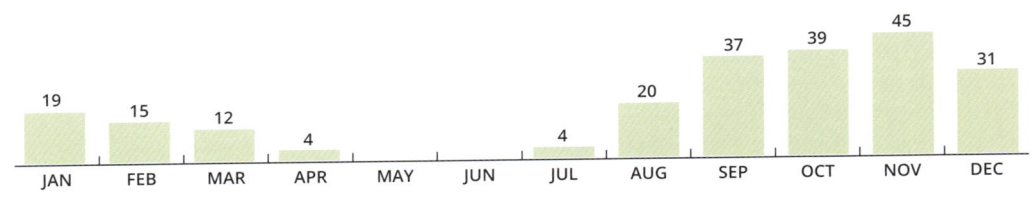

SNIPE | Monthly maxima (average) 1965-2015.

The annual maxima graph shows that numbers increased during the 1960s and early 1970s to a peak of 341 on 8 November 1975; this was followed by another high count of 255 on 4 November 1978. Both these counts were made during times of low water levels, the birds feeding on the open shoreline. Numbers then declined sharply from 1980 onwards to a low point of just six in 1999 and ten the following year. Counts have never again reached the hundred mark, the highest recent total being 85 in February 2005. This trend reflects a significant population decline nationally, particularly in lowland Britain, where the declines are linked to agricultural intensification and the drainage of wet tussocky grassland (*Bird Atlas* 2007–11).

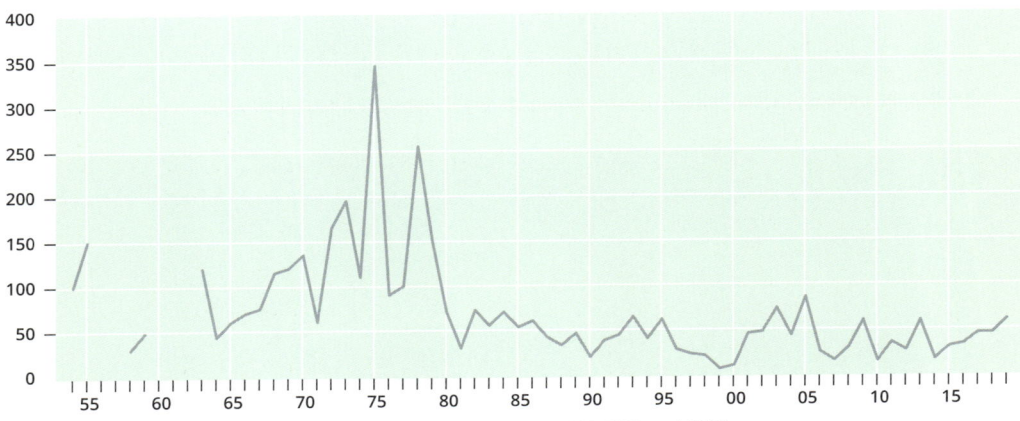

SNIPE | Annual maxima 1954-2019. (No counts in 1956, 1957, 1960, 1961 and 1962).

Snipe | Rich Andrews

WILSON'S PHALAROPE *Phalaropus tricolor*

There was a remarkable run of seven records during 1967–1988, all of which related to birds in juvenile/first-winter plumage. Remarkably, none has been seen since.

- **1967:** one 8–25 September (R. J. Senior, KEV, R. Angles *et al.*).
- **1975:** one 17–18 September (B. Rabbitts *et al.*).
- **1979:** one 20–21 September (J. Aldridge, M. P. Hastings, N. A. & L. A. Tucker *et al.*); another from 29 September to 4 October (A. H. Davis, R. S. Harkness, KEV *et al.*).
- **1980:** one 13–23 September (J. Hole, KEV *et al.*).
- **1985:** one 16–18 October (A. F. A. Hawkins, R. J. Higgins, D. Lawrence, *et al.*).
- **1988:** one 11–12 September (A. J. Merritt, KEV *et al.*).

RED-NECKED PHALAROPE *Phalaropus lobatus*

There have been just three records: the first two were an adult in partial moult on 24 August 1969 (R. J. Lewis) and a male off Moreton Hide on 28 May 1978 (D. Warden).

The rarity of this species at the lake had been a continual source of bewilderment to local birders, but a cracking female in summer plumage turned up swimming on Herriott's Pool on 7 June 2020 (T. Scheen). At the time there were unseasonably strong westerly winds, and a light scattering of inland records in Britain and Ireland.

Interestingly it has recently become apparent that the birds that breed in Shetland, and also those in Iceland, actually migrate westwards, crossing the Atlantic to North America and in fact wintering in the Pacific, off the coast of South America (*British Birds*, August 2018). This migratory divide taken by northern European populations may well explain the extreme rarity of the species at the lake and in southern Britain.

Red-necked Phalarope | Laurel Tucker

GREY PHALAROPE *Phalaropus fulicarius*

First recorded in 1957, it has been seen in 32 years since (to 2018) with 50 individuals in total. Their occurrences are related almost entirely to westerly autumn gales although, presumably, numbers must also be influenced by the summer's breeding productivity. Although they breed on Svalbard and Iceland, they are not numerous there, with around 300 and 50–60 pairs respectively (Hagemeijer and Blair 1997). The vast majority of the birds that arrive in Britain must originate in Greenland and Canada.

As the annual maxima graph shows, records at Chew are erratic, depending on strong westerly gales during their main migration period in September–November. As indicated on the graph, they usually appear singly, but there are six records of two, two records of three (1989 and 2011) and as many as five on 18 October 1987, following the infamous 'hurricane' of that year. The earliest record was one on 30–31 August 1997 and the latest was one on 10–15 December 1972 (in 2011 a very long-staying individual remained from 1 November to 2 December). The most notable record, however, related to a superb summer-plumaged male that was seen in the centre of the lake on 16–17 June 1990 (R. M. Andrews, A. J. Merritt *et al.*). *Bristol Water* very kindly loaned us a fishing boat, instigating the lake's first 'pelagic trip'.

Reference
Hagemeijer, W. J. M. and Blair, .M. J. 1997. *The EBCC Atlas of European Breeding Birds. Their Distribution and Abundance.* T. & A. D. Poyser. London.

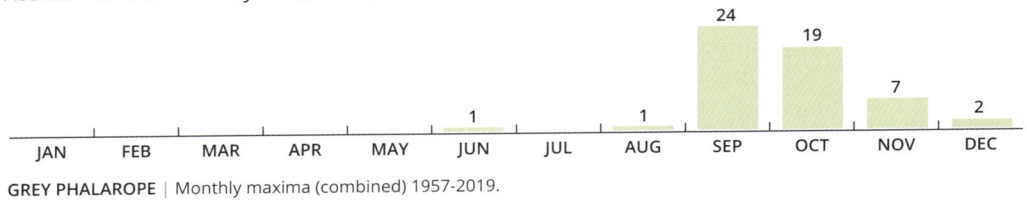

GREY PHALAROPE | Monthly maxima (combined) 1957-2019.

GREY PHALAROPE | Annual maxima 1957-2019.

Grey Phalarope | Rich Andrews

COMMON SANDPIPER *Actitis hypoleucos*

The Common Sandpiper is a summer visitor, breeding along rivers and on lakeside fringes in upland areas of Wales, northern England and Scotland (as well as eastwards across Europe and Asia). It is a common passage migrant at Chew, often to be seen walking along the water's edge on the Main Dam and in Heron's Green Bay. The average arrival date is 13 April, with the earliest being 1 April (in 2001). The combined monthly maxima illustrates that spring passage peaks in April and gradually tails off in May. A low point is reached in June but, even as early as 17th, the first returning adults are already heading back south. The southward migration gets into full swing in July and, although starting with the adults, the first southbound juveniles have been recorded as early as 9 July. As the autumn progresses, the proportion of juveniles inevitably increases, predominating from August onwards. Migration peaks in August and declines through September into October. By November–December, just one or two may remain. These late individuals often go on to spend the entire winter at the lake, a habit that seems to be increasing, and is likely to be related to climate change.

Common Sandpiper | Gary Thoburn

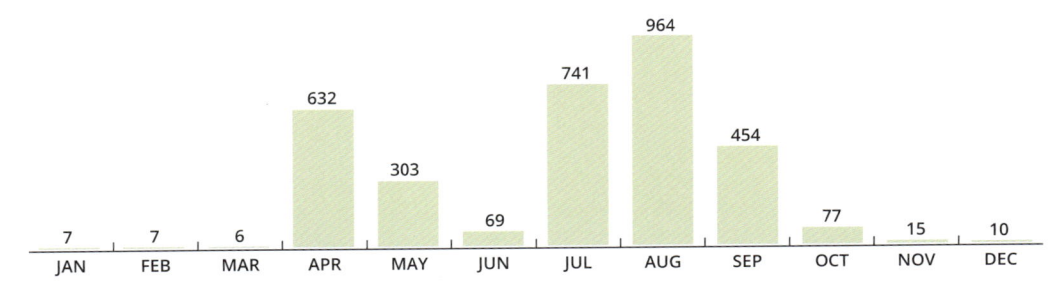

COMMON SANDPIPER | Monthly maxima (combined) 1965-2015.

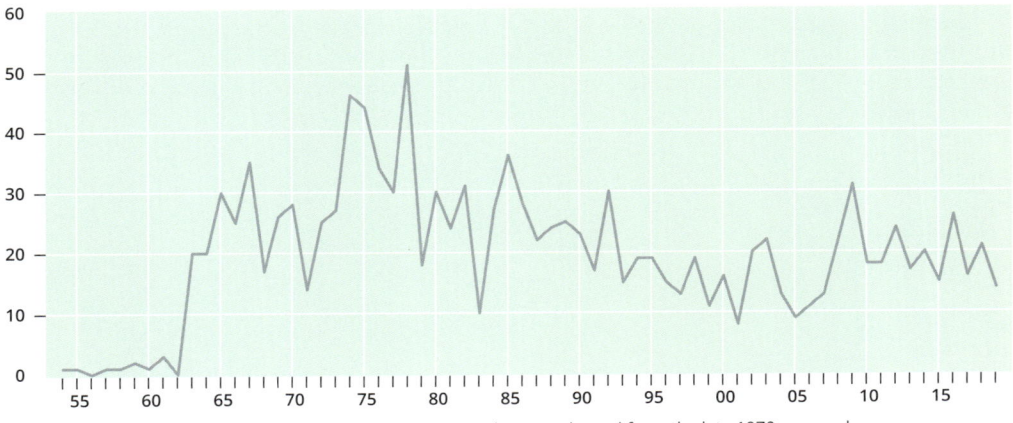

Jan 7, Feb 7, Mar 6, Apr 632, May 303, Jun 69, Jul 741, Aug 964, Sep 454, Oct 77, Nov 15, Dec 10.

COMMON SANDPIPER | Annual maxima 1954-2019. A downward trend from the late 1970s onwards.

SPOTTED SANDPIPER *Actitis macularius*

There have been three records: an adult in Heron's Green Bay on 10 and 13 October 1982 (A. H. Davis, T. A. Guyatt *et al.*); an adult in summer plumage on the Main Dam 7–9 August 2007 (KEV *et al.*); and another adult from 24 September 2011 to 21 April 2012 (A. H. Davis *et al.*). Initially, the last bird was in summer plumage and it regained it before it left in April. It departed following a fall of Common Sandpipers *A. hypoleucos*.

Spotted Sandpiper | Rich Andrews

GREEN SANDPIPER *Tringa ochropus*

The first record was one on 28 June 1953, and they were described as 'frequent July to October' in 1954, with a maximum of 7 on 15 August. On 28 August 1955, 22 were recorded, prompting the comment 'exceptionally numerous' in the 1955 *Report on Somerset Birds*. The combined monthly maxima indicates that the first adults return from Scandinavia in June, with the earliest reliable date being the 16th (in 1998). They nest in trees: usually in the old nests of thrushes or Woodpigeons *Columba palumbus* or in old squirrel dreys (*BWP*). They arrive back in Britain so early because the females often migrate before the young have fledged, leaving the males to stay behind and look after them. The earliest juveniles recorded at Chew have been on 15 July (2011). Numbers increase sharply from that point onwards, peaking in August – the maxima being 30 on 24 July 1964 and 29 on 9 August 1974. Numbers fall considerably from September onwards, although small numbers remain to winter, reaching a low point in January–February, when one or two are normally present, sometimes up to four. In December 2011, however, as many as ten were counted in Heron's Green Bay and one wonders whether some of these were feeding in streams away from the lake.

The annual maxima graph shows numbers were at their highest from the mid-1950s to the late 1970s, with a distinct downward trend since then.

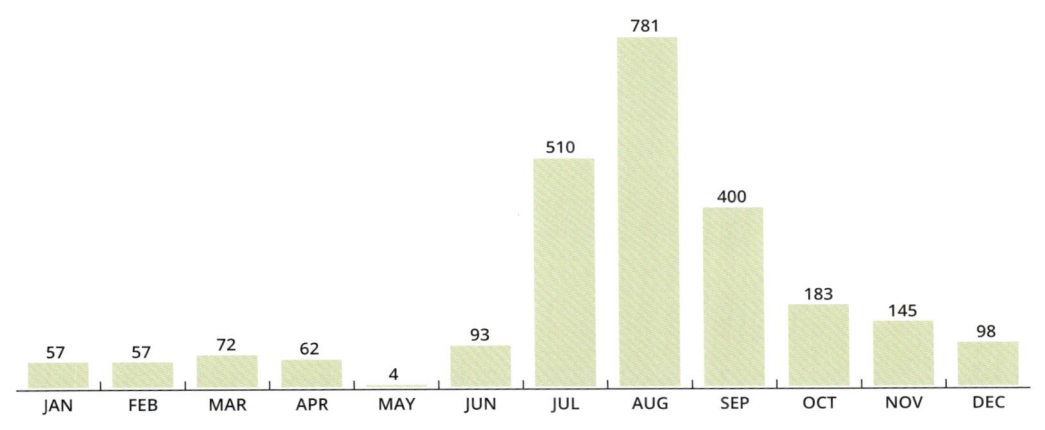

GREEN SANDPIPER | Monthly maxima (combined) 1954-2015.

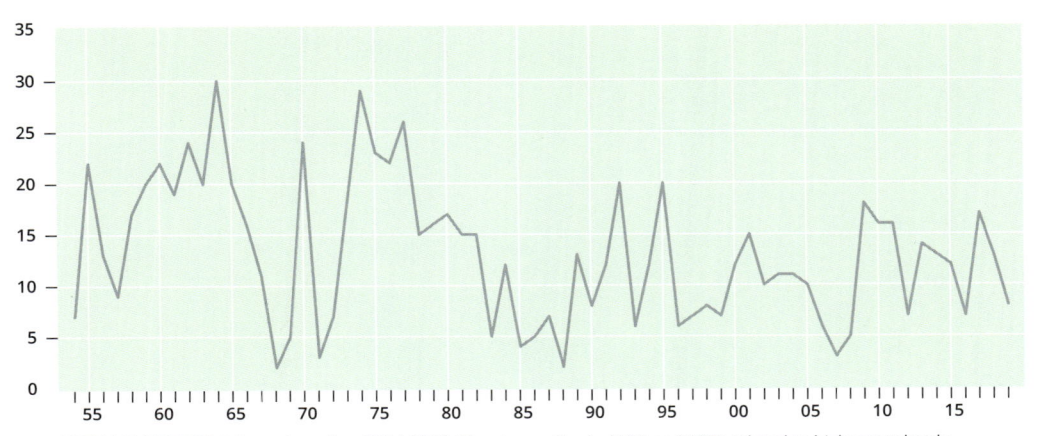

GREEN SANDPIPER | Annual maxima 1954-2019. The strong dips in 1968 and 1971 related to high water levels.

LESSER YELLOWLEGS *Tringa flavipes*

There are three records.
- **1967:** one Moreton Bank 9 September. (R. J. Johns, E. T. Welland).
- **2011:** an adult in summer plumage was seen on Herriott's Pool on 8 July, moving to Herriott's End during the evening (KEV *et al.*).
- **2020:** a juvenile was found at Stratford Bay on 1 October (R. J. Higgins *et al.*), staying until at least 2 November.

The record in 1967 has been highly controversial locally for the last 53 years. If you refer to the account by Dick Senior in Memorable Birding Moments ('Being an account of finding a rare bird') you will see that he and Keith found a wader that they could not identify, none of the possibilities being in their simple bird books, but after consulting it was put out as a Marsh Sandpiper. The next day, however, it was identified as a Wilson's Phalarope, in part because, among other features, this species has yellow legs and a square white rump, not going up between the wings as in a Marsh Sandpiper. So when a Lesser Yellowlegs was reported, a bird also with yellow legs and a squared-off rump, and then never seen again, the assumption was that this was a misidentification of the phalarope. Commonly known derogatively as the 'two bird' theory. This is despite the fact that the finders, Ron Johns and Ed Welland, were probably among the most eminent birders of the time. The record was omitted from Keith's original manuscript. So, we thought it only fair to investigate further for this book and found the report from *Proceedings of the Bristol Naturalists' Society, Bristol Bird Report*, for 1967. Not only was there an excellent description of the Lesser Yellowlegs, but under the record of the Wilson's Phalarope it was clear that Ron and Ed had seen both birds within a short time (although not together) and provided a detailed description of the differences between them. The record has always been accepted by BBRC, and we therefore acknowledge this here. (Ed.)

Lesser Yellowlegs | Paul Dunham

Lesser Yellowlegs | Paul Dunham

Lesser Yellowlegs | Karen Ash

Lesser Yellowlegs | Gary Thoburn

REDSHANK *Tringa totanus*

Although one of our commoner coastal waders, it is generally scarce inland and, at Chew, it is now entirely a passage migrant. But it was not always the case. In the early days of the lake, there was not the woodland that we have now, and much of the shoreline was covered in marshy grassland. Redshank was then a noisy and conspicuous breeding bird, having first bred in 1954 when two or three pairs were present. Numbers rose to at least six pairs the following year and the peak was in 1959, with ten pairs. Thereafter, numbers gradually declined to nine pairs in 1962, six pairs in 1964 and a single pair in 1965, when they last bred on the East Shore.

Since then the species has become a regular but somewhat erratic passage migrant, often sitting out the day on the concrete walls at the Main Dam or Heron's Green Bay or, in recent years when the water level is low, on Herriott's Pool. Most records involve ones and twos, but double-figure counts sometimes occur, although these have become much less frequent since the 1970s. This, no doubt, reflects a general decline in breeding numbers in this country at least. The highest counts since 1965 involved 16 in August 1976, 15 in September 1992, 11 in 1996, ten in 2006 and 17 in early July 1998.

There is an irregular spring passage from March to May but records become more frequent in June, when the first returning failed or post-breeding adults appear. Such records have occurred from the 12th onwards. It is, however, impossible to separate the dates of the last returning spring migrants from the first returning 'autumn' ones and this, of course, is complicated further by the movements of failed breeders. It is possible, however, that the first returning adults have appeared as early as 27 May (in 2014).

The annual maxima graph illustrates the rather erratic nature of their occurrences, the birds rarely staying at the lake for very long. Note the gradual decline in numbers, particularly from about 2000 onwards.

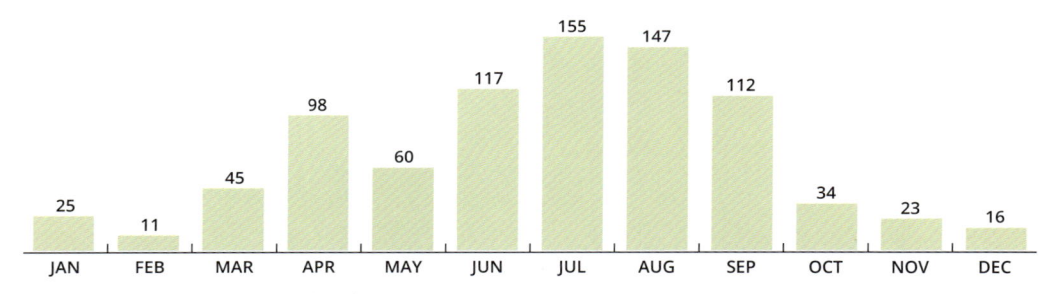

REDSHANK | Monthly maxima (combined) 1954-2015.

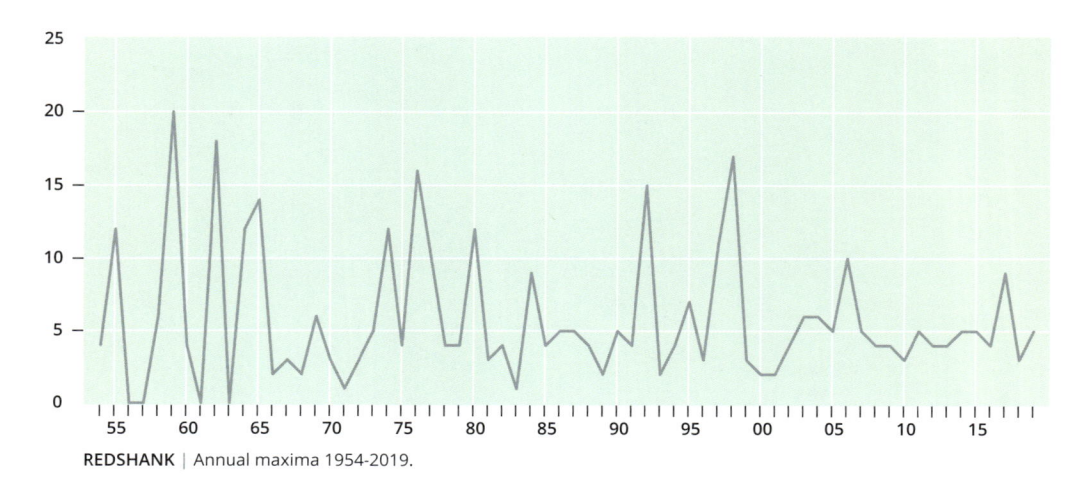

REDSHANK | Annual maxima 1954-2019.

MARSH SANDPIPER *Tringa stagnatilis*

There are two records: an adult on 3–4 October 1982, relocating to Blagdon Lake on 5–12 October (I. R. Machin, D. J. Manns, J. Taylor *et al.*) and a juvenile on 20–27 August 1984, being located and identified by call (KEV *et al.*) and moving between Chew and Blagdon. This individual had originally been seen at Cheddar Reservoir, Somerset, on the morning of 20 August (T. A. Box).

WOOD SANDPIPER *Tringa glareola*

The first Wood Sandpipers to be recorded at Chew were two, sometimes three, during 7–28 August 1954. Since then, they have missed only ten years (to 2019). They occur in small numbers – usually five or less – but higher numbers were present the 1960s, with up to seven during 6–27 August 1960 and a record eight on 11 August 1967. In more recent years, the highest counts were six on 9 September 1978 and five on 14 August 2000.

The annual maxima graph shows that the highest counts were from the late 1950s into the 1960s, and it is clear that numbers have fallen since the turn of the century. Although five were seen in 2000, it has since occurred in just 12 of the 19 years to 2019, all these records relating to single birds, with the exception of two in August and another two in September 2005.

All the autumn records have related to juveniles, with the exception of single adults on 29 July 1967, 6 July 1998, with three the following day, and 28 June 2011. Inevitably, all these were much earlier than the pulse of August juveniles.

The following combined monthly maxima graph also shows the small number of spring records: two in April (one on 28th in 1963 and another on 27th in 1996), three in May (four individuals) and two in early June (both on the 1st, in 1966 and 1970). There is a distinct increase in July, rising to a large peak in August and falling sharply through September into October, when there have been just four records. The latest was one on 5–11 October 1962.

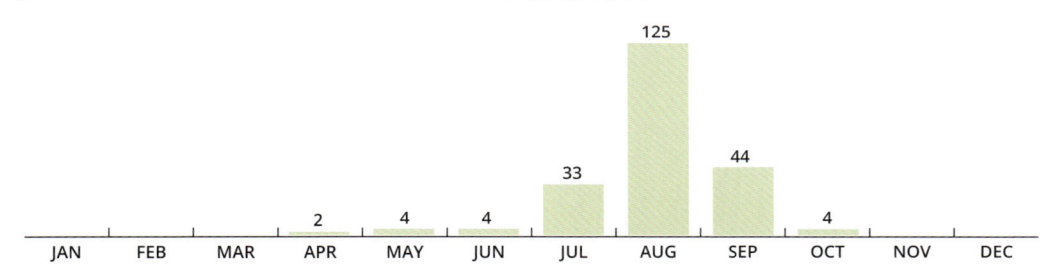

WOOD SANDPIPER | Monthly maxima (combined) 1954-2015.

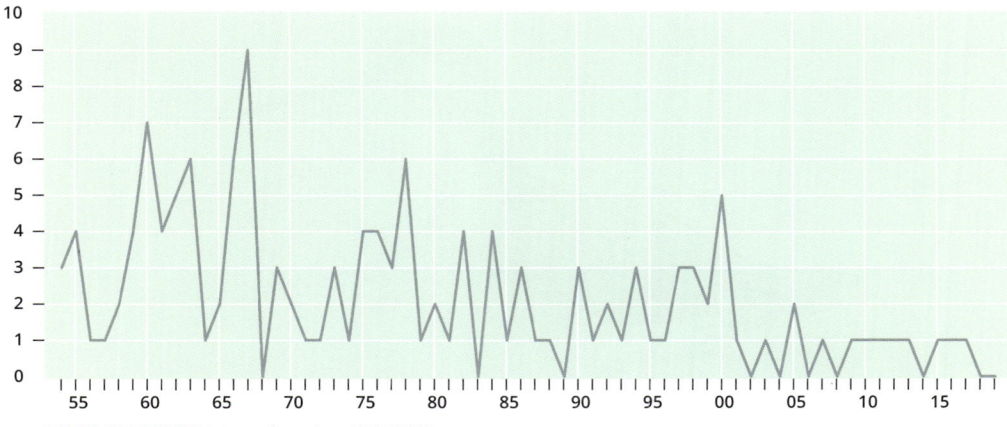

WOOD SANDPIPER | Annual maxima 1954-2019.

SPOTTED REDSHANK *Tringa erythropus*

The first records were up to five in late August and September 1955; single-figure maxima then became the norm until 1963, when 12 were counted on 6 October. In 1964, there was an even higher count of 18 on 3–4 October. Apart from 12 in August 1966, single-figure totals once again became the norm. However, as the graph below shows, annual maxima increased significantly from 1973, reaching a peak of 29 on 16 September 1978 (six winter-plumaged adults and 23 juveniles). Nineteen were recorded in September 1979, followed by yet another high count of 24 on 20 September 1980 and 36 the next day. Annual totals then declined sharply, single figures becoming the norm. There were, however, two further isolated peaks: 11 juveniles on 14 September 1991 (with ten remaining into October) and a flock of 24 on the very late date of 24 November 2011.

As the combined monthly maxima graph clearly shows, numbers peak strongly from August to October, with September being the best month. If the water levels are low, small numbers remain into November (although the average count for that month is skewed by the aforementioned flock of 24 in 2011). If the water levels are low, small numbers have sometimes remained into December (nine individuals in four winters) one of which was 'shot in error' on 21 December 1957. Three have been seen in the New Year: singles from 15 January to 12 February 1956, 24 February to 17 March 1957 and 17 December 1973 to 13 February 1974.

Small numbers have also occurred in spring. There are five for March (to 17th in 1957, 18 March 1962(2), 27 March1964 and 18 March 1986) and there have been ten recorded in April, six in May and seven in June. The June records have all involved birds still in summer plumage and they are thought to have involved early returning migrants.

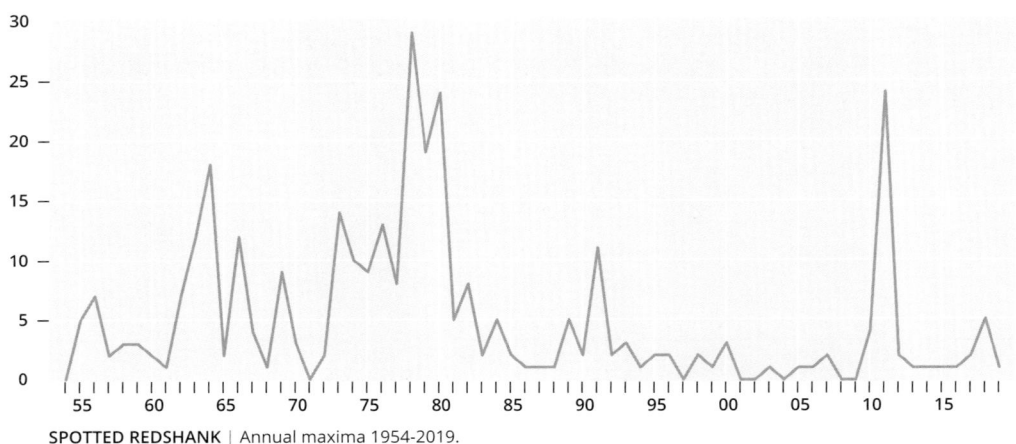

SPOTTED REDSHANK | Annual maxima 1954-2019.

Spotted Redshank | Laurel Tucker

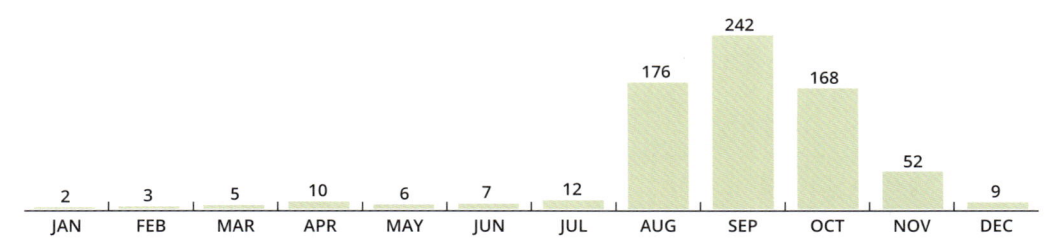

SPOTTED REDSHANK | Monthly maxima (combined) 1955-2015.

Jan 2, Feb 3, Mar 5, Apr 10, May 6, Jun 7, Jul 12, Aug 176, Sep 242, Oct 168, Nov 52, Dec 9.

GREENSHANK *Tringa nebularia*

There are records in every month except February and March. The earliest spring date is one on 2 April 2011. It is, however, infrequent in spring, with 13 records in April and 31 in May. Fourteen have been recorded in June, these appearing to relate to a mixture of late spring migrants (recorded up to 9th) and the first returning adults (recorded from 23rd), with just a two-week gap between them. Autumn passage picks up in July and peaks strongly in August, dropping slightly in September before a significant decline in October. There are only sixteen November records, with the latest on 29th (in 1964). Two have been reported in December: on 10th in 1978 and on 24th in 1973. In 1962, one was also one reported on the unusual date of 28 January, perhaps related to the severe Arctic weather at that time.

The annual maxima graph shows that numbers vary considerably from year to year. The highest counts were in 1963 (28), 1966 (25), 1974 (29), 1978 (27), 1979 (30) and 1984 (a record 33 on 18 August). The graph shows a distinct downturn from the mid-1990s onwards, to some extent probably reflecting higher summer water levels during that period.

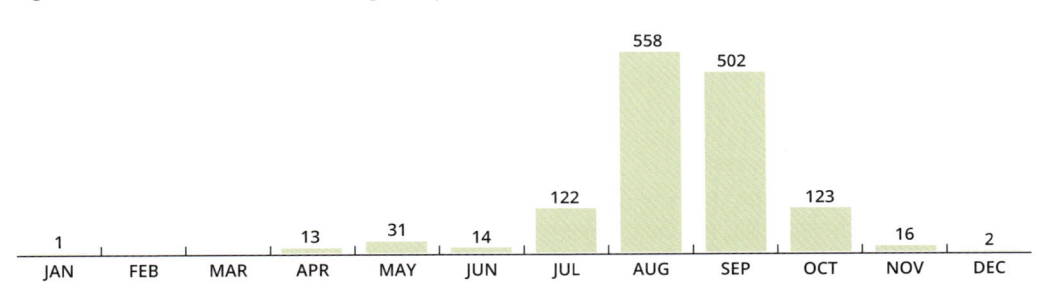

GREENSHANK | Monthly maxima (combined) 1954-2015.

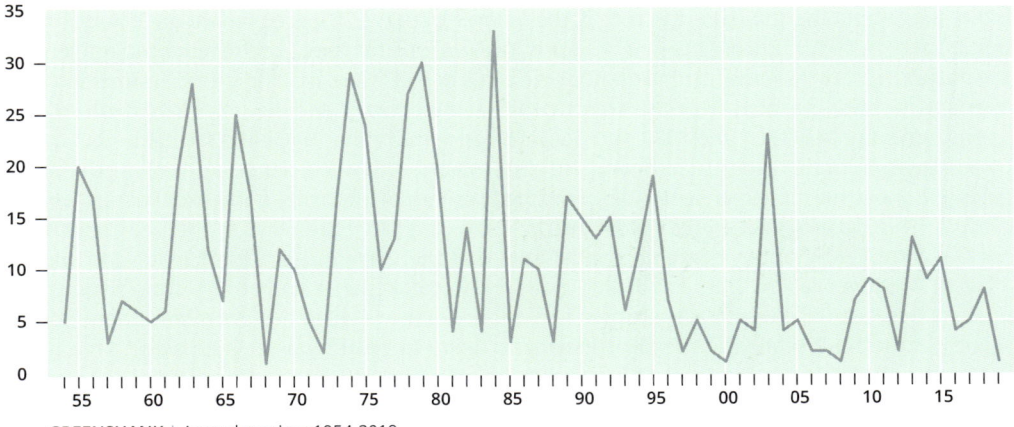

Jan 1, Apr 13, May 31, Jun 14, Jul 122, Aug 558, Sep 502, Oct 123, Nov 16, Dec 2.

GREENSHANK | Annual maxima 1954-2019.

Greenshank | Laurel Tucker

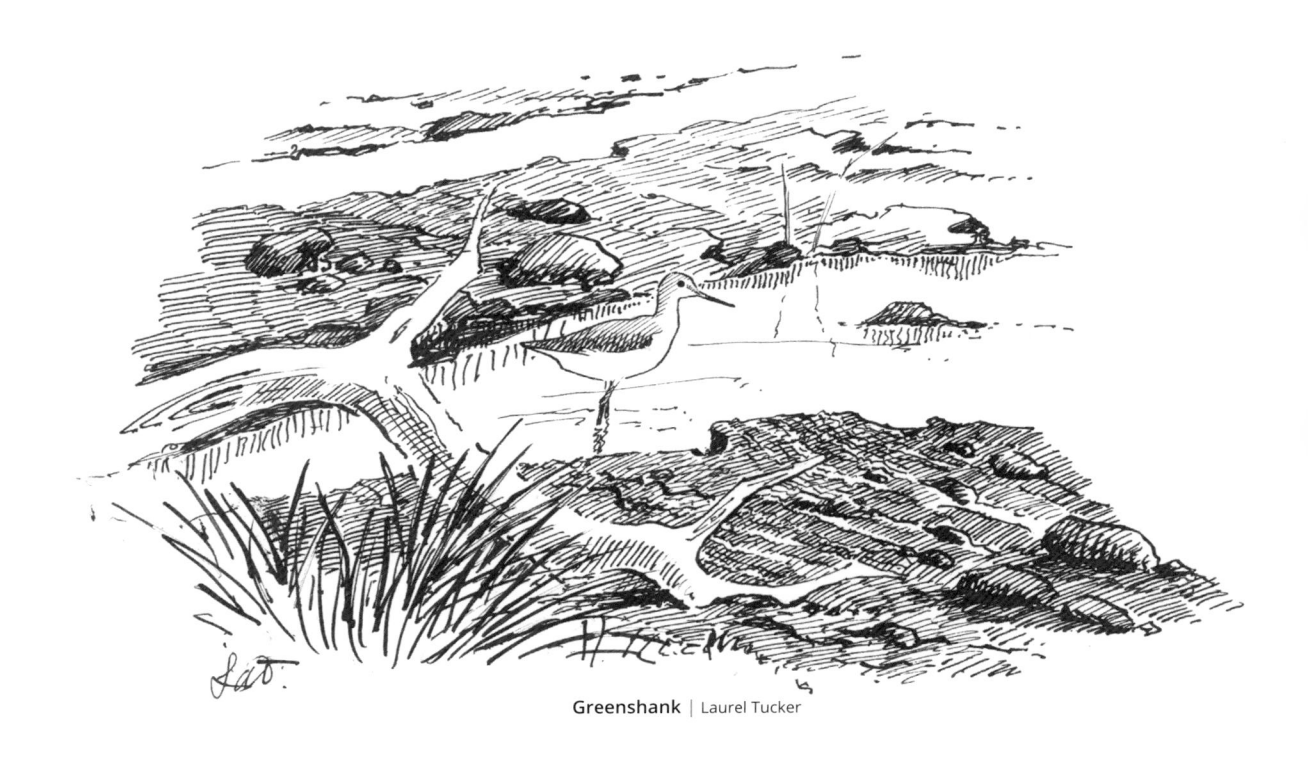

BLACK-WINGED PRATINCOLE *Glareola nordmanni*

A juvenile was present on 6–9 September 1964 (M. Latham, J. E. Squire *et al.*) and another juvenile on 28 August 1993 (S. Preddy *et al.*). The latter was originally discovered earlier in the day at Blagdon Lake (R. Abram, R. M. Andrews, A. Bone *et al.*).

KITTIWAKE *Rissa tridactyla*

As the annual maxima graph shows, Kittiwake is an irregular visitor, recorded in 48 years out of the 62 from 1954 to 2015 (77%). The vast majority of records are in single figures, with the average 'normal' maxima being five. However, on 25 October 1980 a remarkable event occurred. Two were seen during the morning but, from 17.00 hrs to 18.50 hrs a steady passage took place, with small groups flying west through Heron's Green Bay. The final total reached 72, with the largest flock being 16. These consisted of 58 adults and 14 juveniles (C. J. Newman, KEV). What was particularly interesting about this movement was that, the following spring, 50 were present on 26 April (mostly adults) and, in 1982, 18 were seen on 13 April. The reasons for these unprecedented movements are not known, but it seems highly likely that the birds in 1980 were making a deliberate east to west overland crossing, perhaps from the Wash to the Severn Estuary, and that the birds involved in the spring movements in 1981 and 1982 perhaps involved some of the 1980 birds taking the same route back. However, to contradict that theory, the birds in April 1981 occurred on a day of north-easterly gales and snow, the movement coinciding with the presence of the lake's fourth ever Fulmar *Fulmarus glacialis*. This may suggest an east–west overland crossing from the Wash to the Severn Estuary.

The combined monthly maxima graph shows that there are three records in July (an adult on 4th and two juveniles on 24th and 29th). The monthly totals then slowly rise through August to a peak in October (80 individuals) dropping to a low point in December. Numbers then increase slightly in the New Year, when records inevitably relate to winter gales. As an aside, an adult on 9–10 November 2014 spent most of its stay sitting on a flagpole at Woodford Lodge – not exactly typical habitat for an inland Kittiwake!

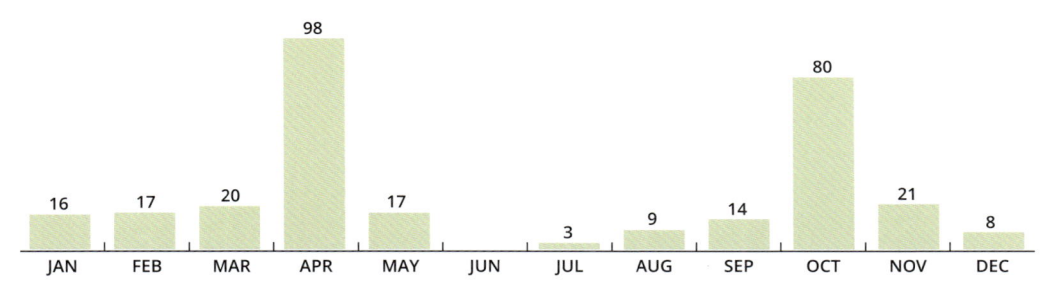

KITTIWAKE | Monthly maxima (combined) 1954-2015.

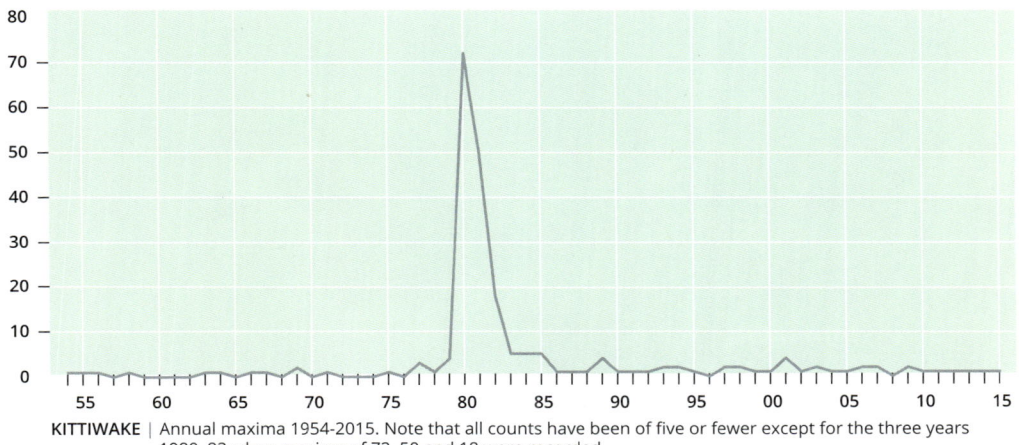

KITTIWAKE | Annual maxima 1954-2015. Note that all counts have been of five or fewer except for the three years 1980–82 when maxima of 72, 50 and 18 were recorded.

SABINE'S GULL *Xema sabini*

The first record was of an adult on 6 September 1970 (J. B. O. Rossetti, P. Andrew, R. J. Senior, KEV and R. Hemmings). Another 18 were recorded between then and 2007, all records during the period 26 August to 3 November, with most in September. The latest date involved an adult that was present from 1 to 3 November 1987. As the annual individuals graph shows, records have been erratic, dependent largely on the severity of autumnal storms, which blow them in from the Atlantic. The records have involved seven adults and 12 juveniles.

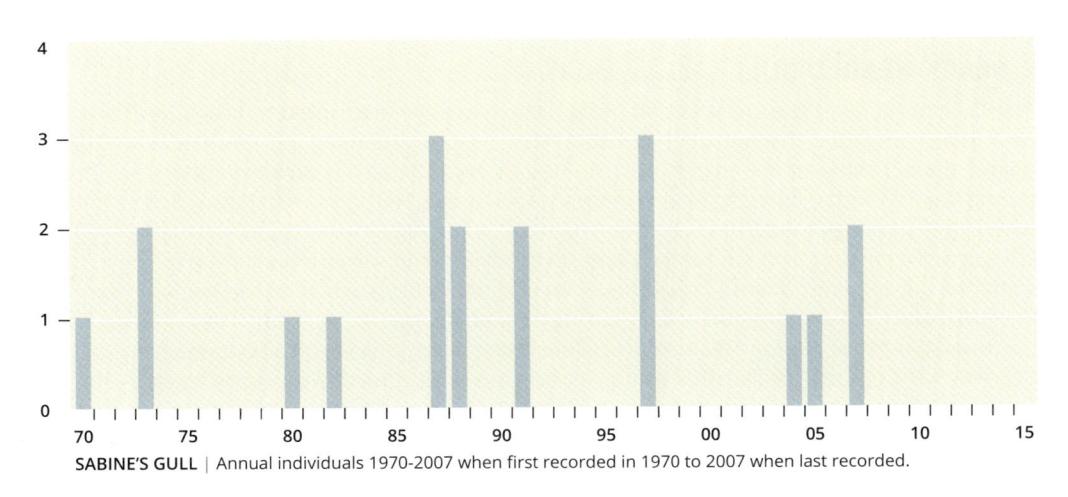

SABINE'S GULL | Annual individuals 1970-2007 when first recorded in 1970 to 2007 when last recorded.

COMPLETE SPECIES LIST AND CHARTS

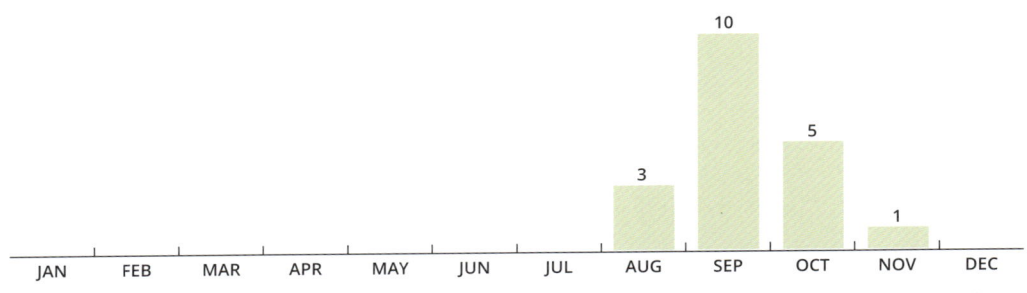

SABINE'S GULL | Monthly individuals 1970-2007. All records from 1970, when first recorded, to 2007, when last recorded.

Sabine's Gull | David Cottridge

BONAPARTE'S GULL *Chroicocephalus philadelphia*
There has been one record: an adult in summer plumage on 27 April 2013 (C. J. Stone, KEV *et al.*).

BLACK-HEADED GULL *Chroicocephalus ridibundus*
In 1954, shortly after the construction of the lake, two pairs attempted to breed, with an empty nest found on 2 June. There have been no further nesting attempts, but Black-headed Gull now enjoys the accolade of the lake's most numerous bird. Relatively small numbers are present during the day, with most hanging around Herriott's Bridge, Heron's Green Bay and the Picnic Site, where they scrounge food from the visiting public. But from late morning onwards, larger numbers start to arrive, mainly from an easterly and southerly direction. These birds fly in to roost, having spent the day feeding on farmland. Although many feed locally, such as on the Mendips, very large numbers make a daily commute from much further afield, such as Salisbury Plain. Indeed, driving north-west from the Warminster area on a winter's afternoon, one soon starts to see flocks of Black-headed and Common Gulls *Larus canus* heading resolutely north-westwards towards the lake. This movement must involve a daily round trip of 50–60 miles. They then leave the roost first thing in the morning, as it starts to get light.

These are mainly winter visitors from the Continent, with ringing recoveries often involving birds from the Baltic. The roost develops from mid-June, soon after the birds have finished breeding, and numbers increase from then onwards. There can be little doubt that Black-headed Gull has increased considerably since the construction of the lake but, even as long ago as 1962, there were roost counts of up to 7,000. Subsequent winter counts have produced very approximate totals of 17,650 in December 1979, 28,800 in January 1983, 36,350 in January 1993 and 29,800 in January 2004. These counts were made as the birds flew in to roost.

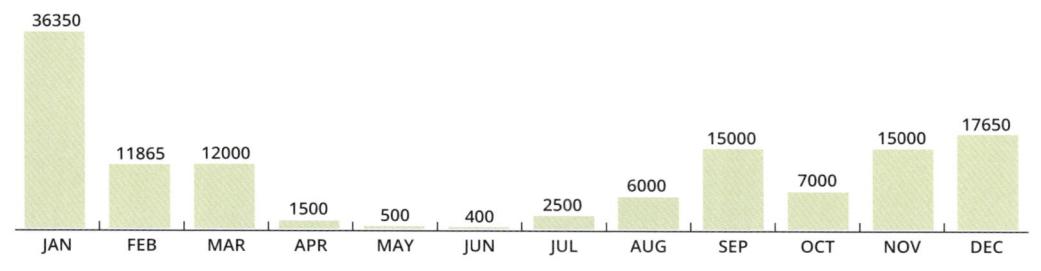

JAN	FEB	MAR	APR	MAY	JUN	JUL	AUG	SEP	OCT	NOV	DEC
36350	11865	12000	1500	500	400	2500	6000	15000	7000	15000	17650

BLACK-HEADED GULL | Monthly maxima 1954-2015.

Black-headed Gull | Laurel Tucker

LITTLE GULL *Hydrocoloeus minutus*

This was a scarce species during the 1950s and early 1960s. The first record was of a first-winter on 26 December 1957, rather surprisingly remaining to 23 March 1958. Later that year, a juvenile was seen on 2–3 September, but was found dead on 8th. Following two in 1960, it became annual from 1963 onwards, but it was not until 1971 that the first double-figure counts were made, when up to 13 were present in April–May. Subsequently, double-figure counts were made in 15 of the next 45 years, with maxima of 74 on 1 May 1984 – during a fresh to moderate easterly wind – and 67 the following day during an evening thunderstorm. These were considered to have been additional to the 74 the day before (J. Aldridge, A. H. Davis).

Further high counts involved, 38 on 28 April 1995, 25 on 6 and 10 April 2010 and 34 on 25 April 2012.

The combined monthly maxima graph shows that it has been recorded in every month, but with a spring passage from March to May (with a strong peak in April). Small numbers have occurred in May and June, slowly increasing from July to a late summer/autumn peak in August and September, tailing off through October and November to a low point in December.

Of those aged, 39% were adults, 30% were juveniles, 28% were first-years but just 3% were second-years.

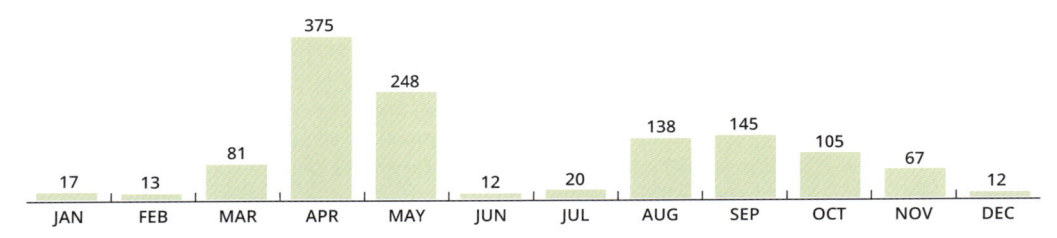

LITTLE GULL | Monthly maxima (combined) 1957-2016.

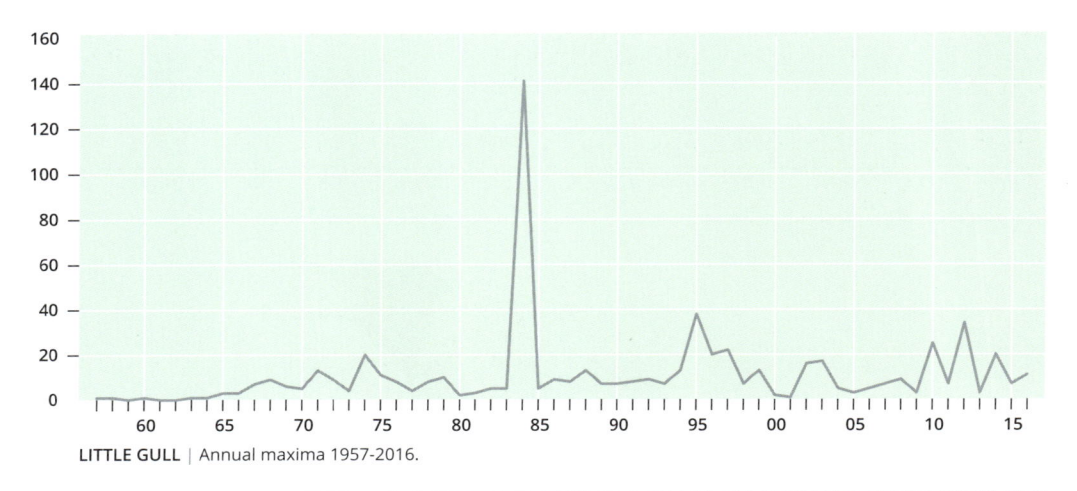

Jan 17, Feb 13, Mar 81, Apr 375, May 248, Jun 12, Jul 20, Aug 138, Sep 145, Oct 105, Nov 67, Dec 12.

LITTLE GULL | Annual maxima 1957-2016.

Little Gull | Ian Stapp

ROSS'S GULL *Rhodostethia rosea*

A second-winter was seen in the gull roost from Nunnery Point on 3 March 1985 before flying across the lake and landing off the East Shore (R. J. Higgins, L. A. Tucker, KEV *et al.*).

This record was adjudged 'Not Proven' by BBRC, but given the observers, has been included. *(Ed.)*

LAUGHING GULL *Leucophaeus atricilla*

An adult in summer plumage was located and identified by call as it flew from the main lake and over Herriott's Bridge at 09.00 hrs on 17 April 2006. It then circled around before gradually drifting off to the south-east (B. Laughton, R. Mielcarek, C. J. Stone, KEV). It was seen during a remarkable influx of the species during the winter of 2005–2006, when 73 were recorded nationally. This was caused by Hurricane Wilma, an intense storm that wreaked havoc in the Caribbean and the Gulf of Mexico before sweeping up the American Eastern Seaboard at the end of October, reaching the south-west approaches at the end of the month (Fraser *et al.* 2007).

Another, this time a first-winter, was discovered and photographed by B. Thompson on 10 March 2020. It was seen again the following day and was greatly appreciated by large numbers of birders, some of whom had travelled some distance. Last seen on 15th, it was relocated on Cheddar Reservoir in Somerset the next day.

Reference:
Fraser, P. A., Rogers, M. J. and the Rarities Committee. 'Report on rare birds in Great Britain in 2005'. Part 1: non-passerines. *British Birds* 100: 16–61.

Laughing Gull | Brian Thompson

FRANKLIN'S GULL *Leucophaeus pipixcan*

A second-winter was seen on Herriott's Pool on 19 January 2008 (J. C. C. Oliver). News of this bird did not reach the local birding community but it was relocated independently the following day, again on Herriott's Pool (KEV *et al.*). It was seen again on 29–31 January, 12–17 February and 23–24 and 27–28 March. Its movements were in fact well monitored as it wandered around and eventually moved north through the country:

13 January:	Torr Reservoir, Somerset.
17 January:	Wareham, Dorset.
15–16 March:	Royal Portbury Dock.
18–23 March:	Somerdale, near Keynsham.
25 March:	Torr Reservoir, Somerset.
26 March:	Blagdon Lake.
7 April:	Newnham-on-Severn, Gloucestershire.
16–21 April:	Brandon Marsh and Draycote Water, Warwickshire.

MEDITERRANEAN GULL *Icthyaetus melanocephalus*

Although there had been reports of this species since 1966, the next authenticated record was an adult in the roost from 4 November to 27 December 1977 (KEV *et al.*). Since then, it has been recorded annually, numbers gradually increasing from the single in 1977 to double figure counts of 11 in March 2005 and 14 in February 2015.

As the combined monthly maxima graph shows, it has been recorded in every month, with a low point in May (just five records) gradually rising through June to a post-breeding peak in July. Numbers then dip slightly, levelling off from August to October, but increasing through the winter to a late winter/early spring peak in February and March. At that time of year, summer-plumaged adults in the roost can frequently be heard giving their atmospheric calls, and displaying pairs have also been seen. Numbers then drop sharply into April.

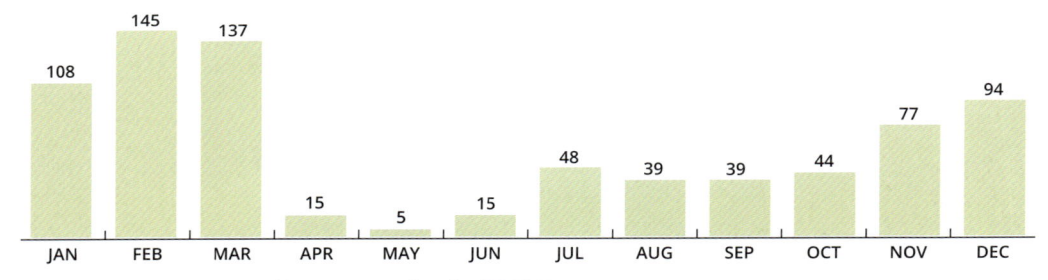

MEDITERRANEAN GULL | Monthly maxima (combined) 1977-2016.

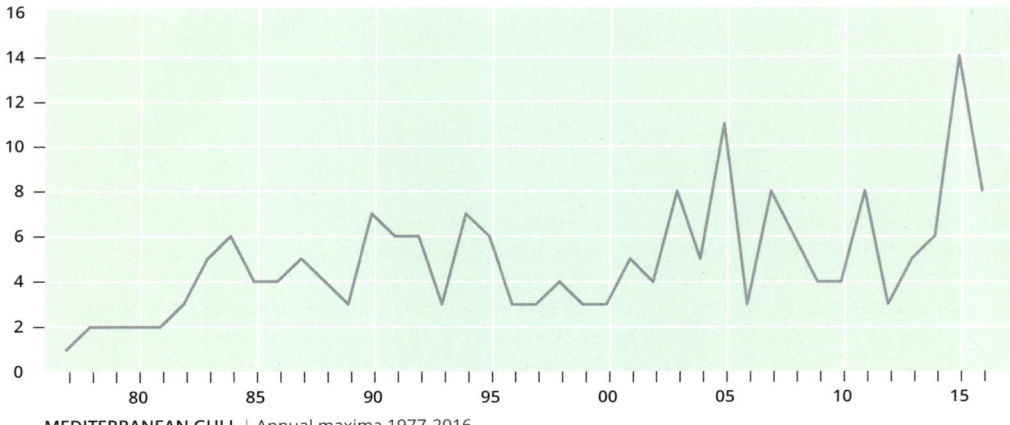

JAN	FEB	MAR	APR	MAY	JUN	JUL	AUG	SEP	OCT	NOV	DEC
108	145	137	15	5	15	48	39	39	44	77	94

MEDITERRANEAN GULL | Annual maxima 1977-2016.

The reason for the February–March peak is difficult to understand, but it has been suggested that it may involve birds that have wintered in Ireland and Wales returning to their colonies in southern England and/or the continent. There have, however, been four interesting sightings of colour-ringed individuals, which illustrate how the birds wander outside the breeding season:

1. A first-winter on 18 January 1986 had been ringed on the Baltic island of Langen Werder, Germany, in the period 17–23 June 1985 (*per* K. J. Hall/*ABR*).
2. A juvenile on 12–15 July 1995 was ringed as a chick at Noordplaat, Zeeland, The Netherlands, on 18 May and was subsequently seen in Finistère, France, on 6 March 1996.
3. A first-summer on 12–15 July 1996 was ringed as a chick at Noordplaat, Zeeland, on 24 June 1994; it was seen subsequently in Plymouth on 8 January 1995, back in Zeeland on 18–25 May 1995, at Poole Harbour, Dorset, on 21 October 1995 and at Radipole Lake, Dorset, on 10 December 1995 (*ABR*).
4. An adult on 20 January 2020 had been ringed at Solvesbourg in Southern Sweden on 11 June 2019 (the first from Sweden).

Of 285 that have been aged, 55% were adults, 9.5% were juveniles, 19.6% were first-years and 16.1% were second-years.

Mediterranean Gull | Ian Stapp

COMMON GULL *Larus canus*

This rather gentle medium-sized gull is basically a winter visitor, originating in northern Europe: Scotland, Scandinavia, Finland and eastwards into Russia. The first point to make is that it is not called 'Common Gull' because it is the commonest gull – it is so called simply because of its tendency to feed on common land. Unlike the larger 'seagulls', the vast majority of the Common Gulls at Chew spend the day on pasture, mainly on the Mendips, and possibly coming from as far away as the Cotswolds or even Salisbury Plain, where they feed on earthworms and other invertebrates.

After feeding, they start to return to the lake from late morning onwards and, during the late afternoon, very large numbers can be seen flying in to roost along well-established flight lines, mainly from the south. In winter, it is usually the second most abundant bird at the lake after Black-headed Gull *Chroicocephalus ridibundus*, and the Chew roost is one of the most important in the country for this species.

As early as 1962 there had been roost counts of 2,000 and, by 1966, totals had reached 5,000. By 1974, 10,000 were estimated and, by 1977, the total had risen to 15,000. These early estimates proved to be surprisingly accurate as, in December 1979, a coordinated roost count took place, with teams of counters strategically stationed under incoming flight lines. This produced a much more accurate total of 12,800, followed by an amazingly similar 12,900 four years later. By January 1993, the total had reached a record 18,710, with a very similar count of 18,200 in January 2004.

Wintering birds return to the continent in early spring and the vast majority have left by the end of March. In 1986, for example, there were still 2,000 in early April but an abrupt final departure took place on 11th–12th. Very small numbers remain into May but all the June counts are in single figures, the majority at this time relating to first-summers that did not migrate. The first returning adults have appeared as early as 18 June (2002) and the first juveniles from 22 July (1991). The winter visitors start to appear in force from as early as 20 September.

In August 2004 a ringed adult was photographed at Herriott's Bridge. It has since been seen every year to at least 2017, meaning that it was at that point at least 15 years old.

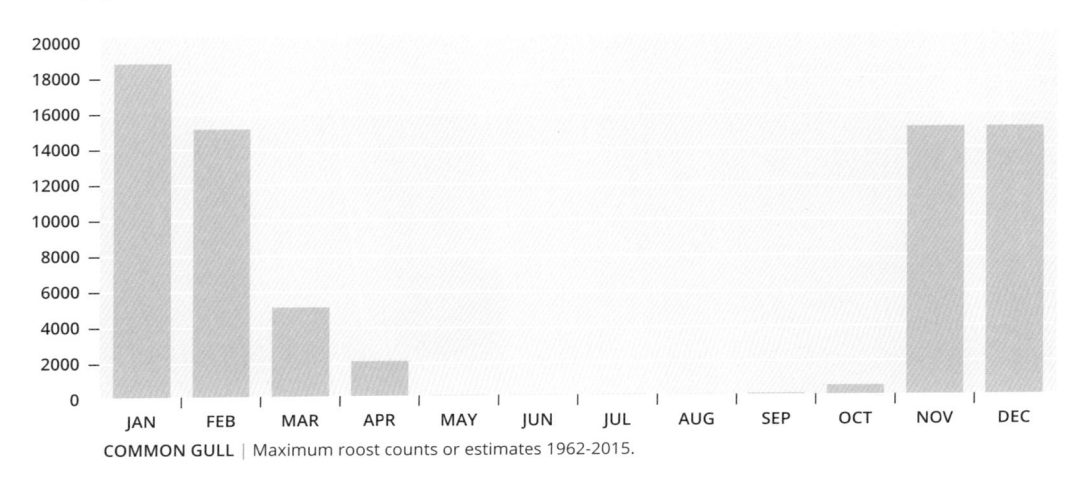

COMMON GULL | Maximum roost counts or estimates 1962-2015.

Common Gull | Ian Stapp

RING-BILLED GULL *Larus delawarensis*

The first British record was in 1973 but it seems highly likely that the species had been overlooked prior to then. The first Chew record was an adult on 22 March 1980 (C. J. Newman, KEV) followed eight days later by a first-winter on 30 March (T. P. Andrews, R. A. Barrett, S. A. Webb). The species was then recorded in 28 of the next 37 years. As the annual individuals graph shows, most of the records relate to single birds but 12 years produced two and there were three in 1985, 1986 and 1988, as well as three adults in 2017.

Working out the number of individuals is difficult, but the age ratios are: 73% adults, 13% 1st-years and 14% 2nd-years, although it is highly likely that some of these non first-years were returnees from previous years. The most famous such bird was a first-winter that first appeared on Herriott's Pool on Boxing Day in 1986. It then returned every winter until 1 April 1992, when he was almost six years old. For some reason he was nick-named 'Harvey', but the reason for this has long been lost in the ether! Harvey's earliest arrival date was 12 November and his latest spring date was 13 May, but he was a first-summer then. In his adult years his spring departure dates spanned the period 25 March to 6 April.

Ring-billed Gull | Rich Andrews

Another interesting record involved an adult that was discovered walking along the road to Woodford Lodge on 3 January 2012. By its size and structure it was clearly a rather small and petite female, but she had an injury to the underside of her left wing. She eventually took up residence at the Picnic Site, where she remained until 23 February, by which time she had fully recovered. She was not seen subsequently until March 2017, when she returned to the Picnic Site – photographs suggest that it was the same individual.

One was recorded in 2018 and two in 2019.

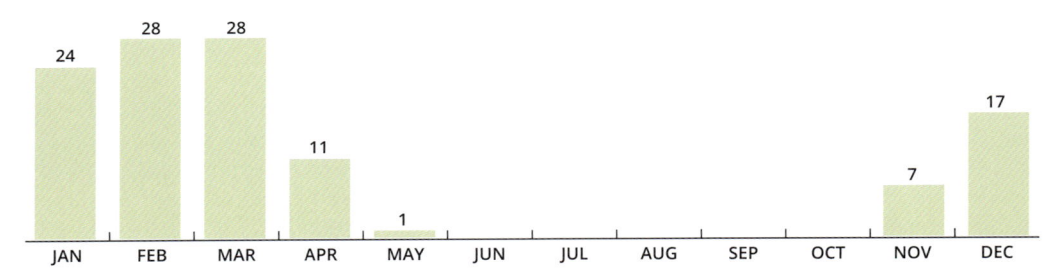

RING-BILLED GULL | Monthly totals of individuals (combined) 1980-2019.

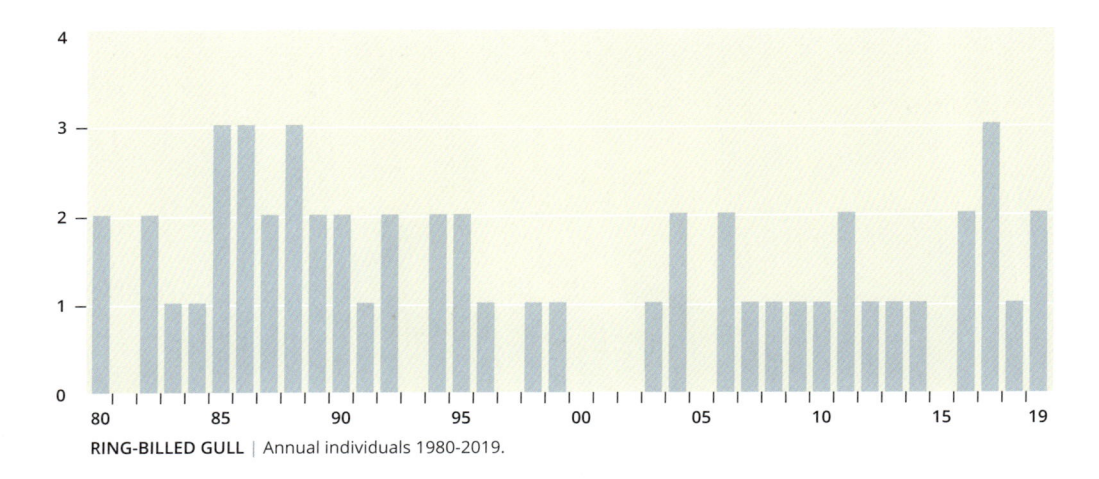

RING-BILLED GULL | Annual individuals 1980-2019.

| GREAT BLACK-BACKED GULL *Larus marinus*

The combined monthly maxima graph shows that this species is present all year, with a distinct peak in August–September. This corresponds with the annual increase in numbers caused by the year's influx of juveniles. Also, at this time of year, the water levels drop to their lowest levels, which concentrates the fish.

As the annual maxima graph shows, numbers from the mid-1970s until recently were in single figures with a peak of eight in 1995. Since 2005, however, numbers have suddenly increased, reaching a record 36 in September 2011. This up-turn is thought to be due entirely to the introduction of Pike, some of which are enormous (the current record is 44lb 6oz, in February 2014). The Great Black-backs do not kill the fish, but they scavenge on the dead ones that float to the surface. The birds are, of course, opportunists and, since the introduction of Pike, the numbers of breeding grebes, wildfowl and coots have plummeted, and it is thought likely that the increase in Great Black-backs – as well as other predators – has exacerbated this problem.

There has been a successful breeding attempt, on Herriott's Pool in 2013.

The pie graph age ratios relate to the period 1990–2015.

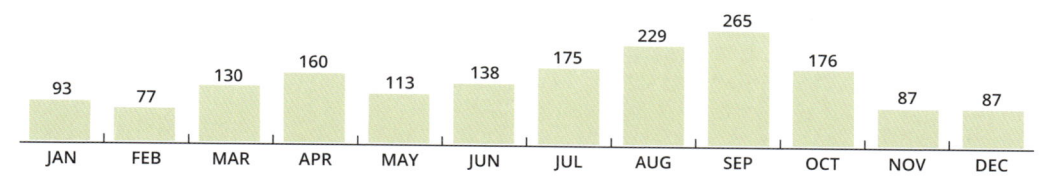

GREAT BLACK-BACKED GULL | Monthly maxima (combined) 1954-2016.

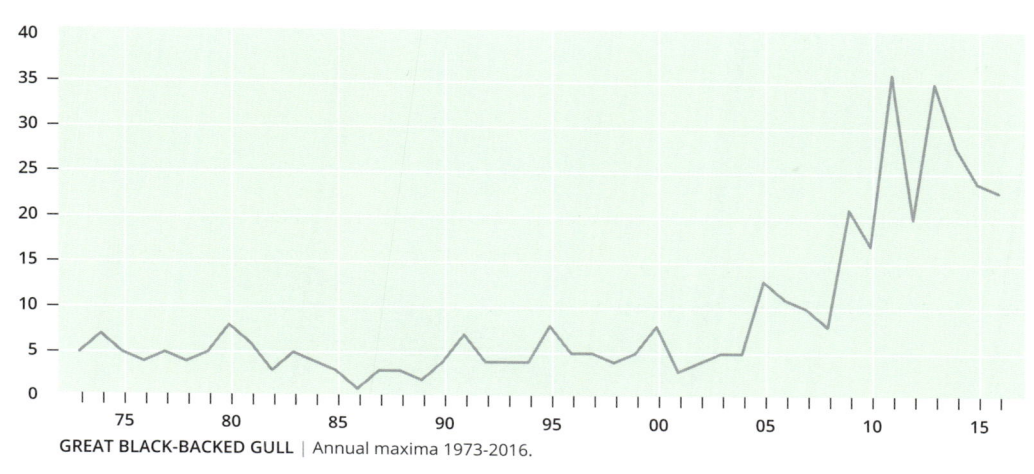

GREAT BLACK-BACKED GULL | Annual maxima 1973-2016.

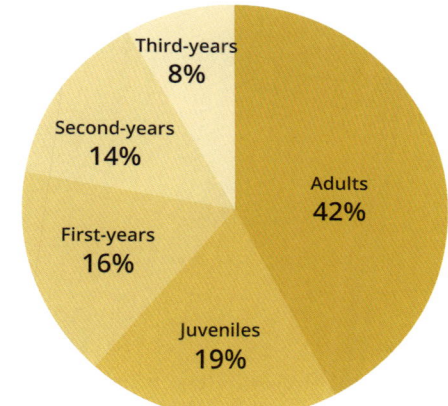

GREAT BLACK-BACKED GULL | Age ratios in the period 1990–2015.

GLAUCOUS GULL *Larus hyperboreus*

This is a rare bird at Chew, with 15 records. The first, probably a third-year, was seen on 13 March 1955 (B. King). There was then a 14-year gap before the next: a juvenile on 16 February 1969. Since then there have been a further 13 records to 2014. As the combined monthly maxima graph indicates, records have occurred from 11 December (1977) to 28 April (2002), with peaks of four in December, February and five in March.

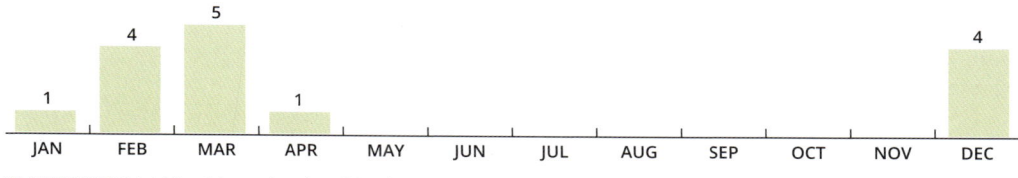

GLAUCOUS GULL | Monthly maxima (combined) 1955-2014.

COMPLETE SPECIES LIST AND CHARTS

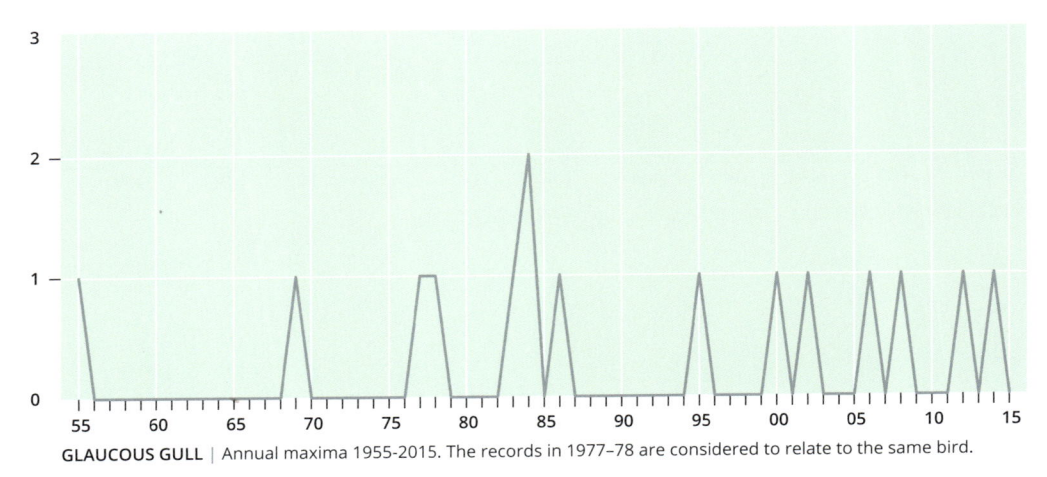

GLAUCOUS GULL | Annual maxima 1955-2015. The records in 1977–78 are considered to relate to the same bird.

Glaucous Gull | Laurel Tucker

ICELAND GULL *Larus glaucoides*

The annual maxima graph indicates that Iceland Gull is an erratic winter visitor, with 42 records in total. There are definite influx years that, to some extent, seem to relate to the frequency of north-westerly gales in late winter. The first record involved an immature on 31 March and 1 April 1961 (P. J. Chadwick, M. A. Wright). Thirteen of the subsequent records have related to singles, but with two in February 1983, four in February 1984, three in 1990, two in January 2002 and three in February 2014. Only 6 of the birds were adults, one of which was in 2019.

As the combined monthly maxima graph shows, there are two records of singles in November and December but the peak time is from January to April, with a peak in February and March. The earliest date was a juvenile on 28 November 1987 and the latest was a second-year on and off from 11 April to 19 May 1973.

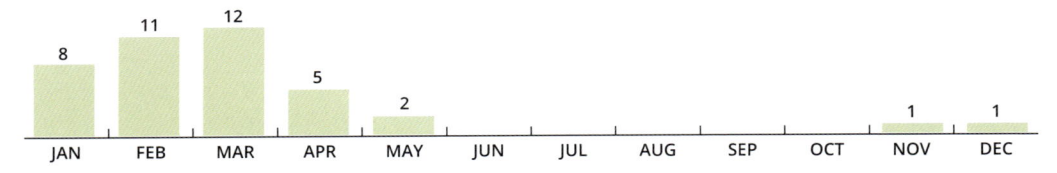

ICELAND GULL | Monthly maxima (combined) 1961-2019.

ICELAND GULL | Annual maxima 1961-2019.

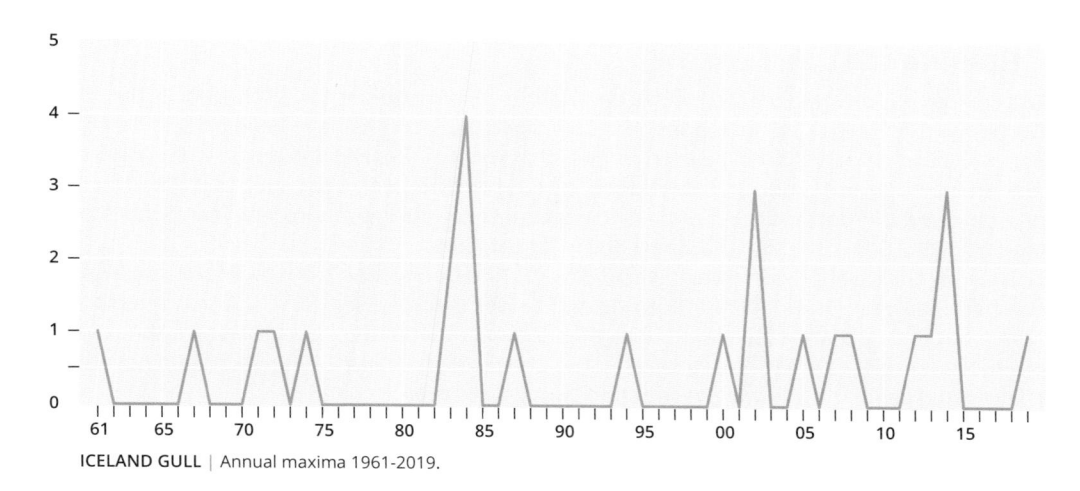

Iceland Gull | Keith Vinicombe

KUMLIEN'S GULL *Larus glaucoides kumlieni*

Kumlien's Gull is the North American race of the Iceland Gull, breeding in north-eastern Canada on Baffin Island as well as on the north-west Ungava Peninsula. The first accepted British record at the time was an adult seen from Moreton Hide on the evening of 16 April 1982 (A. J. Merritt, KEV *et al.*). A second-winter was then seen on 13 and 31 December 1997. An adult then appeared in January 2002, February–March 2003, February–March and December 2004, February and December 2005 and January–February 2006. Between 2003 and 2011, what was almost certainly the same individual was also seen at various sites in Gloucestershire, sometimes roosting at the Cotswold Water Park. What was presumably the same adult was seen again at Chew in February-March 2011 and in March 2014. Other records include a second-winter in 2000 and an adult in 2017.

In addition one Kumlien's/Thayer's Gull *L. (g.) thayeri* type has been seen: a juvenile in Heron's Green Bay on 4 February 1990 (R. J. Higgins, A. J. Merritt).

HERRING GULL *Larus argentatus*

The first records involved roost counts of up to 750 in 1954, increasing to 1,000 in June 1956, 2,000 in December 1962 and 3,000 in September 1969. Since then, counts have been erratic, the highest being 3,400 in January 2004. Unlike other gulls that roost at the lake, most of the Herring Gulls fly in from the north, indicating that they spend the day in Bristol, where the species is now a common breeding bird on rooftops around the city. Peak roost counts in more recent years were 1,000 in March 2002, 2,000 in March 2011 and 3,400 in January 2004.

Herring Gulls were reported to have bred in 1957 on Denny Island, but no figures are available. The following year, 30–50 pairs of Herring and Lesser Black-backed Gulls *L. fuscus* attempted to breed, but the eggs were collected. It was then 57 years before the next breeding attempt: a pair produced two chicks in 2015 on a small island on Herriott's Pool, but the young did not survive. They nested again the following year but no young were seen.

Herring Gulls of the nominate Scandinavian race (*L. a. argentatus*) have been identified in the roost, with up to three in January–February 1984, but such birds are undoubtedly overlooked. They were then seen almost annually until 2012, but with only one record since, on 18 February 2019.

CASPIAN GULL *Larus cachinnans*

There have been 12 records of this species, which breeds from the Black Sea into central Asia:
- **2002:** a second-summer/third-winter on 25 September (KEV).
- **2004:** an adult on 26 September.
- **2006:** a third-winter intermittently from 4 to 28 January and an adult on 17 January and 9 February.
- **2007:** a first-winter on 13 and 20 January and again on 24 February.
- **2008:** a first-winter on 12 October.
- **2013:** a first-winter on 11 January.
- **2016:** a second-summer/third-winter on 9 August.
- **2017:** a first-winter on 17 and 26 January and a second-winter on 14 November.
- **2018:** a second calendar year bird on 31 May and 1 June.
- **2019:** a third calendar year bird on 21 March.

YELLOW-LEGGED GULL *Larus michahellis*

The first report was of an adult in the roost on 7 February 1978 (KEV), although thought to be possibly a Herring Gull / Lesser Black-backed Gull hybrid, the search for this species having been prompted by a paper by R. A. Hume entitled 'Variations in Herring Gulls at a Midland roost' (*British Birds* 71: 338–345). From that date onwards, Yellow-legged Gulls have been seen annually. Although the first records were in the winter gull roost, from 1980 onwards, the species began to be seen mainly from July to September, with a peak in August, and this has proved to be its main period of occurrence (see combined monthly maxima graph). The species can, however, be seen throughout the year, with small numbers from November to January, fewer from February to May, with numbers rising significantly in June to the August peak. Numbers remain high into October but gradually decrease during the winter to a low point in April.

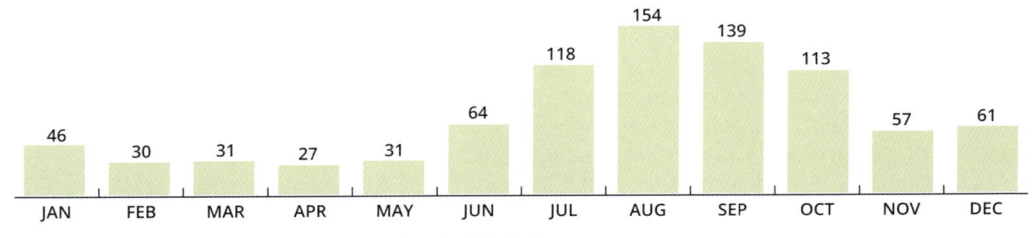

JAN	FEB	MAR	APR	MAY	JUN	JUL	AUG	SEP	OCT	NOV	DEC
46	30	31	27	31	64	118	154	139	113	57	61

YELLOW-LEGGED GULL | Monthly maxima (combined) 1978-2016.

Yellow-legged Gull   Ian Stapp

The annual maxima graph shows the maxima from 1978 to 2016. Once people began to identify the species with increased confidence, including those in immature plumages, the numbers seen annually increased significantly, reaching a peak of 12 in 1992. There are also counts of 15 in 2002 and 10 in 2013.

From 1999, an analysis of specifically aged Yellow-legged Gulls seen at the lake yielded the results as shown in the pie chart below.

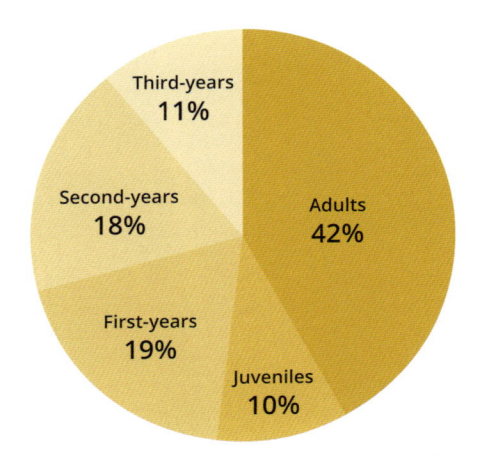

YELLOW-LEGGED GULL | Analysis of specifically aged Yellow-legged Gulls.

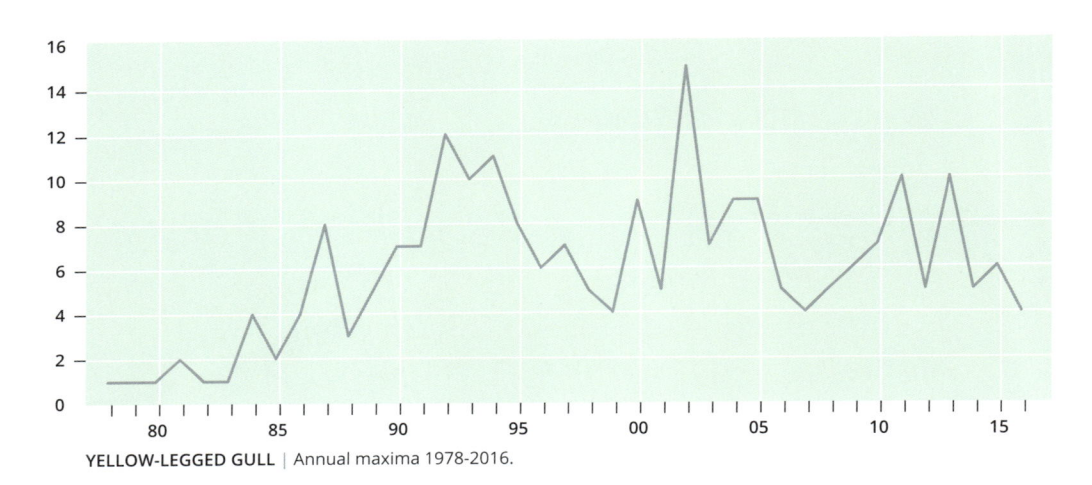

- Adults 42%
- Third-years 11%
- Second-years 18%
- First-years 19%
- Juveniles 10%

YELLOW-LEGGED GULL | Annual maxima 1978-2016.

On 1 September 1997, a second/third-year type showed an extensive and heavily streaked grey head, and an adult on 18 September 2016 also showed a hood of fine grey streaking. A similar adult was seen well and photographed in Heron's Green Bay on 22 November 2017. It is thought quite likely that all these birds were of the Azorean race *atlanticus,* although the 2017 bird has been deemed 'not proven' by BBRC. This suggests that the identification of this race is not yet fully understood.

However, one that was seen from 2016 to at least February 2020 was ringed as a chick at Sempech in Switzerland on 25 May 2016, giving an indication of the origin of at least some of the Yellow-legged Gulls seen at Chew.

Since 2005, there have also been nine records of Yellow-legged Gulls that have shown characters of the south-west Iberian form '*lusitanius*'. This small, short-legged, stubby-billed form has not currently been given sub-specific status.

LESSER BLACK-BACKED GULL *Larus fuscus*

In the early years (1955–1979) this species quite frequently bred, with mixed success, on the ephemeral 'Little Denny Island' and, occasionally, on Denny Island itself:

- **1955:** 12 pairs, but only three young were reared.
- **1956:** a maximum of 17 occupied nests.
- **1957:** breeding reported again.
- **1958:** 30–50 pairs of Herrings *L. argentatus* and Lesser Black-backs but only two juveniles were seen, most of the eggs being collected by the then Bristol Waterworks Company.
- **1962:** three pairs bred.
- **1963:** adult with three chicks.
- **1976:** at least six pairs with five large chicks on 1 August.
- **1977:** about 15 pairs present.
- **1978:** pair with three young.
- **1979:** an incubating female was seen.

The monthly maxima graph shows the maximum recorded count for the respective months but note that the February and November counts are much too low, there being no reliable estimates for those months. Nevertheless, the graph shows a large peak in January.

Since the roost counts are erratic, the table below shows the decadal maxima. The species has clearly increased significantly, this being related to the large roof top colonies that are now well established in central Bristol and Bath.

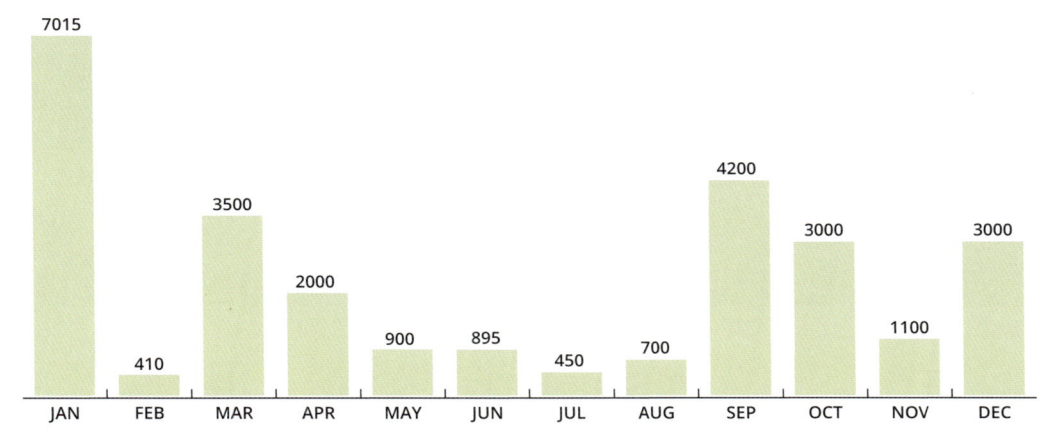

LESSER BLACK-BACKED GULL | Monthly maxima 1954-2015.

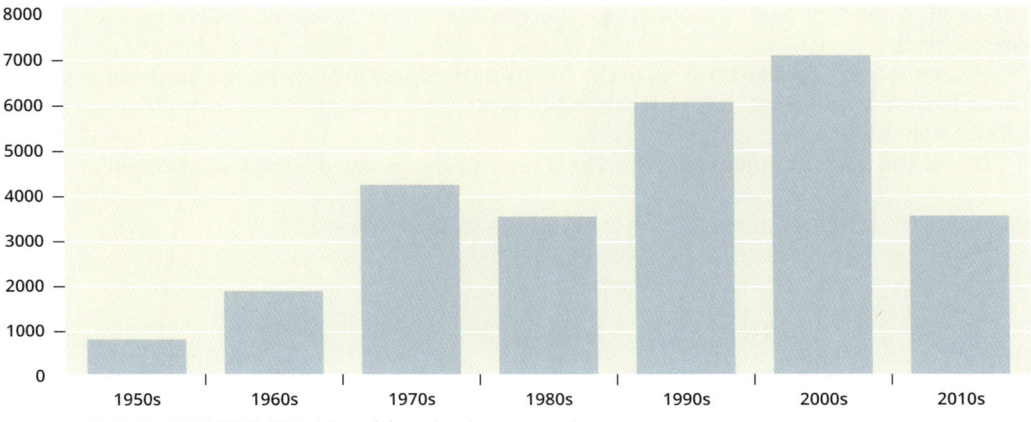

Month	JAN	FEB	MAR	APR	MAY	JUN	JUL	AUG	SEP	OCT	NOV	DEC
Max	7015	410	3500	2000	900	895	450	700	4200	3000	1100	3000

LESSER BLACK-BACKED GULL | Decadal maxima (roost counts).

Decade	1950s	1960s	1970s	1980s	1990s	2000s	2010s
Max	~800	~1900	~4300	~3600	~6100	~7100	~3600

Scandinavian race *L. f. intermedius*

Lesser Black-backs showing characters of the Scandinavian race *intermedius* have been reported regularly, particularly in the roost, with double figure counts in some years. The occurrence of this sub-species is proven by the following ringing recoveries:

A colour-ringed juvenile on 26 Sep 2003 had been ringed 69 days previously at Søgne, Vest-Agder, at the southern tip of Norway (*ABR*).

One on 11 Aug 2005 had been ringed at Farsund, Vest-Agder, Norway, on 3 July 2001 (*ABR*).

Then recently there was one on 2 July 2017, when an adult was seen well and photographed on Herriott's Pool (KEV), followed by later records in 2017 and several in 2018 (refer to *ABR*, 2018 and 2019).

Lesser Black-backed Gull *L. f. intermedius* | Keith Vinicombe

BALTIC GULL *L. f. fuscus*

The status of Baltic Gull in the UK, and its identification, are still developing. BBRC note that, while Baltic Gull has a distinctive appearance, its separation from the Scandinavian race of Lesser Black-backed Gull is problematic. Currently the only accepted British records are of ringed birds.

However black-backed birds from the colony at Horsvaer in Norway are regarded as Baltic Gulls. It should be noted that several ringed birds from there have been seen at the large Gloucester rubbish tip.

Under the current guidelines, the Chew records below are deemed 'not proven'.

Birds showing the characters of this race have been seen as follows:

- **1980:** one found dead on 11 January had been ringed in Estonia (J. Garrigan, Bristol Ornithological Club *Bird News*).
- **1998:** adult on 21 October (KEV).
- **1999:** one 3 August. (Article on this in *ABR* 2003)
- **2003:** adult on 23 and 24 April (KEV).
- **2005:** adult on 1 November (small individual with long 'crossed' wings and all-dark primaries).

2007: adult 17 April
2010: adult 30 March.
2011: adult 14 March.
2015: adult 23 May (A. H. Davis, KEV).
2016: adult 8 August.
2017: adult 8 January, one on 18 January, two adults and a third calendar year bird 1 May.
2018: a third winter on 10 January (KEV).
2019: recorded on 28 February, 18 April and 17 May. (Note that these were published in *ABR* as '*intermedius* but with *fuscus* not excluded'.)

The 1998–2015 birds were all well studied on Herriott's Pool. Note that the spring and autumn dates suggest that these were passage migrants, presumably en route to or from Africa, where they spend the winter.

Baltic Gull | Keith Vinicombe

CASPIAN TERN *Hydroprogne caspia*

There have been two records, both of adults. One was seen in flight off Herriott's Bridge on 13 August 1988. It was then seen in Stratford Bay before flying off over Hollow Brook (R. M. Curber, P. Luxton and T. Riddle). Another was seen on Herriott's Pool on 2 July 2017, before flying off low to the west (S. Isgar).

SANDWICH TERN *Thalasseus sandvicensis*

Being a sea tern, Sandwich Terns are scarce and irregular inland. However, as the annual maxima graph illustrates, small numbers pass through Chew on migration. The first record related to one on 20 June 1955 (B. K. Brooke) but, from then until 1972, there were only 11 subsequent records. During the 43 years from 1973 to 2015, however, it was recorded in 38 of them. All records were in single figures, apart from a party of ten on 12 September 1989.

SANDWICH TERN | Annual maxima 1955-2016.

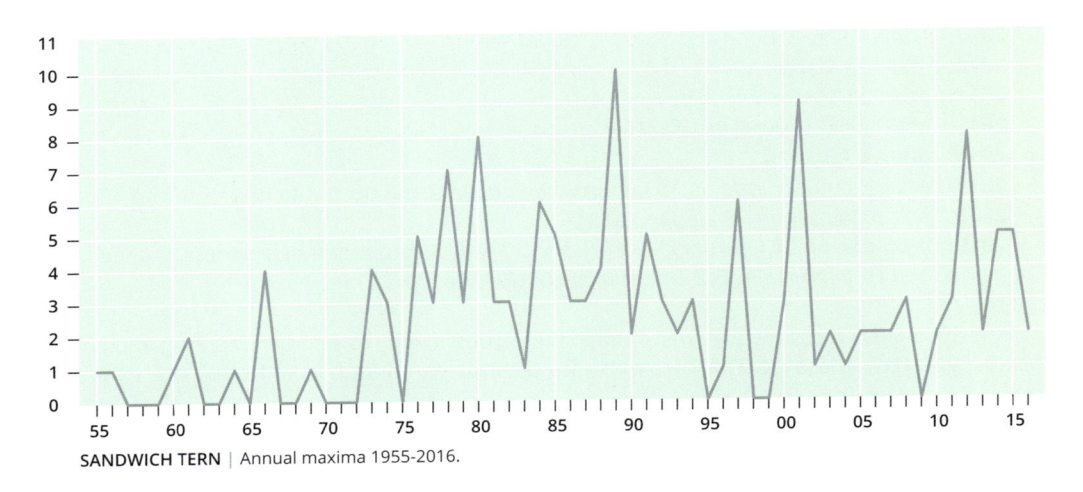

The first Sandwich Terns usually appear around our coasts in March and there is a single Chew record for that month: one on 12 March 1960. They are in fact scarce at the lake in spring, with 25 recorded in April and ten in May. Just seven have been recorded in June but the records increase though July and August to a peak in September, when a total of 101 has been recorded. There is just one October record: three on 10th in 1981.

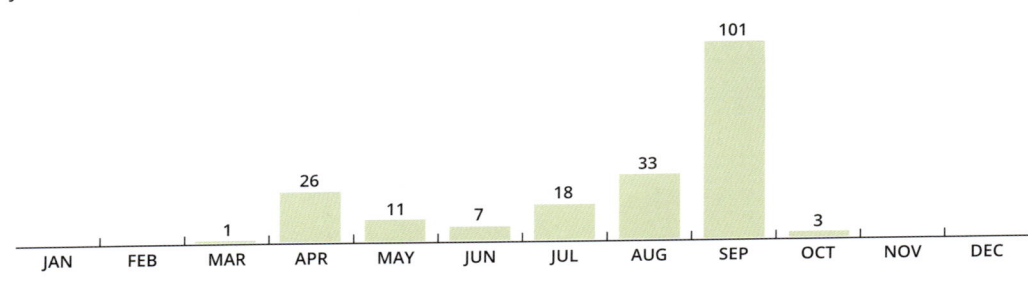

SANDWICH TERN | Monthly maxima (combined) 1956-2016.

LITTLE TERN *Sternula albifrons*

The first record was of one on 2 May 1954 (B. King). This was followed by two on 2 September 1956, with another on 8th. From 1960 onwards, the species became quite regular, recorded in 48 of the 62 years to 2015. As the annual maxima graph indicates, annual maxima usually relate to ones and twos, but sometimes threes and fours. The highest counts were five adults on 8 August 1969, six on 14 September 1970, six on 7 August 1995 and five on 11 September 2006. There were also six, possibly nine, on 11 August 2016. Very few of these autumn birds were aged, but family parties have occurred on at least five occasions and there are at least seven records of unattached juveniles.

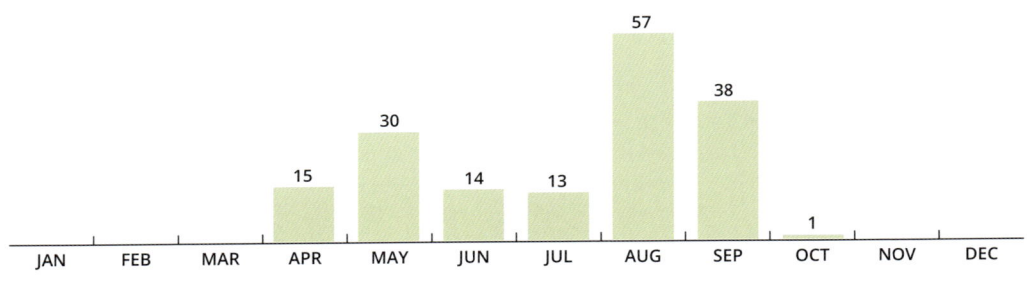

LITTLE TERN | Monthly maxima (combined) 1954-2016.

Spring migrants have appeared as early as 16 April (1988, 2003 and 2015 (3)) while the latest date in autumn was a juvenile on 4–7 October 1975. There are also nine records (11 individuals) in June, but it is difficult to know which way they were heading. However, given that they start breeding in early May (*BWP*) it perhaps seems most likely that these were mainly failed breeders already heading back south.

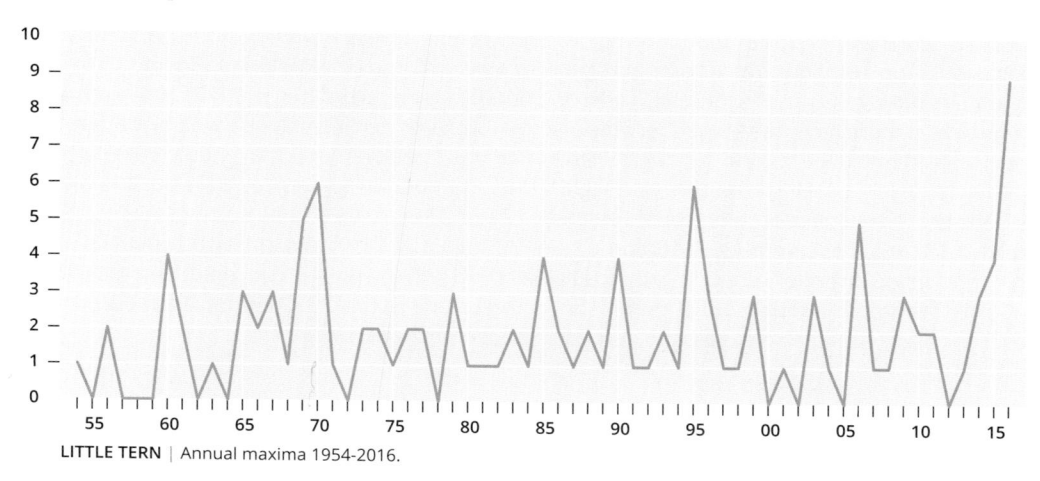

LITTLE TERN | Annual maxima 1954-2016.

Little Terns | Laurel Tucker

ROSEATE TERN *Sterna dougallii*

Only one record, a welcome addition to the Chew list in 2019. However, there had been several earlier sightings that had been dismissed following a review (see *ABR* 2016).

The 2019 record involved an adult on 21 May, watched by many observers and photographed while sat on the 'fish traps'. It was relocated a short time later at Blagdon Lake.

COMMON TERN *Sterna hirundo*

There were several records of Common Terns in the 1950s and 1960s but, at that time, there was considerable uncertainty concerning their separation from Arctic Tern *S. paradisaea*. This was clarified in the early 1970s (see the references listed under Arctic Tern).

As the monthly maxima graph shows, there is a strong spring passage in April–May, the earliest reliable date being 4 April (in 1982). The highest April counts have involved 45 in 1991, 53 in 2003 and 88 in 2013 (on 16th) but overall numbers peak in May, with maxima of 56 in 1990 and 68 in 2001. Numbers dip significantly in June, with only one double figure record (ten in 1977). However, at this time of year there have been seven records of immature birds (ten individuals), which have generally been considered to be second-summers, with as many as three on 7 June 1987. Autumn passage gets underway in July, peaking in August, with slightly lower numbers in September, followed by a big drop in October. The highest autumn counts involved 77 on 13 September 1986, 80 on 19 August 2009, a record 152 on 22 September 2010 and 67 on 19 August 2016. There are also three November records: single juveniles remaining until 1st (1987), 3rd (2002) and one (un-aged) on 14th (1985).

The maximum annual counts graph shows the erratic nature of Common Tern occurrences over the years, but it also suggests a gradual increase since the 1970s.

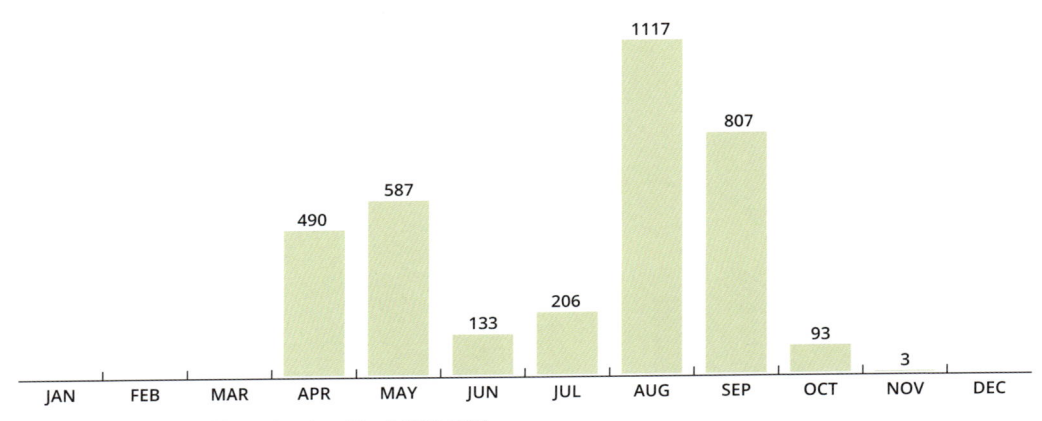

COMMON TERN | Monthly maxima (combined) 1980-2016.

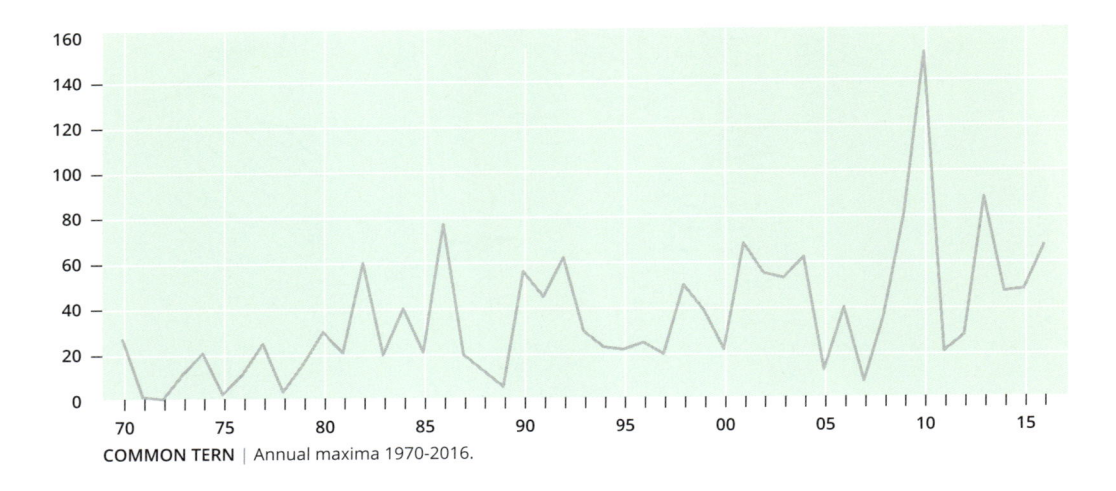

COMMON TERN | Annual maxima 1970-2016.

ARCTIC TERN *Sterna paradisaea*

Prior to the publication of two seminal papers in *British Birds* (Grant and Scott 1969 and Hume and Grant 1974), the criteria for the separation of Common *S. hirundo* and Arctic Terns were not well understood. Since then, the two species have been identified with much more confidence, and this is reflected in the two graphs. Although it regularly occurs inland, Arctic Tern is much more of a pelagic species than Common Tern, with the majority of its spring and autumn migrations being up and down the Atlantic. However, it is also clear that the species routinely migrates overland.

As the combined monthly maxima graph shows, peak numbers occur in April and May, with the earliest arrival date being 12 April and the latest in autumn being 21 November, which is also the latest Avon record (both in 1996). As the annual maxima graph indicates, the largest counts have been 25 in September 1982, 38 on 4 May 1991, 60 on 1 May 1998 and a remarkable 130 on 18 April 2013. The latter count related to westerly gales that also brought large numbers into the Bristol Channel and the Severn Estuary.

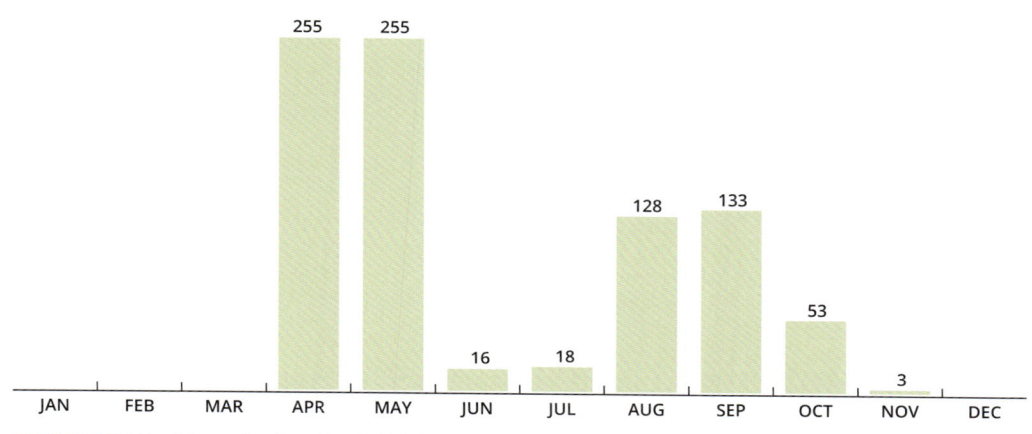

ARCTIC TERN | Monthly maxima (combined) 1965-2016.

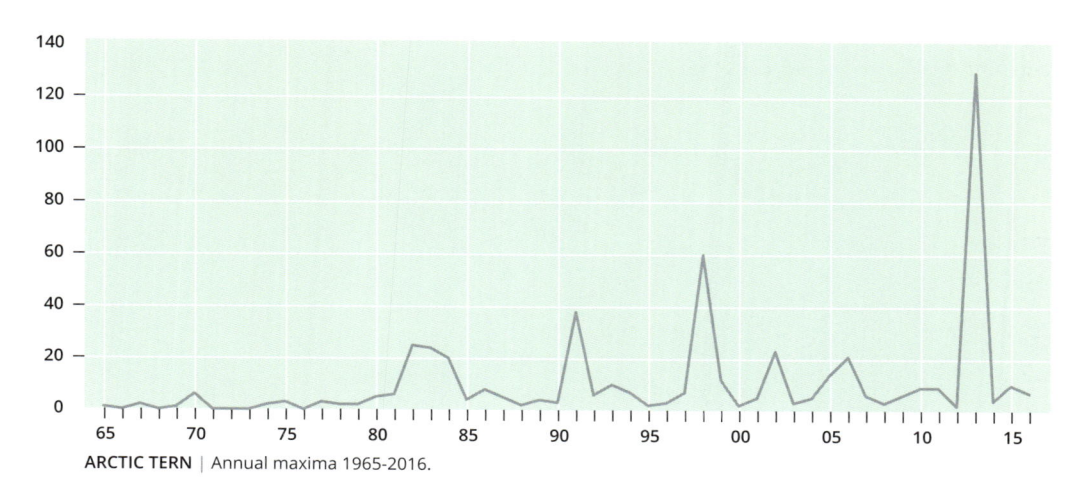

ARCTIC TERN | Annual maxima 1965-2016.

References:
Grant. P. J. and Scott, R. E. (1969). 'Field identification of juvenile Common, Arctic and Roseate Terns'. *British Birds* 62: 297–299.
Hume, R. A. and Grant, P. J. (1974). 'The upperwing pattern of adult Common and Arctic Terns'. *British Birds* 67: 133-136.
Vinicombe, K. E. (2014). 'The migration of Common and Arctic Terns in southern England'. *British Birds* 107: 195–206.

Common and Arctic Terns | Rich Andrews

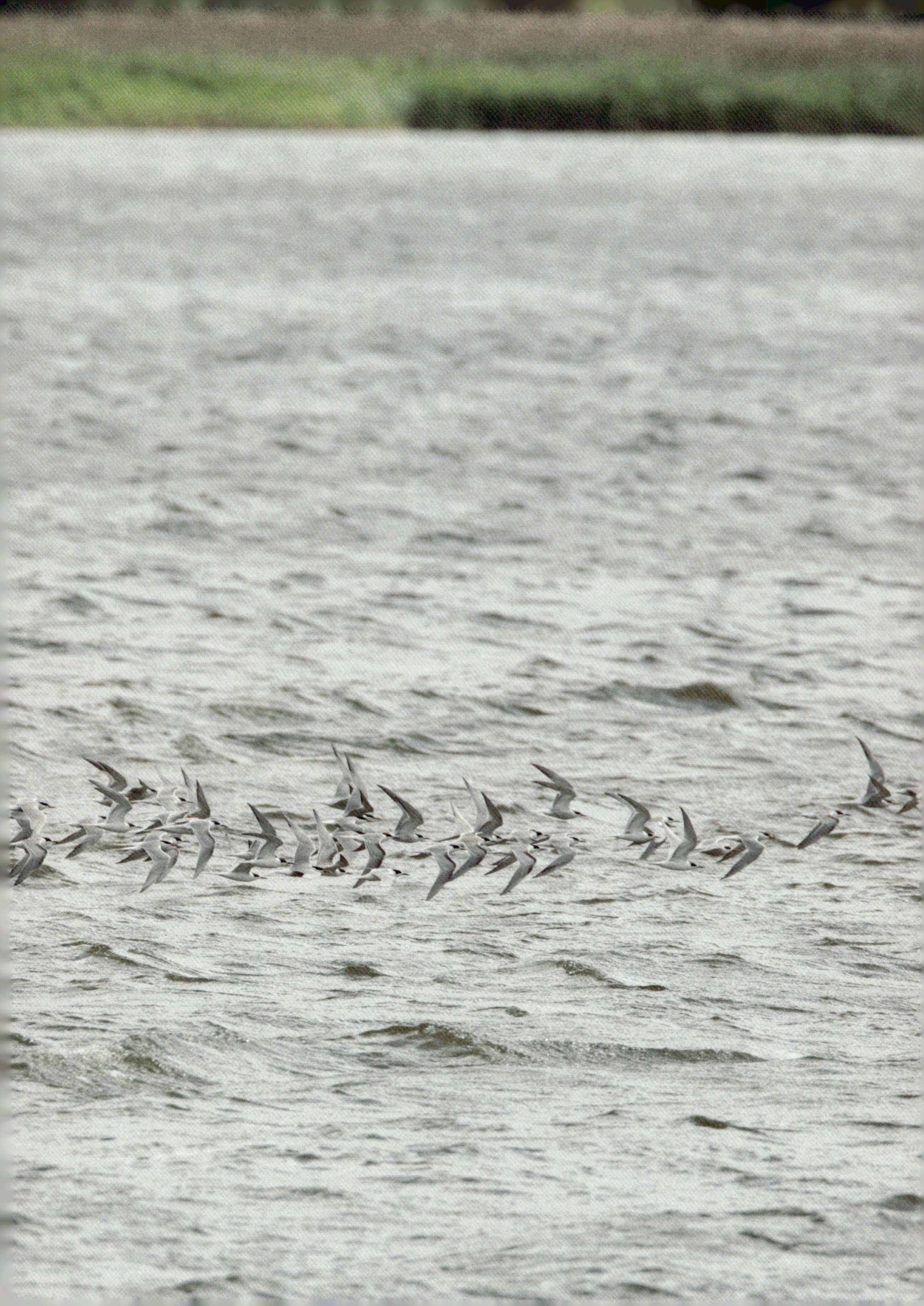

WHISKERED TERN *Chlidonias hybrida*

There have been five records, involving six individuals:
- **1959:** an adult on 23–25 June (H. Highway *et al.*).
- **1983:** two adult types on 29 May, with one until 31st (P. Andrew, L. A. & N. A. Tucker *et al.*).
- **2006:** one, probably a second-summer, on 28–29 April (A. H. Davis, R. Mielcarek *et al.*).
- **2013:** an adult on 23 April (T. Grant *et al.*) and another adult on 25 April (A. Lester *et al.*).

Whiskered Tern *(centre)* | Rich Andrews

WHITE-WINGED BLACK TERN *Chlidonias leucopterus*

The first record was of a juvenile on 27–30 August 1966 (R. M. Curber, B. King, D. Warden *et al.*). The species then occurred in sixteen years to 2014, the records totaling 24 individuals. As the annual maxima graph shows, most (20) occurred in the period 1966–1984, with just four since. Surprisingly, none was recorded during the 17 years from 1997 to 2013 inclusive, this long barren spell being broken by a juvenile on 10–13 September 2014.

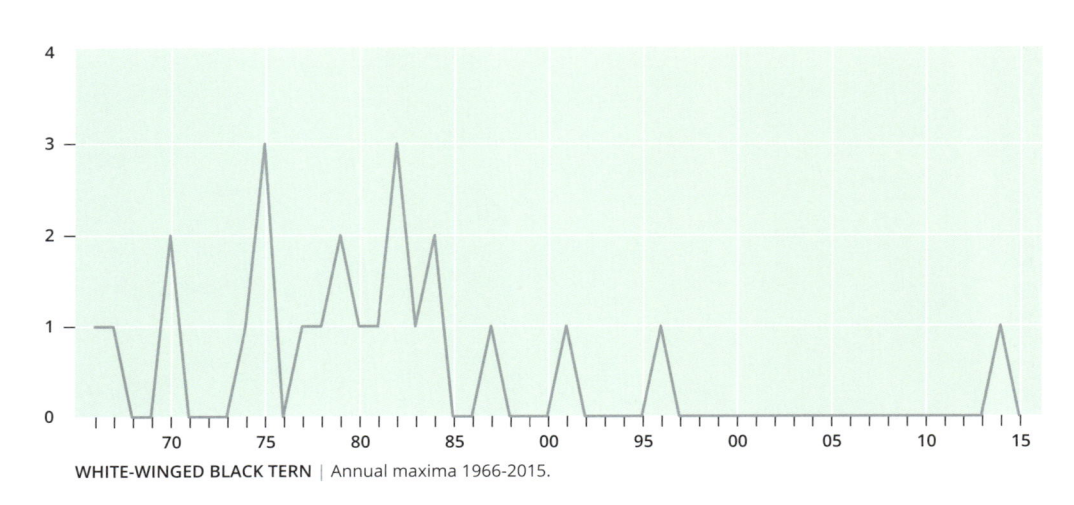

WHITE-WINGED BLACK TERN | Annual maxima 1966-2015.

There have been three June records: two in summer plumage on Herriott's Pool on 14 June 1975 and a second-summer on 9–11 June 1996; there have also been three July records, but the peaks months are August and September, with six and twelve records respectively. The only October record was of a juvenile on the 1st in 1983, this bird originally being present at Barrow Gurney Reservoirs earlier in the day.

The records have involved 14 juveniles, two second-years (July 1991 and June 1996) and eight adults.

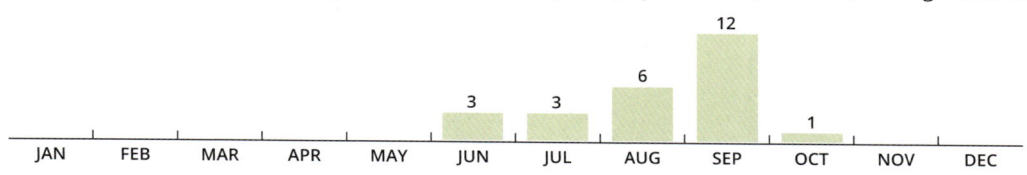

WHITE-WINGED BLACK TERN | Monthly maxima (combined) 1966-2014.

BLACK TERN *Chlidonias niger*

First recorded in 1954, the Black Tern has been a regular spring and autumn passage migrant, peaking in May and in August–September. The earliest spring record involved 12 on 10 April 1965 and the latest in autumn were two that stayed until 13 November 1977.

There have been six counts of 200 or over:
- **1957:** 480 on 21 September (M. W. Pickering).
- **1963:** 200 on 30–31 August (S. E. Chapman, B. King).
- **1965:** 200 on 10 August (T. R. Cleeves, KEV) and 600 the following day (H. Highway).
- **1988:** 350 on 7 September (P. D. Bowerman).
- **1989:** 270 on 8 May (J. R. Best).
- **2019:** 210 on 24 August (ABR 2019).

As the annual maxima graph shows, annual totals vary considerably from year to year, from the record 600 in 1965 to a peak of just four in 2012. A remarkable influx took place on 24 August 2019, some hawking high overhead, when a total of 210 was counted. This was the first count over 100 since 2004, but the totals since the turn of the century still reflect a worrying long-term decline on the Continent.

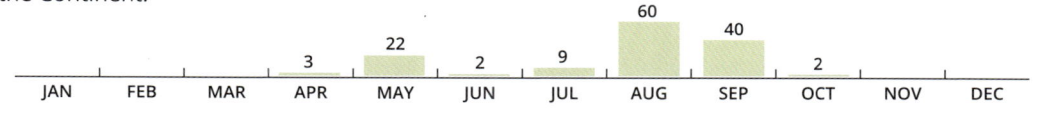

BLACK TERN | Monthly maxima (average) 1954-2015.

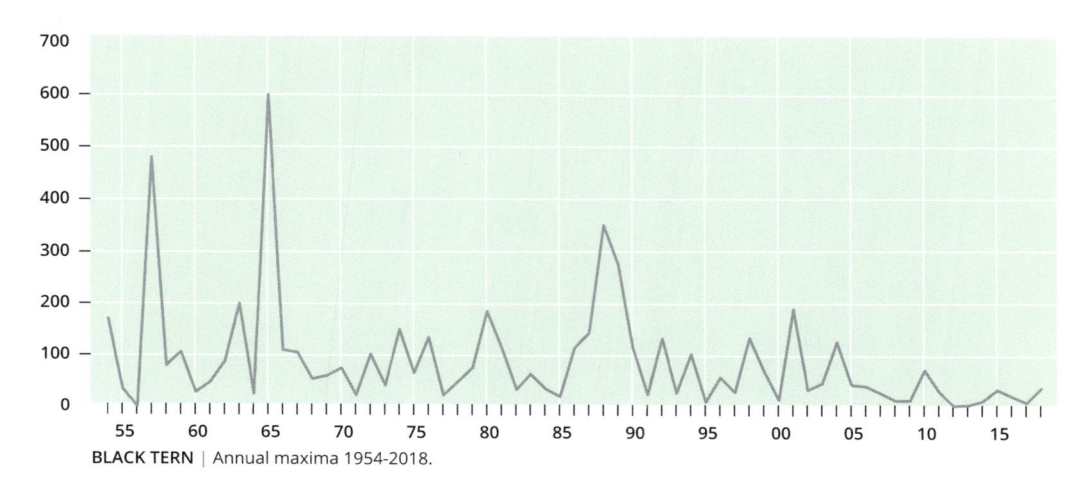

BLACK TERN | Annual maxima 1954-2018.

Black Tern | Gary Thoburn

GREAT SKUA *Stercorarius skua*

Also known by most birders by the colloquial name of Bonxie, the first record was of one on 13–14 September 1969 (B. Rabbitts). The next were two in 1977. Ones and twos were then seen in nine subsequent years to 2009, with a cluster of four records during 1981–1984 when the species was annual. Then, on 26 September 2013, a remarkable passage took place, with a total of 18 flying from east to west over the lake between 10.05 and 15.15, in parties of five, five, seven and one. As with most records of this species, this exceptional total occurred in gloomy anticyclonic weather conditions and undoubtedly involved birds deliberately crossing the country from east to west, presumably taking a short cut to the open ocean via the Severn Estuary.

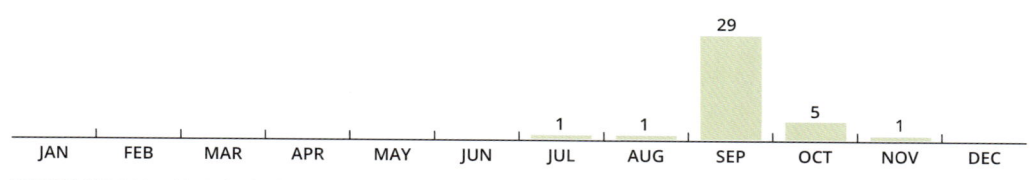

GREAT SKUA | Monthly individuals (combined) 1969-2018.

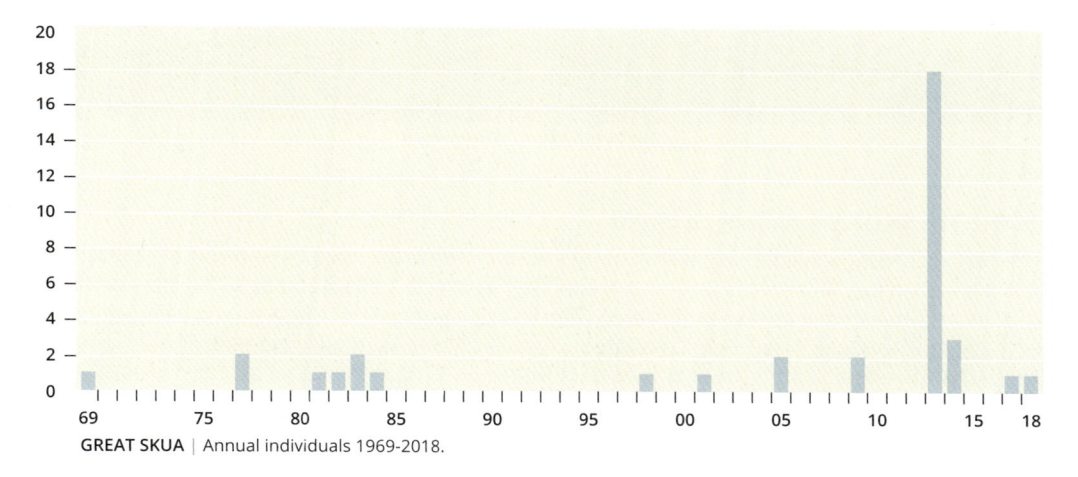

GREAT SKUA | Annual individuals 1969-2018.

POMARINE SKUA *Stercorarius pomarinus*

There have been at least five records, involving six individuals (we have also been informed of one found dead in Chew Magna in 1879!):

- **1999:** two juveniles flew high to the west over Stratford Bay at 15.20 on 4 December (R. J. Higgins).
- **2009:** a pale morph adult on 22 November (J. Thomas); then a second-year from 29 November to 7 December (D. J. Angell, R. Mielcarek *et al.*). During its nine-day stay, this bird killed and ate several Common Gulls *Larus canus*.
- **2012:** an adult with full 'spoons' on 12–13 May. On the latter date it flew off shortly after dawn (M. Jenkins, R. Mielcarek *et al.*). On the 12th, a 'pelagic trip' was organised and the bird was approached in a boat down to a range of two metres. It was even heard calling!
- **2013:** a pale morph adult flew through at 11.05 on 28 September (R. Mielcarek).

In addition, a dark juvenile skua on 5 January 2012 flew in high over Woodford Lodge, spooked the gull roost, and then flew off south-west (S. Mackie, KEV). It was not conclusively identified but was thought most likely to have been a 'Pom'.

Pomarine Skua | Rich Andrews

ARCTIC SKUA *Stercorarius parasiticus*

The first records involved a juvenile on 19 September 1963, followed by another on 26 October. There were no further records until two adults flew south on 19 September 1974, after which the species became almost annual until 1983, when its appearances once again became more erratic. Fifty-seven individuals have been recorded in total: 23 adults, eight juveniles and 26 un-aged. There have been two spring records (two dark phase on 31 May 1980 and an intermediate phase adult on 6 June 2020) but the others involved seven in August, 29 in September and seven in October. Most records have involved birds clearly on an east – west overland route, probably from the Wash to the Severn Estuary. Rather than being windblown, many of the sightings have occurred in calm, gloomy conditions when, presumably, the birds have become somewhat disorientated. The most surprising record was of a well-observed and photographed juvenile that was present off the sailing club on 7–11 December 2001. More recently there was a flock of 4 on 14 September 2017, two intermediate adults on 25 August 2019 and the spring bird in 2020.

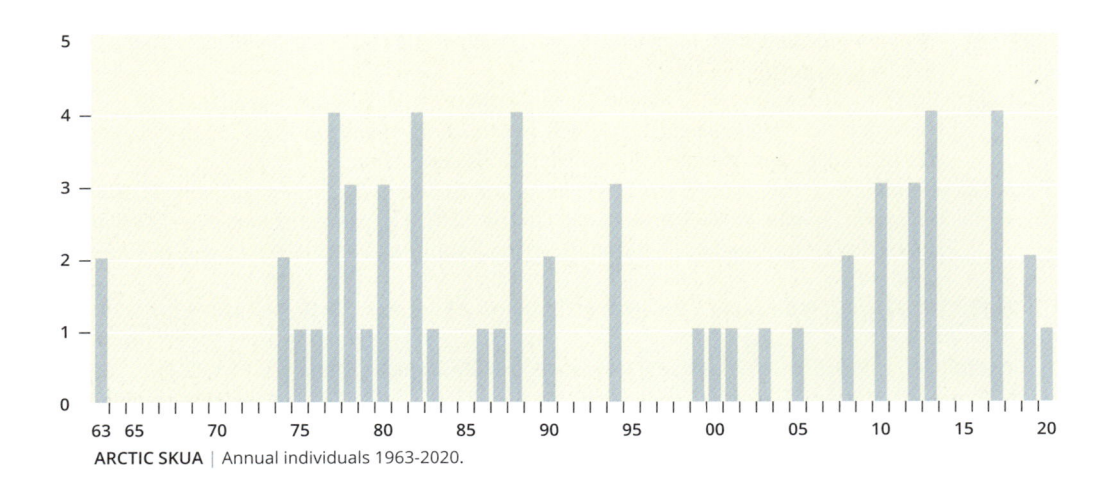

ARCTIC SKUA | Annual individuals 1963-2020.

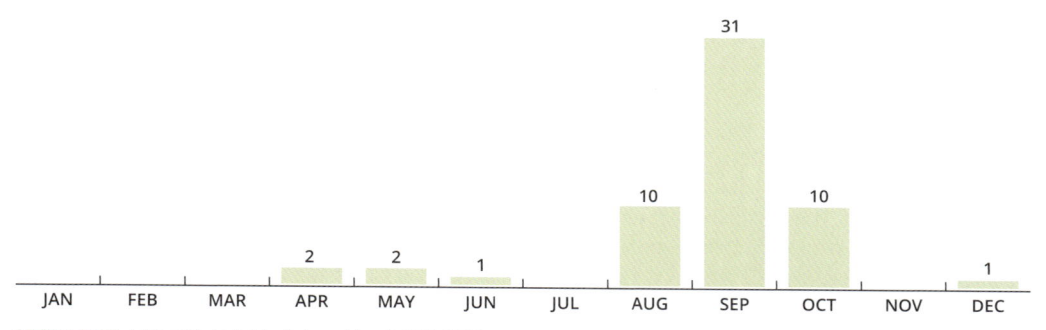

ARCTIC SKUA | Monthly individuals (combined) 1963-2020.

Jan 0, Feb 0, Mar 0, Apr 2, May 2, Jun 1, Jul 0, Aug 10, Sep 31, Oct 10, Nov 0, Dec 1.

LONG-TAILED SKUA *Stercorarius longicaudus*

There have been at least six records:

- **1976:** a pale phase adult in the Denny Island area on 19 June (R. M. Curber, R. Manvell).
- **1982:** a pale phase adult flew west on 10 August (P. A. Amies, C. F. Dibble).
- **1991:** a dark phase juvenile on 6–17 September (A. H. Davis, R. J. Palmer, KEV *et al.*). This bird was watched down to a range of two metres during a 'pelagic trip' in a fishing boat, kindly lent to us by *Bristol Water*.
- **1999:** a juvenile on the water and in flight during the afternoon of 24 August (A. H. Davis, R. J. Higgins, G. Suter *et al.*).
- **2015:** a sub-adult, probably a second-summer, flew west through Heron's Green Bay during the evening of 29 May (KEV). A juvenile flew west through Villice Bay on 7 September, briefly landing amongst a flock of Tufted Ducks *Aythya fuligula* (KEV).

In addition, a small skua that flew west on 25 September 2013 was thought likely to have been this species (A. H. Davis, R. Mielcarek).

Long-tailed Skua | Barry Mitchell

RED-THROATED DIVER *Gavia stellata*

There have been 16 records, the first in 1958 (16 March to 2 April) and the second involving a slightly oiled individual on 24 March 1963 (R. J. Prytherch). This was followed by one on 26 February 1966. One was seen on 2 March and 1 April 1980. There have since been a further 12, from 1983 to 2019 (see annual individuals graph).

As the combined monthly maxima graph shows, all the records have been during the period September to April, the earliest date relating to an adult in summer plumage from 18 September to 12 October 1977. The peak months are November and March, with five and four records respectively. Of those aged, three were adults. Two of the records related to birds that were oiled – one 19–21 February 1983, which was taken into captivity, where it unfortunately died – and another 24–26 November 2007. A further interesting record concerned one that arrived during a heavy downpour on 4 November 2005, but left after only 3½ hours.

A juvenile present 3–28 November 2019 was seen by many observers and photographed.

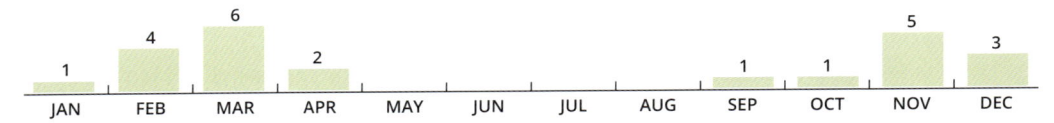

RED-THROATED DIVER | Monthly maxima (combined) 1958-2015.

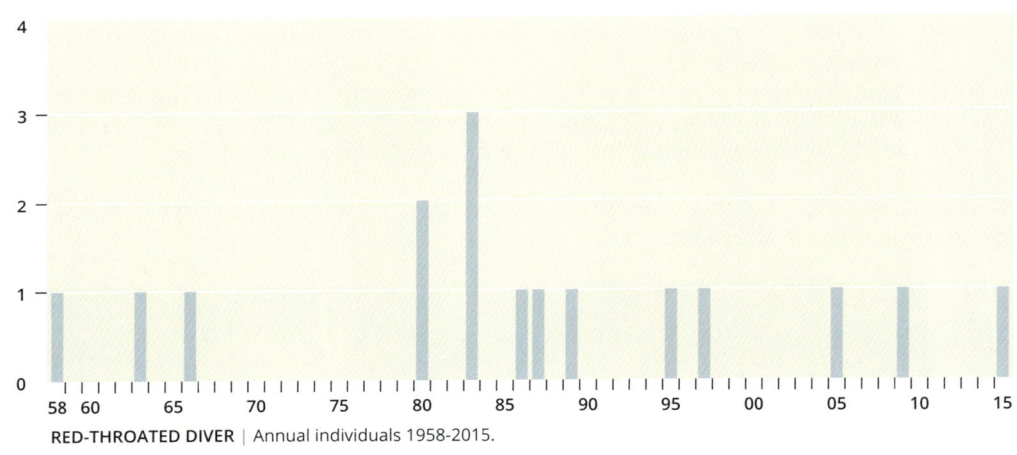

RED-THROATED DIVER | Annual individuals 1958-2015.

Red-throated Diver | Laurel Tucker

BLACK-THROATED DIVER *Gavia arctica*

There are twelve records, involving thirteen individuals:
- **1957:** 17 November.
- **1958:** a bird seen on 19 January and 16 February.
- **1971:** one flew south past Wick Green Point on 17 January.
- **1974:** one from 21 November to 8 December.
- **1982:** 18 January.
- **1985:** one, probably a juvenile, 1–9 November.
- **1986:** two on 17 January dropped in briefly before flying off north.
- **1988:** singles on 7 April and 22 October, the latter eventually flying off south.
- **1994:** a juvenile from 13 November to 4 December.
- **2003:** a first-winter on 11 January, present for an hour and extremely vocal, and a second calendar year bird on 31 May.
- **2013:** a confiding juvenile off Woodford Bank from 16 November to 24 December.

Black-throated Diver | Gary Thoburn

GREAT NORTHERN DIVER *Gavia immer*

Unlike Black-throated *G. arctica* and Red-throated Divers *G. stellata*, the Great Northern Divers that winter in Britain come from the west: Canada, Greenland and also Iceland, the latter hosting about 300 pairs (Hagemeijer and Blair 1997).

The first record was of one on 10 January 1956 (H. H. Davis, B. King and I. J. Ferguson-Lees) and, since then, it has been seen in 25 out of 61 years (to 2015). As the annual maxima graph shows, the records tend to be in clusters, the species being seen annually from 1974 to 1978 and with eight in the nine years 2007–2015.

The earliest arrival date is 26 October (both in 1974 and 2008) but the peak months are November (20) and December (18), dropping from January onwards. This late winter decline is undoubtedly related to higher water levels at this time, which diminish the density of the fish on which they feed. Five have remained into April, but the latest was a juvenile/first-year in 1975 that remained until 10 May. Of those aged, 15 were juveniles and seven were adults. One of the latter – from 18 November 1976 to 4 December 1977 – was in summer plumage. A juvenile off Wick Green Point in December 2002 was heard giving its evocative wailing call. One was seen on 10 and 11 November 2019.

Reference
Hagemeijer, W. J. M and Blair, M. J. (Eds) (1997). *The EBCC Atlas of European Breeding Birds: Their distribution and abundance.* T. & A. D. Poyser, London.

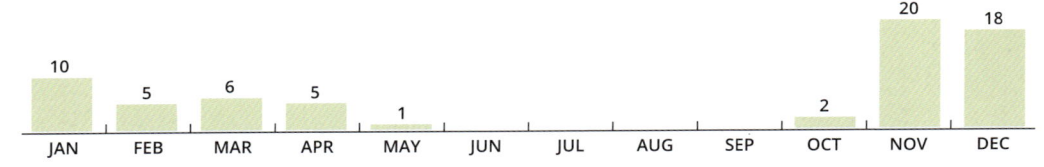

GREAT NORTHERN DIVER | Monthly maxima (combined) 1956-2015.

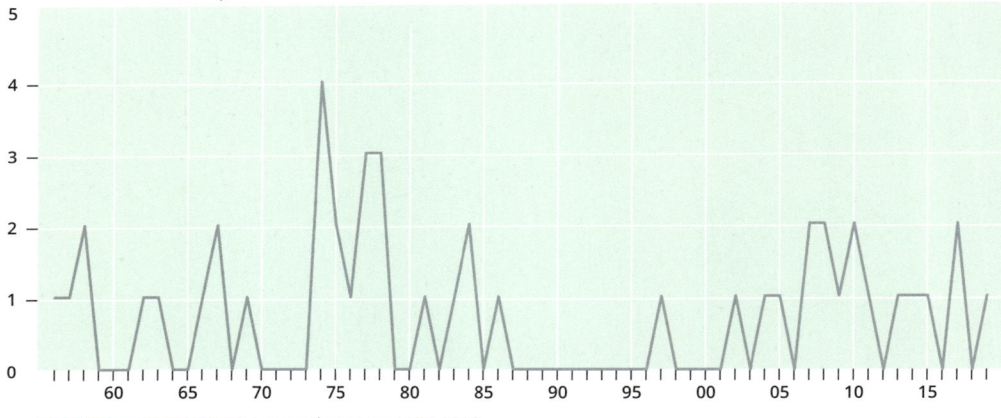

GREAT NORTHERN DIVER | Annual maxima 1956-2019.

Great Nortrhern Diver | Laurel Tucker

STORM PETREL *Hydrobates pelagicus*
There are six records, involving nine or ten individuals:
- 1977: one on 13 November (L. A. Tucker).
- 1983: one, possibly two, on 3 September (KEV), one on 5th and one on 17th (BOC *Bird News*).
- 2000: three on 30 October (R. M. Andrews *et al.*).
- 2012: three on 9 June (R. M. Andrews, R. Mielcarek *et al.*).

All these records occurred after strong westerly gales, the 2012 records being associated with large numbers (c.105) in the Severn Estuary.

LEACH'S PETREL *Oceanodroma leucorhoa*
There are eleven records, involving nineteen individuals. All were associated with strong westerly gales:
- 1978: one on 30 September (K. J. Hall, R. J. Prytherch).
- 1983: seven on 3 September (KEV *et al.*); one on 16 October and one on 29–30 December (K. F. Blake, C. J. Stone, A. Whatley).
- 1987: one on 19 October (R. J. Palmer).
- 1989: one on 27 September (A. H. Davis, A. J. Merritt, KEV); one on 17 December, coinciding with a large influx of 48 into the Severn Estuary (A. J. Merritt).
- 1993: one on 6 December (R. J. Palmer).
- 2000: two with three Storm Petrels on 30 October (R. J. Higgins).
- 2006: one on 7 December (R. M. Andrews).
- 2018: one on 21 September (M. Jenkins *et al.*).

Leach's Petrel | Brian Thompson

FULMAR *Fulmarus glacialis*

There have been nine records, involving ten individuals:
- **1970:** one on 31 May (S. B. Edwards).
- **1975:** one on 4 April (J. Barber).
- **1978:** one on 6 August (R. N. Staples).
- **1981:** one 26–29 April (J. Aldridge, J. Humphris, A. Whatley *et al.*).
- **2007:** one 4 July (D.J. Angell, A. H. Davis, R. Mielcarek).
- **2008:** one on 26–27 May and another on 30 May (A. H. Davis, R. Mielcarek).
- **2012:** two on 5 April (R. Mielcarek *et al.*); another on 29th (R. M. Andrews).

What is surprising about these records is that all but two have occurred in spring, with five in April and one in May. In addition, at least three of the records (1981, 2008 and 2012) occurred during moderate to gale force north-easterly winds. This would suggest an origin in the North Sea, rather than the Atlantic. One of the birds on 5 April 2012 was last seen circling high over Woodford Lodge.

MANX SHEARWATER *Puffnus puffinus*

There have been five records, involving six individuals. All appeared after strong westerly gales and it is likely that they were all juveniles.
- **1974:** one resting in the centre of the lake on 29 September (G. E. Fordham, R. B. H. Smith).
- **1983:** one on 5 September and another on 17th (KEV).
- **1986:** one on 27 August (KEV).
- **1995:** one on 9 October (C. Trott, R. J. Palmer *et al.*).
- **2017:** two juveniles on 11 September (R. J. Higgins *et al.*).

BLACK STORK *Ciconia nigra*

One on 10 April 1988 was watched for nearly 40 minutes as it flew high over Herriott's Bridge, mobbed by a Buzzard *Buteo buteo*. It then drifted south-west towards the Mendips (C. & G. Hughes *et al.*).

WHITE STORK *Ciconia ciconia*

One on 28 May 2000 circled over Herriott's Pool 12.00-12.15 and again 12.50-13.00 (J. P. Martin *et al.*).

In 2019 there were two records of birds that were from the Knepp introduction scheme in Sussex, and therefore not classed as wild birds. One on 30 August was found, on examining photographs (by B. Thompson) to be carrying a transmitter. A second bird on 20 September carried the blue ring GB58 and was traced to be a Polish bird that was released from Knepp in 2018.

GANNET *Morus bassanus*

There have been 19 records: singles in January, April and May, three in July, two in August, six in September, two in October and one in November. Six were adults, three were juveniles, one was a second-year and, remarkably, four were not aged. Most of the records related to strong westerly gales. However at least two juveniles appeared in September in settled anticyclonic conditions, suggesting an overland movement from the Wash. The first was recorded in 1962 and the last in 2018.

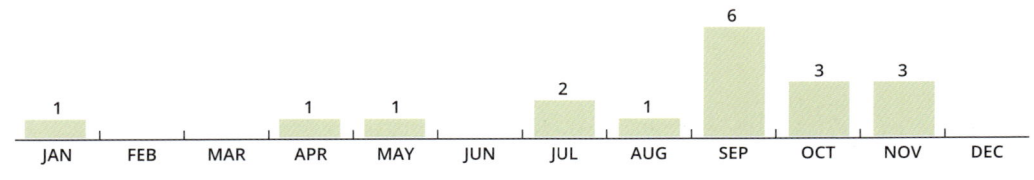

JAN	FEB	MAR	APR	MAY	JUN	JUL	AUG	SEP	OCT	NOV	DEC
1			1	1		2	1	6	3	3	

GANNET | Monthly totals 1962-2016.

GANNET | Annual totals 1962–2016.

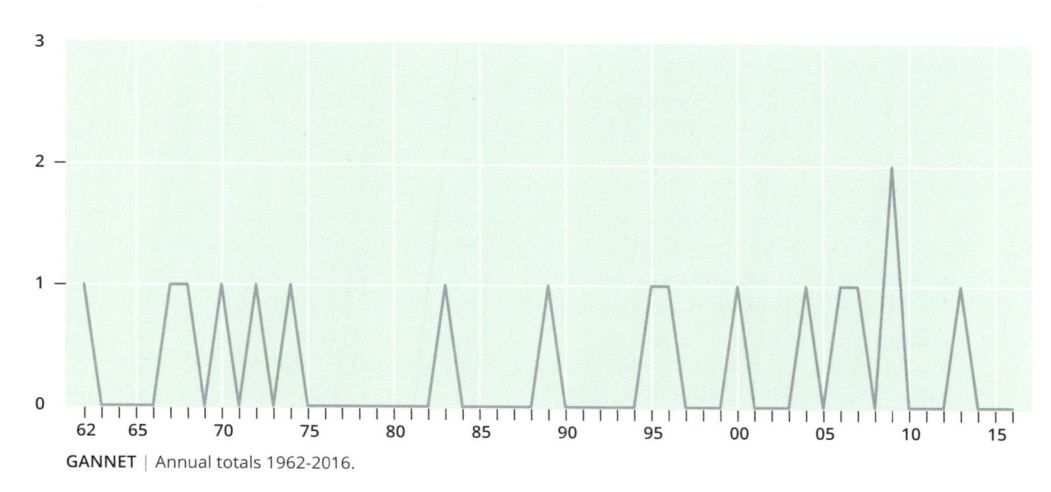

Gannet | Laurel Tucker

SHAG *Phalacrocorax aristotelis*

There are twelve records of at least 23 individuals as follows:
- 1955: one found dead on 3 October had been ringed on Lundy, Devon, on 30 June (R. H. Poulding).
- 1973: two adults and a juvenile 7 August.
- 1974: three on 7 August.
- 1978: singles on 26 March and 26 December.
- 1979: two on 31 October and also two 2–3 December, then one until 15th, when it was found dead.
- 1980: three at the Sailing Club on 2 November, with one still there on 22nd.
- 1988: one off Sutton Wick on 8 October.
- 1998: one on the Main Dam on 12 September.
- 2005: five on 31 August, with one remaining to 1 September.
- 2009: one on 26 November.
- 2017: one 2–17 October.

CORMORANT *Phalacrocorax carbo*

As the maximum monthly counts graph shows, numbers of Cormorants reach a peak in autumn and winter, with the largest numbers being present in November. They gradually decline during the late winter, presumably because the high water levels reduce the density of the fish, rendering them more difficult to catch, and also because of the gradual reduction in fish stocks.

The first record involved two on 9 May 1954 but, of the small number of counts in the 1950s, none exceeded five. It was described as 'scarce or absent' during the cold winter of 1962–63, but eleven were counted in December 1963. There was then a record 19 in February 1964, followed by up to ten in 1965, but the peak count in 1966 was just three. From 1967 onwards, numbers began to slowly increase, reaching 55 in 1972. Around this time, however, complaints from fishermen concerning the species' predation on the lake's trout stocks led the then Bristol Waterworks Company to start shooting them. Despite this controversial action, the Cormorants continued to increase, reaching a new peak of 90 in January 1977. From this high point, numbers declined significantly through the 1980s, with a maximum count of just 13 in 1982. From that low point, numbers once again began to recover, reaching a record 150 in December 1990. A new record of 305 was reached in November 1995 and, since then, three figure maxima have become the norm, culminating in a record 540 in October 2014, followed by 510 in November 2015, and the same number in 2017. In both these years there were very large numbers of coarse fish present and it seems that it was these, rather than the trout, that instigated this phenomenal rise in Cormorant numbers.

Another interesting phenomenon is the occurrence at the lake of the continental subspecies *sinensis*. Unlike the nominate *carbo*, which breeds on rocky islands and cliffs around the British coast, the slightly smaller *sinensis* breeds inland in trees. The first *sinensis* at Chew were confirmed in May 2000, and at least five were counted on 6 July of that year. The differences from *carbo* are subtle but, in March 2011, 40 Cormorants on a small island at Stratford Hide appeared to be all – or nearly all – *sinensis*, while in January 2014, about two-thirds of a flock of 140 also appeared to be of this race. Also of interest was a *sinensis* seen on 12 July 2004 that had been colour-ringed in the Netherlands in June 1997. This was cast-iron proof that this sub-species really is occurring at the lake. A further one on 31 October 2016 had been ringed in the Netherlands on 1 June that year, with another on 7 October 2020.

Cormorant | Rich Andrews

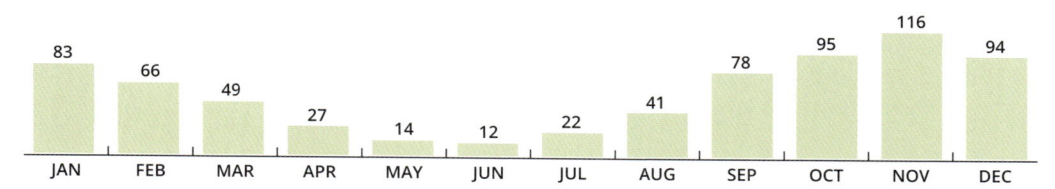

CORMORANT | Monthly maximum counts 1965–2015.

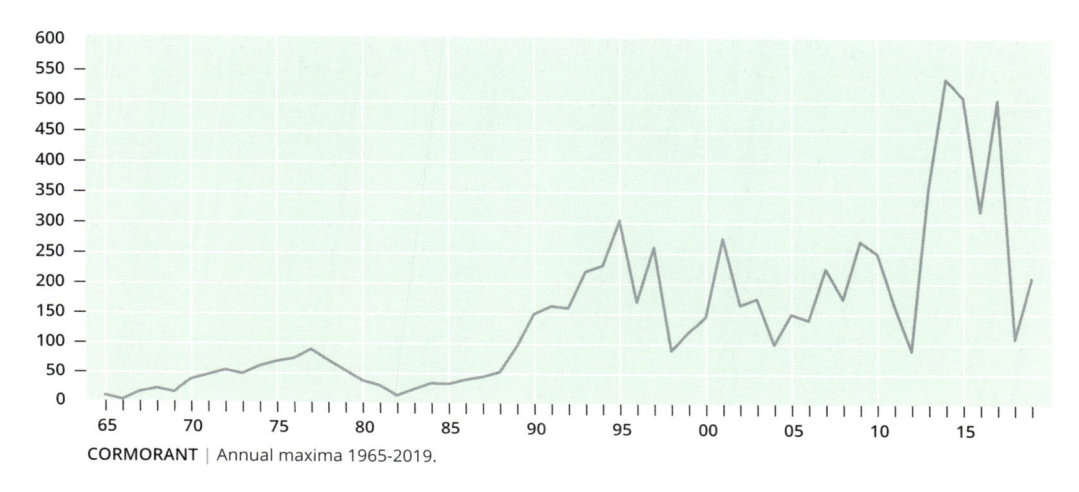

Month	JAN	FEB	MAR	APR	MAY	JUN	JUL	AUG	SEP	OCT	NOV	DEC
Count	83	66	49	27	14	12	22	41	78	95	116	94

CORMORANT | Annual maxima 1965-2019.

GLOSSY IBIS *Plegadis falcinellus*

There have been seven records (11 individuals) as follows:

2007: a first-winter roosted in willows in front of Stratford Hide on 2–3 November (A. H. Davis, G. Thoburn *et al.*). On the 3rd, it landed briefly on Herriot's Pool before it flew south-west and was subsequently seen at Catcott Lows and Greylake RSPB, Somerset, then at Prawle and Bowling Green Marsh in Devon.

2009: an immature fed in front of the Main Reeds 6–12 September (R. Mielcarek *et al.*), then four on 26th (R. M. Andrews *et al.*). Two of the latter were colour ringed: one as a nestling in the Petite Camargue, France, on 15 May 2009, and the other in Donana, Spain (ringing date unknown).

2013: a juvenile flew north over Heron's Green Bay on 27 September before moving to Blagdon Lake (R. Brewer *et al.*). A male and female appeared high over the lake on 26 November and then landed in the Hollow Brook area (KEV); one was then seen in the Moreton Bank area on 28–30 November (R. Mielcarek, I Stapp *et al.*).

2016: one in flight over Herriott's Pool on 11 January (J. McSorley).

2017: one in flight over Stratford Bay 27 May (J. Horsey).

SPOONBILL *Platalea leucorodia*

The first record was of one on 2 May 1954 (B. King). The next was an adult on 13 and 21 April 1969. As the individuals recorded graph shows, the species has since become an erratic visitor, but records have clearly increased since the turn of the century. In total 25 have been recorded (to 2018). All the records have been of single birds apart from a pair on 15 July 2011 and a flock of five (one adult, one juvenile and three immatures) on 14–15 September 2011.

The monthly individuals graph shows that the species has been recorded in every month from April to October, with a strong peak in September and smaller peaks in May, July and October. The latest record was one on 24 October 2010.

One seen from 19 to 23 June 1990 had been ringed as a chick on 28 July 1987 on the Dutch island of Texel. It is generally assumed that Spoonbills arrive from the east, but a colour-ringed first-summer on 30 July 1992 had worked its way south through Wales. It was previously seen on 28–29 July at Llyn Coron, Anglesey, Rhymney Wharf, Glamorgan, and Sluice Farm, Gwent.

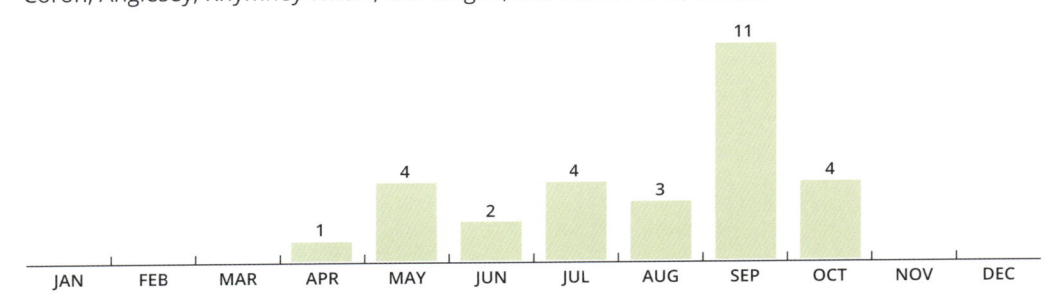

SPOONBILL | Monthly maxima (combined) 1954-2015.

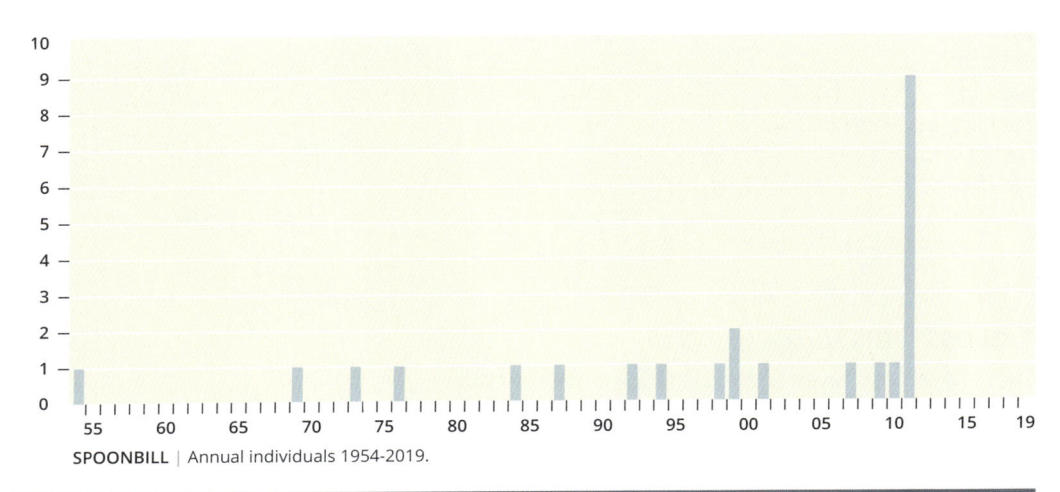

SPOONBILL | Annual individuals 1954-2019.

Spoonbill | Rich Andrews

BITTERN *Botaurus stellaris*

The first record was one from 14 December 1963 to 13 February 1964 (B. King). From that point onwards, the species became a fairly regular winter visitor, occurring in 20 years out of the next 28, with as many as three in March 1982. Since 1993 it has been annual, with a peak of at least five on 13 March 1999. As the combined monthly maxima graph shows, the peak months are from October to March, with the highest totals in January.

In 1997, a male boomed from 27 February to 19 April, with a female display flighting from 13 to 29 March. Subsequently, feeding flights were seen regularly in May and June, a juvenile was seen on 8 June (A. H. Davis) and a used nest was found in September. After a blank year in 1998, booming resumed in 1999 and, remarkably, at least five birds, possibly six, were seen on 13 March. Disappointingly, however, there was no subsequent evidence of breeding.

In 2000, one appeared on 8 January and booming was again heard regularly from February until 5 May. It is thought likely that a female nested in April but failed, probably as a result of rising water levels, which related to some appalling spring weather. She is then thought likely to have re-nested in May, leading to feeding flights from 2 to 15 July. In 2001, the male boomed again from 17 February to 11 May but there was no subsequent evidence of breeding.

In 2008, Bitterns bred at Ham Wall in Somerset, a result of significant habitat creation for the species. Since then, the Somerset population has flourished. It would be nice to think that the breeding at Chew in 1997 and 2000 provided a stepping stone for the subsequent colonisation of the Somerset Levels. One was heard booming on 7, 8 and 9 May 2015, and in 2016, two were again heard booming on 12 April and one on 17th.

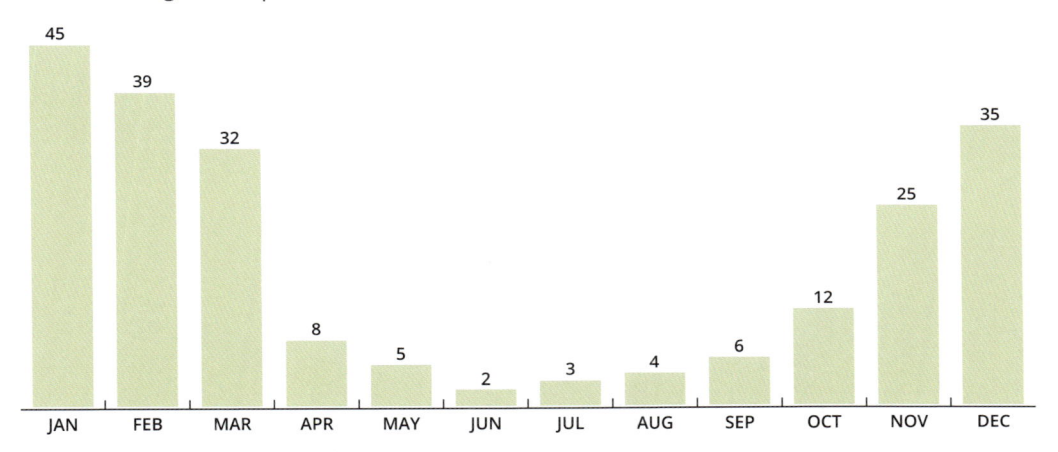

BITTERN | Monthly maxima (combined) 1963-2015.

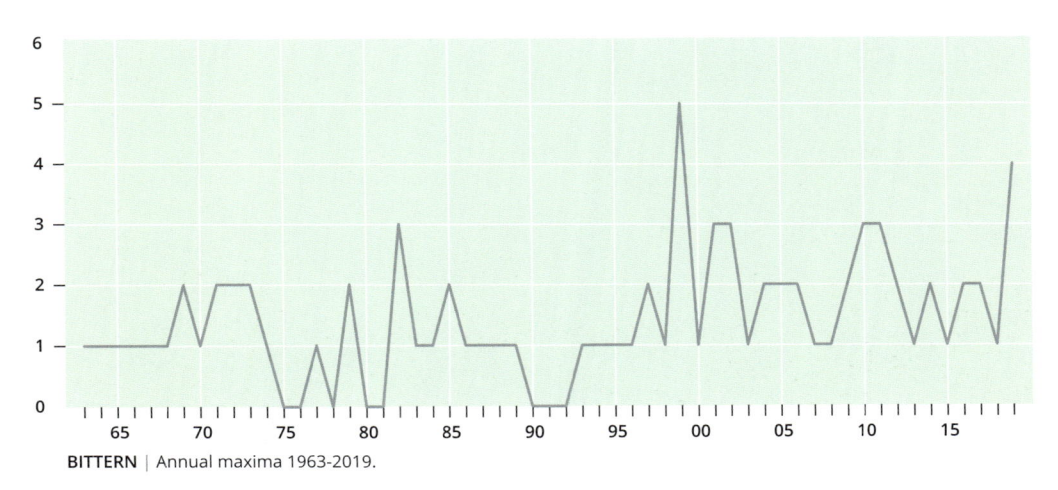

BITTERN | Annual maxima 1963-2019.

Bittern   Rich Andrews

LITTLE BITTERN *Ixobrychus minutus*

There is one record: an adult male on 23 June 1993 was first seen in flight at Herriott's End and then seen well in the reeds on the east side of Herriott's Pool, where it was heard giving its 'barking' advertising call (KEV *et al.*).

NIGHT HERON *Nycticorax nycticorax*

The first record involved a juvenile that was found inside a factory on Severnside on 19 November 1971. It was fed in captivity until it was released at Chew on 28 November, where it remained until 19 December (mainly in the alders on the west side of Herrriott's Pool) (G. Youdale *et al.*). There have since been four 'proper' records as follows:

- 1983: a juvenile at Hollow Brook 6–30 November (J. Aldridge, M. A. & T. B. Silcocks *et al.*).
- 1992: a second-summer in Stratford Bay on 4 June (M. A. Bailey J. M. B. King).
- 1999: a first-summer at Hollow Brook 10–12 June (K. J. Hall *et al.*).
- 2001: an adult or second-year flew from bushes on the east side of Herriott's Pool on the evening of 10 May and appeared to fly south along the River Chew (R. M. Andrews, A. H. Davis, N. R. Milbourne *et al.*).

SQUACCO HERON *Ardeola ralloides*

There are two records.

An adult was seen in Heron's Green Bay on 26 May 1973 (A. R. Ashman, A. J. Bundy, D. E. Ladhams *et al.*).

One was seen distantly on 2 May 2012, flying across the lake from the East Shore towards Heron's Green Bay (KEV). Fortunately, it was relocated later in the day and confirmed as an adult Squacco Heron (A. H. Davis, M. Jenkins *et al.*). It was seen again from 4 to 7 May before relocating to Blagdon Lake from the 6th to the 17th, where it showed very well, revealing itself as a stunning adult in full summer plumage. (The overlap in dates on 6–7 May was because, at that point, it was flying back and forth between the two lakes.)

Squacco Heron | Rich Andrews

CATTLE EGRET *Bubulcus ibis*

The first record involved an escaped summer-plumaged individual of the Asian race (now species) *B. (i.) coromandus*. It was seen from 17 July to 20 November 1994, from 28 January to 29 April 1995 and again on 16 July 1995, and another on 7 July 1997. Records of wild individuals of the nominate race are as follows:

- **2007:** one on 11–13 October 2007, present in Heron's Green Bay and also feeding in the Parkland (R. M. Andrews *et al.*).
- **2009–2010:** three (two adults in summer plumage plus a juvenile) from 30 July to 6 August 2009, the juvenile remaining until 11 August. Another was then seen from 27 December to 3 January 2010.
- **2010:** one was seen on 5 November.
- **2016:** one on 19 and 30 November.
- **2017:** a dramatic increase in records begins, starting with one in February and three in March, then nine arrived on 9 April later joined by 2 more. These eleven were also seen on 10th and 11th. Ten in summer plumage were seen feeding on grassland in front of Heron's Green Cottage on 12th. There was one roosting on 9 May, two then in September and October, with a single adult in December.
- **2018:** the adult from 2017 was seen until 24 February. An autumn influx started with one on 13 August, with 13 on 31st, 5 in September on 4th, rising to 24 on 16th and then a county record of 29 on 21st. This dropped to 8 in October, then up to 11 in November, with ten remaining to the end of the year.
- **2019:** the ten from 2018 reduced to 4 by mid-January, with the last 2 from the flock seen on 3 February. The only other spring record was one on 22 April. The autumn birds started with two in the morning of 23 August which were joined later by 8 more. There was just one on 25th, then 3 in September, and 5 in October and November.

Cattle Egret | Rich Andrews

GREY HERON *Ardea cinerea*

The first published record was of 28 in July 1955, followed by 35 the following month. There were then few counts until 1966, after which it was monitored on a regular basis. Apart from relatively minor fluctuations, the annual maxima have normally varied between 20 and 40, with a record 61 on 24 September 1989, followed by 56 in September 1990 (see annual maximum counts graph).

As the average monthly maximum graph shows, counts are at their lowest from March to May, when they are breeding, but they increase steadily from June through late summer and autumn to a peak in November. This late summer/autumn peak relates to the low water levels at this time of year, which concentrate the fish fry on which they feed.

On 18 April 1981, two were seen entering the wood on Denny Island and this was the first indication that they may have started nesting at the lake. What appeared to be a nest was then seen in May 1983 and breeding was confirmed the following year. This has since been annual, rising to 33 pairs in 1997 and a record 51 in 2008, but since declining to 22 in 2015. Although some of these birds feed around the lake, most feed away from it and, when feeding young, they can often be seen flying in from some distance, no doubt having fed in the streams and rivers in the lake's catchment area.

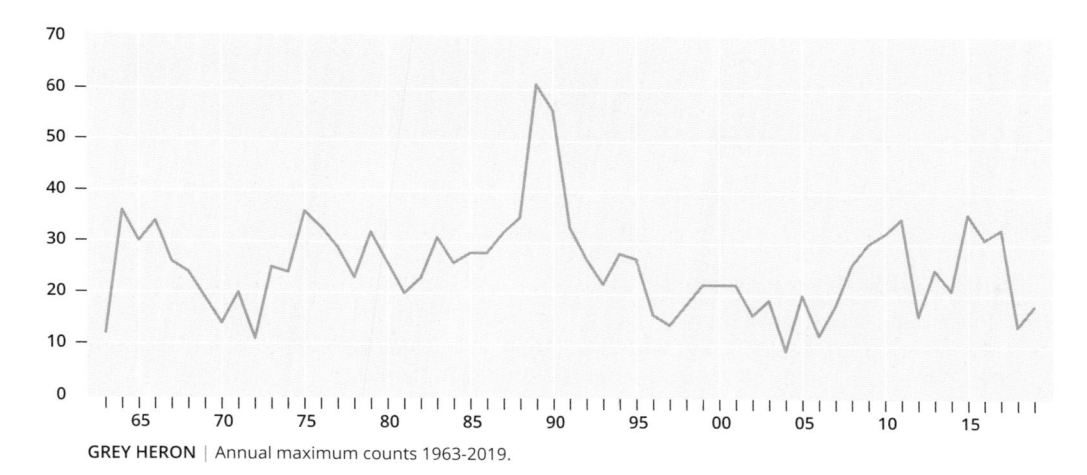

GREY HERON | Annual maximum counts 1963-2019.

Grey Heron | Laurel Tucker

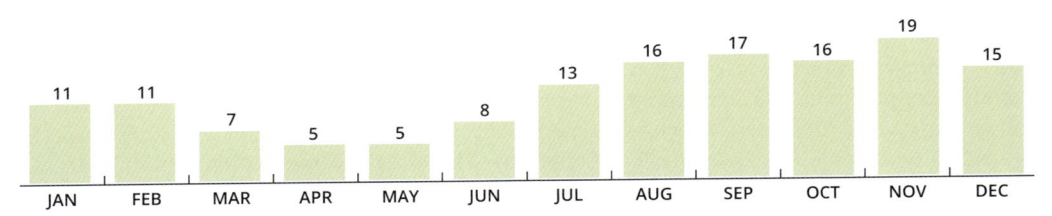

GREY HERON | Monthly maxima (average) 1966-2015.

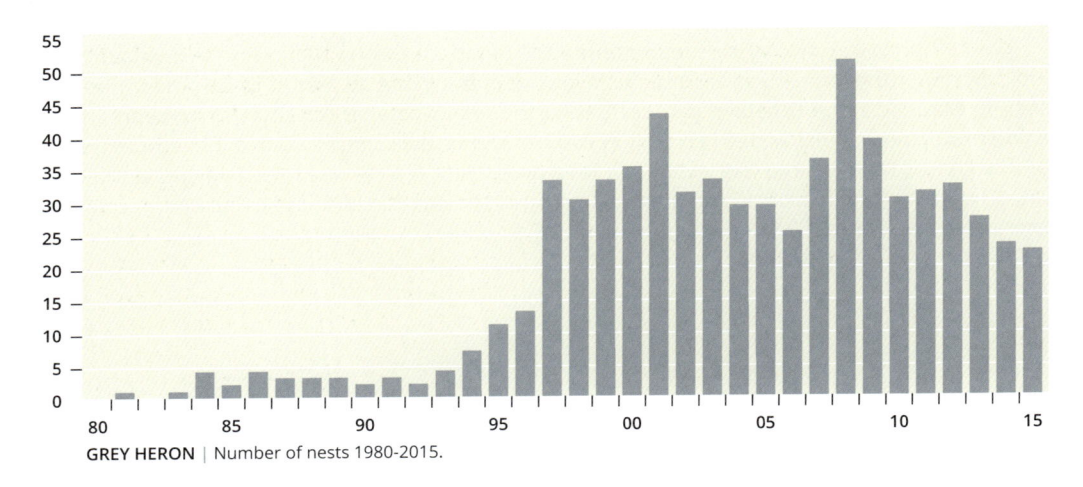

GREY HERON | Number of nests 1980-2015.

PURPLE HERON *Ardea purpurea*

There have been seven records:

- **1970:** one at Herriott's Pool on 20 April and again on 2–3 May (A. Heathcote, A. J. Parsons *et al.*).
- **1975:** one seen briefly on 28 September (D. Buffery, P. Denning).
- **1977:** one in flight on 23 April (K. J. Hall, A. J. Merritt, R. B. H. Smith).
- **1983:** a first-summer on Herriott's Pool from 25 June to 2 July (R. M. Curber, KEV *et al.*).
- **2001:** a sub-adult on 12 May (D. J. Angell *et al.*).
- **2009:** a sub-adult (probably a first-summer) at Heron's Green Pool on 10 May (M. G. Rowan *et al.*).
- **2019:** a first-summer on 17 May (R.J. Higgins *et al.*) was seen a short time later at Stanton Wick as it flew north-east (R. M. Andrews).

Purple Heron | Laurel Tucker

GREAT WHITE EGRET *Ardea alba*

By the late 19th century and the early part of the 20th century, the European range of the Great White Egret was confined to south-eastern Europe. This was the result of Victorian women wearing hats decorated with, amongst other things, exotic plumes. In both Europe and North America this led to the mass slaughter of egrets for the plume trade. By 1917, the European population was almost exterminated and restricted to the Volga Delta and Kazakhstan. In 1889, an organisation to stop this trade was founded in Manchester by Emily Williamson. The group quickly gained popularity, eventually morphing into the Society for the Protection of Birds, which went on to become the RSPB.

Great White Egret was a great rarity in Britain, but years of protection on the continent have gradually led to an increase in records, culminating in the first breeding in Britain in 2012, on the Somerset Levels. Since 1994, extensive wetlands had been created out of old peat workings and this led to the colonisation of the area by many wetland species, including the Great White Egret.

The first Chew record was an adult in summer plumage on 20–21 June 2003 (A. H. Davis *et al.*), which was seen again on 11 and 12 July. The next was in October 2011 and the species has since been annual, with a record 28 on 11 November 2016, feeding together in Heron's Green Bay – a remarkable spectacle that, even a few years ago, one simply could not have imagined. As of June 2019 the record count was 37 (1 November 2017). As the combined monthly maxima graph shows, numbers are at their highest in October–November, when the water levels are at their lowest. Numbers soon drop as the water level rises in early winter.

The annual maxima graph shows the occurrence patterns from 2003, when first recorded, to 2017.

Great White Egret   Lucy Masters

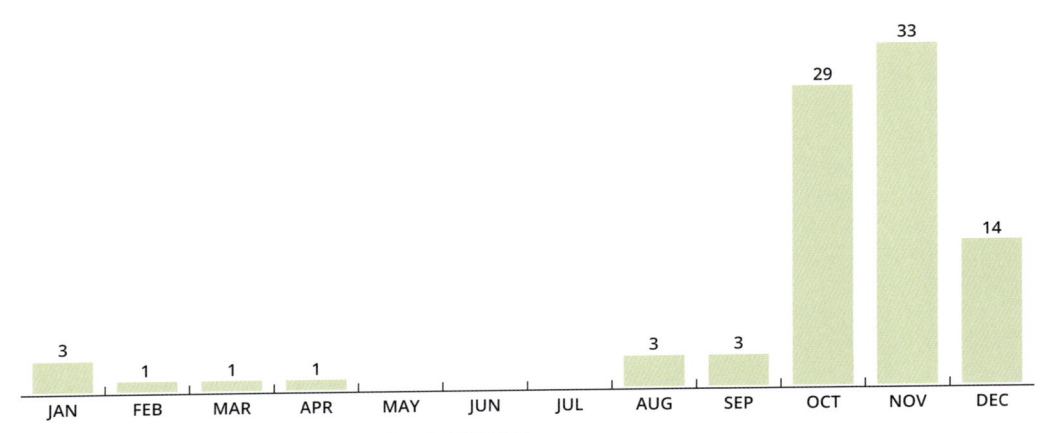

GREAT WHITE EGRET | Monthly maxima (combined) 2003-2016.

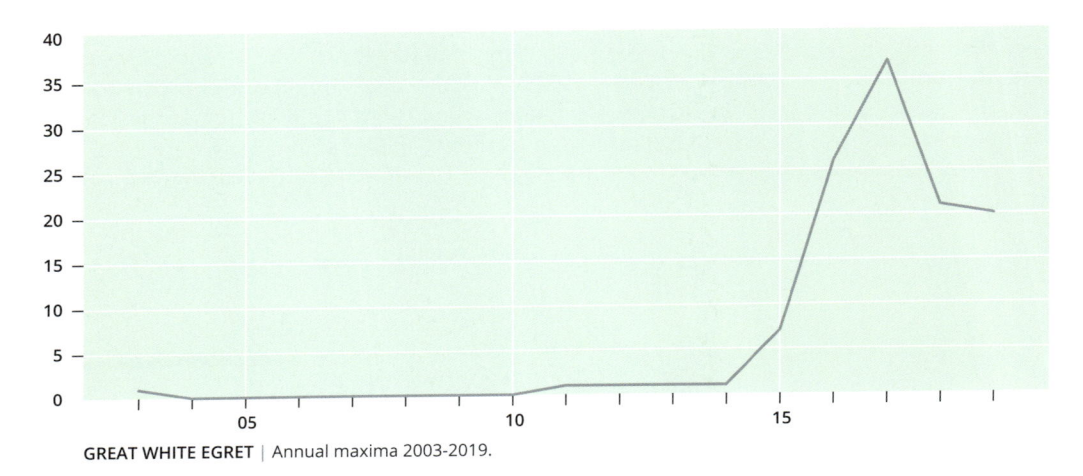

Jan 3, Feb 1, Mar 1, Apr 1, May 0, Jun 0, Jul 0, Aug 3, Sep 3, Oct 29, Nov 33, Dec 14.

GREAT WHITE EGRET | Annual maxima 2003-2019.

LITTLE EGRET *Egretta garzetta*

The first record was of a juvenile on 10 October 1990 which stayed until 21st (R. J. Higgins *et al.*). This record was accepted by BBRC; amazing now that this was a rare UK bird in those days. The next was again a juvenile on 9 August 1992 (D. J. Horlick, R. F. Reader *et al.*). More records were anticipated, reflecting the remarkable northward spread of the species during the 1990s. Throughout that decade, however, the maximum counts at Chew were of just ones and twos. But, from 2000 onwards, they increased significantly, with peaks of nine in 2005 and ten in 2007, the first double figure count. From that point onwards, the numbers gradually increased to a record 27 in December 2015. It should be stressed, however, that the Little Egret is a very mobile species and, therefore, it can be very difficult to accurately count. Counts at evening roosts usually produce the most reliable numbers, Denny Island being the best location to check.

Interestingly, although the species feeds around the lake itself – catching mainly small fish – the largest numbers often appear in wet conditions when they gather in lakeside fields where, quite clearly, they feed on earthworms.

As the combined monthly maxima graph shows, relatively few are present in the New Year, and there is then an obvious dip in May–June, when they are off breeding. Numbers increase significantly to an August–September peak, gradually reducing in late autumn and early winter as the water levels rise.

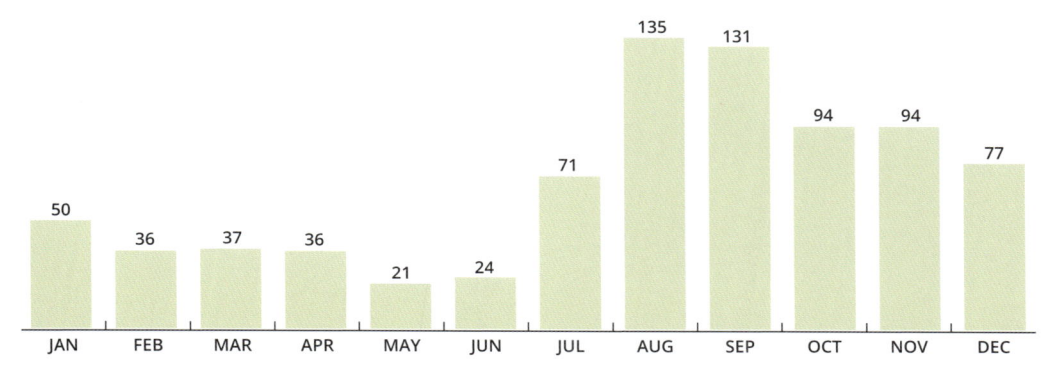

LITTLE EGRET | Monthly maxima (combined) 1992-2015.

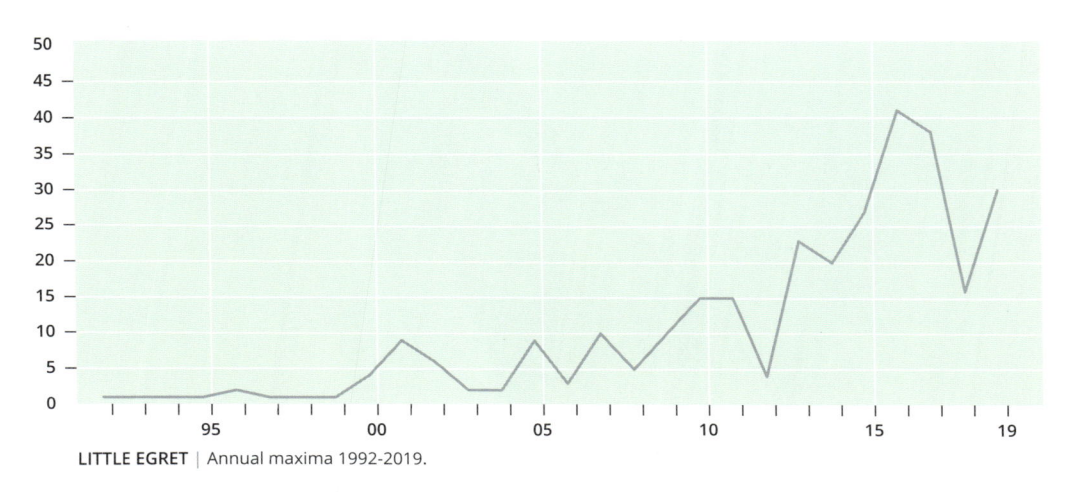

JAN	FEB	MAR	APR	MAY	JUN	JUL	AUG	SEP	OCT	NOV	DEC
50	36	37	36	21	24	71	135	131	94	94	77

LITTLE EGRET | Annual maxima 1992-2019.

Littel Egret | Rich Andrews

COMPLETE SPECIES LIST AND CHARTS 345

Osprey | Gary Thoburn

OSPREY *Pandion haliaetus*

The first records were of one on 16 August 1965 (H. W. Neal), followed by another from 7 September to 4 October 1965 (T. B. Silcocks *et al.*). As the annual individuals graph shows, with the exception of blank years in 1989 and 2003, it has been recorded annually since 1980, with a conservative estimate of 97 individuals during that period. This upsurge reflects the increase and spread of the species since it recolonised Scotland in 1954 or 1955 (*BWP*). Ospreys have become increasingly regular and several nesting platforms have recently been erected in the vicinity of both Chew and Blagdon in the hope that species can be persuaded to remain and breed in the area.

The peak months are April–May and August–October. There have been four March records, with the earliest being one in 2009 on 22nd. The latest was a well-watched individual that commuted between Chew and nearby Litton Reservoirs from 19 October to 6 November 1988 (*ABR*).

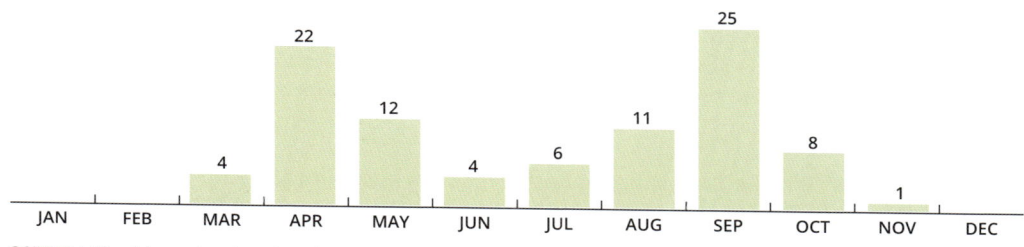

OSPREY | Monthly maxima (combined) 1965-2015.

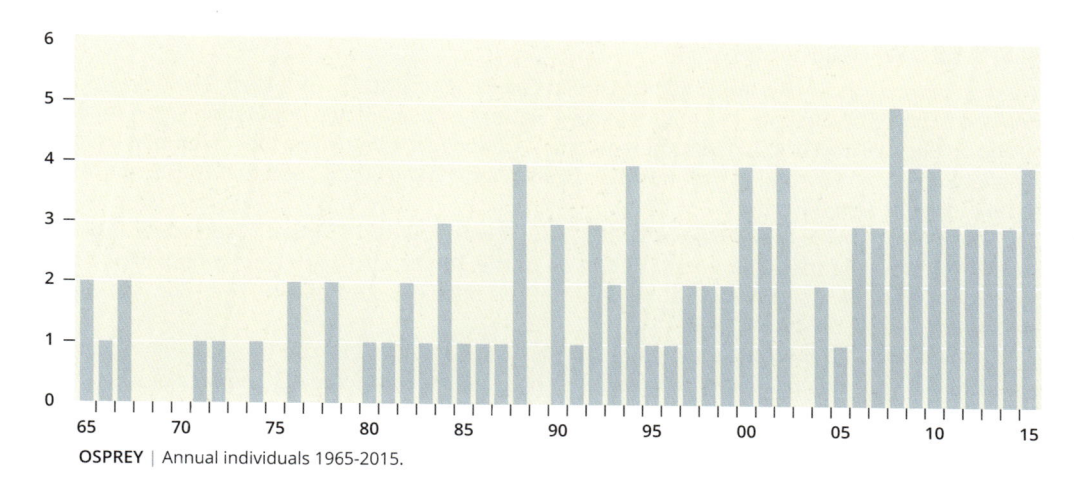

OSPREY | Annual individuals 1965-2015.

HONEY-BUZZARD *Pernis apivorus*

There are four records:

- **1970:** one flew over the lake on 22 May 1970 (J. G. Hole), the first Somerset record since 1917 (*Somerset Birds* 1970).
- **2000:** on 28 September a dark morph juvenile flew south over Burledge Hill before reappearing and drifting slowly south-westwards (A. H. Davis, G. M. Dicker, KEV). Another dark morph juvenile flew south later the same afternoon (R. M. Andrews). These records were part of an unprecedented influx into Britain from mid-September to early October 2000, involving a very rough estimate of 1,975 birds (Fraser & Rogers 2002).
- **2010:** one flew east at Herriott's Bridge on 1 June (A. H. Davis).

Reference
Fraser, P. and Rogers, M. J. (2002). 'Report on scarce migrant birds in Britain in 2000'. *British Birds* 95: 610–612.

BOOTED EAGLE *Aquila pennata*

A pale phase second-winter was present from 11 to 15 February 2000, being first located over Heron's Green Bay by R. M. and M. H. Curber. It was relocated in the afternoon over Burledge Hill, where it remained until the following day, when it flew down to Herriott's Pool and killed and ate a Coot *Fulica atra*. Needless to say, being a first for Britain, it attracted a large number of birders.

Its movements, both prior to and after its appearance at Chew, are interesting. It was first seen at the North Slob, Co. Wexford, in late February 1999, having presumably arrived in Ireland the previous autumn. It was then seen at Rogerstown, Co. Dublin, on 6 March, near Broadway and Killinick, Co. Wexford, on 2–4 April, and on Rathlin Island, Co. Antrim, in late August. It then moved to Britain, being discovered in Cornwall at Porthgwarra and Drift Reservoir, before moving to Marazion and Tremethick Cross (also in Cornwall) from late August to 28 November. It was then seen at Meare Heath and Westhay Heath, Somerset, on 6–9 February 2000, before moving to Chew.

After it left Chew, it was seen in Kent at Dungeness on 7 April and at Cliffe, on 8th. Amazingly, what was presumed to have been the same bird was last seen on North Ronaldsay, Orkney, on 22 June.

This, if it had been accepted, would have been (and would still be) the only British record.

Note:
This record, while clearly a Booted Eagle, has never been accepted as a wild bird by BBRC and to date is not on the British List. Please see also the section in 'Memorable Birding Moments and Tales' on 'The ones that got away'.

SPARROWHAWK *Accipiter nisus*

The first record was of one that caught a Dunlin *Calidris alpina* on 17 April 1955. The next were two in March 1961. The absence in the intervening years was caused by a population crash related to pesticide use, particularly DDT, but there was also under-recording in the bird reports at that time. Single birds were recorded in five months in 1963, but it wasn't until 1965 that the species began to be recorded annually.

The first confirmed breeding was in 1971, but it wasn't until 1978 that it became established, successful breeding then being recorded in 34 of the 38 years to 2015 (see annual brood totals graph). Breeding has occurred at a minimum of ten different sites around the lake. The highest ever count was six on 4 April 1993.

As the combined monthly maxima graph shows, Sparrowhawks can be seen throughout the year, but with a spring peak in April, when they are often seen displaying. They are elusive in May and June, when nesting, but numbers increase in July when the young become particularly noisy, peaking in August after they have fledged. Sightings then gradually decline into the winter.

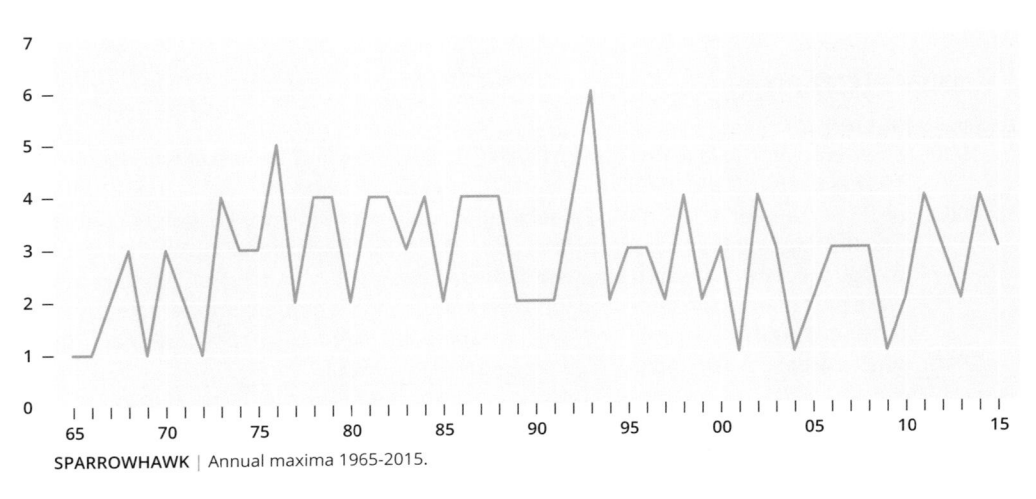

SPARROWHAWK | Annual maxima 1965-2015.

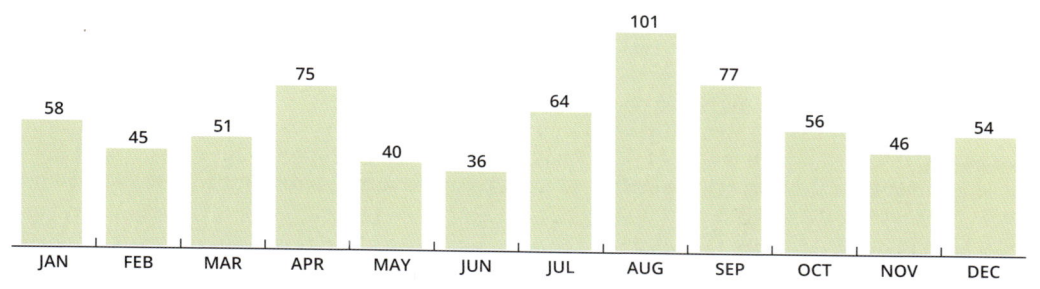

SPARROWHAWK | Monthly maxima (combined) 1963-2015.

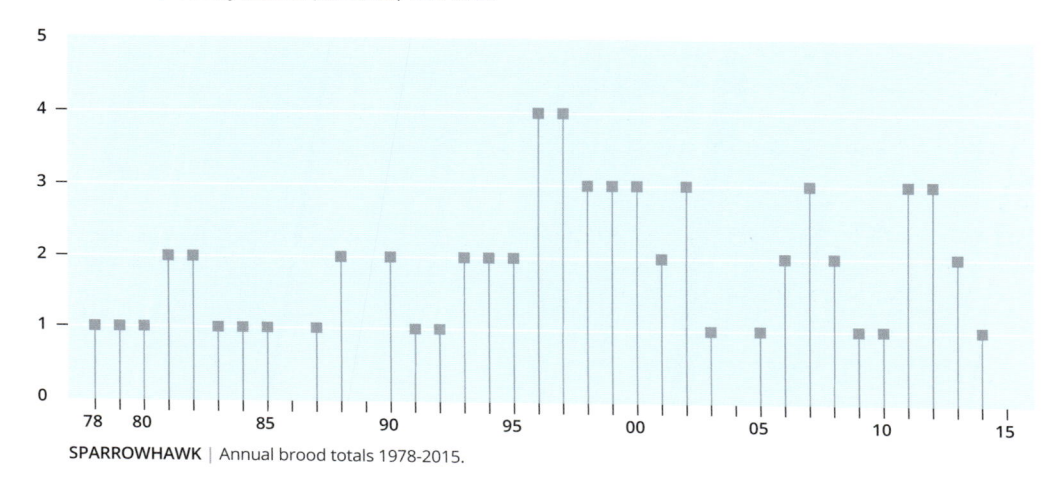

JAN	FEB	MAR	APR	MAY	JUN	JUL	AUG	SEP	OCT	NOV	DEC
58	45	51	75	40	36	64	101	77	56	46	54

SPARROWHAWK | Annual brood totals 1978-2015.

MARSH HARRIER *Circus aeruginosus*

The first records were all of females or juveniles: one 16–31 August 1954 (B. K. Brook *et al.*) with a second bird on 19 September (B. King, R. H. Poulter), one on 22–23 October 1960 (J. R. Best, B. King, C. Lachlan and K. B. Young), and singles on 15 September 1963, 27 May 1964 and 18 April and 6 July 1966. There was then an eight-year gap until a 'female-type' on 27 May 1975. The species occurred in 34 of the 42 years to 2016, and there have been several records in 2017, 2018, 2019 and 2020. This increase reflected an enormous rise in the British breeding population, from just one pair in 1971 to an estimated 363–429 pairs in 2005, these birds fledging a minimum of 796 young (Holling *et al.* 2008). This upward trend is clearly reflected in the Chew records. In light of the recent colonisation of the Avalon Marshes in Somerset, there are indications that the species is starting to appear at the lake on a fairly regular basis and it must now be considered a potential colonist. Conversely, they have also over-wintered, with a juvenile present from 17 December 2008 to 8 February 2009, and two juveniles present from 28 December to 11 January.

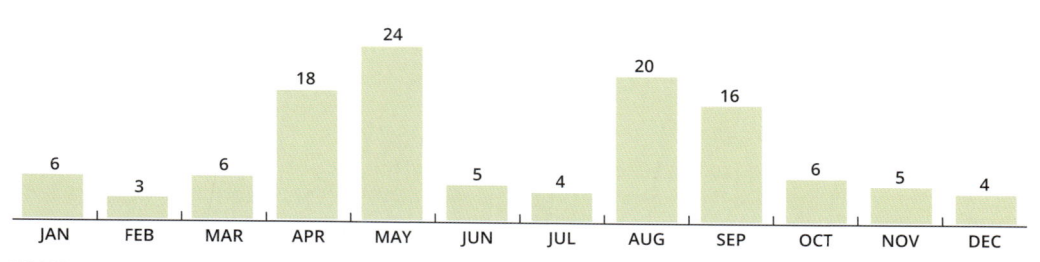

JAN	FEB	MAR	APR	MAY	JUN	JUL	AUG	SEP	OCT	NOV	DEC
6	3	6	18	24	5	4	20	16	6	5	4

MARSH HARRIER | Monthly maxima (combined) 1954-2015. It has occurred in all months, but with strong peaks in April–May and August–September.

An indication of a more distant origin for some of our birds came in 2012, when a wing-tagged second calendar year male was seen on 17 November. It had been tagged as a nestling at Sculthorpe Moor, Norfolk, on 10 June 2011 and was seen subsequently on the Isle of Sheppey, Kent, on 31 October 2011 and at the Newport Wetlands, Gwent, on 11 September 2012.

Reference
Holling, M. and the Rare Breeding Birds Panel (2008). 'Rare breeding birds in the United Kingdom in 2005'. *British Birds* 101: 276-316.

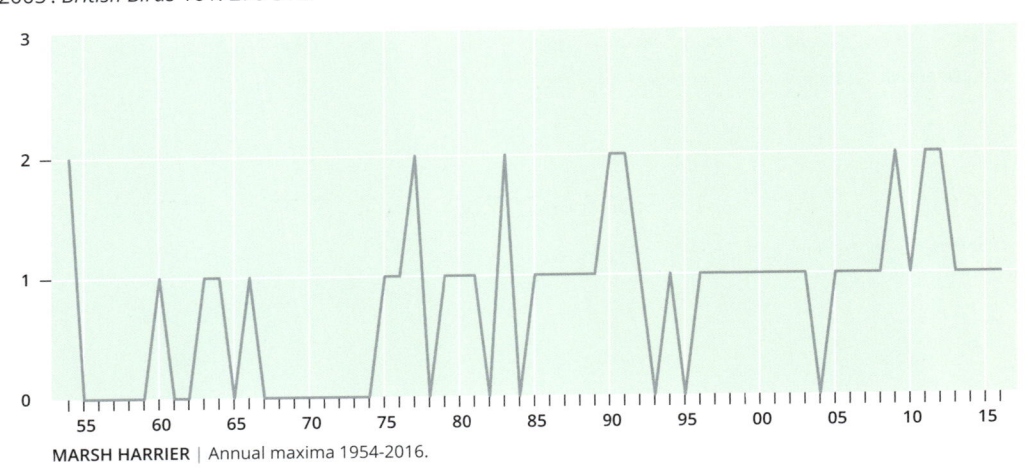

MARSH HARRIER | Annual maxima 1954-2016.

Marsh Harrier | Gary Thoburn

| HEN HARRIER *Circus cyaneus*

A rare and irregular visitor to the lake, recorded in 19 of the 62 years to 2015. As the annual maxima graph indicates, the first records were of singles in 1956 (21, 25 and 26 February – E. G. Brain, G. L. Boyle and B. King) and in January 1957. There was then a ten-year gap until a third, in November 1967. A 12-year gap then followed until a female/juvenile was seen in January 1979. From that point onwards, the species was recorded in 16 of the next 36 years to 2015.

As the combined monthly maxima graph shows, they occur from October to April, January being the peak month with seven records. All the records related to single individuals, apart from two on 1 December 1984. Of those sexed, nine were males and 21 were females or juveniles. The first recorded October date is 14th (in 2007) and the latest date is 13 April (2018). A second calendar year bird on 3 April 1991 carried wing tags that indicated that it had been marked as a chick in Highland Scotland in the summer of 1990. From there it had moved 675 km to Chew, and it was also seen there again the following winter on 9 November 1991(*ABR*). A male was also seen on 13 April 2018.

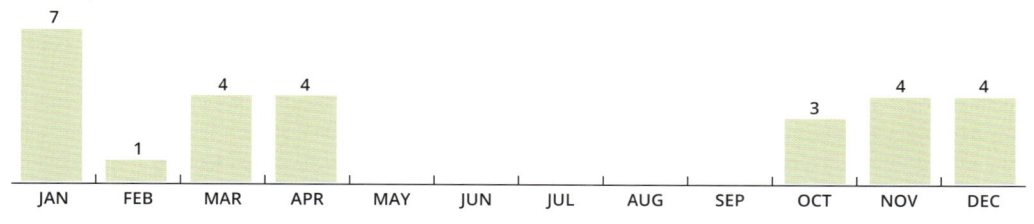

HEN HARRIER | Monthly maxima (combined) 1956-2018.

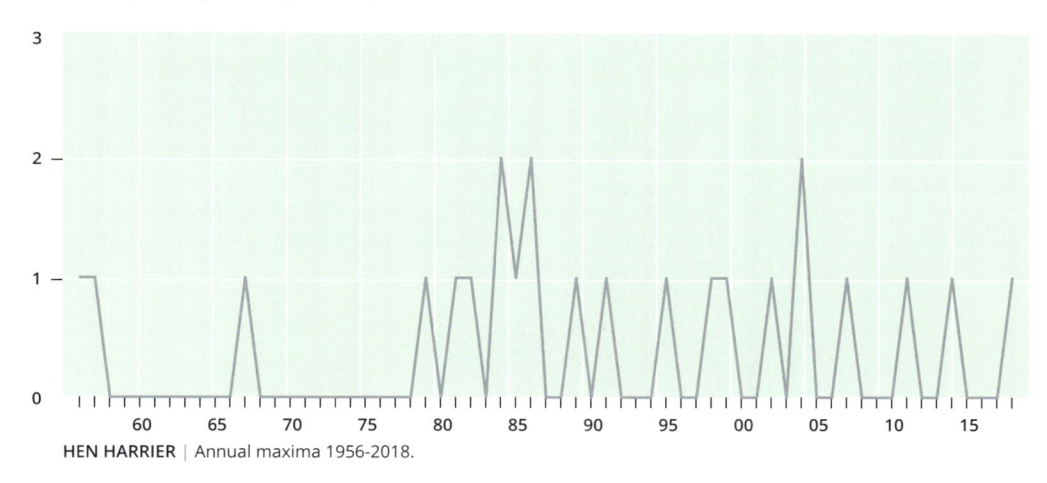

HEN HARRIER | Annual maxima 1956-2018.

Hen Harrier | Brian Thompson

MONTAGU'S HARRIER *Circus pygargus*

1962: A juvenile flew along the north-east shore on 4 August (B. King).
Also, on 13 October 2001, a female or juvenile harrier flew south over the lake at 12.30 hrs. It was considered to have been either a Montagu's or a Pallid Harrier *C. macrourus*, probably the former (A. H. Davis).

RED KITE *Milvus milvus*

The story of the fall and rise of the Red Kite is well known. Following years of persecution, it became a very rare breeding bird, reduced to just a handful of pairs in the early part of the 20th century, confined to central Wales. Following legal protection, the species began to recover and a series of reintroductions in England and Scotland in the late 1980s and 1990s boosted the population to its current high levels. It is now positively common in parts of central England, as well as in parts of Scotland.

Despite this positive state of affairs, the species remains a scarce bird in the Bristol area, although records have increased considerably in recent years, with a total of 273 bird-days recorded in the county of Avon in 2015 (*ABR*). Records at Chew have reflected this upward trend. The first was one over Nunnery Point on 10 March 1990 (G. L. Scott) and the next was one in February 2002. From 2004, this striking bird has been annual. Most records have related to ones and twos, but four were reported on 7 April 2015 (*ABR*).

As the combined monthly maxima graph indicates, most records are in spring, with March and April being the peak months, but there are also several records from May and June, with a smaller peak in September.

It seems highly likely that sightings will continue to increase, and there would seem to be no reason why the species should not eventually breed in the area. The *ABR* for 2016 gives a count of three on 6 May and a total of 38 bird-days during the year.

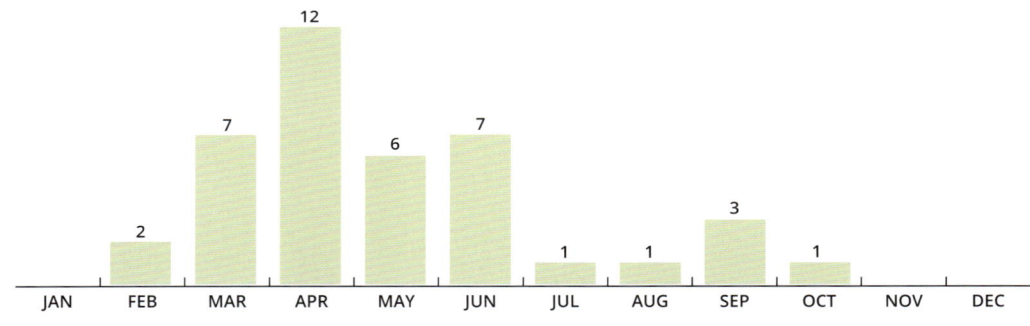

RED KITE | Monthly maxima (combined) 2002-2015.

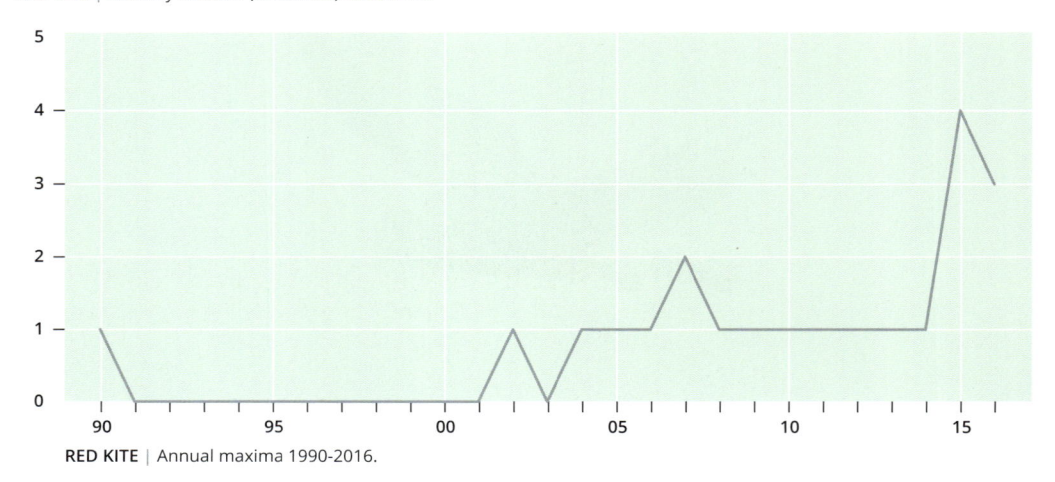

RED KITE | Annual maxima 1990-2016.

Red Kite | Ian Stapp

ROUGH-LEGGED BUZZARD *Buteo lagopus*

There is a single record: one flew south-west over Moreton Bank on 9 November 1974 (A. J. Merritt). It was part of a record influx of the species into Britain in 1974–75, with an estimated 250 individuals recorded. There had also been 170 in the previous winter (Scott 1978).

Reference
Scott, R. E. (1978). 'Rough-legged Buzzards in Britain in 1973/74 and 1974/75'. *British Birds* 71: 325–338.

BUZZARD *Buteo buteo*

It is not clear whether Buzzards were present during the early years of the lake but Palmer and Ballance (1968) stated that the species was scarce, a result of decades of persecution followed by the outbreak of myxomatosis in Rabbits in the 1950s. Apparently, however, it was still present in small numbers on Mendip and in the valleys around Bath. There were at least six sightings at the lake in 1963 and, from 1965 at least, the species was recorded annually, often to be seen soaring over Burledge Hill, just to the south-east. Numbers slowly increased from the 1970s through to the 1990s and the first double figure count was made in September 1991, when 12 were counted. Numbers have continued to rise, with 29 counted in a single scan on 1 April 2001. Since then the species has become a common sight, most obvious when soaring and displaying on fine days in March and April. Further high counts were made: 24 on 19 April 2004, 26 on 16 April 2012 and a remarkable 46 in a single flock on 30 April 2013. These birds were attracted to a recently ploughed field along Denny Lane, just to the north of the Main Dam, the species feeding extensively on earthworms.

It first bred within the lake's perimeter in 1994 and breeding has occurred there and in the immediate surroundings in most years since, with up to nine pairs present and as many as seven broods (in 2009, 2011 and 2015).

Reference
Palmer, E. M. and Ballance, D. K. (1968). *The Birds of Somerset.* Longmans.

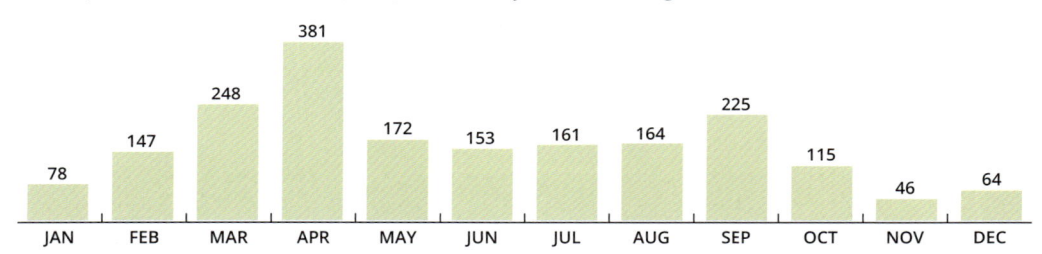

BUZZARD | Monthly maxima (combined) 1963-2015.

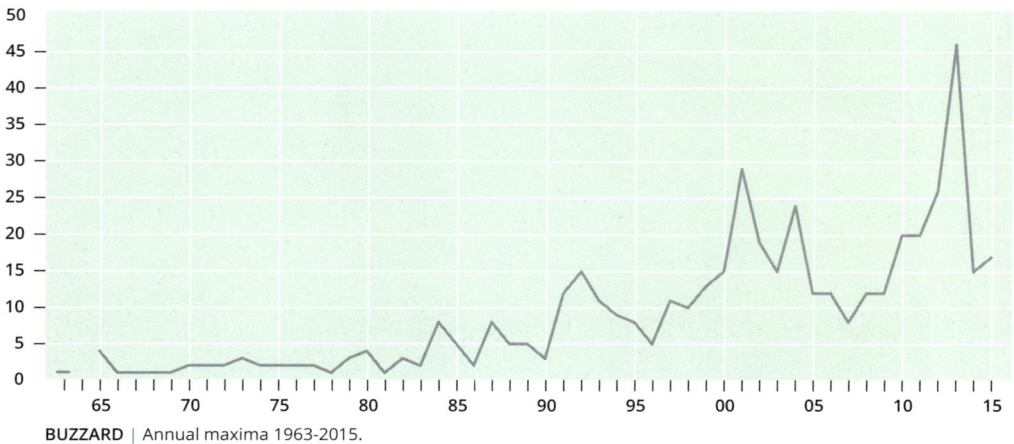

BUZZARD | Annual maxima 1963-2015.

BARN OWL *Tyto alba*

The annual maxima chart is most useful for seeing the absent years. It will always be likely that the figures will be underestimates. For example in 2016, 2 pairs bred and 5 young were ringed, but the 9 birds would never have been seen together.

This elusive species has been recorded in all but 14 of the 63 years from 1954 to 2016. Some of the gaps (e.g. 1962–63) were due to cold winter weather, but wet and windy conditions during the fledging period can also be detrimental to chick survival. In recent years, Barn Owl nest boxes have been installed at four sites around the lake and, as indicated in the combined monthly maxima graph, they have been influential in keeping the population going. The species is present all year round, but they are surprisingly elusive. Note however that between 1961 and 2018, 88 Barn Owls were ringed at the lake. As the combined monthly maxima graph indicates, they are most easily seen during late winter afternoons and are most difficult from April to June, when breeding.

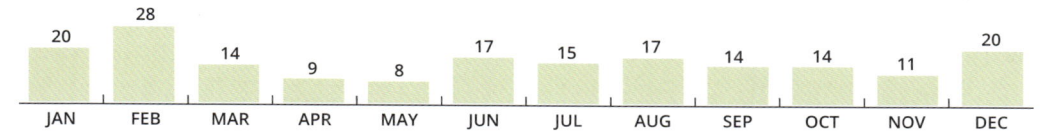

BARN OWL | Monthly maxima (combined) 1954-2016.

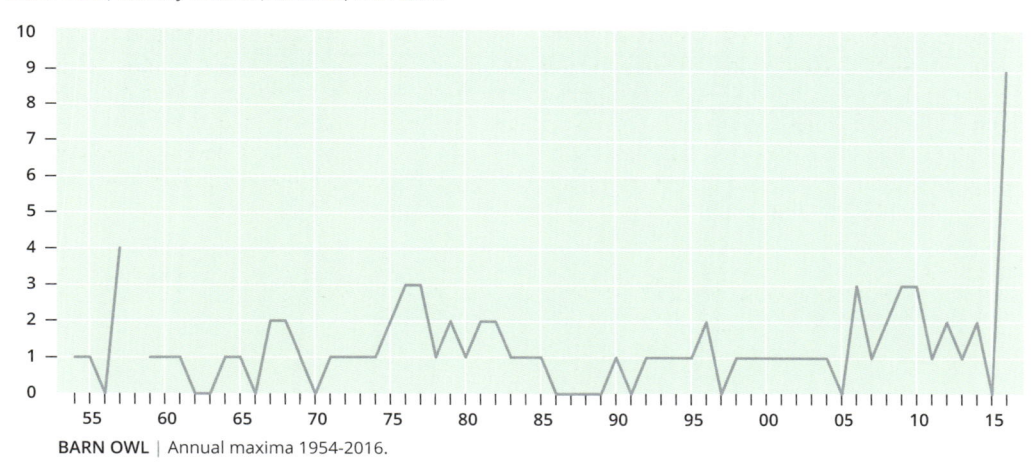

BARN OWL | Annual maxima 1954-2016.

Barn Owl | Gary Thoburn

TAWNY OWL *Strix aluco*

The first traceable record is of one calling on 23 July 1967, but it seems inconceivable that this elusive species was not present before that date. It has to be remembered, however, that, in the early days, the lakeside plantations were in their infancy and so would not have been suitable for hole-nesting Tawny Owls. The annual maxima graph shows that numbers apparently increased from the mid 1980s into the early 2000s, reaching a record eight calling males in 2013. This total was counted on the still evening of 29 September, when five were heard calling from Nunnery Point. Separate calling birds at three other sites along the east shore indicated that there were probably at least 8–10 pairs present. Breeding was actually proved in 1992, 1993 (two broods), 1999, 2000 and 2001.

As befitting a fairly sedentary species, the combined monthly maxima graph indicates that the records are fairly evenly spread, apart from the high September total, which is largely the result of the aforementioned count in 2013. The dip in calling from June to August no doubt relates to their late summer moult period. Note that 45 Tawny Owls have been ringed.

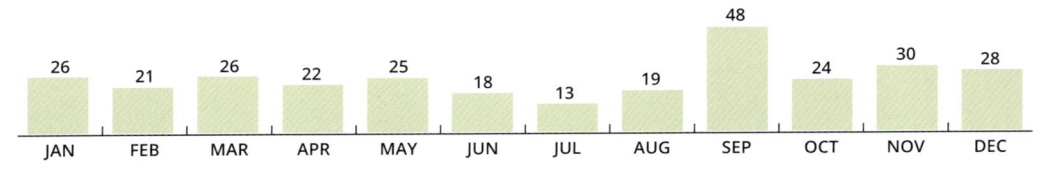

TAWNY OWL | Monthly maxima (combined) 1967-2015.

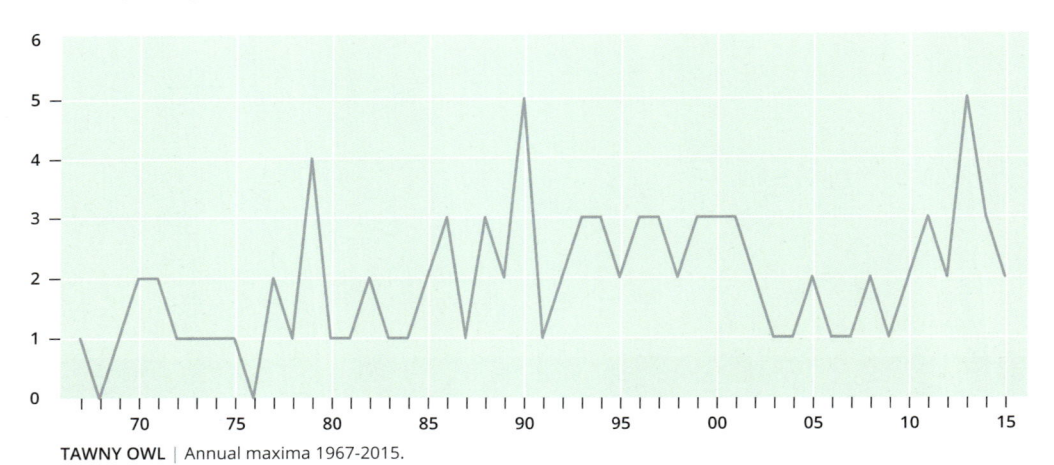

JAN	FEB	MAR	APR	MAY	JUN	JUL	AUG	SEP	OCT	NOV	DEC
26	21	26	22	25	18	13	19	48	24	30	28

TAWNY OWL | Annual maxima 1967-2015.

LITTLE OWL *Athene noctua*

As this species was formerly quite common, there were no published Chew records until October 1965. However the 1963 *ABR* simply lists it as one of the 'other species', and the 1964 *ABR* says 'reported from 18 localities', this being from the whole county of Avon. The annual maxima graph shows that just single sightings were the norm until 1975, when two were recorded on 7 November. Records increased from that point onwards, with counts of five in October 1990 and six in November 1994. Numbers then declined ,with single birds seen up to at least 11 April 2019. As would be expected for a resident species, the combined monthly maxima graph shows that numbers were fairly static throughout the year, but with peaks of activity in March and again from September to December.

The reasons for the decline of the Little Owl are not clear, but one theory is that it is being out-competed by the Buzzard *Buteo buteo*, which not only feeds on similar prey items, but has increased significantly in recent years. The trend shown on the Buzzard annual maxima graph shows the increase in Buzzards. Contrast this with those for the Little Owl annual maxima graph.

Tawny Owls | Gary Thoburn

However, an article by David Warden in the 2016 *Avon Bird Report* entitled 'The Changing Status of the Little Owl in and near the Chew Valley' was based on over 700 sightings of Little Owls from 1963-2016. Ten nest sites were found in an area of 100 sq km and, in fact, the main suspected reason for the recent decline was changes in agricultural practices, with permanent pasture being replaced by arable crops, including biofuels. Only one Little Owl has ever been ringed at the lake.

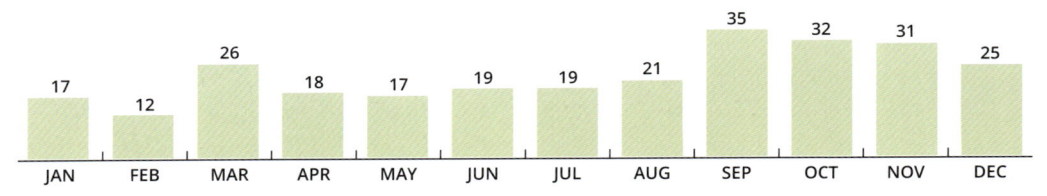

JAN	FEB	MAR	APR	MAY	JUN	JUL	AUG	SEP	OCT	NOV	DEC
17	12	26	18	17	19	19	21	35	32	31	25

LITTLE OWL | Monthly maxima (combined) 1965-2019.

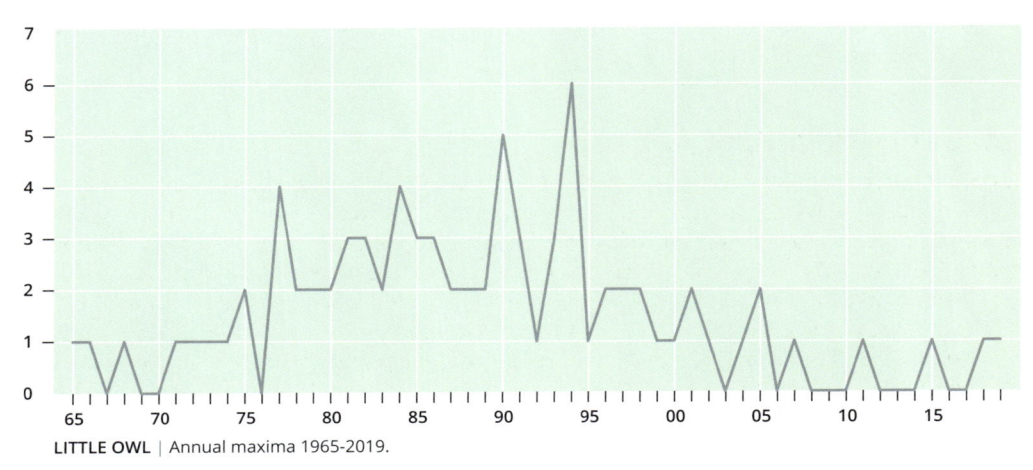

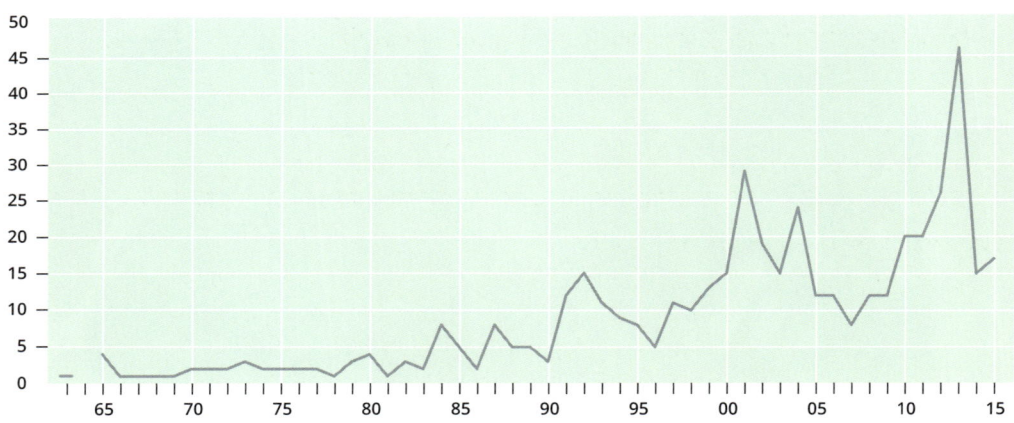

LITTLE OWL | Annual maxima 1965-2019.

BUZZARD | Annual maxima 1963-2015. The Little Owls declined just as the Buzzards increased.

Littel Owl | Laurel Tucker

LONG-EARED OWL *Asio otus*

There have been at least seven records involving eight individuals:
- **1967:** one in a hedgerow and in flight on 5 September (D. E. Ladhams).
- **1976:** one that was seen in a hedgerow on 31 March and 1 May is likely to have been a bird that was found exhausted in Frenchay, Bristol, in January and subsequently released at the lake (D. Warden).
- **1979:** one behind the Main Reeds from 21 April to 2 May (C. J. Newman, KEV *et al.*). Another was seen in a hawthorn on the East Shore on 19 May (N. A. & L. A. Tucker).
- **1989:** two in willows at Stratford Pool on 8 January (R. Mielcarek, KEV), one of which had been trapped and ringed, and one subsequently in Stratford Bay on 5 and 8 February (R. Palmer, R. N. Staples, R. Mielcarek).
- **2006:** one on 11 June was watched in broad daylight for at least 3 hours, sitting on a fence post on Moreton Bank (KEV *et al.*).
- **2008:** another, also seen on a fence post in broad daylight, was at Heron's Green Pool on 4 June (J. Aldridge *et al.*).

SHORT-EARED OWL *Asio flammeus*

The Short-eared Owl is a rare and erratic visitor to the lake. The first record was one on 4 January 1959 (K. B. Young) but it was eight years before the second (12–14 November 1967). There was then a reasonable run of records from 1974 to 1989, involving 13 individuals. All were singles except for two on 8–9 May 1976 (one of which was trapped and ringed) and two on 11 December 1982. The maximum total of three individuals in 1976 (in May, September and November) was related to that year's drought when, in the very low water levels, the lake's banks were colonised by large areas of weedy plants. This, of course, provided excellent feeding conditions for the owls. Apart from one that flew north over Denny Island on 20 October 2001, all the records, where specified, have been along the west shore from Moreton Bank to the Sailing Club. Subsequent records were from 12 to 15 April 2002 and on 30 October 2008. Since then the only ones have been on 1 November 2016 and singles on 17 and 26 November 2018. Only one has been ringed at the lake.

There was also a record of an unidentified *Asio* owl in Villice Bay on 8–9 October 1995.

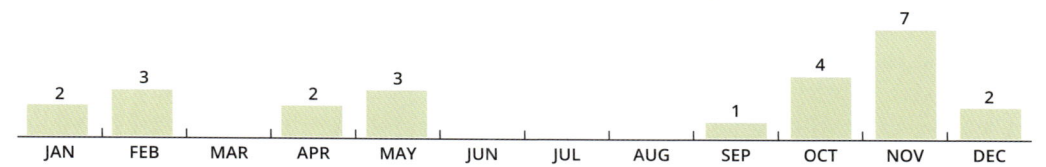

SHORT-EARED OWL | Monthly maxima (combined) 1959-2018.

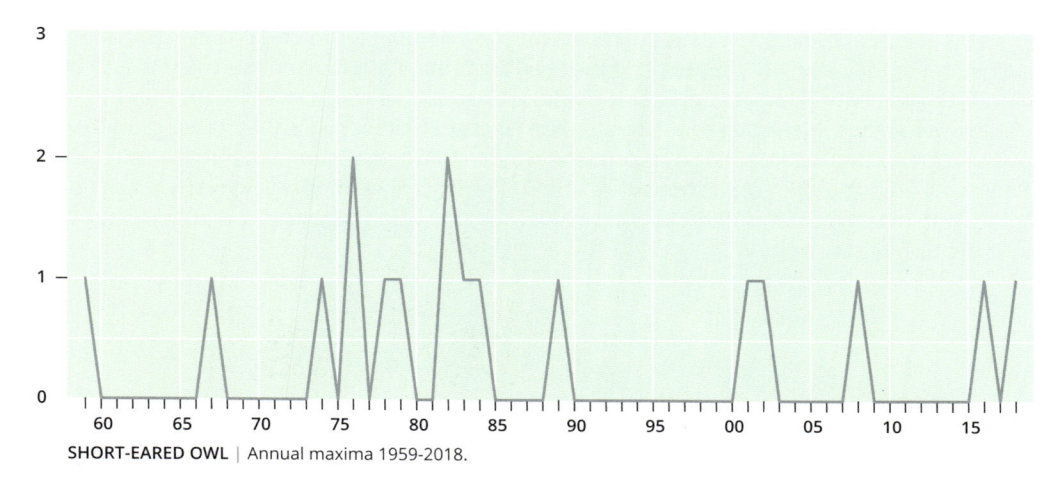

SHORT-EARED OWL | Annual maxima 1959-2018.

Short-eared Owl | Laurel Tucker

HOOPOE *Upupa epops*

One was seen at Woodford Lodge on 2 July 1968 (C. Pollock). A second record on 14 May 1979, reported via Robin Prytherch, was thought to have been seen by John Sparks of the BBC Natural History Unit.

KINGFISHER *Alcedo atthis*

Kingfishers are present around the lake in small numbers all year but they become increasingly difficult to see from January through to April–May. This is because the water levels at this time are high, reducing the density of the fish. Also, later in the winter and spring, the adults move up the incoming streams to nest. Numbers start to increase from June, as the water levels start to fall, rising to a peak in August when the young start to disperse, before gradually dropping through the autumn as the water levels start to rise again.

As the annual maxima graph shows, numbers were at a very low ebb in 1963, following the infamous hard winter of that year, but they bounced back by September 1967, when there was a peak of six. Annual maxima have fluctuated ever since, with peak counts of seven in 1975, 1977 and 1978.

However, what is interesting about the status of Kingfishers at the lake is that, although the highest count ever recorded is seven, ringing totals reveal that much higher numbers actually visit the lake. The annual ringing totals graph shows that totals of birds caught annually regularly reach double figures, with maxima of 33 in 1993 and 31 in 1999. The graph also suggests that numbers have fallen since the turn of the century.

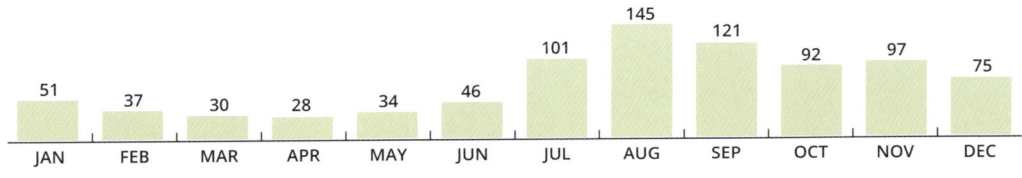

JAN	FEB	MAR	APR	MAY	JUN	JUL	AUG	SEP	OCT	NOV	DEC
51	37	30	28	34	46	101	145	121	92	97	75

KINGFISHER | Monthly maxima (combined) counts 1965-2015.

KINGFISHER | Annual maxima 1965-2015.

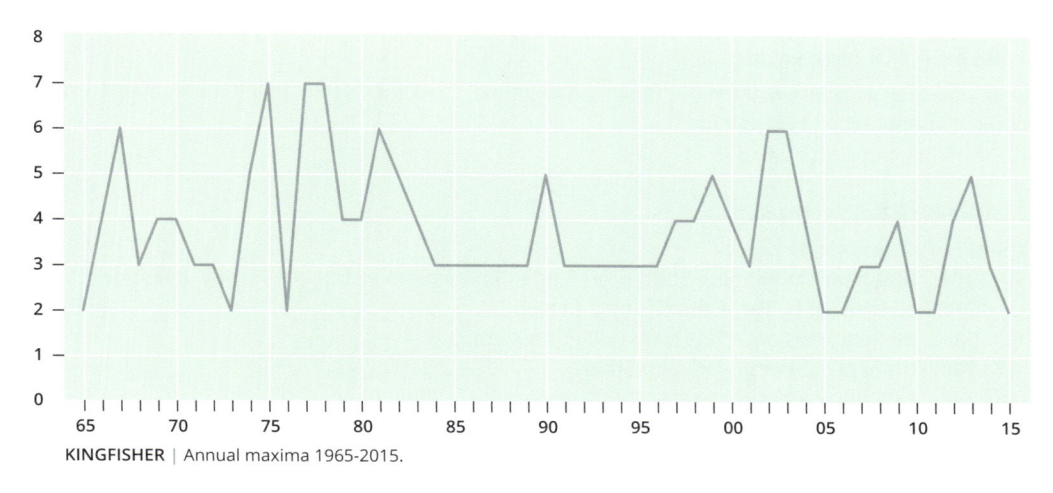

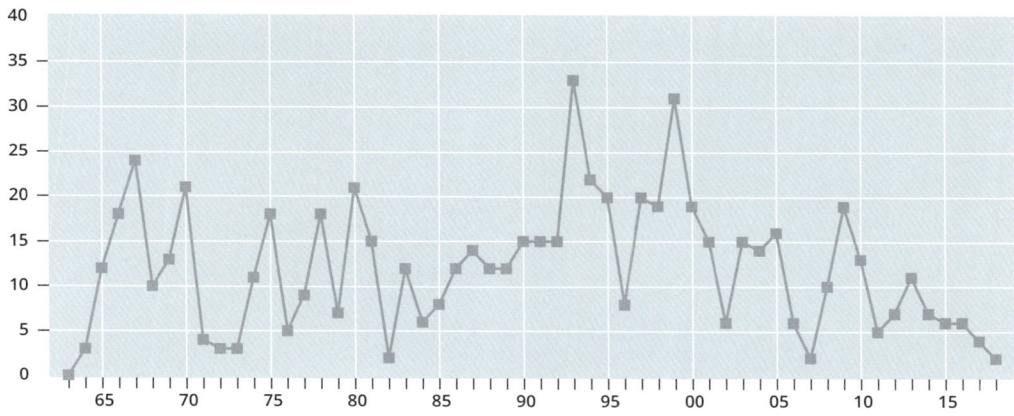

KINGFISHER | Annual ringing totals 1963-2018. Note the peaks of 33 in 1993 and 31 in 1999.

Kingfisher | Gary Thoburn

BEE-EATER *Merops apiaster*
One was seen and heard from the Ringing Station on 15 August 1966, flying north over Herriott's End (D. Shepherd, R. F. Thearle).

WRYNECK *Jynx torquilla*
There have been six records:
- **1974:** one near the Ringing Station on 8 and 16 September (D. & M. Haddy, J. Holmes).
- **1977:** one heard by Roy Curber on 12 March.
- **1981:** one trapped on 7 September (D. J. Evered).
- **1988:** one seen 29 August (Terry Smith)
- **1997:** one trapped on 20 September (no observer details).
- **2012:** one trapped on 29 September (M. Bailey *et al.*).

Wryneck | Rich Andrews

LESSER SPOTTED WOODPECKER *Dryobates minor*
The first record was of two in April 1959, followed by one in June 1960. They were then recorded from 1965, and in May 1969 a pair was seen excavating a nest hole near Moreton Cottage. Unfortunately, they were ousted by a pair of Tree Sparrows *Passer montanus*, a scenario that would now be hard to imagine. Thereafter, that species was recorded almost annually until 1974, the run of records being entirely linked to the outbreak of Dutch Elm Disease which, during the 1970s, killed more than 25 million elm trees in the UK. But one small benefit was that the Lesser Spotted Woodpecker population increased, as they were able to exploit the huge upsurge in elm bark beetles.

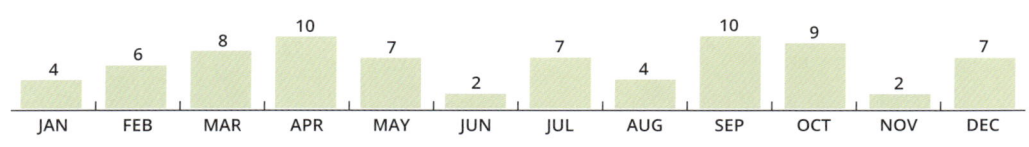

JAN	FEB	MAR	APR	MAY	JUN	JUL	AUG	SEP	OCT	NOV	DEC
4	6	8	10	7	2	7	4	10	9	2	7

LESSER SPOTTED WOODPECKER | Monthly maxima (combined) 1959-2019.

There were then no records at Chew from 1980 to 1985, but in 1986 a pair was seen with two fledged young on 1 July (M. A. Bailey). After this, the species was seen in 19 of the next 26 years (up to and including 2012) with a ringed male drumming from 18 March to 13 April 2009 and another male drumming at two sites in 2012. It was wondered whether one of these enigmatic species would be seen again, when one was heard calling and seen briefly on 5 March 2019.

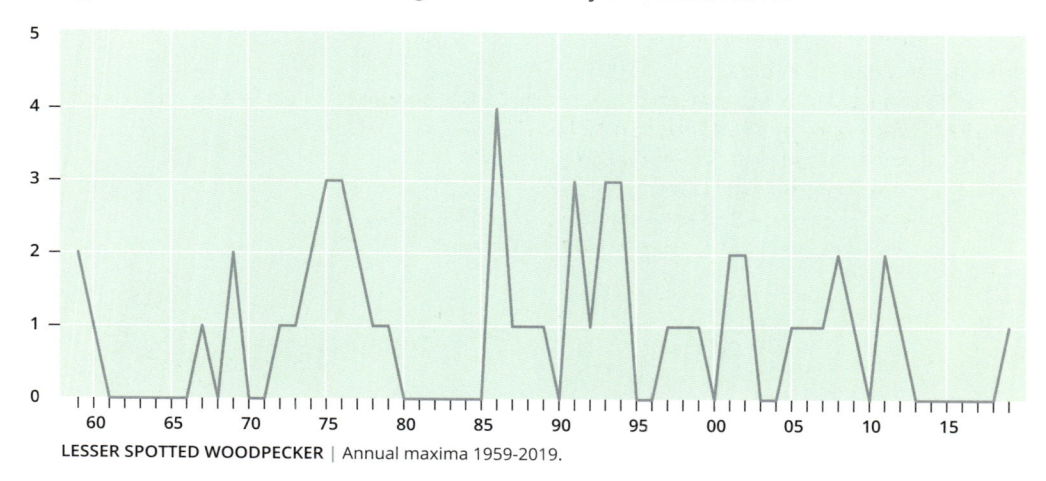

LESSER SPOTTED WOODPECKER | Annual maxima 1959-2019.

GREAT SPOTTED WOODPECKER *Dendrocopos major*

This species is now fairly common around the lake and, being a rather noisy resident species, the birds are easily detected. The numbers remain fairly constant throughout the year, although there is a slight increase in April–June, peaking when the adults are busy feeding their noisy young.

The annual maxima graph shows how the species has increased since the mid 1960s, this being related to the gradual maturation of the lakeside woodland. The number of pairs graph shows the number of drumming males or pairs located around the lake from 1985 to 2015 – again this shows the clear increase in recent years.

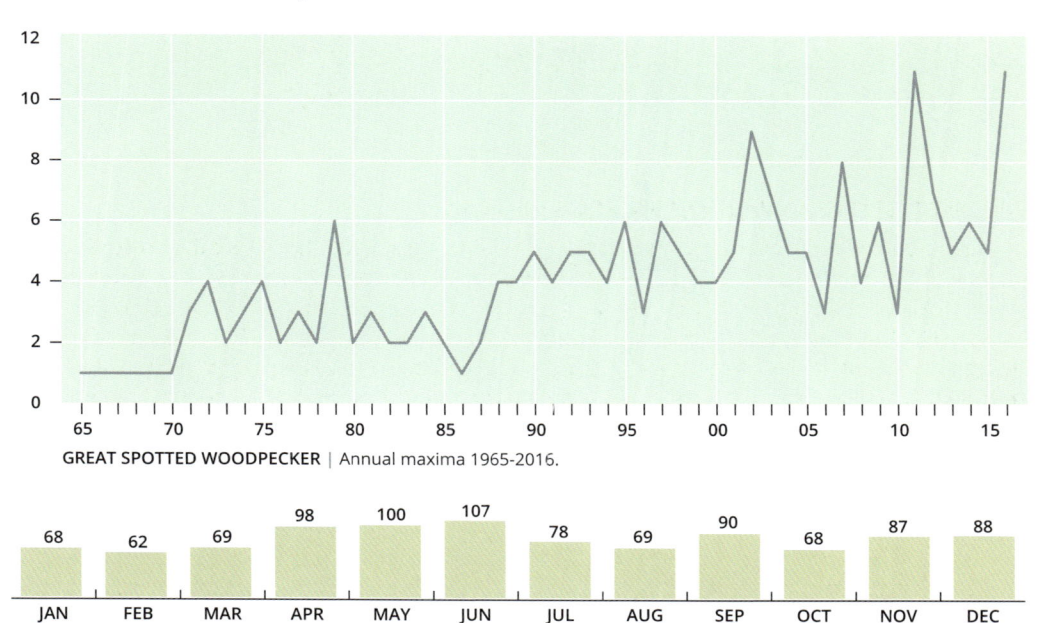

GREAT SPOTTED WOODPECKER | Annual maxima 1965-2016.

JAN	FEB	MAR	APR	MAY	JUN	JUL	AUG	SEP	OCT	NOV	DEC
68	62	69	98	100	107	78	69	90	68	87	88

GREAT SPOTTED WOODPECKER | Monthly maxima (combined) 1965-2015.

Great Spotted Woodpecker | Lucy Masters

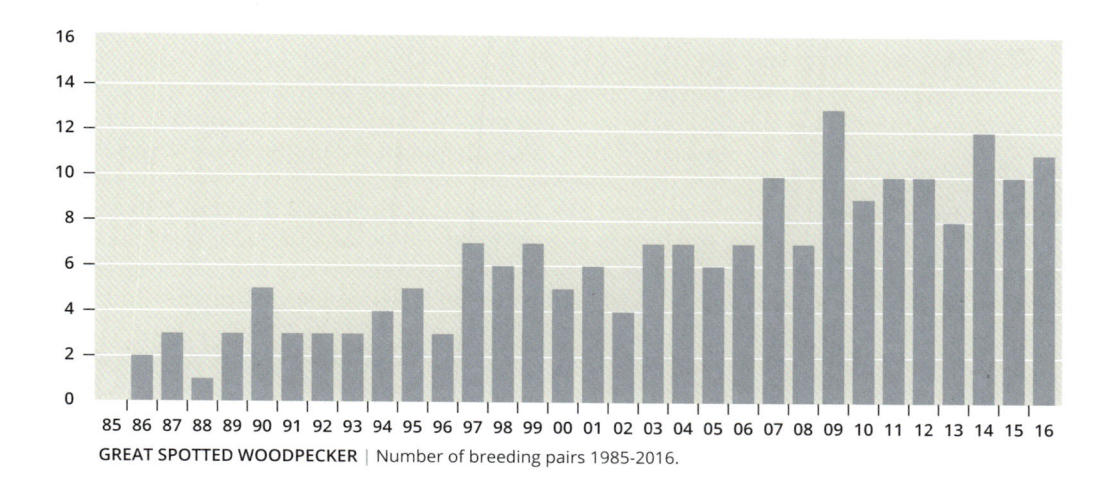

GREAT SPOTTED WOODPECKER | Number of breeding pairs 1985-2016.

GREEN WOODPECKER *Picus viridis*

This species is present throughout the year around the lake and its immediate surroundings. There are, however, small peaks in March and April, when the males are most vocal, and again from July to September, after the young have fledged.

The number of 'yaffling' males suggests that there are around five pairs in the immediate vicinity of the lake, but as many as six were heard in 1991, 1997 and 2005, seven on 14 March 1992 and eight in 2011.

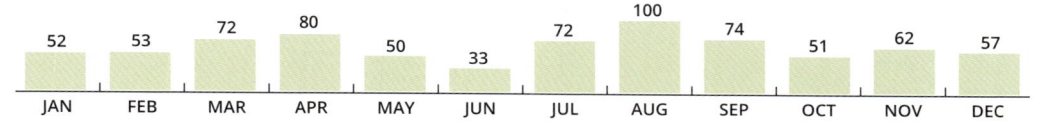

JAN	FEB	MAR	APR	MAY	JUN	JUL	AUG	SEP	OCT	NOV	DEC
52	53	72	80	50	33	72	100	74	51	62	57

GREEN WOODPECKER | Monthly maxima (combined) counts 1965-2015.

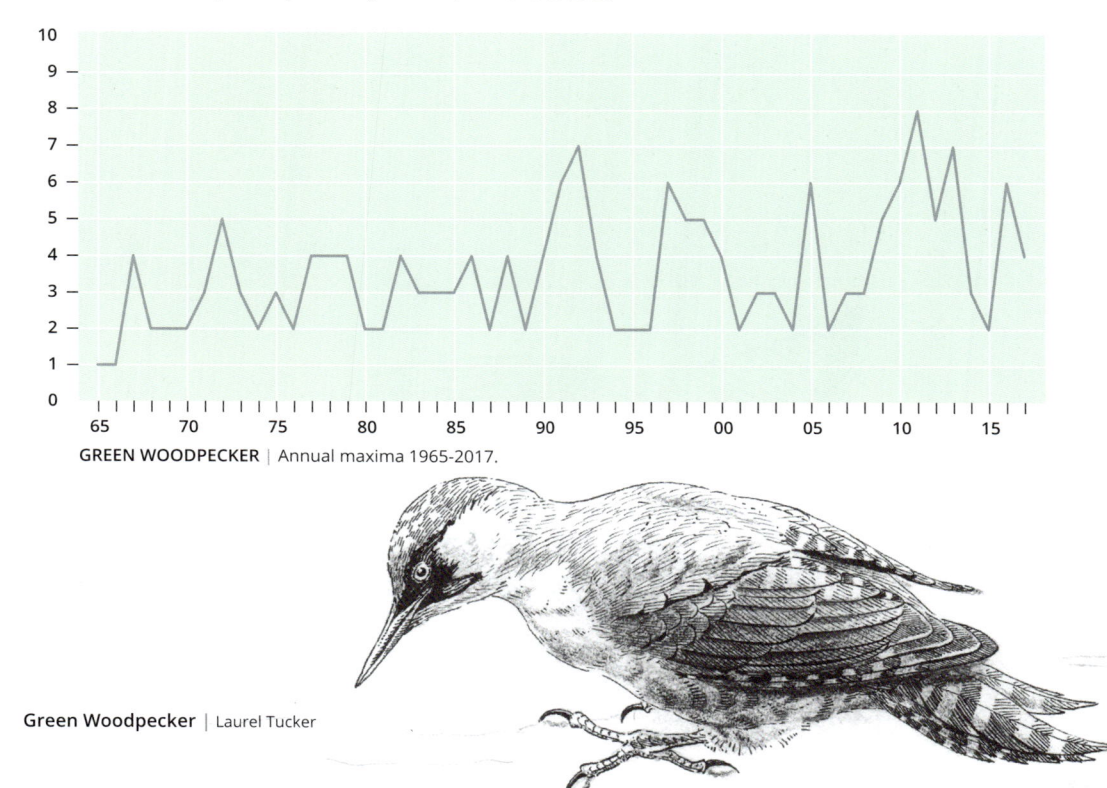

GREEN WOODPECKER | Annual maxima 1965-2017.

Green Woodpecker | Laurel Tucker

KESTREL *Falco tinnunculus*

There are no published records prior to 1963 but in, the mid 1960s, Kestrels were a familiar sight, hovering over the rough ground along the lake's margins. The highest counts were six in 1963 and 1964, seven in 1973 and a record eight in 1976. The latter count was in the drought year, when large swathes of rough vegetation – ideal for Kestrels – developed around the lake's margins. Numbers were distinctly lower through the 1980s and 1990s with a further decrease at the turn of the century. It is thought possible that the relentless rise in the local Buzzard *Buteo buteo* population may have contributed to this recent decline. As the maximum annual counts graph indicates, Kestrels were reasonably numerous during the 1960s and 1970s but their numbers plateaued through the 1980s and 1990s with a further down-turn after 2000.

The combined monthly maxima graph shows that numbers are at their lowest through the winter, but they increase in March and April. There is a dip in June when, presumably, they are settling down to breed, but this is followed by a late summer/early autumn peak, with September being the best month. It seems likely that a lot of the autumn birds are juveniles.

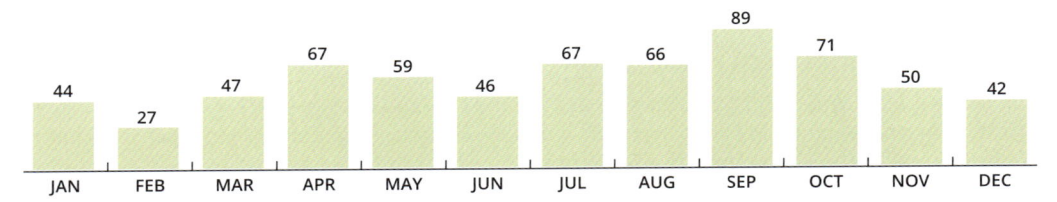

KESTREL | Monthly maxima (combined) 1965-2015.

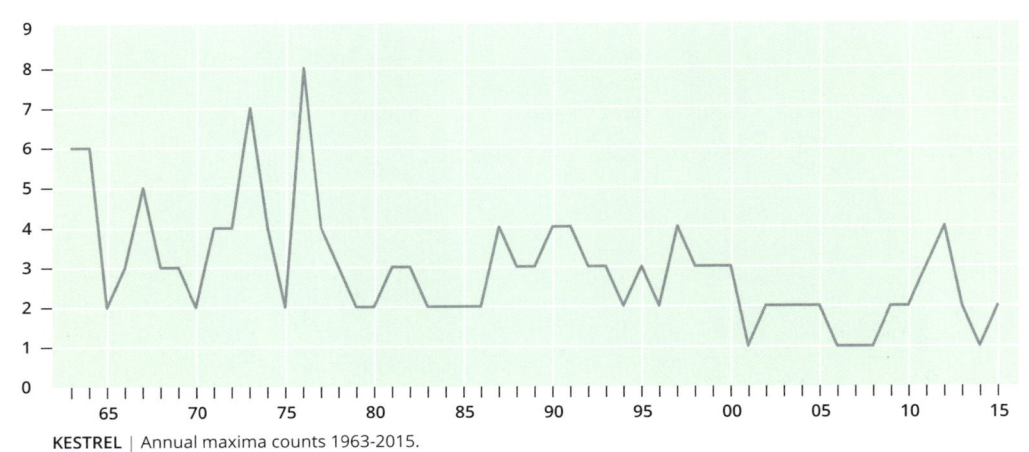

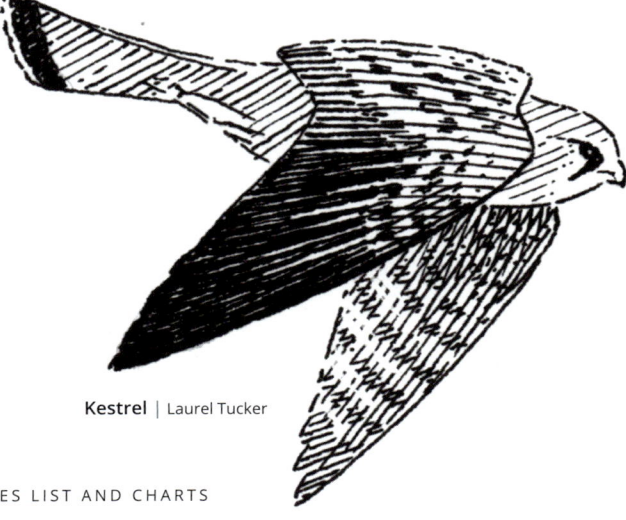

JAN	FEB	MAR	APR	MAY	JUN	JUL	AUG	SEP	OCT	NOV	DEC
44	27	47	67	59	46	67	66	89	71	50	42

KESTREL | Annual maxima counts 1963-2015.

Kestrel | Laurel Tucker

MERLIN *Falco columbarius*

The Merlin is an erratic visitor, recorded in 35 of the 61 years from 1954 to 2015. Most records relate to fly-bys and, as such, they are prone to misidentification: low-flying, fast-moving, pointy-winged male Sparrowhawks *Accipiter nisus* are a particular source of confusion. As the combined monthly maxima graph illustrates, they occur from September (the earliest date being the 5th in 1966) but the peak months are October–November, January and March. The latest spring date is 9 April (in 1999).

All records have related to single birds, but twelve years have produced two, three years have produced three and, in 1961, four were reported. Of the 65 sightings, in total only 12 (18%) have related to adult males, the majority presumably relating to juvenile/first-winters.

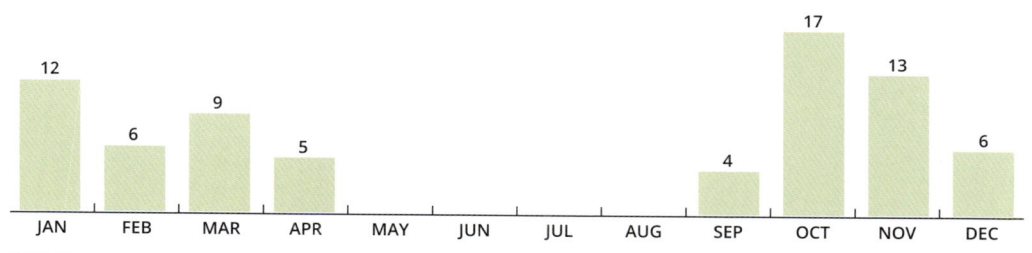

MERLIN | Monthly maxima (combined) 1954-2014.

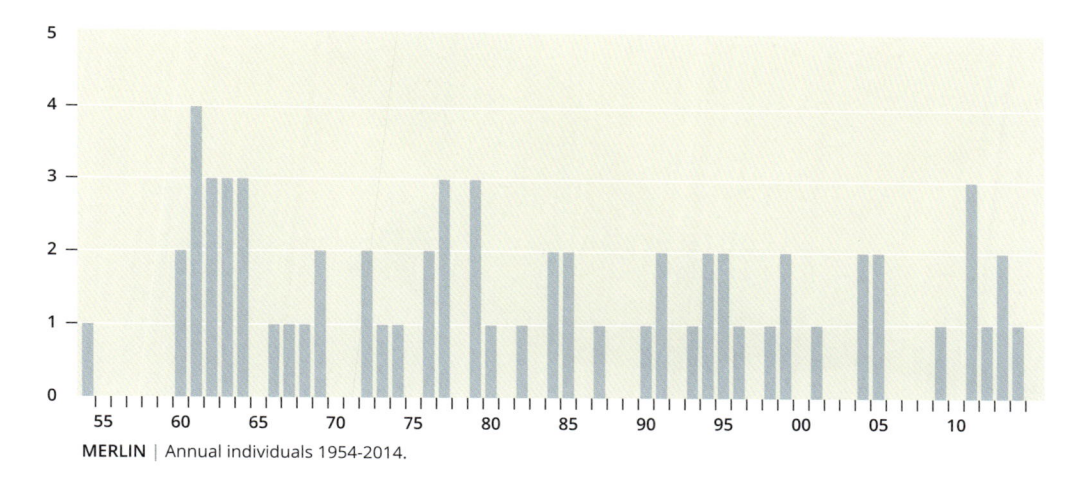

MERLIN | Annual individuals 1954-2014.

HOBBY *Falco subbuteo*

The first record was of one on 24 August 1954 followed by another on 26 April 1956 (B. King). It became an annual summer visitor from 1960 onwards, but just ones and twos were recorded until 1982, when three were seen in June and July. From that point onwards there were regular sightings of up to four, with peak counts of five in September 1997 and 1998 and a record seven on 26 August 2015 which was beaten by 11 in 2019. These higher totals correspond with a national increase and a northward spread in its range, which is thought to be related to climate change. It has bred in or around the lakeside perimeter on at least eight occasions from 1994 onwards.

The first spring records are usually in late April, with 17th probably being the first reliable date. Spring numbers peak in May but then dip in June as the adults become very elusive whilst nesting. Numbers then increase to a peak in August–September, when the juveniles have fledged and the Hobbys can be easily seen. Most are gone by the end of September but there have been 21 October records, with the latest being a juvenile on 13th (in 2009).

Hobby | Gary Thoburn

The species usually feeds on aerial insects, as well as hirundines and swifts. However, one in 1985 caught a juvenile Curlew Sandpiper *Calidris ferruginea* and another in September 1983 was seen chasing a Storm Petrel *Hydrobates pelagicus*.

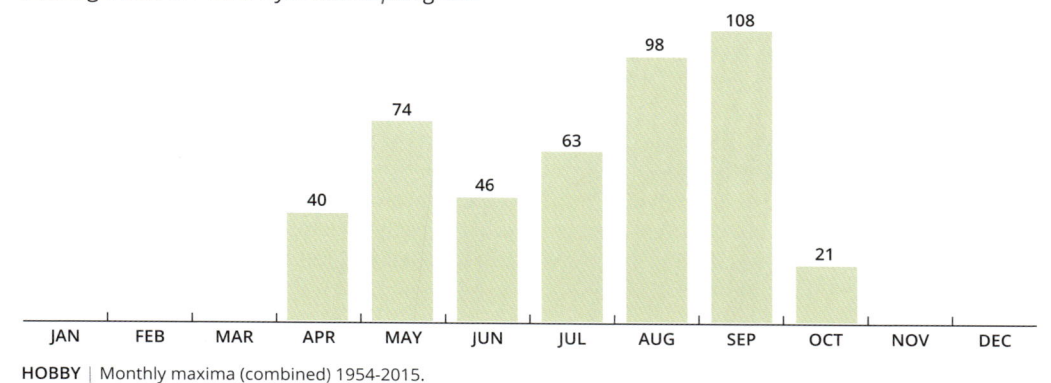

HOBBY | Monthly maxima (combined) 1954-2015.

HOBBY | Annual maxima 1954-2015.

GYR FALCON *Falco rusticolus*

One was present from 5 November 1961 to 13 January 1962 (P. J. Chadwick, M. A. Wright, G. Sweet *et al.*). It was seen by many of the local birders of the day. Recent information from Paul Chadwick indicates that it had brownish wings and body with darker primaries. In addition, no facial markings or moustachial stripes were noted. It was therefore considered most likely to have been a first-winter dark or intermediate phased individual (*per* H. E. Rose). Such birds are prevalent in Scandinavia.

PEREGRINE *Falco peregrinus*

The first records were on 29 August and 19 September 1954 (R. H. Poulding). There were blank years in 1959, 1961, 1964–1968 and 1974 but, apart from these, the species has been annual. The earlier absences were related to the use of persistent pesticides, as a consequence of which the British breeding population plummeted to just 68 breeding pairs in 1962. The annual maxima graph reflects this sorry state of affairs. The decline was halted following restrictions on pesticide use, enabling a slow recovery to get underway (*BWP*). Apart from 1974, Peregrines have been recorded annually at Chew from 1969 to the time of writing, although, until recently, the numbers recorded at any one time have never exceeded two. On 30 November 2017, however, three adults were seen together, rather bizarrely standing in a line on the mud at Twycross. Peregrines have now become a welcome regular occurrence at the lake.

Most records are from August to January, sightings slowly declining in the new year as the birds start to return to their breeding sites. They reach a low point from May to July before increasing again during the late summer and autumn.

A small juvenile, photographed in a tree on Moreton Point on 28 December 2010, was thought likely to have been of the tundra race *tundrius*, this form breeding in north-east Canada and Greenland (KEV). An adult at the lake between 28 November and 8 December 2017 was also thought to have been of this race (A. H. Davis).

A bird seen at the lake in December 2018 carrying an orange ring had been ringed as chick near Northwich, Cheshire on 18 May 2016.

Peregrines at Chew feed on a variety of bird species; those recorded include Wigeon *Mareca penelope*, Teal *Anas crecca*, Ruddy Duck *Oxyura jamaicensis*, Moorhen *Gallinula chloropus*, Coot *Fulica atra*, Curlew Sandpiper *Calidris ferruginea*, Starling *Sturnus vulgaris* and Pied Wagtail *Motacilla alba*.

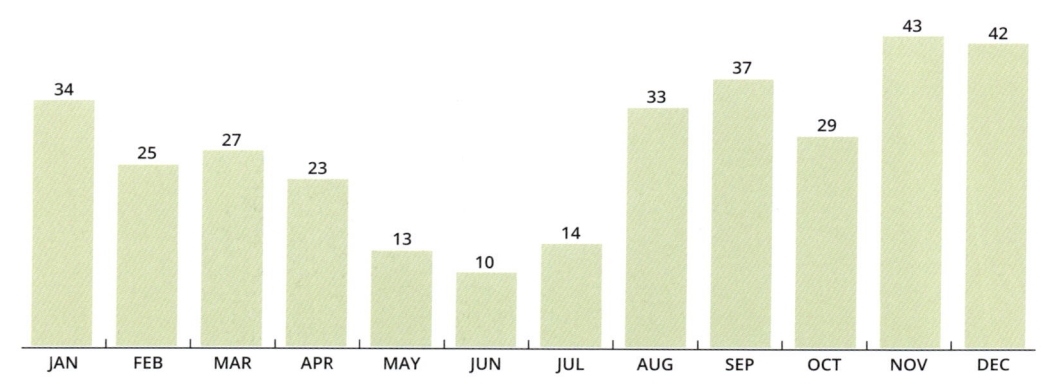

PEREGRINE | Monthly maxima (combined) 1954-2015.

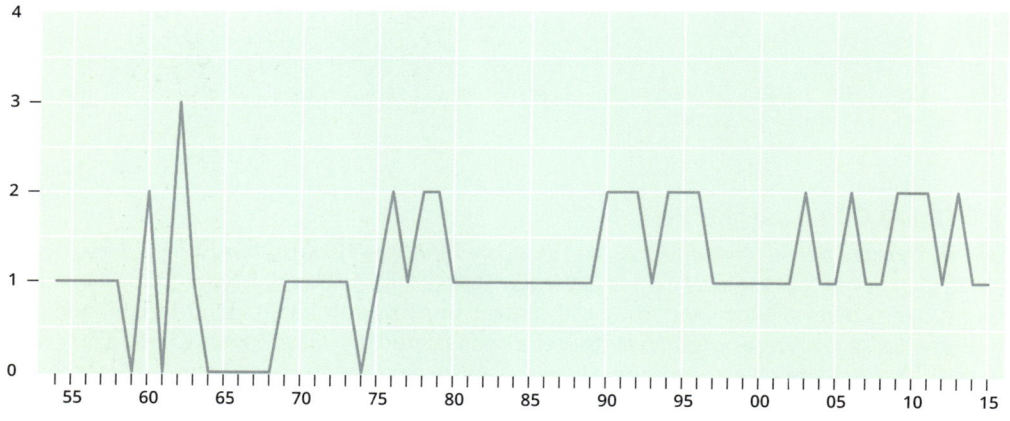

PEREGRINE | Annual maxima 1954-2015. Note the absences in the late 1950s and 1960s, these being related to pesticide use. It has now been recorded annually since 1975.

| RING-NECKED PARAKEET *Psittacula krameri*

The only record for the lake is of two on 25 April 2015 (D. Warden).

Note that the *ABR* only included this species in the main section of its report from 2006, prior to which records were treated as relating to escapes.

Ring-necked Parakeet is classified as Category C1E* on the British list, a naturalised introduced species. As such it does form part of the British list.

Peregrine | Laurel Tucker

RED-BACKED SHRIKE *Lanius collurio*
There have been four records:
- 1969: a male on 28 August (M. Sainsbury).
- 1973: a very confiding female at Sutton Wick car park and Spring Bay from 6 July to 2 August (M. W. A. Martin, KEV *et al.*).
- 1976: a juvenile/first-winter trapped on 10 October (R. J. Prytherch *et al.*).
- 2006: a male on 29 May (D. Warden).

Red-backed Shrike | Laurel Tucker

GREAT GREY SHRIKE *Lanius excubitor*
There have been two records: one on Moreton Bank on 3 January 1973 (A. J. Merritt, T. Nichols) and another was watched for 20 minutes from Stratford Hide on 8 November 1987 (M. Hayes).

WOODCHAT SHRIKE *Lanius senator*
A very confiding second-year female was present at North Widcombe Common on 21–30 April 2013 (C. Hunt *et al.*).

Note:
This bird was visible from and even on the boundary fence of the lake, although not within the lake boundary itself. Some local birders may not include it on their 'Chew List'.

GOLDEN ORIOLE *Oriolus oriolus*
There have been two records:
The first record was of a male on 4 May 1962 (R S Harkness).
A male was repeatedly calling and seen briefly in flight in the poplars at Spring Bay on 25 May 2003 (KEV).

Woodchat Shrike | Gary Thoburn

JAY *Garrulus glandarius*

As the combined monthly maxima chart indicates, Jays are present in small numbers throughout the year, but they are most conspicuous from March to April and, in particular, from October to December, when they are busy caching acorns for the winter. All counts have been in single figures apart from 11 on 14 October 1995. Breeding birds have been estimated annually from 1967 to 2017, the average being six pairs, with a maximum of 11 pairs in 2011.

On 19 May 1984, what was presumably a high-flying migrant was seen heading south about 100 feet above Herriott's Bridge. Interestingly, several migrants were also seen at Portland, Dorset, during the same week.

As the annual maxima graph indicates, the population has increased since the mid-1960s presumably as a result of the maturation of the lakeside woodlands.

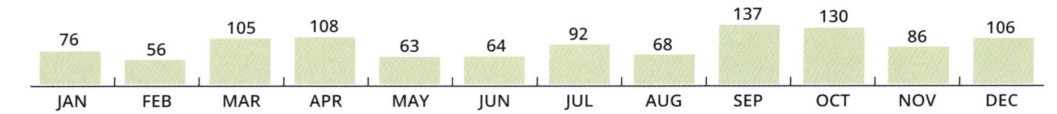

JAN	FEB	MAR	APR	MAY	JUN	JUL	AUG	SEP	OCT	NOV	DEC
76	56	105	108	63	64	92	68	137	130	86	106

JAY | Monthly maxima (combined) 1967-2015.

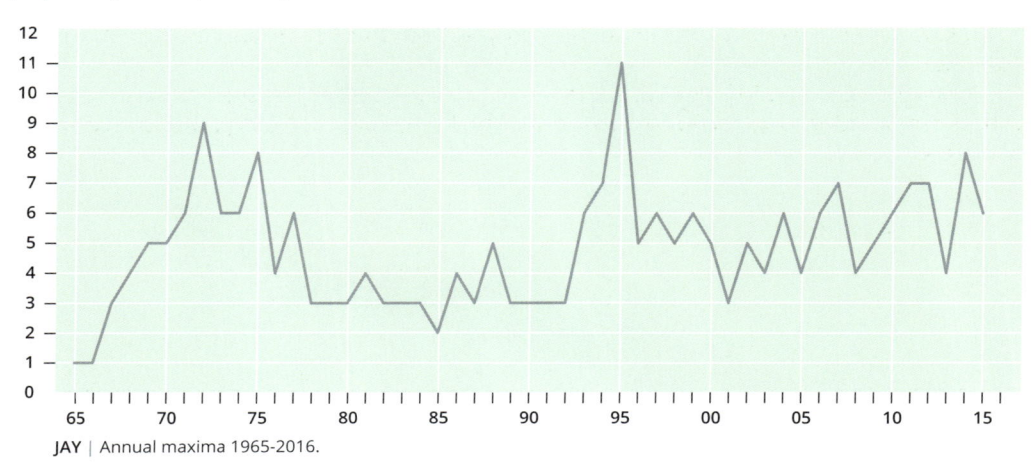

JAY | Annual maxima 1965-2016.

Jay | Laurel Tucker

MAGPIE *Pica pica*

Magpies are present in small numbers around the lake and its immediate vicinity, but there have been few counts and no meaningful estimates of the breeding population. My own counts have been extremely erratic, but I have thirteen double figure counts, with maxima of 20 in September 1977 (including a flock of 11 in Villice Bay), a record 25 on 4 August 1991 and 22 in February 1992. Perhaps five pairs would be a reasonable guess at the current population. Being a wily bird, surprisingly few have been ringed, with a grand total of 59 between 1963 and 2015, with maxima of six in 1990 and seven in 2012.

JACKDAW *Coloeus monedula*

Jackdaws breed at two or three sites around the lake, all nests being in holes in trees. The species is not monitored regularly but at least eight pairs were located in 2011.

Outside the breeding season, however, it is one of the most abundant species. This is because there is a huge nocturnal roost on Denny Island, with large flocks often gathering in the lakeside fields and woods. Rough estimates are all that can be achieved, but most counts have been in the range of 1,000–2,000 with higher totals of 3,000 in October 1982, an estimate of 5,000 in January 2013, 4,000 in February 2014 (an impressive congregation in the Parkland) and 4,000 again in March 2015.

From 6 February to 29 March 2008, one with a white neck collar was seen. It was accepted as subspecies *monedula*, which breeds in parts of Norway, Sweden and Denmark and is a scarce migrant to the UK.

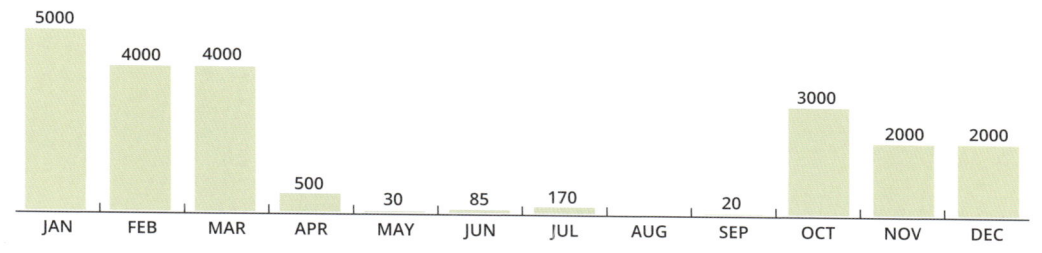

JAN	FEB	MAR	APR	MAY	JUN	JUL	AUG	SEP	OCT	NOV	DEC
5000	4000	4000	500	30	85	170		20	3000	2000	2000

JACKDAW | Monthly maxima 1967-2015. Based on erratic maximum counts, most of which are roost counts.

Jackdaw | Ian Stapp

ROOK *Corvus frugilegus*

The Rook is a fairly common resident in the area and is monitored by a five-yearly rookery survey in Avon. In the past, some large counts were made and there would appear to be no reason why such totals should not be present today. The largest are as follows:

- 1967: 120 on 4 April.
- 1982: 500 roosting on Denny Island on 24 October.
- 1990: 500 roosting on Denny Island on 20 January and 150 feeding in a field at Heron's Green Bay on 10 March.
- 1991: 80 in a newly cut hayfield behind Stratford Bay on 2 June.

In 2017 there were 56 nests either within the lake boundary or in close proximity to it:
- Poplar plantation behind the Main Dam (seven nests).
- The Ringing Station Wood (15 nests).
- Villice Bay (19 nests).
- North of the Blue Bowl Inn (15 nests)

In the late 1960s and 1970s, Rooks were a very familiar sight at Herriott's Bridge, where they used to scrounge food from the visitors, many of the birds becoming extremely tame. It is not known why this behaviour no longer persists.

Rook | Gary Thoburn

CARRION CROW *Corvus corone*

This is a common and widespread species in the adjacent area and small numbers are present at the lake all year round, with a few pairs breeding within the lake's enclosure. However, as a consequence of its familiarity, few counts have ever been made. The largest numbers occur from March to May, with a record 125 in May 1994, 65 in April 2010, 60 in April 2013 and 70 in April 2015. There was also a count of 80 in fields behind Woodford Lane on 10 June 2019 (a mixture of adults and juveniles). The timing of the late April/early May peak suggests that the vast majority of crows seen at this time are non-breeders. Numbers can remain relatively high into August.

Carrion Crow | Gary Thoburn

RAVEN *Corvus corax*

The only record from the early days was of a party of four that crossed the lake on 27 September 1962, disappearing south towards Litton (G. C. and S. I. Buxton). At that time, the nearest breeding pair was at Brean Down, Somerset, where they raised three young in 1961 (*Somerset Birds* 1961). It was 26 years before the next Chew record: one flying south on 15 August 1988 (J. J. Packer). It was then regular up to 1995, with four juveniles seen over the Parkland on 25 August 1992. Most of the sightings came from Burledge Hill, just to the south-east of the lake, with display seen there in the late winters of both 1994 and 1995, with as many as six on 22 August 1995. Then, after three records in 1998, the species became annual from 2000, although most sightings continued to be over Burledge Hill.

In 2002, a pair took up residence on Denny Island and they were thought possibly to be breeding there. In 2005, breeding was confirmed within the lake boundary, but at a different site. Breeding has occurred in every year since, with two pairs using two out of four different nesting sites. During that period, there have been peak counts of 14 on 3 September 2006 and a record 19 four days later. Seventeen were also seen on 22 September 2016.

The combined monthly maxima graph shows that numbers are relatively stable throughout the year, but with a spring peak in March–April, when the birds are very vocal, and a more definite peak in August and September, following the recruitment of the year's young.

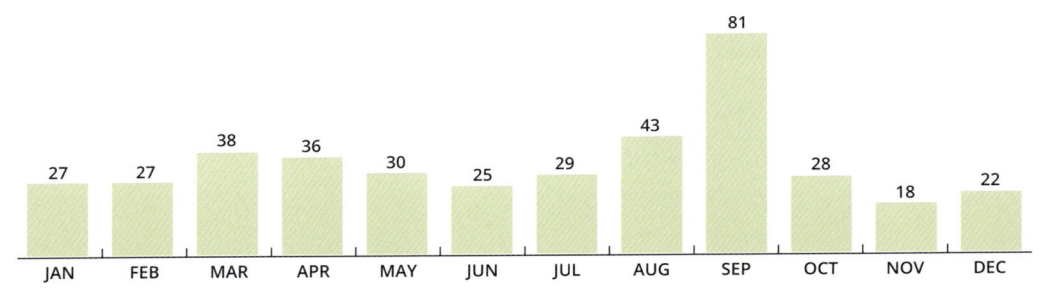

RAVEN | Monthly maxima (combined) 1992-2016.

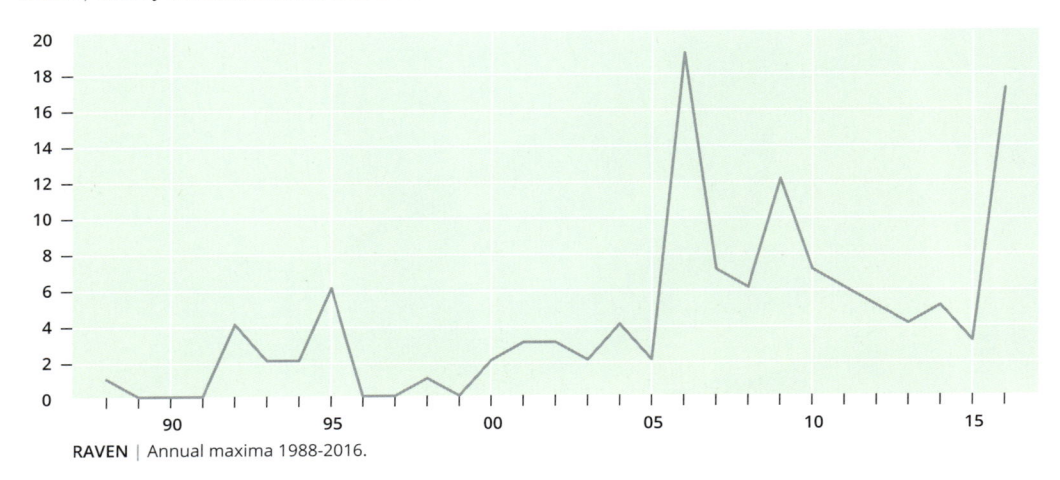

RAVEN | Annual maxima 1988-2016.

| WAXWING *Bombycilla garrulus*

Two were present in a cherry tree along the A368 at Bishop Sutton on 27 November 2010 (G. Thoburn et al.). Although just outside the Chew boundary, these birds were so close to the lake that it would have been churlish to omit them.

This is another record that was outside the lake boundary, and questionable if it would appear on a 'Chew List'. (Ed.)

| COAL TIT *Periparus ater*

Coal Tit is not a common species at the lake, with counts in most years barely reaching double figures. It is, however, under-recorded. They are most frequently encountered from August (when they become peculiarly vocal) into the autumn and winter, double figure counts being made from September to December. The species is, however, prone to occasional irruptions, the most obvious examples being in 1971, when there were up to 30 from September to December, and also in 1975 when there was a count of 25+ on 7 October. The latter coincided with a movement at New Passage (on the Severn Estuary) that reached 92 on 11 October and 80 on 12th. Annual ringing totals indicate a steady increase since the early 1980s, no doubt related to the gradual maturation of the lakeside woodlands, but these figures too suggest periodic surges in the population, with high ringing totals of 31 in 1988 and 37 in both 2009 and 2011.

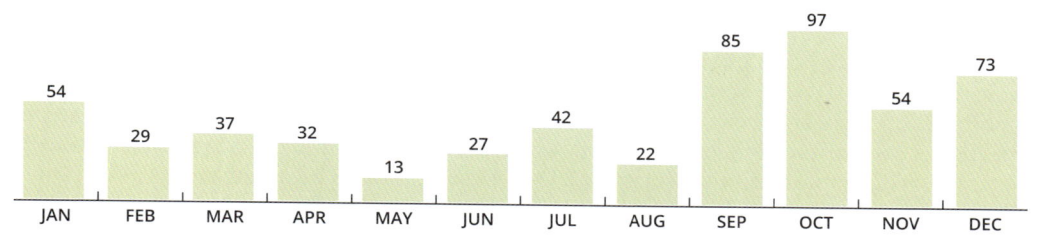

JAN	FEB	MAR	APR	MAY	JUN	JUL	AUG	SEP	OCT	NOV	DEC
54	29	37	32	13	27	42	22	85	97	54	73

COAL TIT | Monthly maxima (combined) 1962-2015.

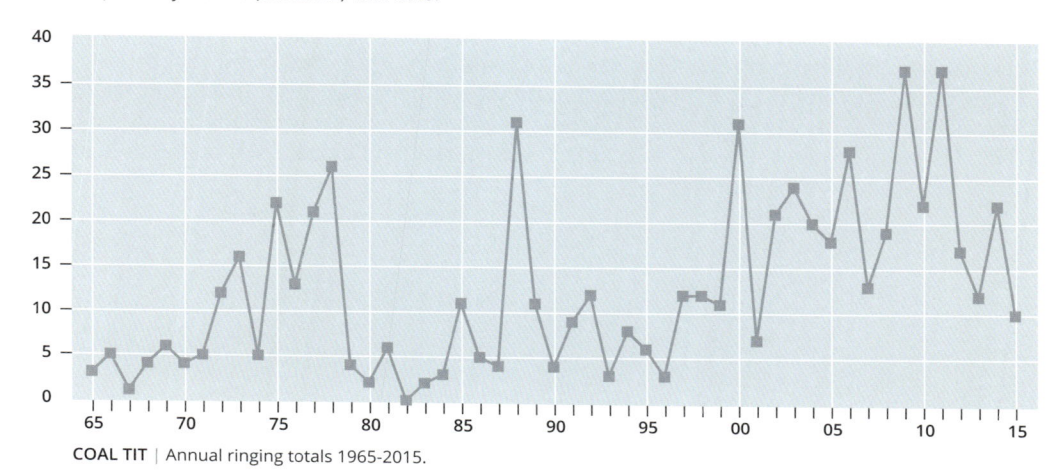

COAL TIT | Annual ringing totals 1965-2015.

Western Palearctic Coal Tits with British race (top) | Laurel Tucker

MARSH TIT *Poecile palustris*

Amazingly, there were no published records from the years 1954–1965. There are two possible reasons for this: (a) they were present but were deemed too common to mention in the bird reports or (b) they were not present owing to the relative immaturity of the lakeside plantations. The former seems much the more likely as the annual ringing totals in the years 1965–1968 were eight, ten and eight respectively, suggesting that they had indeed been present all along. There was another ringing peak in 1975 when six were trapped. In recent years, there were none in 2009 or 2010, but two in April and one in July 2011, and one in both June and December 2013. There have since been spring records (February to April) in 2014, four in 2015 (two in September and two in November), one in June and two in October 2016 and three in 2017 (two in September and one in November). A pair also bred in a bat box in 2017 with 9 young ringed.

The combined monthly maxima graph shows that numbers reach a spring peak in April when, presumably, the birds are most vocal. Few have been recorded in May, when they are no doubt breeding, but they increase again from June onwards, reaching a peak in September. Numbers then gradually decline into the winter.

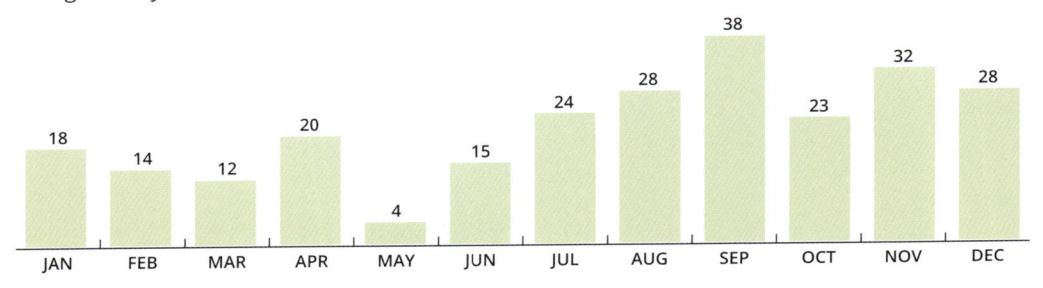

JAN	FEB	MAR	APR	MAY	JUN	JUL	AUG	SEP	OCT	NOV	DEC
18	14	12	20	4	15	24	28	38	23	32	28

MARSH TIT | Monthly maxima (combined) 1966-2017.

Marsh Tit (with Willow Tit) | Laurel Tucker

MARSH TIT | Annual maxima 1966-2017.

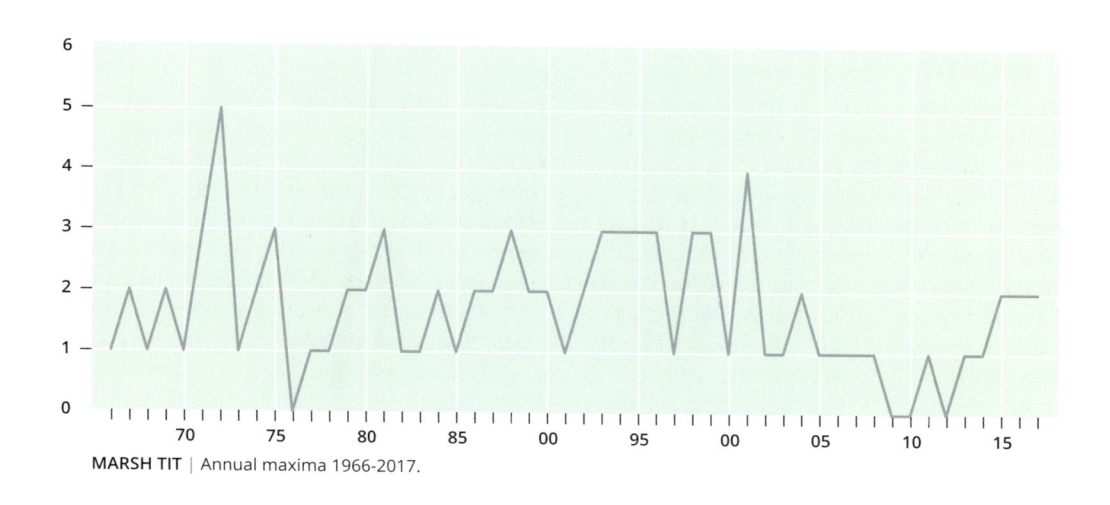

WILLOW TIT *Poecile montanus*

There have been nine records (ten individuals):
- **1968:** one trapped 24 July.
- **1969:** one trapped on 7 April (CVRS).
- **1971:** two at Hollow Brook on 26 September and 5 December (KEV).
- **1972:** one on 27 July.
- **1975:** one in dogwood at Herriott's Bridge on 2 July (KEV).
- **1976:** one on 25 January and one on 18 July (A. J. Merritt).
- **1978:** one trapped on 2 September (CVRS) and re-trapped on 8 and 15 October, last noted 24 November; perhaps the same individual was seen in Stratford Bay on 8 October (R. B. H. Smith).
- **1997:** a juvenile was trapped on 15 July (CVRS).

Given the recent decline in Britain, it seems highly unlikely that this species will be recorded again.

Western Palearctic Willow Tits with British race (top) | Laurel Tucker

BLUE TIT *Cyanistes caeruleus*

The Blue Tit is a common breeding species around the lake but the most useful data is of birds trapped at the Ringing Station. The annual ringing totals graph shows that numbers have risen steadily from the mid-1960s to the present time, with annual maxima of 590 in 1988, 609 in 2002 and 623 in 2011. In the early days, the species was probably still recovering from the hard winter of 1962–63, coupled with the fact that the ringing station was only just getting started. The seemingly relentless increase since then presumably relates to the general maturation of the lake's woodlands, coupled with the provision of nest boxes in the ringing area and elsewhere as well as, in more recent years, the provision of food.

It is also very notable that in 2018, of the 69 nests monitored at the lake, 48 were successful. Moreover, the calculated juvenile to adult ratio was 12.06, which is not only more than twice that in any recent year, it is in fact the highest since this data series started in 1976. The previous highest was 9.82 in 1978 (*ABR* 2018, page 116).

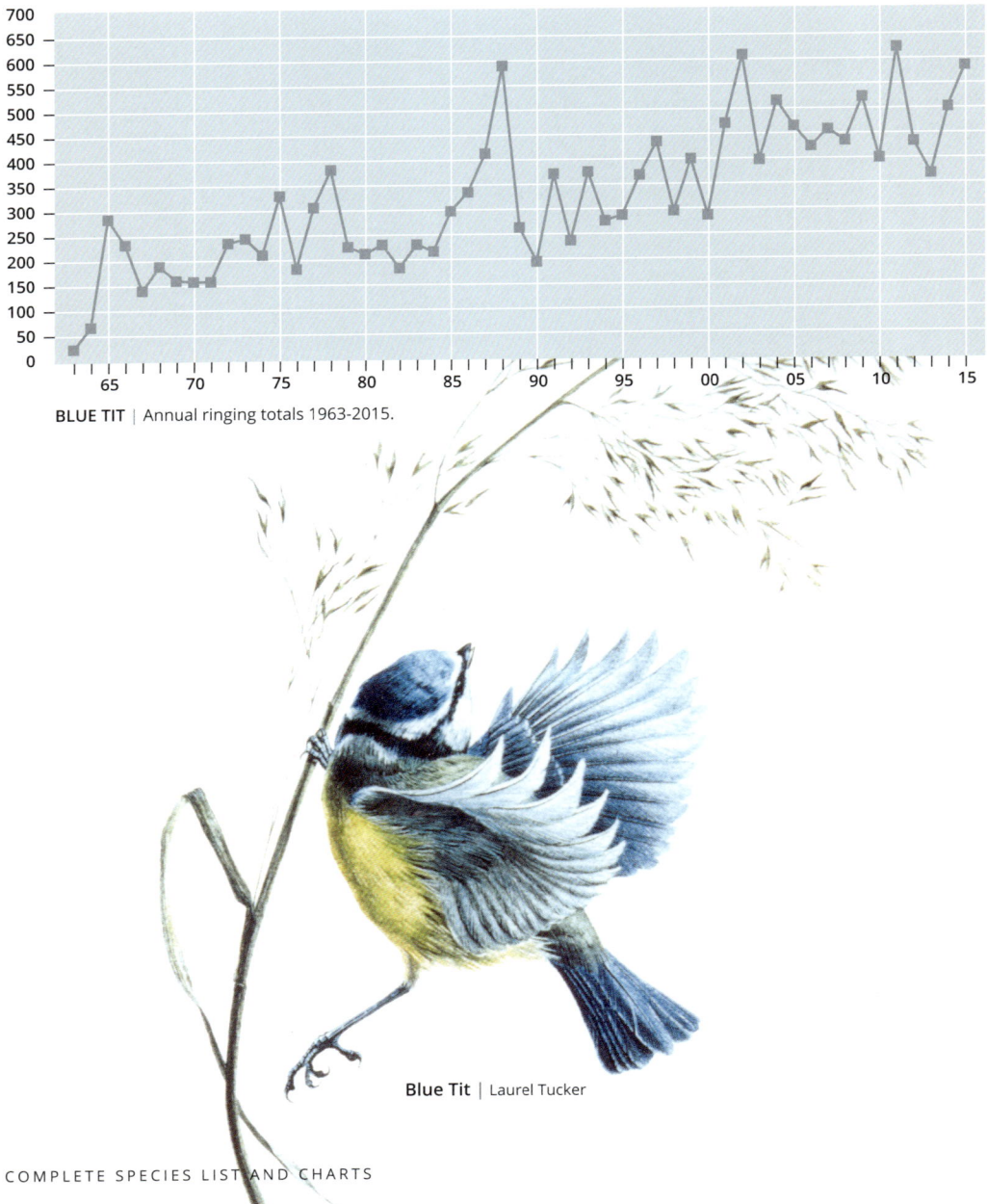

BLUE TIT | Annual ringing totals 1963-2015.

Blue Tit | Laurel Tucker

GREAT TIT *Parus major*

The graph for the numbers of Great Tits ringed annually is similar to that for the Blue Tit *Cyanistes caeruleus* in that it too shows a gradual long-term increase. However, unlike the Blue Tit, Great Tits were in much lower numbers from the 1960s to the end of the century. Since then, numbers have rocketed, with three years having annual totals of over 400 (2005, 2007, 2008 and 2011) with a peak of 436 trapped in 2007. The long-term trend shows that, like the Blue Tits, Great Tits have increased almost exponentially from the mid-1960s to the mid-2000s. As with the Blue Tit, in more recent years the provision of nest boxes and feeding stations has presumably attributed significantly to this.

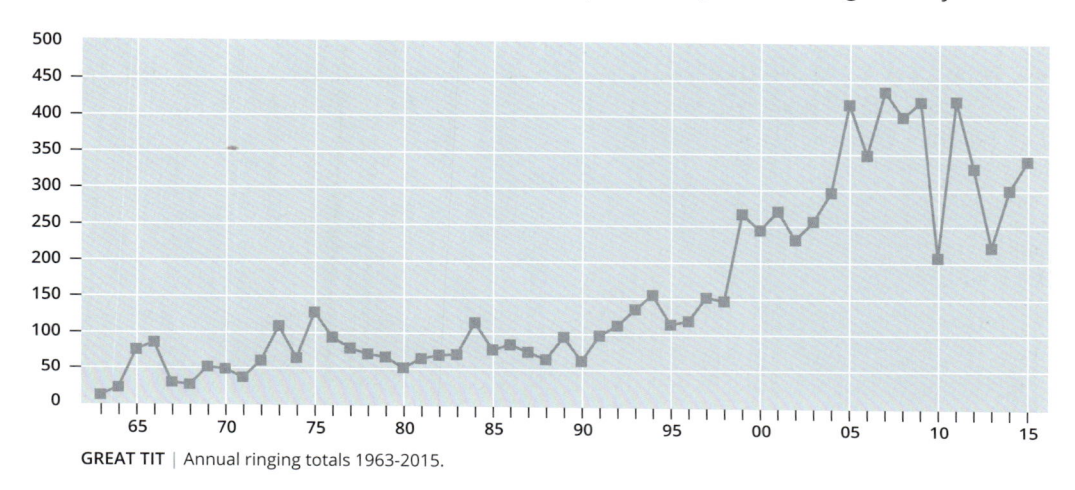

GREAT TIT | Annual ringing totals 1963-2015.

BEARDED TIT *Panurus biarmicus*

Bearded Tits were first recorded on 17 October 1965 and, by 12 November, at least 50 were present. This unprecedented influx was linked to the reclamation of the Ijsselmeer in the Netherlands. This resulted in the creation of large areas of reed beds that in turn led to a huge increase in the Dutch population of Bearded Tits. When the area eventually dried out, a major eruption of Bearded Tits then ensued. Thirty-seven were caught at Chew in October 1965, two of which had been ringed a week previously at Portland, Dorset; another of the Chew birds was re-trapped at Chichester, Sussex, in January 1966 (*Somerset Birds* 1965). At least two lingered until March 1966 with another seen in December. The next record involved a male in November 1970, after which the species' status reverted to that of an erratic autumn and winter visitor. From 1987 onwards, however, there were erratic summer sightings, culminating in a pair rearing six young from two broods in the summer of 1991.

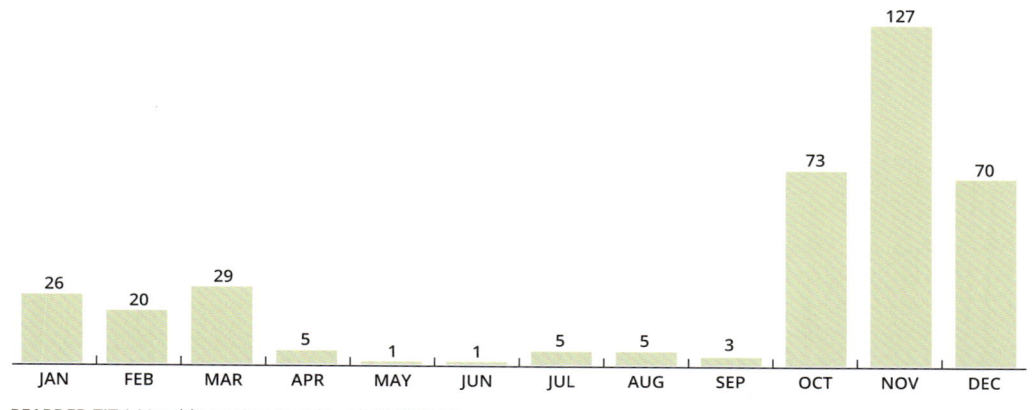

JAN	FEB	MAR	APR	MAY	JUN	JUL	AUG	SEP	OCT	NOV	DEC
26	20	29	5	1	1	5	5	3	73	127	70

BEARDED TIT | Monthly maxima (combined) 1965-2019.

Bearded Tit | Gary Thoburn

There was no further sign of breeding until 2003 when one trapped on 1 June had a brood patch. Disappointingly, there has been no indication of breeding since then and the species has reverted to its status as an erratic autumn and winter visitor.

A pair in December 2017 were seen again in January 2018 with other single records up to 15 March. In 2019, none were seen until 3 on 22 October, with 2 pairs up to the end of the year.

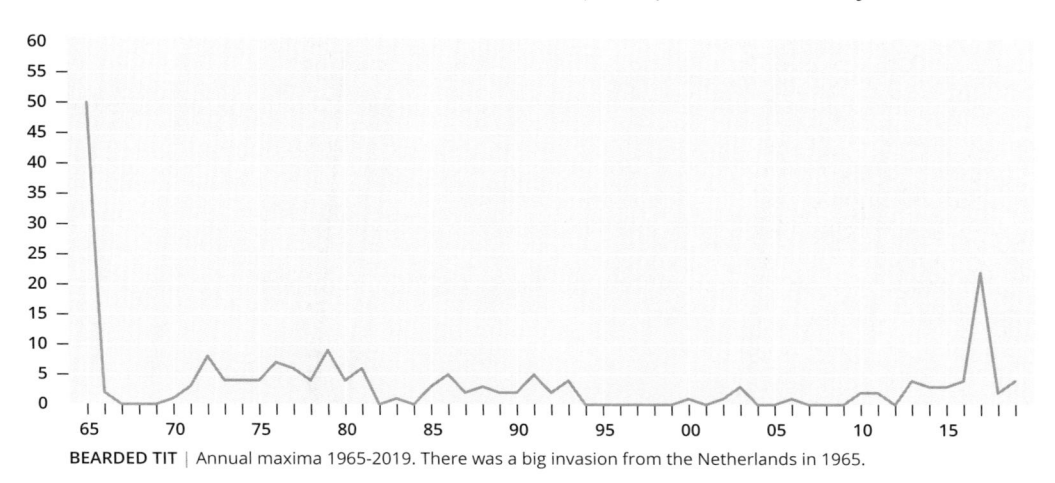

BEARDED TIT | Annual maxima 1965-2019. There was a big invasion from the Netherlands in 1965.

SKYLARK *Alauda arvensis*

Skylarks traditionally bred along the north-east shore and in the lakeside fields behind, and in fields behind Walley Bank (along the north-west shore). It was always regarded as a common bird and it was not until 1970 that attempts were made to census them. Only one was heard singing in that year, but numbers increased to a peak of seven singing males in both 1976 and 1977, with four singing in 1979. Small numbers continued to sing each year but, apart from three singing in both 1989 and 1992, only ones and twos were then recorded. They had stopped breeding along the north-east shore itself when a footpath was opened between the two picnic sites. In addition, the ones in the fields behind the north-west shore (behind Walley Bank) also disappeared when those fields were planted with trees. It now seems highly unlikely that this iconic bird will ever return to the lake as a breeding species, although the song has been heard in 2014 and 2017.

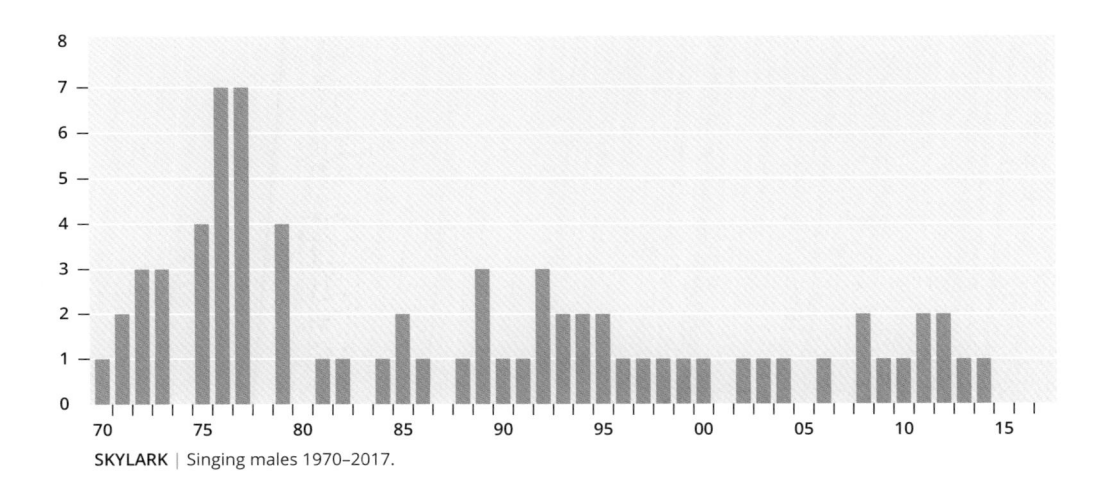

SKYLARK | Singing males 1970–2017.

The combined monthly maxima graph reveals low numbers from March to September, but with a small peak in January and a low point in June. By far the best month is October, but this is due almost entirely to overhead visible migration, the birds usually flying in a westerly or south-westerly direction. The highest such counts are as follows:

- **1967:** 95 flying west on 22 October.
- **1970:** 86 in November.
- **1971:** 65 but no date given.
- **1975:** 75 flying south-west on 7 October.
- **1978:** an exceptional cold weather movement of an estimated 1,000 birds on 31 December (CVRS).
- **2002:** 50 flying south-east on 17 October.
- **2011:** 45 flying south or south-west on 25 October.
- **2017:** the highest recent count was 65 flying over on 17 October.

The annual maxima graph shows how the species has mostly declined in numbers from 1967, apart from occasional fly-over flocks.

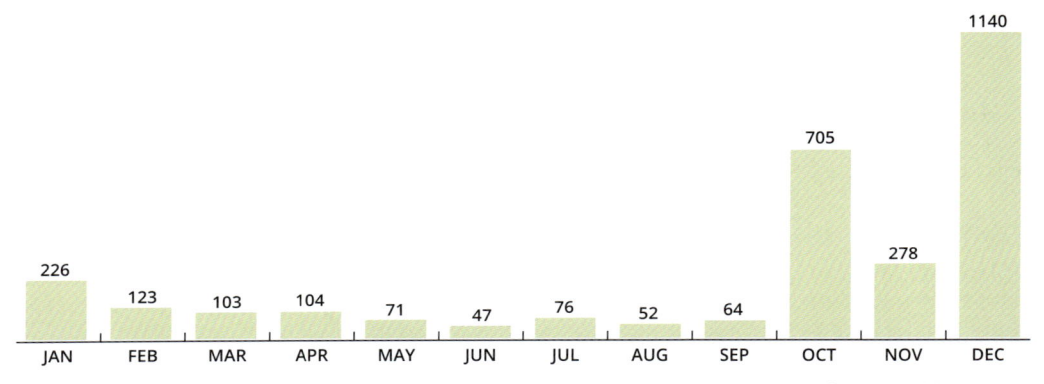

SKYLARK | Monthly maxima (combined) 1967-2017. Note the December figure includes the estimated 1000 in 1978.

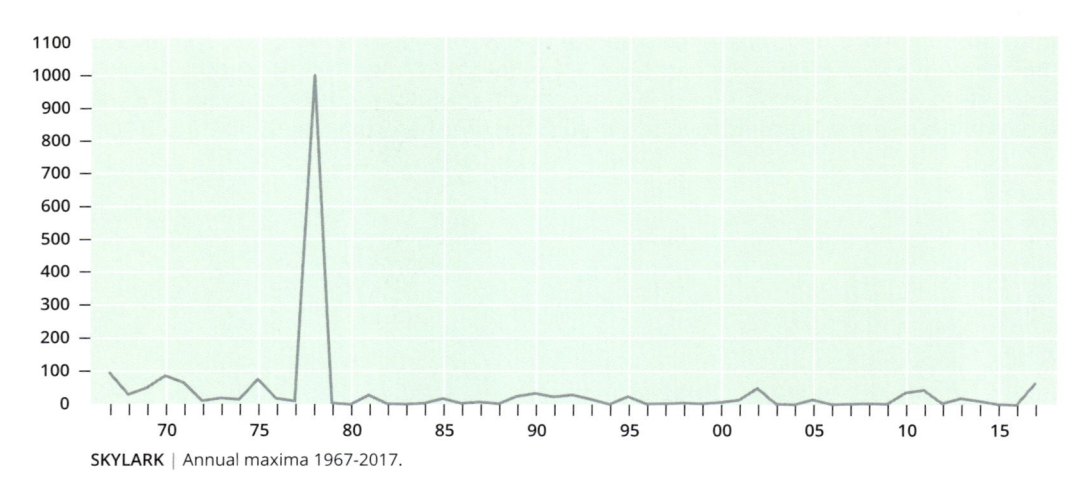

SKYLARK | Annual maxima 1967-2017.

| SHORE LARK *Eremophila alpestris*

One, probably a first-winter, was present from 3 February to 10 March 1963. It was seen by 'at least a dozen observers'. Credited to P. Chadwick and R. M. Curber (*Bristol Bird Report*).

SAND MARTIN *Riparia riparia*

The Sand Martin is a common passage migrant from March to September, but the earliest records were two on 25 February 1990, and an even earlier one on 23 February 2008. As the average monthly maxima graph shows, the main arrival begins in March, reaching a peak in April before dropping sharply in May. Very few are seen in June but it is difficult at this time to differentiate between late spring migrants and early autumn ones. It is possible that the first autumn migrants appear as early as 25 May, there being a small cluster of records in the last week of the month. Small numbers continue to be seen in June, with five double figure counts, the highest being 20 in 1995. Autumn migration really gets under way in July, increasing to a peak in September, but with only a very few seen in October. The highest October count was 25 on 4th in 1981 and the latest date involved one roosting on 14th (in 1994).

As the annual maxima graph indicates, numbers showed a marked increase from the mid-1990s. In the 29 years from 1964 to 1992, the average maximum count was 234 but, in the 22 years from 1993 to 2015, the average was 1,180. However, this increase involved four exceptional influxes:

1994: 5,000 on 31 March.
1996: 2,000 on 16 April, roosting in the Main Reeds during a spell of cold wind and rain.
2001: 3,000 on 7 April in cool conditions.
2008: 7,000 on 7 April, numbers having built up after several days of cold wet weather.

It is clear that large build-ups of migrating hirundines are usually the result of cold wet weather. In warm and sunny conditions there is no need for them to stop, so they simply pass through undetected, presumably at some height.

Sand Martin | Gary Thoburn

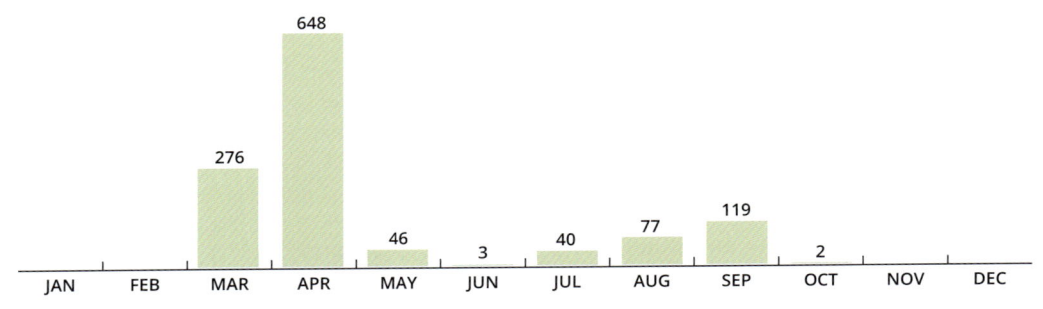

SAND MARTIN | Monthly maxima (average) 1965-2015.

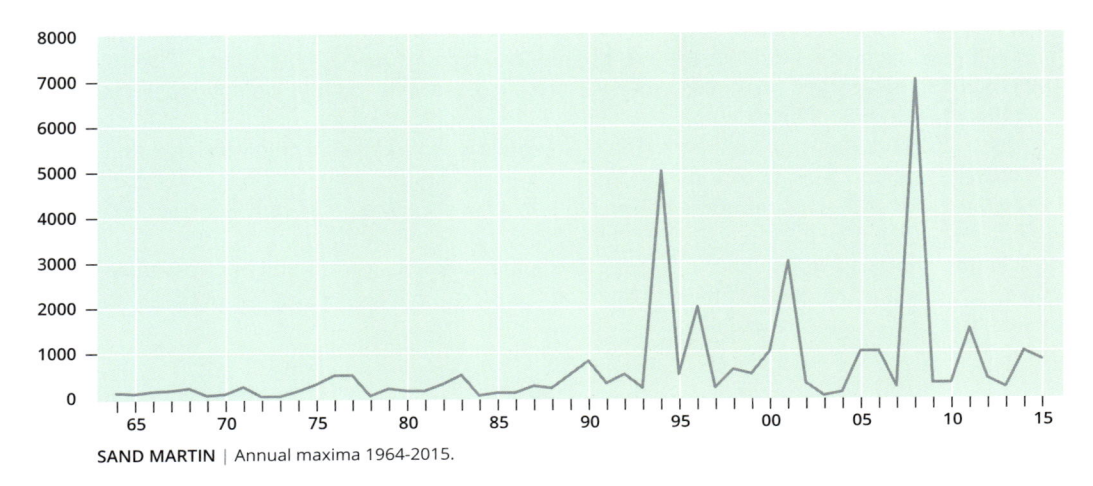

Jan —, Feb —, Mar 276, Apr 648, May 46, Jun 3, Jul 40, Aug 77, Sep 119, Oct 2, Nov —, Dec —

SAND MARTIN | Annual maxima 1964-2015.

SWALLOW *Hirundo rustica*

The first Swallows usually appear in March, the average first date being 28th, and the earliest had been 5 March 1989 until a bird on 18 February 2019. The average last date is 9 October but there have been six November records, with the latest being on 28th (in 2001).

As the average monthly maxima graph indicates, the peak spring passage is in April and May, while the autumn passage gets under way in July and peaks in August and September, dropping sharply in October.

As the annual maxima graph shows, annual totals vary considerably, these fluctuations being directly linked to the weather. As with Swifts *Apus apus* and with hirundines, the highest counts are in cool, wet and windy weather, when the birds find it difficult to find food over the land. They then congregate at the lake to take advantage of the chironomids that hatch in vast numbers during the spring and summer. As with Swifts, overall numbers are difficult to assess, but the highest recorded estimates were 4,000 roosting on 14 August 1975, 3,000 roosting on 12 August 1981 and 3,500 feeding in May 1997.

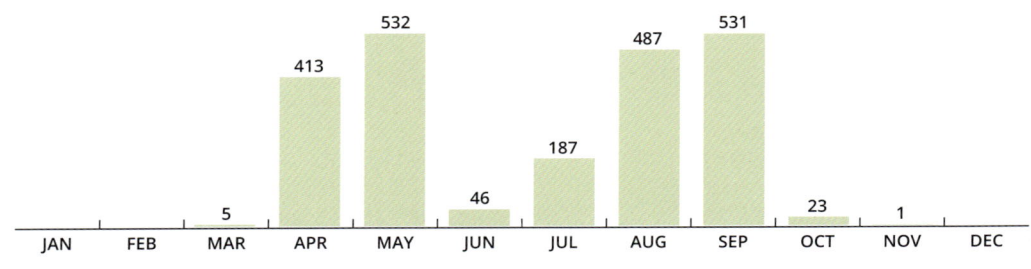

Jan —, Feb —, Mar 5, Apr 413, May 532, Jun 46, Jul 187, Aug 487, Sep 531, Oct 23, Nov 1, Dec —

SWALLOW | Monthly maxima (average) 1967-2015.

The species breeds quite commonly in the various farm buildings, out-houses and porches in the area but, from 1994 to 1999, a pair bred under the arch to the valve tower on the Main Dam, raising eleven broods during that period. The earliest flying juvenile was seen on 9 June (in 2011).

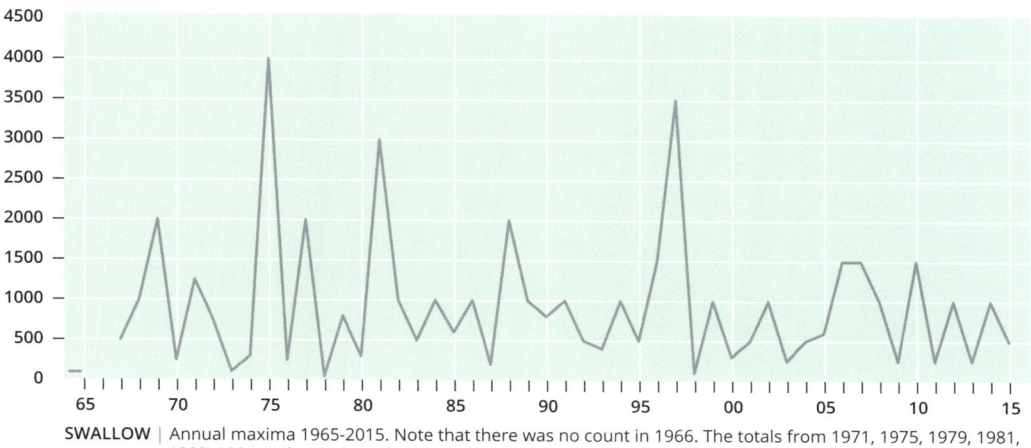

SWALLOW | Annual maxima 1965-2015. Note that there was no count in 1966. The totals from 1971, 1975, 1979, 1981, 1982, 1984 and 2006 are related to roost counts.

Swallow | Gary Thoburn

HOUSE MARTIN *Delichon urbicum*

As the average monthly maxima graph shows, the first spring House Martins often appear in March, the earliest date being one in fine spring weather on 24 March 1990. There have been seven March records in total, all of singletons except for one count of five (on 31 March 2000). Numbers rise slowly through April, increasing month on month to a peak in September. There is then a sharp drop in October. The latest records were one on 17 November 1982 and singles, perhaps the same bird, on 3, 10 and 16 November 1986.

This regular monthly increase, shown in the graph, is interesting, suggesting that there is an incremental increase in numbers throughout the summer and into the autumn. Obviously, the recruitment of the summer's young largely accounts for this, but it has been suggested that House Martins that breed first in southern Europe may then breed again as they make their way north through the summer. The average monthly maxima graph does nothing to dispel such a theory.

As the annual maxima graph shows, annual totals vary considerably, with peak counts ranging from as few as 500 to a maximum of 5,000 (in 1982, 1986, 1989, 1992, 2001 and 2008). The largest numbers relate to cold wet weather, when thousands of Swifts *Apus apus* and House Martins gather over the lake to feed on the emerging insects which, in those kind of conditions, are scarce over the towns, villages and countryside.

House Martins breed quite commonly on suitable local houses, as well as in the villages around the lake, but, when the very large numbers occur, they clearly arrive from much further afield.

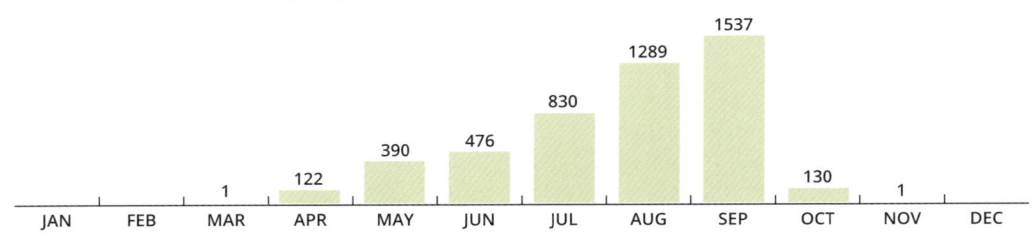

HOUSE MARTIN | Monthly maxima (average) 1968-2015.

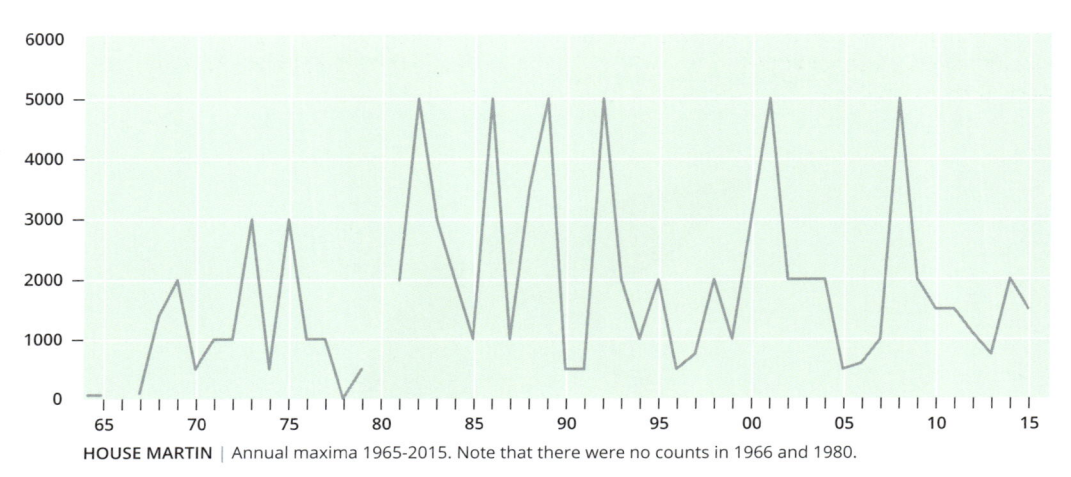

HOUSE MARTIN | Annual maxima 1965-2015. Note that there were no counts in 1966 and 1980.

House Martin | Gary Thoburn

COMPLETE SPECIES LIST AND CHARTS

RED-RUMPED SWALLOW *Cecropis daurica*

One was seen at Herriott's Bridge on 20 October 1990 (R. J. Palmer, D. J. Angell *et al.*). Considering the huge numbers of hirundines that regularly pass through the lake in both spring and autumn, it is astonishing that there have not been further records.

CETTI'S WARBLER *Cettia cetti*

The first record, not previously published, was of one repeatedly calling in the Main Reeds on 27 October 1973 (KEV). Occurrences were then erratic, the next being one trapped on 25 February 1975 and present until 20 April. There was then a five-year gap until the third, one trapped on 29 December 1982 and present until at least 20 February 1983, then one seen on 6 October that year. One was then trapped on 1 April 1990 and the next was on 31 October 1992, when three were recorded. From that point onwards, the species established a toehold at the lake, with the first breeding in 1995, when three females reared eleven young, followed by nine more juveniles from second broods (*ABR per* CVRS). However, a juvenile on 23 July 1994 was thought to have been born at the lake. Since then, numbers have continued to increase, with a record 31 singing males in 2010. Unfortunately, the species was then badly hit by the cold winter of 2011/12, with only six singing males present in the summer of 2012 and just three in 2013. But again numbers bounced back, with 14 singing males in 2015, 22 in 2016 and 28 in 2017.

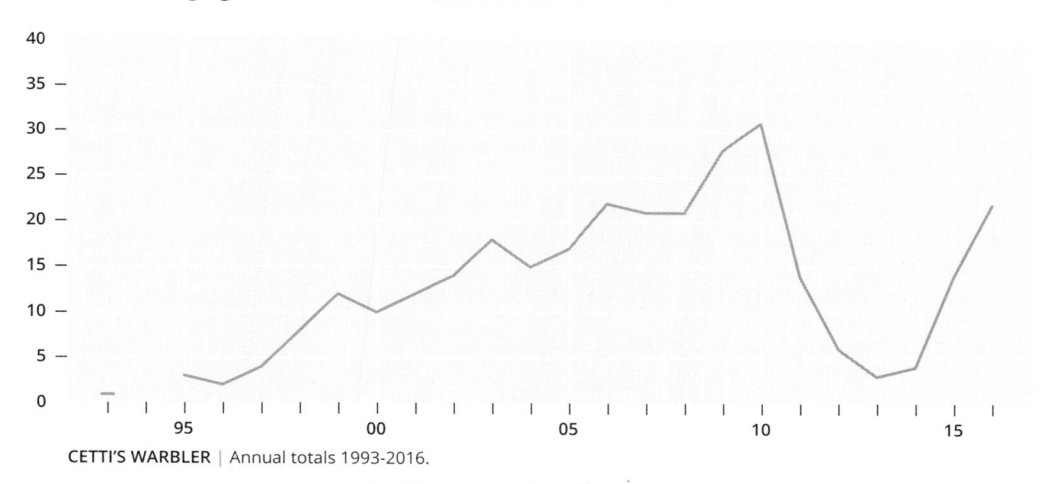

CETTI'S WARBLER | Annual totals 1993-2016.

Cetti's Warbler | Laurel Tucker

The annual ringing totals graph shows the numbers of Cetti's Warblers caught annually, the peaks being 67 in 2009 and 52 in 2016.

Note that in total 774 were caught between 1975 and 2018.

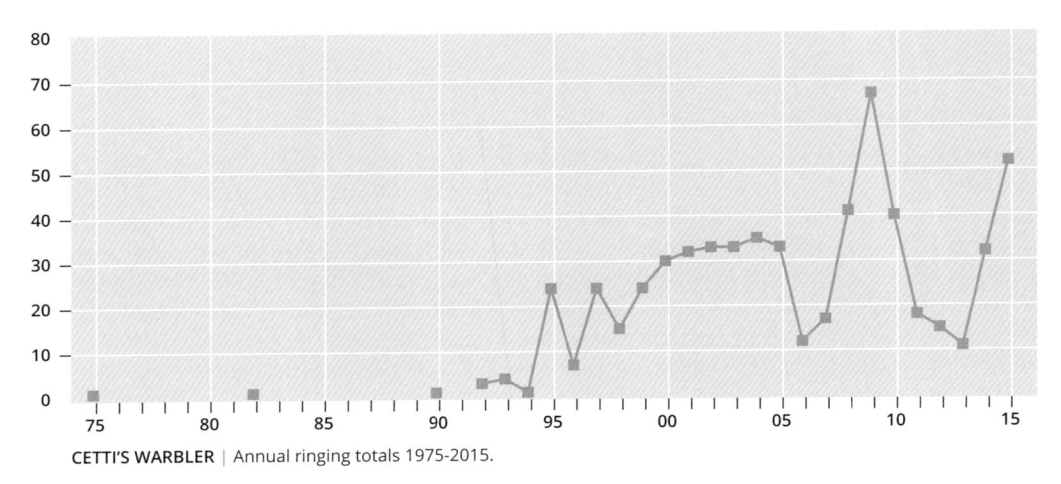

CETTI'S WARBLER | Annual ringing totals 1975-2015.

LONG-TAILED TIT *Aegithalos caudatus*

This is a common resident and small parties can be located almost anywhere around the lake, although the eastern side (particularly Twycross and the East Shore boardwalk) is perhaps the most likely area to come across them. The highest numbers are in summer when the flocks are heavily augmented by the year's young.

Between 1961 and 2018, 3,757 Long-tailed Tits were ringed at the lake. There were none in either 1963 or 1964 – it seems likely that their absence then was related to high mortality rates in the severe winter of 1962–63. Numbers since have varied considerably, with the fewest in 1982 (14) and the highest in 1975 (168). However, the overall trend seems to be upward.

Long-tailed Tit | Laurel Tucker

WOOD WARBLER *Phylloscopus sibilatrix*

The first record was of a male singing at Hollow Brook on 27 April 1969 (KEV). Since then, there have been a further 30 spring records, all in the period 18 April to 15 May, except for an unusually early individual on 9 April 1999. All these have related to singing males on migration and all have been along the east shore, with a large concentration of 11 in the area of the Sutton Wick car park, the birds seemingly attracted to the adjacent silver birches. By contrast, there have been only three recorded on autumn migration, all of which were trapped by CVRS: singles on 25 July 1976 and 12 and 13 August 1984.

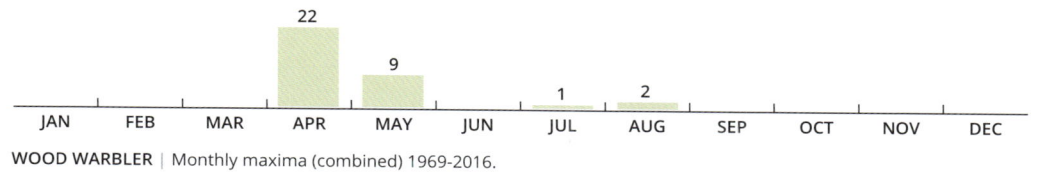

WOOD WARBLER | Monthly maxima (combined) 1969-2016.

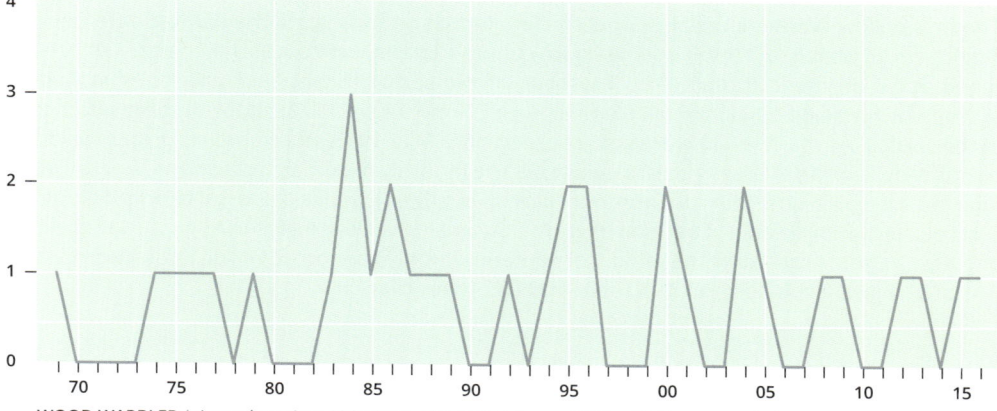

WOOD WARBLER | Annual maxima 1969-2016. The best year was 1984, with three recorded.

Wood Warbler | Laurel Tucker

YELLOW-BROWED WARBLER *Phylloscopus inornatus*

There have been eight records:
- **1986:** one along the East Shore 15 November (A. J. Merritt).
- **1988:** one with a tit flock in Stratford Bay on 9 October (KEV).
- **2005:** one at the back of Herriott's Pool on 24 September (KEV).
- **2008:** one at Chew Stoke Sewage Treatment Works from 29 January to 21 February (R. Mielcarek *et al.*).
- **2011:** one trapped on 29 December, retrapped on 1 January 2012 and remaining to 12 February 2012 (CVRS).
- **2014:** one trapped on 25 October (CVRS).
- **2016:** one ringed on 8 October and re-trapped on 16 October; another on the Bittern Trail on 13 October (M. Davis *et al.*).

WILLOW WARBLER *Phylloscopus trochilus*

The first Willow Warblers usually appear in late March or early April, the earliest date being one singing on 18 March (in 1990). Double figure counts sometimes occur at the end of March, with as many as 18 on the 28th (in 2010). The peak of the spring migration, however, is in April, the average count being 15, but with a fall of at least 70 on 19 April 1970, and with three other counts in the forties. As many as 40 were also counted on 5 May 1968, but numbers drop considerably during May, with an average peak of eleven. As the monthly maxima graph shows, few are seen in June (an average of just four) but numbers pick up in July as juvenile dispersal takes place, plus the first southerly movements of autumn migrants. Surprisingly few are seen in August and September, and the species is rare after the middle of September (only five records). The latest recorded date was of one giving sub-song on 4 October 1980 (C. J. Newman).

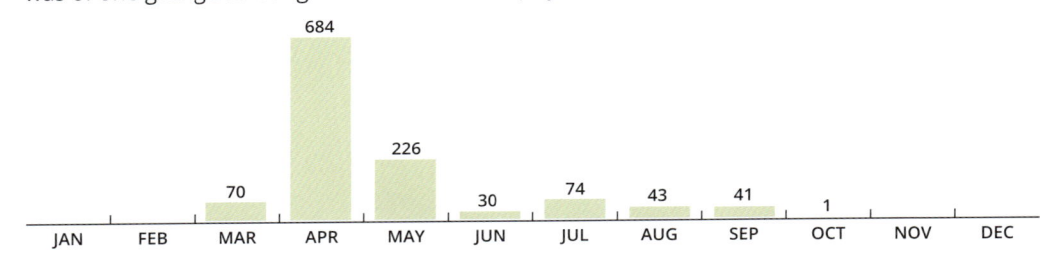

JAN	FEB	MAR	APR	MAY	JUN	JUL	AUG	SEP	OCT	NOV	DEC
		70	684	226	30	74	43	41	1		

WILLOW WARBLER | Monthly maxima (combined) 1965-2015.

Willow Warbler | Laurel Tucker

Attempts at working out the breeding population have been fraught with difficulty, it being extremely difficult to differentiate migrants, which often sing on migration, from those birds actually on territory. Because of this problem, there is no doubt that, in the past, the numbers of breeding birds have been significantly overestimated. Having said that, there were probably more breeding birds in the early years than there are now, simply because the newly planted lakeside woodland was much better suited to them. Since then, the plantations have matured and this habitat is now utilized by 'proper' woodland species, particularly Chiffchaff *Ph. collybita* and Blackcap *Sylvia atricapilla*.

Both graphs – which show the number of singing males (1984–2017) and the annual ringing totals (1963–2015) – show a similar trend. Note the very low numbers since the turn of the century.

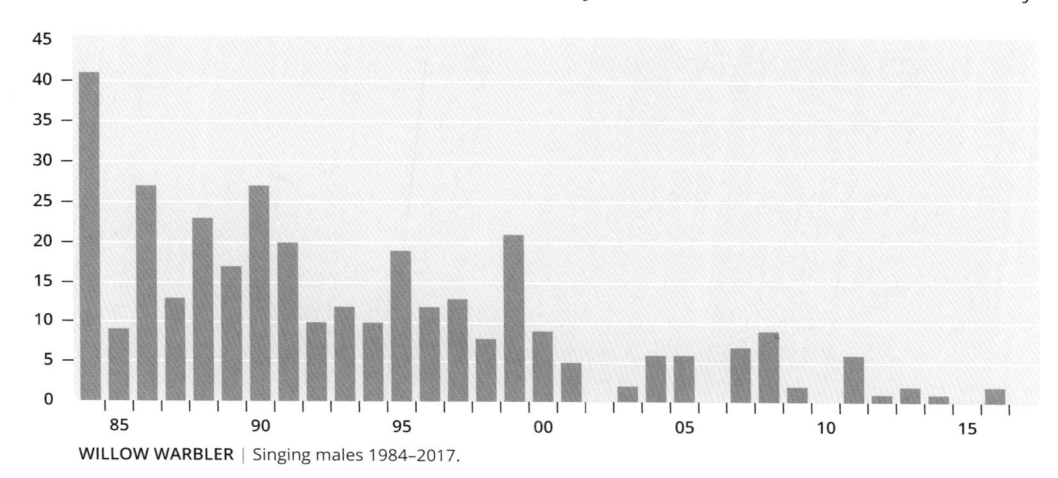

WILLOW WARBLER | Singing males 1984–2017.

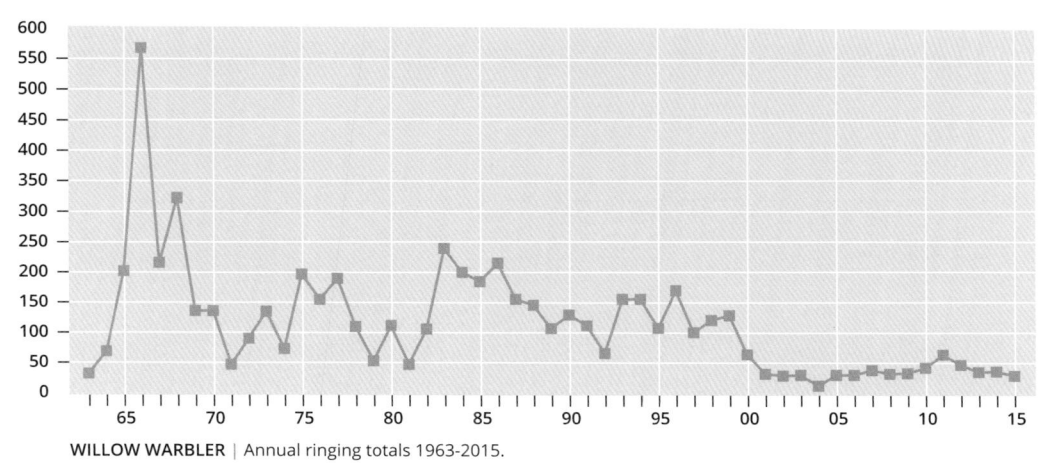

WILLOW WARBLER | Annual ringing totals 1963-2015.

CHIFFCHAFF *Phylloscopus collybita*

As the combined monthly maxima graph shows, Chiffchaffs are present throughout the year, but the highest numbers are in March and April, when the first summer migrants appear. The *average* first date (1966–2011) is 20 March but there has been a cluster of first dates around the period 2–5 March, these involving birds in full song, which are assumed to relate to the first spring migrants. As the graph shows, spring numbers peak in April, with a marked fall in May, dropping to a low point in June when the birds are breeding. Autumn numbers peak in September and, surprisingly, this is followed by a small but gradual increase to a lesser peak in December, as small numbers of winter visitors arrive.

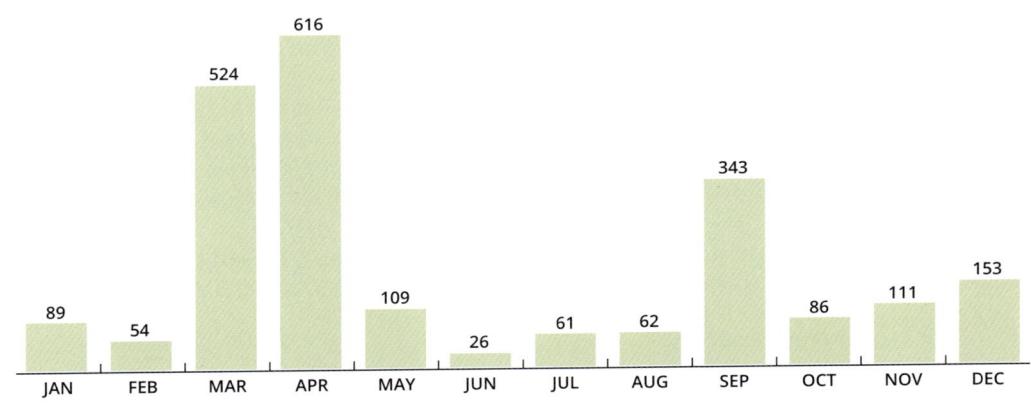

CHIFFCHAFF | Monthly maxima (combined) 1967-2015.

Month	JAN	FEB	MAR	APR	MAY	JUN	JUL	AUG	SEP	OCT	NOV	DEC
Max	89	54	524	616	109	26	61	62	343	86	111	153

As the lakeside woodlands have gradually matured, the numbers of breeding Chiffchaffs have increased accordingly. The graph shows a gradual rise in the numbers of singing males, to a record 83 in 2012. The annual ringing graph shows a vaguely similar pattern for the period 1984–2016

One trapped on 3 December 2016 proved to be of the Scandinavian race *abietinus*. This was confirmed by DNA analysis (*ABR* 2016). This was only the ninth confirmed British record of this race. In fact a second Chew record occurred on 25 November 2017 (*ABR* 2018).

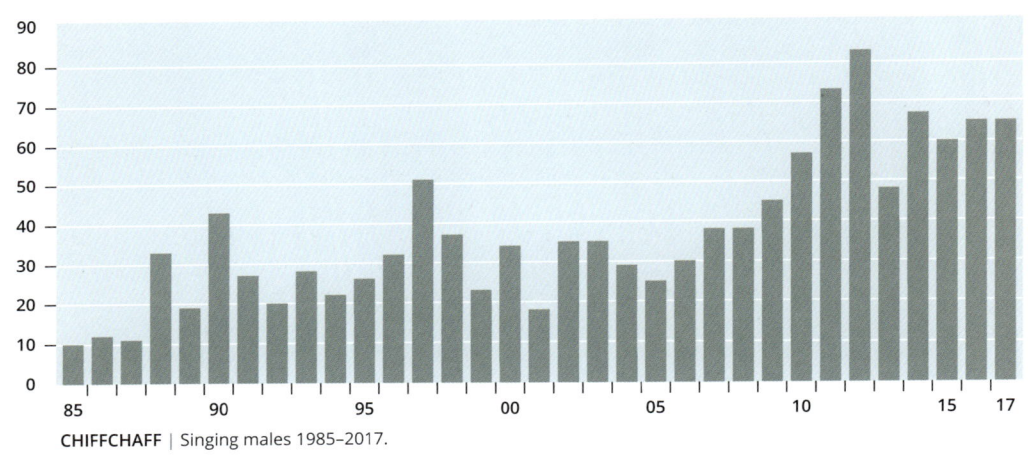

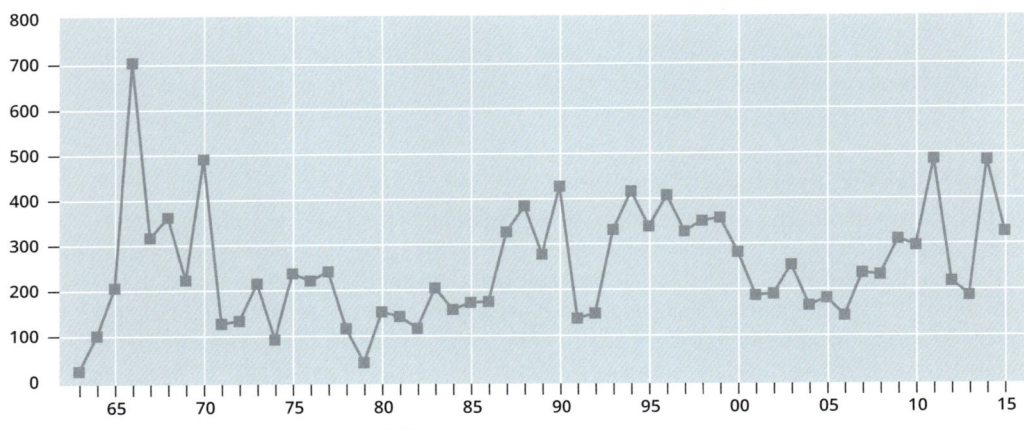

CHIFFCHAFF | Singing males 1985–2017.

CHIFFCHAFF | Annual ringing totals 1963-2015.

Chiffchaff | Gary Thoburn

Siberian Chiffchaff *Phylloscopus (c.) tristis*

The first record was of one on 5 November 1976 (A. J. Merritt) but it was twelve years before the next: two on 27 November 1988, with one seen again on 10 December (KEV). It has since been recorded in 15 of the 27 years to 2015.

From 1990 to 2012, all the records involved single birds, but two were seen in 2013 and as many as four in March 2014. In fact, a total of at least eight individuals were thought to have been present in 2014. Numbers were again high in 2015, with five recorded. In 2016, four individuals trapped between 23 October and 3 December were confirmed as *tristis* from DNA analysis.

It has been seen at several sites around the lake, but the main ones have been the Chew Stoke Sewage Treatment Works (behind the Main Dam, not run by Bristol Water but very close to the lake), Twycross/East Shore and the Herriott's Bridge area.

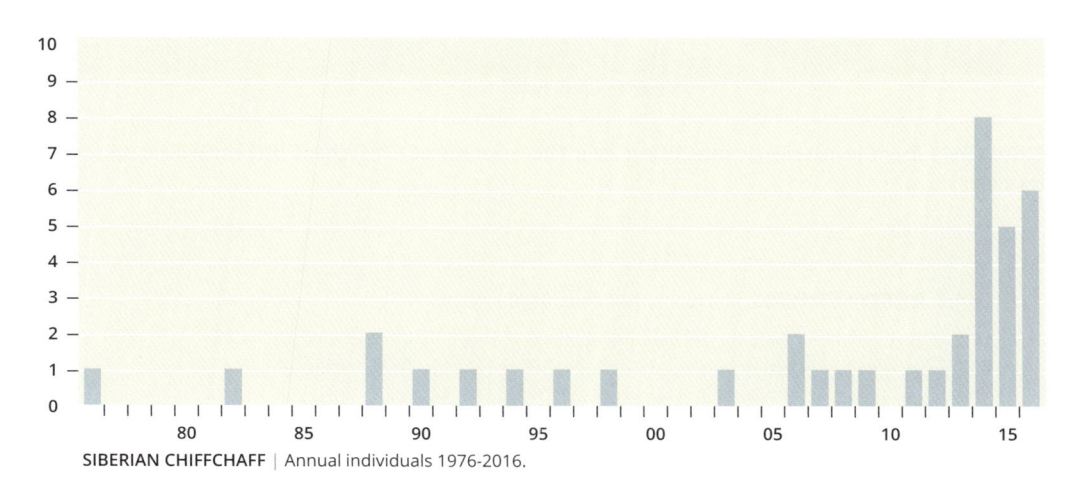

SIBERIAN CHIFFCHAFF | Annual individuals 1976-2016.

As the combined monthly maxima graph indicates, the species has been recorded from 2 November (1998) to 10 April (2014), with a distinct peak in December (12 individuals).

Further records occurred in December 2018 with 2 into February 2019, then one in December 2019 and a different one from December into 2020.

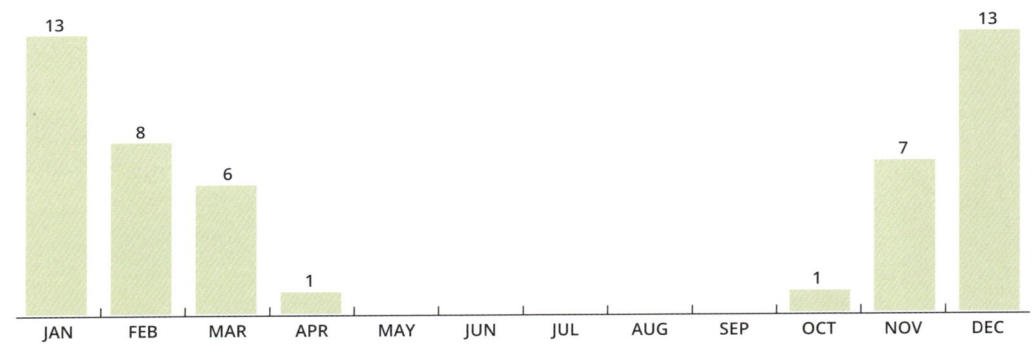

SIBERIAN CHIFFCHAFF | Monthly maxima (combined) 1976-2016.

JAN	FEB	MAR	APR	MAY	JUN	JUL	AUG	SEP	OCT	NOV	DEC
13	8	6	1						1	7	13

Siberian Chiffchaff | Gary Thoburn

Note: This form is currently classified as a sub-species of Chiffchaff but may be a species in its own right.

GREAT REED WARBLER *Acrocephalus arundinaceus*

There have been three records, all involving singing males that were seen well:
- **1992:** one on the east side of Herriott's Pool on 18 May (J. Aldridge *et al.*).
- **2008:** one in front of Herriott's Bridge on 12 May (A. H. Davis *et al.*).
- **2014:** one also in front of Herriott's Bridge on 24–26 May (S. Davies *et al.*).

Great Reed Warbler | Keith Vinicombe

AQUATIC WARBLER *Acrocephalus paludicola*

There have been twelve records of this critically endangered species, which breeds in eastern Europe. All the following were singles, all were juveniles and all except two were trapped.

- **1965:** 15 August (R. J. Prytherch, P. T. Sims, R. F. Thearle *et al.*). The bird was released on 16th.
- **1966:** 13 August (D. M. Crampton, D. Shepherd, R. F. Thearle).
- **1972:** 20 August (R. J. Prytherch, F. R. Smith, K. T. Standring).
- **1976:** one was seen in the field on 16 August (P. R. Baber).
- **1977:** 3 August (D. Buffery, R. Webber, S. J. Wilkinson).
- **1984:** singles on 12 and 13 August (CVRS); another was found on Moreton Bank on 20 August (KEV) and was subsequently trapped on 21st (A. J. Merritt *et al.*).
- **1990:** one on 14 August had been ringed in Poland (CVRS).
- **1994:** 13 August (CVRS, R. J. Higgins, KEV).
- **1995:** 9 August (CVRS).
- **1999:** Herriott's Pool on 3 September (J. P. Martin, T. McGrath).

None has been recorded since 1999.

Aquatic Warbler | Laurel Tucker

SEDGE WARBLER *Acrocephalus schoenobaenus*

The Sedge Warbler breeds around the lake but, unlike the Reed Warbler *A. scirpaceus*, it is not so much a bird of reed beds but more a bird of drier, scrubbier, weedier, and rougher habitats. As the first chart shows, it was much more abundant in the mid-1960s than it is now, there being a crash in numbers following the 1968–69 winter. This was caused by a sub-Saharan drought that badly affected a number of trans-Saharan migrants, most notably the Whitethroat *Sylvia communis*. Numbers of singing Sedge Warblers appear to have fallen even further since the mid-1990s, but with something of an upsurge in the late 2000s.

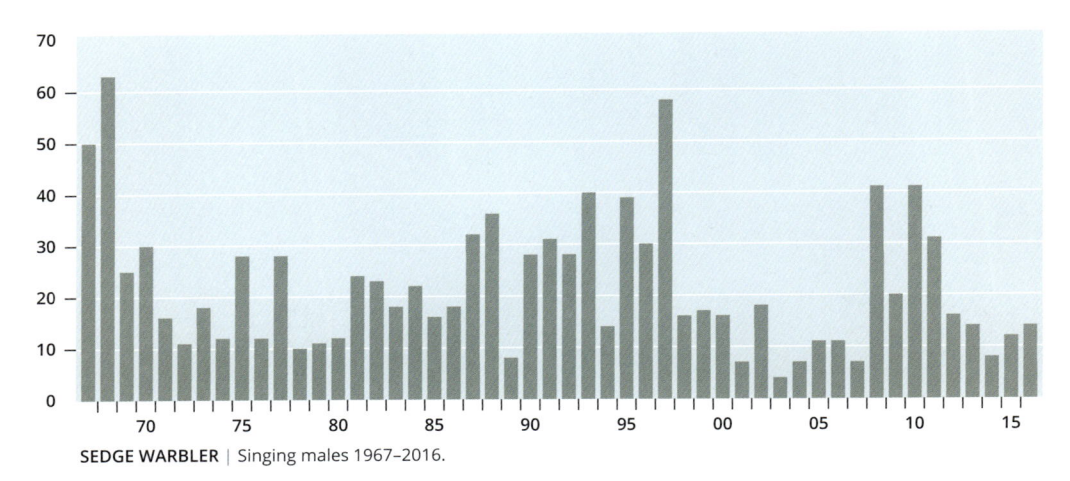

SEDGE WARBLER | Singing males 1967–2016.

Another reason for the decline is the relentless spread of reeds around the lake. This favours Reed Warblers but reduces the amount of suitable breeding habitat for Sedge Warblers. A more prosaic factor is that Sedge Warblers are not easy to monitor. For one thing, there is a strong peak in their singing when they first arrive and, also, the peak of their singing is around dawn, well before most birders have arrived at the lake. That being the case, singing Sedge Warblers are likely to be under-counted. Yet another problem is that they also seem to sing whilst on migration, making it difficult to separate birds on territory from those passing through.

Interestingly, the graph which shows the annual ringing totals, reveals a remarkably similar pattern to the chart of singing males: high numbers ringed in the 1960s, a steep decline following the 1968–69 sub-Saharan drought, a slow recovery to the mid-1970s, another down-turn in the mid-1980s, followed by a recent up-turn during 2008–2011.

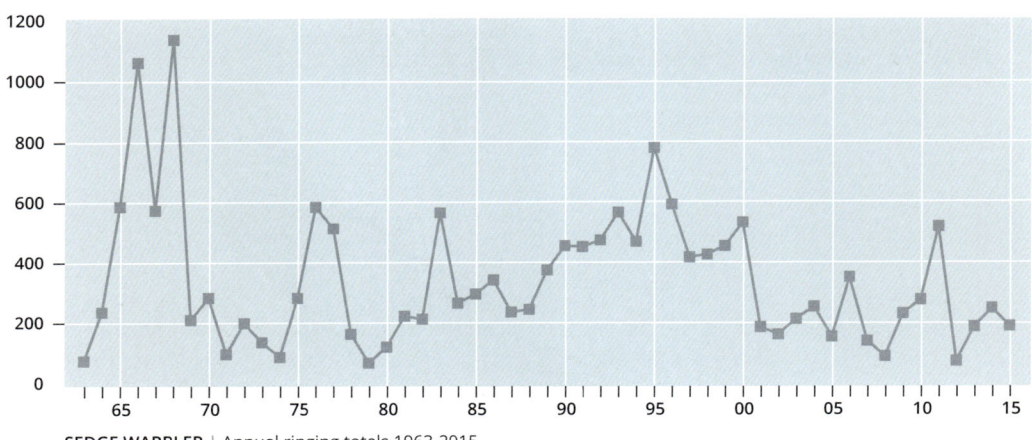

SEDGE WARBLER | Annual ringing totals 1963-2015.

As the annual ringing totals graph also indicates, the totals for Sedge Warbler were 587 in 1965, rising to 1,062 in 1966 and 1,138 in 1968, but falling to just 68 in 1979. Despite an upsurge to 780 in 1995 and a smaller peak of 517 in 2011, numbers have never recovered to the earlier peak in the late 1960s.

The combined monthly maxima graph shows the bulk of the spring arrivals are in April, the earliest arrival date being 2nd (in 1988) and the average being the 16th. The latest autumn record was one on 16 October (in 1976).

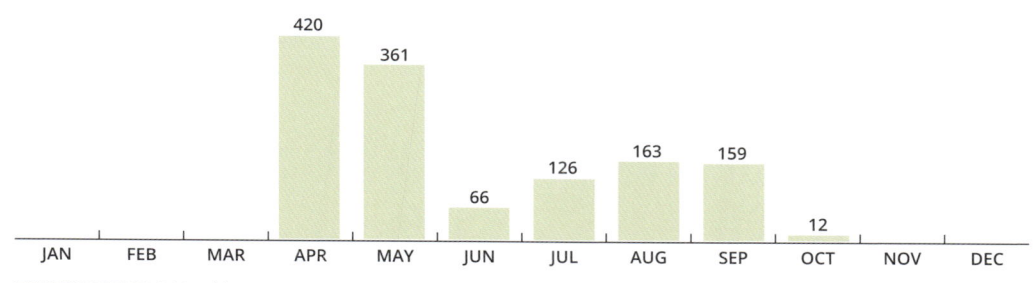

JAN	FEB	MAR	APR	MAY	JUN	JUL	AUG	SEP	OCT	NOV	DEC
			420	361	66	126	163	159	12		

SEDGE WARBLER | Monthly maxima (combined) 1965-2015.

Sedge Warbler | Gary Thoburn

REED WARBLER *Acrocephalus scirpaceus*

It is not known when the first Reed Warblers were recorded at Chew, but there were two or more singing on 3 July 1958. This was followed by a record of '4+ singing' in 1959 and 20 singing on 1 July 1962. It has to be remembered that, in the early days of the lake, there were no reeds, but it seems as though they were becoming established by the late 1950s and early 1960s. However, in *The Birds of Somerset* (1968) there is an aerial photograph which shows that the only significant reeds were in the south-east corner – the area that is now referred to as the 'Main Reeds'. This photograph also shows that the reeds were colonising the area immediately to the south of Wick Green Point. Nowadays, there are extensive areas of reed right around the lake, being absent only where there are steep banks and along the stone causeways.

The Reed Warbler is now by far the commonest breeding bird, although it is impossible to know how many pairs there are. Twenty-seven nests were found in 1981, 61 in 1987, 227 in 1996 and 282 in 2004, but these represent only minimum totals. Most of the counts are the result of survey work by David Warden. In a paper in the 2003 *Avon Bird Report*, he states that his 'estimates of the population breeding at the lake have varied from about 530 pairs in 1968 to about 900 pairs in 2000. For the six years that estimates of the population have been made, the average is over 800 pairs.' He goes on to say that 'Bearing in mind the potential for errors these figures can only be approximations. Even so, it seems that a very considerable number of Reed Warblers now breed at the lake.'

The graph, based on annual ringing totals, clearly shows the increase from 1963 (when 69 were caught) to a peak of 1,781 in 1995. There have now been 16 years between 1993 and 2015 when annual ringing totals have exceeded a thousand.

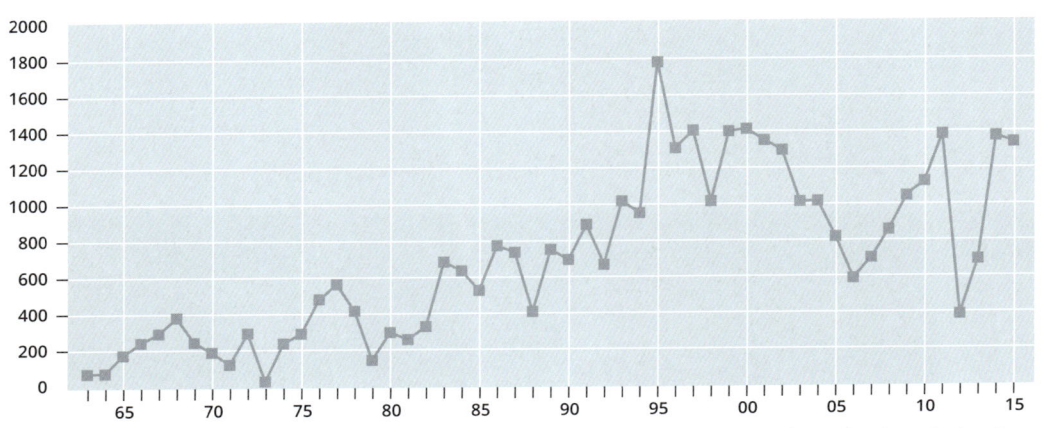

REED WARBLER | Annual ringing totals 1963-2015. It is important to stress that these totals are also dependent on the levels of ringing activity.

Another interesting feature is that, based on observations, their first arrival dates have in general become earlier. The following shows the earliest arrival dates for the six decades from the 1960s to the 2010s, plus 2011–2015 and the latest decadal dates.

EARLIEST ARRIVAL	
1960s:	25 April (based on just one year – 1968)
1970s:	24 March (1973)
1980s:	16 April
1990s:	8 April
2000s:	10 April
2010–2015:	1 April

LATEST DEPARTURE	
1970s:	16 October
1980s:	4 October
1990s:	23 October
2000s:	16 December
2010–2019:	26 December

Given that the earliest dates are getting earlier and the latest dates are getting later, it seems hardly surprising that one was recently trapped in winter: on 30 January 2015. A DNA sample confirmed that it was of the nominate race (CVRS, *ABR* 2015).

MARSH WARBLER *Acrocephalus palustris*

There have been two records:

A male in full song was discovered on 19 May 1979 in osiers along the East Shore. It was frequently to be seen singing in full view on the tops of the bushes (KEV *et al.*). It remained until early July when it was still singing strongly (A. H. Davis). Another was trapped on 5 June 1994 (CVRS).

Reed Warbler | Lucy Masters

GRASSHOPPER WARBLER *Locustella naevia*

This peculiar, secretive bird was first recorded in 1965, but it is not known whether it was seen prior to this. The average arrival date is 24 April, but the earliest was on 6 April (in 2011). As the combined monthly maxima graph indicates, numbers peak in April–May and again in July, gradually tailing off through August and September, with the latest date being 24 September (in 2005).

As the annual maxima graph shows, it was virtually annual from 1965 to 1982, but it has been much more erratic since, with significant gaps in 1983–86 inclusive and 1998–2004 inclusive. It is thought that this is related to the gradual maturation of the lakeside vegetation: reeds, woodland and willows replacing the scrub, young plantations and grassland that used to be there. Interestingly, however, a concerted effort to find Grasshopper Warblers in late August/early September 2011 led to the discovery of four individuals, presumably migrants.

The annual ringing totals in the graph show a remarkably similar trend to the annual maxima graph, with most in 1964–76, a resurgence in 1987–95, and fairly erratic occurrences since.

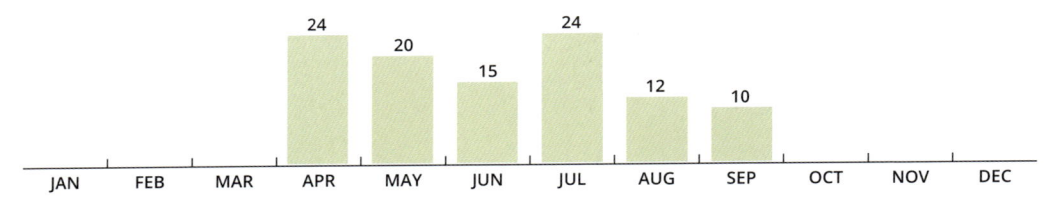

GRASSHOPPER WARBLER | Monthly maxima (combined) 1965-2015.

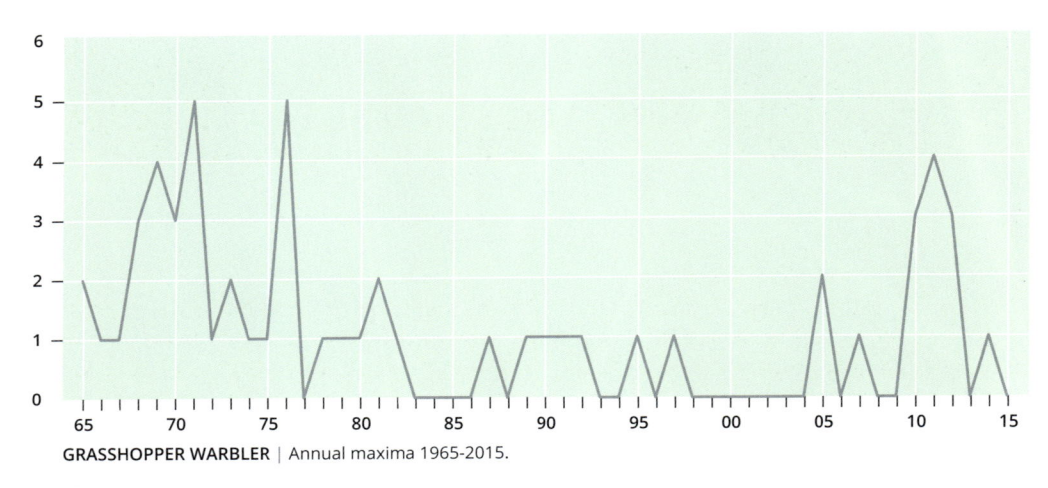

GRASSHOPPER WARBLER | Annual maxima 1965-2015.

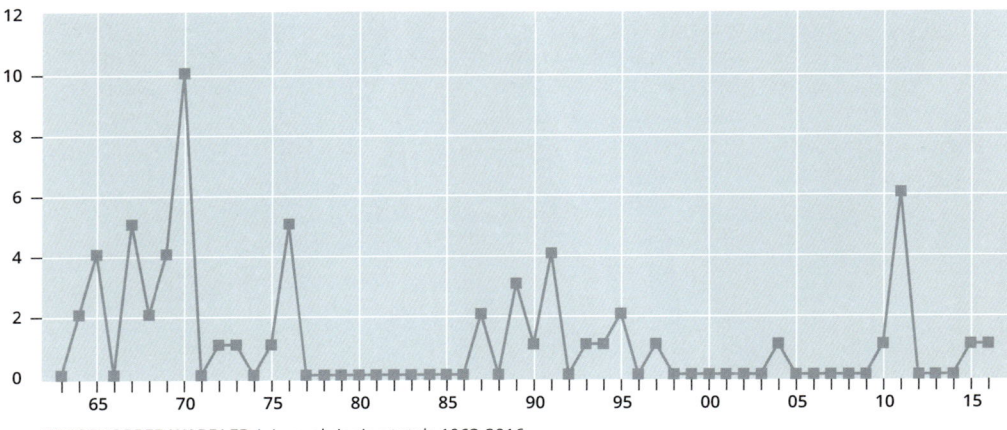

GRASSHOPPER WARBLER | Annual ringing totals 1963-2016.

SAVI'S WARBLER *Locustella luscinioides*
There have been four records:
- **1960:** a male reeling 24–30 July (B. King, K. B. Young).
- **1980:** a male reeling on 16 April (C. J. Newman, R. Unite).
- **1986:** a juvenile/first-winter trapped on 31 August (A. J. Merritt, C. J. Newman, KEV).
- **2001:** a male reeling and seen briefly on the east side of Herriott's Pool on 9–10 May (KEV *et al.*).

Savi's Warbler | Keith Vinicombe

BLACKCAP *Sylvia atricapilla*
There were no March records prior to 1997, when two were singing on 30th, but records in that month have now been recorded in 12 of the 20 years since, a clear indication that Blackcaps are arriving earlier (the current earliest date relates to a male on 20 March 2012). As the combined monthly maxima graph shows, the highest totals are recorded in April, when the males are in full song and defending a territory. The subsequent decline shown there simply reflects a decrease in their song into the summer. The number of singing males graph shows that numbers have increased significantly since the 1980s, reaching a record 80 singing males in 2016. By 2017 it was the second most numerous breeding warbler after Reed Warbler *Acrocephalus scirpaceus*. This increase is undoubtedly related to the gradual maturation of the lakeside woodland, which clearly favours this species. Ringing totals also reflect this upward trend, with annual maxima reaching a record 453 in 2011. There are a few winter records, mostly ringed, and also a male photographed in the Picnic Site Number 1 car park on 1 December 2017 and one at Woodford Lodge 7 February 2018 (I. Stapp).

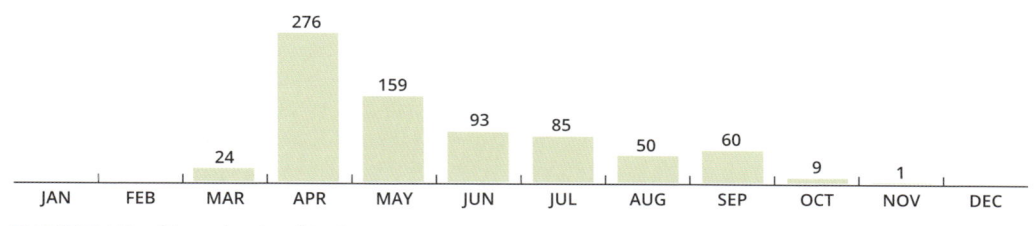

JAN	FEB	MAR	APR	MAY	JUN	JUL	AUG	SEP	OCT	NOV	DEC
		24	276	159	93	85	50	60	9	1	

BLACKCAP | Monthly maxima (combined) 1965-2015.

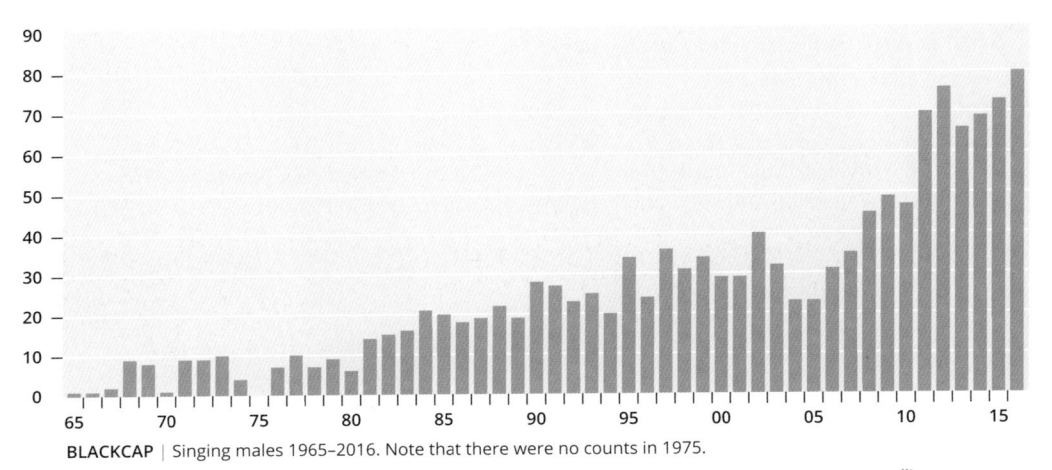

BLACKCAP | Singing males 1965–2016. Note that there were no counts in 1975.

Blackcap | Laurel Tucker

| GARDEN WARBLER *Sylvia borin*

This is one of the later spring migrants, with the earliest arrival date being 17 April (in both 2014 and 2015). Numbers peak in May, when the species is easily located by its remarkable and beautiful song. Once the singing subsides, they become much more difficult to locate, hence the abrupt fall in numbers from June to August, shown in the graph on page 408. It is uncommon in September, being recorded in just seven years, the latest being one on 20th in 1981.

As the combined monthly maxima graph shows, the breeding population has increased significantly from 1977, when first surveyed, to 2016, with a peak of 58 singing males in 2011 and 51 in 2013. However, numbers fell to 35 in 2016, but rose again to 48 in 2017.

Garden Warbler | Gary Thoburn

Annual ringing totals show a steady increase from 1963 through to the ten years from 1985-1996, when totals of over a hundred were caught in six of those years. The maxima were 173 in 1986, 150 in 1987 and 153 in 1993.

The discrepancy between the graph showing the ringing data and the one showing the number of singing males is obvious. However, Garden Warblers are birds of bushes, thick hedgerows and well-vegetated woodland understorey, particularly along east and west shores. These habitats are not as prevalent in areas where the ringing activities take place, at the southern end of the lake.

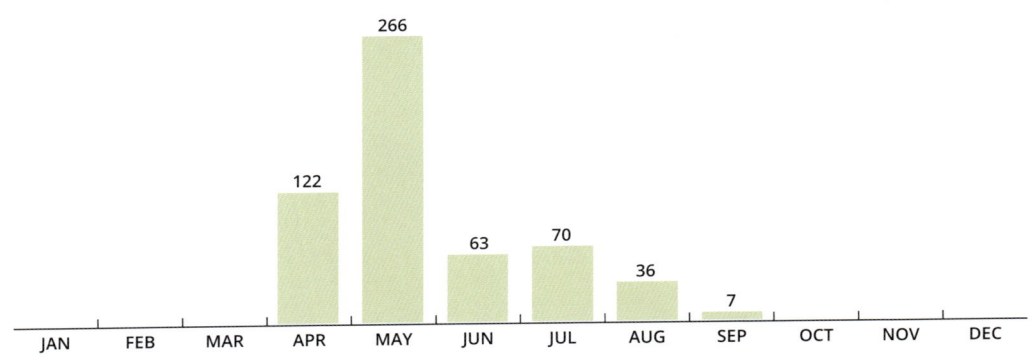

GARDEN WARBLER | Monthly maxima (combined) 1966-2015. The high spring peak is simply due to the fact that the males sing at this time.

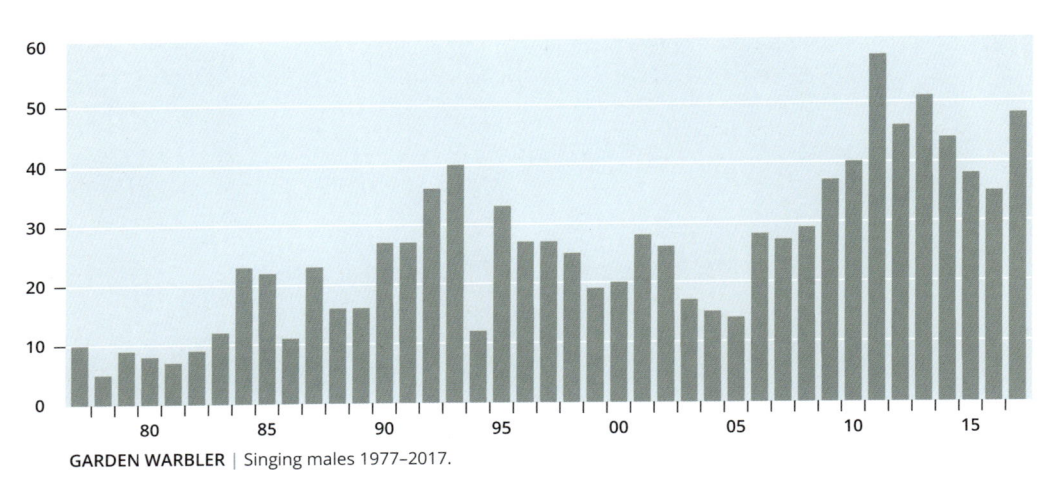

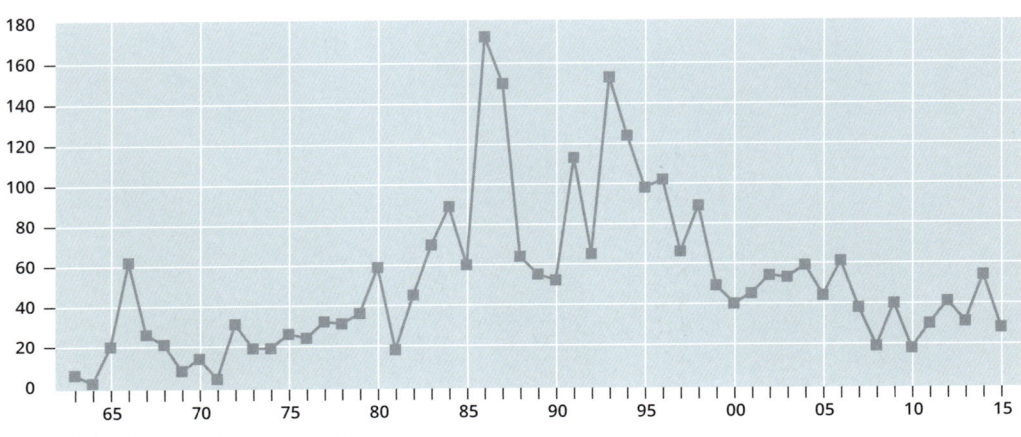

GARDEN WARBLER | Singing males 1977–2017.

GARDEN WARBLER | Annual ringing totals 1963-2015.

LESSER WHITETHROAT *Sylvia curruca*

As the combined monthly maxima graph shows, Lesser Whitethroats appear in April. Traditionally, the first date has been from 20th onwards but, in 2014, one was heard singing as early as the 12th. Numbers increase markedly in May before dipping in June when they are breeding. Numbers peak as early as July, remaining high into August, before dropping in September, the latest date being 26th (in 1994). However, in 2014 one was trapped on 29 November and, at the time, it was thought possibly to have been one of the Asian races, examples of which sometimes winter in Britain. However, the bird's DNA was analysed and it proved it to have been a nominate *curruca*.

The graph below shows the number of singing males from 1976 to 2016. Annual totals are erratic, no doubt relating to the fact that Chew is close to the western edge of its European breeding range, but, since the 1980s, the overall trend appears to be downward.

The annual ringing totals graph indicates a long-term decline since the turn of the century. Peak annual totals were 164 in 1966, 88 in 1978, 97 in 1985 and 88 in 1983. However, the average for the years 2006–2015 was just 12. The ringing totals also show that the species is significantly under-recorded by general birding activities.

Unlike most of our summer migrants, this species winters in Sudan and Ethiopia, migrating in spring around the eastern end of the Mediterranean before crossing Europe. The winter range has, in recent years, been affected by droughts, while the trapping of the species for food – particularly in Lebanon – may also be a significant factor in the decline.

An interesting point concerning Lesser Whitethroat and Whitethroat is that most birders would probably think that (Common) Whitethroat is much the commoner bird. The Chew ringing totals for the two species in the 1960s certainly confirmed this, with 70% of the whitethroats caught being Common and 30% Lesser. However, following the 1968–69 population crash, the figures for the 1970s reversed, with 35% of those trapped being Common and 65% Lesser. But what is surprising is that these ratios have not fully reversed, as the pie charts on page 411 show. Only in the last few years are the ratios starting to revert to the historical position.

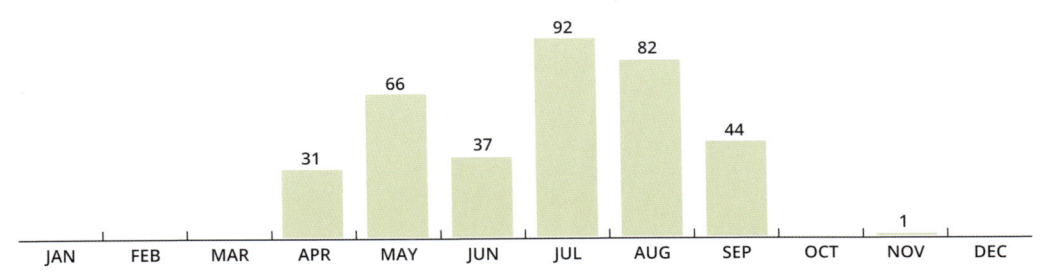

LESSER WHITETHROAT | Monthly maxima (combined) 1965-2015.

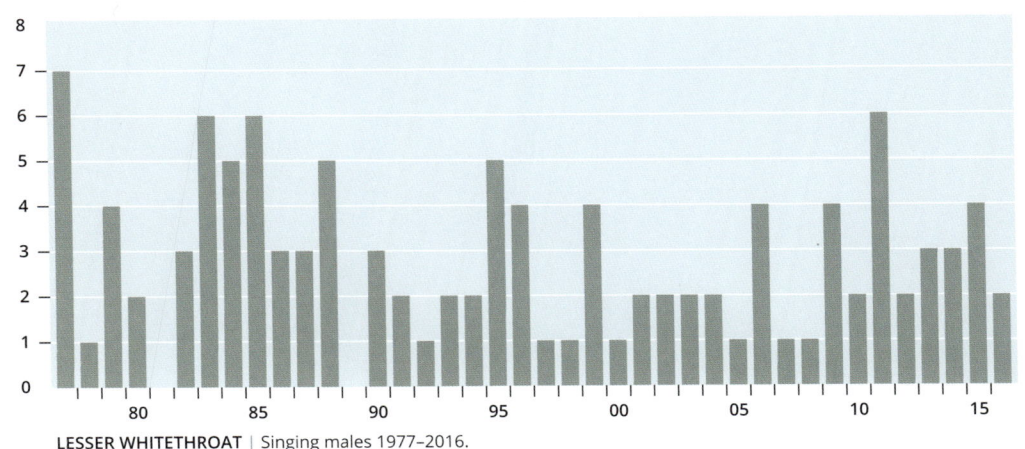

LESSER WHITETHROAT | Singing males 1977–2016.

Lesser Whitethroat | Lucy Masters

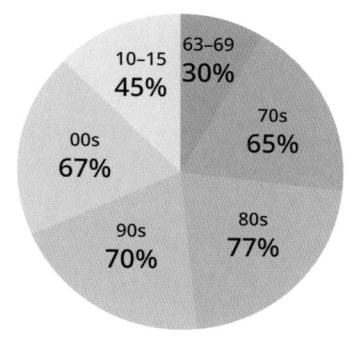

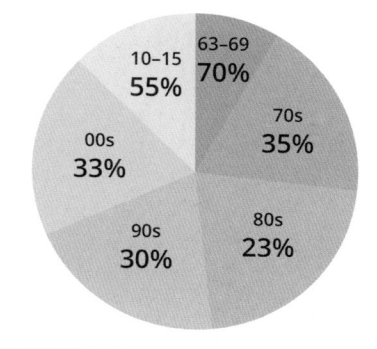

LESSER WHITETHROAT | Ringing totals ratios 1963-2015.

- 63–69: 30%
- 70s: 65%
- 80s: 77%
- 90s: 70%
- 00s: 67%
- 10–15: 45%

WHITETHROAT | Ringing totals ratios 1963-2015.

- 63–69: 70%
- 70s: 35%
- 80s: 23%
- 90s: 30%
- 00s: 33%
- 10–15: 55%

LESSER WHITETHROAT | Annual ringing totals 1963-2015.

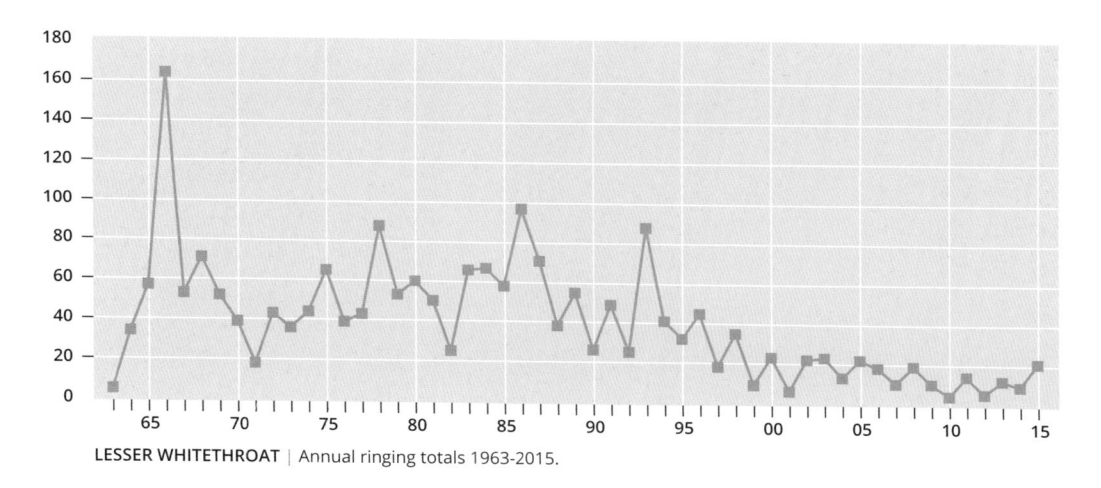

WHITETHROAT *Sylvia communis*

Historically, the Whitethroat was a common breeding species throughout much of the British countryside, but numbers crashed during the winter of 1968–69. This was the result of severe droughts on their wintering grounds in the Sahel Zone south of the Sahara. To this day, numbers have never fully recovered (*Bird Atlas* 2007–11). The annual ringing totals graph clearly shows the decline from peaks of 253 ringed in 1965 and 262 in 1966 to just 38 in 1969, with the numbers falling further to just six in 1971. The annual maxima graph, which relates to numbers counted in the field, shows a similar pattern, falling from a peak of 35 in May 1968 to 11 in 1969 and four in 1972. Both graphs, however, hint at a small increase in the late 1970s and early 1980s and again from the mid-1990s, but numbers are still nowhere near the totals in the mid-1960s.

Encouragingly, the graph, which is based on surveys of singing males from 1977 to 2017, strongly indicates an increase in breeding numbers since 2005.

As the combined monthly maxima graph shows, the first Whitethroats appear in April, the average arrival date being 22nd; the earliest was a singing male on 8th (in 2011). The peak numbers are in May, when the males are singing and display flighting. Once their song period is over, they become quiet whilst breeding in mid-summer, but they increase again in July to a peak in August, most of which, presumably, are south-bound migrants. A few may remain into September and there are two October records, the latest being one on 6th (in 2012).

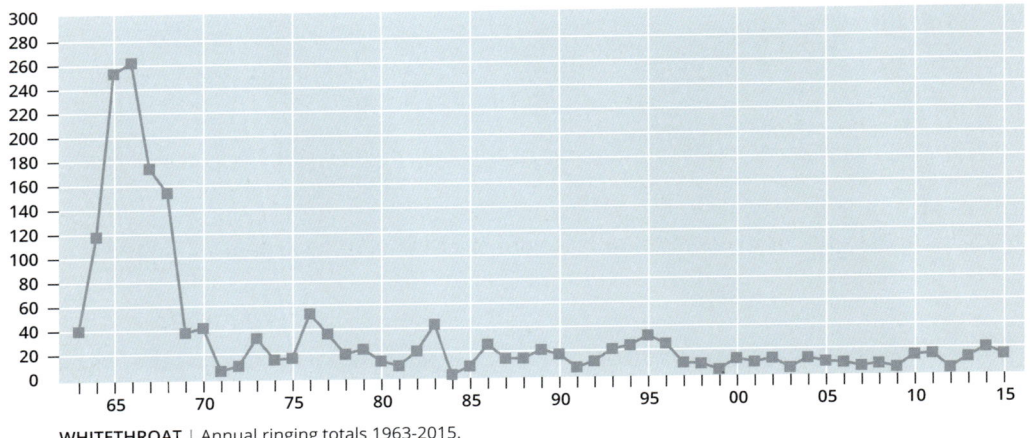

WHITETHROAT | Annual ringing totals 1963-2015.

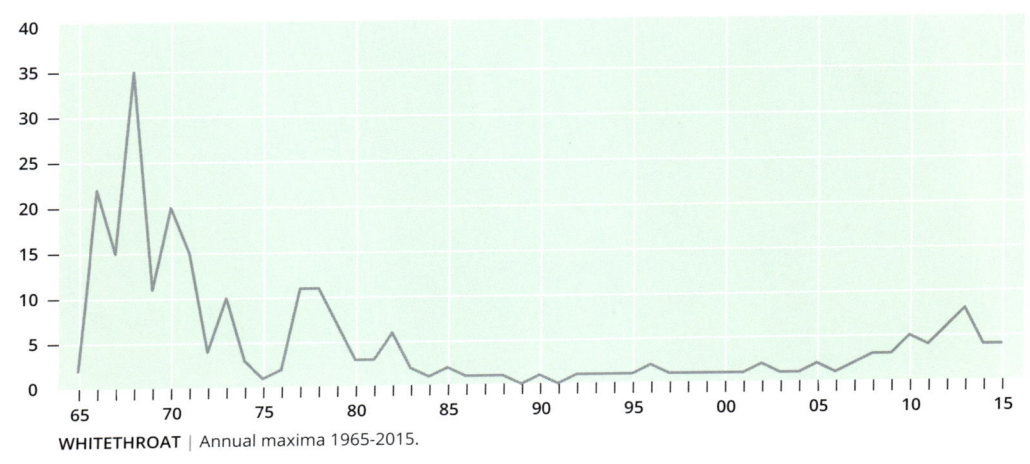

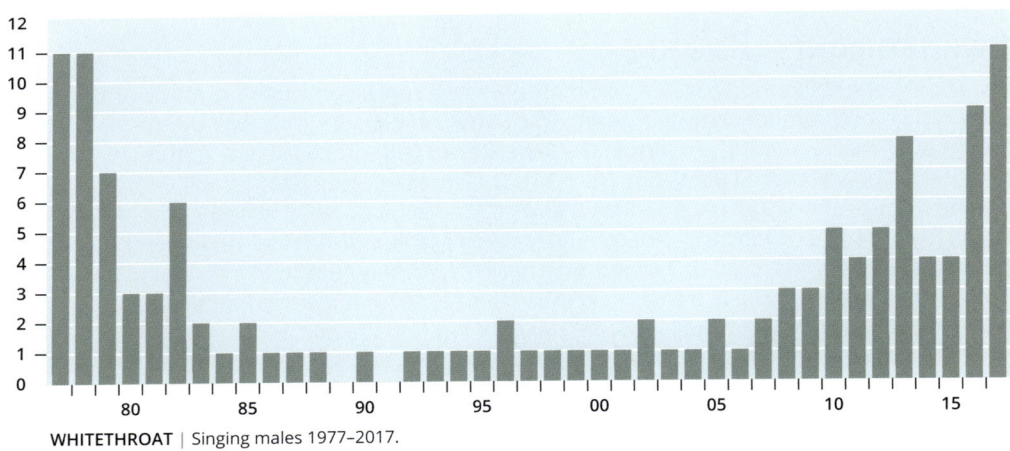

WHITETHROAT | Annual maxima 1965-2015.

WHITETHROAT | Singing males 1977–2017.

WHITETHROAT | Monthly maxima (combined) 1963-2015.

FIRECREST *Regulus ignicapilla*

The first record was of one in 1 January 1968 (T. Cook, KEV), after which it occurred in five of the next seven years until 1975. There was then a six-year gap until 1982, after which it occurred in 18 of the next 33 years (to 2016).

The earliest autumn record was of one trapped on 3 September 2015 and, as can be seen from the combined monthly maxima graph, numbers rise to a December peak but drop in February and March; the latest was one on 4 April 1996. As the annual maxima graph shows, annual totals normally involve ones and twos, but three were recorded in 1990, 1993 and 2015.

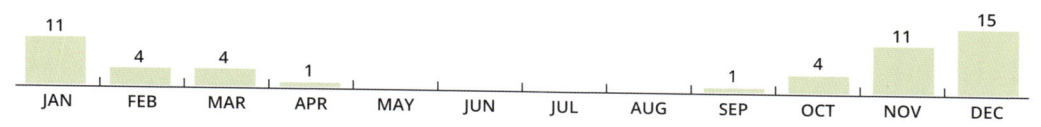

FIRECREST | Monthly maxima (combined) 1968-2016.

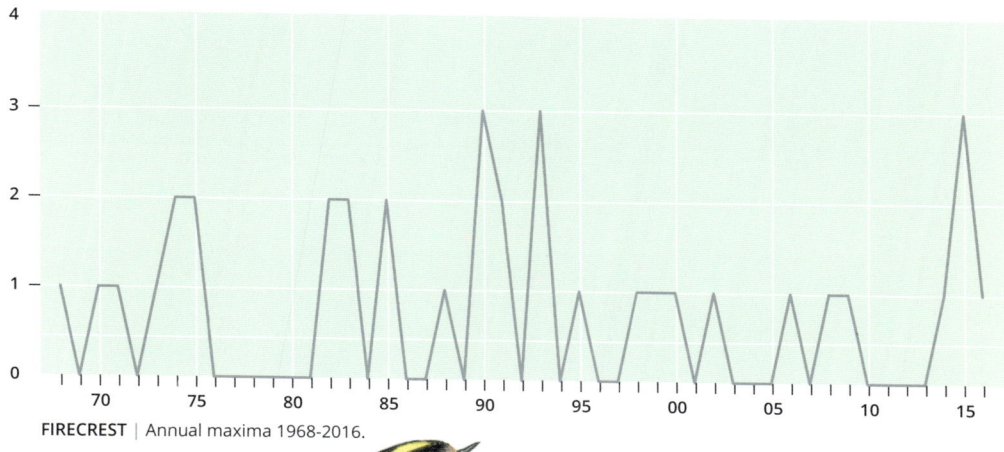

FIRECREST | Annual maxima 1968-2016.

Firecrest (left top, centre and bottom) | Laurel Tucker

GOLDCREST *Regulus regulus*

This is a secretive bird that is difficult to detect, particularly by older birders who struggle to hear their high-pitched song and calls. As the combined monthly maxima graph shows, numbers decline from January to a low point in June–July when, presumably, they are in moult, which lasts from late June to October (*BWP*). This makes them difficult to detect at that time of year. Sightings increase from August to a peak in October when, presumably, numbers are inflated by migrants.

Goldcrests breed quite commonly in the coniferous plantations around the lake, with a peak of 19 singing males in 2000. However, as the species is easily overlooked, the figures shown in the annual numbers of singing males must be regarded as minima.

A better indication of numbers is given by the annual ringing totals (see the graph). The first thing to note is that none was ringed in 1963 and 1964, an indication of how hard the species was hit during the severe winter of 1962–63. Similar low numbers were ringed in 1979 (2), 1981 (7), 1982 (4), 1991 (3) and 2013 (8). By contrast, the highest annual totals were 100 in 1999 and a record 111 in 2015. The graph shows well these regular fluctuations in its population levels.

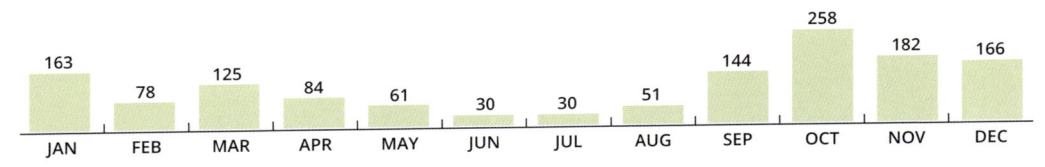

GOLDCREST | Monthly maxima (combined) 1965-2015.

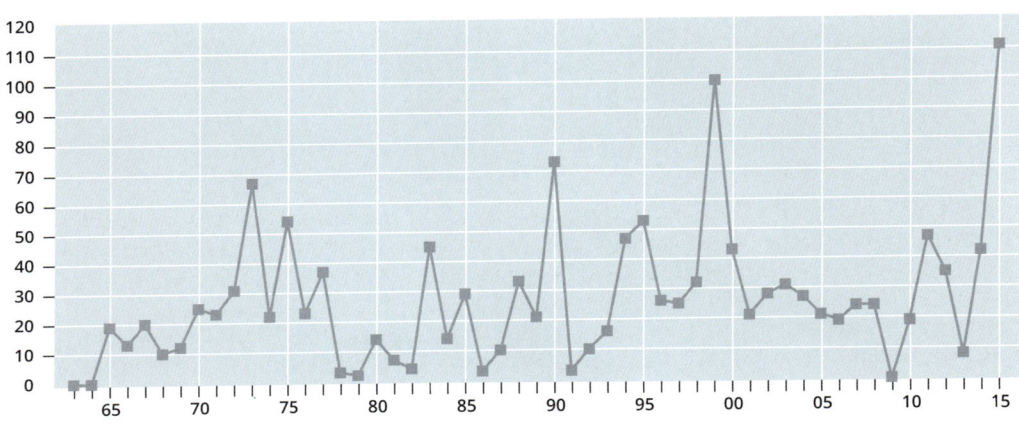

GOLDCREST | Annual ringing totals 1963-2015.

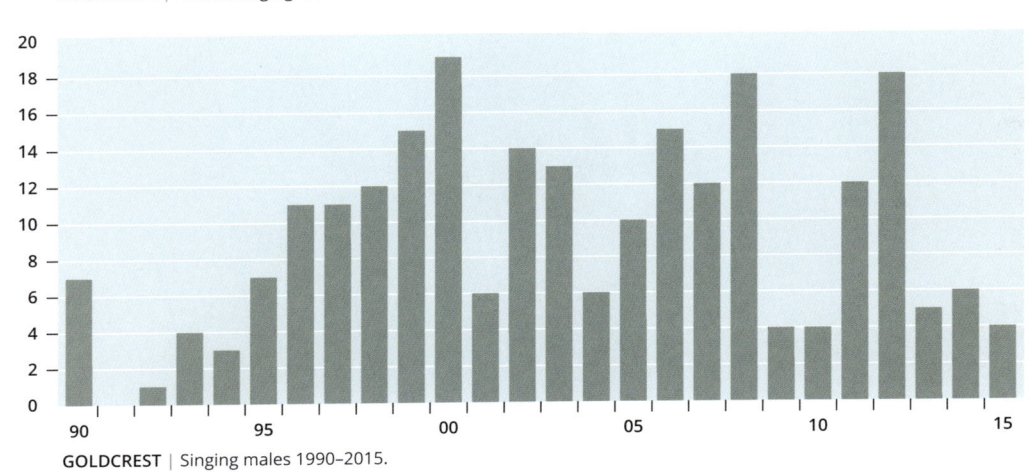

GOLDCREST | Singing males 1990–2015.

COMPLETE SPECIES LIST AND CHARTS

Goldcrest | Laurel Tucker

WREN *Troglodytes troglodytes*

The Wren is a common bird around the lake but it is difficult to census. The only available data that reveals its trends are the annual ringing totals. As the annual ringing totals graph shows, it was hit very hard by the severe winter of 1962–63 but it soon started to bounce back from the mid-1960s into the early 1970s. However, it then took another dip after some hard winters in the late 1970s and early 1980s before increasing again to a record peak in 1993, when 195 were trapped. However, as the graph suggests, numbers have once again declined since the turn of the century, followed by yet another distinct upturn since 2010. It must be stressed, however, that these figures are also related to the levels of ringing activity.

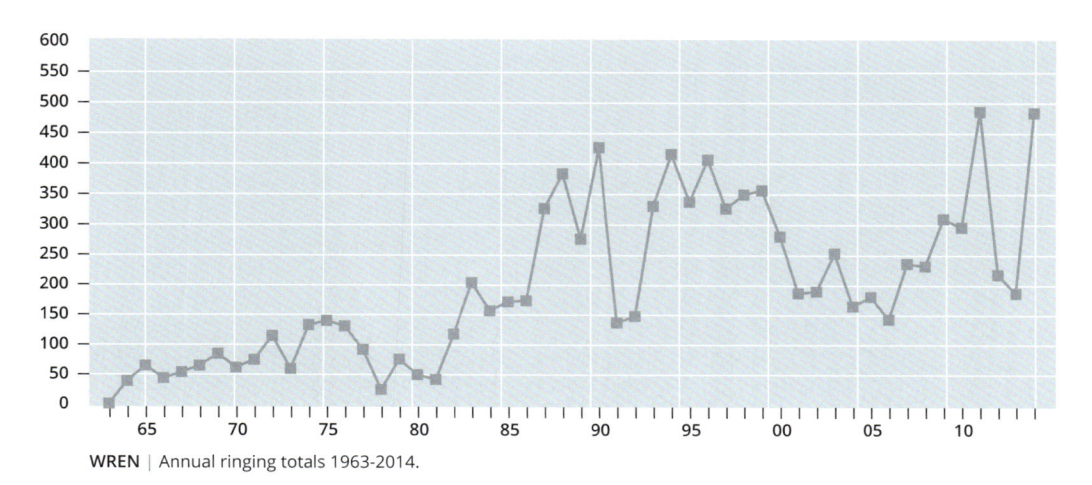

WREN | Annual ringing totals 1963-2014.

COMPLETE SPECIES LIST AND CHARTS

NUTHATCH *Sitta europaea*

The first records were of one trapped in 1963 (CVRS) and a juvenile seen on 23 July 1967 (KEV). The absence of records prior to this was undoubtedly related to the immaturity of the lakeside woodland. As the annual maxima graph shows, there were just four records in the 1960s and 1970s, but sightings increased from the early 1980s, with the species recorded annually from 2008.

In April 2010, a pair was present behind the Main Dam and, in 2011, a pair was seen courtship feeding there, with another male in the East Shore poplars. In 2012, Nuthatches were seen in the breeding season at four sites and breeding was finally confirmed in 2014, when a female on 27 May was seen carrying food in the East Shore poplars. There were also further pairs behind the Dam and at Hollow Brook. Two pairs were seen in 2015 – with a female feeding young in a nest hole on 23 May – and another nest was found in both 2017 and 2018. It is clear that the species is now an established resident at the lake, albeit in small numbers.

The combined monthly maxima graph indicates that Nuthatches are most numerous in April, but this peak undoubtedly relates to the fact that they are highly vocal in spring, and thus easily detected. The late summer/early autumn peak presumably relates to wandering juveniles and first-winters, combined with greater ringing activity at this time.

Nuthatch | Lucy Masters

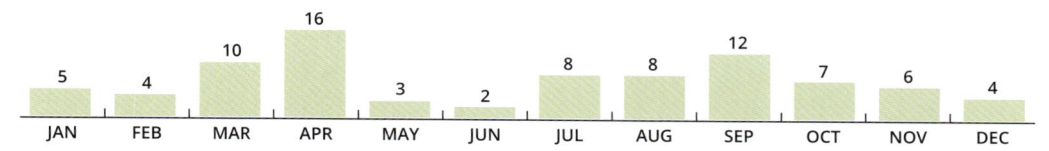

NUTHATCH | Monthly maxima (combined) 1967-2017.

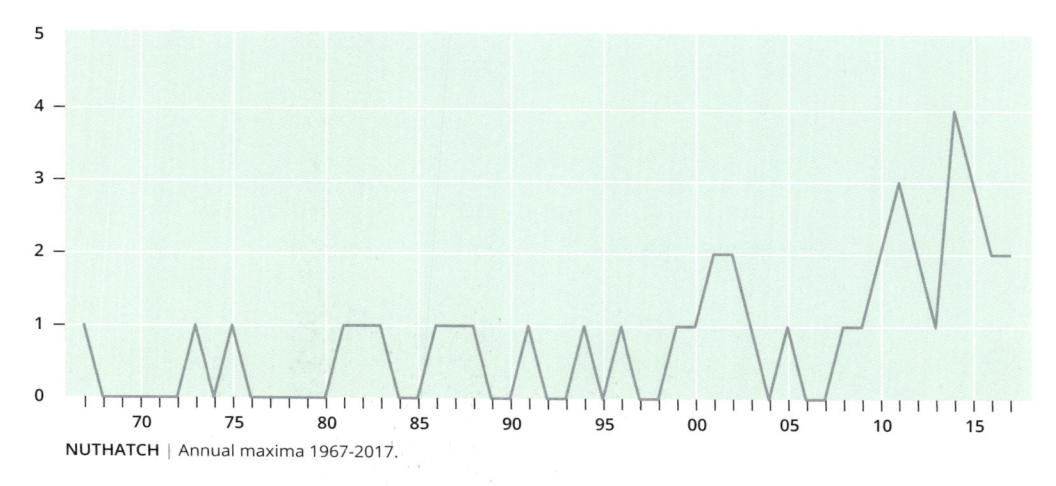

NUTHATCH | Annual maxima 1967-2017.

TREECREEPER *Certhia familiaris*

There were no published records of Treecreepers during the 1950s and early 1960s (up to and including 1965). Since then, its numbers have undoubtedly risen as the lakeside plantations slowly matured. The annual maxima graph shows a distinct increase from the mid-1960s to a peak of 13 in July 2000, but numbers appear to have declined since then. It is likely, however, that this apparent decline is related to the fact that older birders can no longer hear their extremely high-pitched song and calls.

The annual ringing totals graph does not show the apparent decline in recent years that is shown by the annual maxima graph. What it does show, however, is a peak of 40 ringed in 1999, clearly indicating that the species is grossly underestimated during normal birding activities.

The combined monthly maxima graph shows that Treeceepers are present all year with a low point in May–June, when they are breeding, and a high point in July–September following the recruitment of the year's juveniles.

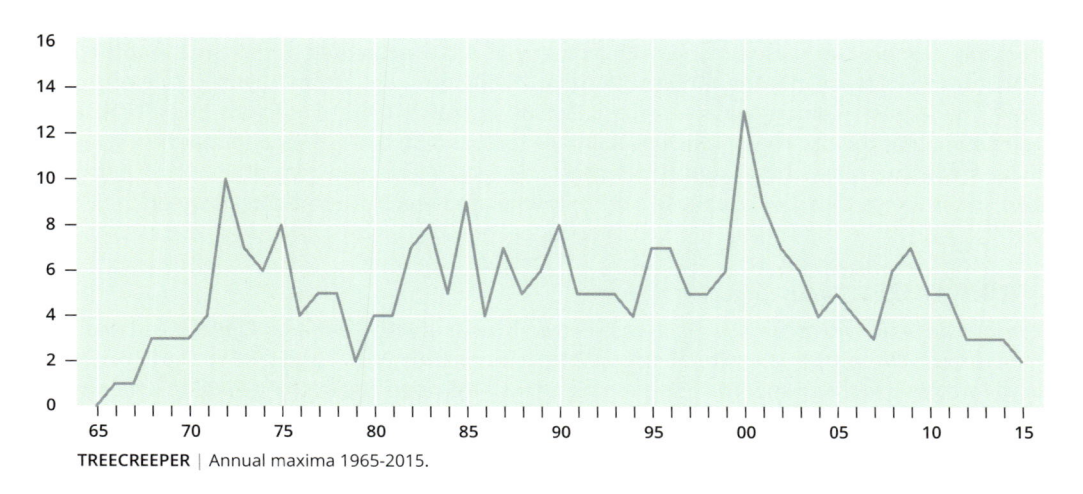

TREECREEPER | Annual maxima 1965-2015.

TREECREEPER | Annual ringing totals 1963-2015.

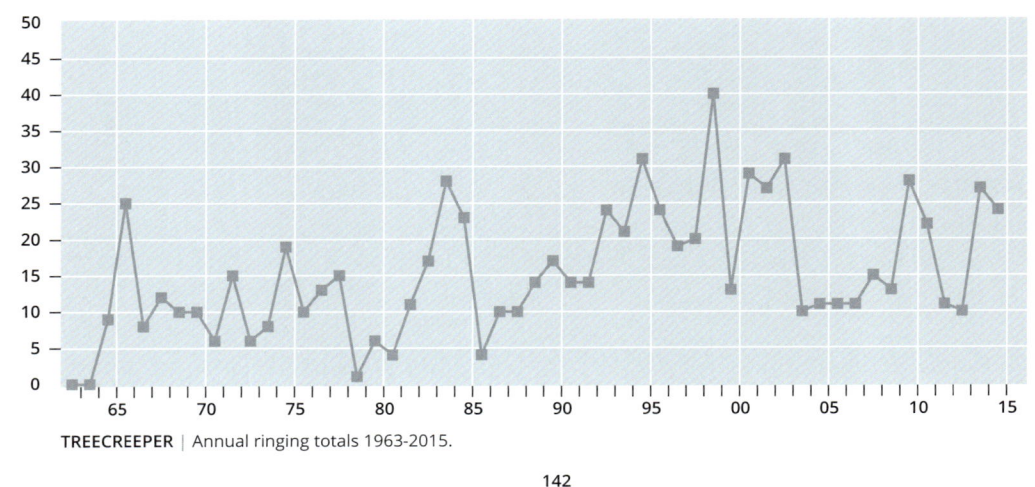

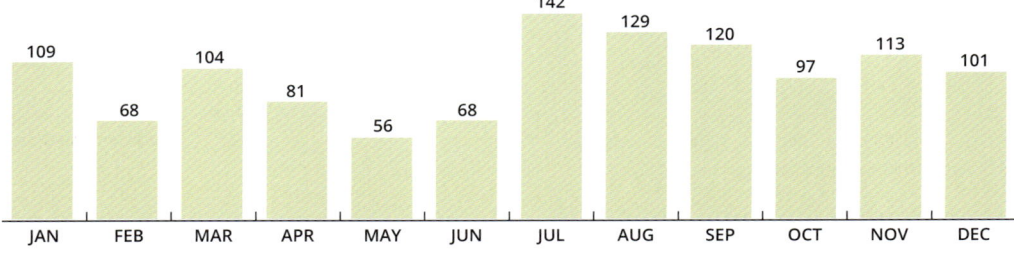

TREECREEPER | Monthly maxima (combined) 1966-2015.

STARLING *Sturnus vulgaris*

Starling counts have to be divided into daytime counts and roosting counts. The species breeds around the lake's perimeter in small numbers, usually in holes in trees, a frequently used site being the East Shore poplar plantation.

After breeding, they often form large flocks in the lakeside fields, mainly from late spring into the summer. The highest such counts included a pre-roosting flock of 750 on 30 May 1971 (c. 75% juveniles) and 800 feeding in a newly cut hay field on 2 June 1991. In 1979, a roosting estimate of 5,000 was made on 27 June and it was also estimated that three-quarters of these were juveniles. Winter counts include 1,000 feeding in a field at Villice Bay on 16 March 1985.

Nocturnal roosts have developed as early as late April, with an estimated 3,000 on 25 April 1984 (with a similar number the following month). Presumably, these related to non-breeders. Roosting numbers increase in June, with as many as 5,000 estimated at this time, but the roost continues to increase into the winter with up to 20,000 estimated from August to the end of the year. The largest estimate was of perhaps 50,000 in March 1993, this figure being reached by estimating that the pre-roost flock was half mile long and 50 birds deep and that they averaged three feet apart. Most of the large winter roosts develop in the reed beds at the south end of the lake, but it seems that they use these sites only when the reeds are standing in water.

RING OUZEL *Turdus torquatus*

There have been two records: a male was seen well feeding with Fieldfares *T. pilaris* and Redwings *T. iliacus* in hawthorns on Moreton Bank on 2 November 1985 (L. A. Tucker, KEV). On 17 April 2007 a well-watched first-summer male spent most of the afternoon and evening feeding under a large willow bush at the Picnic Site adjacent to the Main Dam (D. Nevitt *et al.*). Not exactly classic habitat for a Ring Ouzel!

BLACKBIRD *Turdus merula*

The Blackbird is a common breeding species around the lake but, largely because of this, the numbers of singing males have never been counted. The only useful statistic is ringing data (see graph below). It is likely that it has increased since the 1950s, simply because the lakeside woodland has matured since then.

About 40–60 are ringed annually but with a large peak of 103 in 1983.

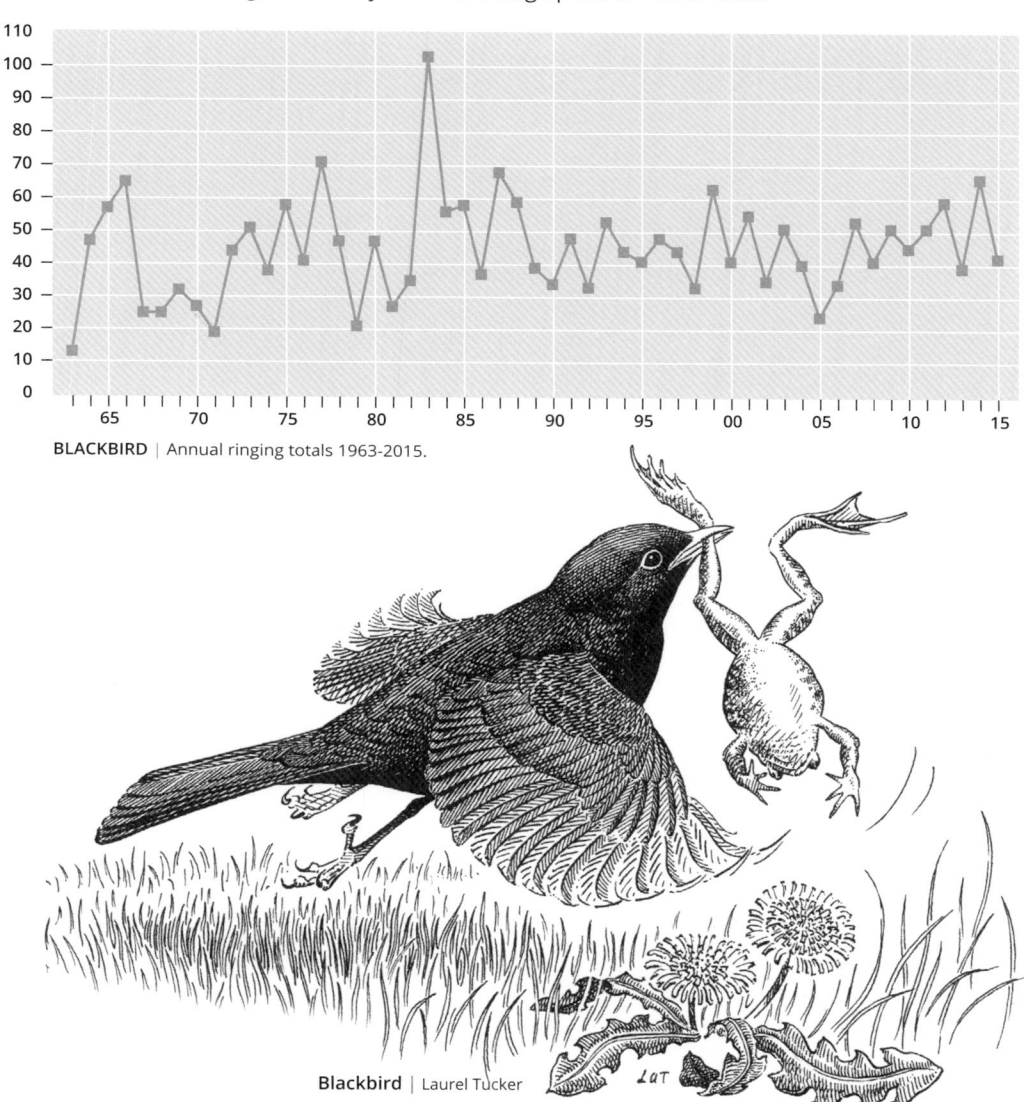

BLACKBIRD | Annual ringing totals 1963-2015.

Blackbird | Laurel Tucker

FIELDFARE *Turdus pilaris*

Fieldfare is normally a fairly common winter visitor but numbers fluctuate from year to year. The earliest autumn date is 13 October (in 2011) and the latest spring date is 24 April (in 1976). The average winter maximum is 176, but with a minimum of just three in 1997 and a maximum of 2,000 in 1981. The latter involved an exceptionally heavy westerly movement on 22 November. A similarly high count involved 1,100 on 13 November 1999, which, presumably, were also overhead migrants. Prior to their spring departure, large flocks often gather in the Parkland, where, presumably, they feed up on earthworms.

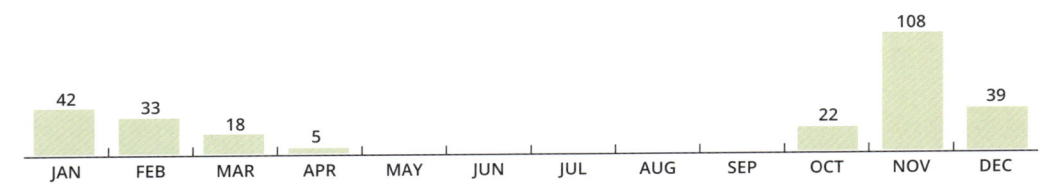

FIELDFARE | Monthly counts (average) 1965-2015.

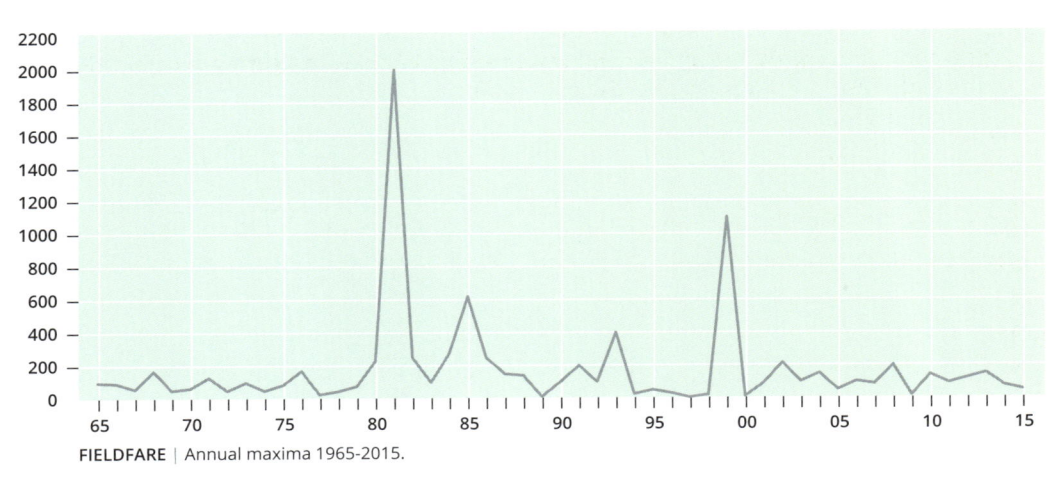

- JAN: 42
- FEB: 33
- MAR: 18
- APR: 5
- MAY:
- JUN:
- JUL:
- AUG:
- SEP:
- OCT: 22
- NOV: 108
- DEC: 39

FIELDFARE | Annual maxima 1965-2015.

Fieldfare | Rich Andrews

| REDWING *Turdus iliacus*

The Redwing is a common winter visitor in variable numbers, which largely depend on the various berry crops, particularly hawthorn. Prior to their spring migration, large numbers often feed on earthworms in the Parkland, the large area of 'unimproved' pasture between Heron's Green and Villice Bays. Annual totals also depend on cold weather; in hard winters, hundreds can sometimes be seen flying south to escape the cold.

As the monthly totals graph indicates, the first autumn migrants usually appear in mid-October, the earliest date being the 7th (in 1984). The last in spring are usually in March, but small numbers sometimes remain into April, the latest date being 8 April (five in 1996 and 30 in 2013).

As the annual maxima graph shows, twenty-nine years have produced counts of a hundred or more and there have been eight years when over 500 have been seen. The highest totals were 800 in March 1976, feeding in just three fields behind the 'toe' of Heron's Green Bay – described at the time as 'a very impressive sight'. On 22 November 1981, there was a heavy overhead passage from the east, estimated at about a thousand. Thirdly, there was another high count on 17 October 2002, involving about 750 in about six large flocks, flying east at dusk from Stratford Bay.

The graph clearly shows that annual numbers are erratic, but it also suggests a general reduction since the early 1990s, perhaps a result of milder winters.

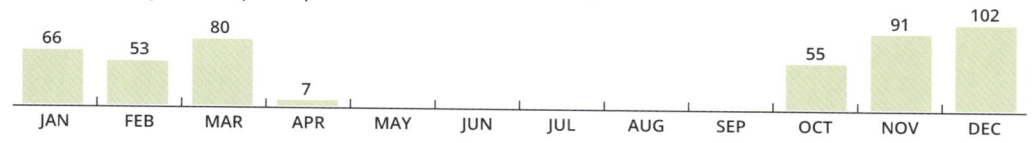

REDWING | Average monthly totals 1965–2015.

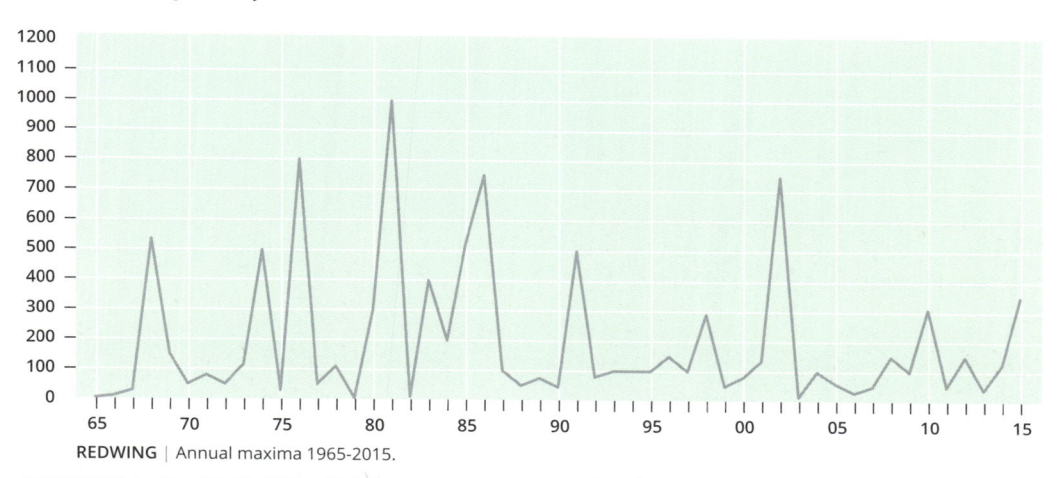

REDWING | Annual maxima 1965-2015.

Redwing | Rich Andrews

COMPLETE SPECIES LIST AND CHARTS

SONG THRUSH *Turdus philomelos*

As the number of singing males graph shows, Song Thrushes have slowly increased since the mid-1980s, when singing males were monitored for the first time. Numbers during the 1990s averaged 11 singing males, increasing to 16 during the 2000s and 22 during 2010–2017. The highest annual total was 29 in 2013. This increase is likely to be related to the gradual maturation of the lakeside woodlands, fewer cold winters and, perhaps, better censusing. Interestingly, the graph – which shows annual ringing totals – also indicates an increase in recent years.

The earliest song was heard on 6 December (in 2015) and the highest individual count was of ten together in a field behind Woodford Bank on 18 December 2012. The highest annual ringing total was 39 (in 1983).

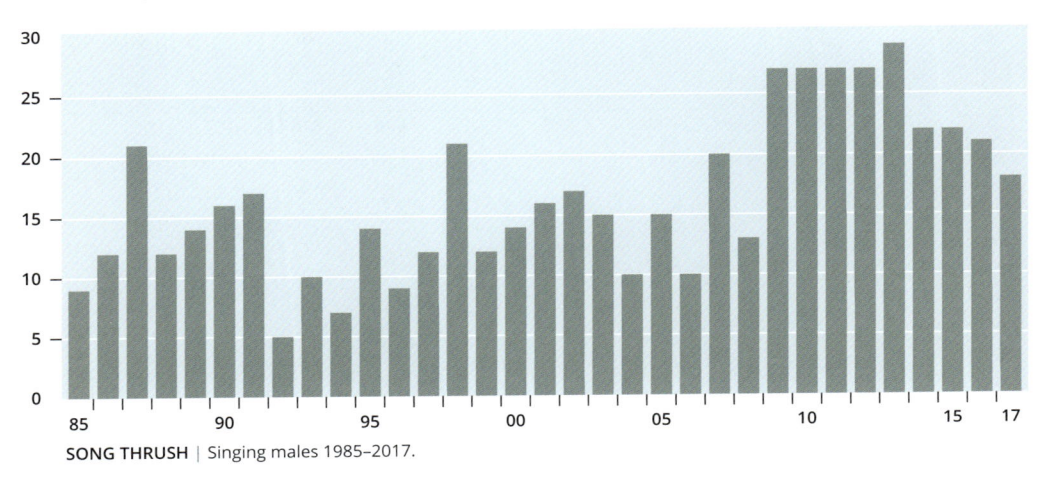

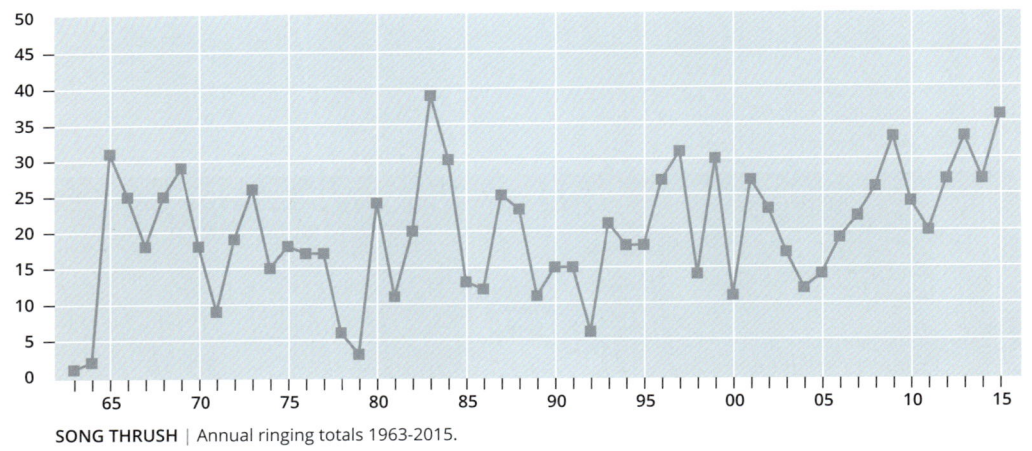

SONG THRUSH | Singing males 1985–2017.

SONG THRUSH | Annual ringing totals 1963-2015.

MISTLE THRUSH *Turdus viscivorus*

Mistle Thrushes are present around the lake in small numbers, the average number of pairs being 1.7, but with as many as five in 1993, 1995 and 2014 and with six singing males in February 1976. In some years, however, none have been recorded at all (1980, 1981, 1983, 1986 and 2003). The most reliable place to see them is in the Woodford Lodge area, most of the others being seen in various random fields around the lake. They start singing in mid-winter, with the earliest song recorded on 14 December (in 2015). In urban areas, they can nest as early as January but, at Chew, the earliest flying juveniles have been on 23 April; conversely, a pair in 1978 was feeding newly fledged young as late as 22 July.

The combined monthly maxima graph shows relatively stable numbers throughout the year, but with a small peak in December–January (when they start singing), another from March to May (when they are breeding) and another slight peak from July to September when family parties may occur.

The annual maxima graph below shows an interesting trend. There were high numbers in the late 1960s and 1970s but with a crash in the early to mid-1980s, followed by a slight resurgence in the late 1980s to the mid-1990s. Numbers have been very low since the mid-1990s, but with recent peaks of five in 2012 and nine in 2013. It is, however, a difficult bird to monitor, it being highly mobile around the lake and its hinterland. Ringing data do not shed much light on their status, only 17 having been ringed up to 2015. However, a large count of 14 was seen at Heron's Green Pool on 17 July 2018.

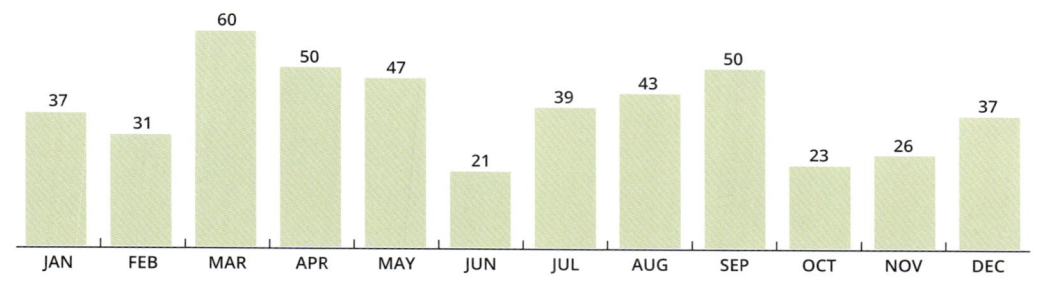

MISTLE THRUSH | Monthly maxima (combined) 1967-2015.

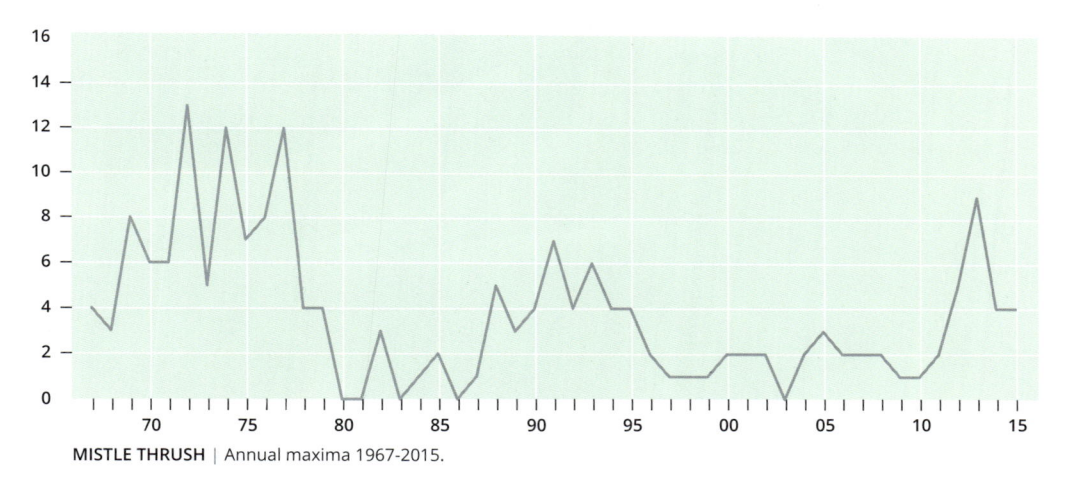

MISTLE THRUSH | Annual maxima 1967-2015.

SPOTTED FLYCATCHER *Muscicapa striata*

The Spotted Flycatcher is a scarce summer visitor at the lake. The earliest recorded date is 20 April (in 2016) and the latest is 6 October (in 2010). Most arrive in May with similar numbers in June. Numbers increase significantly in July as the year's young start to appear, but the peak month is August when, presumably, southward bound migrants raise the totals. Reasonable numbers have been recorded in September and there is a single October record: on 6th in 2010.

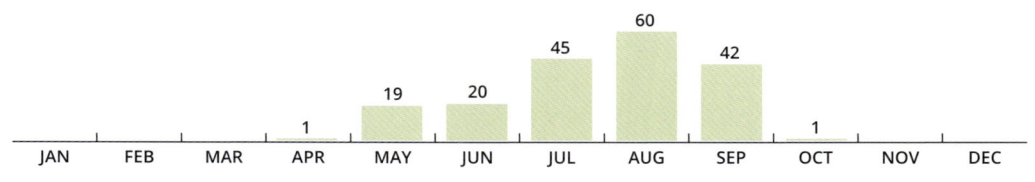

SPOTTED FLYCATCHER | Monthly maxima (combined) 1965-2016.

Spotted Flycatcher | Gary Thoburn

Spotted Flycatchers are notoriously elusive, but singing males and/or broods have been recorded in 25 of the 52 years from 1965 to 2016. However, the annual maxima graph shows a long and gradual decline from the late 1960s, when the highest counts were nine on 23 August 1966 and ten (seven juveniles) on 15 August 1968. None were recorded from 2003–2007, but there has since been a resurgence.

The annual ringing totals graph is the most shocking. It shows the annual ringing totals from 1963 to 2015, illustrating how the species has declined from a peak of 39 in 1966 to 16 in 1969, 12 in 1976 and ten in 1987. In the 18 years from 1998 to 2015, only three were ringed in total.

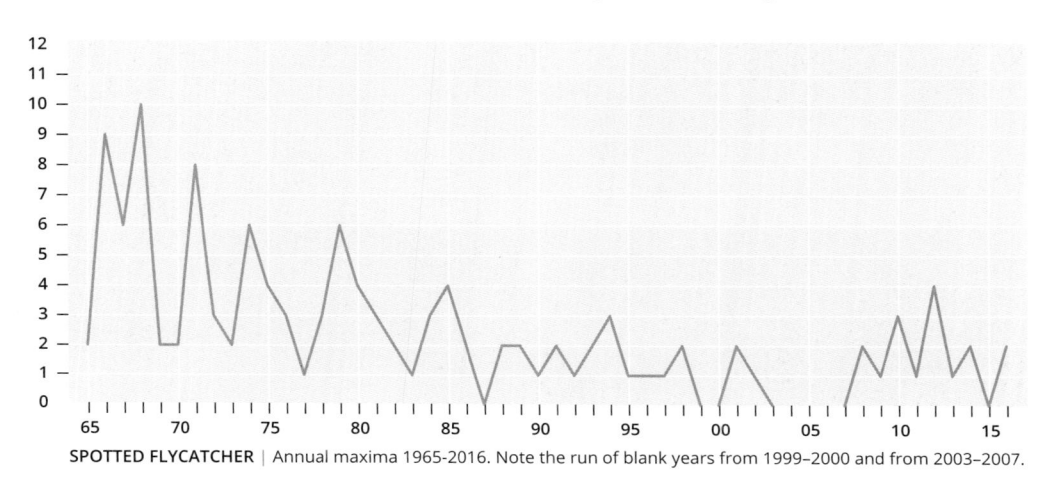

SPOTTED FLYCATCHER | Annual maxima 1965-2016. Note the run of blank years from 1999–2000 and from 2003–2007.

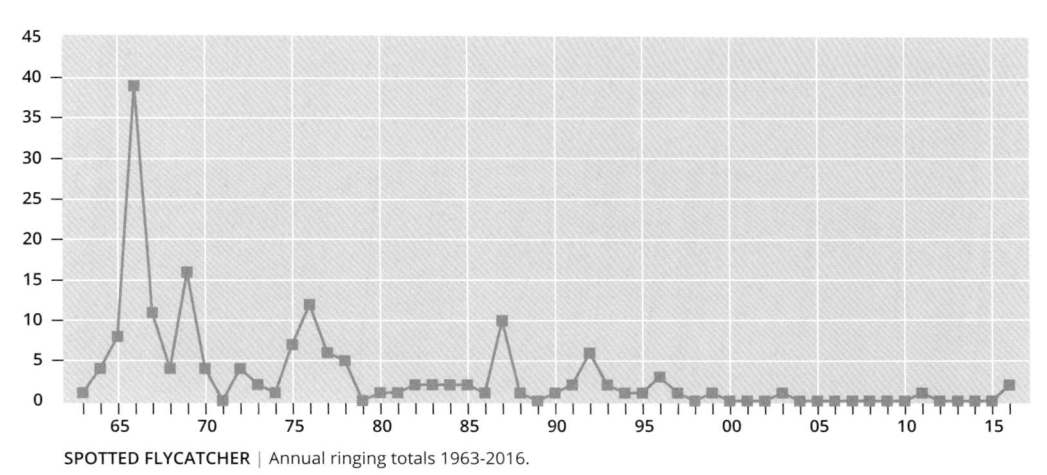

SPOTTED FLYCATCHER | Annual ringing totals 1963-2016.

ROBIN *Erithacus rubecula*

There have been no surveys of Robins around the lake, the only useful data being the annual ringing totals, shown in the graph. The numbers were clearly low after the hard winter of 1962–63 but they gradually increased during the 1970s and 1980s, though with further dips in 1971 and 1979, after cold winter weather. Numbers peaked during the mid to late 1990s with three-figure totals in four of the five years from 1993 to 1997, with a maximum of 112 caught in 1994. However, numbers then dipped before reaching a new peak of 132 in 2015. It should be stressed, however, that the levels of ringing activity also affect these numbers.

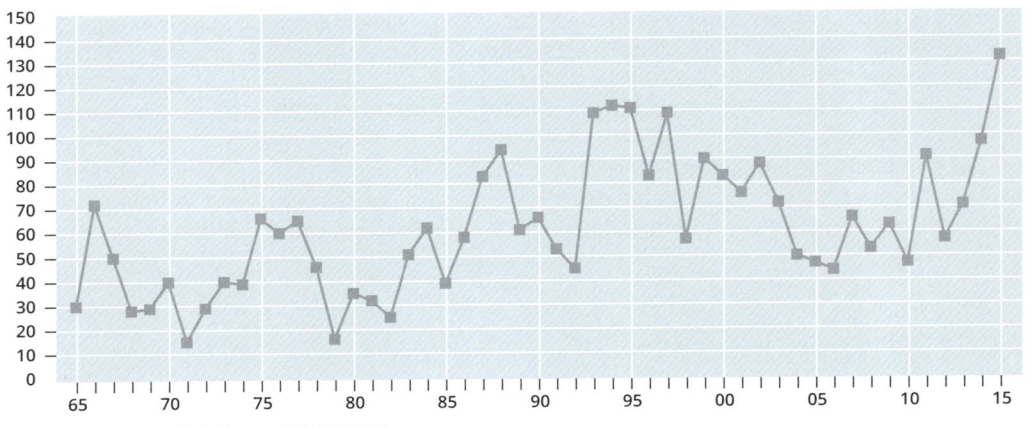

ROBIN | Annual ringing totals 1965-2015.

Robin | Rich Andrews

| BLUETHROAT *Luscinia svecica*

A first-winter male of the red-spotted nominate race was trapped and ringed on 22 September 1968 (R. J. Prytherch, M. Tibbles, KEV *et al.*).

| NIGHTINGALE *Luscinia megarhynchos*

There have been twelve records involving 14 individuals:
- **1966:** one trapped on 17 April during the 'blizzard' (see 'The Great Fall of 1966' in 'Memorable birding moments and tales').
- **1971:** a juvenile at Twycross on 30 July and an adult in the same place on 20 August (KEV).
- **1972:** two singing behind the Main Dam on 23 April, with one still singing there on 30th (KEV); two adults at Twycross on 15 August (KEV).
- **1975:** one trapped on 25 August (CVRS).

1980: one trapped on 30 April and still present on 1 May (CVRS).
1986: one ringed on 20 July.(CVRS).
1994: a juvenile trapped on 30 July (CVRS) was re-trapped on 8 August.
2006: one singing (and seen) in an alder wood in Villice Bay on 10 May (R. J. Palmer *et al.*).
2011: one trapped on 14 June (CVRS).
2013: one trapped on 20 April (CVRS).

Despite the presence of an adult and a juvenile in 1971, there was never any indication that the species bred at the lake.

PIED FLYCATCHER *Ficedula hypoleuca*

There have been 22 records: 16 in spring between 16 April and 16 May and six in autumn between 2 and 30 August. It has been recorded in 20 of the 51 years since the first record (one on 16–17 April 1966). The total number of individuals has been 24. Remarkably, only 11 of the spring records were sexed: six males and five females. The most likely area in which to encounter them is along the East Shore from Twycross to Sutton Wick. At least one of the males was heard singing.

BLACK REDSTART *Phoenicurus ochruros*

There have been six records:
1971: a first-year male singing by the Parkland car park on 7 April (KEV).
1983: an adult male on 13 March flew across Herriott's Bridge and landed on the roof of Herriott's Cottage (KEV).
1987: one on 3 January (*ABR*).
1993: one at Woodford Lodge on 20 November (P. R. Baber *et al.*).
2001: a female type at the Main Dam on 1–3 January (R. M. Curber *et al.*).
2010–2011: an adult male at Woodford Lodge and the Sailing Club from 22 November to 12 February (D. J. Angell, R. Hansford *et al.*).

Black Redstart | Laurel Tucker

REDSTART *Phoenicurus phoenicurus*

This is a scarce migrant at Chew, recorded in 31 of the 51 years from 1965 to 2015. By far the best month is April, with 35 recorded, but this high total includes an unprecedented fall of 20 during an unseasonal blizzard on 14 April 1966. All the other records have related to ones and twos, apart from four on 26 July 1965 that were feeding along a fence at the Ringing Station Wood. The earliest spring date is of a female on 5 April 1999 and the latest were two on 2 May (in 1992 and 2002). The first autumn migrant was one on 12 July (in 1981) and the latest was one on 24 September (in 1975). Sixty-two were ringed between 1965 and 2015, the highest totals being 17 in 1966, five in 1968 and seven in 1995.

As the annual totals graph indicates, the species seems to have become scarcer since the turn of the century.

Single juveniles seen on 31 July 1966 and 22 July 1975 perhaps suggested a local origin, such as the Mendips, where the species breeds in small numbers.

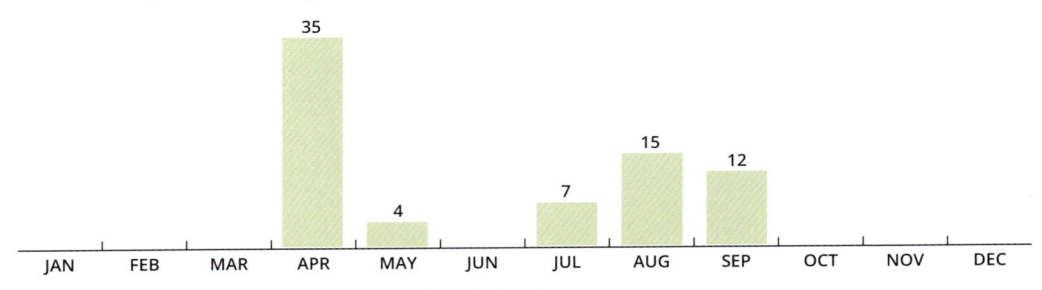

REDSTART | Monthly maxima (combined) 1965-2015 (excluding ringing totals).

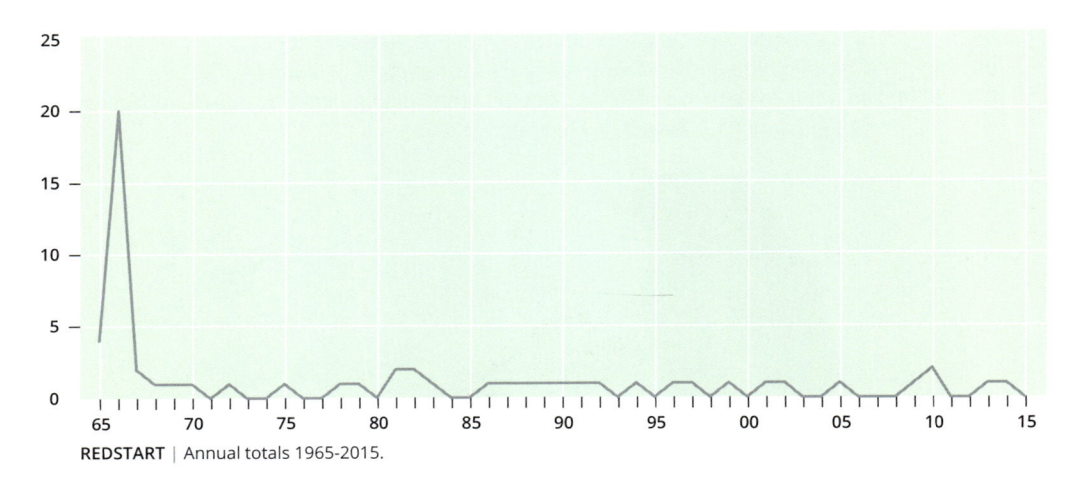

REDSTART | Annual totals 1965-2015.

WHINCHAT *Saxicola rubetra*

The first record in any of the bird reports was one in 1959 (no exact date). Presumably, there were records prior to this, but it can only be assumed that the species was not considered worthy of publication. It then bred in every year from 1960 to 1970, with four pairs breeding successfully in 1965, two pairs in 1968, three pairs in 1969 and two pairs in 1970. The highest counts were ten on both 1 August 1967 and 29 July 1970.

What finished them off was the decision by the then Bristol Waterworks Company to cut the grass short in mid-summer on Moreton Bank, the exact area in which they were nesting. Since then, the species has become a regular but scarce passage migrant, the spring dates spanning the period 21 April (1982) to 15 May (1992) and the autumn dates from 23 July (1989) to 23 October (1988) – but see below. Since 1971, all the records have been in single figures, with maxima of five on 5 September 1973 and 6 September 1997, and six from 9 to 11 September 2010. There have been fourteen recorded in October (to 23rd) but a very late individual was seen in Villice Bay on 14 November 2012 (C. & H. Craig, R. Mielcarek).

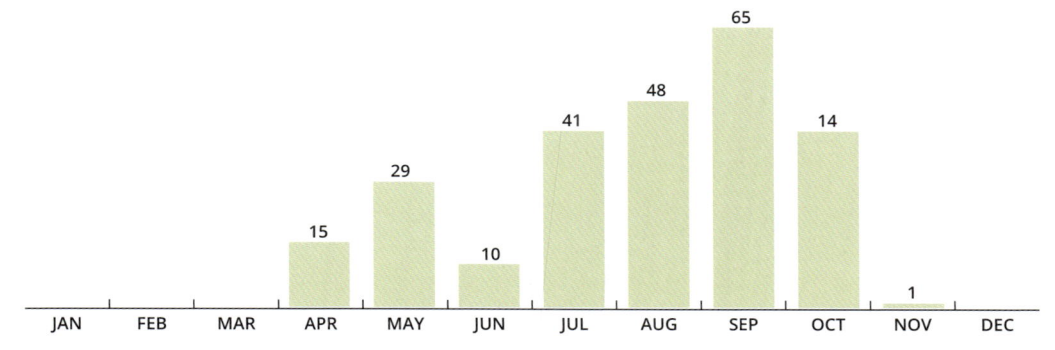

WHINCHAT | Monthly maxima (combined) 1965-2015.

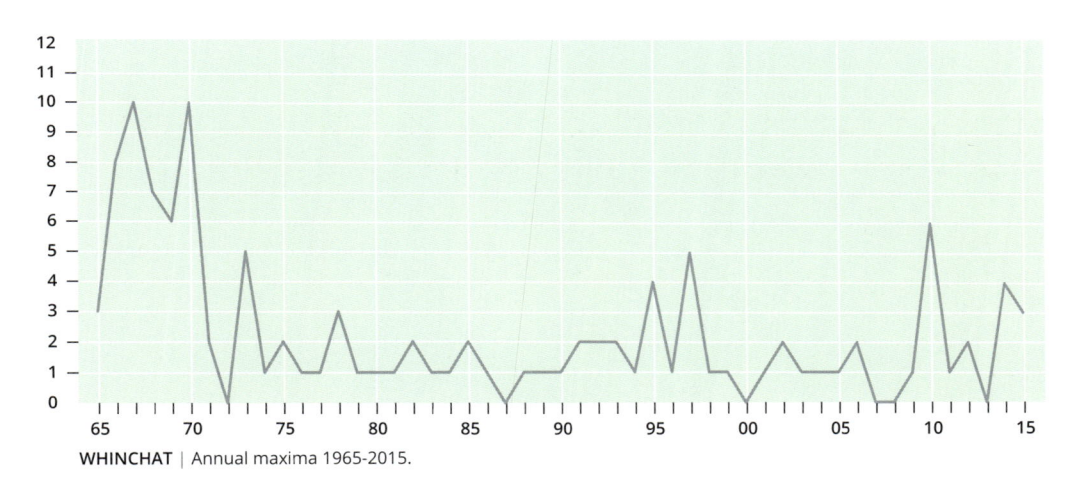

WHINCHAT | Annual maxima 1965-2015.

Whinchat | Laurel Tucker

STONECHAT *Saxicola rubicola*

Stonechat is basically a winter visitor. The first appear in September, the earliest date being the 7th (in 2006). Numbers rise in October to a peak in November and December. Totals then decline until March but a secondary peak in February may involve early returning migrants. The latest spring record was of a single on 5 April (in 1987). The first 'returning birds' have been seen as early as 29 May (1976), 3 July (1982), 24 July (1999) and 25 July (2011). Apart from the 1982 bird, which wasn't aged, all of these were juveniles. It seems highly likely that they were locally dispersing individuals, no doubt from the Mendips.

The counts have normally been in single figures, there being as many as eight on 14 October 1995; but the highest numbers occurred during the drought year of 1976, when the lake margins were swathed in large areas of fresh vegetation. Numbers reached 16 in November and a record 17+ on 26 December.

Stonechats are badly affected by cold winter weather and the annual maxima graph shows that numbers were low in the mid-1960s, following the infamous cold winter of 1962–63. Numbers were again low in the late 1970s and early 1980s, again the result of a series of cold winters.

Stonechat | Rich Andrews

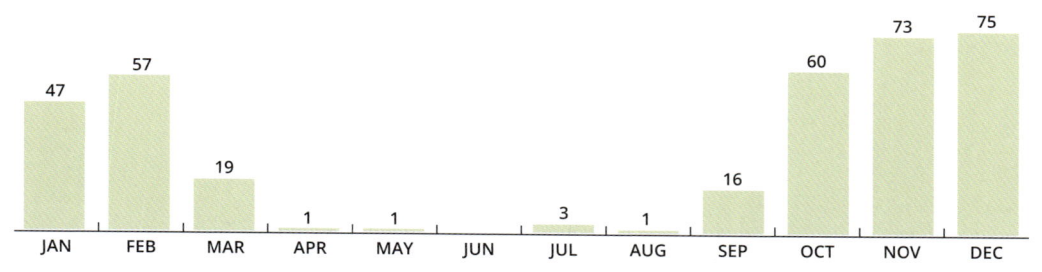

STONECHAT | Monthly maxima (combined) 1965-2015.

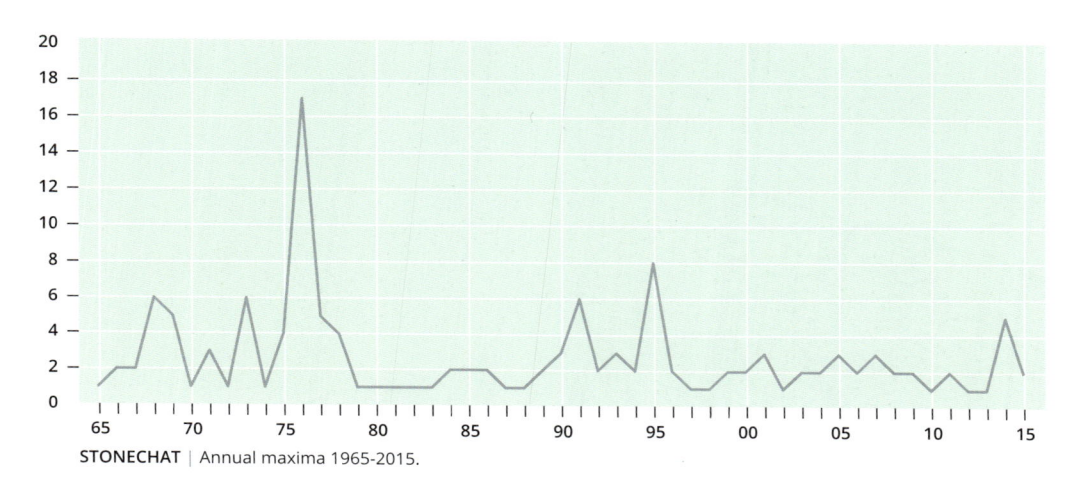

STONECHAT | Annual maxima 1965-2015.

WHEATEAR *Oenanthe oenanthe*

The first Wheatears appear in March, the earliest date being the 10th (in 1996); the latest in spring was on 25 May (in 1997). As the combined monthly maxima graph shows, the peak spring month is April. There are no June records but the first returning adults have appeared in July, the earliest date being 24th (in 1983). There are, however, two July records of juveniles: one on 8 July 1998 and two on 25 July 1992. These are best treated as dispersing birds, presumably with a relatively local origin (perhaps South Wales). The main autumn passage is from July to October, with a peak in September. The latest date was one on 2 November in 1980.

As the annual maxima graph shows, with the exception of 13 (eight males) on 4 April 1968, none of the records has exceeded four. The above figures hide the fact that the turnover of birds is often considerably higher than the monthly maxima. For example, although a maximum of four Wheatears was recorded in August 2000, there were 13 bird-days in that month, so the monthly maximum may have been under-recorded.

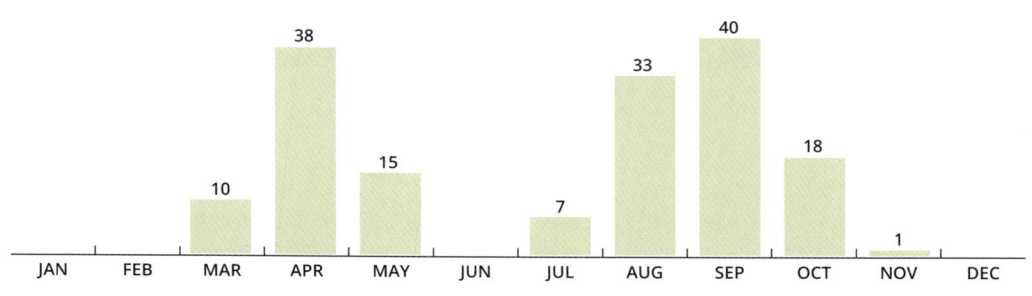

WHEATEAR | Monthly maxima (combined) 1965-2015.

WHEATEAR | Annual maxima 1965-2015.

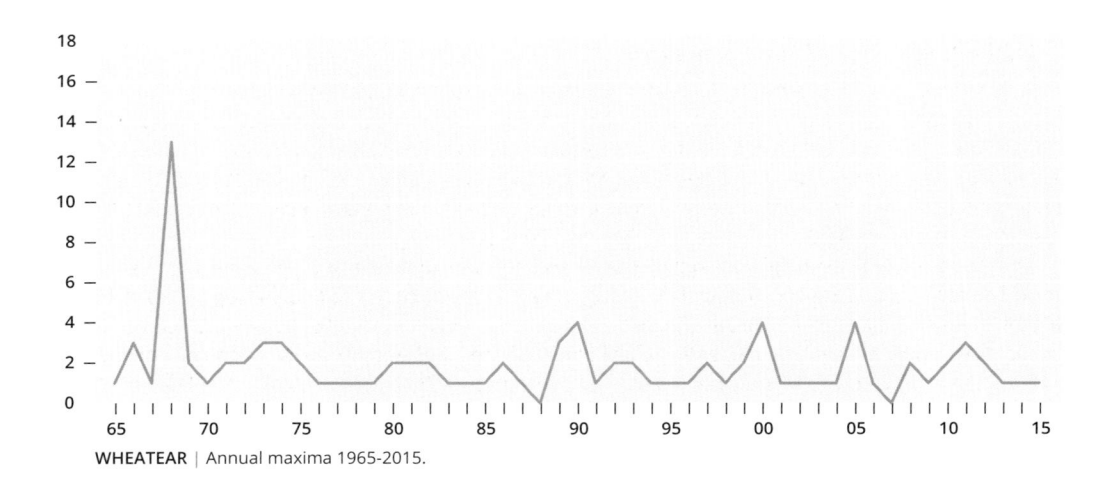

Wheatear | Laurel Tucker

| DIPPER *Cinclus cinclus*

One on 14 December 2001 flew across Herriott's Pool, landed on the spillway, then flew across the lake (R. J. Palmer). Given that the species breeds on the River Chew both up-stream and down-stream from the lake, it is perhaps surprising that there have not been more records.

HOUSE SPARROW *Passer domesticus*

House Sparrows were formerly fairly common around the lake, particularly at Herriott's Bridge and Heron's Green Bay, where people used to feed them. Large numbers also sometimes gathered on stubble or in adjacent weedy fields. But, because the species was so common, few counts were ever made. The annual totals shown in the graph relate to the 25 years from 1991 to 2015. It clearly shows how scarce it has become, although there have been three years (1993, 2003 and 2012) when high numbers were again recorded (56, 60 and 100 respectively).

As the monthly maxima graph shows, House Sparrow numbers are at their highest in the summer months from April to September, with a strong peak in August, partly due to a flock of 250 in 1968 at Heron's Green Bay. High counts at this time were traditionally related to the annual harvest. More recent high counts have been 56 at Stratford Lane in June 1993 and 60 in two separate cornfields in August 2003. In August–September 2012, however, about 100 were discovered at Heron's Green Farm, which is about half a mile to the north-west of Heron's Green Bay. This farm is clearly the source of the small numbers (up to 23 in recent years) that still regularly feed along the dam wall at Heron's Green Bay. This is now the only site for the species at the lake, although they also breed nearby at the Blue Bowl Inn near West Harptree.

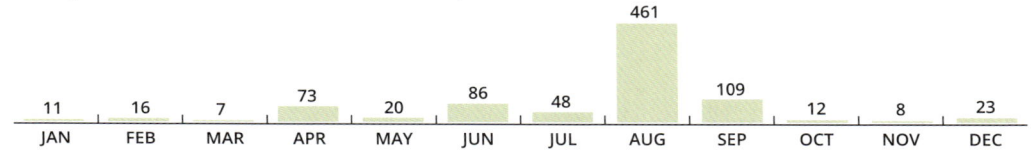

JAN	FEB	MAR	APR	MAY	JUN	JUL	AUG	SEP	OCT	NOV	DEC
11	16	7	73	20	86	48	461	109	12	8	23

HOUSE SPARROW | Monthly maxima 1968-1971 and 1991-2015.

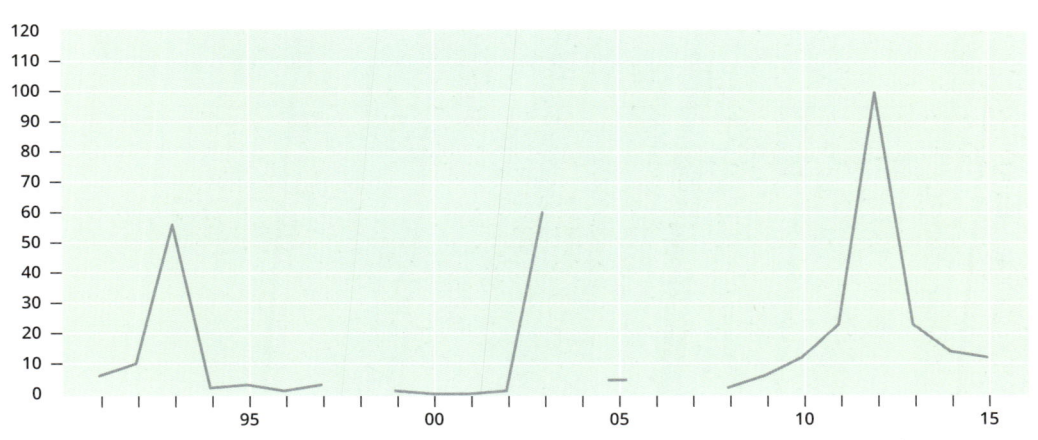

HOUSE SPARROW | Annual maxima 1991-2015. Note that there were no counts in 1998, 2004, 2006 and 2007.

House Sparrow | Laurel Tucker

TREE SPARROW *Passer montanus*

Records of Tree Sparrows were not mentioned in the bird reports prior to 1960. The species was, however, undoubtedly present during this period but was presumably considered too common to warrant a mention. In 1960 it was reported at Chew from mid-September to November, with at least ten on 16 November. Two pairs bred in 1961 and a single pair bred in an orchard in 1962, with a family party of 14 seen on 30 July (*BBR*).

The annual maxima graph shows that it was recorded almost annually from 1960 to 1985, with just two blank years: 1963 and 1982. What stands out, however, is the huge total of 150 in January 1976. These birds gathered in a large weedy field immediately to the south-west of Herriott's Pool. This field also attracted many finches and buntings, including the lake's first Little Bunting *Emberiza pusilla*. Apart from 40 on 25 October 1983 (BOC *Bird News*) numbers from 1981 onwards were low or non-existent, and in the 31 years from 1986 to 2016, it was recorded in only six, with a small peak of eight in 1991. The last to be recorded were one on 22 December 2007 (CVRS) and a recent isolated record of one at Woodford Lodge on 23 November 2015 (I. Stapp, A. Chard). It seems hard to imagine that the species will ever be recorded at the lake again.

As the combined monthly maxima graph shows, the peak months were January and October, with secondary peaks in July and November. The numbers depended on the presence of suitable weedy fields around the lake, the like of which no longer exist.

In May 1969, a pair of Tree Sparrows ousted a pair of Lesser Spotted Woodpeckers *Dryobates minor* from a nest hole in a tall tree at Moreton Cottage.

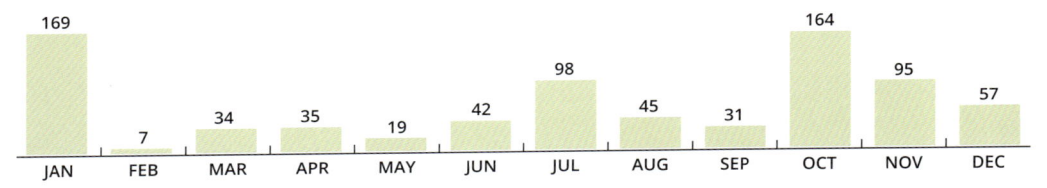

TREE SPARROW | Monthly maxima (combined) 1960-2015.

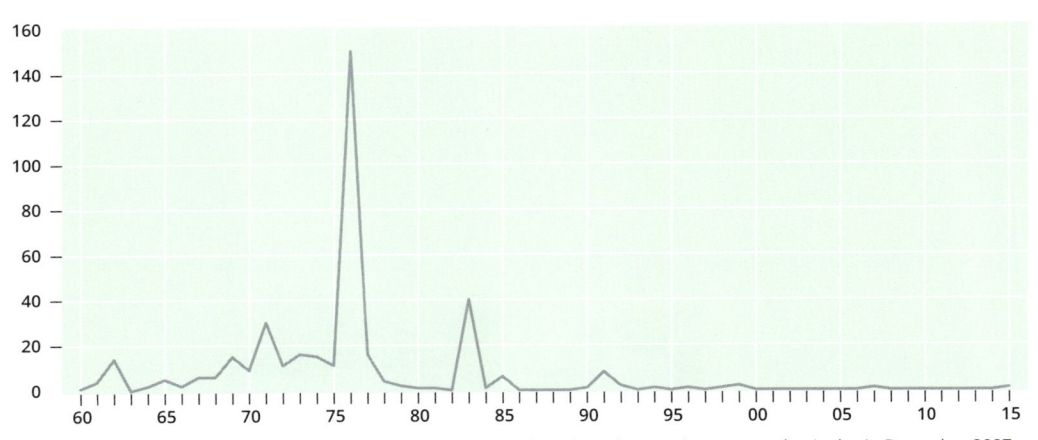

TREE SPARROW | Annual maxima 1960-2015. Since 2000 there have been only two records: singles in December 2007 and November 2015.

DUNNOCK *Prunella modularis*

This is a fairly common bird at the lake but one that has never been surveyed. The only data that exist are from ringing. The annual ringing totals graph indicates a gradual increase from the cold winter of 1962–63 to the turn of the century, presumably associated with the general maturation of the lakeside woodland. There has, however, been a slight decline since then. There were annual ringing totals of 101 in 1995 and 100 in 1997 but what is particularly striking is the large total of 160 in 1976. The reasons for this are unknown but may be linked to the very low water levels in that year, coupled with the large areas of colonising bankside vegetation.

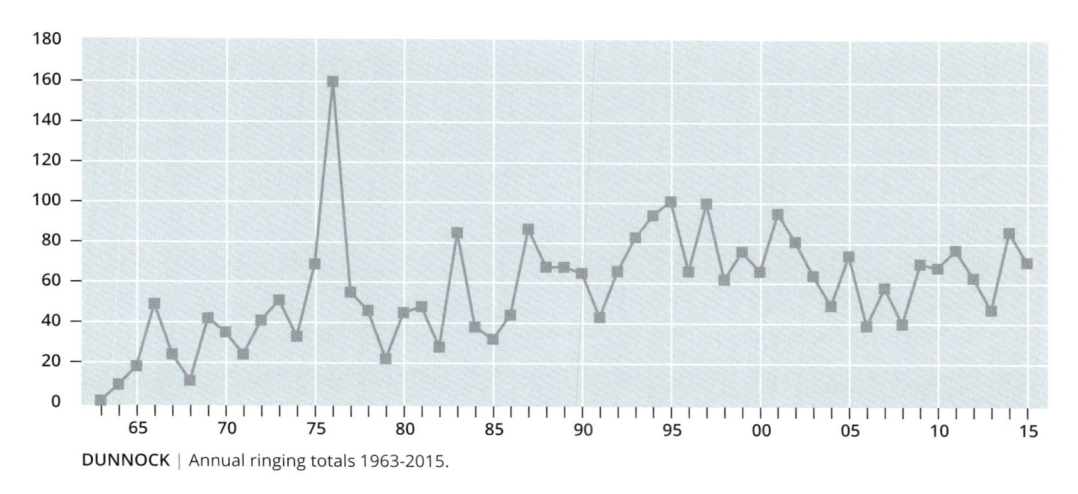

DUNNOCK | Annual ringing totals 1963-2015.

YELLOW WAGTAIL *Motacilla flava flavissima*

The first traceable record is of 50 roosting on 11 September 1958. The next meaningful count was of 14 pairs on 9 June 1962, half of which were feeding young (W. J. Stone). It seems likely that the species was an early colonist at the lake, the marshy margins providing ideal breeding habitat. Breeding continued until 1976, the reason for the extinction being related to the gradual maturation of the lakeside vegetation. However, an undoubted factor in their demise was the opening up to the public of much of the northern part of the lake.

The depressing downward trend is shown well in the annual maxima graph. Double-figure counts were normal until 1989, with peaks of 200 in April 1966 (during the spring blizzard of that year), 110 on 23 August 1970 and 100 in the Parkland on 30 August 1982. As the annual maxima graph shows, numbers then declined rapidly and, since the turn of the century, single figures have become the norm. The highest totals since 2000 have been 14 in September 2005 and ten in August 2011. Personally, I saw just one single individual in both 2015 and 2016.

Traditionally, the first spring arrivals are in early April, although there have been two March records: males on 31st in 1968 and on 27th in 1993. Spring numbers peak in April, declining through May to a low point in June (see combined monthly maxima graph). Autumn migrants appear through July, increasing to a strong peak in August and declining in September, with just a few occasionally remaining into October, the latest date being one on 22nd (in 1983). However, on 18 November 1984, one was heard twice in Heron's Green Bay but the call had a distinct 'z' in it, so there is a strong possibility that it may have been one of the eastern races or species (L. A. Tucker, KEV). Surprisingly, there have also been two winter records: a male at Herriott's Bridge on 12–13 December 1968 and one in the Old Picnic Site/Denny Island area from 8 December 1979 to 5 January 1980 (KEV).

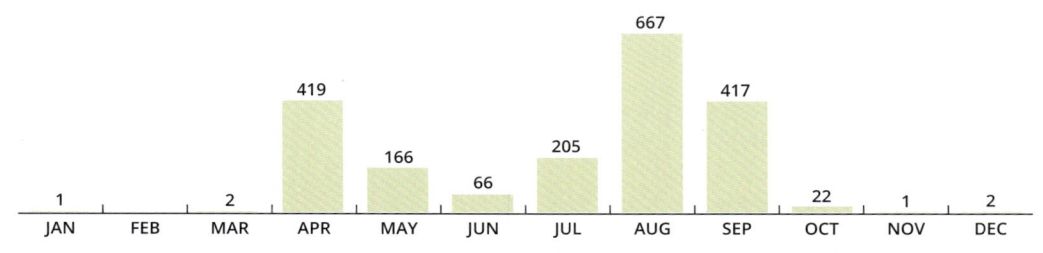

YELLOW WAGTAIL | Monthly maxima (combined) 1965-2015.

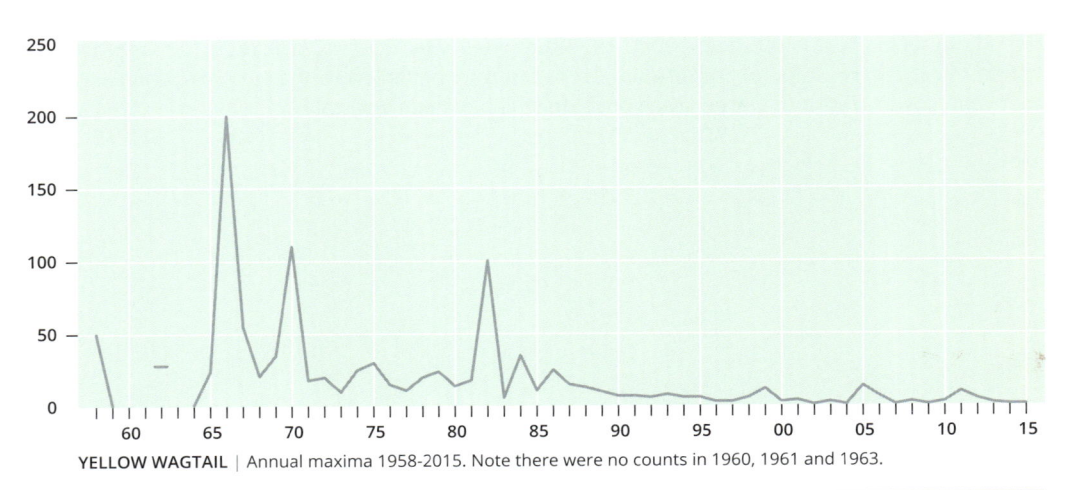

YELLOW WAGTAIL | Annual maxima 1958-2015. Note there were no counts in 1960, 1961 and 1963.

Yellow Wagtail | Gary Thoburn

Blue-headed Wagtail *Motacilla flava flava*

Mainly a rare spring migrant, with sixteen records of at least 24 individuals, including breeding records in 1972 and 1974. All records as follows:

- **1960:** male on 1 May (B. E. Slade).
- **1965:** male on 23 April and another on 23 May.
- **1968:** five: male on 4 April, three [one male] on 5 and 9 May; female on 30 July.
- **1969:** one trapped 28 August.
- **1972:** female 30 April, one 27 July, male 19 September
- **1973:** a pair bred and raised at least 2 young (*Somerset Bird Report*).
- **1974:** a pair bred – see facing page.
- **1976:** male from 10 April to 29 May.
- **1992:** male on 25 April.
- **1995:** male on 26 August.
- **1999:** female on 29 April.
- **2003:** male on 19–20 April.

The following are details of the 1974 breeding record. A male was seen on Moreton Bank on 10 April (KEV). Over a month later, on 18 May, what is assumed to have been the same male was found singing in the then newly developing Picnic Site, next to the Main Dam. A pair was found there on 28 May, with the male seen again on 9 July and 5 August. On 9 August the pair was seen carrying food and, on 10 August, a nest with five chicks was found at the base of a small, newly planted pine tree. On 12 August the nest was found to contain five half-grown chicks and also present were the male, the female and a juvenile, presumably from an earlier brood. The female and a juvenile were seen on 22 August, a male plus two juveniles on 24 August (one of the juveniles being from the first brood), a juvenile on 26 August and, finally, three (male, female and juvenile) on 9 September.

Other variants

The Yellow Wagtail group is quite complicated. There is an 'intergrade zone' in northern France where Yellow and Blue-headed interbreed, the hybrids of which are now called 'Channel Wagtail'. These were formerly thought to be the Asian subspecies *Motacilla flava beema*. Records at the lake showing these characteristics are:

- **1963:** 1 May
- **1972:** a male, 11 June.
- **1973:** one, 29 June.
- **1974:** one 20 April and one 1 August.

Additionally, a bird with the features of Spanish Wagtail *Motacilla flava iberiae*, a male at the Main Dam, was seen on 27 April 2018 (C. Craig, A. H. Davis, R. Mielcarek). BBRC adjudged that the identification was 'not conclusive'.

CITRINE WAGTAIL *Motacilla citreola*

There have been two records of first-winters: one at Heron's Green Pool on 15 September 1996 (N. R. Milbourne, P. Vowles *et al.*) and another first-winter flew over Herriott's Bridge, calling, on the evening of 7 September 2010. It then landed in the reeds on the eastern side of Herriott's Pool, where it was seen quite well in the wagtail roost before dropping out of view (R. J. Higgins, KEV).

GREY WAGTAIL *Motacilla cinerea*

Grey Wagtails occur at the lake in small numbers, most reliably at the Main Dam, where a pair often breeds. Numbers gradually decrease to a minimum in May but, from then on, numbers are boosted by the presence of the summer's young. The peak month is September, this being the result of a small autumn passage. At this time of year, they can be encountered more widely around the lake. The highest counts have been 12 in September 1978, 13 in August 1990 and ten in July 1996. The annual maxima graph suggests a small decrease in numbers from the mid-1990s.

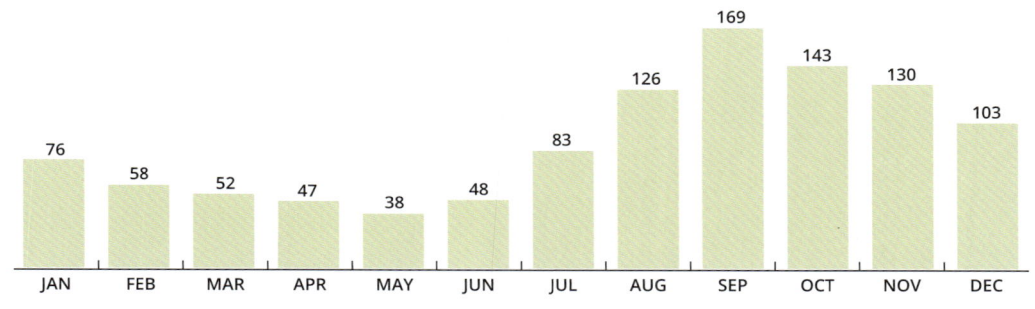

JAN	FEB	MAR	APR	MAY	JUN	JUL	AUG	SEP	OCT	NOV	DEC
76	58	52	47	38	48	83	126	169	143	130	103

GREY WAGTAIL | Monthly maxima (combined) 1965-2015.

Grey Wagtail | Gary Thoburn

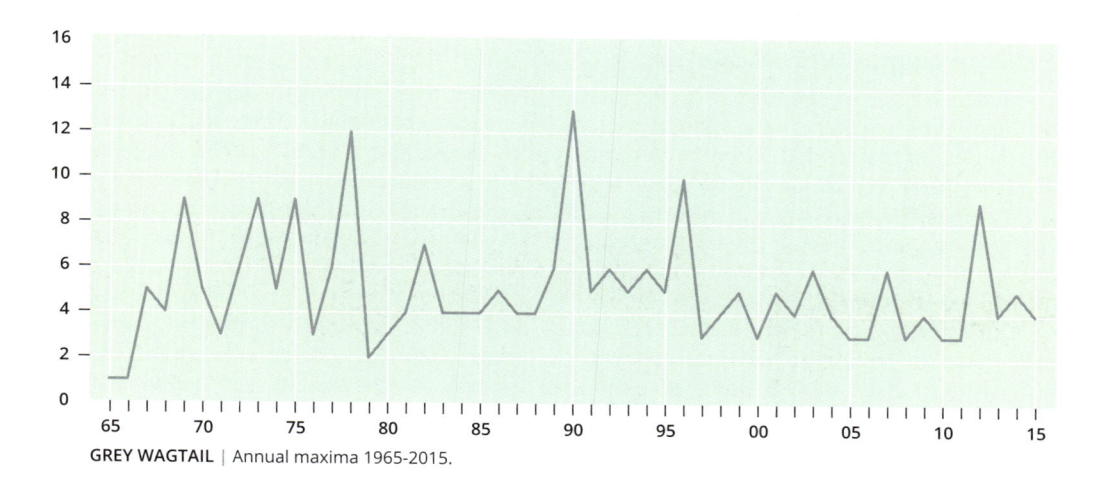

GREY WAGTAIL | Annual maxima 1965-2015.

PIED WAGTAIL *Motacilla alba yarrelli*

Pied Wagtail is a common bird around the lake. The average monthly maxima graph shows that numbers are low in winter, when a large proportion of the British population heads south to the Continent, mainly to Brittany, western Iberia and Morocco (*BWP*). The first returning migrants appear as early as 2 March, with passage birds still moving through as late as 11 May. The largest spring counts were in the Parkland, with 85 in both March and April 1993, these flocks consisting almost entirely of males. The latest date for obvious spring passage was 3 May 2000, when a flock of 20 was seen on Moreton Bank.

Numbers drop considerably in May and June, when the birds settle down to breed. In most years only one or two pairs breed, but as many as four pairs were seen in 1990 and 2012. Undoubtedly, there are more pairs nesting in nearby farm buildings and other suitable sites. Adults have been seen carrying food on 28 April but the earliest date for the first fledged juveniles is 24 May.

Large roosts develop from August through to at least January, with most counts being in the region of 100–250, but with larger estimates of 400 on 21 September 2006 and 300 on 3 November 2007. Most roost in the reeds at Herriott's Bridge, but there may also be a large roost at Heron's Green Bay.

The average monthly maxima graph reflects the large August to October peak, with September being the best month. Numbers reduce considerably in winter, but as many as 100 were roosting in January 1969 and 150 in January 2007. In the depths of winter, smaller numbers feed at the sewage works behind the Main Dam, with counts there of up to 30 in January 2001.

JAN	FEB	MAR	APR	MAY	JUN	JUL	AUG	SEP	OCT	NOV	DEC
50	39	33	28	10	7	37	78	111	76	64	33

PIED WAGTAIL | Monthly maxima (average) 1966-2015.

Pied Wagtails | Laurel Tucker

White Wagtail *Motacilla alba alba*

The White Wagtail is essentially a spring passage migrant, those moving through western Britain heading north to Iceland, where they breed. As the combined monthly maxima graph shows, the first appear in March, usually in the third and fourth weeks. There have, however, been several atypically early records: a male on 8 March in 1992 and an exceptionally early female seen well in a maize field behind Moreton Bank on 1 March 2007 (KEV). There is a large peak in April, numbers falling away sharply in May. The latest spring record is of three on 24th (in 1989). There is, however, a single June record: a male photographed on 14 June 2008. He had only one foot, which no doubt explained his tardiness.

The earliest autumn record was a first-winter on 18–20 August 2003; surprisingly, when first seen it was still retaining a few traces of juvenile plumage (KEV). Oddly, a very similar bird was seen on 24 August 2017 (KEV). September is the peak autumn month, with 58 recorded in total, but numbers at this time of year are much lower than in spring. There are just four October records and one in November, which was seen well and photographed on 20th and 23rd in 2014 (KEV).

Interestingly, the number of autumn records is far lower than the number of spring records. It has been discovered that, in autumn, Icelandic Whimbrel *Numenius phaeopus* fly direct to Iberia and Western Africa, explaining the lower numbers seen in Britain in autumn. Could it be that Icelandic White Wagtails also take a trans-oceanic route direct to Iberia? Interestingly, Flood *et al.* (2007) list three records of a hundred in the Isles of Scilly (in September 1995, 2003 and 2004). Could these high totals at this south-western extremity support this theory?

As the annual maxima graph shows, White Wagtails normally occur at Chew in single figures, with just six double figure counts: 20 on 14 April 1966 during the infamous 'spring blizzard', 14 on the Main Dam on 1 May 1982, 11 in April 1990 (no precise date) and ten on 9 September 2011. There has also been a count of 18 in 2019. The largest total, however, was a loose flock of at least 45 on 23 April 1977 (A. H. Davis).

Reference
Flood, R. L., Hudson, N. and Thomas, B. (2007). *Essential Guide to Birds of the Isles of Scilly*. Privately published.

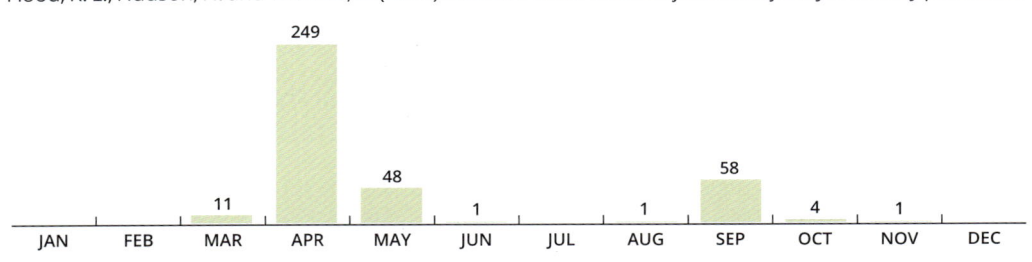

WHITE WAGTAIL | Monthly maxima (combined) 1965-2015.

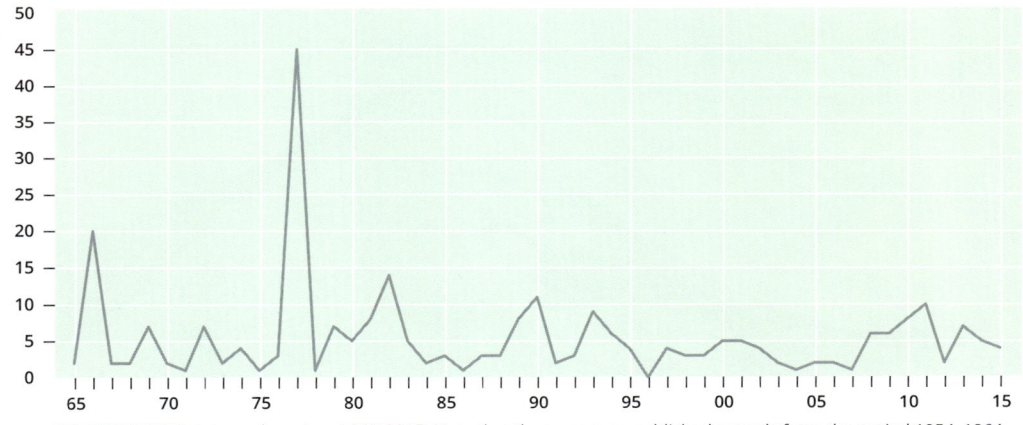

WHITE WAGTAIL | Annual maxima 1965-2015. Note that there were no published records from the period 1954–1964.

TAWNY PIPIT *Anthus campestris*
One was seen in front of Moreton Hide on 2 October 1982 (N. A. Lethaby, A. F. Silcocks).

MEADOW PIPIT *Anthus pratensis*
As the combined monthly maxima graph shows, Meadow Pipits are present in the winter but numbers are small, with an average January total of just eight. Numbers start to increase in February, gaining momentum through March to a strong peak in April (averaging 31) but with counts sometimes reaching three figures. Maximum totals have been 290 on 4 April 1968 and 190 on 11 April 1973. The average last April date is 14th, but records have continued to 25th, with the latest recorded being one on 3 May (in 2000).

On 1 and 7 April 1971, two were seen display flighting behind the Main Dam, with at least one present into May and two again on 20 June, with a male still singing as late as 8 July. They returned in 1972 with song flights seen again on 11 and 16 April; two birds remained until 18 June, with one until 15 August. On 30 April 1972 another pair was also seen on Moreton Bank. There have been no other summer records apart from a single on 8 July 1980. Unfortunately, there was no evidence of successful breeding in any of these years.

The first autumn migrants appear in September, the earliest date being 2nd (seven in 1978) rising through the month to a peak in October, dropping in November–December to the January minimum.

What is surprising from the annual maxima graph is the extent to which the species has declined since the maximum count of 290 in 1968. There has been a notable decline, with annual maxima being just eight in 1997 and three in 2004. However, with counts of 130 in 2016, 80 in 2017 and 80 in 2018, there are signs of a recent revival.

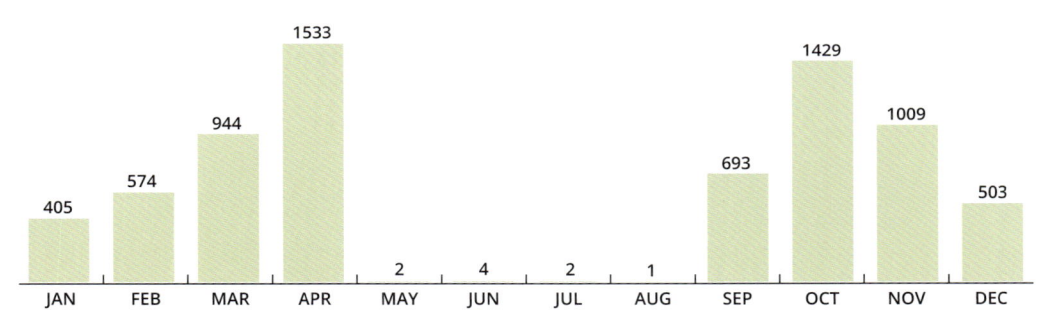

MEADOW PIPIT | Monthly maxima (combined) 1966-2015.

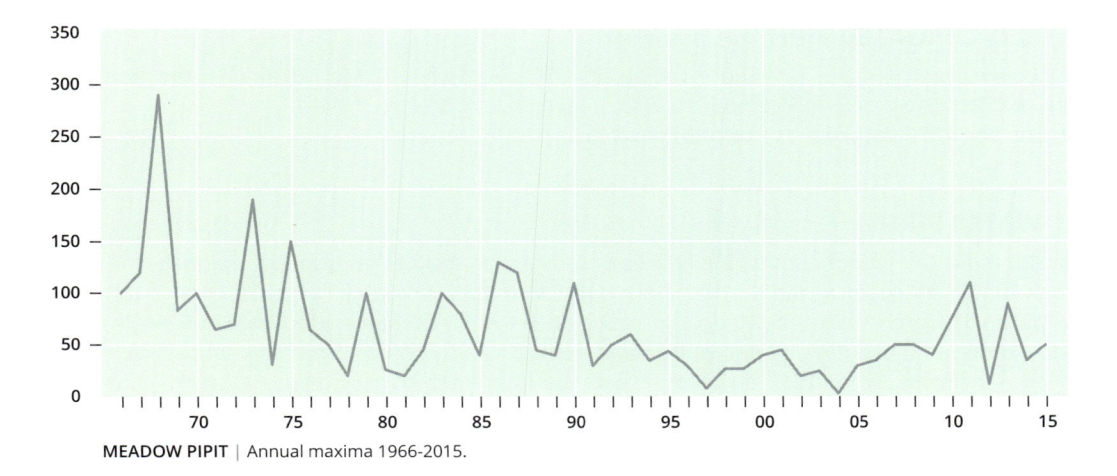

MEADOW PIPIT | Annual maxima 1966-2015.

TREE PIPIT *Anthus trivialis*

Tree Pipits used to breed at the lake in the early years, but there are no published records apart from a comment in the 1957 *Report on Somerset Birds*, which stated 'plentiful in the breeding season'. This was attributed to Bernard King. In those years, the banks were planted with young trees, mainly conifers, which would have provided ideal – but temporary – habitat for the species.

They had virtually gone by 1965, when the only record was one on 18 July (KEV) but, in 1966, one was seen carrying food on 30 May (P. L. Garvey). Since then, the species has occurred on migration in 34 of the 50 years to 2015. As the annual maxima graph shows, there have been several blank years and these have undoubtedly increased since the mid-1990s. It is, in fact, now a rare bird at the lake.

As the combined monthly maxima graph shows, the peak spring month is April, with 49 recorded, but 20 of those were on 17 April 1966, during the unseasonal blizzard. Since then, there have been 56 spring records between 10 April and 19 May and 41 autumn records between 6 July and 3 October (the peak autumn month being August, with 25 records).

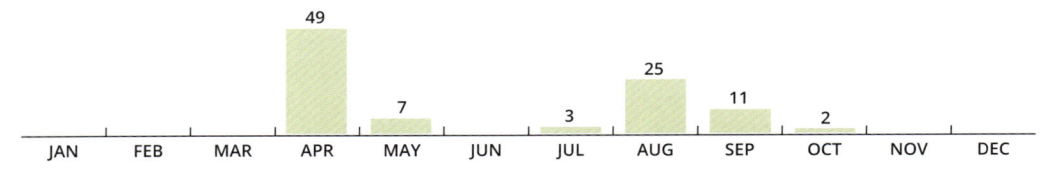

TREE PIPIT | Monthly maxima (combined) 1965-2015.

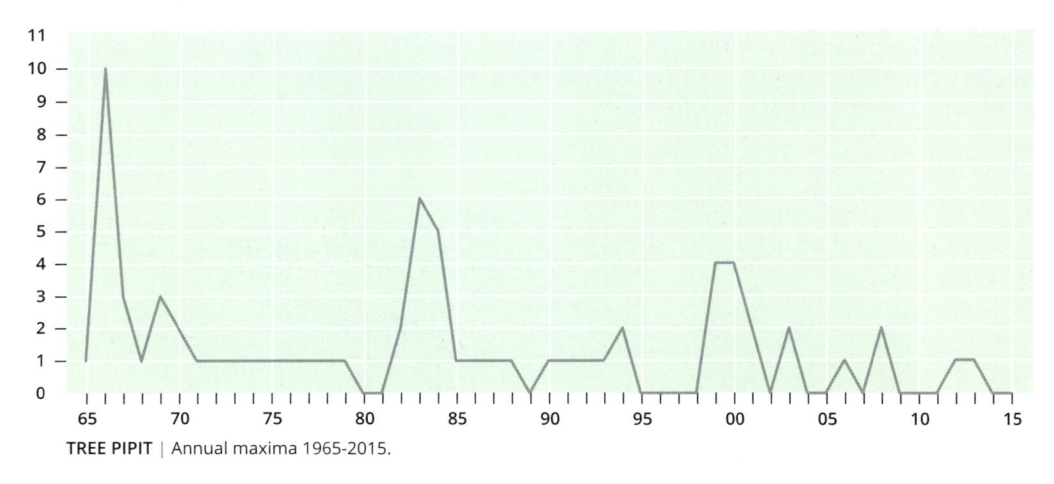

TREE PIPIT | Annual maxima 1965-2015.

RED-THROATED PIPIT *Anthus cervinus*

One flew over the North-east Shore, calling, on 4 October 1976 (A. J. Merritt) and another was seen on the East Shore on 16 December 1979 (A. J. Merritt, L. A. & N. A. Tucker).
Note: the 1976 record was not published in the BBRC report.

WATER PIPIT *Anthus spinoletta*

Water Pipits breed in the mountain ranges of central and southern Europe so, uniquely, the birds that winter at Chew migrate north or north-west from their breeding range. The first record was of six on 31 March 1958 (S. G. Madge) with nine on 3–4 April. These were followed by a single on 29 November. In those days, Water Pipit wasn't treated as a full species, it being lumped with Rock Pipit *A. petrosus*. From 1958 onwards, it was seen annually, usually in single figures, but their numbers were badly affected by cold winters, there being very few from 1964 to 1967, following the cold winter of 1962–63 (see annual maxima graph on page 444).

Water Pipit | Rich Andrews

As the graph also shows, there was a distinct up-turn in 1969–1974 with 17 in both 1970 and 1971 and a record 21 on 28 March 1972, 20 of which were between the Dam and Hollow Brook (a favoured spot in those days). From 1975 onwards, single-figure maxima again became the norm, with just six years producing double figure counts, but with a peak of 17 on 15 November 2003; these were seen coming into roost in the reed beds at Herriott's Bridge. In recent years (2006–2017) the species has once again become scarce, with an annual average of three, and just one seen in 2014, but with a slight upturn in the 2015–16 and 2016–17 winters (6 and 7 respectively).

The average monthly graph shows that Water Pipits usually arrive in October, the earliest recorded date being 10th (in 1971); the last spring date is 21 April (in 1996). The highest numbers have been in November–December and again in March. By the time they migrate in spring, they have usually acquired their distinctive summer plumage, with a bluish head and a strong pink wash to the underparts. At this time, they often feed in grassy lakeside fields, particularly on Moreton Bank or in the Parkland.

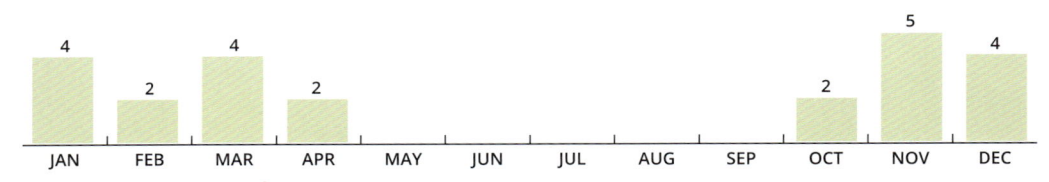

WATER PIPIT | Monthly maxima (average) 1958-2016.

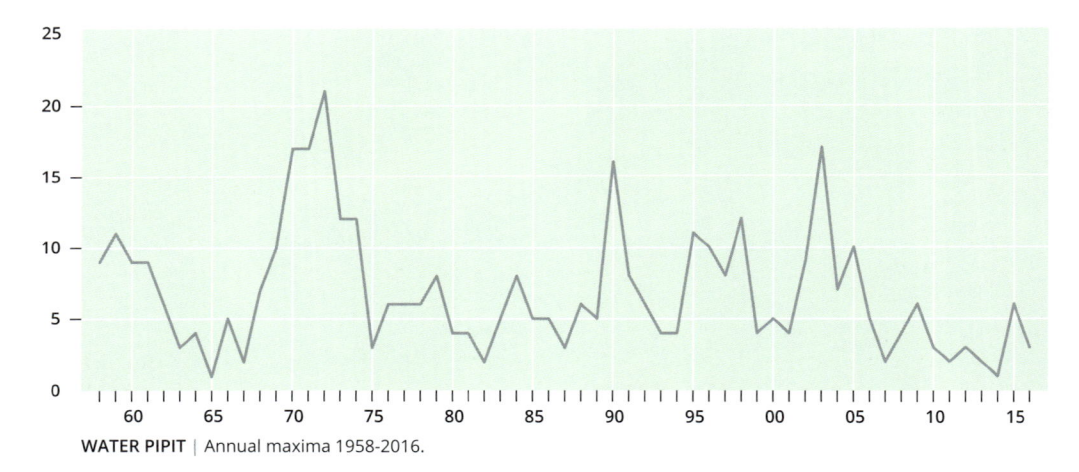

WATER PIPIT | Annual maxima 1958-2016.

| ROCK PIPIT *Anthus petrosus*

As the annual maxima graph clearly indicates, Rock Pipit is an erratic visitor, recorded in 34 of the 60 years from 1958 (when first recorded) to 2017. The records relate mostly to single birds, but there have been eight records of twos, and as many as four in both 1987 and 1992.

The peak times are March (with nine records) and in late September and October (13 and 33 records respectively). There is also a single December record (on 5th in 1958) but it has not been recorded in January. One on 28 February and 12 March 1960 was presumably an early spring migrant.

As most records involve birds in winter plumage, it is impossible to know whether they are of the nominate race, which breeds quite commonly around our rocky coastlines, or whether they relate to birds of the more migratory Scandinavian race *littoralis*. Their separation can be attempted only in spring, when they are acquiring summer plumage – *littoralis* have been recorded at the lake as follows:

2005: two on 23 March (A. H Davis, R. Mielcarek) and one on 4 April (A. H. Davis).
2001: one on 24 March (J. P. Martin *et al.*).
2012: one on 25 March (S. Curtis, R. Mielcarek *et al.*).

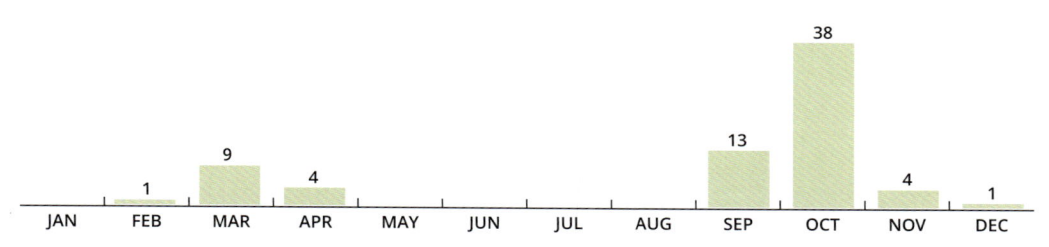

ROCK PIPIT | Monthly chart of all records 1958-2017.

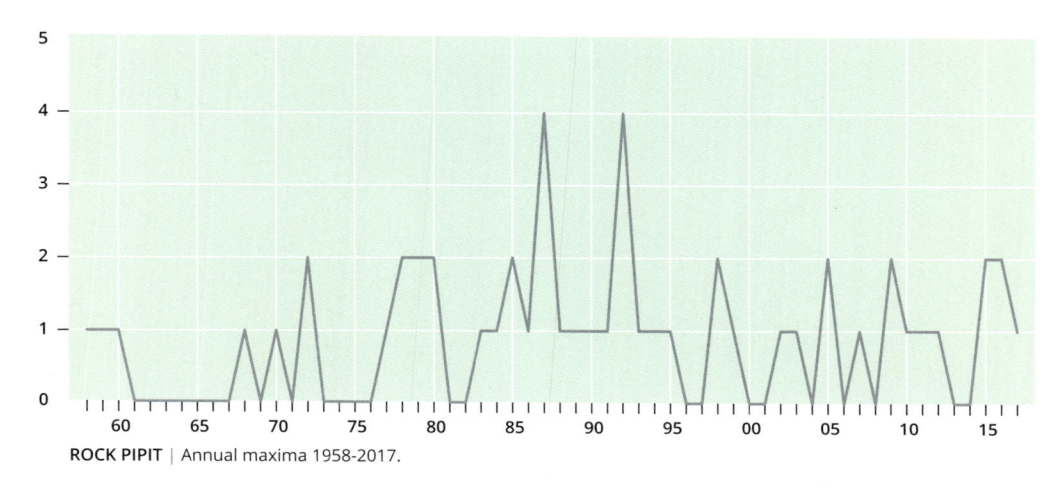

ROCK PIPIT | Annual maxima 1958-2017.

CHAFFINCH *Fringilla coelebs*

This common breeding species is one of the harbingers of spring, with the first song usually heard in mid-February, but sometimes as early as January (the earliest date being 13th in 2001). Because it is so common, breeding numbers have never been surveyed, the only data relating to ringing totals. As the graph below indicates, it has increased steadily since the mid-1960s, no doubt as a consequence of the gradual maturation of the lakeside woodland.

Winter numbers vary, but in some years large flocks have gathered in suitable weedy lakeside fields. Counts of a hundred or more have occurred in ten years, with maxima of 150 in 1972, 1983 and 2011, and as many as 200 in January 1999 (in a maize field behind Moreton Bank) and in December 2012 (in a field near Villice Bay). Totals of over a hundred have been trapped in 14 years, with a maximum of 234 ringed in 1994.

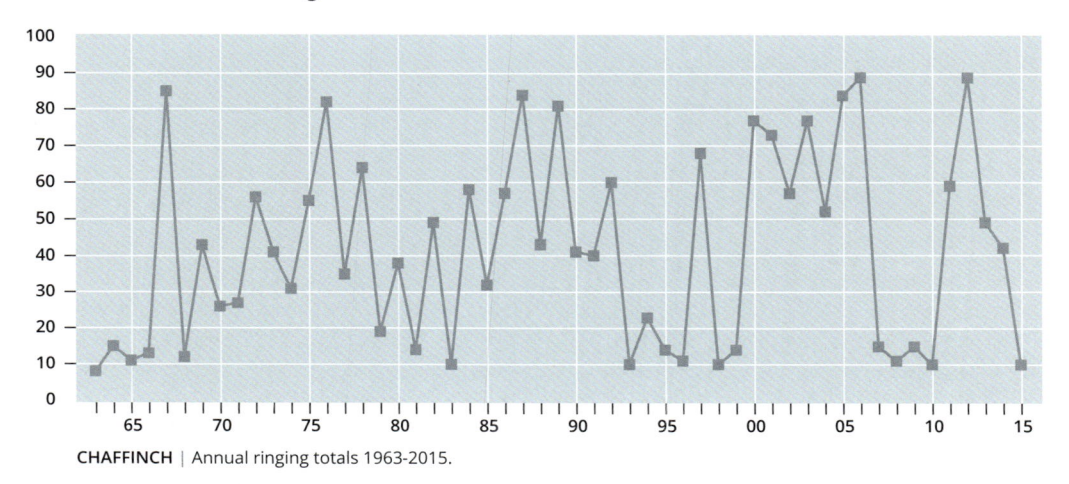

CHAFFINCH | Annual ringing totals 1963-2015.

Chaffinch | Lucy Masters

BRAMBLING *Fringilla montifringilla*

This species breeds mainly in sub-Arctic birch woods in northern Europe and also in open coniferous forests immediately to the south. Its annual occurrences here are closely related to food availability in these areas: chiefly seeds of the beech (*BWP*). In years when the crop is poor, the birds tend to move southwards, with large numbers often reaching Britain and other European countries. The sporadic nature of their annual movements is well reflected in the lower chart.

Bramblings were first recorded at Chew on 18 December 1955, when 60 were seen, increasing to a record 100 from 5 February to 19 March 1956. Although seen since then, the next published records were of up to 15 in January–February 1965. It has since occurred in 39 of the 51 years to 2015. Most annual maxima have been in single figures, but there have been eight counts of up to 23, with 50 in November–December 1963, when a large finch flock was attracted to a weedy field along Sutton Wick Lane. The highest counts since then were up to 19 in a maize field behind Moreton Bank from December 1998 to January 1999, 23 in pines in the Second Picnic Site on 14 April 2011 and up to 12 in the Woodford Lodge/Nunnery Point area from December 2012 to January 2013. The earliest ever autumn record involved two on 6 October 2000 and the latest in spring was one on 22 April 2006.

References
Palmer, E. M. and Ballance, D. K. (1968). *The Birds of Somerset.* Longmans.

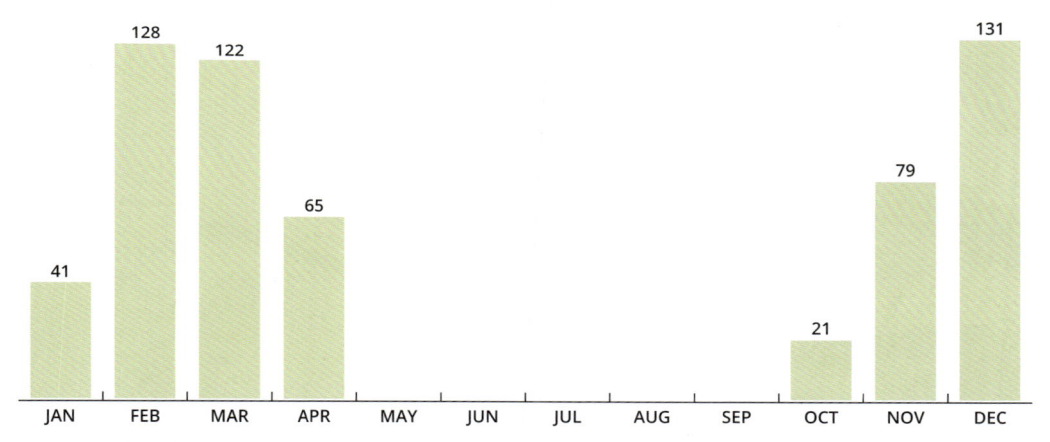

BRAMBLING | Combined monthly maxima 1955-2015.

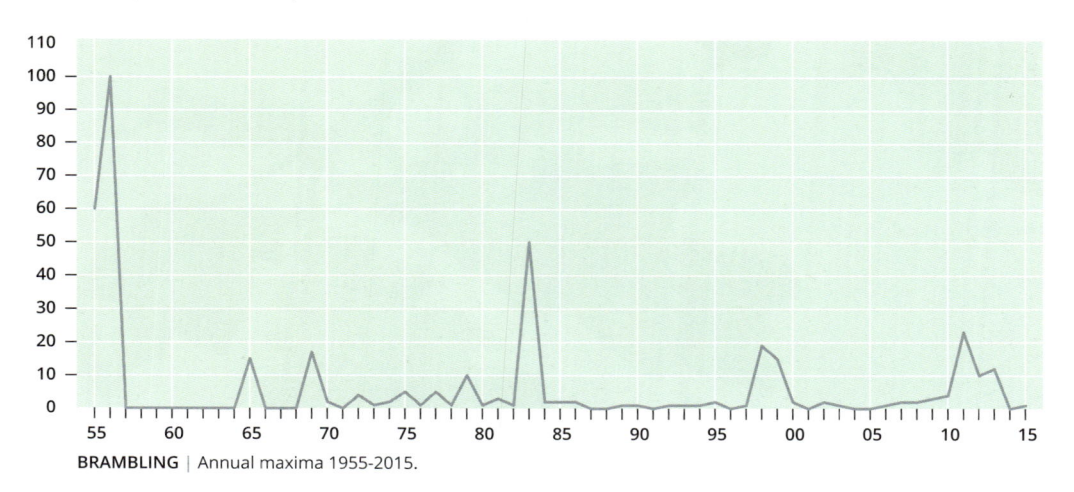

BRAMBLING | Annual maxima 1955-2015.

HAWFINCH *Coccothraustes coccothraustes*

There have been twelve records (at least 14 individuals):

- **1974:** two on 4 April along the road to Woodford Lodge (R. Aston, M. I. Avery, J. F. Ryan, D. Titcomb).
- **1979:** one on 5 February (P. J. Dolton); female on the East Shore on 31 March (KEV).
- **1989:** one on 13 April at Stratford Lane (M. C. Powell).
- **1994:** one on the Bittern Trail on 21 November (R. J. Palmer).
- **1997:** two along the Bittern Trail on 6 January (*ABR* but no observer details).
- **2009:** one in flight over Moreton Hide on 2 April (KEV).
- **2017:** one along the Parkland Track between 15 and 27 November. Together with the records for 2018 below, these records were part of a huge national invasion during the autumn and winter of 2017–18, which is thought to have originated in eastern Europe.
- **2018:** one 3 January (KEV), three 11 January (I. Stapp) and one 16 February (D. Brooke-Taylor).

Hawfinch | Laurel Tucker

BULLFINCH *Pyrrhula pyrrhula*

As the annual maxima graph shows, Bullfinches are present around the lake in small numbers, with most counts being in single figures. There have, however, been eleven counts in double figures, the highest totals being 15 on 19 January and 26 September 1972, and 15 on 16 November 2002.

However, the numbers of birds seen are undoubtedly much lower than the numbers actually present, as confirmed by the annual ringing totals graph, which shows totals from 1965 to 2015. The highest totals were 56 in 1966, 57 in 1969 and 53 in 1976, but numbers since the early 1980s have been lower, with maxima of 41 in 1997 and 39 in 2011.

The combined maximum monthly graph counts indicates that the species is most numerous from November to January, with a low point in May and June when they are breeding. The dips in February and October are difficult to explain, but may simply relate to lower coverage.

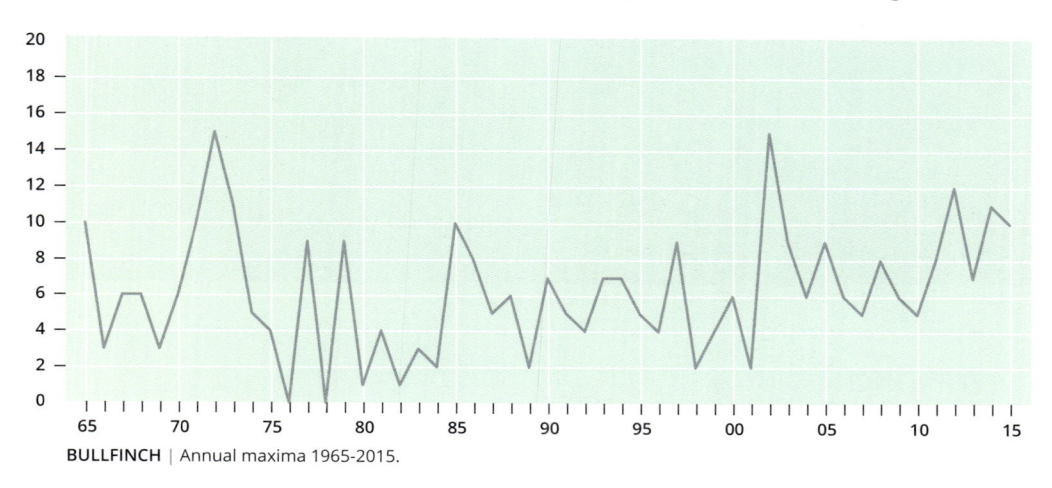

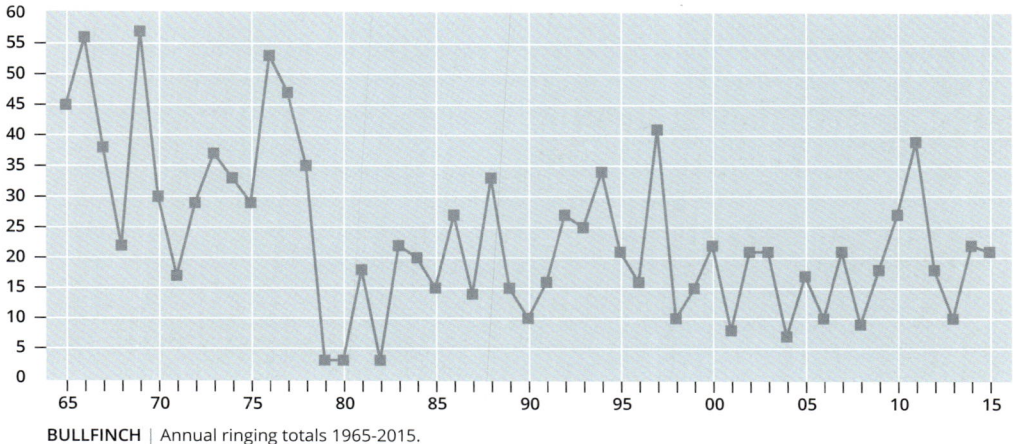

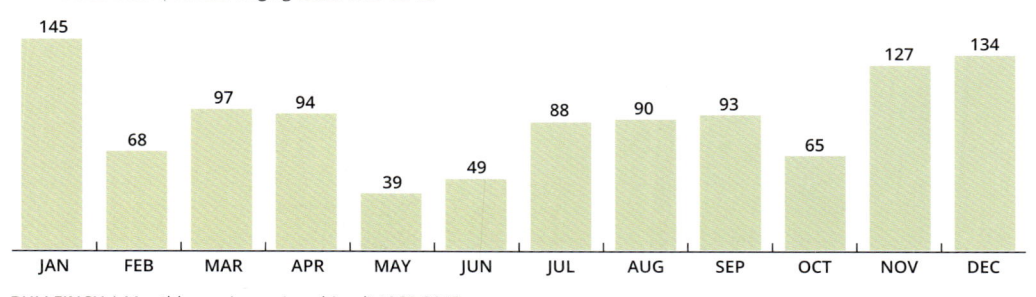

BULLFINCH | Annual maxima 1965-2015.

BULLFINCH | Annual ringing totals 1965-2015.

BULLFINCH | Monthly maximum (combined) 1965-2015.

Month	JAN	FEB	MAR	APR	MAY	JUN	JUL	AUG	SEP	OCT	NOV	DEC
Max	145	68	97	94	39	49	88	90	93	65	127	134

COMPLETE SPECIES LIST AND CHARTS

Bullfinch | Lucy Masters

GREENFINCH *Chloris chloris*

The Greenfinch is not particularly common at the lake but, in the past, large numbers were occasionally attracted to weedy lakeside fields. However, such fields no longer exist. The largest counts were 200 in January 1976 and up to 300 from December 1973 to January 1974. The first chart shows that the peak months are December and January, but these are the result of a large winter roost in a line of tall cypress trees adjacent to Moreton Cottage. The roost was present every winter from 1994 to 1998, peaking at 150 in February 1997. However, the trees were then severely lopped and the roost no longer exists. The largest recent count was 55 in September 2011, the birds feeding on cotoneaster berries along the Dam overflow.

The graph shows the annual maxima but note that there were no meaningful counts in seven of the years from 1977 to 1986. Nevertheless it shows that the species has declined. In recent years, this has been exacerbated by a disease called trichomonosis, which is caused by a protozoan parasite, *Trichomonas gallinae*. This has severely affected the Greenfinch population from the late summer of 2006 onwards (per British Trust for Ornithology).

The annual ringing graph shows the totals from 1963–2015. This indicates that the species was scarce at the lake until the mid-1970s, but increased considerably from the mid-1990s. However, these higher totals were undoubtedly affected by the fact that the ringers were putting out food to attract the species. The graph also shows a distinct crash in 2010–2011, this presumably relating to the aforementioned outbreak of trichomonosis.

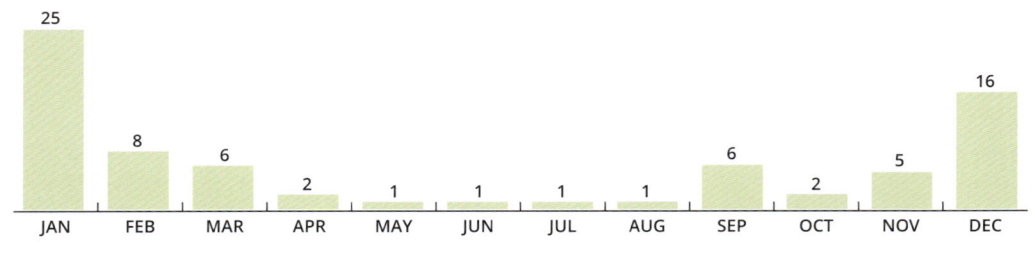

JAN	FEB	MAR	APR	MAY	JUN	JUL	AUG	SEP	OCT	NOV	DEC
25	8	6	2	1	1	1	1	6	2	5	16

GREENFINCH | Monthly maxima (average) 1967-2015.

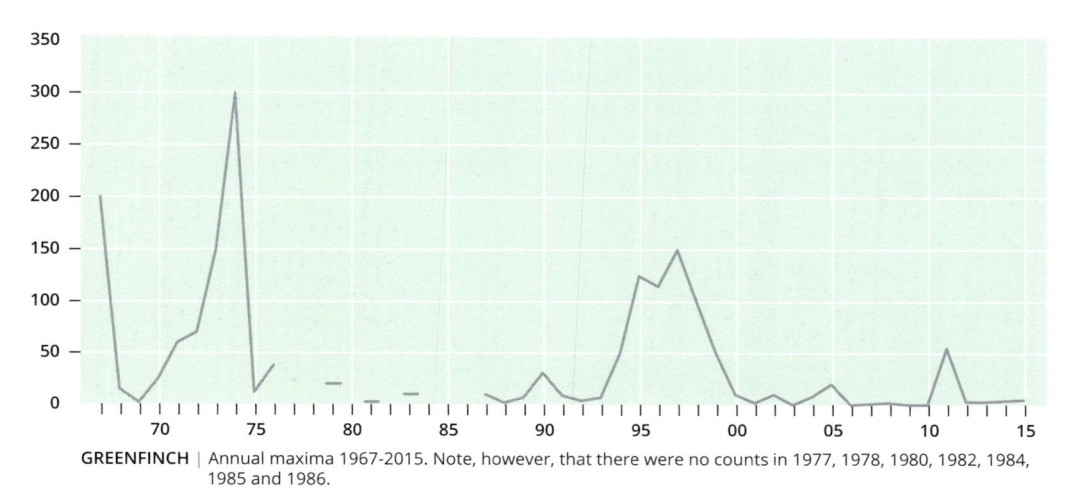

GREENFINCH | Annual maxima 1967-2015. Note, however, that there were no counts in 1977, 1978, 1980, 1982, 1984, 1985 and 1986.

GREENFINCH | Annual ringing totals 1963-2015.

TWITE *Linaria flavirostris*

On 28 January 1979, two were seen well feeding with a large mixed finch flock (about 170 birds) in a field at North Widcombe (KEV). What was no doubt one of these birds was subsequently seen on 24 February, feeding with finches in Villice Bay (N. A. & L. A. Tucker). Large numbers were seen elsewhere in the area in the February of that year, including two at Severn Beach, 22 at Portbury Wharf, 38 at Portishead, 20 at Clevedon, 20+ at Sand Bay and three at Steart.

LINNET *Linaria cannabina*

As the combined monthly maxima graph shows, numbers of Linnets peak in January, declining sharply in February and March, with the lowest numbers during the breeding season in May and June. They start to increase in July, leading to high numbers in the autumn and early winter, with a peak in October.

However, as the annaul maxima graph indicates, winter numbers vary considerably from year to year, depending on the availability of weedy fields and/or years with low winter water levels. In such years, ideal feeding habitat often develops as ruderal plants colonise the lakeside margins. There have been eleven years with flocks of more than a hundred, the highest totals being 290 in September 1973, 200 in December 1983 and 260 in January 2011, with 250 in November of that year. It is possible, however, that in October–November 2011, an autumn of low water levels, as many as 450 were present, with flocks of 200 on the East Shore on 31 October and 250 in Spring Bay on 3 November.

Traditionally, small numbers have bred in the vicinity of the lake, particularly during 1968–1976 and again in 1988–1999, but the numbers have been small, usually just one or two pairs, though with maxima of four in 1976 and 1997. Given that the lakeside fields are now predominantly pastoral, these low breeding numbers are hardly surprising.

In December 2014, a small roost developed in the bushes at Woodford Lodge, with a peak of 24 on 28th.

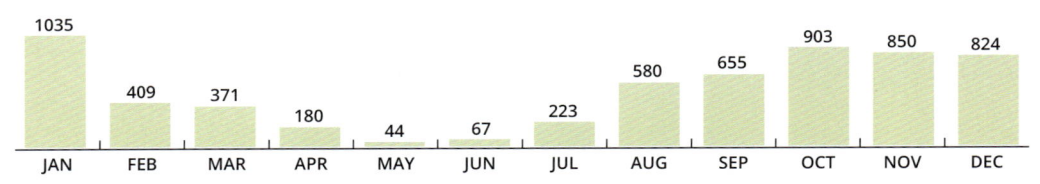

LINNET | Monthly maxima (combined) 1967-2015.

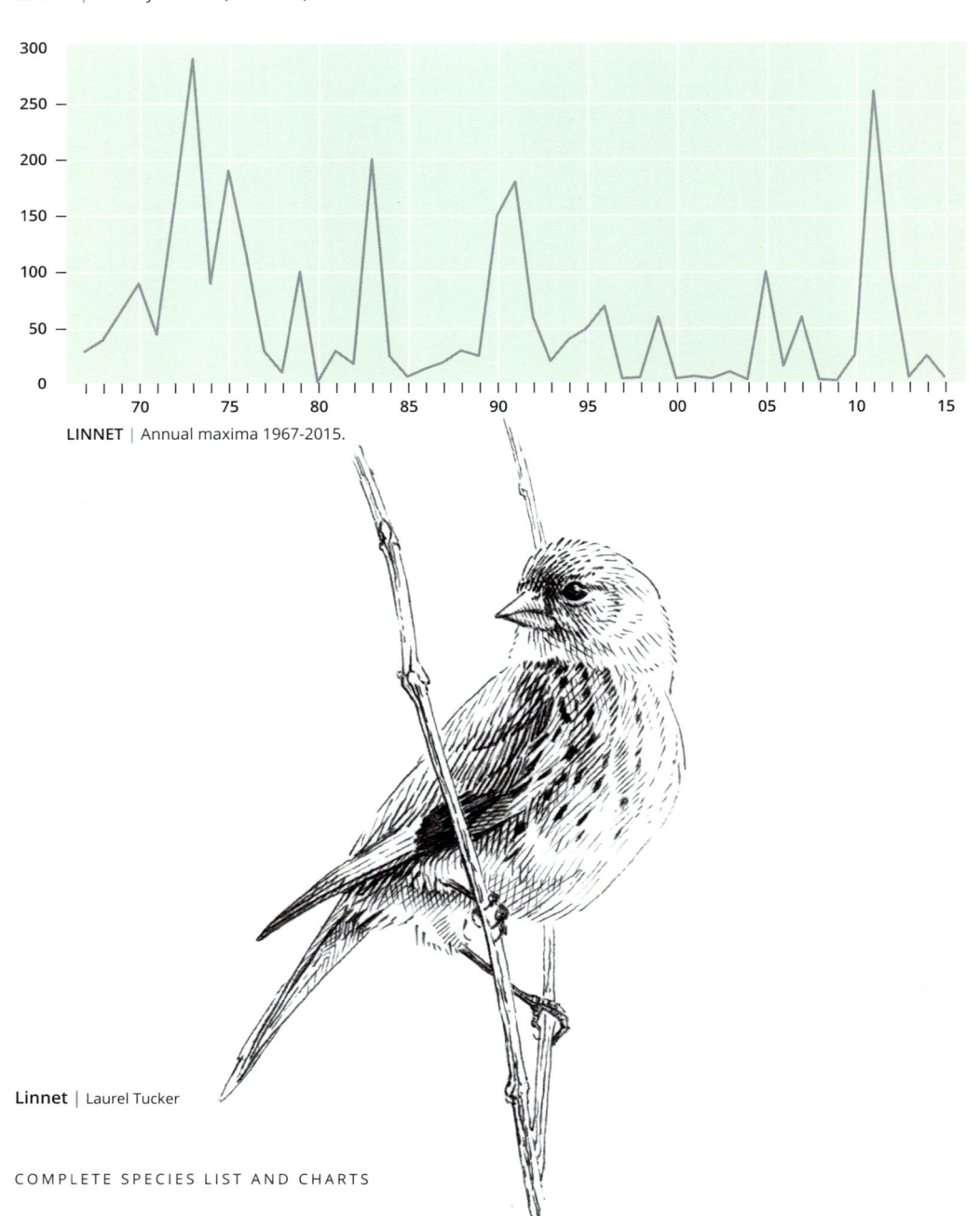

LINNET | Annual maxima 1967-2015.

Linnet | Laurel Tucker

COMMON REDPOLL *Acanthis flammea*

There have been five records:
- **1965:** one in Stratford Bay with Lesser Redpolls *A. cabaret* on 31 October and 1 November (K. L. Fox. P. A. Roscoe, D. Shepherd).
- **1996:** one at Sutton Wick on 12–13 April (A. H. Davis, J. P. Martin *et al.*). This bird appeared during an exceptional influx into Britain during the winter of 1995–96 (Riddington *et al.* 2000).
- **2001:** a male on 16 March was seen feeding under a willow at Herriott's Bridge (A. H. Davis, I. Stapp).
- **2013:** one on 17 April (R. Mielcarek).
- **2015:** a first-winter was trapped on 25 October (CVRS); a photograph can be found in the 2015 *Avon Bird Report*.

Reference
Riddington, R., Votier, S. C. and Steele, J. (2000). 'The influx of redpolls into Western Europe, 1995/96'. *British Birds* 93: 59–67.

LESSER REDPOLL *Acanthis cabaret*

This species is fundamentally a winter visitor, from September to April, but, as the annual maxima graph shows, numbers fluctuate significantly from year to year. This is because annual totals depend largely on the birch crop, there being higher numbers when the crop is good (Newton 1972). The best years at Chew were 1966, 1967 and 1986, all of which had maxima between 20 and 26. However some of these numbers may be low, as shown by total ringing numbers of 186 with 33 between October and December 2012.

The first autumn records occur in September with one on 10th (in 1966) being the earliest date. Numbers then rise sharply from October to January, followed by a late winter dip in February and March. There is then a spring peak in April, presumably relating to migrating birds, some of which, no doubt, will have wintered on the continent. There are three May records, with the latest being one on 17th (in 2013). Eleven days prior to this (on 6 May) one had been heard singing. There is also a single June record: on 29th in 1986.

Reference
Newton, I. (1972). *Finches*. Collins.

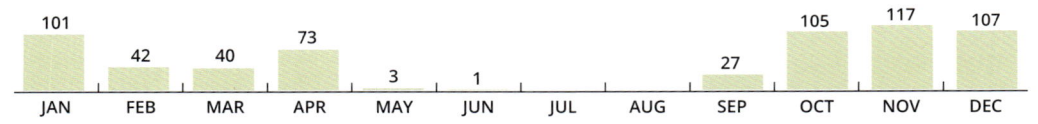

JAN	FEB	MAR	APR	MAY	JUN	JUL	AUG	SEP	OCT	NOV	DEC
101	42	40	73	3	1			27	105	117	107

LESSER REDPOLL | Monthly maxima (combined) 1965-2015.

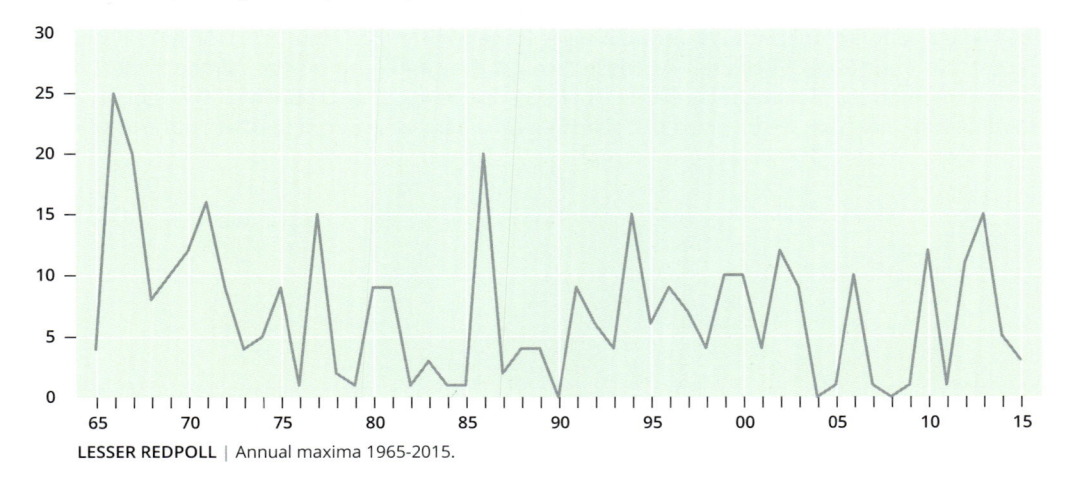

LESSER REDPOLL | Annual maxima 1965-2015.

CROSSBILL *Loxia curvirostra*

This irruptive species is a rare and irregular visitor. The first record was of one on 10 November 1963. The next were 23 in 1972, which was an irruption year, with three on 25 July, 17 on 20 August and singles on three dates from 4 to 30 November. The next record related to an early juvenile on 18 June 1978 and, from then until 2016, there have been a further 16 records involving 30 individuals. As the combined monthly maxima graph shows, the peak months are July–August, which are typical for irruptive Crossbills. Ten were seen near Moreton Cottage on 8 October 2019.

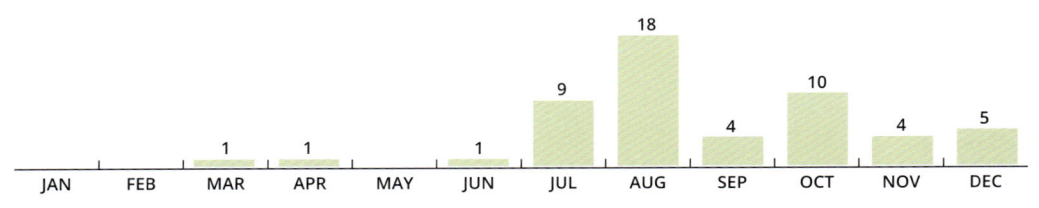

CROSSBILL | Monthly maxima (combined) 1963-2016.

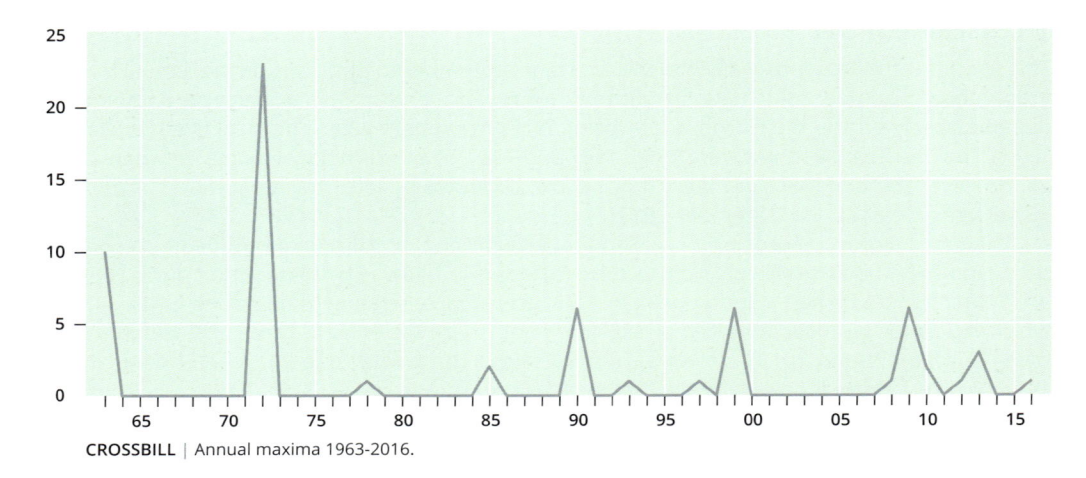

JAN	FEB	MAR	APR	MAY	JUN	JUL	AUG	SEP	OCT	NOV	DEC
		1	1		1	9	18	4	10	4	5

CROSSBILL | Annual maxima 1963-2016.

GOLDFINCH *Carduelis carduelis*

The Goldfinch breeds at the lake in small numbers, with an average of four pairs during 1993–2015, but with a recent increase to a maximum of about ten pairs in 2015. As the combined monthly maxima graph shows, numbers are fairly low in summer, rising to a strong peak from August to October, with the highest counts at this time relating to birds feeding on thistles: 170 in 1970, 150 in 1990 and 250 in both 2011 and 2015. They then decrease through the early winter, large numbers presumably having migrated south onto the continent. There was, however, a high count of 100 in February 1981 and this was likely to have involved birds feeding on alders, a favoured food at this time of year.

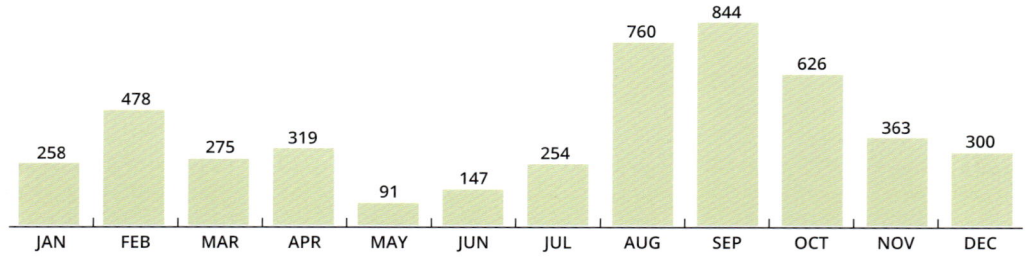

JAN	FEB	MAR	APR	MAY	JUN	JUL	AUG	SEP	OCT	NOV	DEC
258	478	275	319	91	147	254	760	844	626	363	300

GOLDFINCH | Monthly maxima (combined) 1967-2015.

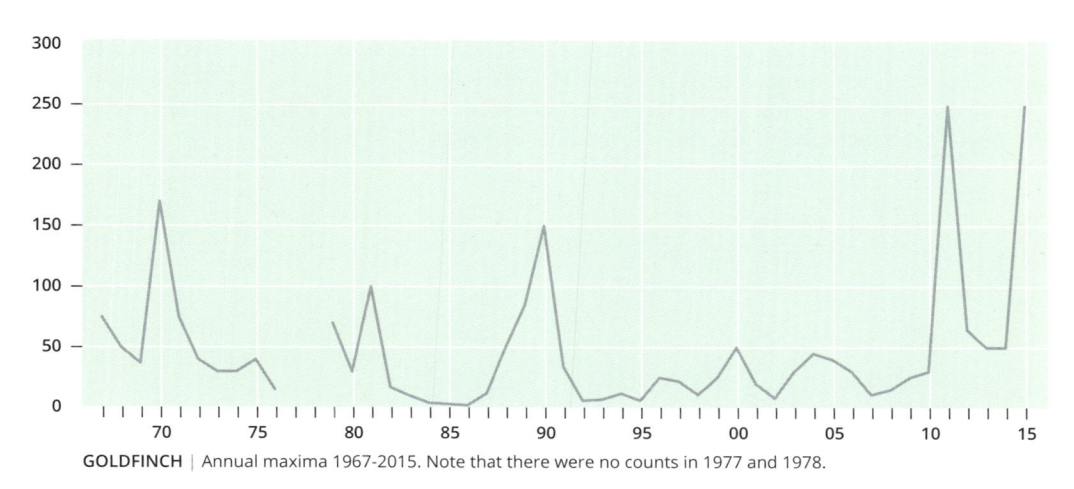

GOLDFINCH | Annual maxima 1967-2015. Note that there were no counts in 1977 and 1978.

Goldfinch | Gary Thoburn

SERIN *Serinus serinus*

One was seen and heard briefly at Twycross on 22 October 1983 (P. J. Hopkin, C. J. Newman).

SISKIN *Spinus spinus*

The only record from the early years was of two on 7 November 1959. Presumably, the species was recorded prior to this but the records did not appear in the bird reports. Since 1965, it has been recorded in every year, although the numbers vary considerably. These fluctuations relate to the availability of the seed crops on which they depend – primarily birch and alder. The annual maxima graph illustrates these fluctuations, with virtually none recorded in some years but large numbers in others. Just single birds were seen in 1976 and 1987 but, by contrast, the largest counts were 120 on 28 November 1981 and 150 on 14 December 2015.

The earliest record was one on 16 August 2015, followed by six on 2 September; autumn/early winter records increase to a peak between November and January, steadily falling away from February to April. The latest spring dates were three on 3 May 1986 and one on 17 May 2012. It has never been recorded in July, but there is one June record of 3 in 2018.

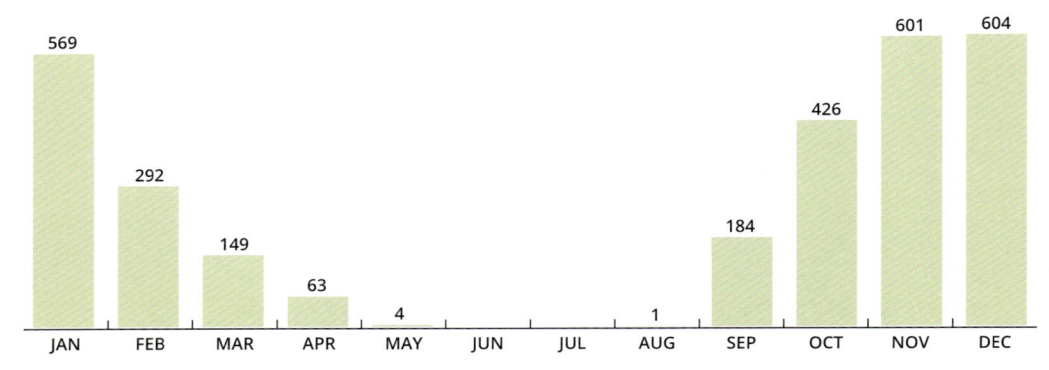

SISKIN | Monthly maxima (combined) 1965-2015.

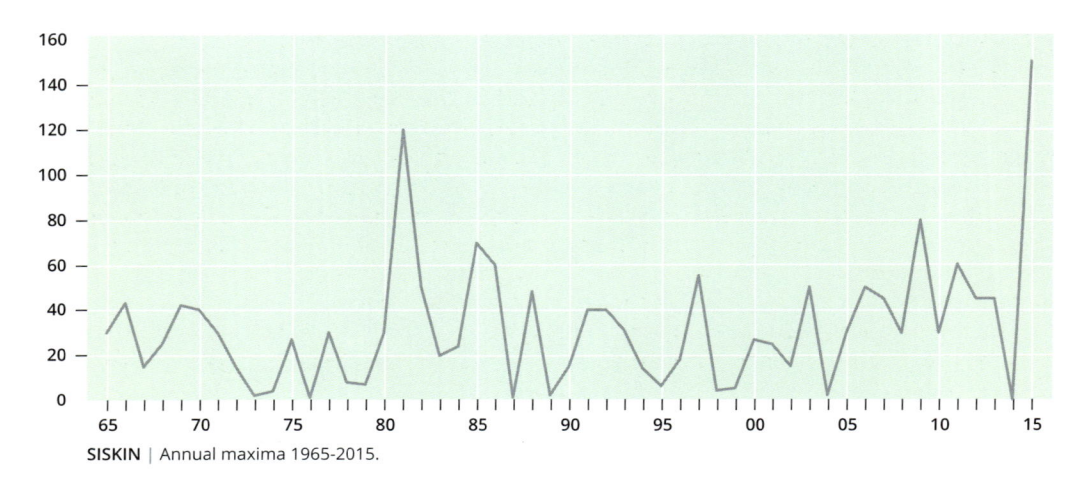

SISKIN | Annual maxima 1965-2015.

| LAPLAND BUNTING *Calcarius lapponicus*

There have been two records: a male at Sutton Wick on 11 November 1990 (A. J. Merritt) and one flew west over Hollow Brook and Denny Island on 17 November 1991 (KEV). It was calling, at a height of about 50 feet.

| SNOW BUNTING *Plectrophenax nivalis*

There have been nine records:
- **1969:** singles on 12 November (R. Angles) and 9 December (B. Rabbitts).
- **1977:** one flew south over Picnic Site No. 1 on 17 November (KEV).
- **1984:** one seen and heard overhead on 11 November (A. J. Merritt).
- **1987:** one in flight at Twycross on 28 November (KEV).
- **1992:** one at Hollow Brook on 31 October (R. M. Andrews, A. J. Merritt).
- **2010:** one on 4 December in the Hollow Brook area (J. Delve).
- **2011:** one over Stratford Hide on 12 December (A. H. Davis).
- **2013:** one at Picnic Site No. 1 on 28 November (*ABR*, but no observer details).

CORN BUNTING *Emberiza calandra*

There have been seven records as follows:
- **1964:** one on 7 November (R. J. Lewis).
- **1967:** one on 7 May (A. H. Davis, K. L. Fox).
- **1970:** one singing in fields behind the North-east Shore on 17 May (KEV).
- **1973:** one on 8 September (B. Rabbitts).
- **1977:** one on 18 May singing alongside the road behind the North-east Shore. It later flew off north over the hill (KEV).
- **1978:** one on 28 October flew out of a large willow at the bottom of Stratford Lane, calling, and then flew north along Moreton Bank (KEV).
- **1979:** one on 9 June (R. J. Palmer).

Given the long-term national decline in this species, it seems highly unlikely that it will ever occur again.

YELLOWHAMMER *Emberiza citrinella*

Yellowhammers used to breed around the lake in small numbers. Unfortunately, there were no published records during 1954–1964. It seems highly probable that they were present in the early years but were considered too common to warrant a mention in the bird reports.

As the annual maxima graph shows, they were present annually in small numbers from 1965 to 1996 inclusive, with the highest totals being 35 in a stubble field behind the East Shore in January 1969, 50 on 22 March 1981 and at least 16 at Heron's Green Farm on 19 March 1995. None was recorded from 2003 to 2009 but, ironically, given the species' decline, the highest ever count was 60 on 23 February 2012. This flock was present from 9 February to 23 March in a stubble field just to the north-west of the Main Dam. Where these birds came from is of course unknown, but small numbers of breeding Yellowhammers still persist on Dundry Hill, to the north of the lake.

The combined monthly maxima graph shows that numbers were highest from January to March, but with much smaller peaks in July and from October to December.

The graph, which shows the numbers of singing males, also illustrates how the Yellowhammer has declined as a breeding species since the mid-1980s, with just two singing in 1995 and one in 2012.

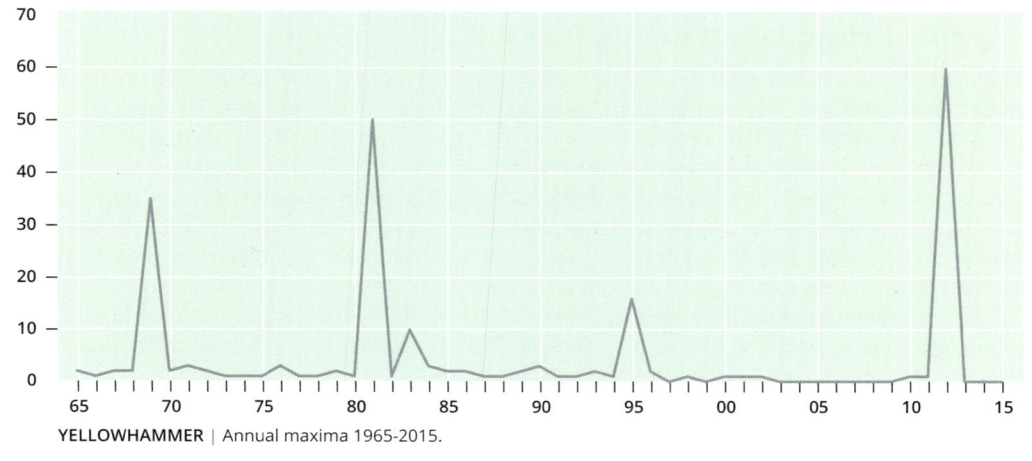

YELLOWHAMMER | Annual maxima 1965-2015.

YELLOWHAMMER | Monthly maxima (combined) 1965-2015.

JAN	FEB	MAR	APR	MAY	JUN	JUL	AUG	SEP	OCT	NOV	DEC
49	73	82	12	12	6	18	7	2	20	23	20

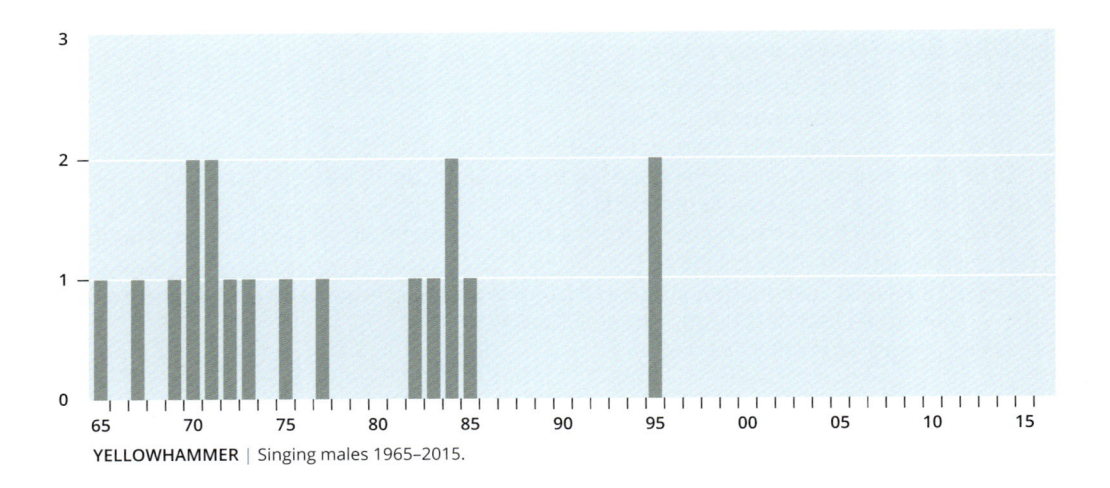

YELLOWHAMMER | Singing males 1965–2015.

CIRL BUNTING *Emberiza cirlus*

Having been a regular bird of the Chew Valley up to the earlier half of the last century, this species is no longer present. They are reported to have bred in Chew Magna and Compton Martin prior to 1955. There are two confirmed records.

1960: one 6 August (B. King).
1966: one 1 May (D.J. Perriman).

LITTLE BUNTING *Emberiza pusilla*

There have been two records. One was trapped on 4 January 1976 amongst a large flock of finches and Tree Sparrows *Passer montanus* in a field behind Herriott's Pool (A. R. Ashman, D. Buffery, R. Webber *et al.*). A first-winter male was seen at Sutton Wick from 31 March to 21 April 1996 (A. G. Duff *et al.*). It was sometimes heard sub-singing towards the end of its stay.

REED BUNTING *Emberiza schoeniclus*

The Reed Bunting is a common breeding species. The third graph shows the numbers of singing males from 1990 to 2016. It must be stressed, however, that, living as it does in reeds and other lakeside vegetation, numbers are difficult to monitor, apart from the occasional mid-winter flocks.

Numbers of singing males appear to have dipped slightly from the late 1990s into the early 2000s, but the numbers increased to as many as 51 in 2012 and 53 the year after. However, these counts were undoubtedly related to better coverage from 2011 onwards. The graph based on annual ringing totals also shows a similar pattern from 1990 onwards, suggesting that the recent increase may well be real. It could, perhaps, be related to milder winters.

The combined monthly maxima graph shows high numbers from January to April, but the high January total is skewed by the fact that a flock of 75 was present behind Herriott's Pool during 1-4 January 1976 (along with a Little Bunting *E. pusilla*), while a flock of 35 in fields at Sutton Wick Lane on 13 January 1985 further increases this total. The earliest date for the first song is 6 February (in 2012) and the increase shown on the chart in March and April reflects the start of the species' main song period. The high July total is perhaps related to the continuation of the male's song period into early July, plus, no doubt, the addition of the lake's young during the course of the summer.

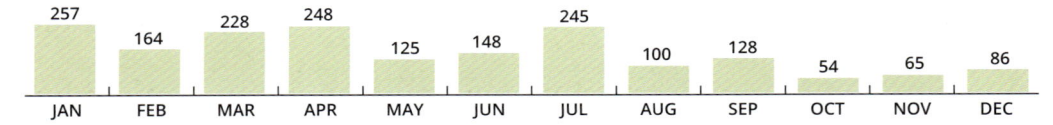

JAN	FEB	MAR	APR	MAY	JUN	JUL	AUG	SEP	OCT	NOV	DEC
257	164	228	248	125	148	245	100	128	54	65	86

REED BUNTING | Monthly maxima (combined) 1965-2014.

REED BUNTING | Annual ringing totals 1963-2015.

REED BUNTING | Singing males 1990–2016.

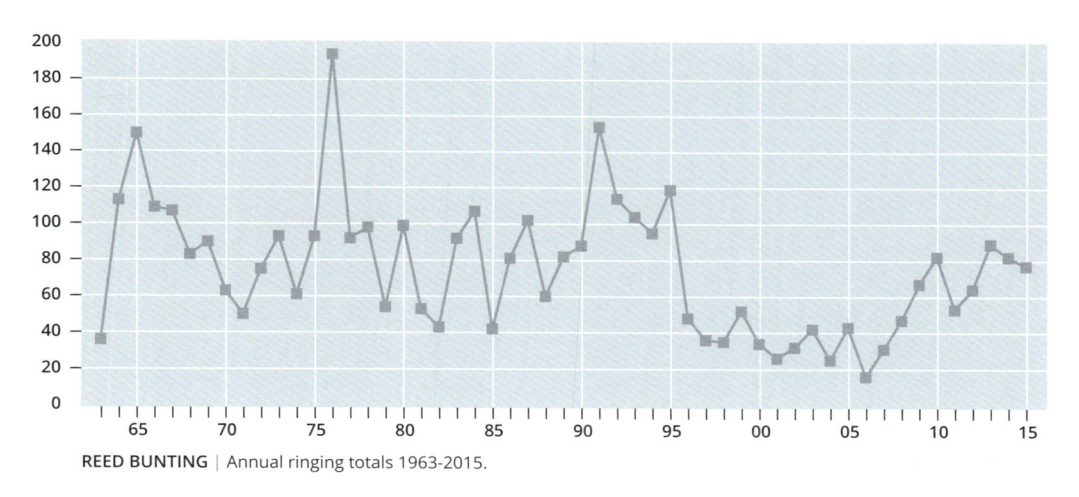

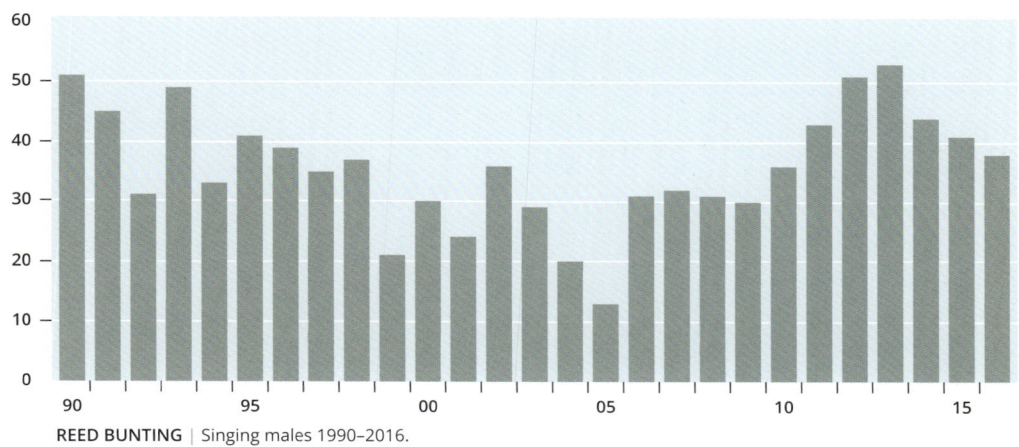

Reed Bunting | Ian Stapp

COMPLETE SPECIES LIST AND CHARTS

Index

to the full species list

This index, in alphabetical order by British (English) vernacular name, refers to birds within the section 'Complete species list and charts'. We hope you will also have enjoyed encountering some of these wonderful birds in other chapters of the book.

We have aimed this index at both birders as well as at the general readership who may have less knowledge of bird family groups. For many birders, the frequent recent changes in the order of the systematic list has meant that different publications are in different bird orders, depending on when they were published. This list is in line with the Ninth edition of the British list as of 24 January 2020.

There is no simple solution, so we have chosen to give an alphabetic list by name. Some publications may use well-known groupings with, for example, Reed Bunting under 'B' as in '**Bunting,** *Reed'*, although Yellowhammer, also a bunting, will be under 'Y'. Our approach has other problems, in that '***Blue-headed wagtail'*** will be a long way from its conspecific ***'Yellow Wagtail'***. But either will get you to the wagtail section, as you would of course with **Pied Wagtail**. *(Ed).*

Alpine Swift	229
American Golden Plover	257
American Wigeon	200
Aquatic Warbler	399
Arctic Skua	326
Arctic Tern	319
Avocet	254
Baltic Gull	314
Barn Owl	355
Barnacle Goose	178
Bar-tailed Godwit	264
Bearded Tit	383
Bee-eater	362
Bewick's Swan	188
Bittern	337
Black Redstart	427
Black Stork	332
Black Tern	323
Blackbird	419
Blackcap	405
Black-headed Gull	298
Black-necked Grebe	250
Black-tailed Godwit	266
Black-throated Diver	329
Black-winged Pratincole	296
Black-winged Stilt	253
Blue Tit	382
Blue-headed Wagtail	436
Bluethroat	426
Blue-winged Teal	195
Bonaparte's Gull	298
Booted Eagle	348
Brambling	447
Brent Goose	176
Buff-breasted Sandpiper	279
Bufflehead	220
Bullfinch	449
Buzzard	354
Cackling Goose	180
Canada Goose	177
Carrion Crow	377
Caspian Gull	310
Caspian Tern	315
Cattle Egret	340
Cetti's Warbler	391
Chaffinch	445
Chiffchaff	395
Cirl Bunting	458
Citrine Wagtail	437
Coal Tit	378
Collared Dove	235
Common Gull	303
Common Redpoll	453
Common Sandpiper	287
Common Scoter	217
Common Tern	318
Coot	241
Cormorant	334
Corn Bunting	457
Corncrake	238
Crane	243
Crossbill	454
Cuckoo	231
Curlew	263
Curlew Sandpiper	272
Dipper	432
Dunlin	275
Dunnock	434
Egyptian Goose	189
Eider	216
Feral Pigeon	232
Ferruginous Duck	209
Fieldfare	419
Firecrest	413
Franklin's Gull	302
Fulmar	332
Gadwall	197
Gannet	332
Garden Warbler	406
Garganey	193
Glaucous Gull	307
Glossy Ibis	335
Goldcrest	414
Golden Oriole	372
Golden Plover	256
Goldeneye	220
Goldfinch	454
Goosander	224
Grasshopper Warbler	404
Great Black-backed Gull	306
Great Bustard	231
Great Crested Grebe	248
Great Grey Shrike	372
Great Northern Diver	330
Great Reed Warbler	398
Great Skua	325
Great Spotted Woodpecker	363
Great Tit	383
Great White Egret	343
Greater Flamingo	251
Greater Sand Plover	261
Green Sandpiper	289

Green Woodpecker	365	Little Stint	277
Greenfinch	450	Little Tern	316
Greenland White-fronted Goose	185	Long-billed Dowitcher	281
Greenshank	295	Long-eared Owl	359
Green-winged Teal	204	Long-tailed Duck	219
Grey Heron	341	Long-tailed Skua	327
Grey Partridge	174	Long-tailed Tit	392
Grey Phalarope	285	Magpie	375
Grey Plover	257	Mallard	200
Grey Wagtail	437	Mandarin Duck	192
Greylag Goose	180	Manx Shearwater	332
Gyr Falcon	369	Marbled Duck	205
Hawfinch	448	Marsh Harrier	349
Hen Harrier	350	Marsh Sandpiper	293
Herring Gull	310	Marsh Tit	380
Hobby	367	Marsh Warbler	402
Honey-buzzard	347	Meadow Pipit	441
Hoopoe	360	Mediterranean Gull	302
House Martin	389	Merlin	367
House Sparrow	433	Mistle Thrush	422
Iceland Gull	308	Montagu's Harrier	352
Jack Snipe	282	Moorhen	240
Jackdaw	375	Mute Swan	187
Jay	374	Night Heron	339
Kentish Plover	260	Nightingale	426
Kestrel	366	Nightjar	229
Killdeer	260	Nuthatch	416
Kingfisher	360	Osprey	347
Kittiwake	296	Oystercatcher	252
Knot	269	Pectoral Sandpiper	279
Kumlien's Gull	309	Peregrine	369
Lapland Bunting	456	Pheasant	175
Lapwing	255	Pied Flycatcher	427
Laughing Gull	301	Pied Wagtail	439
Leach's Petrel	331	Pied-billed Grebe	246
Lesser Black-backed Gull	313	Pink-footed Goose	182
Lesser Redpoll	453	Pintail	202
Lesser Scaup	215	Pochard	207
Lesser Spotted Woodpecker	362	Pomarine Skua	325
Lesser White-fronted Goose	185	Purple Heron	342
Lesser Whitethroat	409	Purple Sandpiper	277
Lesser Yellowlegs	290	Quail	175
Linnet	451	Raven	377
Little Bittern	339	Red Kite	352
Little Bunting	458	Red-backed Shrike	372
Little Crake	238	Red-breasted Merganser	226
Little Egret	344	Red-crested Pochard	206
Little Grebe	243	Red-legged Partridge	174
Little Gull	299	Red-necked Grebe	246
Little Owl	356	Red-necked Phalarope	285
Little Ringed Plover	260	Red-rumped Swallow	391

Redshank	292
Redstart	428
Red-throated Diver	328
Red-throated Pipit	442
Redwing	420
Reed Bunting	458
Reed Warbler	401
Ring Ouzel	418
Ring-billed Gull	305
Ringed Plover	259
Ring-necked Duck	211
Ring-necked Parakeet	370
Robin	425
Rock Pipit	444
Rook	376
Roseate Tern	317
Ross's Gull	300
Rough-legged Buzzard	354
Ruddy Duck	227
Ruddy Shelduck	192
Ruff	271
Sabine's Gull	297
Sand Martin	387
Sanderling	274
Sandwich Tern	315
Savi's Warbler	405
Scaup	214
Sedge Warbler	400
Semipalmated Sandpiper	281
Serin	455
Shag	333
Sharp-tailed Sandpiper	272
Shelduck	191
Shore Lark	386
Short-eared Owl	359
Shoveler	195
Siberian Chiffchaff	397
Siskin	455
Skylark	385
Slavonian Grebe	250
Smew	222
Snipe	283
Snow Bunting	456
Song Thrush	422
Sparrowhawk	348
Spoonbill	335
Spotted Crake	238
Spotted Flycatcher	423
Spotted Redshank	294
Spotted Sandpiper	288
Squacco Heron	339
Starling	418
Stock Dove	232
Stone Curlew	251
Stonechat	430
Storm Petrel	331
Swallow	388
Swift	230
Tawny Owl	356
Tawny Pipit	441
Teal	203
Temminck's Stint	273
Tree Pipit	442
Tree Sparrow	434
Treecreeper	417
Tufted Duck	212
Tundra Bean Goose	183
Turnstone	268
Turtle Dove	234
Twite	451
Velvet Scoter	216
Water Pipit	442
Water Rail	237
Waxwing	378
Wheatear	431
Whimbrel	261
Whinchat	428
Whiskered Tern	322
White Stork	332
White Wagtail	440
White-fronted Goose	185
White-headed Duck	229
White-rumped Sandpiper	278
Whitethroat	411
White-winged Black Tern	322
Whooper Swan	189
Wigeon	199
Willow Tit	381
Willow Warbler	394
Wilson's Phalarope	285
Wood Sandpiper	293
Wood Warbler	393
Woodchat Shrike	372
Woodcock	282
Woodpigeon	233
Wren	415
Wryneck	362
Yellow Wagtail	435
Yellow-browed Warbler	394
Yellowhammer	457
Yellow-legged Gull	310

Laurel Tucker

We are especially pleased that this book is able to showcase over 70 drawings by Laurel, many previously unpublished.

Early self-portrait | Laurel Tucker

John Rossetti

John started birdwatching in his teens, initially with a group of friends and then also as part of the Bristol Grammar School field club. He met Keith at Chew in the late 60's. After studying Pure Mathematics at Sussex and Leeds Universities, he and his then wife Kate were selected by the BBC to be one of six couples to take part in the first ever reality TV program, 'Living in the Past'. They lived for 13 months cut off from civilisation, living in the technology and farming practices of Iron Age Britain of 300 BC. Four of the couples, now with partners, children and even grandchildren, still meet up regularly for reunions.

John abandoned an academic career and set up his own software (and later logistics) business Swift Computing in 1982. From 1997 he also owned and ran the Prom music bar in Bristol, which staged live music six nights a week, as well as supporting younger artists in the local arts trail.

He managed the occasional birding trips, including to the Scillies and North Ronaldsay, the latter with his great friend, the inimical and charismatic late Tim Cleeves. He survived a collapse of his businesses in the recession of 2008 to 2011. He has a son Will and Daughter Polly, and two young granddaughters that live in London. John lives in Bristol and enjoys playing football (mostly with his local team 'Barely Athletic'), tennis and discussing philosophy. He is also renovating a derelict cottage in the highlands, in a stunning and under watched location.

This is the first book that he has been involved with.

John, on the right, with Keith, exhibiting some of Ray Scally's paintings for the book | Jane Vinicombe

Bar-tailed Godwit | Laurel Tucker